The Very Best CANADA Baby Name Book

The Very Best CANADIAN Baby Name Book

Bruce Lansky

Meadowbrook Press
Distributed by Simon & Schuster
New York

ISBN-10: 0-88166-540-1
ISBN-13: 978-0-88166-540-6

Editors: Angela Wiechmann, Alicia Ester
Researcher: David Rochelero
Production Manager: Paul Woods
Graphic Design Manager: Tamara Peterson
Cover Photography: Sergei Chumakov and Elnur

Published by Meadowbrook Press, 5451 Smetana Drive, Minnetonka, Minnesota 55343

www.meadowbrookpress.com

BOOK TRADE DISTRIBUTION by Simon and Schuster, a division of Simon and Schuster, Inc., 1230 Avenue of the Americas, New York, New York 10020

14 13 12 11 10 09   10 9 8 7 6 5 4 3 2 1

Printed in the United States of America

Contents

Introduction 1

How to Pick a Name You and Your Baby Will Like 3

How to Pick a Unique Version of a Popular Name 8

The Most Popular Names in Select Provinces 10

The Most Popular Names around the World 14

Names from Canadian Ethnic Origins 17

The Impressions Names Make 21

Names of Notable Canadians 27

Names Inspired by People, Places, and Things 43

Star Kids 65

How to Register Your Baby's Birth in Canada 75

Girls' Names 81

Boys' Names 235

Introduction

Searching for the right baby name can be a pleasure—if you have the right book. Let me tell you why I think *The Very Best Canadian Baby Name Book* is right for you.

It contains 50,000 popular and uncommon names—complete with origins, meanings, variations, fascinating facts, and famous namesakes. You'll find thousands of names from the major ethnic groups that make up Canadian heritage, including English, French, Scottish, Irish, and German names. You'll also find names from dozens of other ethnic origins, including East Indian, Chinese, Dutch, and North American Indian.

More importantly, *The Very Best Canadian Baby Name Book* lives up to its title. It's simply the best book to help Canadian parents find the best name for their baby. Whereas many books on the market are intended primarily for American or British readers (and this includes many books I myself have authored), this book is for *you*. Where else can you find the following features?

- The most popular names from select provinces

- Highlighted names from Canada's fifteen largest ethnic groups

- Hundreds of names inspired by notable Canadians from entertainment, sports, history, and other areas of interest

- Celebrity baby names featuring famous Canadians

- Information about registering your baby's birth and name in each province

In addition to the Canadian-focused content, you'll also find the following:

- Interesting and informative articles about how to pick a name you and your baby will like and how to pick a unique version of a popular name

- The most popular names from countries all around the world

- Survey data about the impressions names make

- Hundreds of names inspired by people, places, and things beyond Canada

As you can see, this isn't an American or British baby name book that's found its way to Canadian bookstores. It was created specifically for you. I hope you find it fun, helpful, and easy to use as you search for the best name for your little Canuck.

Bruce Lansky

How to Pick a Name You and Your Baby Will Like

The first edition of *The Best Baby Name Book in the Whole Wide World*, which I wrote back in 1978, had about 10,000 names on 120 pages. So, you could browse all the main listings (and even pause to read the origins, meanings, and variations for names that appealed to you) in a few hours. It's something a couple could do together.

The Very Best Canadian Baby Name Book has more than 50,000 names on 404 pages. I don't know how long it would take you and your partner to browse all the main listings and pause to read more about your favorites, but it could be a daunting task. If you're up to the challenge, go for it. You'll certainly find your favorite names and discover some new names as well.

But if the idea of wading through a sea of 50,000 names sounds overwhelming, I'd like to propose another method. The method I suggest involves generating lists of names you and your partner love and then narrowing down the lists based on how well the names might work for your baby. It's a fun, easy way to come up with a name that has special meaning but is practical as well. Let's get started.

Step 1: Make a List of Names with Special Meaning

Make a list of names to consider by writing down your answers to the following questions. (You each will make your own list.) These questions are based on the lists starting on page 10. Browse those lists to help you answer the questions and to brainstorm other questions specific to your background, preferences, and experiences.

The Most Popular Names in Select Provinces (pages 10–13)
What are your favorite names from the most popular names in your province or any province? If you feel these names are *too* popular, do you like any of their less-common variations? (To learn how to pick a unique version of a popular name, see page 8.)

Names around the World (pages 14–16) and Names from Canadian Ethnic Origins (pages 17–20)

What country are your parents or grandparents from? If you or your partner are not Canadian born, what country are you from?

What are your favorite names that are currently popular in other countries?

What language(s) do you speak?

Where did you go on your honeymoon?

Where do you like to vacation?

Where did you conceive?

Impressions Names Make (pages 21–26)

What might your baby's personality be like?

How might your baby look physically?

What impression would you like your baby's name to make about him/her?

Names of Notable Canadians (pages 27–42) and Names Inspired by People, Places, and Things (pages 43–64)

Who are your favorite literature figures?

Who are your favorite historical figures?

Who are your favorite figures from religion and mythology?

Who are your favorite figures from movies and television?

Who are your favorite musicians? What are your favorite songs?

Who are your favorite sports figures?

What are your favorite natural elements and places?

What are your favorite other ideas for names (virtue names, old-fashioned names, etc.)?

Once you answer these questions, turn to the Girls' Names and Boys' Names sections to find interesting spellings or variations based on the names from your list. As you flip through the book, you might stumble across a few new names that capture your attention, too. That will give you a long list of names to consider for the next step.

Step 2: Narrow the List Based on What Will Work Best for Your Baby

Now that you've each created a list based on personal considerations, it's time to narrow them down based on practical considerations. This way, you'll choose a name that works well for you and for your baby. You may love a particular name, but if it doesn't hold up to these basic criteria, your baby probably won't love it. It can be unpleasant going through life with a name that for whatever reason doesn't work for you.

Make enough copies of the table on the following page for each name on your list. Have your partner do the same. Rate each name on twelve factors. Example: Consider the popularity of the name Jacob—if you think there might be too many Jacobs in his school, check "too popular." Consider nicknames—if you love Jake, check "appealing." Another example: Consider the way Rafael sounds to you—if it's music to your ears, check "pleasing." Consider its fit with your last name—if you don't think it goes so well with Abramovitz, check "doesn't fit."

When you've completed the table, add up the score by giving three points for every check in the Positive column, two points for every check in the Neutral column, and one point for every check in the Negative column. Scoring each name might help make the subjective process of selecting a name more objective to you.

(Note: If you're pinched for time, mentally complete the table for each name, keeping track of a rough score. The important part is to narrow the list to your top five boys' and girls' names.)

Name:_____

Factors	Positive	Neutral	Negative
1. Spelling	❏ easy	❏ medium	❏ hard
2. Pronunciation	❏ easy	❏ medium	❏ hard
3. Sound	❏ pleasing	❏ okay	❏ unpleasing
4. Last Name	❏ fits well	❏ fits okay	❏ doesn't fit
5. Gender ID	❏ clear	❏ neutral	❏ unclear
6. Nicknames	❏ appealing	❏ okay	❏ unappealing
7. Popularity	❏ not too popular	❏ popular	❏ too popular
8. Uniqueness	❏ not too unique	❏ unique	❏ too unique
9. Impression	❏ positive	❏ okay	❏ negative
10. Namesakes	❏ positive	❏ okay	❏ negative
11. Initials	❏ pleasing	❏ okay	❏ unpleasing
12. Meaning	❏ positive	❏ okay	❏ negative

Final Score:_____

Step 3: Make the Final Choice

List your top five boys' and girls' names in the chart below, and have your partner do the same. It's now time to share the names. If you have names in common, compare your scores; perhaps average them. If you have different names on your lists, swap names and rate them using the same table as before. In the end, you'll have a handful of names that work well for you, your partner, and your baby. Now all you have to do is make the final decision. Good luck!

Mom's Top Five Names

1. _____ Mom's Score: _____ Dad's Score: _____
2. _____ Mom's Score: _____ Dad's Score: _____
3. _____ Mom's Score: _____ Dad's Score: _____
4. _____ Mom's Score: _____ Dad's Score: _____
5. _____ Mom's Score: _____ Dad's Score: _____

Dad's Top Five Names

1. _____ Dad's Score: _____ Mom's Score: _____
2. _____ Dad's Score: _____ Mom's Score: _____
3. _____ Dad's Score: _____ Mom's Score: _____
4. _____ Dad's Score: _____ Mom's Score: _____
5. _____ Dad's Score: _____ Mom's Score: _____

How to Pick a Unique Version of a Popular Name

Many parents-to-be like the security and familiarity of popular names. They see them as the "best of the best."

However, it's important to note that the popularity issue cuts two ways: Psychologists say a child with a popular name seems to have better odds of success than a child with an uncommon name, but a child whose name is at the top of the popularity poll may not feel as unique and special as a child whose name is less common. Looking from a child's perspective, nothing contributes quite so much to the feeling that you're not unique as when you share your name with several classmates. Then again, it's one thing for a name to make you feel "different" and "odd."

Perhaps a good compromise is to select a unique version of a popular name for your baby. This involves taking a popular name and customizing it with a touch of individuality. Here are some tips to help you do just that:

1. Choose a Variation.

One easy way to select a unique version of a popular name is to look for variations of a popular name you like. In the Girls' Names and Boys' Names sections of this book, you can find variations in two ways. One, look for italicized names listed under a main entry. Two, look for bold main entries that have "a form of [root name]" as their meaning. For example, Jake and Kobi are variations you might want to consider for Jacob. If you're worried that William is too popular, you might want to consider less-popular variations Will and Liam. For girls, Emilia and Emmaline are forms of Emily. (It's interesting to point out that Emma is also a variation of Emily. As Emily became more popular, parents viewed Emma as a fresh variation. But as it turned out, thousands of parents had the same idea, so now this "unique" variation is ironically a popular name in its own right.)

2. Choose a "Name-Book Neighbor."

Go to the Girls' Names or Boys' Names section, find your favorite name from the popularity lists, and scan the names on the page before, the facing page, or the page after. You'll probably come across variations of the name (which we discussed above), but you'll also find "name-book neighbors." These names contain some of the same letters and sounds as the popular name, but they may have different origins and meanings and are often more unique. Sticking with the example of Emily, you'll find the name-book neighbor Emory (a name so good they used it for a top-flight university). For Olivia, you'll find Olinda and Olympia. For fellas, a name-book neighbor of Matthew is Mathias, and a name-book neighbor of Michael is Micah.

3. Change the Spelling.

If you like the sound of a popular name but want to give it a unique treatment, an easy trick is to change the spelling. You can make the change as subtle (Hannah to Hanna) or dramatic (Michael to Mikkel) as you wish. One interesting study in spelling is the name Haley, for which you can mix-and-match *Ha-*, *Hae-*, *Hai-*, and *Hay-* with *-lea*, *-lee*, *-leigh*, *-ley*, *-lie*, *-li*, and *-ly*. As if that weren't enough, you can also double the *l* in any one of these options. The main concern with the spelling approach is that people may not spell or pronounce the name correctly—a daily inconvenience that could frustrate your child. That said, sometimes variant spellings become common names on their own.

4. Combine Names.

An additional way to put a unique twist on a popular name is to combine it with another name. You can make a double name separated by a space or a hyphen, such as John Paul or Mary Kate, or you can also make a single name, such as Michaelangelo or Emmalee (which you can also pronounce as "Emma Lee" or

Emily"). This technique is especially easy with girls' names, because names like Lyn, Lee, Ann, Tina, Lisa, and Ella blend well with other names. For boys, names like Jay, Bert, and Shawn combine well. If you want to add a personal touch to a combination name, combine your own names or the names of special relatives. If your names are Mary and Lee, combine them to get Marlee. If the grandfathers' names are William and Tony, combine them to get Wilton. The possibilities are endless—but keep in mind that sometimes the results can be quite silly (for example, combining Raymond with Darla can produce Raydar).

5. Add a Prefix or Suffix.

In addition to combining a popular name with another name, you can also add a prefix or suffix to it. This is especially prevalent with names of American origin used by African American families. Common prefixes are *Da-*, *De-*, *Le-*, *La-*, *Sha-*, *Ja-*, and *Ta-*. Common suffixes are *-a*, *-ia*, *-ina*, *-ita*, *-la*, *-en*, *-o*, *-ta*, *-te*, *-us*, and *-y*. When you add these to popular names, you get unique versions of popular names such as Lakayla, Deanthony, Sarita, and Josephus. Throughout history, the suffix *-son* has been used to link a father's name to a son's name, as in the case of Jackson and Jameson. These names have since become last names, but they're still commonly used as first names for boys *and* girls. Borrowing from this custom, you can add a twist to a popular name (or perhaps your own name) by adding *-son*.

6. Use an Ethnic Variation.

If you like the name John but find it too popular, consider giving it an ethnic spin: Sean (Irish), Zane (English), Gian (Italian), Hans (Scandinavian) Janne (Finnish), Honza (Czech), Ian (Scottish), Janek (Polish), Jan (Dutch and Slavic), Jean (French), Johann (German), Jens (Danish), Juan (Spanish), or even Keoni (Hawaiian). For girls, Katherine has many interesting ethnic variations, including Ekaterina (Russian), Kasia (Polish), and Kathleen (Irish). You may choose an ethnic variation to reflect your heritage, or perhaps you'll simply choose an ethnic name on its own merits. (Just be careful when you pair the first name with your last name; you might get strange results like Juan Kowalski.)

As you can see, there are several ways to find or create a unique version of a popular name. With these techniques, you can stray a little or a lot from a popular name, depending on your comfort level and your imagination. In the end, you may come up with a name that's the best of both worlds.

The Most Popular Names in Select Provinces

The popularity of names, like the length of hemlines and width of ties, is subject to change every year. When choosing a name for your baby, it's wise to consider whether its popularity is rising, declining, or holding steady.

To help you assess name trends, we present the latest popularity rankings of names given to baby girls and boys in Alberta, British Columbia, Nova Scotia, Ontario, Quebec, and Saskatchewan. (Name popularity data is not available for other provinces.) The rankings come from information collected by the vital statistics offices in each of these provinces.

Most Popular Names in Alberta

Girls

2007 Rank	Name	2006 Rank	Rank Change
1	Ava	1	—
2	Emma	2	—
3	Emily	3	—
4	Olivia	8	+4
5	Sarah	6	+1
6	Hannah	4	−2
7	Madison	5	−2
8	Abigail	7	−1
9	Sophia	20	+11
10	Hailey	12	+2
11	Brooklyn	16	+5
12	Isabella	17	+5
13	Chloe	13	—
14	Ella	10	−4
15	Taylor	14	−1
16	Brooke	19	+3
17	Grace	9	−8
18	Addison	70	+52
19	Sophie	41	+22
20	Samantha	11	−9
21	Avery	26	+5
22	Elizabeth	18	−4
23	Anna	35	+12
24	Lily	46	+22
25	Alyssa	36	+11

Boys

2007 Rank	Name	2006 Rank	Rank Change
1	Ethan	1	—
2	Jacob	3	+1
3	Logan	4	+1
4	Noah	6	+2
5	Joshua	2	−3
6	Owen	14	+8
7	Alexander	11	+4
8	Liam	8	—
9	Matthew	5	−4
10	Nathan	7	−3
11	Samuel	25	+14
12	Ryan	19	+7
13	Austin	13	—
14	Evan	12	−2
15	William	10	−5
16	Benjamin	15	+1
17	Jack	18	+1
18	Lucas	16	−2
19	Daniel	26	+7
20	Carter	9	−11
21	Jayden	32	+11
22	Zachary	27	+5
23	Riley	24	+1
24	Dylan	29	+5
25	Nicholas	28	+3

Most Popular Names in British Columbia

Girls

2007 Rank	Name	2006 Rank	Rank Change
1	Ava	3	+2
2	Emily	2	—
3	Sophia	7	+4
4	Olivia	4	—
5	Emma	1	−4
6	Hannah	5	−1
7	Ella	8	+1
8	Isabella	9	+1
9	Sarah	6	−3
10	Chloe	12	+2
11	Madison	10	−1
12	Sophie	18	+6
13	Lily	23	+10
14	Grace	11	−3
15	Abigail	13	−2
16	Brooklyn	16	—
17	Taylor	15	−2
18	Julia	19	+1
19	Samantha	14	−5
20	Claire	44	+24
21	Elizabeth	26	+5
22	Kaitlyn	25	+3
23	Hailey	22	−1
24	Maya	17	−7
25	Jessica	29	+4

Boys

2007 Rank	Name	2006 Rank	Rank Change
1	Ethan	1	—
2	Jacob	2	—
3	Noah	12	+9
4	Liam	6	+2
5	Matthew	3	−2
6	Joshua	4	−2
7	Logan	9	+2
8	Owen	16	+8
9	Ryan	8	−1
10	Lucas	13	+3
11	Alexander	11	—
12	Benjamin	7	−5
13	Nathan	5	−8
14	Daniel	10	−4
15	Jack	20	+5
16	William	15	−1
17	James	14	−3
18	Nicholas	17	−1
19	Jayden	39	+20
20	Tyler	19	−1
21	Aiden	27	+6
22	Dylan	29	+7
23	Samuel	18	−5
24	Evan	22	−2
25	Gavin	41	+16

Most Popular Names in Nova Scotia

Girls

2006 Rank	Name	2005 Rank	Rank Change
1	Emma	1	—
2	Ava	9	+7
3	Madison	2	-1
4	Olivia	3	-1
5	Hannah	5	—
6	Abigail	6	—
7	Emily	4	-3
8	Sarah	7	-1
9	Ella	12	+3
10	Chloe	11	+1
11	Lily	n/a	n/a
12	Grace	8	-4
13	Brooke	14	+1
14	Sophia	n/a	n/a
15	Sophie	18	+2
16	Faith	n/a	n/a
17	Elizabeth	n/a	n/a
18	Brooklyn	20	+2
19	Julia	13	-6
20	Rachel	n/a	n/a

Boys

2006 Rank	Name	2005 Rank	Rank Change
1	Ryan	12	+11
2	Jacob	1	-1
3	Ethan	2	-1
4	Noah	9	+5
5	Liam	18	+13
6	Owen	14	+8
7	Alexander	3	-4
8	Matthew	10	+2
9	Jack	5	-4
10	Benjamin	15	+5
11	Nathan	11	—
12	Evan	17	+5
13	Cole	n/a	n/a
14	William	13	-1
15	Joshua	6	-9
16	Logan	4	-12
17	Lucas	n/a	n/a
18	Connor	7	-11
19	Cameron	19	—
20	Nicholas	8	-12

Most Popular Names in Ontario

Girls

2006 Rank	Name	2005 Rank	Rank Change
1	Emma	1	—
2	Olivia	3	+1
3	Emily	2	-1
4	Ava	8	+4
5	Sarah	4	-1
6	Isabella	11	+5
7	Hannah	6	-1
8	Abigail	10	+2
9	Madison	5	-4
10	Ella	9	-1
11	Julia	7	-4
12	Sophia	19	+7
13	Grace	12	-1
14	Samantha	13	-1
15	Chloe	21	+6
16	Victoria	15	-1
17	Lauren	17	—
18	Maya	22	+4
19	Jessica	14	-5
20	Hailey	18	-2
21	Rachel	16	-5
22	Alyssa	20	-2
23	Mackenzie	24	+1
24	Elizabeth	26	+2
25	Avery	33	+8

Boys

2006 Rank	Name	2005 Rank	Rank Change
1	Ethan	2	+1
2	Matthew	1	-1
3	Joshua	3	—
4	Jacob	4	—
5	Ryan	5	—
6	Noah	8	+2
7	Nathan	7	—
8	Daniel	6	-2
9	Alexander	10	+1
10	Owen	9	-1
11	Nicholas	11	—
12	William	16	+4
13	Lucas	15	+2
14	Michael	14	—
15	Benjamin	12	-3
16	Andrew	17	+1
17	Liam	13	-4
18	Logan	21	+3
19	Evan	20	+1
20	Jack	19	-1
21	Tyler	18	-3
22	Adam	26	+4
23	James	25	+2
24	Samuel	24	—
25	Dylan	23	-2

Most Popular Names in Quebec

Girls

2006 Rank	Name	2005 Rank	Rank Change
1	Lea	1	—
2	Jade	2	—
3	Rosalie	4	+1
4	Florence	7	+3
5	Laurie	15	+10
6	Gabrielle	11	+5
7	Sarah	3	-4
8	Camille	8	—
9	Oceane	13	+4
10	Laurence	6	-4
11	Noemie	5	-6
12	Emma	23	+11
13	Emilie	19	+6
14	Juliette	17	+3
15	Maika	27	+12
16	Coralie	10	-6
17	Justine	18	+1
18	Megane	9	-9
19	Ariane	16	-3
20	Emy	25	+5
21	Chloe	20	-1
22	Audrey	14	-8
23	Annabelle	31	+8
24	Marianne	22	-2
25	Charlotte	24	-1

Boys

2006 Rank	Name	2005 Rank	Rank Change
1	William	2	+1
2	Samuel	1	-1
3	Alexis	3	—
4	Nathan	8	+4
5	Thomas	9	+4
6	Antoine	5	-1
7	Gabriel	4	-3
8	Justin	11	+3
9	Olivier	7	-2
10	Felix	6	-4
11	Zachary	18	+7
12	Xavier	10	-2
13	Jeremy	12	-1
14	Alexandre	15	+1
15	Mathis	13	-2
16	Anthony	14	-2
17	Jacob	17	—
18	Raphael	16	-2
19	Emile	21	+2
20	Vincent	19	-1
21	Nicolas	20	-1
22	Benjamin	22	—
23	Maxime	23	—
24	Tristan	27	+3
25	Noah	33	+8

Most Popular Names in Saskatchewan

Girls

2007 Rank	Name	2006 Rank	Rank Change
1	Ava	1	—
2	Emma	3	+1
3	Hannah	6	+3
4	Olivia	9	+5
5	Emily	4	-1
6	Madison	2	-4
7	Hailey	7	—
8	Brooklyn	5	-3
9	Sarah	17	+8
10	Taylor	14	+4
11	Abigail	11	—
12	Chloe	8	-4
13	Nevaeh	n/a	n/a
14	Addison	n/a	n/a
15	Alexis	n/a	n/a
16	Alyssa	n/a	n/a
17	Sophia	n/a	n/a
18	Ella	16	-2
19	Avery	13	-6
20	Grace	n/a	n/a

Boys

2007 Rank	Name	2006 Rank	Rank Change
1	Ethan	1	—
2	Logan	9	+7
3	Matthew	10	+7
4	Noah	3	-1
5	Carter	7	+2
6	Alexander	8	+2
7	Jacob	13	+6
8	William	12	+4
9	Chase	n/a	n/a
10	Aiden	15	+5
11	Hunter	6	-5
12	Samuel	20	+8
13	Liam	2	-11
14	Owen	5	-9
15	Lucas	16	+1
16	Brody	n/a	n/a
17	Hayden	n/a	n/a
18	Jayden	4	-14
19	Joshua	11	-8
20	Dylan	n/a	n/a

The Most Popular Names around the World

Want to track popularity trends across the globe? Want to give your baby a name that reflects your heritage, language, or favorite travel destination? Here are the most popular names around the globe, as compiled by official statistics organizations from select countries.

Most Popular Names in Argentina

Female	Male
Sofía	Santiago
Camila	Lautaro
Valentina	Matías
Martina	Tomás
Agustina	Lucas
Micaela	Joaquín
Lucía	Franco
Milagros	Agustín
Victoria	Thiago
Julieta	Nicolás

Most Popular Names in Austria

Female	Male
Lena	Lukas
Leonie	Tobias
Sarah	David
Anna	Florian
Julia	Simon
Katharina	Maximilian
Hannah	Fabian
Sophie	Alexander
Laura	Sebastian
Lisa	Julian

Most Popular Names in Belgium

Female	Male
Emma	Noah
Marie	Thomas
Laura	Nathan
Julie	Lucas
Louise	Louis
Clara	Arthur
Manon	Milan
Léa	Hugo
Sarah	Maxime
Luna	Mohamed

Most Popular Names in Chile

Female	Male
Martina	Benjamín
Constanza	Vicente
Catalina	Matías
Valentina	Martín
Sofía	Sebastián
Javiera	Joaquín
Antonia	Diego
Maria	Nicolas
Isidora	Jose
Francisca	Cristobal

Most Popular Names in England/Wales

Female	Male
Grace	Jack
Ruby	Thomas
Olivia	Oliver
Emily	Joshua
Jessica	Harry
Sophie	Charlie
Chloe	Daniel
Lily	William
Ella	James
Amelia	Alfie

Most Popular Names in Finland

Female	Male
Aino	Eetu
Emma	Veeti
Sara	Aleksi
Venla	Elias
Ella	Joona
Anni	Onni
Aada	Arttu
Iida	Leevi
Emilia	Juho
Helmi	Lauri

Most Popular Names in France

Female	Male
Emma	Enzo
Léa	Mathis
Manon	Lucas
Clara	Hugo
Chloe	Mathéo
Inès	Nathan
Camille	Théo
Sarah	Noah
Océane	Mattéo
Jade	Thomas

Most Popular Names in Germany

Female	Male
Hannah, Hanna	Leon
Leonie, Leoni	Lukas, Lucas
Lena	Luca, Luka
Anna	Fynn, Finn
Lea, Leah	Tim, Timm
Lara	Felix
Mia	Jonas
Laura	Luis, Louis
Lilly, Lilli	Maximilian
Emily, Emilie	Julian

Most Popular Names in Ireland

Female	Male
Sarah	Sean
Emma	Jack
Katie	Conor
Aoife	Adam
Sophie	James
Ava	Daniel
Grace	Luke
Ella	Cian
Leah	Michael
Ciara	Jamie

Most Popular Names in Italy

Female	Male
Giulia	Andrea
Alessia	Lorenzo
Alice	Simone
Chiara	Paolo
Gaia	Marco
Ginevra	Francesco
Emma	Luca
Ilaria	Tommaso
Viola	Christian
Ludovica	Alessandro

Most Popular Names in Mexico

Female	Male
Gabriela	Alejandro
María Carmen	Juan Carlos
Adriana	Miguel Angel
Alejandra	Eduardo
María Guadalupe	Fernando
Mariana	Carlos
Claudia	Rodrigo
Monica	Ricardo
María Teresa	Javier
María Elena	Jose Luis

Most Popular Names in NSW, Australia

Female	Male
Isabella	Jack
Ella	William
Emily	Joshua
Chloe	Lachlan
Mia	Thomas
Olivia	Riley
Charlotte	Cooper
Sophie	James
Sienna	Noah
Jessica	Ethan

Most Popular Names in New Zealand

Female	Male
Ella	Jack
Sophie	James
Olivia	Joshua
Emma	Daniel
Charlotte	William
Emily	Oliver
Lily	Samuel
Grace	Benjamin
Hannah	Ethan
Isabella	Ryan

Most Popular Names in Norway

Female	Male
Thea	Jonas
Emma	Mathias
Julie	Magnus
Ida	Elias
Emilie	Emil
Nora	Henrik
Ingrid	Sander
Anna	Martin
Sara	Tobias
Sofie	Daniel

Most Popular Names in Russia

Female	Male
Elena	Aleksandr
Olga	Sergey
Tatiana	Vladimir
Irina	Andrey
Natalia	Aleksey
Anna	Dmitriy
Svetlana	Mikhail
Maria	Igor
Marina	Yuri
Ludmilla	Nikolai

Most Popular Names in Scotland

Female	Male
Sophie	Lewis
Emma	Jack
Lucy	Ryan
Katie	James
Erin	Callum
Ellie	Cameron
Amy	Daniel
Emily	Liam
Chloe	Jamie
Olivia	Kyle

Most Popular Names in Spain

Female	Male
Lucia	Alejandro
Maria	Daniel
Paula	Pablo
Laura	David
Claudia	Adrian
Irene	Alvaro
Marta	Javier
Alba	Sergio
Sara	Hugo
Carla	Diego

Most Popular Names in Sweden

Female	Male
Wilma	William
Maja	Lucas
Ella	Elias
Emma	Oscar
Julia	Hugo
Alice	Viktor
Alva	Filip
Linnea	Erik
Ida	Emil
Ebba	Isak

Most Popular Names in the U.S.

Female	Male
Emily	Jacob
Isabella	Michael
Emma	Ethan
Ava	Joshua
Madison	Daniel
Sophia	Christopher
Olivia	Anthony
Abigail	William
Hannah	Matthew
Elizabeth	Andrew

Names from Canadian Ethnic Origins

Canadians are proud of their heritage, no matter what their origins may be. If you're interested in giving your baby a name that reflects your heritage, the following lists include names from the fifteen most common ethnic origins in Canada, as identified by Statistics Canada's 2006 Census. You'll find even more names from these origins—and dozens of other origins—in the Girls' Names (page 81) and Boys' Names (page 235) sections.

English—21% of the population

Female	Male
Addison	Alfie
Ashley	Ashton
Beverly	Baxter
Britany	Blake
Cady	Chip
Chelsea	Cody
Ellen	Dawson
Evelyn	Edward
Hailey	Franklin
Holly	Gordon
Hope	Harry
Janet	Jamison
Jill	Jeffrey
Julie	Jeremy
Leigh	Lane
Maddie	Maxwell
Millicent	Ned
Paige	Parker
Piper	Rodney
Robin	Scott
Sally	Slade
Scarlet	Ted
Shelby	Tucker
Sigourney	Wallace
Twyla	William

French—16% of the population

Female	Male
Angelique	Adrien
Annette	Alexandre
Aubrey	Andre
Belle	Antoine
Camille	Christophe
Charlotte	Donatien
Christelle	Edouard
Cosette	François
Desiree	Gage
Estelle	Guillaume
Gabrielle	Henri
Genevieve	Jacques
Juliette	Jean
Jolie	Leroy
Lourdes	Luc
Margaux	Marc
Maribel	Marquis
Michelle	Philippe
Monique	Pierre
Nicole	Quincy
Paris	Remy
Raquel	Russel
Salina	Sébastien
Sydney	Stéphane
Yvonne	Sylvian

Scottish—15% of the population

Female	Male
Aili	Adair
Ailsa	Alastair
Ainsley	Angus
Berkley	Boyd
Blair	Bret
Camden	Caelan
Connor	Cameron
Christal	Dougal
Davonna	Duncan
Elspeth	Geordan
Greer	Gregor
Isela	Henderson
Jeana	Ian
Jinny	Kennan
Keita	Kenzie
Kelsea	Lennox
Leslie	Leslie
Maisie	Macaulay
Marjie	Malcolm
Mckenzie	Morgan
Mhairie	Perth
Paisley	Ronald
Rhona	Seumas
Roslyn	Stratton
Tavie	Tavish

Irish—14% of the population

Female	Male
Aileen	Aidan
Alanna	Brenden
Blaine	Clancy
Breanna	Desmond
Brigt	Donovan
Carlin	Eagan
Colleen	Flynn
Dacia	Garret
Dierdre	Grady
Erin	Keegan
Fallon	Keenan
Ilene	Kevin
Kaitlin	Liam
Keara	Logan
Kelly	Mahon
Kyleigh	Makenzie
Maura	Nevin
Maureen	Nolan
Moira	Owen
Quincy	Phinean
Raleigh	Quinn
Reagan	Reilly
Sinead	Ryan
Sloane	Seamus
Taryn	Sedric

German—10% of the population

Female	Male
Adelaide	Adler
Amelia	Adolf
Christa	Arnold
Edda	Bernard
Elke	Claus
Elsbeth	Conrad
Emma	Derek
Frederica	Dieter
Giselle	Dustin
Gretchen	Frederick
Heidi	Fritz
Hetta	Gerald
Hilda	Harvey
Ida	Johan
Johana	Karl
Katrina	Lance
Klarise	Louis
Lisele	Milo
Lorelei	Philipp
Margret	Roger
Milia	Roland
Monika	Sigmund
Reynalda	Terrell
Velma	Ulrich
Wanda	Walter

Italian—5% of the population

Female	Male
Adrianna	Adriano
Bianca	Alberto
Camila	Alessandro
Capri	Antonino
Carlita	Carlo
Chiara	Dante
Ciana	Dino
Clarice	Domenico
Contessa	Edoardo
Fiorella	Emilio
Francesca	Enzo
Gabriela	Federico
Giovanna	Flavio
Giulia	Gian
Graziella	Giorgio
Lucia	Giuseppe
Lucrezia	Leonardo
Marietta	Lucio
Mia	Marco
Nicola	Octavio
Patrizia	Paolo
Rosetta	Pietro
Teresina	Rafael
Valentia	Romeo
Zola	Salvatore

Chinese—4% of the population

Female	Male
An	Chen
Bo	Cheung
Chi	Chi
Chulua	Chung
Hua	De
Jun	Dewei
Lee	Fai
Lian	Gan
Lien	Guotin
Lin	Ho
Ling	Hu
Mani	Jin
Martim	Keung
Meiying	Kong
Nuwa	Lei
Ping	Li
Shu	Liang
Syá	On
Tao	Park
Tu	Po Sin
Ushi	Quon
Xiang	Shing
Xiu Mei	Tung
Yang	Wing
Yen	Yu

North American Indian—4% of the population

Female	Male
Aiyana	Ahanu
Cherokee	Anoki
Dakota	Bly
Dena	Delsin
Halona	Demothi
Heta	Elan
Imala	Elsu
Izusa	Etu
Kachina	Hakan
Kanda	Huslu
Kiona	Inteus
Leotie	Istu
Magena	Iye
Netis	Jolon
Nina	Knoton
Olathe	Lenno
Oneida	Mingan
Sakuna	Motega
Sora	Muraco
Taima	Neka
Tala	Nodin
Utina	Pawin
Wyanet	Sahale
Wyoming	Songan
Yenene	Wingi

Ukrainian—4% of the population

Female	Male
Akalena	Aleksandr
Alyona	Andrij
Aneta	Bohdan
Anichka	Bohomir
Ekaterina	Borysko
Elena	Burian
Galechka	Chtoma
Galina	Danya
Galyunja	Evgeni
Halyna	Fadeyushka
Inga	Fedir
Inna	Gennadi
Irisha	Hadeon
Ivanna	Harasym
Katya	Ilko
Kejan	Ivas
Klarsa	Jakiv
Palahna	Josyp
Tanechka	Juriy
Tatjana	Lyaksandro
Tomochka	Osip
Valechka	Samiilo
Valyusha	Slavo
Victoriya	Svietlana
Yeva	Yuri

Dutch—3% of the population

Female	Male
Aleene	Adriaan
Aleida	Andries
Anouk	Bartel
Carolien	Caspar
Catharina	Deman
Elke	Diederik
Evelien	Gerrit
Floortje	Govert
Godelieve	Hendrick
Hendrika	Jaan
Hester	Jilt
Janneke	Joost
Jonanneke	Joris
Katelijn	Jurrien
Katrijn	Kees
Liesbeth	Kerstan
Loris	Klef
Mariel	Kort
Mena	Laurens
Minikin	Maarten
Sanne	Pieter
Trudel	Ramond
Tryne	Schuyler
Viona	Skelton
Willemijn	Zeeman

Polish—3% of the population

Female	Male
Ania	Andros
Aniela	Andrzej
Anka	Aurek
Bryga	Bronislaw
Dalya	Cerek
Ela	Crystek
Elizaveta	Danek
Elka	Dawid
Gita	Dobry
Imber	Garek
Jasia	Gwidon
Jula	Heniek
Kasia	Iwan
Krysta	Janek
Macia	Jedrek
Manka	Karol
Morela	Krzysztof
Nata	Liuz
Otylia	Machas
Pela	Marcin
Tola	Mateusz
Waleria	Patek
Wera	Pawel
Zali	Szczepan
Zusa	Tomasz

East Indian—3% of the population

Female	Male
Aditi	Ajay
Adya	Amandeep
Aja	Amir
Amlika	Amritpal
Anala	Anoop
Ananda	Gagan
Baka	Gurdeep
Bakula	Harjot
Bel	Harpreet
Chandani	Harvir
Daru	Jaspal
Deva	Jaspreet
Gagandeep	Málik
Ganesa	Mandeep
Gurpreet	Noor
Hara	Onkar
Mandeep	Palash
Navdeep	Paramesh
Ramandeep	Pavit
Sharday	Purdy
Sherika	Raheem
Simran	Rajah
Sukhdeep	Sandeep
Thanh	Sundeep
Tosha	Vijay

Russian—2% of the population		Welsh—1% of the population		Filipino—1% of the population	
Female	**Male**	**Female**	**Male**	**Female**	**Male**
Alena	Alexi	Beranne	Bevan	Amihan	Adan
Annika	Christoff	Bronwyn	Bowen	Bituin	Agapito
Breasha	Dimitri	Carys	Broderick	Chesa	Bagwis
Duscha	Egor	Deryn	Bryce	Dakila	Balagtas
Galina	Feliks	Enid	Caddock	Dalisay	Bayani
Irina	Fyodor	Guinevere	Cairn	Daraga	Dakila
Katina	Gena	Gwendolyn	Davis	Divata	Datu
Katia	Gyorgy	Gwyneth	Dylan	Erlat	Fermin
Lelya	Igor	Idelle	Eoin	Hilaria	Gwapo
Liolya	Ilya	Isolde	Gareth	Imee	Hagibis
Marisha	Iosif	Linette	Gavin	Ligaya	Heherson
Masha	Ivan	Mab	Griffith	Liwanag	Huyla
Natasha	Kolya	Meghan	Howell	Liwayway	Igme
Natalia	Leonid	Meredith	Jestin	Lualhati	Jejomar
Nikita	Maxim	Olwen	Kynan	Luzviminda	Kalinga
Olena	Michail	Owena	Lewis	Maganda	Kidlat
Orlenda	Panas	Rhiannon	Llewellyn	Mahal	Lauro
Raisa	Pasha	Rhonda	Lloyd	Malaya	Luzvimindo
Sasha	Pavel	Ronelle	Maddock	Malea	Mabait
Shura	Pyor	Rowena	Price	Marikit	Magtanggol
Svetlana	Sacha	Sulwen	Rhett	Marilag	Makisig
Tanya	Sergei	Teagan	Rhys	Mutya	Ramil
Valera	Valeri	Vanora	Tristan	Ofelyn	Rizalino
Yekaterina	Viktor	Wenda	Vaughn	Sampaguita	Rommel
Yelena	Vladimir	Wynne	Wren	Tala	Rosito

The Impressions Names Make

Consciously or unconsciously, we all create pictures or impressions when we hear certain names. These impressions come from images we absorb from the mass media as well as from personal experience. You may think of voluptuous femininity when you hear the name Marilyn—until you think of Marilyn your neighbor with the ratty bathrobe, curlers, and a cigarette dangling from her mouth.

Over the years, researchers have been fascinated by this question of the "real" meanings of names and the effect those impressions can have on a child's life. If people think someone named Alissa is charming, does that influence a girl named Alissa to become charming? If people imagine someone named Randy is loud, does that mean a boy named Randy will be loud? Experts agree that names don't guarantee instant success or certain failure, but they do affect self-images, influence relationships with others, and help (or hinder) success in work and school. For that reason, it's important to pick a name that has a positive impression so it gives your child a head start in life.

I surveyed over 100,000 parents about the impressions names make. Results of this survey are presented in my book, *The New Baby Name Survey*. It details the images people associate with nearly 1800 popular and uncommon names. The following are lists of boys' and girls' names that were found to have particular image associations. To learn more about the impressions people create for each name, be sure to check out the book.

Arty

Female	Male
Dena	August
Frida	Dominic
Gillian	Timothy
Jenay	
Lia	
Mia	
Odera	
Taryn	
Veda	
Zola	

Athletic

Female	Male
Callie	Carrick
Jodi	Chad
Martina	Jerome
Nike	Tommy

Beautiful

Female

Alisha, Alyssa, Bonita, Chantal, Chaya, Claire, Clara, Ebony, Ella, Estelle, Gabriella, Harmony, Jana, Jillian, Jolie, Kali

Beautiful (cont.)

Female

Kayla, Lilah, Maddie, Mallory, Michaela, Morgan, Nailah, Raquel, Selena, Stella, Sydney, Tyra

Blond

Female	Male
Blythe	Ken
Caitlin	Tyler
Cassidy	
Natalie	
Nicolette	

Calm

Female	Male
Belinda	Austin
Charlotte	
Iolanthe	
Lynette	
Patrice	
Patricia	
Rosalyn	
Serena	

Charming

Female	Male
Alissa	Gabe
Babette	Hayden

Charming (cont.)

Female	Male
Charisma	Julian
Darla	Nicholas
Diane	Oliver
	Omar
	Rhett
	Rodrigo
	Steven
	Thaddeus

Cheerful

Female	Male
Amanda	Dustin
Autumn	Dylan
Becca	Kelly
Betsy	Ramon
Bliss	Sam
Britany	Tanner
Cheyenne	
Daisy	
Doris	
Dottie	
Emma	
Florida	
Glenda	
Jenny	
Lila	
Lulu	
Marjorie	
Montana	
Olivia	
Shirley	
Stormy	
Summer	
Sunny	
Sunshine	
Taylor	

Cheerful (cont.)

Female

Terri, Toni

Compassionate

Female	Male
Breena	Bryson
Elizabeth	Gavin
Grace	Hunter
Maire	Jonah
Maxine	
Rhiannon	
Thea	
Virginia	

Confident

Female	Male
Andrea	Abram
Antonia	Carson
Ava	Hugh
Bianca	Rico
Cannyn	Simba
Judith	
Koren	
Lonna	
Maura	
Michelle	
Reese	
Regina	
Tatum	
Torie	

Cranky

Female	Male
Doreen	Grover
Fleta	Leroy
Myrna	Wayne

Cranky (cont.)

Female
Prudence
Rhea
Sharon

Male
Wilson

Cute

Female
Alice
Brenna
Evie
Katelyn
Katy
Mindy
Molly

Male
Cory

Dark Haired

Female
Alexandria
Carmen
Demi
Hazel
Jocelyn
Phylicia
Sonya

Male
Arturo
Santos
Sergio
Vince

Driven

Female
Greta
Hanna
Iman
Ingrid
Jaclyn
Josephine
Katherine
Lane
Octavia
Roma
Sarina

Male
Douglas
Garrett
Lamar
Raheem
Vladimir

Driven (cont.)

Female
Shonda
Suzanne
Vanessa

Elegant

Female
Audrey
Cora
Eleanor
Helene
Julianne
Katarina
Verena

Male
Alden
Benson
Grayson

Friendly

Female
Adelaide
Akiko
Amy
Becky
Capri
Carina
Danica
Dee Dee
Denise
Dolly
Jaime
Jasmine
Jelena
Kari
Katina
Lauren
Lindsey
Lynn
Maisie
Marcy
Nadia

Male
Adriel
Brant
Breck
Casper
Duncan
Kenley
Kenneth
Leon
Lonnie
Lyle
Ty
Will

Friendly (cont.)

Female
Norell
Rita
Savanna
Sophia
Sue
Susannah

Funny

Female
Angie
Bridget
Celeste
Fran
Janine

Male
Alec
Asher
Hilario
Hugo
Humphrey
Leif
Monty
Nathan
Terry
Vaughn
Wilbert

Goofy

Female
Kimmy
Mickie
Sherry
Zizi
Zoe

Male
Archie
Carl
Chandler
Corey
Darren
Eddie
Elmo
Gordon
Luis
Ollie
Poni
Sammy

Handsome

Male
Antoine
Braden
Brian
Collin
Devin
Evan
Fabio
Jackson
Jason
Nick
Nigel
Raphael
Taylor
Tristan

Intelligent

Female
Amelia
Cathleen
Clare
Eileen
Eldora
Gretchen
Iris
Jean
Jennifer
Justine
Kass
Larissa
Lina
Marit
Nancy
Nevaeh
Nyssa
Paula
Paulette
Sierra

Male
Aaron
Abraham
Armen
Avery
Barak
Barton
Brady
Carter
Charles
Colin
Constantine
Deangelo
Donald
Emery
Franklin
Garrison
Harry
Irving
Isaac
Kadar

Intelligent (cont.)

Female: Tatiana, Therese, Trinity

Male: Kane, Keelan, Lionel, Lloyd, Marion, Maxwell, Mervin, Myles, Neal, Noel, Owen, Phineas, Rashad, Rick, Sebastian, Sheldon, Soloman, Theodore, Todd, Wood

Kind

Female: Abigail, Ali, Angela, Anna, Annette, Aubrey, Bernadette, Beth, Britta, Caley, Chavi, Christina, Claudia, Deirdre

Male: Adon, Carmel, Charlie, Chris, Daryl, Eric, Fred, Jay, Jimmy, Joe, Lorne, Mateo, Paul, Reggie

Kind (cont.)

Female: Della, Dominique, Dorothy, Eve, Francine, Hermosa, Irene, Ivy, Janna, Juliana, Kacey, Karen, Kathleen, Kona, Marietta, Megan, Mimi, Miriam, Rosa, Serenity, Shelly, Siobhan, Tisha

Male: Robert, Rodney, Stevie, Trevor

Loud

Female: Carla, Carlene, Kitra, Krystal, Lindsay, Marcia, Mercedes, Nidia, Priscilla, Rachael, Wanda

Male: Geraldo, Jan, Jibril, Randy, Regis, Steve, Tom, Zeke

Macho

Male: Alfonso, Beau, Fernando, Hector, Rocky, Steel

Female:

Perky

Female: Allie, Ashley, Christa, Cicely, Cynthia, Dani, Jeri, Judy, Kanika, Katie, Kelly, Kim, Marilyn, Piper, Polly, Stephanie, Suzette, Suzie, Taffy, Tasha, Tierney, Tina, Trish, Trista, Vivian

Male: Bailey, Jules

Nerdy

Female: Adele, Eliza

Male: Albert, Arnie, Bart, Cornelius, Dennis, Elvin, Flynn, Gideon, Kenny, Larry, Marvin, Melvin, Norman, Oswald, Preston, Quintin, Ross, Stuart, Warren, Wilbur

Old

Female: Ada, Agatha, Agnes, Beatrice, Bernice, Beverly, Blanche, Edith, Ester, Heloise, Irma, Mabel, Maureen, Odele, Winifred

Male: Dan, Earl, Eldon, Lincoln, Maurice, Orson, Otis, Roger, Senior

Popular

Female	Male
Alicia	Andre
Cadence	Dale
Candace	Jayden
Casey	Jeremy
Jackie	King
Kaylee	Mike
Mandy	Scott
Shanna	
Sheena	
Shoshana	
Tricia	
Winona	

Prim

Female
Adeline
Alexandra
Angelique
Blair
Isabella
Kristen
Marsha
Norma

Quiet

Female	Male
Amber	Fynn
Aolani	Bern
Bette	Fletcher
Clementine	Harold
Cordelia	Hubert
Ela	Ike
Enid	Kim
Gwendolyn	Mandek
Helen	Nodin
Jody	Peter
Laurel	Sullivan

Quiet (cont.)

Female	Male
Lillian	Tariq
Meka	Trenton
Rhoda	Zedekiah
Riona	
Romola	
Sofia	
Sylvana	

Rich

Female	Male
Caitlyn	Allen
Evelyn	Bartholomew
Leigh	Beaman
Madeline	Edward
Monique	Gilbert
Sable	Mason
	Park
	Parker
	Sinclair
	Sutherland
	Weston

Sexy

Female	Male
Alexis	Brad
Brigitte	Marc
Chloe	Paolo
Lana	
Simone	

Shy

Female	Male
Akina	Chuck
Aubrey	Elton
Colleen	Lenny
Donna	Marcel
Emily	Skipper

Shy (cont.)

Female	Male
Gail	Tymon
Ghita	
Kalare	
Lizina	
Mariel	
Marta	
Mauve	
Mead	
Myra	
Nadine	
Nia	
Nora	
Othelia	
Patience	
Qadira	

Snobby

Female	Male
Anais	Alcott
Buffy	Ballard
Delia	Barrett
Erica	Basil
Italia	Brandon
Jessamine	Edmund
Margot	Kipp
Meredith	Palmer
	Percy
	Pierece
	Scotty
	Thornton
	Upton

Strong

Female	Male
Aretha	Angelo
Lilith	Axel
Lorena	Darrion
Pavla	Gage

Strong (cont.)

Female	Male
Thema	Heath
Zelia	Kent
	Kiros
	Lorenzo
	Nolan
	Roscoe
	Sherman
	Vinny

Sweet

Female	Male
Adora	Ace
Adrienne	Aubrey
Allison	Ben
Baka	Bruce
Belle	Buddy
Bethany	Drew
Briana	Francis
Callidora	Justin
Camille	Luther
Cheryl	Michael
Corinne	Ralph
Diana	Tim
Ellen	Tomlin
Ellie	Tucker
Faith	
Ginny	
Hannah	
Holly	
Jill	
Kyla	
Kyra	
Leandra	
Louisa	
Natalia	
Petula	
Sabina	
Shelby	

26

Talented

Female	Male
Aria	Forrest
Marley	Elvis
	Ephraim
	Marcus
	Marshall
	Pascale

Talkative

Female	Male
Carly	Carlos
Chiara	
Destiny	
Gaby	
Kalinda	
Kaliska	
Kristi	
Lawanda	
Mary Ellen	

Wild

Female	Male
Avril	Chance
Chiquita	Cole
Janis	Cooper
Liza	Gerard
Loretta	Kelsey
Margarita	
Sage	
Shannon	
Stacia	

Witty

Female	Male
Barbara	Cedric
Lucille	Guy
	Ron
	Shakir

Names of Notable Canadians

What inspires parents to name their child after someone? Many people name their baby after special relatives, but others look beyond their family to find inspiring namesakes. Some sports buffs name their children after legendary athletes, and some bookworms name their children after their favorite authors. Here are several lists featuring famous Canadians from movies and TV, literature, music, sports, and other areas of interest. You may want to focus on your favorite areas to find a special namesake, or you may want to simply browse each list for interesting names. (To learn more about choosing a name with special meaning, check out the "How to Pick a Name You and Your Baby Will Like" feature on page 3.)

Movies and TV

Movie Stars

Female	Male
Carrie-Anne (Moss)	Anthony (Sherwood)
Catherine (O'Hara)	Barry (Pepper)
Deanna (Durbin)	Christopher (Plummer)
Elisha (Cuthbert)	Corey (Haim)
Fay (Wray)	Dan (Aykroyd)
Fiona (Reid)	Donald (Sutherland)
Genevieve (Bujold)	Gene (Lockhart)
Gloria (Reuben)	Glenn (Ford)
Jackie (Burroughs)	Harold (Russell)
Jayne (Eastwood)	Jack (Carson)
Joy (Coghill)	Jason (Priestley)
Kate (Nelligan)	Jay (Silverheels)
Margot (Kidder)	Jim (Carrey)
Marie (Dressier)	John (Candy)
Mary (Pickford)	Keanu (Reeves)
Meg (Tilly)	Leslie (Nielsen)
Neve (Campbell)	Lou (Jacobi)
Norma (Shearer)	Mike (Myers)
Rachel (McAdams)	Peter (Aykroyd)
Rae Dawn (Chong)	Rick (Moranis)
Ruby (Keeler)	Ryan (Gosling)
Sarah (Polley)	Scott (Speedman)
Sharon (Acker)	Tom (Green)
Susan (Clark)	Walter (Huston)
Wendy (Crewson)	William (Shatner)

Comedians

Female and Male

Bruce (McCulloch)	
Caroline (Rhea)	
Catherine (O'Hara)	
Dan (Aykroyd)	
Dave (Foley)	
David (Steinberg)	
Frank (Shuster)	
Howie (Mandel)	
John (Candy)	
Johnny (Wayne)	
Kevin (McDonald)	
Leslie (Nielsen)	
Lorne (Michaels)	
Luba (Goy)	
Martin (Short)	
Mary (Walsh)	
Mike (Myers)	
Norm (MacDonald)	
Phil (Hartman)	
Rich (Little)	
Rick (Moranis)	
Samantha (Bee)	
Sandra (Shamas)	
Tom (Green)	
Tommy (Chong)	

Directors

Female and Male

Anne (Wheeler)
Arthur (Hiller)
Bonnie (Sherr Klein)
Christopher (Newton)
Claude (Jutra)
Daniel (Petrie)
David (Cronenberg)
Deepa (Mehta)
Denys (Arcand)
Diana (Leblanc)
Diane (Dupuy)
Donna (Feore)
Edward (Dmytryk)
George (Dunning)
Ivan (Reitman)
James (Cameron)
Jean (Gascon)
Jennifer (de Silva)
John (Hirsch)
Judith (Crawley)
Léa (Pool)
Mack (Sennett)
Norman (Jewison)
Richard (Monette)
Ted (Kotcheff)

TV Stars and Personalities

Female	Male
Camilla (Scott)	Al (Waxman)
Emily (VanCamp)	Alan (Thicke)
Erica (Durance)	Alex (Trebek)
Gabrielle (Miller)	Brendan (Fraser)
Helen (Shaver)	Chris (Potter)
Helene (Winston)	Conrad (Bain)
Janet (Wright)	Donnelly (Rhodes)
Jennifer (Dale)	Eric (McCormack)
Jessica (Steen)	Eugene (Levy)
Jill (Hennessy)	Fred (Ewanuick)
Julie (Khaner)	Gordon (Pinsent)
June (Havoc)	Harvey (Atkin)
Kim (Cattrall)	James (Doohan)
Megan (Follows)	Kiefer (Sutherland)
Michelle (Latimer)	Lorne (Greene)
Nancy (Robertson)	Martin (Short)
Nia (Vardalos)	Matt (Frewer)
Pamela (Anderson)	Matthew (Perry)
Rachel (Blanchard)	Michael (J. Fox)
Rosemary (Forsyth)	Mike (Myers)
Sandra (Oh)	Monty (Hall)
Sara (Botsford)	Paul (Gross)
Shirley (Douglas)	Phil (Hartman)
Vanessa (Lengies)	Raymond (Burr)
Yvonne (De Carlo)	Tommy (Chong)

News Anchors

Female	Male
Alison (Smith)	Bernard (Derome)
Anne (Petrie)	Bill (Haugland)
Barbara (Frum)	Don (Newman)
Betty (Kennedy)	Earl (Cameron)
Carole (MacNeil)	Evan (Solomon)
Céline (Galipeau)	Gordon (Sinclair)
Diana (Swain)	Hal (Yerxa)
Hana (Gartner)	Harvey (Kirck)
Heather (Hiscox)	Henry (Champ)
Jacquie (Perrin)	Hudson (Mack)
Kate (Wheeler)	Keith (Morrison)
Keri (Adams)	Kevin (Newman)
Lisa (LaFlamme)	Knowlton (Nash)
Lynne (Russell)	Larry (Henderson)
Marci (Ien)	Lloyd (Robertson)
Mary Lou (Finlay)	Lorne (Saxberg)
Merella (Fernandez)	Mark (Kelley)
Monita (Rajpal)	Max (Keeping)
Pamela (Wallin)	Mike (Duffy)
Robin (Gill)	Morley (Safer)
Sandie (Rinaldo)	Peter (Jennings)
Tara (Nelson)	Robert (MacNeil)
Thalia (Assuras)	Sheldon (Turcott)
Valerie (Pringle)	Stephen (Andrew)
Wendy (Mesley)	Tony (Parsons)

Stage Stars

Female	Male
Alexis (Smith)	Arthur (Hill)
Beatrice (Lillie)	Barry (Morse)
Catherine (McKinnon)	Berton (Churchill)
Charmion (King)	Bob (Frazer)
Colleen (Dewhurst)	Brent (Carver)
Cynthia (Dale)	Bruce (Gray)
Diane (D'Aquila)	Christopher (Plummer)
Eva (Tanguay)	Colm (Feore)
Fifi (D'Orsay)	Donovan (King)
Frances (Hyland)	Douglas (Campbell)
Jane (Mallett)	Duncan (Regehr)
Joanna (Gleason)	Eric (Peterson)
Kate (Reid)	Graham (Abbey)
Lally (Cadeau)	Gratien (Gélinas)
Linda (Thorson)	Hume (Cronyn)
Lynne (Griffin)	John (Colicos)
Marie (Dressler)	Lorne (Cardinal)
Martha (Henry)	Louis (Negin)
Maude (Eburne)	Nicholas (Pennell)
Moya (O'Connell)	Raymond (Massey)
Roberta (Maxwell)	Sean (McCann)
Sheila (McCarthy)	Tom (Kneebone)
Susan (Coyne)	Victor (Garber)
Yvette (Brind'Amour)	Walter (Huston)
	William (Hutt)

Literature

Authors

Female	Male
Adele (Wiseman)	Alberto (Manguel)
Anne (Hébert)	Alistair (MacLeod)
Barbara (Gowdy)	Arthur (Hailey)
Carol (Shields)	Bruce (Hutchison)
Charlotte (Vale Allen)	C. P. (Stacey)
Constance (Beresford-Howe)	David (Adams Richards)
Cora (Taylor)	Guy (Vanderhaeghe)
Dorothy (Livesay)	Hugh (MacDonald)
Elizabeth (Smart)	James (Powell)
Elspeth (Cameron)	John (Robert Colombo)
Gabrielle (Roy)	Louis-Honore (Fréchette)
Janette (Oke)	Mordecai (Richler)
Jean (Little)	Paul (Quarrington)
June (Callwood)	Raymond (Fraser)
Kelly (Armstrong)	Robert (Munsch)
Lucy (Maude Montgomery)	Roch (Carrier)
Lynn (Crosbie)	Rohinton (Mistry)
Margaret (Atwood)	Rudy (Wiebe)
Marian (Engel)	Saul (Bellow)
Marie-Claire (Blais)	Silver (Donald Cameron)
Mavis (Gallant)	Sinclair (Ross)
Maxine (Trottier)	Thomas (Head Raddall)
Mazo (de la Roche)	Tim (Wynne-Jones)
Miriam (Toews)	W. O. (Mitchell)
Tanya (Huff)	W. P. (Kinsella)

Poets

Female and Male

A. H. (Reginald Buller)
A. M. (Klein)
Al (Purdy)
Anne (Hecht)
Annie (Louisa Walker)
Archibald (Lampman)
Bill (Bissett)
Bliss (Carman)
Caroline (Hayward)
Douglas (Lochhead)
Duncan (Campbell Scott)
E. Pauline (Johnson Tekahionwake)
Earle (Birney)
Frederick (George Scott)
George (Woodcock)
Gwendolyn (MacEwen)
Irving (Layton)
James (McIntyre)
Marjorie (Pickthall)
Raymond (Knister)
Robert (Priest)
Rosanna (Eleanor Leprohon)
Stephen (Leacock)
Susan (Ioannou)
William (Wilfred Campbell)

Journalists

Female and Male

Allan (Fotheringham)
Barrie (Wallace Zwicker)
Betty (Kennedy)
Camilla (Di Giuseppe)
Charles (Lynch)
Claude (Ryan)
Clyde (Gilmour)
Conrad (Black)
Douglas (Mason Fisher)
Gillis (Purcell)
Gwyn ("Jocko" Thomas)
J. D. (MacFarlane)
Joe (Schlesinger)
June (Callwood)
Morley (Safer)
Peter (Jennings)
Pierre (Berton)
Richard (Doyle)
Robert (MacNeil)
Steve (Armitage)
Stuart (Keate)
Sue (Gardner)
Tara (Singh Hayer)
Terry (Mosher)
Valerie (Pringle)

Fine Arts

Artists

Female

Asheyak (Kenojuak)
Betty (Goodwin)
Christine (Montague)
Daphne (Odjig)
Emily (Carr)
Florence (Carlyle)
Francine (Bradette)
Gigi (Hoeller)
Isabel (McLaughlin)
Joan (Pain)
Joyce (Wieland)
Kim (Ondaatje)
Lilias (Torrance Newton)
Marian (Bantjes)
Martina (Shapiro)
Mary (Pratt)
Maya (Kulenovic)
Mona (Yousef)
Paula (Franzini)
Prudence (Reward)
Richelle (Nontell)
Sarah (Theophilus)
Shirley (Cheechoo)
Tracey (Costescu)
Yvonne (McKague-Housser)

Male

Alex (Cohlile)
Alexander (Young Jackson)
Arthur (Lismer)
Charles (Pachter)
Christopher (Pratt)
Clarence (Gagnon)
Cornelius (Krieghoff)
Edwin (Holgate)
Frank (Johnston)
Franklin (Carmichael)
Frederick (Varley)
Harold (Town)
Homer (Watson)
J. E. H. (MacDonald)
Jack (Shadbolt)
Jean-Paul (Riopelle)
Ken (Danby)
Lawren (Harris)
Lionel (LeMoine FitzGerald)
Michael (Snow)
Norval (Morrisseau)
Paul (Kane)
Robert (Bateman)
Tom (Thomson)
William (Kurelek)

Cartoonists

Female and Male

Albéric (Bourgeois)
Ben (Wicks)
Chester (Brown)
David (Sim)
Doug (Wright)
George (Feyer)
Graeme (MacKay)
Gregory (Gallant)
Hal (Foster)
J. D. (Frazer)
Joe (Shuster)
John (Wilson Bengough)
Len (Norris)
Lynn (Johnston)
Marie-Louise (Gay)
Paul (Szep)
Peter (Whalley)
Rand (Holmes)
Ryan (North)
Sandra (Bell-Lundy)
Scott (Ramsoomair)
Terry (Mosher)
Todd (McFarlane)
Walter (Ball)
Win (Mortimer)

Dancers

Female and Male

Annette (av Paul)
Brian (Macdonald)
Chan (Hon Goh)
Christopher (Gillis)
Denise (Fujiwara)
Edna (Malone)
Evelyn (Hart)
Frank (Augustyn)
Grant (Strate)
Jean-Marc (Genereux)
Karen (Kain)
Kimberley (Glasco)
Lois (Smith)
Louise (Lecavalier)
Margaret (Illman)
Margie (Gillis)
Marie (Chouinard)
Melissa (Hayden)
Patricia (Beatty)
Rex (Harrington)
René (Highway)
Shelagh (McKenna)
Vanessa (Harwood)
Veronica (Tennant)
Wendy (Arena)

Models

Female and Male

Andi (Muise)
Andrea (Muizelaar)
Andrew (Stetson)
Coco (Rocha)
Daria (Werbowy)
Debbie (Wong)
Ehrinn (Cummings)
Ève (Salvail)
Gabriel (Aubry)
Heather (Marks)
Irina (Lazareanu)
Julia (Dunstall)
Kevin (Zegers)
Linda (Evangelista)
Lisa (Cant)
Melyssa (Ford)
Monika (Schnarre)
Natasha (Henstridge)
Rebecca (Hardy)
Saira (Mohan)
Shalom (Harlow)
Stacey (McKenzie)
Tasha (Tilberg)
Tricia (Helfer)
Yasmin (Warsame)

Music

Singers

Female
Alannah (Myles)
Amanda (Marshall)
Anne (Murray)
Carole (Pope)
Catherine (McKinnon)
Céline (Dion)
Cookie (Rankin)
Deborah (Cox)
Diane (Dufresne)
Fiona (MacGillivray)
Holly (Cole)
Jully (Black)
K. D. (Lang)
Lois (Marshall)
Luba (Kowalchyk)
Marie (Denise Pelletier)
Mary (Rose-Anna Bolduc)
Michelle (Wright)
Monique (Leyrac)
Nelly (Furtado)
Rita (MacNeil)
Susan (Aglukark)
Tanya (Tagaq Gillis)
Toya (Alexis)
Véronique (Béliveau)

Male
Bernie (Toorish)
Bobby (Curtola)
Brad (Roberts)
Bryan (Adams)
Corrado ("Connie" Codarini)
David (Clayton-Thomas)
Ed (Robertson)
Frank (Busseri)
Geddy (Lee)
George (Evans)
Gino (Vannelli)
Gordon (Downie)
Hank (Snow)
Jimmy (Arnold)
John (Kay)
Kyp (Harness)
Louis (Quilico)
Nick (Gilder)
Paul (Anka)
Raffi (Cavoukian)
Raymond (Berthiaume)
Robert (Goulet)
Sebastian (Bach)
Steven (Page)
Wilf ("Montana Slim" Carter)

Singer/Songwriters

Female
Alanis (Morissette)
Anna (McGarrigle)
Avril (Lavigne)
Buffy (Sainte-Marie)
Carolyn (Dawn Johnson)
Carroll (Baker)
Chantal (Kreviazuk)
Connie (Kaldor)
Jann (Arden)
Jill (Barber)
Joni (Mitchell)
Julie (Doiron)
Kate (McGarrigle)
Kim (Bingham)
Kinnie (Starr)
Kristy (Thirsk)
Lisa (Brokop)
Maren (Ord)
Sarah (McLachlan)
Shania (Twain)
Shirley (Eikhard)
Sue (Foley)
Sylvia (Tyson)
Tara (MacLean)
Veda (Hille)

Male
Andy (Kim)
Bruce (Cockburn)
Burton (Cummings)
Charles (Thomas "Stompin' Tom" Connors)
Claude (Gauthier)
Corey (Hart)
Dan (Hill)
Daniel (Lanois)
Denny (Doherty)
Félix (Leclerc)
Gordon (Lightfoot)
Ian (Tyson)
Jimmy (Rankin)
Leonard (Cohen)
Matthew (Barber)
Neil (Young)
Oscar (Brand)
Robbie (Robertson)
Ron (Sexsmith)
Rufus (Wainwright)
Spencer (Krug)
Steve (Poltz)
Terry (Jacks)
Tom (Cochrane)
Travis (MacRae)

Musicians

Female

Beverly (Breckenridge)
Christina (Petrowska-Quilico)
Christine (Yoshikawa)
Diana (Krall)
Emily (Haines)
Evelyne (Datl)
Fallon (Bowman)
G. B. (Jones)
Ingrid (Jensen)
Jane (Bunnett)
Jennifer (Scott)
Joni (Mitchell)
Liona (Boyd)
Loreena (McKennitt)
Lorraine (Desmarais)
Melanie (Doane)
Melissa (Auf der Maur)
Natalie (MacMaster)
Ofra (Harnoy)
Renee (Rosnes)
Ruth (Lowe)
Sara (Quin)
Talena (Atfield)
Tegan (Quin)
Yati (Kathryn Root)

Male

Alex (Lifeson)
Ashley (Macisaac)
Brent (Fitz)
Dal (Richards)
Dan (Roberts)
Devin (Townsend)
Domenic (Troiano)
Garth (Hudson)
Guy (Lombardo)
Jeff (Healey)
John (Morris Rankin)
Kevin (Hearn)
Lenny (Breau)
Maynard (Ferguson)
Mitch (Dorge)
Morris ("Moe" Koffman)
Neil (Peart)
Norman (Byron "Dutch" Mason)
Oscar (Peterson)
Pat (Travers)
Paul (Schaffer)
Randy (Bachman)
Rick (Danko)
Rob (McConnell)
Stan (Rogers)

Classical Musicians

Female and Male

Alan (Monk)
Alexina (Louie)
Angela (Hewitt)
Ben (Heppner)
Catherine (Manoukian)
Emma (Albani)
Gilles (Tremblay)
Glenn (Gould)
Harold (Sumberg)
Harry (Somers)
James (Ehnes)
Jon Kimura (Parker)
Judith (Forst)
Lee (Kum-Sing)
Mario (Bernardi)
Maureen (Forrester)
Maurice (Zbriger)
Micheline (Coulombe Saint-Marcoux)
Peter (Oundjian)
Pierrette (Alarie)
Rex (Liu)
Richard (Margison)
Russell (Braun)
Teresa (Stratas)
Violet (Archer)

Sports

Hockey Players—1900s

Male

Art (Ross)
Arthur (Farrell)
Billy (McGimsie)
Bouse (Hutton)
Bruce (Stuart)
Didier (Pitre)
Edouard ("Newsy" Lalonde)
Ernie (Russell)
Fred ("Cyclone" Taylor)
Frederick (Whitcroft)
Georges (Vézina)
Harry (Trihey)
Hughie (Lehman)
Jack (Laviolette)
Jimmy (Gardner)
Joe (Hall)
Lester (Patrick)
Marty (Walsh)
Newsy (Lalonde)
Paddy (Moran)
Percy (LeSueur)
Riley (Hern)
Silas (Griffis)
Tom (Phillips)
Tommy (Smith)

Hockey Players—1910s

Male

Art (Ross)
Barney (Stanley)
Buck (Boucher)
Cy (Denneny)
Dick (Irvin)
Duke (Keats)
Eddie (Gerard)
Ernest ("Moose" Johnson)
Frank (Rankin)
Fred ("Steamer" Maxwell)
George (Richardson)
Georges (Vezina)
Gordon (Roberts)
Harold ("Bullet Joe" Simpson)
Harry (Hyland)
Herb (Gardiner)
Jack (Darragh)
Joe (Malone)
Lester (Patrick)
Reg (Noble)
Rusty (Crawford)
Scotty Davidson
Si (Griffis)
Sprague (Cleghorn)
Tommy (Gorman)

Hockey Players—1920s

Male

Albert ("Babe" Siebert)
Aurel (Joliat)
Bill (Cook)
Billy (Burch)
Cecil ("Babe" Dye)
Charlie (Gardiner)
Clarence ("Hap" Day)
Eddie (Shore)
Francis ("King" Clancy)
Frank (Fredrickson)
George (Hainsworth)
Gordon ("Phat" Wilson)
Harry (Oliver)
Harry (Watson)
Howie (Morenz)
Irvine ("Ace" Bailey)
Ivan ("Ching" Johnson)
Mervyn (Dutton)
Mickey (MacKay)
Nels (Stewart)
Ralph ("Cooney" Weiland)
Red (Homer)
Roy (Worters)
Sylvio (Mantha)
Wilfred ("Shorty" Green)

Hockey Players—1930s

Male

Alex (Connell)
Art (Coulter)
Aubrey ("Dit" Clapper)
Bill (Cowley)
Charlie (Conacher)
David ("Sweeney" Schriner)
Earl (Seibert)
Ebbie (Goodfellow)
Frank (Boucher)
Frederick ("Bun" Cook)
Gordon (Drillon)
Harvey ("Busher" Jackson)
Hector ("Toe" Blake)
Herbie (Lewis)
Joe (Primeau)
Lionel (Conacher)
Lynn (Patrick)
Marty (Barry)
Milt (Schmidt)
Neil (Colville)
Reginald ("Hooley" Smith)
Roy (Conacher)
Syd (Howe)
Syl (Apps)
Walter ("Turk" Broda)

Hockey Players—1940s

Male

Bill (Mosienko)
Bobby (Bauer)
Chuck (Rayner)
Clint (Smith)
Doug (Bentley)
Edgar (Laprade)
Elmer (Lach)
Emile (Bouchard)
Fernie (Flaman)
Gordie (Howe)
Harry ("Apple Cheeks" Lumley)
Hector ("Toe" Blake)
John ("Black Jack" Stewart)
Johnny (Bower)
Kenny (Reardon)
Maurice (Richard)
Max (Bentley)
Neil (Colville)
Roy (Conacher)
Sid (Abel)
Ted (Lindsay)
Teeder (Kennedy)
Turk (Broda)
Walter ("Babe" Pratt)
Woody (Dumart)

Hockey Players—1950s

Male

Alex (Delvecchio)
Allan (Stanley)
Andy (Bathgate)
Bernie (Geoffrion)
Bert (Olmstead)
Bob (Pulford)
Bryan (Hextall)
Doug (Harvey)
Frank (Mahovlich)
George (Armstrong)
Glenn (Hall)
Harry (Howell)
Henri (Richard)
Jacques (Plante)
Jean (Béliveau)
Johnny (Bucyk)
Leo (Boivin)
Leonard ("Red" Kelly)
Lorne ("Gump" Worsley)
Marcel (Pronovost)
Norm (Ullman)
Pierre (Pilote)
Terry (Sawchuk)
Tim (Horton)
Tom (Johnson)

Hockey Players—1960s

Male

Bernie (Parent)
Bobby (Orr)
Brad (Park)
Dave (Keon)
Dick (Duff)
Dickie (Moore)
Eddie (Giacomin)
Edward ("Terrible Ted" Green)
Gary (Bergman)
Gerry (Cheevers)
Jacques (Lemaire)
Jean (Beliveau)
Jean-Claude ("J.C." Tremblay)
Jim (Pappin)
John (McKenzie)
Pat (Stapleton)
Paul (Henderson)
Phil (Esposito)
Pierre (Pilote)
Rod (Gilbert)
Ron (Ellis)
Serge (Savard)
Stan (Mikita)
Ted (Harris)
Yvan (Cournoyer)

Hockey Players—1970s

Male

Bill (Barber)
Bill (Goldsworthy)
Bob (Gainey)
Bobby (Clarke)
Bryan (Trottier)
Clark (Gillies)
Daryl (Sittler)
Don (Awrey)
Gilbert (Perreault)
Gordon ("Red" Berenson)
Guy (Lafleur)
Reggie (Leach)
Jocelyn (Guevremont)
Ken (Dryden)
Lanny (McDonald)
Larry (Robinson)
Marcel (Dionne)
Mark (Messier)
Mike (Bossy)
Paul (Henderson)
Ray (Bourque)
Rick (Martin)
Steve (Shutt)
Tony (Esposito)
William ("Battlin' Billy" Smith)

Hockey Players—1980s

Male

Al (MacInnis)
Bernie (Federko)
Brendan (Shanahan)
Brett (Hull)
Dale (Hawerchuk)
Darryl (Sutter)
Denis (Potvin)
Ed (Belfour)
Grant (Fuhr)
Guy (Lapointe)
Joe (Sakic)
Larry (Murphy)
Mario (Lemieux)
Mark (Messier)
Michel (Goulet)
Mike (Bossy)
Pat (LaFontaine)
Patrick (Roy)
Paul (Coffey)
Ray (Bourque)
Rod (Langway)
Ron (Francis)
Steve (Yzerman)
Theoren (Fleury)
Wayne (Gretzky)

Hockey Players—1990s

Male

Adam (Foote)
Brian (Bellows)
Byron (Dafoe)
Chris (Pronger)
Christopher (Osgood)
Curtis (Joseph)
Daren (Puppa)
Denis (Savard)
Ed (Jovanovski)
Éric (Desjardins)
Eric (Lindros)
Jarome (Iginla)
Kirk (McLean)
Luc (Robitaille)
Mark (Recchi)
Martin (Brodeur)
Michael (Peca)
Mike (Vernon)
Owen (Nolan)
Paul (Kariya)
Rick (Tocchet)
Ryan (Smyth)
Scott (Niedermayer)
Simon (Gagne)
Theoren (Fleury)

Hockey Players—2000s

Male

Alexander (Steen)
Andrew (Raycroft)
Barret (Jackman)
Bradley (Richards)
Brian (Campbell)
Cam (Ward)
Dany (Heatley)
David (Perron)
Dion (Phaneuf)
Eric (Staal)
Jason (Spezza)
Jay (Bouwmeester)
Jonathan (Toews)
Jordan (Staal)
Kris (Letang)
Kyle (Wellwood)
Marc (Staal)
Paul (Stastny)
Rick (Nash)
Ryan (Getzlaf)
Sam (Gagner)
Shea (Weber)
Sydney (Crosby)
Taylor (Pyatt)
Todd (White)

Hockey Players

Female

Becky (Kellar)
Carla (Macleod)
Caroline (Ouellette)
Cassie (Campbell)
Charline (Labonté)
Cherie (Piper)
Cheryl (Pounder)
Colleen (Sostorics)
Danielle (Goyette)
Gillian (Apps)
Gina (Kingsbury)
Haley (Wickenheiser)
Jayna (Hefford)
Jennifer (Botterill)
Katie (Weatherston)
Kelly (Bechard)
Kim (St-Pierre)
Lori (Dupuis)
Manon (Rhéaume)
Meghan (Agosta)
Sarah (Vaillancourt)
Stacy (Wilson)
Tammy (Lee Shewchuk)
Therese (Brisson)
Vicky (Sunohara)

Baseball Players

Male

Aaron (Guiel)
Bill (Atkinson)
Chris (Reitsma)
Corey (Koskie)
Dick (Fowler)
Eric (Gagne)
Erik (Bedard)
Ferguson (Jenkins)
Jason (Bay)
Jeff (Zimmerman)
Jesse (Crain)
Joey (Votto)
Justin (Morneau)
Larry (Walker)
Matt (Stairs)
Nigel (Wilson)
Paul (Quantrill)
Pete (Laforest)
Reggie (Cleveland)
Rheal (Cormier)
Rich (Harden)
Russell (Martin)
Ryan (Dempster)
Scott (Mathieson)
Terry (Puhl)

Basketball Players	Football Players	Golfers	Soccer Players
Male	**Male**	**Female and Male**	**Female and Male**
Bill (Wennington)	Amis (Stukus)	Ada (Mackenzie)	Amber (Allen)
Bob (Houbregs)	Bronko (Nagurski)	Al (Balding)	Andrea (Neil)
Bobby (Croft)	Danny (Kepley)	Dan (Halldorson)	Atiba (Hutchinson)
Brian (Heaney)	Dave (Ridgeway)	Dave (Barr)	Bobby (Lenarduzzi)
Eli (Pasquale)	David (Sapunjis)	Dawn (Coe-Jones)	Charmaine (Hooper)
Ernie (Vandeweghe)	Gerry (James)	Florence (Harvey)	Christine (Sinclair)
Gerald (Kazanowski)	Jason (David)	Gail (Graham)	Dale (Mitchell)
Gino (Sovran)	Joe (Krol)	Gary (Cowan)	David (Edgar)
Hank (Biasatti)	Lionel (Conacher)	George (Knudson)	Dwayne (De Rosario)
Jamaal (Magloire)	Mark (Rypien)	Jennifer (Wyatt)	Jim (Brennan)
James (Naismith)	Mike (Vanderjagt)	Jim (Nelford)	Jimmy (Nicholl)
Jim (Zoet)	Nate (Burleson)	Jocelyne (Bourassa)	John (Catliff)
Joel (Anthony)	Normie (Kwong)	Judy (Sams)	Jonathan (de Guzman)
Lars (Hansen)	Peter (Dalla Riva)	Jules (Huot)	Julian (de Guzman)
Leo (Rautins)	Ray (Elgaard)	Keith (Alexander)	Kara (Lang)
Mike (Smrek)	Rocky (Dipietro)	Laurie (Kane)	Kevin (McKenna)
Norm (Baker)	Roger (Aldag)	Marlene (Streit)	Otto (Christman)
Rick (Fox)	Royal (Copeland)	Mike (Weir)	Owen (Hargreaves)
Ron (Crevier)	Rueben (Mayes)	Moe (Norman)	Paul (Stalter)
Samuel (Dalembert)	Shaun (Suisham)	Nick (Weslock)	Randy (Ragan)
Stan (Nantais)	Teyo (Johnson)	Richard (Zokol)	Rob (Friend)
Steve (Nash)	Tony (Gabriel)	Sandra (Post)	Ryan (Gyaki)
Stewart (Granger)	Troy (Westwood)	Sandy (Somerville)	Sophie (Schmidt)
Todd (MacCulloch)	Vince (Danielson)	Stan (Leonard)	Tomasz (Radzinski)
Trevor (C. Williams)	William (Zock)	Stephen (Ames)	Will (Johnson)

Auto Racers

Male

Al (Pease)
Bernie (Fedderly)
Billy (Kydd)
Craig (Fisher)
Dennis (Grant)
Earl (Ross)
Ed (Leavens)
Gary (Beck)
Gilles (Villeneuve)
Gordon (Jenner)
Greg (Moore)
Harvey (Lennox)
Jacques (Villeneuve)
Jean-Paul (Perusse)
Joe (Cheng)
John (Duff)
Ludwig (Heimrath, Jr.)
Norm (Lelliott)
Patrick (Carpentier)
Paul (Tracy)
Rollie (MacDonald)
Ron (Fellows)
Ross (de St. Croix)
Scott (Goodyear)
Taisto (Heinonen)

Boxers

Female and Male

Jeanine (Garside)
Arturo (Gatti)
Dale (Walters)
Dave (Hilton, Sr.)
Donovan (Ruddock)
Eddie (Carroll)
Eric (Lucas)
Gaétan (Hart)
George (Chuvalo)
Horace (Gwynne)
Jack (Delaney)
Jackie (Callura)
Jessica (Rakoczy)
Kara (Rheault)
Larry (Gains)
Lennox (Lewis)
Otis (Grant)
Sammy (Luftspring)
Shane (Sutcliffe)
Steve (Molitor)
Tommy (Burns)
Walter (Henry)
Wayne (Bourque)
Willie (DeWitt)
Yvon (Durelle)

Curlers

Female and Male

Brad (Gushue)
Cathy (King)
Chris (Schille)
Colleen (Jones)
Dave (Nedohin)
Don (Duguid)
Glenn (Howard)
Guy (Hemmings)
Jamie (Korab)
Jan (Betker)
Jean-Michel (Ménard)
Jeff (Stoughton)
Jenn (Hanna)
Kelly (Scott)
Kerry (Burtnyk)
Marcel (Rocque)
Marcia (Gudereit)
Mark (Dacey)
Mike (Harris)
Randy (Ferbey)
Sandra (Schmirler)
Scott (Patterson)
Sherry (Middaugh)
Suzanne (Gaudet)
Wayne (Middaugh)

Figure Skaters

Female and Male

Barbara (Underhill)
Barbara Ann (Scott)
Brian (Orser)
Cynthia (Phaneuf)
David (Pelletier)
Donald (Jackson)
Elizabeth (Manley)
Elvis (Stojko)
Emanuel (Sandhu)
Isabelle (Duchesnay)
Jamie (Salé)
Jeff (Buttle)
Josée (Chouinard)
Karen (Magnussen)
Kurt (Browning)
Lloyd (Eisler)
Maria (Jelinek)
Otto (Jelinek)
Paul (Martini)
Petra (Burka)
Robert (Paul)
Tanith (Belbin)
Tessa (Virtue)
Toller (Cranston)
Tracey (Wainman)

Skiers

Female and Male

Anne (Heggtveit)
Beckie (Scott)
Betsy (Clifford)
Dave (Murray)
David (Irwin)
Erik (Guay)
Francois (Bourque)
Gerry (Sorensen)
Horst (Bulau)
Jean-Luc (Brassard)
Jennifer (Heil)
Karen (Percy)
Kathy (Kreiner)
Ken (Read)
Kerrin (Lee-Gartner)
Laurie (Graham)
Liisa (Savijarvi)
Lucille (Wheeler)
Mélanie (Turgeon)
Nancy (Greene)
Pierre (Harvey)
Ross (Rebagliati)
Steve (Podborski)
Sue (Holloway)
Thomas (Grandi)

Speed Skaters

Female and Male

Angela (Cutrone)
Annie (Perreault)
Catherine (Priestner-Allinger)
Catriona (LeMay Doan)
Charles (Gorman)
Christine (Boudrias)
Cindy (Klassen)
Clara (Hughes)
Derrick (Campbell)
Erik (Bedard)
Francois (Drolet)
Francois-Louis (Tremblay)
Frank (Stack)
Gaétan (Boucher)
Jeremy (Wotherspoon)
Jonathan (Guilmette)
Justin (Warsylewicz)
Kevin (Scott)
Lela (Brooks)
Marc (Gagnon)
Mathieu (Turcotte)
Nathalie (Lambert)
Steven (Elm)
Susan (Auch)
Sylvie (Daigle)

Swimmers

Female and Male

Alex (Baumann)
Andrea (Nugent)
Anne (Ottenbrite)
Carolyn (Waldo)
Cindy (Nicholas)
Clay (Evans)
Cliff (Lumsdon)
Elaine (Tanner)
George (Hodgson)
Helen (Vanderburg)
Jessica (Deglau)
Karen (Clark)
Leslie (Cliff)
Marianne (Limpert)
Marilyn (Bell)
Mark (Tewksbury)
Michelle (Cameron)
Nancy (Ellen Garapick)
Phyllis (Dewar)
Ron (Jacks)
Sylvie (Fréchette)
Vicki (Keith)
Victor (Davis)
William (Mahony)
Winnie (Leuszler)

Track Athletes

Female and Male

Abby (Hoffman)
Angela (Bailey)
Ben (Johnson)
Bruny (Surin)
Chantal (Petitclerc)
Charmaine (Crooks)
Debbie (Brill)
Diane (Jones Konihowski)
Donovan (Bailey)
Duncan (McNaughton)
Ethel (Catherwood)
Fanny (Rosenfeld)
Glenroy (Gilbert)
Graham (Hood)
Greg (Joy)
Harry (Jerome)
Jacqueline (Gareau)
Jane (Bell)
Leah (Pells)
Mark (McCoy)
Mike (Smith)
Myrtle (Cook)
Robert (Esmie)
Tom (Longboat)
Tony (Sharpe)

Professional Wrestlers

Female and Male

Adam ("Edge" Copeland)
Bret ("The Hitman" Hart)
Chris (Benoit)
Christian (Cage)
Claude (Giroux)
Eric (Young)
Gail (Kim)
Gene (Kiniski)
Jacques (Rougeau)
Lance (Storm)
Larry ("Abdulla the Butcher" Shreve)
Owen (Hart)
Petey (Williams)
Raymond (Rougeau)
Rene (Dupree)
Robert (Roode)
Rocky (Johnson)
Roderick ("Rowdy Roddy" Piper)
Stu (Hart)
Sylvain (Grenier)
Tracy (Brooks)
Trish (Stratus)
Val (Venis)
William ("Whipper Billy Watson" Potts)
Yvon (Cormier)

Religion

Religious Figures

Female and Male

Aimee (Semple McPherson)
Albert (Lacombe)
Alexandre-Antonin (Taché)
Alexis (André)
Aloysius (Ambrozic)
André (Bessette)
Anthony (Daniel)
Aviel (Barclay)
Charles (Garnier)
David (Mainse)
Franklin (Pyles)
Gabriel (Lallemant)
Hugh (B. Brown)
Isaacs (Jogues)
Jean (de Brébeuf)
John (Taylor)
Kateri (Tekakwitha)
Lionel (Groulx)
Marguerite (Bourgeoys)
Marie-Marguerite (d'Youville)
Merlin (Lybbert)
Nathan (Eldon Tanner)
Noel (Chabanel)
Paul-Émile (Cardinal Léger)
Rene (Goupil)

History

Prime Ministers

Female and Male

Alexander (Mackenzie)
Arthur (Meighen)
Brian (Mulroney)
Charles (Joseph Clark)
Charles (Tupper)
Jean (Chrétien)
John (A. MacDonald)
John (Abbott)
John (Diefenbaker)
John (Thompson)
John (Turner)
Kim (Campbell)
Lester (B. Pearson)
Louis (St. Laurent)
Mackenzie (Bowell)
Paul (Martin)
Pierre (Elliott Trudeau)
Richard (Bennett)
Robert (Borden)
Stephen (Harper)
Wilfrid (Laurier)
William (Lyon Mackenzie King)

Politicians

Female	Male
Adrienne (Clarkson)	Allan (Studholme)
Agnes (Macphail)	Brock (Chisholm)
Audrey (McLaughlin)	Clarence ("C. D." Howe)
Barbara (McDougall)	Daniel (Roland Michener)
Beverley (McLachlin)	Ed (Broadbent)
Catine (Wilson)	Edward (Schreyer)
Catherine (Callbeck)	Charles (Fitzpatrick)
Deborah (Grey)	Francis (Hincks)
Ellen (Fairclough)	George-Étienne (Cartier)
Ethel (Blondin-Andrew)	Georges (Vanier)
Flora (MacDonald)	Henri (Bourassa)
Grace (MacInnis)	Jack (Layton)
Jeanne (Sauvé)	Joseph (Howe)
Joyce (Fairbairn)	Jules (Léger)
Judy (LaMarsh)	Lloyd (Axworthy)
Louise (Frechette)	Louis-Hippolyte (Lafontaine)
Marie (Thérèse Casgrain)	Louis-Joseph (Papineau)
Marion (Dewar)	Lucas (Stone)
Michaëlle (Jean)	Perrin (Beatty)
Monique (Bégin)	Pierre (Bourgault)
Muriel (McQueen Fergusson)	Ramon (Hnatyshyn)
Nellie (Cournoyea)	Robert (Baldwin)
Rosemary (Brown)	Roméo (LeBlanc)
Sharon (Carstairs)	Thomas (Bain)
Suzanne (Tremblay)	Tim (Buck)
	Vincent (Massey)

Supreme Court Justices

Female and Male

Antonio (Lamer)
Bertha (Wilson)
Beverley (McLachlin)
Bora (Laskin)
Brian (Dickson)
Charles (Fitzpatrick)
Francis (Alexander Anglin)
Frank (Iacobucci)
Gérald (Fauteux)
Henri (Elzéar Taschereau)
John (Robert Cartwright)
Louis (Henry Davies)
Louis (LeBel)
Louise (Charron)
Lyman (Poore Duff)
Marie (Deschamps)
Marshall (Rothstein)
Michel (Bastarache)
Morris (J. Fish)
Patrick (Kerwin)
Robert (Taschereau)
Rosalie (Abella)
Samuel (Henry Strong)
Thibaudeau (Rinfret)
William (Buell Richards)

Military Figures

Female and Male

Alan (Arnett McLeod)
Andrew (McNaughton)
Arthur (Currie)
Billy (Bishop)
Francis (Pegahmagabow)
Frank (Pickersgill)
George (Lawrence Price)
Gustave (Biéler)
Harry (Crerar)
Henry (Norwest)
Isaac (Brock)
James (Ralston)
John (Kenneth Macalister)
Kenneth (Stuart)
Leonard (Birchall)
Lewis (MacKenzie)
Lionel (Guy D'Artois)
Maurice (Baril)
Peter (Dmytruk)
Roméo (Sabourin)
Roy (Brown)
Sam (Steele)
Tommy (Prince)
Wendy (Clay)
William (Hall)

Trades

Business Moguls

Male

Bob (Young)
Conrad (Black)
Craig (Dobbin)
David (Asper)
Edward (Rogers)
Guy (Laliberté)
Hartland (Molson)
Jack (Kent Cooke)
Jean (Pouliot)
John (Kenneth Galbraith)
Kenneth (Thomson)
Lino (Saputo)
Max (Aitken)
Michael (Lee-Chin)
Nat (Taylor)
Percy (Girouard)
Pete (Luckett)
Peter (Munk)
Ron (Joyce)
Roy (Thompson)
Sam (McLaughlin)
Samuel (Bronfman)
Timothy (Eaton)
Victor (Li)
William (Cornelius Van Horne)

Educators

Female and Male

Adelaide (Hoodless)
Aleksis (Dreimanis)
Anthony (J. Naldrett)
Charles (R. Stelck)
Colin (Simpson)
David (Strangway)
Egertron (Ryerson)
Eric (W. Mountjoy)
Francis (Reginald "F. R." Scott)
Frank (Hawthorne)
Gerald (V. Middleton)
Henry (C. Gunning)
James (E. Gill)
John (Ross Mackay)
Michael (John Keen)
Petr (Cerny)
Richard (Lee Armstrong)
Roger (G. Walker)
Rose (Sheinin)
Ruth (Collins-Nakai)
Stephen (E. Calvert)
Sue (Johanson)
Thomas (H. Clark)
Tom (Symons)
William (Richard Peltier)

Inventors

Female and Male

Abraham (Gesner)
Archibald (G. Huntsman)
Arthur (Sicard)
Chris (Haney)
Cluny (MacPherson)
Donald (L. Hings)
Edward (Samuel Rogers)
Elijah (McCoy)
George (Klein)
Gerald (Bull)
Gideon (Sundback)
Henry (Woodward)
Hugh (Le Caine)
James (Naismith)
John (Connon)
Joseph-Armand (Bombardier)
Lewis (Urry)
Mathew (Evans)
Reginald (Fessenden)
Robert (Foulis)
Sandford (Fleming)
Scott (Abbott)
Thomas (Carroll)
Wilbur (Franks)
Wilfred (Bigelow)

Doctors

Female and Male

Anna (Hilliard)
Charles (Best)
Charles (Brenton Huggins)
Daniel (David Palmer)
David (Hubel)
Edgar (Randolph Parker)
Elizabeth (Bagshaw)
Emily (Stowe)
Frederick (Banting)
Harry (Bain)
Henry (Morgentaler)
Jean (Davignon)
Jeanne (Mance)
Jennie (Trout)
Jessie (Gray)
John (Callaghan)
Maude (Abbott)
Mira (Ashby)
Norman (Bethune)
Salluste (Duval)
T. Douglas (Kinsella)
Thomas (Chang)
Wilder (Penfield)
Wilfred (Bigelow)
William (Osler)

Architects

Female and Male

Andrew (R. Cobb)
Arthur (Erickson)
Bing (Thom)
Blanche (van Ginkel)
Bruce (Kuwabara)
Catherine (Wisnicki)
Dan (Hanganu)
Douglas (Cardinal)
Edward (J. Lennox)
Ernest (Cormier)
Esther (Hill)
Étienne (Gaboury)
Francis (Rattenbury)
Frank (Gehry)
Gregory (Henriquez)
Jack (Diamond)
John (M. Lyle)
Louis (Bourgeois)
Macy (DuBois)
Moshe (Safdie)
Phyllis (Lambert)
Raymond (Moriyama)
Ron (Thom)
Sidney (Badgley)
Stephen (Irwin)

Scientists

Female and Male

Bertram (Brockhouse)
Biruté (Galdikas)
Charles (Best)
David (H. Hubel)
Doreen (Kimura)
Edward (A. Irving)
Ernest (McCulloch)
Frederick (G. Banting)
Gerhard (Herzberg)
Harold (Williams)
Helen (Battles Hogg-Priestley)
Henry (Taube)
Hubert (Reeves)
Irene (Ayako Uchida)
J. Tuzo (Wilson)
James (Hillier)
John (Polanyi)
Julia (Levy)
Maud (Menten)
Michael (Smith)
Richard (E. Taylor)
Rudolph (A. Marcus)
Sidney (Altman)
Ursula (Franklin)
William (Giauque)

Names Inspired by People, Places, and Things

What's in a name? Some parents choose names that carry special meaning. They're sports buffs who name their children after legendary athletes, bookworms who name their children after beloved characters, and nature lovers who name their children after the things they see in their favorite vistas. Then again, some people choose names not because they carry personal significance but simply because they fall in love with them. They may not be sports buffs, bookworms, or nature lovers, but they still choose names like Jordan, Bridget, and Willow.

However you approach it, here are several lists of girls' and boys' names inspired by people, places, and things. (To learn more about choosing names with special meaning, check out the "How to Pick a Name You and Your Baby Will Like" feature on page 3.)

Literature

Fictional Characters

Female	Male
Anna (Karenina)	Atticus (Finch)
Anne (Shirley)	Billy (Coleman)
Antonia (Shimerda)	Boo (Radley)
Bridget (Jones)	Cyrus (Trask)
Cosette (Valjean)	Edmond (Dantés)
Daisy (Buchanan)	Ethan (Frome)
Dorothea (Brooke)	Frodo (Baggins)
Edna (Pontellier)	Guy (Montag)
Elizabeth (Bennet)	Harry (Potter)
Emma (Woodhouse)	Heathcliff
Hermione (Granger)	Henry (Fleming)
Hester (Prynne)	Holden (Caulfield)
Isabel (Archer)	Huck (Finn)
Jane (Eyre)	Jake (Barnes)
Josephine (March)	Jay (Gatsby)
Juliet (Capulet)	Jean (Valjean)
Junie (B. Jones)	John (Proctor)
Mary (Lennox)	Odysseus
Meg (Murry)	Owen (Meany)
Ophelia	Pip (Philip Pirrip)
Phoebe (Caulfield)	Rhett (Butler)
Pippi (Longstocking)	Robinson (Crusoe)
Scarlett (O'Hara)	Romeo (Montague)
Scout (Finch)	Santiago
Serena (Joy)	Victor (Frankenstein)

Dramatic Characters

Female and Male

Abigail (Williams)
Algernon ("Algy" Moncrieff)
Bella (Kurnitz)
Blanche (DuBois)
Christine (Daaé)
Cosette
Edmund (Tyrone)
Eliza (Doolittle)
Emily (Webb)
George (Gibbs)
Gwendolen (Fairfax)
Henry (Higgins)
Jean (Valjean)
Jim (O'Connor)
John (Proctor)
Juliet (Capulet)
Laura (Wingfield)
Linda (Loman)
Mary (Tyrone)
Odysseus
Raoul (de Chagny)
Romeo (Montague)
Stanley (Kowalski)
Vladimir
Willy (Loman)

Shakespearean Characters

Female	Male
Adriana	Angelo
Beatrice	Antony
Cleopatra	Balthasar
Cordelia	Bertram
Emilia	Cicero
Gertrude	Claudio
Helena	Cromwell
Hermia	Duncan
Hero	Edmund
Imogen	Hamlet
Isabella	Iachimo
Juliet	Iago
Katharina	Julius (Caesar)
Lavinia	Lysander
Mariana	Malcolm
Miranda	Oberon
Olivia	Orlando
Ophelia	Othello
Paulina	Paris
Portia	Puck
Regan	Richard
Rosalind	Romeo
Titania	Titus
Ursula	Tybalt
Viola	Vincentio

British Literature Characters

Female and Male

Alice
Beowulf
Bob (Cratchet)
Catherine (Earnshaw)
Clarissa (Dalloway)
Dorian (Gray)
Ebenezer (Scrooge)
Edward (Ferrars)
Elinor (Dashwood)
Eliza (Doolittle)
Elizabeth (Bennet)
Emma (Woodhouse)
Gloriana
Harry (Potter)
Heathcliff
Henry (Higgins)
Hermione (Granger)
Jane (Eyre)
Jim (Hawkins)
Lemuel (Gulliver)
Oliver (Twist)
Robinson (Crusoe)
Samuel (Pickwick)
Victor (Frankenstein)
Winston (Smith)

French Literature Characters

Female and Male

Aramis
Armand (Richelieu)
Athos
Bishop Myriel
Captain Nemo
Claude (Frollo)
Cosette
d'Artagnan
Dom (Juan)
Edmund (Dantes)
Éponine (Thenardier)
Esmeralda
Fantine
Figaro
Jean (Valjean)
Jules (Mazarin)
Marius (Pontmercy)
Milady (de Winter)
Otto (Lidenbrock)
Panurge
Passepartout
Philéas (Fogg)
Porthos
Quasimodo
Tom (Ayrton)

Nursery Rhyme Characters	Picture Book Characters	Comic Strip Characters	Comic Book Superhero Alter Egos
Female and Male	**Female and Male**	**Female and Male**	**Female and Male**
Bo (Peep)	Alexander	Andy (Capp)	Arthur (Curry, "Aquaman")
Bobby (Shaftoe)	Alice	Blondie (Bumstead)	Barbara (Gordon, "Bat Girl")
Bonnie	Arthur	Brenda (Starr)	Ben (Grim, "The Thing")
Elsie (Marley)	Babar	Calvin	Bruce (Wayne, "Batman")
Fred	Cinderella	Cathy	Charles (Xavier, "Professor X")
Georgie (Porgie)	Clifford	Charlie (Brown)	Clark (Kent, "Superman")
Jack	Elmo	Dennis (Mitchell)	Diana (Prince, "Wonder Woman")
Jerry (Hall)	Ferdinand	Dick (Tracy)	Dick (Grayson, "Robin")
Jill	Frances	Dolly	Emma (Frost, "White Queen")
John (Jacob Jingleheimer Schmidt)	George	Elly (Patterson)	Frank (Castle, "The Punisher")
King Cole	Harold	Florrie (Capp)	Hal (Jordan, "Green Lantern")
Lou	Horton	Garfield	Henry (McCoy, "Beast")
MacDonald	Imogene	George (Wilson)	Jean (Gray, "Phoenix")
Margery (Daw)	Lilly	Hägar (the Horrible)	Logan (Howlett, "Wolverine")
Mary	Madeline	Heathcliff	Matt (Murdock, "Daredevil")
Michael	Maisy	Helga	Oliver (Queen, "Green Arrow")
Nancy (Etticoat)	Max	Hiram ("Hi" Flagston)	Peter (Parker, "Spider-Man")
Peter (Piper)	Olivia	Jeffy	Reed (Richards, "Mr. Fantastic")
Polly (Flinders)	Paddington	Lois (Flagston)	Scott (Summers, "Cyclops")
Robin	Pat	Luann	Selina (Kyle, "Catwoman")
Taffy	Peter	Michael (Doonesbury)	Steve (Rogers, "Captain America")
Tommy (Tittlemouse)	Ping	Odie	Susan (Richards, "Invisible Woman")
Simon	Sal	Rex (Morgan)	Tony (Stark, "Iron Man")
Solomon (Grundy)	Tikki	Sally (Forth)	Wally (West, "Flash")
Willie (Winkie)	Winnie	Ziggy	Warren (Worthington III, "Archangel")

History

Arthurian Legend Characters	Harry Potter Characters		Kings	Queens
Female and Male	Female	Male	Male	Female
Anna	Alicia (Spinnet)	Albus (Dumbledore)	Albert	Anna
Arthur	Angelina (Johnson)	Blaise (Zabini)	Alexander	Anne
Bors	Bellatrix (Lestrange)	Cedric (Diggory)	Arthur	Beatrix
Ector	Cho (Chang)	Colin (Creavey)	Canute	Candace
Emmeline	Dolores (Umbridge)	Dean (Thomas)	Charles	Catherine
Gaheris	Fleur (Delacour)	Draco (Malfoy)	Cormac	Charlotte
Galahad	Ginny (Weasley)	Dudley (Dursley)	Cyrus	Christina
Gareth	Hermione (Granger)	Fred (Weasley)	David	Cleopatra
Gawain	Katie (Bell)	George (Weasley)	Edgar	Elizabeth
Guinevere	Lavender (Brown)	Harry (Potter)	Edmund	Esther
Igraine	Lily (Potter)	James (Potter)	Edward	Filippa
Iseult	Luna (Lovegood)	Kingsley (Shacklebolt)	Ferdinand	Ingrid
Isolde	Minerva (McGonagall)	Lucius (Malfoy)	Frederick	Isabella
Kay	Molly (Weasley)	Neville (Longbottom)	George	Jeanne
Lancelot	"Moaning" Myrtle	Oliver (Wood)	Harold	Juliana
Lot	Narcissa (Malfoy)	Percy (Weasley)	Henry	Louise
Mark	Nymphadora (Tonks)	Peter (Pettigrew)	James	Margaret
Merlin	Padma (Patil)	Remus (Lupin)	John	Marie
Mordred	Pansy (Parkinson)	Ron (Weasley)	Louis	Mary
Morgan (le Fey)	Parvati (Patil)	Rubeus (Hagrid)	Magnus	Matilda
Morgause	Penelope (Clearwater)	Seamus (Finnigan)	Malcolm	Silvia
Nimue	Petunia (Dursley)	Severus (Snape)	Niall	Sofia
Percival	Poppy (Pomfrey)	Sirius (Black)	Phillip	Tamar
Tristan	Rita (Skeeter)	Tom (Riddle)	Richard	Victoria
Uther (Pendragon)	Sibyll (Trelawney)	Viktor (Krum)	William	Zenobia

Religion and Mythology

Members of the British Royal Family	Old Testament Figures	New Testament Figures	Biblical Women
Female and Male	**Male**	**Male**	**Female**
Alexander	Abel	Agrippa	Abigail
Alexandra	Abraham	Andrew	Bathsheba
Alice	Adam	Annas	Deborah
Andrew	Cain	Aquila	Delilah
Anne	Caleb	Gabriel	Dinah
Beatrice	Daniel	Herod	Eden
Birgitte	David	James	Elizabeth
Camilla	Eli	Jesus	Esther
Charles	Esau	John	Eve
Davina	Ezekiel	Joseph	Hagar
Diana	Ezra	Judas	Hannah
Edward	Isaac	Jude	Jezebel
Elizabeth	Isaiah	Luke	Judith
Eugenie	Jacob	Mark	Julia
Frederick	Jeremiah	Matthew	Leah
George	Job	Nicolas	Maria
Helen	Joel	Paul	Martha
Henry (Harry)	Joshua	Peter	Mary
Louise	Moses	Philip	Miriam
Michael	Nemiah	Simon	Naomi
Nicholas	Noah	Stephen	Phoebe
Peter	Samson	Thomas	Rachel
Philip	Samuel	Timothy	Rebekah
Richard	Saul	Titus	Ruth
William	Solomon	Zechariah	Sarah

Saints		Popes	Christmas-Themed	Heavenly and Angelic	Jewish Figures
Female	**Male**	**Male**	**Female and Male**	**Female and Male**	**Female and Male**
Agatha	Ambrose	Adrian	Angel	Angel	Aaron
Agnes	Andrew	Alexander	Bell	Angela	Akiva
Bernadette	Anselm	Benedict	Carol	Angellica	Abraham
Bridget	Anthony	Boniface	Claus	Angelo	Daniel
Candida	Augustine	Celestine	Ebenezer	Asención	David (Ben Gurion)
Catherine	Bartholomew	Clement	Emmanuel	Beulah	Deborah
Cecilia	Benedict	Constantine	Garland	Celeste	Esther
Clare	Christopher	Cornelius	Gloria	Divinity	Golda (Meir)
Florence	Felix	Eugene	Holly	Eden	Hillel
Genevieve	Francis	Felix	Jesus	Faith	Isaac
Hilary	Gregory	Gregory	Joseph	Gabriel	Jacob
Ingrid	Ignatius	Innocent	Joy	Gloria	Joseph
Joan	Jerome	John Paul	King	Heaven	Judah (Maccabee)
Julia	John	Julius	Kris	Jannah	Leah
Louise	Jude	Leo	Manger	Lani	Maimonides
Lucy	Leo	Linus	Mary	Mary	Miriam
Lydia	Linus	Peter	Merry	Michael	Mordechai
Margaret	Nicholas	Pius	Nicholas	Nevaeh	Moses
Maria	Patrick	Romanus	Noel	Paradise	Nachmanides
Mary	Paul	Sixtus	Peace	Paradiso	Rachel
Monica	Peter	Stephan	Rudolf	Raphael	Rashi
Regina	Sebastian	Theodore	Shepherd	Seraphim	Rebecca
Rose	Stephen	Urban	Star	Seraphina	Ruth
Sylvia	Thomas	Valentine	Wenceslas	Tian	Sarah
Teresa	Valentine	Zachary	Yule	Trinity	Yochanan (ben Zakkai)
	Vincent			Zion	

Muslim Figures	Hindu Figures	Greek Mythology Figures		Roman Mythology Figures	
Male	**Female and Male**	**Female**	**Male**	**Female**	**Male**
Adam	Agni	Aphrodite	Achilles	Aurora	Aeneas
Al-Yasa	Arjuna	Artemis	Adonis	Bellona	Aesculapius
Ayub	Bali	Athena	Apollo	Camilla	Amor
Daud	Brahma	Calliope	Ares	Ceres	Bacchus
Harun	Buddha	Calypso	Atlas	Clementia	Cupid
Hud	Chandra	Chloe	Dionysus	Concordia	Faunus
Ibrahim	Devi	Daphne	Eros	Decima	Honos
Idris	Dharma	Demeter	Hades	Diana	Inuus
Ilyas	Indra	Echo	Hector	Fauna	Janus
Isa	Kali	Electra	Helios	Felicitas	Jove
Ishaq	Kama	Europa	Hercules	Flora	Jupiter
Ismail	Krishna	Gaea	Hermes	Fortuna	Liber
Lut	Maya	Helen	Icarus	Hippona	Mars
Muhammad	Nala	Hera	Jason	Juno	Mercury
Musa	Parvati	Hestia	Midas	Juventus	Neptune
Nuh	Rama	Io	Morpheus	Levana	Orcus
Saleh	Ravi	Leda	Narcissus	Luna	Pluto
Shoaib	Sati	Medusa	Odysseus	Mania	Remus
Sulayman	Shiva	Nike	Orion	Minerva	Romulus
Yahya	Sita	Pandora	Pan	Pax	Saturn
Yaqub	Surya	Penelope	Paris	Roma	Silvanus
Yunus	Uma	Persephone	Perseus	Venus	Sol
Yusuf	Ushas	Phoebe	Poseidon	Veritas	Somnus
Zakariya	Vishnu	Psyche	Prometheus	Vesta	Ulysses
Zulkifl	Yama	Rhea	Zeus	Victoria	Vulcan

Egyptian Mythology Figures	Norse Mythology Figures	African Mythology	Japanese Mythology
Female and Male	**Female and Male**	**Female and Male**	**Female and Male**
Aker	Aegir	Abuk	Amaterasu
Anouke	Astrild	Agé	Amida
Anubis	Atla	Aja	Benten
Atum	Balder	Astar	Bishamon
Bastet	Bragi	Buku	Daikoku
Bes	Edda	Deng	Dosojin
Buto	Forseti	Edinkira	Ebisu
Geb	Freya	Enekpe	Fujin
Hapi	Freyr	Eshu	Gama
Hathor	Frigg	Faro	Gongen
Horus	Hel	Gun	Hachiman
Isis	Hermod	Inkosazana	Hiruko
Ma'at	Hod	Kiru	Hoderi
Min	Idun	Loko	Inari
Neith	Loki	Mawu	Isora
Nun	Mimir	Mugasa	Jimmu
Ninet	Njord	Osawa	Kaminari
Osiris	Odin	Oshun	Kishijoten
Ptah	Ran	Oya	Marisha-Ten
Ra	Saga	Shango	Onamuji
Seb	Sif	Tamuno	Raiden
Seth	Thor	Wele	Sengen
Shu	Thrud	Woto	Susanowa
Sobek	Tyr	Xamaba	Tsuki-Yumi
Thoth	Ull	Yemaja	Uzume

Entertainment

Movie Characters

Female

Amélie (Poulain)
Annie (Hall)
Bonnie (Parker)
Bridget (Jones)
Clarice (Starling)
Clementine (Kruczynski)
Dorothy (Gale)
Elaine (Robinson)
Eliza (Doolitle)
Ellen (Ripley)
Erin (Brockovich)
Holly (Golightly)
Ilsa (Lund)
Jean Louise ("Scout" Finch)
Lara (Croft)
Leia (Organa)
Louise (Sawyer)
Marge (Gunderson)
Maria (von Trapp)
Mary (Poppins)
Norma Rae (Webster)
Sandy (Olsson)
Scarlett (O'Hara)
Thelma (Dickerson)
Trinity

Male

Atticus (Finch)
Austin (Powers)
Billy (Madison)
Charles (Foster Kane)
Forrest (Gump)
Frodo (Baggins)
George (Bailey)
Hannibal (Lector)
Harry (Potter)
Indiana (Jones)
Jack (Sparrow)
Jacques (Clouseau)
James (Bond)
Jerry (Maguire)
Judah (Ben-Hur)
Lloyd (Dobler)
Luke (Skywalker)
Maximus (Decimus Meridius)
Napoleon (Dynamite)
Neo
Norman (Bates)
Rhett (Butler)
Rick (Blaine)
Rocky (Balboa)
Vito (Corleone)

TV Characters

Female

Abby (Lockhart)
Ally (McBeal)
Buffy (Summers)
Carmela (Soprano)
Carrie (Bradshaw)
Daphne (Moon Crane)
Elaine (Benes)
Erica (Kane)
Felicity (Porter)
Fran (Fine)
Gabrielle (Solis)
Grace (Adler)
Kelly (Bundy)
Kimberly (Shaw Mancini)
Lacey (Burrows)
Lucy (Ricardo)
Marcia (Brady)
Margaret ("Hot Lips" Houlihan)
Michelle (Tanner)
Molly (McGuire)
Rachel (Green)
Rebecca (Howe)
Sally (Ross)
Sydney (Bristow)
Vanessa (Huxtable)

Male

Al (Bundy)
Alex (P. Keaton)
Archie (Bunker)
Arthur ("Fonzie" Fonzarelli)
Brent (LeRoy)
Chandler (Bing)
Cliff (Huxtable)
Cosmo (Kramer)
David (Sandstrom)
Dylan (McKay)
Fox (Mulder)
Frasier (Crane)
Gil (Grissom)
Grant (Jansky)
Jack (McCoy)
J. B. (Dixon)
Jean-Luc (Picard)
Joey (Tribbiani)
John Ross ("J. R." Ewing, Jr.)
Kevin (Arnold)
Ricky (Ricardo)
Sam (Malone)
Tony (Soprano)
Will (Truman)
Zack (Morris)

Disney Cartoon Characters

Female	Male
Alice	Aladdin
Ariel	Bambi
Aurora	Bob (Parr)
Belle	Buzz (Lightyear)
Boo	Chip
Cinderella	Christopher (Robin)
Daisy (Duck)	Dale
Esmeralda	Dash (Parr)
Fauna	Dewey
Flora	Donald (Duck)
Helen (Parr)	Eric
Jane (Porter)	Gaston
Jasmine	Hercules
Jessie	Huey
Lilo	Ichabod (Crane)
Marian	Jafar
Mary (Poppins)	Louie
Megara	Merlin
Minnie	Mickey
Mulan	Mufasa
Nala	Peter (Pan)
Pocahontas	Robin (Hood)
Ursula	Sebastian
Violet (Parr)	Simba
Wendy	Timon

Musical Terms

Female and Male
Allegro
Aria
Cadence
Canon
Carol
Chante
Clef
Coda
Diva
Fermata
Harmony
Harp
Hymn
Lyric
Major
Medley
Musika
Opus
Piano
Reed
Rococo
Sonata
Symphony
Viola

Notorious Celebrity Baby Names

Female and Male

Ahmet Emuukha Rodan (son of Frank and Gail Zappa)
Apple Blythe Alison (daughter of Gwyneth Paltrow and Chris Martin)
Audio Science (son of Shannyn Sossamon and Dallas Clayton)
Coco Riley (daughter of Courteney Cox Arquette and David Arquette)
Daisy Boo (daughter of Jamie and Jools Oliver)
Dweezil (son of Frank and Gail Zappa)
Elijah Bob Patricus Guggi Q (son of Bono and Alison Stewart)
Fifi Trixiebelle (daughter of Paula Yates and Bob Geldof)
Hazel Patricia (daughter of Julia Roberts and Danny Moder)
Heavenly Hirani Tiger Lily (daughter of Paula Yates and Michael Hutchence)
Lourdes Maria Ciccone (daughter of Madonna and Carlos Leon)
Moon Unit (daughter of Frank and Gail Zappa)
Moxie Crimefighter (daughter of Penn and Emily Jillette)
Peaches Honeyblossom (daughter of Paula Yates and Bob Geldof)
Phinnaeus Walter (son of Julia Roberts and Danny Moder)
Pilot Inspektor (son of Jason Lee and Beth Riesgraf)
Pirate Howsmon (son of Jonathan and Deven Davis)
Poppy Honey (daughter of Jamie and Jools Oliver)
Prince Michael (son of Michael Jackson and Debbie Rowe)
Prince Michael II (son of Michael Jackson)
Rocco (son of Madonna and Guy Ritchie)
Rumer Glenn (daughter of Demi Moore and Bruce Willis)
Scout LaRue (daughter of Demi Moore and Bruce Willis)
Seven Sirius (son of Andre 3000 and Erykah Badu)
Tallulah Belle (daughter of Demi Moore and Bruce Willis)

One-Name Wonders

Female and Male

- Ann-Margret
- Beck
- Björk
- Bono
- Brandy
- Cher
- Dido
- Enya
- Fabio
- Iman
- Jewel
- Liberace
- Madonna
- Moby
- Nelly
- Pelé
- Prince
- Roseanne
- Sade
- Seal
- Shakira
- Sinbad
- Tiffany
- Twiggy
- Yanni

Songs with Names in the Titles

Female

- "Alison" (Elvis Costello)
- "Angie" (The Rolling Stones)
- "Annie's Song" (John Denver)
- "Beth" (Kiss)
- "Billie Jean" (Michael Jackson)
- "Come On Eileen" (Dexy's Midnight Runners)
- "Georgia on My Mind" (Ray Charles)
- "Good Golly Miss Molly" (Little Richard)
- "Help Me Rhonda" (The Beach Boys)
- "Jack and Diane" (John Mellencamp)
- "Janie's Got a Gun" (Aerosmith)
- "Jenny from the Block" (Jennifer Lopez)
- "Kathy's Song" (Simon & Garfunkel)
- "Layla" (Derek and the Dominos)
- "Lucy in the Sky with Diamonds" (The Beatles)
- "Maggie May" (Rod Stewart)
- "Mandy" (Barry Manilow)
- "Mary Jane's Last Dance" (Tom Petty and the Heartbreakers)
- "Mustang Sally" (Wilson Pickett)
- "My Sharona" (The Knack)
- "Rosalita (Come Out Tonight)" (Bruce Springsteen)
- "Rosanna" (Toto)
- "Roxanne" (The Police)
- "Sweet Caroline" (Neil Diamond)
- "Wake Up Little Susie" (The Everly Brothers)

Male

- "Achilles Last Stand" (Led Zeppelin)
- "Adam's Song" (blink-182)
- "Bad, Bad Leroy Brown" (Jim Croce)
- "Bennie and the Jets" (Elton John)
- "Billy, Don't Be a Hero" (Paper Lace)
- "Buddy Holly" (Weezer)
- "Calling Elvis" (Dire Straits)
- "Daniel" (Elton John)
- "Fernando" (ABBA)
- "Galileo" (Indigo Girls)
- "Goodbye Earl" (Dixie Chicks)
- "Hey Joe" (Jimi Hendrix)
- "Hey Jude" (The Beatles)
- "James Dean" (The Eagles)
- "Jeremy" (Pearl Jam)
- "Jessie's Girl" (Rick Springfield)
- "Jim Dandy" (Black Oak Arkansas)
- "Johnny B. Goode" (Chuck Berry)
- "Jumpin' Jack Flash" (The Rolling Stones)
- "Louie, Louie" (The Kingsmen)
- "Me and Bobby McGee" (Janis Joplin)
- "Mickey" (Toni Basil)
- "Stan" (Eminem)
- "What's the Frequency, Kenneth?" (R.E.M.)
- "You Can Call Me Al" (Paul Simon)

Nature and Places

Flowers	Rocks, Gems, Minerals	Natural Elements		Celestial Names
Female	**Female and Male**	**Female**	**Male**	**Female and Male**
Angelica	Beryl	Amber	Ash	Andromeda
Calla	Clay	Autumn	Branch	Antares
Dahlia	Coal	Breezy	Bud	Aries
Daisy	Coral	Blossom	Canyon	Cassiopeia
Fern	Crystal	Briar	Cliff	Castor
Flora	Diamond	Brook	Crag	Cloud
Flower	Esmerelda	Delta	Dale	Corona
Holly	Flint	Gale	Eddy	Draco
Hyacinth	Garnet	Hailey	Field	Étoile
Iris	Gemma	Heather	Ford	Leo
Jasmine	Goldie	Ivy	Forest	Luna
Laurel	Jade	Marina	Heath	Moona
Lavender	Jasper	Rain	Lake	Nova
Lilac	Jewel	Rainbow	Marsh	Orion
Lily	Mercury	Savannah	Moss	Pollux
Marigold	Mica	Sequoia	Oakes	Rigel
Pansy	Opal	Sierra	Thorne	Saturn
Poppy	Pearl	Skye	Ridge	Scorpio
Posy	Rock	Star	River	Skye
Rose	Ruby	Summer	Rye	Soleil
Sage	Sandy	Sunny	Rock	Star
Tulip	Sapphire	Terra	Stone	Starling
Verbena	Steele	Tempest	Storm	Sunny
Vine	Stone	Willow	Woody	Ursa
Violet	Topaz	Windy		Venus

Animals

Water-Themed Names

Places

Trades

Trade Names

Animals — Female and Male	Water-Themed Names — Female and Male	Places — Female	Places — Male	Trade Names — Female and Male
Billy	Bay	Africa	Afton	Baker
Birdie	Brooke	Asia	Austin	Butcher
Buck	Chelsea	Brooklyn	Boston	Carver
Bunny	Delmar	Cheyenne	Chad	Chandler
Cat	Delta	China	Cleveland	Cooper
Colt	Dewey	Dakota	Cuba	Cutler
Crane	Eddy	Florence	Dakota	Draper
Cricket	Ice	Georgia	Dallas	Fletcher
Drake	Lake	Holland	Denver	Fowler
Fawn	Marin	India	Diego	Gardner
Fox	Marina	Italia	Indiana	Hunter
Hawk	Marisol	Jamaica	Israel	Marshall
Jaguar	Meri	Kenya	Kent	Mason
Jay	Misty	Lourdes	Laramie	Miller
Joey	Nile	Madison	London	Painter
Kitty	Oceana	Montana	Montreal	Porter
Lark	Rain	Olympia	Nevada	Ranger
Newt	Rio	Paris	Orlando	Sawyer
Phoenix	River	Regina	Phoenix	Scribe
Raven	Seabert	Savannah	Reno	Shepherd
Robin	Spring	Siena	Rhodes	Slater
Starling	Storm	Sydney	Rio	Smith
Tiger	Tempest	Tijuana	Sydney	Stockman
Wolf	Tigris	Victoria	Tennessee	Tailor
Wren	Wade	Vienna	Washington	Tanner

Other Ideas for Names

Leadership Titles	Double Names		Easily Shortened Names		Names Based on Letters
Female and Male	**Female**	**Male**	**Female**	**Male**	**Female and Male**
Baron	Anne-Marie	Aaronjames	Abigail	Andrew	Ajay
Bishop	Billie-Jean	Billijo	Angela	Anthony	Alpha
Caesar	Billie-Jo	Giancarlo	Barbara	Benjamin	Bea
Chancellor	Bobbi-Jo	Gianluca	Caroline	Christopher	Bebe
Deacon	Bobbi-Lee	Gianpaolo	Christine	Daniel	Bee
Duke	Brandy-Lynn	Jaylee	Deborah	Donald	Beta
Earl	Brooklyn	Jayquan	Elizabeth	Edward	Cee
Khan	Carolanne	Jean-Claude	Gwendolyn	Frederick	Ceejay
King	Clarabelle	Jean-Luc	Jacqueline	Gregory	Dee
Lord	Emmylou	Jean-Paul	Jennifer	Jacob	Dee Dee
Major	Hollyann	Jean-Sebastien	Jessica	Jeffery	Delta
Marquis	Jody-Ann	Jimmyjo	Jillian	Jonathan	Elle
Nagid	Julie-Anne	John-Paul	Josephine	Joseph	Em
Oba	Katelyn	Joseluis	Katherine	Kenneth	Gigi
Pasha	Kellyann	Juancarlos	Lillian	Leonardo	Jay
Pharaoh	Krystalynn	Kendarius	Margaret	Michael	Jaycee
Priest	Leeann	Keyshawn	Nicole	Nicholas	Jaydee
Prince	Mary-Kate	Markanthony	Pamela	Peter	Kay
Princess	Marylou	Michaelangelo	Rebecca	Richard	Kaycee
Queen	Raeann	Miguelangel	Samantha	Robert	Kaydee
Rabbi	Raelynn	Quindarius	Stephanie	Samuel	Ojay
Shah	Roseanne	Rayshawn	Suzanne	Thomas	Omega
Shaman	Ruthann	Tedrick	Valerie	Timothy	Theta
Sharif	Saralyn	Tyquan	Victoria	Walter	Vijay
Sultan	Terry-Lynn	Tyshawn	Vivian	William	Zeta

Names Based on Numbers

	Virtue Names	Palindrome Names	Names Used for Both Genders		
Female and Male	**Female**	**Female and Male**	**More for Girls**	**More for Boys**	**About Equal**
Decimus	Amity	Ada	Alexis	Alex	Britt
Deuce	Blythe	Anna	Ariel	Cameron	Addison
Dixie	Charity	Ara	Ashley	Carson	Ashton
Nona	Chastity	Asa	Bailey	Chandler	Berwyn
Octavia	Constance	Ava	Billie	Chase	Blair
Octavious	Faith	Aviva	Dominique	Chris	Carey
Osen	Felicity	Aya	Guadalupe	Christian	Casey
Primo	Fidelity	Aziza	Holland	Cody	Charley
Quartilla	Grace	Bob	Jade	Dakota	Derian
Quentin	Harmony	Davad	Jadyn	Devin	Devyn
Quincy	Honora	Elle	Jamie	Drew	Dylan
Quintana	Hope	Emme	Kelly	Evan	Gentry
Reva	Innocence	Eve	Madison	Hunter	Harley
Septima	Joy	Hallah	Morgan	Jaime	Jessie
Septimus	Justice	Hannah	Payton	Jaylin	Jody
Sextus	Love	Idi	Reagan	Jesse	Kristen
Tan	Mercy	Iggi	Reese	Jordan	London
Tertia	Modesty	Lil	Ricki	Logan	Maddox
Tertius	Passion	Nan	Robin	Parker	Pat
Trent	Patience	Natan	Shannon	Quinn	Peyton
Trey	Prudence	Nayan	Shea	Riley	Quincey
Triana	Purity	Olo	Sidney	Ryan	Skylar
Trinity	Temperance	Otto	Stacy	Skyler	Sunny
Una	Unity	Pip	Taylor	Terry	Tory
Uno	Verity	Viv	Tegan	Tyler	Tristyn

Anagram Names

Female	Male	Female and Male
Adria, Daria	Alec, Cale	Abe, Bea
Aileen, Elaine	Andrej, Darien	Aden, Edna
Alice, Celia	Andres, Sander	Adlar, Darla
Alli, Lila	Arnold, Ronald	Agni, Gina
Amy, Mya	Blake, Kaleb	Amir, Mira
Anise, Siena	Byron, Robyn	Brady, Darby
Ann, Nan	Chaz, Zach	Brion, Robin
April, Pilar	Darnell, Randell	Clay, Lacy
Ashanti, Tanisha	Daryn, Randy	Daly, Lyda
Ashlee, Sheela	Enzo, Zeno	Dashaun, Shaunda
Blaise, Isabel	Eric, Rice	Dylan, Lynda
Dana, Nada	Ernest, Nester	Edwyn, Wendy
Diana, Nadia	Jason, Jonas	Etta, Tate
Easter, Teresa	Kale, Lake	Hale, Leah
Elsa, Sela	Leo, Ole	Ian, Nia
Gem, Meg	Mason, Osman	Jason, Sonja
Gina, Inga	Moore, Romeo	Karl, Lark
Hallie, Leilah	Nero, Reno	Kory, York
Lena, Nela	Percy, Pryce	Leon, Noel
Leta, Teal	Roth, Thor	Liam, Mila
Marta, Tamra	Royce, Corey	Rico, Cori
Mary, Myra	Ryder, Derry	Ryker, Kerry
Nita, Tina	Santo, Aston	Sayid, Daisy
Norah, Rhona	Seaton, Easton	
Sita, Tisa	Thane, Ethan	

Rhyming Names

Female	Male	Female and Male
Addison, Madison	Aaron, Darren	Bessie, Jesse
Alyssa, Melissa	Abe, Gabe	Beth, Seth
Ann, Jan	Ace, Chase	Brandy, Randy
Anna, Hannah	Aidan, Jaiden	Cady, Brady
Candy, Mandy	Alvin, Calvin	Cleo, Leo
Carolyn, Marilyn	Barrett, Garrett	Doris, Morris
Celia, Delia	Barry, Larry	Erin, Darren
Chloe, Zoe	Brandon, Landon	Gayle, Dale
Ellen, Helen	Brian, Ryan	Grace, Chase
Erin, Karen	Cade, Jade	Gwen, Ken
Gracie, Stacie	Chance, Lance	Jeanne, Dean
Jane, Elaine	Cody, Brody	Jen, Ben
Jen, Gwen	Craig, Greg	Jodie, Cody
Kailey, Bailey	Devin, Evan	Joy, Roy
Karen, Sharon	Donald, Ronald	Kamie, Jamey
Lori, Tori	Dustin, Justin	Kate, Nate
Mae, Rae	Eric, Derek	Kay, Jay
Maura, Laura	Frank, Hank	Kim, Tim
Molly, Holly	Heath, Keith	Lori, Corey
Rhonda, Shonda	Hogan, Logan	Mandy, Andy
Sara, Kara	Jack, Mack	Mariah, Josiah
Sherry, Carrie	Jake, Blake	Mary, Harry
Stella, Bella	Jason, Mason	Millie, Billy
Valerie, Mallory	Phil, Will	Paige, Gage
Winnie, Minnie	Sean, John	Zoe, Joey

Fun Nicknames

Female	Male
Anka	Binky
Babs	Buddy
Bertie	Chaz
Biddy	Che
Birdie	Chip
Buffy	Danno
Bunny	Deano
Coco	Fonzie
Dodie	Fritz
Fannie	Gino
Fifi	Jimbo
Flo	Jobo
Gigi	Joop
Ginger	Junior
Hattie	Kit
Jas	Lucky
Kiki	Mango
Kitty	Paco
Madge	Paddy
Sissy	Pepe
Steffi	Pinky
Stevie	Rafi
Tottie	Rollo
Trixie	Skip
Xuxa	Ziggy

Old-Fashioned Names

Female	Male
Abigail	Abraham
Alice	Alexander
Anna	Dominic
Ava	Elijah
Caroline	Ethan
Charlotte	Gabriel
Claire	Hector
Elizabeth	Isaac
Emily	Isaiah
Emma	Ivan
Evelyn	Jasper
Genevieve	Julian
Grace	Maxwell
Hannah	Nathaniel
Hazel	Noah
Isabella	Oscar
Jacqueline	Owen
Katherine	Remy
Madeline	Samuel
Margaret	Sebastian
Maria	Vernon
Olivia	Vincent
Rebecca	Wesley
Sarah	Xavier
Sofia	Zachary

One-Syllable Names

Female	Male
Ann	Blake
Bea	Chad
Belle	Chen
Brie	Drew
Chai	Gabe
Cher	Hugh
Claire	Jack
Dawn	Jake
Eve	John
Gayle	Juan
Gwen	Lee
Jade	Luke
Jane	Max
Jill	Paul
Kate	Pierce
Lane	Raj
Ling	Ralph
Lynn	Reece
Mae	Sage
Maude	Spence
Paige	Tad
Rose	Tate
Rue	Todd
Skye	Wade
Trish	Will

Two-Syllable Names

Female	Male
Anna	Ashton
Ashley	Brian
Ava	Christian
Carmen	Dante
Carrie	David
Cheyenne	Dylan
Chloe	Eric
Diane	Garrett
Emma	Jacob
Heidi	Jesse
Jada	Jordan
Jasmine	Joseph
Jody	Landon
Juana	Latrell
Kaitlyn	Luis
Kayla	Maddox
Leah	Matthew
Mary	Michael
Maura	Miguel
Megan	Noah
Rachel	Owen
Rosa	Ryan
Sadie	Sanjay
Sydney	William
Zoe	Wyatt

Three-Syllable Names

Female	Male
Aaliyah	Adrian
Andrea	Anthony
Brianna	Benjamin
Claudia	Christopher
Desirae	Deondre
Emily	Diego
Evelyn	Dominic
Gloria	Elijah
Gwendolyn	Francisco
Jacqueline	Gabriel
Kimberly	Gregory
Lakeisha	Isaiah
Mackenzie	Jeremy
Madeline	Jonathan
Madison	Joshua
Makayla	Julian
Olivia	Marcellus
Pamela	Mathias
Rhiannon	Muhammad
Sierra	Nathaniel
Sophia	Nicholas
Stephanie	Orlando
Sylvia	Sebastian
Tabitha	Timothy
Vanessa	Tobias

Four Syllable Names

Female	Male
Alejandra	Alejandro
Amelia	Antonio
Anastasia	Aristotle
Angelina	Bartholomew
Arianna	Benicio
Carolina	Cornelius
Damonica	Deanthony
Dominica	Demetrius
Eleanora	Ebenezer
Elizabeth	Ezekiel
Evangeline	Geronimo
Frederica	Giovanni
Guadalupe	Immanuel
Isabella	Indiana
Josephina	Jebediah
Julianna	Jeremiah
Katarina	Leonardo
Penelope	Macallister
Samuela	Napolean
Serafina	Odysseus
Serenity	Quindarius
Tatiana	Santiago
Valentina	Thelonius
Veronica	Valentino
	Zachariah

Names of Famous Pairs

Female and Male
Adam and Eve
Amos and Andy
Bert and Ernie
Bill and Ted
Bonnie and Clyde
Brooks and Dunn
Cain and Abel
Castor and Pollux
David and Goliath
Dick and Jane
Ebony and Ivory
Hansel and Gretel
Jack and Jill
Lancelot and Guenevere
Laurel and Hardy
Laverne and Shirley
Lewis and Clark
Mario and Luigi
Milo and Otis
Romeo and Juliet
Romy and Michele
Samson and Delilah
Siegfried and Roy
Sonny and Cher
Thelma and Louise

Names Ending with "A"

Female	Male
Alexandra	Abdula
Amanda	Akiva
Amelia	Aquila
Andrea	Baptista
Brianna	Barretta
Carmela	Bela
Fiona	Bubba
Gabriella	Columbia
Jana	Cuba
Julia	Dakota
Kayla	Dana
Kendra	Daytona
Maria	Elisha
Mia	Ezra
Michaela	Garcia
Pamela	Indiana
Roxanna	Joshua
Sara	Krishna
Selma	Luca
Sonja	Montana
Sophia	Mustafa
Tyra	Nevada
Uma	Santana
Viola	Shea
Wanda	Zacharia

Names Ending with "E"

Female	Male
Angie	Abe
Ashlee	Andre
Bette	Blake
Brooke	Blaze
Chloe	Boone
Claire	Cole
Gabrielle	Dale
Grace	George
Jane	Ike
Jasmine	Jade
Josie	Jake
Julie	Jerome
Juliette	Jesse
Kate	Jose
Kylie	Jude
Belle	Kayne
Marie	Lane
Nicole	Lee
Paige	Louie
Rose	Mike
Sadie	Ozzie
Stephanie	Pierre
Winnie	Reece
Yvonne	Vince
Zoe	Zebedee

Names Ending with "L"

Female	Male
Abigail	Abdul
Angel	Abel
April	Carl
Ariel	Cyril
Bell	Daniel
Carol	Darrell
Chantal	Denzel
Crystal	Earl
Ethel	Emmanuel
Gail	Gabriel
Hazel	Hershel
Isabel	Jamal
Jewel	Joel
Jill	Lionel
Laurel	Marshall
Mabel	Maxwell
Meryl	Michael
Muriel	Nathaniel
Nell	Neil
Noel	Paul
Pearl	Phil
Rachel	Russell
Sheryl	Samuel
Sybil	Terrell
Val	Will

Names Ending in "N"

Female	Male
Allison	Aidan
Ann	Alan
Ashlyn	Ashton
Autumn	Benjamin
Caitlin	Colin
Carmen	Darren
Ellen	Donovan
Erin	Evan
Fran	Flynn
Gwendolyn	Hayden
Jillian	Holden
Karen	Ian
Kathryn	Jordan
Kirsten	Justin
Lauren	Keenan
Lillian	Kevin
Magdalen	Llewellyn
Megan	Logan
Morgan	Marvin
Reagan	Mason
Rosalyn	Nathan
Shannon	Quentin
Teagan	Steven
Vivian	Tristan
Yasmin	Warren

Names Ending with "O"

Female	Male
Aiko	Alberto
Bayo	Alejandro
Calypso	Alfonzo
Cameo	Angelo
Charo	Antonio
Cleo	Benicio
Clio	Bo
Coco	Bruno
Domino	Carlo
Doro	Cisco
Echo	Eduardo
Flo	Falco
Gerardo	Fredo
Indigo	Georgio
Jo	Leo
Juno	Marco
Kameko	Mario
Koto	Mo
Mariko	Orlando
Marlo	Pablo
Maryjo	Pedro
Orino	Sancho
Ryo	Theo
Tamiko	Waldo
Yoko	Yao

Names Ending with "R"

Female	Male
Amber	Alexander
Blair	Arthur
Briar	Carter
Cedar	Chandler
Cher	Christopher
Easter	Connor
Eleanor	Evander
Ester	Homer
Ginger	Hunter
Harper	Jasper
Heather	Junior
Jennifer	Oliver
Kashmir	Oscar
Kimber	Parker
Lavender	Peter
Pier	River
Pilar	Roger
Piper	Sawyer
September	Spencer
Skyler	Trevor
Star	Tyler
Summer	Victor
Taylor	Walker
Tipper	Walter
Zephyr	Xavier

Names Ending with "Y"

Female	Male
Ashley	Anthony
Audrey	Bailey
Becky	Barry
Bethany	Bradley
Carly	Cody
Courtney	Corey
Dorothy	Darcy
Ebony	Farley
Emily	Gary
Felicity	Gordy
Hailey	Hardy
Jenny	Huey
Josey	Humphrey
Kelsey	Jeffrey
Lily	Jeremey
Mallory	Jerry
Molly	Koby
Polly	Manny
Shelly	Ozzy
Sidney	Randy
Stacy	Riley
Tiffany	Roy
Wendy	Timothy
Whitney	Westley
Zoey	Zachary

Names Inspired by "Ann"

Female
Ana
Anci
Anezka
Anica
Anik
Anisha
Anissa
Anita
Anja
Anka
Anna
Annabel
Annah
Annaliese
Anne
Anneka
Annette
Annie
Annika
Anya
Hannah
Nan
Nancy
Nanette
Nina

Names Inspired by "Elizabeth"

Female
Bess
Beth
Betsy
Betty
Elisa
Elise
Elizabet
Elizaveta
Elizabeth
Elka
Elsa
Ilse
Libby
Liese
Liesel
Lisa
Lisabeth
Liset
Lissie
Liz
Liza
Lizabeta
Lizbeth
Lizzie
Yelisbeta

Names Inspired by "Jacob"	Names Inspired by "Jane"	Names Inspired by "John"	Names Inspired by "Joseph"	Names Inspired by "Katherine"
Male	**Female**	**Male**	**Male**	**Female**
Akiva	Chavon	Evan	Beppe	Cat
Chago	Ciana	Gian	Che	Catherine
Coby	Giovanna	Handel	Cheche	Catheryn
Diego	Jalena	Hans	Chepe	Cathleen
Giacomo	Jan	Ian	Giuseppe	Cathy
Iago	Jana	Ivan	Iokepa	Catrina
Iakobos	Janae	Jack	Iosif	Catriona
Jack	Janelle	Jan	Jobo	Ekaterina
Jaco	Janessa	Janek	Jody	Kari
Jacobi	Janet	Jean	Joe	Kasen
Jacobo	Janica	Jens	Joeseph	Kasia
Jacobson	Janice	Joao	Joey	Kat
Jacorey	Janie	Johann	Joop	Katalina
Jacques	Janiqua	John Paul	José	Kate
Jaime	Jasa	Johnson	Josef	Katelyn
Jake	Jasia	Jon	Jupp	Kathleen
Jakob	Jean	Jonas	Osip	Kathlyn
James	Jenine	Jonathan	Pepa	Kathryn
Jock	Juana	Jones	Pepe	Kathy
Kobe	Maryjane	Jonny	Peppe	Katia
Kuba	Seana	Jovan	Pino	Katie
Tiago	Shana	Juan	Sepp	Katja
Yakov	Sinead	Sean	Yeska	Katrina
Yasha	Zanna	Yanni	Yosef	Kay
Yoakim	Zhane	Zane	Zeusef	Yekaterina

Names Inspired by "Margaret"	Names Inspired by "Mary"	Names Inspired by "Michael"	Names Inspired by "Peter"	Names Inspired by "William"
Female	**Female**	**Male**	**Male**	**Male**
Gita	Maija	Carmichael	Boutros	Bill
Greta	Mara	Demichael	Ferris	Billy
Gretchen	Mare	Machas	Panos	Guglielmo
Gret	Maren	Makel	Parnell	Guilherme
Madge	Mari	Mhichael	Pearson	Guillaume
Maggie	Maria	Micael	Peder	Guillermo
Maisey	Mariah	Micah	Pedro	Gwilym
Mamie	Marian	Michael	Peers	Liam
Maretta	Mariana	Michaelangelo	Pekelo	Uilliam
Margarita	Maribel	Michel	Per	Vasyl
Margaux	Maribeth	Mick	Perico	Vilhelm
Marge	Marice	Mickey	Perkin	Viljo
Margery	Marie	Miguel	Perry	Welfel
Margie	Mariel	Migel	Pete	Wilek
Margo	Marietta	Mihail	Peter	Wilhelm
Marguerite	Marigold	Mika	Peterson	Wilkins
Marjorie	Marika	Mike	Petr	Wilkinson
Marjorie	Marilyn	Mikel	Petru	Will
Markita	Marjorie	Mikhail	Petter	Willem
Meg	Maura	Mikko	Pier	Williams
Megan	Maureen	Miko	Pierce	Willie
Meta	Miriam	Miles	Piero	Willis
Peg	Molara	Milko	Pierre	Wills
Peggy	Molly	Misael	Pierson	Wilson
Reet	Muriel	Miska	Pieter	Wylie
Rita		Mitchell	Takis	
		Mychael		

Star Kids

What Celebrities Are Naming Their Kids

Ace Shane
son of Jennie Finch and Casey Daigle

Adelaide Rose
daughter of Rachel Griffiths and Andrew Taylor

Agnes Charles
daughter of Elisabeth Shue and David Guggenheim

Ahmet Emuukha Rodan
son of Frank Zappa and Gail Zappa

Aidan Rose
daughter of Faith Daniels

Alabama Gypsy Rose
daughter of Drea de Matteo and Shooter Jennings

Alabama Luella
daughter of Travis Barker and Shanna Moakler Barker

Alaia
daughter of Stephen Baldwin and Kenya Baldwin

Alastair Wallace
son of Rod Stewart and Penny Lancaster

Alex 🍁
son of Howie Mandel and Terry Mandel

Alexa
daughter of Mario Lemieux and Nathalie Asselin

Alexander Pete
son of Naomi Watts and Liev Schreiber

Alexandria Zahra Jones
daughter of David Bowie and Iman Abdulmajid

Alice Ann
daughter of Tom Cavanagh and Maureen Grise

Alina Chiara 🍁
daughter of Dave Foley and Crissy Guerrero

Allegra
daughter of John Leguizamo and Justine Maurer

Allie Colleen
daughter of Garth Brooks and Sandy Mahl

Angel Iris
daughter of Melanie "Scary Spice" Brown and Eddie Murphy

Annaliese 🍁
daughter of Barry Pepper and Cindy Pepper

Anthea 🍁
daughter of Paul Anka and Anne de Zogheb

Apple Bythe Alison
daughter of Gwyneth Paltrow and Chris Martin

Aquinnah Kathleen 🍁
daughter of Tracy Pollan and Michael J. Fox

Arpad Flynn
son of Elle Macpherson and Arpad Busson

Ashby Grace
daughter of Nancy O'Dell and Keith Zubchevich

Atherton Grace
daughter of Don Johnson and Kelley Johnson

Atticus
son of Isabella Hoffman and Daniel Baldwin

Audio Science
son of Shannyn Sossamon and Dallas Clayton

August Anna
daughter of Garth Brooks and Sandy Mahl

August Miklos Friedrich
son of Mariska Hargitay and Peter Hermann

Augustin James 🍁
son of Linda Evangelista

Aurelius Cy Andre
son of Elle Macpherson and Arpad Busson

Aurora Rose
son of Paul "Triple H" Levesque and Stephanie McMahon Levesque

Austin 🍁
son of Mario Lemieux and Nathalie Asselin

Ava 🍁
daughter of Gil Bellows and Rya Kihlstedt

Ava Caroline
daughter of Mia Hamm and Nomar Garciaparra

Ava Elizabeth
daughter of Reese Witherspoon and Ryan Phillippe

Ava Veronica 🍁
daughter of Jason Priestley and Naomi Lowde

Avery Grace
daughter of Angie Harmon and Jason Sehorn

Bailey
son of Tracey Gold and Roby Marshall

Bailey Jean
daughter of Melissa Etheridge and Julie Cypher

Banjo
son of Rachel Griffiths and Andrew Taylor

Barron William
son of Donald Trump and Melania Trump

Basil Patrick 🍁
son of Dave Foley and Tabitha Southey

Beatrice Milly
daughter of Paul McCartney and Heather Mills

Beau
son of Emma "Baby Spice" Bunton and Jade Jones

Bechet
daughter of Woody Allen and Soon-Yi Previn

Beckett
son of Conan O'Brien and Liza O'Brien

Bella
daughter of Steve Nash and Alejandra Amarilla

Belle Kingston 🍁
daughter of Dan Aykroyd and Donna Dixon

Birgen Anika 🍁
daughter of Phil Hartman and Brynn Hartman

Bluebell Madonna
daughter of Geri "Ginger Spice" Halliwell

Bobbi Kristina
daughter of Whitney Houston and Bobby Brown

Braison Chance
son of Billy Ray and Tish Cyrus

Brandon Thomas 🍁
son of Pamela Anderson and Tommy Lee

Brawley King
son of Nick Nolte and Rebecca Linger

Braydon Hart
son of Melissa Joan Hart and Mark Wilkerson

Brennan 🍁
son of Alan Thicke and Gloria Loring

Brighton Rose
daughter of Jon Favreau and Joya Tillem

Brody Jo
daughter of Gabrielle Reece and Laird Hamilton

Bronwyn Golden
daughter of Angela Bassett and Courtney B. Vance

Brooklyn Joseph
son of Victoria "Posh Spice" Beckham and David Beckham

Bryce Thadeus
son of Connie Nielsen and Lars Ulrich

Cannon Edward
son of Larry King and Shawn Southwick-King

Carter 🍁
son of Alan Thicke and Gina Tolleson

Carys
daughter of Catherine Zeta-Jones and Michael Douglas

Cash Anthony
son of Saul "Slash" Hudson and Perla Hudson

Cashel Blake
son of Daniel Day-Lewis and Rebecca Miller

Caspar Matthew
son of Claudia Schiffer and Matthew Vaughn

Castor
son of James Hetfield and Francesca Hetfield

Cayden Wyatt
son of Kevin Costner and Christine Baumgartner

Charles Bernard
son of Jodie Foster

Charles Spencer
son of Russell Crowe and Danielle Spencer

Chase 🍁
son of Joe Sakic and Debbie Sakic

Chelsea Belle
daughter of Rosie O'Donnell

Claudia Rose
daughter of Michelle Pfeiffer

Clementine de Vere Drummond
daughter of Claudia Schiffer and Matthew Vaughn

Coco Riley
daughter of Courteney Cox Arquette and David Arquette

Cole Cameron
son of Matt Leinart and Brynn Cameron

Connor Antony
son of Nicole Kidman and Tom Cruise

Cooper 🍁
son of Kimberley Conrad and Hugh Hefner

Cruz
son of Victoria "Posh Spice" Beckham and David Beckham

Cypress
daughter of Sole

D'Lila Star
daughter of Kim Porter and Sean "Diddy" Combs

Daisy True
daughter of Meg Ryan

Daisy-Boo
daughter of Jamie Oliver and Jools Oliver

Dandelion
daughter of Keith Richards and Anita Pallenberg

Danielle
daughter of Dan Aykroyd and Donna Dixon

Dannielynn Hope
daughter of Anna Nicole Smith and Larry Birkhead

Dante
daughter of Corey Hart and Julie Masse

Darby Galen
son of Patrick Dempsey and Jillian Fink

Darius
son of James Rubin and Christiane Amanpour

De'jan
daughter of Sole

Deacon Reese
son of Reese Witherspoon and Ryan Phillippe

Declyn Wallace
son of Cyndi Lauper and David Thornton

Delilah Belle
daughter of Harry Hamlin and Lisa Rinna

Denim
son of Toni Braxton and Keri Lewis

Denni Montana
daughter of Woody Harrelson and Laura Louie

Destry Allyn
daughter of Kate Capshaw and Steven Spielberg

Devo
son of Maynard James Keenan

Dexter Dean
daughter of Diane Keaton

Dexter Henry Lorcan
son of Diana Krall and Elvis Costello

Dezi James
son of Jaime Pressly and Eric Cubiche

Dhani
son of George Harrison and Olivia Harrison

Diezel
son of Toni Braxton and Keri Lewis

Diva Muffin
daughter of Frank Zappa and Gail Zappa

Dominik
daughter of Andy Garcia and Maria Victoria Garcia

Douglas Paul
son of Mark Messier and Kim Clark

Dream Sarae
daughter of Ginuwine and Sole

Dree Louise
daughter of Mariel Hemingway and Stephen Crisman

Duncan Zowie Heywood
son of David Bowie and Mary Angela Barnett

Dusti Rain
daughter of Rob "Vanilla Ice" and Laura Van Winkle

Dweezil
son of Frank Zappa and Gail Zappa

Dylan Frances
daughter of Sean Penn and Robin Wright Penn

Dylan Jagger
son of Pamela Anderson and Tommy Lee

Dylan Paul
son of Bart Conner and Nadia Comaneci

Eden
daughter of Marcia Cross and Tom Mahoney

Edie
daughter of Samantha Morton and Harry Holm

Edmund
son of Dave Foley and Tabitha Southey

Eja D'Angelo
son of Shania Twain and Robert "Mutt" Lange

Elijah Bob Patricious Guggi Q
son of Alison Stewart and Bono

Eliot Pauline
son of Sting and Trudie Styler

Ella Sofia
daughter of Jeff Gordon and Ingrid Vandebosch

Emerson Rose
daughter of Teri Hatcher and Jon Tenney

Emma Marie
daughter of Wayne Gretzky and Janet Jones

Emme
daughter of Jennifer Lopez and Mark Anthony

Enzo
son of Patricia Arquette and Paul Rossi

Esme
daughter of Samantha Morton and Charlie Creed-Miles

Ever Gabo
daughter of Milla Jovovich and Paul Anderson

Felicity-Amore
daughter of Keisha Castle-Hughes and Bradley Hull

Fifi Trixiebelle
daughter of Paula Yates and Bob Geldof

Finley
son of Chris O'Donnell and Caroline Fentress

Finn
son of Christy Turlington and Ed Burns

Finnigan Holden 🍁
son of Eric McCormack and
Janet Holden

Fiona Eve
daughter of Jennie Garth and
Peter Facinelli

Frances Bean
daughter of Kurt Cobain and
Courtney Love

Frances Pen
daughter of Amanda Peet and
David Benioff

Francesca Nora
daughter of Jason Bateman and
Amanda Anka

Frank Harlan James 🍁
son of Diana Krall and
Elvis Costello

Frederick 🍁
son of Patrick Roy and
Michèle Piuze

Freedom
daughter of Ving Rhames and
Deborah Reed

Fuschia Katherine
daughter of Sting and
Frances Tomelty

Gaia
daughter of Emma Thompson and
Greg Wise

Gianna Maria-Onore
daughter of Kobe Bryant and
Vanessa Bryant

Gilbran 🍁
son of Tommy Chong and
Shelby Chong

Giovanni 🍁
son of Gil Bellows and
Rya Kihlstedt

Gisele
daughter of Jeri Ryan and
Christophe Émé

Giulia Isabel
daughter of Debi Mazar and
Gabriele Corcos

God'iss Love
daughter of Lil' Mo and Al Stone

Grace Elisabeth
daughter of Elisabeth Hasselbeck
and Tim Hasselbeck

Grace Isabella
daughter of Mia Hamm and
Nomar Garciaparra

Gracie Katherine
daughter of Faith Hill and
Tim McGraw

Grier Hammond
daughter of Brooke Shields and
Chris Henchy

Griffin Arthur 🍁
son of Brendan Fraser and
Afton Smith

Gulliver Flynn
son of Gary Oldman and
Donya Fiorentino

Hannah 🍁
daughter of Paul Gross and
Martha Burns

Harlow Olivia
daughter of Patricia Arquette and
Thomas Jane

Harlow Winter Kate
daughter of Nicole Richie and Joel
Madden

Hazel Patricia
daughter of Julia Roberts and
Danny Moder

Heaven Rain
daughter of Brooke Burke and
David Charvet

Heavenly Hirani Tiger Lily
daughter of Paula Yates and
Michael Hutchence

Henry 🍁
son of Martin Short and
Nancy Dolman

Henry Chance
son of Rachel Weisz and
Darren Aronofsky

Henry Daniel
son of Julia Roberts and
Danny Moder

**Henry Günther Ademola
Dashtu Samuel**
son of Heidi Klum and Seal

Henry Lee
son of Jack White and
Karen Elson

Holden Fletcher 🍁
son of Brendan Fraser and
Afton Smith

Homer James Jigme
son of Richard Gere and
Carey Lowell

Honor Marie
daughter of Jessica Alba and
Cash Warren

Hopper
son of Sean Penn and
Robin Wright Penn

Hudson Harden
son of Marcia Gay Harden and
Thaddeus Scheel

Ignatius Martin
son of Cate Blanchett and
Andrew Upton

India 🍁
daughter of Corey Hart and
Julie Masse

India Ann Sushil 🍁
daughter of Sarah McLachlan and
Ashwin Sood

Indiana August
son of Summer Phoenix and
Casey Affleck

Indio
son of Deborah Falconer and
Robert Downey, Jr.

Ireland Eliesse
daughter of Kim Basinger and
Alec Baldwin

Isabella
daughter of Matt Damon and Luciana Damon

Isabella Jane
daughter of Nicole Kidman and Tom Cruise

Isabella Katherine
daughter of Lisa Brennan and Steve Yzerman

Isadora
daughter of Björk and Matthew Barney

Jack 🍁
son of Paul Gross and Martha Burns

Jack John Christopher
son of Johnny Depp and Vanessa Paradis

Jackie 🍁
daughter of Howie Mandel and Terry Mandel

Jackson Phillip Devereaux
son of Poppy Montgomery and Adam Kaufman

Jacob Emerson
son of Courtney Thorne-Smith and Roger Fishman

Jacqueline Jean 🍁
daughter of Mark Messier and Kim Clark

Jagger Joseph Blue
daughter of Soleil Moon Frye and Jason Goldberg

James Padraig
son of Colin Farrell and Kim Bordenave

Jamison Leon
daughter of Billy Baldwin and Chynna Phillips

Jana 🍁
daughter of Patrick Roy and Michèle Piuze

Jane Erin 🍁
daughter of Jim Carrey and Melissa Carrey

Jaya
daughter of Ben Harper and Laura Dern

Jayden James
son of Britney Spears and Kevin Federline

Jelani Asar
son of Wesley Snipes and April Snipes

Jennifer Katharine
daughter of Bill Gates and Melinda Gates

Jesse James
son of Jon Bon Jovi and Dorothea Bon Jovi

Jessie James
daughter of Kim Porter and Sean "Diddy" Combs

Jett
son of Kelly Preston and John Travolta

Joaquin
son of Kelly Ripa and Mark Consuelos

Johan Riley Fyodor Taiwo Samuel
son of Heidi Klum and Seal

John David
son of Nancy Grace and David Linch

John Edward Thomas
son of Bridget Moynahan and Tom Brady

Johnnie Rose
daughter of Melissa Etheridge and Tammy Lynn Michaels

Johnny
son of Mira Sorvino and Chris Backus

Jonas Rocket
son of Tom DeLonge and Jennifer DeLonge

Jonathan 🍁
son of Patrick Roy and Michèle Piuze

Julian Murray
son of Lisa Kudrow and Michel Stern

Julitta Dee
daughter of Marcia Gay Harden and Thaddeus Scheel

Kaiis Steven
son of Geena Davis and Reza Jarrahy

Kal-El
son of Nicholas Cage and Alice Kim

Kamryn 🍁
daughter of Joe Sakic and Debbie Sakic

Karsen
daughter of Ray Liotta and Michelle Grace

Katherine Elizabeth 🍁
daughter of Martin Short and Nancy Dolman

Keelee Breeze
daughter of Rob "Vanilla Ice" and Laura Van Winkle

Kellen 🍁
son of Rueben Mayes and Marie Mayes

Kian William
son of Geena Davis and Reza Jarrahy

Kiefer 🍁
son of Donald Sutherland and Shirley Douglas

Kieran Lindsay
son of Julianna Margulies and Keith Lieberthal

Kingston James McGregor
son of Gwen Stefani and Gavin Rossdale

Kit Bernard
son of Jodie Foster

Knox Leon
son of Angelina Jolie and Brad Pitt

Kyd Miller
son of David Duchovny and Téa Leoni

Landon 🍁
son of Lennox Lewis and Violet Lewis

Langley Fox
daughter of Mariel Hemingway and Stephen Crisman

Lauren 🍁
daughter of Mario Lemieux and Nathalie Asselin

Leland Francis 🍁
son of Brendan Fraser and Afton Smith

Lennon
son of Patsy Kensit and Liam Gallagher

Leo Kipling
son of Kim Raver and Manuel Boyer

Letesha
daughter of Tracy "Ice-T" and Darlene Morrow

Levi Alves
son of Matthew McConaughey and Camila Alves

Liam Aaron
son of Tori Spelling and Dean McDermott

Lily-Rose Melody
daughter of Johnny Depp and Vanessa Paradis

Ling 🍁
daughter of Lennox Lewis and Violet Lewis

Loewy
son of John Malkovich and Nicoletta Peyran

Logan 🍁
son of Rueben Mayes and Marie Mayes

Lola 🍁
daughter of Steve Nash and Alejandra Amarilla

Lola Rose
daughter of Charlie Sheen and Denise Richards

Lola Simone
daughter of Chris Rock and Malaak Rock

London Emilio
son of Saul "Slash" Hudson and Perla Hudson

Lorca 🍁
daughter of Leonard Cohen and Suzanne Elrod

Lourdes Maria Ciccone
daughter of Madonna and Carlos Leon

Lucy Elizabeth
daughter of Nancy Grace and David Linch

Luisa Danbi
daughter of David Alan Grier and Christine Y. Kim

Lyric
daughter of Karla De Vito and Robby Benson

Mackenzie Jean Rowling
daughter of J. K. Rowling and Neil Murray

Maddie Briann
daughter of Jamie Lynn Spears and Casey Aldridge

Maddox
son of Angelina Jolie and Brad Pitt

Madeleine West
daughter of David Duchovny and Téa Leoni

Maeve Frances
daughter of Chris O'Donnell and Caroline Fentress

Maggie Elizabeth
daughter of Faith Hill and Tim McGraw

Maggie Rose
daughter of Jon Stewart and Tracy Stewart

Magnus Hart 🍁
son of Kristy Swanson and Lloyd Eisler

Magnus Paulin
son of Will Ferrell and Viveca Paulin

Makani Ravello
daughter of Woody Harrelson and Laura Louie

Makena'lei
daughter of Helen Hunt and Matthew Carnahan

Malachy
son of Cillian Murphy and Yvonne Murphy

Malu Valentine
daughter of David Byrne and Adelle Lutz

Manzie Tio
daughter of Woody Allen and Soon-Yi Previn

Margaret Heather
daughter of Kellie Martin and Keith Christian

Maria Charlotte
daughter of Lisa Brennan and Steve Yzerman

Marston 🍁
son of Kimberley Conrad and Hugh Hefner

Mason Walter
son of Melissa Joan Hart and Mark Wilkerson

Matalin Mary
daughter of Mary Matalin and James Carville

Mateo Braverly
son of Benjamin Bratt and Talisa Soto

Matilda Rose
daughter of Heath Ledger and Michelle Williams

Mattea Angel
daughter of Mira Sorvino and Chris Backus

Matthias
son of Will Ferrell and Viveca Paulin

Max
son of Jennifer Lopez and Marc Anthony

Max Liron
son of Christina Aguilera and Jordan Bratman

Maxwell Alston
son of Trista Sutter and Ryan Sutter

Maxx
son of Scott Hamilton and Tracie Hamilton

McCanna
son of Gary Sinise and Moira Harris

McKenna Lane
daughter of Mary Lou Retton and Shannon Kelly

Me'arah Sanaa
daughter of Shaquille O'Neal and Shaunie O'Neal

Memphis Eve
daughter of Alison Stewart and Bono

Messiah Lauren
daughter of Allen Iverson and Tawanna Iverson

Michael
son of Mark Wahlberg and Rhea Durham

Miller Steven
son of Melissa Etheridge and Tammy Lynn Michaels

Milo
son of Camryn Manheim

Milo William
son of Liv Tyler and Royston Langdon

Mingus Lucien
son of Helena Christensen and Norman Reedus

Mitchell 🍁
son of Joe Sakic and Debbie Sakic

Moon Unit
daughter of Frank Zappa and Gail Zappa

Moses
son of Gwyneth Paltrow and Chris Martin

Moxie CrimeFighter
daughter of Penn Jillette and Emily Jillette

Nahla Ariela 🍁
daughter of Halle Berry and Gabriel Aubry

Najee
son of LL Cool J and Simone Smith

Nala
daughter of Keenan Ivory Wayans and Daphne Polk

Nana Kwadjo
son of Isaac Hayes and Adjowa Hayes

Natalia
daughter of Adam Corolla and Lynette Corolla

Natashya Lorien
daughter of Tori Amos and Mark Hawley

Nathan Thomas
son of Jon Stewart and Tracey Stewart

Nayib
son of Gloria Estefan and Emilio Estefan

Neve
daughter of Conan O'Brien and Liza Powell O'Brien

Nevis 🍁
daughter of Nelly Furtado and Jasper Gahunia

Nicholas 🍁
son of Shannon Tweed and Gene Simmons

Nolan
son of Molly Shannon and Fritz Chesnutt

Ocean Alexander
son of Forest Whitaker

Olive
daughter of Isla Fisher and Sacha Baron Cohen

Oliver Patrick 🍁
son of Martin Short and Nancy Dolman

Oliver Philip
son of Fred Savage and Jennifer Stone

Orion Christopher
son of Chris Noth and Tara Wilson

Orson
son of Lauren Ambrose and Sam Handel

Owen
daughter of Michelle Branch and Teddy Landau

Paris
son of Blair Underwood and Desiree DeCosta

Paris 🍁
son of Tommy Chong and Shelby Chong

Paris Michael Katherine
daughter of Michael Jackson and Debbie Rowe

Parker Jaren
son of Rosie O'Donnell

Paulina 🍁
daughter of Wayne Gretzky and Janet Jones

Pax Thien
son of Angelina Jolie and Brad Pitt

Peaches Honeyblossom
daughter of Paula Yates and Bob Geldof

Pearl
daughter of Maya Rudolph and Paul Thomas Anderson

Penelope 🍁
daughter of Jessalyn Gilsig and Bobby Salomon

Phinnaeus Walter
son of Julia Roberts and
Danny Moder

Phoenix Chi
daughter of Melanie "Scary Spice"
Brown and Jimmy Gulzar

Pilot Inspektor
son of Jason Lee and
Beth Riesgraf

Piper Maru
daughter of Gillian Anderson and
Clyde Klotz

Pirate Howsmon
son of Jonathan Davis and
Deven Davis

Pixie
daughter of Paula Yates and
Bob Geldof

Poppy-Honey
daughter of Jamie Oliver and Jools
Oliver

Precious 🍁
daughter of Tommy Chong and
Shelby Chong

Presley Tanita
daughter of Tanya Tucker and
Jerry Laseter

Presley Walker
son of Cindy Crawford and
Rande Gerber

Prince Michael
son of Michael Jackson and
Debbie Rowe

Prince Michael II
son of Michael Jackson

Puma
daughter of Erykah Badu

Quinlin Dempsey
son of Ben Stiller and
Christine Taylor

Rae Dawn 🍁
daughter of Tommy Chong and
Maxine Sneed

Rain
son of Corey Hart and
Julie Masse

Rainie
daughter of Andie MacDowell and
Paul Qualley

Ramona
daughter of Maggie Gyllenhaal
and Peter Sarsgaard

Reignbeau
daughter of Ving Rhames and
Deborah Reed

Rene-Charles 🍁
son of Celine Dion and
Rene Angelil

Riley 🍁
daughter of Howie Mandel and
Terry Mandel

Rio Kelly
son of Sean Young and
Robert Lujan

Ripley
daughter of Thandie Newton and
Oliver Parker

River
son of Keri Russell and
Shane Deary

River 🍁
daughter of Corey Hart and
Julie Masse

River Samuel
son of Taylor Hanson and
Natalie Bryant

Roan
son of Sharon Stone and
Phil Bronstein

Robbi 🍁
daughter of Tommy Chong and
Maxine Sneed

Robin
son of Alan Thicke and
Gloria Loring

Rocco
son of Madonna and Guy Ritchie

Roman Robert
son of Cate Blanchett and
Andrew Upton

Romeo
son of Victoria "Posh Spice"
Beckham and David Beckham

Romy
daughter of Sofia Coppola and
Thomas Mars

Ronan Cal
son of Daniel Day-Lewis and
Rebeca Miller

Rory
son of Bill Gates and
Melinda French

Rowan
daughter of Brooke Shields and
Chris Henchy

Ruby
daughter of Charlotte Church and
Gavin Henson

Ruby
daughter of Tobey Maguire and
Jennifer Meyer

Rumer Glenn
daughter of Demi Moore and
Bruce Willis

Ryan Elizabeth
daughter of Rodney Peete and
Holly Robinson Peete

Ryder
son of Monica Treadway and
Ty Treadway

Ryder Russel
son of Kate Hudson and
Chris Robinson

Sadie Madison
daughter of Adam Sandler and
Jackie Titone Sandler

Saffron Sahara
daughter of Simon Le Bon and
Yasmin Le Bon

Sage Florence
daughter of Toni Collette and Dave
Galafassi

Sailor Lee
daughter of Christie Brinkley and Peter Cook

Salome Violetta
daughter of Alex Kingston and Florian Haertel

Sam Alexis
daughter of Tiger Woods and Elin Nordegren Woods

Samantha Jane
daughter of Charlie Sheen and Denise Richards

Samuel Jason
son of Jack Black and Tanya Haden

Samuel Wyatt
son of Elizabeth Vargas and Marc Cohn

Santino
son of Adam Corolla and Lynette Corolla

Saoirse Roisin
daughter of Courtney Kennedy and Paul Hill

Sarah Jude 🍁
daughter of Kiefer Sutherland and Camelia Kath

Sasha Gabriella 🍁
daughter of Vanessa Williams and Rick Fox

Satchel Lewis
daughter of Spike Lee and Tonya Linette Lewis

Savannah
daughter of Marcia Cross and Tom Mahoney

Sawyer
daughter of Sara Gilbert

Scarlett Teresa
daughter of Jack White and Karen Elson

Schuyler Frances 🍁
daughter of Tracy Pollan and Michael J. Fox

Scout LaRue
daughter of Demi Moore and Bruce Willis

Sean Edward
son of Phil Hartman and Brynn Hartman

Selah Louise
daughter of Lauryn Hill and Rohan Marley

Seven Sirius
son of Andre 3000 and Erykah Badu

Shaya
son of Brooke Burke and David Charvet

Shea Joelle
daughter of Kevin James and Steffiana De La Cruz

Shepherd Kellen
son of Jerry Seinfeld and Jessica Seinfeld

Shiloh Nouvel
daughter of Angelina Jolie and Brad Pitt

Sindri
son of Björk and Thor Eldon

Sistine Rose
daughter of Jennifer Flavin and Sylvester Stallone

Slade Lucas Moby
son of David Brenner and Elizabeth Bryan Slater

Slater Josiah
son of Angela Bassett and Courtney B. Vance

Solita Liliana
daughter of Geraldo Rivera and Erica Rivera

Sonnet Noel
daughter of Forest Whitaker and Keisha Whitaker

Sophia Rose 🍁
daughter of Lisa Brennan and Steve Yzerman

Sophie 🍁
daughter of Shannon Tweed and Gene Simmons

Sosie Ruth
daughter of Kyra Sedgwick and Kevin Bacon

Speck Wildhorse
son of John Mellencamp and Elaine Mellencamp

Stella 🍁
daughter of Sass Jordan and Derek Sharp

Stella Doreen
daughter of Tori Spelling and Dean McDermott

Stella Irene August 🍁
daughter of Dan Aykroyd and Donna Dixon

Stellan
son of Jennifer Connelly and Paul Bettany

Stephanie 🍁
daughter of Mario Lemieux and Nathalie Asselin

Story
daughter of Ginuwine and Sole

Story Elias
son of Jenna Elfman and Bodhi Elfman

Sullivan Patrick
son of Patrick Dempsey and Jillian Fink

Sunday Rose
daughter of Nicole Kidman and Keith Urban

Sunny Bebop
daughter of Michael "Flea" Balzary and Frankie Rayder

Suri
daughter of Tom Cruise and Katie Holmes

Sy'Rai
daughter of Brandy Norwood and Robert Smith

Taja Summer 🍁
daughter of Sarah McLachlan and Ashwin Sood

Tali
daughter of Annie Lennox and Uri Fruchtman

Tallulah Belle
daughter of Demi Moore and Bruce Willis

Taylor Mayne Pearl
daughter of Garth Brooks and Sandy Mahl

Taylor Thomas
son of Elisabeth Hasselbeck and Tim Hasselbeck

Tennyson Spencer
son of Russell Crowe and Danielle Spencer

Theodore Norman
son of Bryce Dallas Howard and Seth Gabel

Thijs
son of Matt Lauer and Annette Roque

Thomas Boone
son of Dennis Quaid and Kimberly Quaid

Trevor Douglas 🍁
son of Wayne Gretzky and Janet Jones

Tristan Wayne 🍁
son of Wayne Gretzky and Janet Jones

True
daughter of Forest Whitaker and Keisha Whitaker

True Harlow
daughter of Joely Fisher and Christopher Duddy

Truman Theodore
son of Rita Wilson and Tom Hanks

Tu Simone Ayer Morrow
daughter of Rob Morrow and Debbon Ayre

Ty Robert 🍁
son of Wayne Gretzky and Janet Jones

Valentina 🍁
daughter of Lolita Davidovich and Ron Shelton

Valentina Paloma
daughter of Salma Hayek and Francois Henri Pinault

Vance Alexander
son of Billy Baldwin and Chyna Phillips

Violet Anne
daughter of Jennifer Garner and Ben Affleck

Violet Maye
daughter of Dave Grohl and Jordyn Grohl

Vivienne Marcheline
daughter of Angelina Jolie and Brad Pitt

Weston
son of Nicolas Cage and Kristina Fulton

Wilder Brooks
son of Oliver Hudson and Erinn Bartlett

William Huckleberry
son of Brad Paisley and Kimberly Williams-Paisley

Willow
daughter of Will Smith and Jada Pinkett Smith

Wolfgang William
son of Eddie Van Halen and Valerie Bertinelli

Yeshua Francis Neil
son of Sinead O'Connor and Frank Bonadio

Zahara Marley
daughter of Angelina Jolie and Brad Pitt

Zahra Savannah
daughter of Chris Grohl and Malaak Rock

Zander Ryan
son of Mindy McCready and Billy McKnight

Zeke 🍁
son of Neil Young and Carrie Snodgrass

Zelda
daughter of Robin Williams and Marsha Garces Williams

Zen Scott 🍁
son of Corey Feldman and Susie Sprague

Zephyr
son of Karla De Vito and Robby Benson

Zion David
son of Lauryn Hill and Rohan Marley

Zoe Giordano
daughter of Woody Harrelson and Laura Louie

Zoe Grace
daughter of Dennis Quaid and Kimberly Quaid

Zolten Penn
son of Penn Jillette and Emily Jillette

How to Register Your Baby's Birth

The following are summaries of how to register your baby's birth and name in each province. For more information, contact your province's vital statistics office.

Alberta

It is the responsibility of the mother or, if the parents are married, either parent to complete a Registration of Birth form. In some circumstances, a person who has full knowledge of the facts surrounding the birth may also complete the Registration of Birth form.

The birth registration should be left with the hospital where the child was born, so that the document can be forwarded to Vital Statistics. The birth registration must be sent to the Vital Statistics office within ten days of the date of the child's birth. The Registration of Birth form becomes a permanent legal record of the birth event. The information is used to produce birth certificates, when ordered.

Once a birth is legally registered, corrections or alterations may only be completed with the appropriate documentation and statutory declarations.

Alberta Registries Vital Statistics
Box 2023
Edmonton, Alberta T5J 4W7
780-427-7013
vs@gov.ab.ca
www.servicealberta.gov.ab.ca/VitalStatistics.cfm

—Adapted from www.servicealberta.gov.ab.ca

British Columbia

The birth of every newborn in the province must be registered with the Vital Statistics Agency. Either parent is responsible for registering the birth of the child. Another individual standing in place of the parents may register the birth, if the parents are incapable. If only one parent is being named on the registration, different rules apply.

To register a child's birth, complete and return the Registration of Live Birth form to the Vital Statistics Agency within thirty days of the date of birth. This form is contained in the birth package given to parents during their stay in the hospital. It is also available at any Vital Statistics office.

The information on the birth registration form is collected under the Vital Statistics Act to register a birth, apply for a Social Insurance Number, and produce a birth certificate. It also provides statistical information for British Columbia.

Vital Statistics Agency
818 Fort Street
PO Box 9657, STN PROV GOV'T
Victoria, BC V8W 9P3
250-952-2681 (Victoria) or 604-660-2937 (Vancouver)
www.vs.gov.bc.ca

—Adapted from www.vs.gov.bc.ca

Manitoba

A child's birth must be registered with both a given name and a sur-name, made up of the letters *a* to *z* and accents from the English or French languages, and may include hyphens and apostrophes. If the parents are not married, information about the father can only be included on the birth registration if the parents complete a joint written request and submit it to the Vital Statistics Agency.

Manitoba Vital Statistics
254 Portage Avenue
Winnipeg, MB R3C 0B6
204-945-3701
vitalstats@govmb.ca
www.govmb.ca/cca/vital

—Adapted from www.gov.mb.ca

New Brunswick

You must register your baby's birth with Service New Brunswick's Vital Statistics Office. The document used to record the birth of your baby is called the Registration of Birth, Form C-1. This document establishes the legal identity of your child and becomes a permanent record kept by the Vital Statistics office. The information recorded on this form is used to produce birth certificates.

In person:
Service New Brunswick
435 King Street, Suite 203
Fredericton, NB E3B1E5

By mail:
Vital Statistics Office
Service New Brunswick
PO Box 1998
Fredericton, NB E3B5G4

Phone: 506-453-2385
Fax: 506-453-3245
vitalstatistics@snb.ca
www.snb.ca/e/1000/1000-01/e/index-e.asp

—Adapted from www.snb.ca

Newfoundland and Labrador

To register your newborn child's birth in Newfoundland and Labrador, you may apply in person at any Government Service Cen-tres or departmental offices. Or you can send a form to Vital Statistics at the following mailing address:

Vital Statistics
Government Service Centre
Department of Government Services
5 Mews Place
PO Box 8700
St. John's, NL A1B 4J6
info@gov.nl.ca
www.gs.gov.nl.ca

—Adapted from www.gs.gov.nl.ca

Northwest Territories

The birth of every child in the Northwest Territories must be regis-tered with the Registrar General of Vital Statistics within thirty days after the birth. Registration is required to establish a permanent legal record of a person's birth. Without registration, a birth certifi-cate cannot be obtained.

Registering the birth is the responsibility of the mother of the child; if the mother is incapable, the father of the child; where either parent is incapable, the other parent; and where both parents are incapable, the person standing in the place of the parents.

Registrar-General of Vital Statistics
Department of Health and Social Services
Government of Northwest Territories
Bag #9
Inuvik NT X0E 0T0
Phone: 867-777-7420 or 800-661-0830
Fax: 867-777-3197
hsa@gov.nt.ca
www.hlthss.gov.nt.ca/english/services/vital_statistics/default.htm

—Adapted from www.hlthss.gov.nt.ca

Nova Scotia

Every birth in Nova Scotia must be properly registered for a birth certificate to be issued. The parent receives the registration form in the hospital at the time of the birth. You can you get this registration and/or further information from any local division Registrar of Births and Stillbirths properly authorized by the Government of Nova Scotia. These can be reached through the medical records director at your local hospital.

When the form is completed, it is submitted to the Local Division Registrar at the hospital, who signs it and then forwards it to the Vital Statistics office. The registration form should be submitted within thirty days. Additional forms may be required.

In person:
Vital Statistics Office
Service Nova Scotia and Municipal Relations
Joseph Howe Building
Ground Floor
1690 Hollis Street
Halifax, NS B3J 3J9

By mail:
Vital Statistics Office
Service Nova Scotia and Municipal Relations
PO Box 157
Halifax, NS B3J 2M9

Phone: 902-424-4381 or 877-848-2578
Fax: 902-424-0678
vstat@govns.ca
http://www.govns.ca/snsmr/vstat/

—Adapted from www.govns.ca

Nunavut

An application for registering a birth in Nunavut can be found at www.gov.nu.ca/documents/Vital%20Statistics-Birth-Marriage-Death-Applications.pdf. For more information, please contact the Registrar-General of Vital Statistics.

Registrar-General of Vital Statistics
Nunavut Health & Social Services
Bag #3
Rankin Inlet, NU X0C 0G0
Phone: 867-645-8001 or 888-252-9869
Fax: 867-645-8092
www.gov.nu.ca

—Adapted from www.gov.nu.ca

Ontario

You must register the birth of your child before you can apply for a birth certificate. After the baby is born, you will receive a Statement of Live Birth form from the hospital or midwife. The Statement of Live Birth is your child's permanent legal record.

Return the form as soon as possible to the Division Registrar's Office for the city where your baby was born. The Division Registrar will send the form to the Office of the Registrar General, which will register the birth.

Office of the Registrar General
Ministry of Consumer and Business Services
PO Box 4600 3rd Floor
189 Red River Road
Thunder Bay, Ontario P7B 6L8
416-325-8305 or 800-461-2156
www.serviceontario.ca

—Adapted from www.gov.on.ca

Prince Edward Island

Within thirty days of the birth of a child, the birth must be registered with Vital Statistics. This is usually done in the hospital after the baby is born. After the birth is registered, a follow-up letter is sent out to the parent(s). This letter is called a Confirmation of Birth. If it is returned within thirty days of the birth, the parent can make changes to the information on this form. The letter also provides the opportunity to request a birth certificate.

Vital Statistics
126 Douses Road
Montague, PE C0A 1R0
Phone: 902-838-0880 or 877-320-1253
Fax: 902.833.0883
www.gov.pe.ca/health/

—Adapted from www.gov.pe.ca

Quebec

After a birth, the person who assists in the delivery draws up an Attestation of Birth. The parents will receive a copy of the Attestation as well as a Declaration of Birth, which one or both parents must fill out within thirty days of the child's birth. A witness must sign the Declaration of Birth. Both documents must then be sent to the Directeur de l'état civil.

Le Directeur de l'état civil
2535 Boulevard Laurier
Québec, Québec G1V 5C5
Phone: 418-643-3900 or 800-567-3900
Fax: 418-646-3255
etatcivil@dec.gouv.qc.ca
www.etatcivil.gouv.qc.ca/en/default.html

—Adapted from www.etatcivil.gouv.qc.ca/

Saskatchewan

By law, the birth of every child in Saskatchewan must be registered with Vital Statistics within fifteen days after the birth. Registration is necessary to establish a permanent legal record of a person's birth. Without registration you cannot obtain a birth certificate. Registering the birth is the responsibility of the mother and father of the child; where the father is unacknowledged, or either parent is incapable, the other parent; and where both parents are incapable, the person standing in the place of the parents.

The child's name must be written entirely in characters of the Roman alphabet. If identifiers such as Junior, Jr., II, or III are included in either the given name(s) or surname of the child, it will become part of the child's legal name.

If the birth occurs in a hospital, the hospital requires the completion of the Registration of Live Birth form before the mother is discharged. If the birth does not occur in a hospital, the mother and/or father must contact the Saskatchewan Vital Statistics office to obtain a Registration of Live Birth form for completion. The Registration of Live Birth is to be forwarded to a division registrar, who registers the birth and then forwards it to Saskatchewan Vital Statistics.

Vital Statistics
Saskatchewan Health
100-1942 Hamilton St
Regina, Saskatchewan S4P 4W2
Phone: 306-787-3251 or 800-667-7551
Fax: (306) 787-2288
www.health.gov.sk.ca/vital-statistics

—Adapted from www.health.gov.sk.ca

Yukon Territory

The birth of every child must be registered within thirty days after the birth. The responsibility for registering the birth rests with the mother and the father; where the father is unacknowledged, or either parent is incapable, by the other parent; or where both parents are incapable, by the person standing in place of the parents.

The information on this form is collected under the authority of the Vital Statistics Act. The information provided will be used to register this birth, produce birth certificates, and provide statistical and demographic information.

In person:
Vital Statistics
4th Floor-204 Lambert St.
Whitehorse, Yukon Y1A 3T2

By mail:
Vital Statistics
Health and Social Services
Box 2703
Whitehorse, YT Y1A 2C6

Phone: 867-667-5207 or 800-661-0408 ext. 5207
Fax: 867-393-6486
Vital.Statistics@gov.yk.ca
www.hss.gov.yk.ca/programs/vitalstats/

—Adapted from www.hss.gov.yk.ca

Girls

Aaleyah (Hebrew) a form of Aliya.
Aalayah, Aalayaha, Aalea, Aaleah,
Aaleaha, Aaleeyah, Aaleyiah, Aaleyyah

Aaliah (Hebrew) a form of Aliya.
Aaliaya, Aaliayah

Aalisha (Greek) a form of Alisha.
Aaleasha, Aaliesha

Aaliyah (Hebrew) a form of Aliya.
Aahliyah, Aaeliyah, Aailiyah, Aaleyah,
Aaleeah, Aalia, Aaliayha, Aaliya,
Aaliyaha, Aaliyha, Aalliah, Aaliyah,
Aalyah, Aalyiah

Abagail (Hebrew) a form of Abigale.
Abagail, Abagaile, Abagale, Abagayle,
Abageal, Abagil, Abaigael, Abaigeal

Abbagail (Hebrew) a form of Abigale.
Abbagale, Abbagayle, Abbegail, Abbegale,
Abbegayle

Abbey, Abbie, Abby (Hebrew) famil-
iar forms of Abigail.
Aabbee, Abbe, Abbea, Abbeigh, Abbi,
Abbye, Abbey, Abey, Abi, Abia, Abie, Aby

Abbygail (Hebrew) a form of Abigale.
Abbeygale, Abbygale, Abbygayl,
Abbygayle

Abegail (Hebrew) a form of Abigail.
Abegale, Abegaile, Abegayle

Abelina (American) a combination of
Abbey + Lina.
Abilana, Abilene

Abia (Arabic) great.
Abbia, Abbiah, Abiah, Abya

Abianne (American) a combination of
Abbey + Ann.
Abena, Abeni, Abian, Abinaya

Abida (Arabic) worshiper.
Abedah, Abidah

Abigail (Hebrew) father's joy. Bible:
one of the wives of King David. See
also Gail.
Abagail, Abbagail, Abbey, Abbiegail,
Abbiegayle, Abbigail, Abbigayl, Abbigal,
Abegail, Abgail, Abbigayle, Abbygail,
Abigaile, Abigal, Abigale, Abigayle,
Abigayil, Abigayl, Abigayle, Abigel,
Abigal, Abigayil, Abygail, Avigail

Abinaya (American) a form of
Abiann.
Abenaa, Abenaya, Abinaa, Abinaiya,
Abinayan

Abira (Hebrew) my strength.
Abbira, Abeer, Abeerah, Abeir, Abera,
Aberah, Abhira, Abiir, Abir

Abra (Hebrew) mother of many
nations.
Abree, Abri, Abria

Abria (Hebrew) a form of Abra.
Abréa, Abrea, Abreia, Abriah, Abriéa,
Abrya

Abrial (French) open; secure;
protected.
Abrial, Abreal, Abreale, Abriale, Abrielle

Abriana (Italian) a form of Abra.
Abbrienna, Abbryana, Abreana,
Abrianna, Abreanna, Abreauna,

Abreona, Abriann, Abrianna, Abriannah,
Abrieana, Abrien, Abrienna, Abrienne,
Abrietta, Abrion, Abrionée, Abrionne,
Abrunna, Abryann, Abryanna, Abryona

Abrielle (French) a form of Abrial.
Aabriella, Abriel, Abriell, Abryell

Abril (French) a form of Abrial.
Abrilla, Abrille

Abygail (Hebrew) a form of Abigail.
Abygael, Abygale, Abygayle

Acacia (Greek) thorny. Mythology: the
acacia tree symbolizes immortality
and resurrection. See also Casey.
Acasha, Acatia, Accassia, Acey, Acie,
Akacia, Cacia, Casia, Kasia

Ada (German) a short form of
Adelaide. (English) prosperous; happy.
Adabelle, Adah, Adan, Adaya, Adda,
Auda

Adah (Hebrew) ornament.
Ada, Addah

Adair (Greek) a form of Adara.
Adaire

Adalene (Spanish) a form of Adalia.
Adalena, Adalena, Adalin, Adalina,
Adaline, Adalinn, Adalyn, Adalynn,
Adalynne, Addalyn, Addalynn

Adalia (German, Spanish) noble.
Adal, Adala, Adalea, Adaleah, Adalee,
Adalene, Adali, Adalie, Adaly, Addal,
Addala, Addaly

Adama (Phoenician, Hebrew) a form
of Adam (see Boys' Names).

Adamma (Ibo) child of beauty.

Adana (Spanish) a form of Adama.
Adanya

Adanna (Nigerian) her father's daughter.

Adara (Greek) beauty. (Arabic) virgin.
Adair, Adaira, Adaora, Adar, Adarah, Adare, Adaria, Adarra, Adasha, Adauré, Adra

Adaya (American) a form of Ada.
Adaija, Adajiah, Adaja, Adajah, Adayja, Adayjah, Adejah

Addie (Greek, German) a familiar form of Adelaide, Adrienne.
Aday, Adde, Addee, Addey, Addi, Addia, Addy, Ade, Adee, Adei, Adey, Adeye, Adi, Adie, Ady, Atti, Attie, Atty

Addison, Addyson (English) child of Adam.
Addis, Addisen, Addisson, Adison

Adela (English) a short form of Adelaide.
Adelae, Adelia, Adelista, Adella

Adelaide (German) noble and serene. See also Ada, Adela, Adeline, Adelle, Ailis, Delia, Della, Ela, Elke, Heidi.
Adelade, Adelaid, Adelaida, Adelei, Adelheid, Adeliade, Adelka, Aley, Laidey, Laidy

Adele (English) a form of Adelle.
Adel, Adelie, Adile

Adelina (English) a form of Adeline.
Adalina, Adelena, Adelena, Adellyra, Adeliana, Adellena, Adileena, Adleena

Adeline (English) a form of Adelaide.
Adaline, Adelaine, Adelin, Adelina, Adelind, Adelita, Adeliya, Adelle, Adelyn,

Adelynn, Adelynne, Adilene, Adlin, Adline, Adlyn, Adlynn, Aline

Adelle (German, English) a short form of Adelaide, Adeline.
Adele, Adell

Adena (Hebrew) noble; adorned.
Adeana, Adeen, Adeena, Aden, Adene, Adenia, Adenna, Adina

Adia (Swahili) gift.
Adea, Adéa, Adia, Adiah

Adila (Arabic) equal.
Adeala, Adeela, Adela, Adelah, Adeola, Adilah, Adileh, Adilia, Adyla

Adilene (English) a form of Adeline.
Adilen, Adileni, Adilenne, Adlen, Adlene

Adina (Hebrew) a form of Adena. See also Dina.
Adeana, Adiana, Adiena, Adinah, Adine, Adinna, Adyna

Adira (Hebrew) strong.
Ader, Adera, Aderah, Aderra, Adhira, Adirah, Adirana

Adison, Adyson (English) forms of Addison, Addyson.
Adis, Adisa, Adisen, Adisynne, Adysen

Aditi (Hindi) unbound. Religion: the mother of the Hindu sun gods.
Adithi, Aditi

Adleigh (Hebrew) my ornament.
Adla, Adleni

Adonia (Spanish) beautiful.
Adonica, Adonis, Adonna, Adonnica, Adonya

Adora (Latin) beloved. See also Dora.
Adore, Adoree, Adoria

Adra (Arabic) virgin.
Adara

Adreana, Adreanna (Latin) forms of Adrienne.
Adrean, Adreanne, Adreauna, Adreeanna, Adreen, Adreena, Adreeyana, Adrena, Adrene, Adrenea, Adreona, Adreonia, Adreonna

Adria (English) a short form of Adriana, Adriene.
Adrea, Adriani, Adrya

Adriana, Adrianna (Italian) forms of Adrienne.
Addrianna, Addriyanna, Adreiana, Adreinna, Adria, Adriannea, Adriannia, Adrionna

Adriane, Adrianne (English) forms of Adrienne.
Adrian, Adrianne, Adria, Adrian, Adrienne, Adriann, Adriayon, Adrion

Adrielle (Hebrew) member of God's flock.
Adriel, Adrielli, Adryelle

Adrien, Adriene (English) forms of Adrienne.

Adrienna (Italian) a form of Adrienne. See also Edrianna.
Adreanna, Adrieanna, Adrieaunna, Adriena, Adrienia, Adriennah, Adrieunna

Adrienne (Greek) rich. (Latin) dark. See also Hadriane.
Adie, Adrien, Adriana, Adriane, Adrianne, Adrianne, Adrie, Adrieanne, Adrianna, Adrianne, Adrie, Adrienna, Adriyanna

Adrina (English) a short form of Adriana.
Adrinah, Adrine

Adriyanna (American) a form of Adrienne.
Adriyana, Adriyana, Adriyana, Adryane, Adryanna, Adryanne

Adya (Hindi) Sunday.
Adia

Aerial, Aeriel (Hebrew) forms of Ariel.
Aeriale, Aeriela, Aerielle, Aeril, Aerile, Aeryal

Africa (Irish) pleasant. Geography: one of the seven continents.
Affrica, Afric, Africah, Africaya, Africia, Africiana, Afrika, Afric

Afra (Hebrew) young doe. (Arabic) earth color. See also Aphra.
Affery, Affrey, Affric, Afraa

Afrika (Irish) a form of Africa.
Afrikah

Afrodite, Aphrodite (Greek) Mythology: the goddess of love and beauty.
Afrodita

Afton (English) from Afton, England.
Aftan, Aftine, Aftinn, Afryn

Afi (African) born on Friday.
Affi, Afia, Efi, Efia

Agate (English) a semiprecious stone.
Aggie

Agatha (Greek) good, kind. Literature: Agatha Christie was a British writer of more than seventy detective novels. See also Gasha.
Agace, Agaisha, Agasha, Agata, Agatah,

Adya (Hindi) Sunday.

Agathe (Greek) a form of Agatha.
Agathe, Agathi, Agatka, Agetha, Aggie, Agota, Agotha, Agueda, Atka

Aggie (Greek) a short form of Agatha, Agnes.
Ag, Aggy, Agi

Agnes (Greek) pure. See also Aneesa, Anessa, Anice, Anisha, Ina, Inez, Necha, Nessa, Nessie, Neza, Nyusha, Una, Ynez.
Aganetha, Aggie, Agna, Agne, Agnes, Agnella, Agnella, Agnès, Agnesa, Agnesca, Agnese, Agnesina, Agness, Agnessa, Agnesse, Agneta, Agneti, Agnetta, Agnieszka, Agniya, Agnola, Agnus, Agnés, Aneska, Anka

Ahava (Hebrew) beloved.
Ahavia

Ahliya (Hebrew) a form of Aliya.
Ahlai, Ahlaia, Ahlaya, Ahleah, Ahleeyah, Ahley, Ahleya, Ahlia, Ahliah, Ahliyah

Aida (Latin) helpful. (English) a form of Ada.
Aidah, Aidan, Aide, Aidee

Aidan, Aiden (Latin) forms of Aida.

Aiesha (Swahili, Arabic) a form of Aisha.
Aesha, Aeshia, Aieysha, Aiiesha

Aiko (Japanese) beloved.

Ailani (Hawaiian) chief.
Aelani, Ailana

Aileen (Scottish) light bearer. (Irish) a form of Helen. See also Eileen.
Ailan, Ailena, Ailen, Ailene, Aili, Ailina, Ailinn, Aillen

Aili (Scottish) a form of Alice. (Finnish) a form of Helen.
Aila, Ailee, Ailey, Ailie, Aily

Ailis (Irish) a form of Adelaide.
Ailesh, Ailish, Ailyse, Eilis

Ailsa (Scottish) island dweller. Geography: Ailsa Craig is an island in Scotland.
Ailsa

Ailya (Hebrew) a form of Aliya.
Atliyah

Aimee (Latin) a form of Amy. (French) loved.
Aime, Aimée, Aimey, Aimi, Aimia, Aimie, Aimy

Ainsley (Scottish) my own meadow.
Ainslee, Ainsleigh, Ainslie, Ainsly, Ainsley, Aynslee, Aynsley, Aynslie

Airiana (English) a form of Ariana.
Airianna, Airreanna, Airreanah, Aireanna, Aireona, Aireanah, Airianna, Airianne, Airiona, Airriana, Airrion, Airryon, Airyana, Airyanna

Airiél (Hebrew) a form of Ariel.
Aieral, Aierl, Aiiryel, Aire, Aireal, Aireale, Aireal, Airel, Airele, Airelle, Airi, Airial, Airiale, Airrel

Aisha (Swahili) life. (Arabic) woman. See also Asha, Asia, Iesha, Isha, Keisha, Yiesha.
Aaisha, Aaishah, Aesha, Aeshah, Aheesha, Aiasha, Aiesha, Aieshah, Aisa, Aischa, Aish, Aishah, Aishia, Aishiah, Aiysha, Aisheh, Aishia, Aishiah, Aiysha, Aisheh, Aishia, Ayse, Ayiza

Aislinn, Aislynn (Irish) forms of Ashlynn.
Aishellyn, Aishlinn, Aislee, Aisley, Aislin, Aisling, Aislyn, Aislynne

Aiyana (Native American) forever flowering.
Aiyhana, Aiyona, Aiyonia, Ayana

Aiyanna (Hindi) a form of Ayanna.
Aianna, Aiyannah, Aiyonna, Aiyunna

Aja (Hindi) goat.
Ahjah, Aija, Aijah, Ajá, Ajada, Ajah, Ajana, Ajaran, Ajare, Ajaree, Ajha, Ajia

Ajanae (American) a combination of the letter A + Janae.
Ajahnae, Ajahne, Ajana, Ajanaé, Ajane, Ajané, Ajanee, Ajanique, Ajena, Ajenae, Ajené

Ajia (Hindi) a form of Aja.
Aijia, Ajhia, Aji, Ajia

Akayla (American) a combination of the letter A + Kayla.
Akaela, Akaelia, Akailla, Akailah, Akala, Akaylah, Akaylia

Akeisha (American) a combination of the letter A + Keisha.
Akaesha, Akaisha, Akasha, Akasia, Akeecia, Akeesha, Akeishia, Akeshia, Akisha

Akela (Hawaiian) noble.
Ahkayla, Ahkeelah, Akelah, Akelia, Akeliah, Akeya, Akeyla, Akeylah

Akeria (American) a form of Akira.
Akera, Akerah, Akeri, Akerra, Akerra

Aki (Japanese) born in autumn.
Akeeye

Akia (American) a combination of the letter A + Kia.
Akaja, Akeia, Akeya, Akiá, Akiah, Akiane, Akiaya, Akiea, Akiya, Akiyah, Akya, Akyan, Akyia, Akyiah

Akiko (Japanese) bright light.

Akilah (Arabic) intelligent.
Aikela, Aikeilah, Akeela, Akeelah, Akeila, Akeilah, Akeiyla, Akiela, Akielah, Akila, Akilah, Akila, Akilka, Akillah, Akkila, Akyla, Akylah

Akili (Tanzanian) wisdom.

Akina (Japanese) spring flower.

Akira (American) a combination of the letter A + Kira.
Akeria, Akiera, Akierra, Akirah, Akire, Akiria, Akirrah, Akyra

Alaina, Alayna (Irish) forms of Alana.
Aalaina, Alainah, Alaine, Alainna, Alainnah, Alane, Alaynah, Alayne, Alaynna, Aleine, Alleyna, Alleynah, Alleyne

Alair (French) a form of Hilary.
Alaia, Ali, Allaire

Alamea (Hawaiian) ripe; precious.

Alameda (Spanish) poplar tree.

Alana (Irish) attractive; peaceful. (Hawaiian) offering. See also Lana.
Alaana, Alaina, Alanae, Alanah, Alane, Alanea, Alani, Alania, Alanis, Alanna, Alauna, Alayna, Allana, Allanah, Allyn, Alonna

Alandra, Alandria (Spanish) forms of Alexandra, Alexandria.
Alandrea, Alantra, Aleandra, Aleandrea

Alani (Hawaiian) orange tree. (Irish) a form of Alana.
Alairi, Alainie, Alania, Alanie, Alaney, Alannie

Alanna (Irish) a form of Alana.
Alannah

Alanza (Spanish) noble and eager.

Alaysha, Alaysia (American) forms of Alicia.
Alaysh, Alayshia

Alba (Latin) from Alba Longa, an ancient city near Rome, Italy.
Albana, Albani, Albanie, Albany, Albeni, Albina, Albine, Albinia, Albinka, Elba

Alberta (German, French) noble and bright. See also Auberte, Bertha, Elberta.
Albertina, Albertine, Albertyna, Albertyne, Alverta

Albreanna (American) a combination of Alberta + Breanna (see Breana).
Albré, Albrea, Albreona, Albreonna, Albreyon

Alcina (Greek) strong-minded.
Alceena, Alcine, Alcinia, Alseena, Alsinia, Alsyna, Alzina

Alda (German) old; elder.
Aldina, Aldine

Alden (English) old; wise protector.
Aldan, Aldon, Aldyn

Aldina, Aldine (Hebrew) forms of Alda.
Aldeana, Aldene, Aldona, Aldyna, Aldyne

Alea, Aleah (Arabic) high, exalted. (Persian) God's being.
Aileah, Aleea, Aleeah, Aleia, Aleiah, Allea, Alleah, Alleea, Alleeah

Aleasha, Aleesha (Greek) forms of Alisha.
Aleashae, Aleashia, Aleassa, Aleeshia

Alecia (Greek) a form of Alicia.
Aalecia, Ahlasia, Alacia, Aleacya, Aleasia, Alecea, Aleceea, Aleciya, Aleciyah, Alecy, Aleeya, Aleeceia, Aleecia, Alesia, Aleesiya, Aleicia, Alesha, Alesia, Allecia, Alleecia

Aleela (Swahili) she cries.
Aleelah, Alila, Alile

Aleena (Dutch) a form of Aleene.
Ahleena, Aleana, Aleanna

Aleene (Dutch) alone.
Aleen, Aleena, Alene, Alleen

Aleeya (Hebrew) a form of Aliya.
Alee, Aleea, Aleeyah, Aleya, Aleryah, Aleryah

Aleeza (Hebrew) a form of Aliza. See also Leeza.
Aleiza

Alegria (Spanish) cheerful.
Alegra, Alegra, Allegra, Allegria

Aleisha, Alesha (Greek) forms of Alecia, Alisha.
Aleasha, Aleashea, Aleasia, Alesha, Aleeshah, Aleeshia, Aleeshya, Aleisa, Alesa, Alesah, Aleishia, Aleishia, Aleshya, Alesia, Alessia

Alejandra (Spanish) a form of Alexandra.
Alejandra, Alejandra, Alejandr,

Alejandrea, Alejandria, Alejandrina,
Alejandro

Aleka (Hawaiian) a form of Alice.
Aleeka, Alekah

Aleksandra (Greek) a form of Alexandra.
Alexandra, Aleksasha, Aleksandrija, Aleksandriya

Alena (Russian) a form of Helen.
Alenah, Alene, Alenea, Aleni, Alenia, Alenka, Alenna, Alennah, Alenya, Alyna

Alesia, Alessia (Greek) forms of Alice, Alicia, Alisha.
Alessea, Alesya, Allesia

Alessa (Greek) a form of Alice.
Alessi, Alessa

Alessandra (Italian) a form of Alexandra.
Alessandra, Alessandrea, Alissandra, Alissondra, Allesand, Allessandra

Aleta (Greek) a form of Alida. See also Leta.
Aletta, Alleta

Alethea (Greek) truth.
Alathea, Alathia, Aletea, Aletha, Aletheia, Alethia, Aletia, Alithea, Alithia

Alette (Latin) wing.

Alexa (Greek) a short form of Alexandra.
Aleixa, Aleka, Aleksa, Aleksha, Aleksi, Alexah, Alexsa, Alexxa, Allexa

Aleka (Hawaiian) a form of Alice.
Aleeka, Alekah

Aleksandra (Greek) a form of Alexandra.
Alexandra, Aleksasha, Aleksandrija, Aleksandriya

Alex (Greek) a short form of Alexander, Alexandra.
Aleix, Aleks, Alexe, Alexx, Allex, Allexx

Alexandra (Greek) defender of humankind. History: the last czarina of Russia. See also Lexia, Lexie, Olesia, Ritsa, Sandra, Sandrine, Sasha, Shura, Sondra, Xandra, Zandra.
Alandra, Alaxandra, Alecxandra, Alejandra, Aleksandra, Alessandra, Alex, Alexa, Alexande, Alexandre, Alexas, Alexi, Alexine, Alexis, Alexsandra, Alexis, Alexsis, Alexus, Alexxandra, Alexys, Alexzandra, Alix, Alixandra, Aljexi, Alla, Alyx, Alyxandra, Lexandra

Alexandrea (Greek) a form of Alexandria.
Alexandreana, Alexandria, Alexandriea, Alexandrea

Alexandria (Greek) a form of Alexandra. See also Drinka, Xandra, Zandra.
Alaxandria, Alesandria, Aleczandria, Alexandaria, Alexanderia, Alexanderine, Alexandira, Alexandrena, Alexanderine, Alexandria, Alexandria, Alexandrina, Alexandrya, Alexandrine, Alexia, Alixandria, Alyxandria

Alexandrine (Greek) a form of Alexandra.
Alexandrina

Alexanne (American) a combination of Alex + Anne.
Alexan, Alexanna, Alexane, Alexann, Alexanna, Alexian, Alexiana

Alexas, Alexes (Greek) short forms of Alexandra.
Alexess

Alexi, Alexie (Greek) short forms of Alexandra.
Aleksey, Aleksi, Alexey, Alexy

Alexia (Greek) a short form of Alexandria. See also Lexia.
Aleksia, Aleska, Alexcia, Alexea, Alexsia, Alexsiya, Allexia, Alyxia

Alexis (Greek) a short form of Alexandra.
Aalexis, Ahlexis, Alaxis, Alecis, Aleccis, Aleksis, Alexcis, Alexius, Alexiou, Alexsis, Alexiz, Alexsis, Alixis, Allexis, Elexis, Lexis

Alexius, Alexis (Greek) short forms of Alexandra.
Aalexus, Aalexxus, Aelexus, Ahlexus, Alecsus, Alexsus, Alexxus, Alixus, Allexius, Allexus, Elexus, Lexus

Alexsandra (Greek) a form of Alexandra.
Alexsandria, Alexsandro, Alixsandra

Alexsis, Alexsis (Greek) short forms of Alexandra.
Alexciz

Alexys (Greek) a short form of Alexandra.
Alexyes, Alexyes, Alexyis, Alexyss, Alleexys

Alexzandra, Alexzandra (Greek) forms of Alexandra.
Alexzand, Alexzandrea, Alexzandriah, Alexzandrya, Alixzandria

Aleya, Aleyah (Hebrew) forms of Aliya.
Alayah, Aleayah, Aleeya, Aleyah, Aleyia, Aleyiah

Alfie (English) a familiar form of Alfreda.
Alfi, Alfy

Alfreda (English) elf counselor; wise counselor. See also Effie, Elfrida, Freda, Frederica.
Alfie, Alfredda, Alfredia, Alfreeda, Alfreida, Alfrieda

Ali, Aly (Greek) familiar forms of Alice, Alicia, Alisha, Alison.
Allea, Alli, Allie, Ally

Alia, Aliah (Hebrew) forms of Aliya. See also Aaliyah, Alea.
Aelia, Allia, Alya

Alice (Greek) truthful. (German) noble. See also Aili, Aleka, Alie, Alisa, Alison, Alli, Alysa, Alyssa, Alysse, Elke.
Adelice, Alecia, Aleece, Alesia, Alicie, Aliece, Alise, Alix, Alize, Alla, Alleece, Allie, Allis, Allise, Allix

Alicia (English) a form of Alice. See also Elicia, Licia.
Aelicia, Alaysha, Aleecea, Alecia, Aleecia, Ali, Alicea, Alicha, Alichia, Aliciah, Alician, Aliqja, Alicya, Aliecia, Alisha, Allicea, Allicia, Alycia, Ilysa

Alida (Latin) small and winged. (Spanish) noble. See also Aleta, Lida, Oleda.
Aleda, Aleida, Alidia, Alita, Alleda, Allida, Allidah, Alyda, Alydia, Elida, Elidia

Alie, Allie (Greek) familiar forms of Alice.

Aliesha (Greek) a form of Alisha.
Alieshai, Alieshia, Alliesha

Alika (Hawaiian) truthful. (Swahili) most beautiful.
Aleka, Alica, Alikah, Alike, Alikee, Aliki

Alima (Arabic) sea maiden; musical.

Alina, Alyna (Slavic) bright. (Scottish) fair. (English) short forms of Adeline. See also Alena.
Aliana, Alianna, Alinah, Aline, Alima, Allyna, Alynna, Alyona

Aline (Scottish) a form of Alina.
Alianne, Allene, Alline, Allyn, Allyne, Alyne, Alynne

Alisa, Alissa (Greek) a form of Alice. See also Elisa, Ilisa.
Aalissah, Aaliysah, Aleessa, Alisah, Alisea, Alisia, Alisza, Alissza, Alysa, Allissa, Alyssa

Alise, Allise (Greek) forms of Alice.
Alics, Aliese, Alis, Aliss, Alise, Alisse, Alles, Allesse, Allis, Allisse

Alisha (Greek) truthful. (German) noble. (English) a form of Alicia. See also Elisha, Ilisha, Lisha.
Aalisha, Aaliysah, Aleessa, Alisah, Aleisha, Alesha, Ali, Aliesha, Alisia, Alishah, Alishay, Alishaye, Alishia, Alishya, Alitsha, Allisha, Allysha, Alysha

Alishia, Alisia, Alissia (English) forms of Alisha.
Alishea, Alisheia, Alishiana, Alyssaya, Alisea, Alissya, Alisyia, Allissia

Alison, Allison (English) forms of Alice. See also Lissie.
Ali, Alicen, Alicyn, Alisan, Alisann, Alisanne, Alisen, Alisenne, Alisin, Alison, Alisonn, Alisson, Alison, Alles, Allesse, Alleyson, Allie, Allisson, Allisyn, Allix, Allsun

Alita (Latin) a form of Alida.
Allita

Alivia (Spanish) a form of Alida.
Alivah

Alivia (Latin) a form of Olivia.
Alivah

Alix (Greek) a short form of Alexandra, Alice.
Alixe, Alixia, Allix, Alyx

Alixandra, Alixandria (Greek) forms of Alexandria.
Alixandriya, Alixandra, Allixandria, Allixandrya

Aliya (Hebrew) ascender.
Aaleyah, Aaliyah, Aeliyah, Ahliya, Aiya, Alea, Aleya, Alia, Alieya, Alieyah, Aliyah, Aliyiah, Aliyyah, Allia, Alliyah, Aliy, Alyah

Aliye (Arabic) noble.
Aliyeh

Aliza (Hebrew) joyful. See also Aleeza, Eliza.
Alieza, Aliezah, Alitza, Aliz, Alizah, Alize, Alizee

Alizabeth (Hebrew) a form of Elizabeth.
Alyzabeth

Allana, Allanah (Irish) forms of Alana.
Allanie, Allanna, Allanna

Allegra (Latin) cheerful.
Legra

Allena (Irish) a form of Alana.
Alleen, Alleyna, Alleynah

Alli, Ally (Greek) familiar forms of Alice.
Ali, Alley

Allia, Alliah (Hebrew) forms of Aliya.
Alona, Alonnah, Alorya, Aloryah

Allissa (Greek) a form of Alyssa.
Alisa

Alliyah (Hebrew) a form of Aliya.
Alliya, Alliyha, Alliyiah, Alliya, Alliyah

Allysa, Allyssa (Greek) a form of Alyssa.
Allissa, Allysia, Allysa, Allysah, Allyssah

Allysha (English) a form of Alisha.
Alishia, Allysia

Allyson, Alyson (English) forms of Alison.
Allysen, Allyson, Allysonn, Allysun, Alyson

Alma (Arabic) learned. (Latin) soul.
Almah

Almeda (Arabic) ambitious.
Almeda, Almedah, Almeta, Allmita, Almea, Almedah, Almeda, Almita, Almita

Almira (Arabic) aristocratic, princess; exalted. (Spanish) from Almeira, Spain. See also Elmira, Mira.
Almeera, Allmeira, Almeera, Almeira, Almeira, Almeria, Almira, Almire

Aloha (Hawaiian) loving, kindhearted, charitable.
Alohi

Aloisa (German) famous warrior.
Aloisia, Aloysia

Aloma (Latin) a short form of Paloma.

Alondra (Spanish) a form of Alexandra.
Allandra, Alonda

Alonna (Irish) a form of Alana.
Alona, Alonnah, Alonya, Alonyah

Alonza (English) noble and eager.

Alora (American) a combination of the letter A + Lora.
Alorah, Alorha, Alorie, Alorra, Alouria

Alpha (Greek) first-born. Linguistics: the first letter of the Greek alphabet.
Alpha

Alta (Latin) high; tall.
Altia, Altah, Altaira, Altea, Alto

Althea (Greek) wholesome; healer. History: Althea Gibson was the first African American to win a major tennis title. See also Thea.
Altha, Altheda, Altheya, Althia, Elthea, Elthia

Alva (Latin, Spanish) white; light skinned. See also Elva.
Alvara, Alvanna, Alvannah

Alvina (English) friend to all; noble friend; friend to elves. See also Elva, Vina.
Alveanea, Alveen, Alveena, Alveenia, Alveenea, Alvie, Alvinae, Alvincia, Alvine, Alvinea, Alvinesha, Alvinia, Alvinna, Alvira, Alvona, Alvyna, Aluin, Alvina, Alwyn

Alyah, Alyiah (Hebrew) forms of Aliya.
Aly, Alya, Aleah, Alyia

Alycia, Alyssia (English) forms of Alicia.
Allyce, Alycea, Alyciah, Alyse, Lycia

Alysa, Alyse, Alysse (Greek) forms of Alice.
Allys, Allyse, Allyss, Alys, Alyss

Alysha, Alysia (Greek) forms of Alisha.
Allysia, Allyscia, Alysea, Alyshia, Alyssha, Alyssia

Alyssa (Greek) rational. Botany: alyssum is a flowering herb. See also Alice, Elissa.
Ahlyssa, Alissa, Allissa, Allyssa, Alyesa, Alyessa, Alyissa, Alysah, Ilyssa, Lyssa, Lyssah

Alysse (Greek) a form of Alice.
Allyce, Allyse, Allyss, Alys, Alyss

Alyx, Alyxis (Greek) short forms of Alexandra.

Alyxandra, Alyxandria (Greek) forms of Alexandria.
Alyxandrea, Alyxzandrya

Am (Vietnamese) lunar; female.

Ama (African) born on Saturday.

Amabel (Latin) lovable. See also Bel, Mabel.

Amada (Spanish) beloved.
Amadea, Amadi, Amadia, Amadita

Amairani (Greek) a form of Amara.
Amairaine, Amairane, Amairanie, Amairany

Amal (Hebrew) worker. (Arabic) hopeful.
Amala

Amalia (German) a form of Amelia.
Ahmalia, Amalea, Amaleah, Amaleta, Amalija, Amalina, Amalisa, Amalita, Amaliya, Amalya, Amalyn

Amalie (German) a form of Amelia.
Amalee, Amali, Amaly

Aman, Amani (Arabic) forms of Imani.
Aamani, Ahmani, Amane, Amanee, Amaney, Amanie, Ammanu

Amanada (Latin) a form of Amanda.

Amanda (Latin) lovable. See also Manda.
Amada, Amanada, Amandah, Amandalee, Amandalyn, Amandi, Amandie, Amandine, Amandy

Amandeep (Punjabi) peaceful light.

Amara (Greek) eternally beautiful. See also Mara.
Amar, Amaira, Amairani, Amarah, Amari, Amaria, Amariah

Amaranta (Spanish) a flower that never fades.

Amari (Greek) a form of Amara.
Amaree, Amarie, Amarri, Amarri

Amaris (Hebrew) promised by God.
Amarissa, Amarys, Maris

Amaryllis (Greek) fresh; flower.
Amarillis, Amarylis

Amaui (Hawaiian) thrush.

Amaya (Japanese) night rain.

Ambar (French) a form of Amber.

Amber (French) amber.
Aamber, Ahmber, Ambar, Amberia, Amberise, Amberly, Ambria, Ambur, Ambyr, Ambyre, Ammber, Ember

Amberly (American) a familiar form of Amber.
Amberle, Amberlea, Amberlee, Amberleigh, Amberley, Amberli, Amberlie, Amberly, Amberlye

Amberlyn, Amberlynn (American) combinations of Amber + Lynn.
Amberlin, Amberlina, Amberlyne, Amberlynne

Ambria (American) a form of Amber.
Ambrea, Ambra, Ambriah

Amelia (German) hard working. (Latin) a form of Emily. History: Amelia Earhart, an American aviator, was the first woman to fly solo across the Atlantic Ocean. See also Ima, Melia, Millie, Nuela, Yamelia.
Aemilia, Aimilia, Amalia, Amalie, Amaliya, Ameila, Amelie, Amelina, Ameline, Amelisa, Amelita, Amelia, Amilia, Amilina, Amilisa, Amilita, Amilyn, Amylia

Amelie (German) a familiar form of Amelia.
Amaley, Amalie, Amelee, Ameleigh, Ameley, Amélie, Amely, Amilie

America (Teutonic) industrious.
Americana, Amerika

Ami, Amie (French) forms of Amy.
Aami, Amii, Amiee, Amiie, Ammee, Ammie, Ammiee

Amilia, Amilie (Latin, German) forms of Amelia.
Amilee, Amili, Amillia, Amily, Amiya

Amina (Arabic) trustworthy, faithful. History: the mother of the prophet Muhammad.
Aamena, Aamina, Aaminah, Ameena, Ameenah, Aminah, Aminda, Aminta, Amintah

Amira (Hebrew) speech; utterance. (Arabic) princess. See also Mira.
Ameera, Ameerah, Amirah

Amissa (Hebrew) truth.
Amissah

Amita (Hebrew) truth.
Amitha

Amity (Latin) friendship.
Amitie

Amlika (Hindi) mother.
Amlikah

Amma (Hindi) god, godlike. Religion: another name for the Hindu goddess Shakti.

Amorie (German) industrious leader.

Amparo (Spanish) protected.

Amrit (Sanskrit) nectar.
Amrita

Amy (Latin) beloved. See also Aimee, Emma, Esmé.
Amata, Ame, Amey, Ami, Amia, Amie, Amio, Ammy, Amye, Amylyn

An (Chinese) peaceful.

Ana (Hawaiian, Spanish) a form of Hannah.
Anai, Ania

Anaba (Native American) she returns from battle.

Anabel, Anabelle (English) forms of Annabel.
Anabela, Anabele, Anabell, Anabella

Anahita (Persian) a river and water goddess.
Anahai, Anahi, Anahit, Anahy

Anais (Hebrew) gracious.
Anaise, Anaïse

Anala (Hindi) fine.

Analisa, Analise (English) combinations of Ana + Lisa.
Analic, Analicia, Analis, Analisha, Analisia, Analissa

Anamaria (English) a combination of Ana + Maria.
Anamarie, Anamary

Ananda (Hindi) blissful.

Anastacia (Greek) a form of Anastasia.
Anastace, Anastacie

Anastasia (Greek) resurrection. See also Nastasia, Stacey, Stacia, Stasya.
Anastacia, Anastase, Anastasia, Anastasha, Anastashia, Anastasie, Anastasija, Anastasiya, Anastasya, Anastatia, Anastasiya, Anastazia, Anastice, Anastasia, Annastasjia, Annastazia, Annastasyia, Annastazia, Annstás

Anatola (Greek) from the east.

Anci (Hungarian) a form of Hannah.
Annus, Annushka

Andee, Andi, Andie (American) short forms of Andrea, Fernanda.
Ande, Andea, Andy

Andrea (Greek) strong; courageous. See also Ondrea.
Aindrea, Andee, Andera, Andra, Andrah, Andraia, Andrea, Andrea, Andra, Andreaka, Andreana, Andreane, Andree, Andrea, Andrea, Andreja, Andreka, Andrel, Andrell, Andrey, Andreya, Andrette, Andreya, Andria, Andriana, Andrieka, Andrietta, Andri, Aundrea

Andreane, Andreanne (Greek) forms of Andrea.
Andrean, Andreanne, Andree Anne, Andrene, Andria, Andrienne

Andria (Greek) a form of Andrea.
Andri, Andria

Andriana, Andrianna (Greek) forms of Andrea.

Aneesa, Aneesha (Greek) forms of Agnes.
Alneesha, Alnessha, Anee, Aneesah, Aneese, Aneeslah, Aneesia, Aneisa, Aneisha, Aneesa, Anessia

Aneko (Japanese) older sister.

Anela (Hawaiian) angel.
Anel, Anelle

Anessa (Greek) a form of Agnes.
Anesha, Aneshia, Anesia, Anessia, Annessa

Anetra (American) a form of Annette.
Anitra

Anezka (Czech) a form of Hannah.

Angel (Greek) a short form of Angela.
Angele, Angèle, Angell, Angelle, Angil, Anjel

Angela (Greek) angel; messenger.
Angala, Anganita, Angel, Angelanell, Angelanette, Angelee, Angeleigh, Angeles, Angeli, Angelia, Angelica, Angelina, Angelique, Angelita, Angella, Angellita, Angie, Anglea, Anjela, Anjelica

Angelia (Greek) a form of Angela.
Angelea, Angeleah, Angelie

Angelica, Angelika (Greek) forms of Angela.
Angalic, Angelic, Angelicia, Angelicia, Angelike, Angeliki, Angellica, Angilica

Angelina, Angeline (Russian) forms of Angela.
Angalena, Angalina, Angeleen, Angelena, Angelene, Angeliana, Angeleana, Angellina, Angelyn, Angelyna, Angelyne, Angelynn, Angelynne, Anhelina, Anjelina

Angelique (French) a form of Angela.
Angeliqua, Angélique, Angilique, Anjelique

Angeni (Native American) spirit.

Angie (Greek) a familiar form of Angela.
Ange, Angee, Angey, Angi, Angy

Ani (Hawaiian) beautiful.
Aany, Aanye

Ania (Polish) a form of Hannah.
Alnia, Anaya, Aniah

Anica, Anika (Czech) familiar forms of Anna.
Aanika, Anaka, Aneeky, Aneka, Anekah, Anicka, Anik, Anikah, Anike, Anikka, Anikke, Aniko, Anneka, Annika, Annika, Anouska, Anuska

Anice (English) a form of Agnes.
Anesse, Anis, Anise, Annes, Annice, Annis, Annus

Anila (Hindi) Religion: an attendant of the Hindu god Vishnu.
Anilla

Anisa, Anisah (Arabic) friendly.
Annissah

Anissa, Anisha (English) forms of Agnes, Ann.
Aanisha, Aeniesha, Anis, Anisa, Anissah, Anise, Annisa, Annisha, Annissa, Anyssa

Anita (Spanish) a form of Ann, Anna. See also Nita.
Aneeta, Aneetah, Aneethah, Anetha, Anitha, Anithah, Anitia, Anitra, Anitte

Anjelica (Greek) a form of Angela.
Anjelika

Anka (Polish) a familiar form of Hannah.
Anke

Ann, Anne (English) gracious.
Anissa, Anita, Annchen, Annette, Annie, Annik, Annika, Annze, Anouche

Anna (German, Italian, Czech, Swedish) gracious. Culture: Anna Pavlova was a famous Russian ballerina. See also Anica, Anissa, Nina.
Ahnna, Ana, Anah, Anica, Anita, Annah, Annina, Annora, Anona, Anya, Anya, Aska

Annabel (English) a combination of Anna + Bel.
Amabel, Anabel, Annabal, Annabelle

Annabelle (English) a form of Annabel.
Anabelle, Annabell, Annabella

Annalie (Finnish) a form of Hannah.
Analee, Annalea, Annaleah, Annalee, Annaleigh, Annaleigha, Annali, Anneli, Annelie

Annalisa, Annalise (English) combinations of Anna + Lisa.
Analisa, Analise, Annaliesa, Annaliese, Annalissa, Annalise

Annamarie, Annemarie, Annmarie, Anne-Marie (English) combinations of Anne + Marie.
Annamaria, Anna-Maria, Anna-Marie, Annmaria

Anneka (Swedish) a form of Hannah.
Annaka, Anneke, Annika, Anniki, Anniki

Annelisa (English) a combination of Ann + Lisa.
Analiese, Anelisa, Anelise, Anneliese, Annelise

Annette (French) a form of Ann. See
also Anetra, Nettie.
*Anet, Aneta, Anetra, Anett, Anetta,
Anette, Anneth, Annett, Annetta*

Annie (English) a familiar form of Ann.
Anni, Anny

Annik, Annika (Russian) forms of Ann.
*Aneka, Anekah, Annicke, Annicka,
Annike, Annikka, Anninka, Anouk*

Annjanette (American) a combination
of Ann + Janette (see Janett).
*Angen, Angenett, Angenette, Anjane,
Anjanetta, Anjani*

Anona (English) pineapple.

Anouhea (Hawaiian) cool, soft
fragrance.

Ansley (Scottish) forms of Ainsley.
Anslea, Anslee, Ansleigh, Anslie

Anthea (Greek) flower.
Antha, Anthe, Anthia, Thia

Antionette (French) a form of
Antonia.
Antionet, Antionett, Anntionett

Antoinette (French) a form of Antonia.
See also Netti, Toinette, Toni.
*Anta, Antanette, Antoinella, Antoinet,
Antoinetta, Antonetta, Antoinette,
Antonice, Antonietta, Antonietta,
Antonique*

Antonia (Greek) flourishing. (Latin)
praiseworthy. See also Toni, Tonya,
Tosha.
*Ansonia, Ansonya, Antania, Antinia,
Antoinette, Antonia, Antona, Antonia,*

*Antonice, Antonie, Antonina, Antonine,
Antoniya, Antonnea, Antonnia, Antonya*

Antonice (Latin) a form of Antonia.
*Antanise, Antanisha, Antonesha,
Antonesha, Antonise, Antonisha*

Anya (Russian) a form of Anna.
Aanyah, Aniya, Aniyah, Anja

Anyssa (English) a form of Anissa.
Aryssa, Arysha

'Aolani (Hawaiian) heavenly cloud.

Aphra (Hebrew) young doe. See also
Afra.

April (Latin) opening. See also Avril.
*Aprele, Aprell, Aprelle, Aprila,
Aprile, Apriliette, April, Aprill, Apryl*

Apryl (Latin) a form of April.
Apryle

Aquene (Native American) peaceful.

Ara (Arabic) opinionated.
Ahraya, Aira, Arae, Arah, Araya, Arayah

Arabella (Latin) beautiful altar. See
also Belle, Orabella.
Arabela, Arabele, Arabelle

Ardelle (Latin) warm; enthusiastic.
Ardelia, Ardelis, Ardella

Arden (English) valley of the eagle.
Literature: in Shakespeare, a romantic
place of refuge.
*Ardeen, Ardeena, Ardena, Ardene,
Ardenia, Ardi, Ardin, Ardina, Ardine*

Ardi (Hebrew) a short form of Arden,
Ardice, Ardith.
Ardie, Ardi, Artie

Ardice (Hebrew) a form of Ardith.
Ardis, Artis, Ardiss, Ardyce, Ardys

Ardith (Hebrew) flowering field.
Ardath, Ardi, Ardice, Ardyth

Arella (Hebrew) angel; messenger.
Arela, Arelle, Orella, Orelle

Areli, Arely (American) forms of
Oralee.
*Areli, Arelie, Areli, Arelis, Arelli,
Arellia, Arely*

Aretha (Greek) virtuous. See also
Oretha.
*Areatha, Areetha, Areta, Aretina, Aretta,
Arette, Arita, Aritha, Retha, Ritha*

Ari, Aria, Arie (Hebrew) short forms
of Ariel.
Ariah, Aria, Arya

Ariadne (Greek) holy. Mythology: the
daughter of King Minos of Crete.

Ariana, Arianna (Greek) holy.
*Aeriana, Aerionna, Aeronna, Ahreanna,
Ahriana, Ahrianna, Airiana, Arieana,
Ariona, Arionna, Aryonna*

Ariane (French), Arianne (English)
forms of Ariana, Arianna.
*Aerian, Aeriann, Aerion, Aerionne,
Airiann, Ari, Ariainie, Ariann, Ariannie,
Arieann, Arien, Ariene, Arienne, Arieon,
Arionne, Aryane, Aryann, Aryanne*

Arica (Scandinavian) forms of Erica.
*Aeria, Aericka, Aeryka, Arica, Aricka,
Arika, Ariie, Arikka*

Ariel (Hebrew) lion of God. *Aerial, Aeriale, Aeriel, Aeriela, Aeryal, Ahriel, Aire, Aireal, Airial, Ari, Aria, Arial, Ariale, Arieal, Ariela, Arielle, Arrieal, Arriel, Aryel, Auriel*

Arielle (French) a form of Ariel. *Aeriell, Ariella, Arriele, Arriell, Arrielle, Aryelle, Aurielle*

Arin (Hebrew) enlightened. (Arabic) messenger. See also Erin. *Aaren, Aerin, Aieron, Aieren, Arinn, Aryn*

Arista (Greek) best. *Aris, Arissa, Aristana, Aristen*

Arla (German) a form of Carla.

Arleigh (English) a form of Harley. *Arlea, Arlee, Arley, Arlie, Arly*

Arlene (Irish) pledge. See also Lena, Lina. *Airlen, Arlana, Arleen, Arleene, Arlen, Arlena, Arlenis, Arlette, Arleyne, Arliene, Arlina, Arlinda, Arline, Arlis*

Arlette (English) a form of Arlene. *Arleta, Arletta, Arletty*

Arlynn (American) a combination of Arlene + Lynn. *Arlyn, Arlyne, Arlynne*

Armani (Persian) desire, goal. *Armahni, Arman, Armanee, Armanii*

Armine (Latin) noble. (German) soldier. (French) a form of Herman (see Boys' Names). *Armina*

Arnelle (German) eagle. *Arnell, Arnella*

Artha (Hindi) wealthy, prosperous. *Arthi, Arti, Artie*

Artis (Irish) noble; lofty hill. (Scottish) bear. (English) rock. (Icelandic) follower of Thor. *Arthea, Arthelia, Arthene, Arthette, Arthurette, Arthurina, Arthurine, Artina, Artice*

Aryana, Aryanna (Italian) forms of Ariana. *Aryan, Aryanah, Aryannah*

Aryn (Hebrew) a form of Arin. *Aerryn, Aeryn, Airyn, Aryne, Arynn, Arynne*

Asa (Japanese) born in the morning.

Asha (Arabic, Swahili) a form of Aisha, Ashia.

Ashanti (Swahili) from a tribe in West Africa. *Achante, Achanti, Asante, Ashanta, Ashantae, Ashante, Ashanté, Ashantee, Ashantie, Ashaunta, Ashauntae, Ashauntee, Ashaunti, Ashonti, Ashuntae, Ashunti*

Ashely (English) form of Ashley. *Ashelee, Ashelei, Asheley, Ashelie, Ashelley, Ashelly*

Ashia (Arabic) life. *Asha, Ashya, Ashyah, Ashyia, Ayshia*

Ashlee, Ashli, Ashlie, Ashly (English) forms of Ashley. *Ashle, Ashlea, Ashleah, Ashleeh, Ashliee*

Ashleigh (English) a form of Ashley. *Ahsleigh, Asheleigh, Ashlei, Ashliegh*

Ashley (English) ash tree meadow. See also Lee. *Ahslee, Aishlee, Ashala, Ashalee, Ashalei, Ashaley, Ashely, Ashla, Ashlay, Ashleay, Ashlee, Ashleigh, Ashleye, Ashli, Ashlie, Ashly, Ashlye*

Ashlin (English) a form of Ashlyn. *Ashlean, Ashliann, Ashlianne, Ashline*

Ashlyn, Ashlynn (English) ash tree pool. (Irish) vision, dream. *Ashlan, Ashleann, Ashleen, Ashleene, Ashlen, Ashlene, Ashlin, Ashling, Ashlyne, Ashlynne*

Ashten, Ashtin (English) forms of Ashton. *Ashtine*

Ashton (English) ash-tree settlement. *Ashten, Ashtyn*

Ashtyn (English) a form of Ashton. *Ashtynne*

Asia (Greek) resurrection. (English) eastern sunrise. (Swahili) a form of Aisha. *Ahsia, Aisia, Aisian, Asiah, Asian, Asianae, Asya, Aysia, Aysiah, Aysian, Ayzia*

Aspen (English) aspen tree. *Aspin, Aspyn*

Aster (English) a form of Astra. *Astera, Asteria, Astyr*

Astra (Greek) star. *Asta, Astara, Aster, Astraea, Astrea*

Astrid (Scandinavian) divine strength. *Astri, Astrida, Astrik, Astrud, Atti, Estrid*

Atalanta (Greek) mighty huntress. Mythology: an athletic young woman who refused to marry any man who could not outrun her in a footrace. See also Lani.
Atalaya, Atlanta, Atlante, Atlee

Atara (Hebrew) crown.
Atarah, Ataree

Athena (Greek) wise. Mythology: the goddess of wisdom.
Athenea, Athene, Athina, Atina

Atira (Hebrew) prayer.

Aubree, Aubrie (French) forms of Aubrey.
Aubra, Aubrette, Aubria, Aubric, Aubrj, Aubury, Avery

Aubriana, Aubrianna (English) combinations of Aubrey + Anna.
Aubreyana, Aubreyanna, Aubreyanne, Aubrieyena, Aubrianne

Audey (English) a familiar form of Audrey.
Aude, Audi, Audie

Audra (French) a form of Audrey.
Audria, Audrea

Audreanne (English) a combination of Audrey + Anne.
Audrea, Audreen, Audrianna, Audrienne

Audree, Audrie (English) forms of Audrey.
Audre, Audri

Audrey (English) noble strength.
Adrey, Audey, Audra, Audray, Audree, Audrie, Audrin, Audriya, Audry, Audrye

Audriana, Audrianna (English) combinations of Audrey + Anna.
Audreanna, Audrienna, Audrina

Audris (German) fortunate, wealthy.
Audrys

Auberte (French) a form of Alberta.
Auberta, Aubertha, Auberthe, Aubine

Aubrey, Aubrie (French) forms of Aubrey.
Audrys

Aubie (German) noble; bearlike. (French) blond ruler; elf ruler.
Aubary, Aubery, Aubrey, Aubrea, Aubreah, Aubree, Aubrette, Aubria, Aubric, Aubrj, Aubury, Avery

Augusta (Latin) a short form of Augustine. See also Gusta.
Agusta, August, Auguste, Augustia, Augustus, Austina

Augustine (Latin) majestic. Religion: Saint Augustine was the first archbishop of Canterbury. See also Tina.
Agustina, Augusta, Augustina, Augustyna, Augustyme, Austin

'Aulani (Hawaiian) royal messenger.
Lani, Lanie

Aundrea (Greek) a form of Andrea.
Aundreah

Aura (Greek) soft breeze. (Latin) golden. See also Ora.

Aurelia (Latin) golden. See also Oralia.
Auralea, Auralia, Aurea, Aureal, Aurel, Aurele, Aurelea, Aureliana, Aurelie, Auria, Aurie, Aurilia, Auriia

Aurelie (Latin) a form of Aurelia.
Auralee, Auralei, Aurelee, Aurelei, Aurelle

Aurora (Latin) dawn. Mythology: Aurora was the goddess of dawn.
Aurore, Ora, Ori, Orie, Rora

Austin (Latin) a short form of Augustine.
Austen, Austin, Austyn, Austynn

Autumn (Latin) autumn.

Ava (Greek) a form of Eva.
Avada, Avae, Ave, Aveen

Avalon (Latin) island.
Avallon

Avery (English) a form of Aubrey.
Aivree, Averi, Averie, Avry

Avis (Latin) bird.
Avais, Avi, Avia, Aviana, Avianna, Avi, Avit, Avy

Aviva (Hebrew) springtime. See also Viva.
Aviv, Avivah, Aviva, Avivice, Avni, Avnit, Avrille, Avrilia, Avy

Avril (French) a form of April.
Averil, Averyl, Avra, Avri, Avrilia, Avrill, Avrille, Avrilia, Avy

Axelle (Latin) axe. (German) small oak tree; source of life.
Aixa

Aya (Hebrew) bird; fly swiftly.
Aia, Aiah, Aiya, Aiyah

Ayanna (Hindi) innocent.
Aiyana, Aiyanna, Ayan, Ayana, Ayania, Ayannica, Ayna

Ayesha (Persian) a form of Aisha.
Ayasha, Ayeshah, Ayessa, Ayisha, Ayishah, Aysha, Ayshah, Ayshe, Ayshea, Aysia

Ayita (Cherokee) first in the dance.

Ayla (Hebrew) oak tree.
Aylana, Aylee, Ayleen, Aylene, Aylie, Aylin

Aza (Arabic) comfort.
Aiza, Aizha, Aizia, Azia

Aziza (Swahili) precious.
Azize

Baba (African) born on Thursday.
Aba

Babe (Latin) a familiar form of Barbara. (American) a form of Baby.
Babby

Babette (French, German) a familiar form of Barbara.
Babita, Barbette

Babs (American) a familiar form of Barbara.
Bab

Baby (American) baby.
Babby, Babe, Bebe

Bailee, Bailie (English) forms of Bailey.
Baelee, Baeli, Bailea, Bailei, Baillee, Baillie, Bailli

Baileigh, Baleigh (English) forms of Bailey.
Baeleigh

Bailey (English) bailiff.
Baeley, Bailee, Baileigh, Bailley, Baily, Baily, Bali, Balley, Baylee, Bayley

Baka (Hindi) crane.

Bakula (Hindi) flower.

Bambi (Italian) child.
Bambee, Bambie, Bamby

Bandi (Punjabi) prisoner.
Banda, Bandy

Baptista (Latin) baptizer.
Baptiste, Batista, Battista, Bautista

Bara, Barra (Hebrew) chosen.
Bára, Bari

Barb (Latin) a short form of Barbara.
Barba, Barbe

Barbara (Latin) stranger, foreigner. See also Bebe, Varvara, Wava.
Babara, Babb, Babbie, Babe, Babette, Babina, Babs, Barb, Barbara-Ann, Barbarit, Barbarita, Barbary, Barbeeleen, Barbera, Barbie, Barbora, Barborah, Barborka, Barbra, Barbraann, Barbro, Barbska, Basha, Bebe, Bobbi, Bobbie

Barbie (American) a familiar form of Barbara.
Barbee, Barbey, Barbi, Barby, Baubie

Barbra (American) a form of Barbara.
Barbro

Barrett (German) strong as a bear.

Barrie (Irish) spear; markswoman.
Bari, Barri, Berri, Berrie, Berry

Basia (Hebrew) daughter of God.
Basya, Bathia, Batia, Batya, Bitya, Bithia

Bathsheba (Hebrew) daughter of the oath; seventh daughter. Bible: a wife of King David. See also Sheba.
Bathshua, Batsheva, Bersaba, Bethsabee, Bethsheba

Batini (Swahili) inner thoughts.

Baylee, Bayleigh, Baylie (English) forms of Bailey.
Bayla, Bayle, Baylea, Bayleah, Baylei, Bayli, Bayliee, Bayliegh

Bayley (English) a form of Bailey.
Bayly

Bayo (Yoruba) joy is found.

Bea, Bee (American) short forms of Beatrice.

Beata (Latin) a short form of Beatrice.
Beatta

Beatrice (Latin) blessed; happy; bringer of joy. See also Trish, Trixie.
Bea, Beata, Beatrica, Béatrice, Beatricia, Beatriks, Beatrisa, Beatrise, Beatrissa, Beatriz, Beattie, Beatty, Bebe, Bee, Trice

Beatriz (Latin) a form of Beatrice.
Beatris, Beatriss, Beatrix, Beitris

Bebe (Spanish) a form of Barbara, Beatrice.
BB, Beebee, Bibi

Becca (Hebrew) a short form of Rebecca.
Beca, Becka, Bekah, Bekka

Becky (American) a familiar form of Rebecca.
Beckey, Becki, Beckie

Bedelia (Irish) a form of Bridget.
Bedeelia, Biddy, Bidelia

Bel (Hindi) sacred wood of apple trees. A short form of Amabel, Belinda, Isabel.

Bela (Czech) white. (Hungarian) bright.
Belah, Biela

Belen (Greek) arrow. (Spanish) Bethlehem.
Belina

Belicia (Spanish) dedicated to God.
Beli, Belia, Belica

Bella (Latin) beautiful.
Bellah

Belle (French) beautiful. A short form of Arabella, Belinda, Isabel. See also Billie.
Belita, Bell, Belli, Bellina

Belva (Latin) beautiful view.
Belvia

Bena (Native American) pheasant. See also Bina.
Benea

Benecia (Latin) a short form of Benedicta.
Benecia, Benicia, Benish, Benisha, Benishia, Bennicia

Benedicta (Latin) blessed.
Bendite, Benecia, Benedetta, Benedicte, Benedikta, Bengta, Benicia, Benna, Benni, Bennicia, Benoîte, Binney

Benedicte (Latin) a form of Benedicta.

Belinda (Spanish) beautiful. Literature: a name coined by English poet Alexander Pope in *The Rape of the Lock.* See also Blinda, Linda.
Bel, Belinda, Belle, Belynda

Benita (Spanish) a form of Benedicta.
Beneta, Benetta, Benitta, Neeta, Benite, Benny

Bennett (Latin) little blessed one.
Bennet, Bennetta

Benni (Latin) a familiar form of Benedicta.
Bennie, Binni, Binnie, Binny

Bente (Latin) blessed.

Berenice (Greek) a form of Bernice. See also Bunny, Vernice.
Berenise, Berenisse, Bereniz, Berenize

Berget (Irish) a form of Bridget.
Bergette, Bergit

Berit (German) glorious.
Beret, Berette, Berta

Berkley (Scottish, English) birch-tree meadow.
Berkeley, Berkly

Berlynn (English) a combination of Bertha + Lynn.
Berla, Berlin, Berlinda, Berline, Berling, Berlyn, Berlyne, Berlynne

Bernadette (French) a form of Bernadine. See also Nadette.
Bera, Beradette, Berna, Bernadet, Bernadete, Bernadett, Bernadetta, Bernarda, Bernaderte, Bernadett, Bernedette, Bernessa, Berneta

Bernadine (English, German) brave as a bear.
Bernadene, Bernadin, Bernadina, Bernardina, Bernardine, Berni

Berneta (French) a short form of Bernadette.
Bernatta, Bernetta, Bernette, Bernita

Berni (English) a familiar form of Bernadine, Bernice.
Bernie, Berny

Bertha (German) bright; illustrious; brilliant ruler. A short form of Alberta. See also Birdie, Peke.
Barta, Bartha, Berta, Berthe, Bertille, Bertina, Bertrona, Bertus, Birtha

Bernice (Greek) bringer of victory. See also Bunny, Vernice.
Berenice, Berenike, Bernessa, Berni, Bernicia, Bernise, Nixie

Berti (German, English) a familiar form of Gilberte, Bertina.
Berte, Bertie, Berty

Bertille (French) a form of Bertha.

Bertina (English) bright, shining.
Bertine

Beryl (Greek) sea green jewel.
Beryle

Bess, Bessie (Hebrew) familiar forms of Elizabeth.
Bessi, Bessy

Beth (Hebrew, Aramaic) house of God. A short form of Bethany, Elizabeth.
Betha, Bethe, Bethia

Bethann (English) a combination of Beth + Ann.
Beth-Ann, Bethan, Bethann, Bethanne

Bethani, Bethanie (Aramaic) forms of Bethany.
Bethanee, Bethania, Bethannie, Bethni, Bethnie

Bethany (Aramaic) house of figs.
Beth, Bethanee, Bethaney, Bethani, Bethanie, Bethann, Bethanny, Bethehy

Bethany (Aramaic) house of figs. Bible: the site of Lazarus's resurrection.
Beth, Bethaney, Bethani, Bethanney, Bethanny, Bethena, Betheny, Bethia, Bethina, Bethney, Bethny, Betthany

Betsy (American) a familiar form of Elizabeth.
Betsey, Betsi, Betsie

Bette (French) a form of Betty.
Beta, Beti, Betka, Bett, Betta

Bettina (American) a combination of Beth + Tina.
Betina, Betine, Betti, Bettine

Betty (Hebrew) consecrated to God. (English) a familiar form of Elizabeth.
Bette, Bettey, Betti, Bettie, Bettye, Bettyjean, Betty-Jean, Bettyjo, Betty-Jo, Bettylou, Betty-Lou, Bety, Boski, Bözsi

Betula (Hebrew) girl, maiden.

Beulah (Hebrew) married. Bible: Beulah is a name for Israel.
Beula, Beulla, Beullah

Bev (English) a short form of Beverly.

Bevanne (Welsh) child of Evan.
Bevan, Bevann, Bevany

Beverly (English) beaver field. See also Buffy.
Bev, Bevalee, Beverle, Beverlee, Beverley, Beverlie, Beverlly, Bevlyn, Bevlynn, Bevlynne, Bevvy, Verly

Beverlyann (American) a combination of Beverly + Ann.
Beverliann, Beverlianne, Beverlyanne

Bian (Vietnamese) hidden; secretive.

Bianca (Italian) white. See also Blanca, Vianca.
Biancha, Biancia, Bianco, Bianey, Bianica, Bianka, Bianna, Binney, Biona, Blanca, Blanche, Byanca

Bianka (Italian) a form of Bianca.
Beyanka, Biannka

Bibi (Latin) a short form of Bibiana. (Arabic) lady. (Spanish) a form of Bebe.

Bibiana (Latin) lively.
Bibi

Biddy (Irish) a familiar form of Bedelia.
Biddie

Billi, Billy (English) forms of Billie.
Billye

Billie (English) strong willed. (German, French) a familiar form of Wilhelmina.
Belle, Bileigh, Bili, Bilie, Billee, Billi, Billy, Billye

Billie-Jean (American) a combination of Billie + Jean.
Billiejean, Billyjean, Billy-Jean

Billie-Jo (American) a combination of Billie + Jo.
Billiejo, Billyjo, Billy-Jo

Bina (Hebrew) wise; understanding. (Swahili) dancer. (Latin) a short form of Sabina. See also Bena.
Binah, Binney, Binta, Bintah

Binney (English) a familiar form of Benedicta, Bianca, Bina.
Binnee, Binni, Binnie, Binny

Bionca (Italian) a form of Bianca.
Beonca, Beyona, Beyonka, Bioncha, Bionica, Bionka, Bionnca

Birdie (English) bird. (German) a familiar form of Bertha.
Bird, Birdee, Birdella, Birdena, Birdey, Birdi, Birdy, Byrd, Byrdey, Byrdie, Byrdy

Birgitte (Swedish) a form of Bridget.
Birgit, Birgita, Birgitta

Blaine (Irish) thin.
Blane, Blayne

Blair (Scottish) plains dweller.

Blaire (Scottish) a form of Blair.
Blare, Blayre

Blaise (French) one who stammers.
Blaize, Blasha, Blasia, Blaza, Blaze, Blazena

Blake (English) dark.
Blaque, Blayke

Blakely (English) dark meadow.
Blakelea, Blakelee, Blakeleigh, Blakeley, Blakeli, Blakelyn, Blakelynn, Blakesley, Blakley, Blakli

Blanca (Italian) a form of Bianca.
Bellanca, Blancka, Blanka

Blanche (French) a form of Bianca.
Blanch, Blancha, Blinney

Blinda (American) a short form of Belinda.
Blynda

Bliss (English) blissful, joyful.
Blisse, Blyss, Blysse

Blodwyn (Welsh) flower. See also Wynne.
Blodwen, Blodwynne, Blodyn

Blondelle (French) blond, fair haired.
Blondell, Blondie

Blondie (American) a familiar form of Blondelle.
Blonde, Blondey, Blondy

Blossom (English) flower.

Blum (Yiddish) flower.
Bluma

Blythe (English) happy, cheerful.
Blithe, Blyss, Blyth

Bo (Chinese) precious.

Boacha (Hebrew) blessed.

Bobbette (American) a familiar form of Roberta.
Bobbet, Bobbetta

Bobbi, Bobbie (American) familiar forms of Barbara, Roberta.
Barbie, Bobbe, Bobbey, Bobbisue, Bobby, Bobbye, Bobi, Bobie, Bobina, Bobbie-Jean, Bobbie-Lynn, Bobbie-Sue

Bobbi-Ann, Bobbie-Ann (American) combinations of Bobbi + Ann.
Bobbiann, Bobbi-Anne, Bobbianne, Bobbie-Anne, Bobby-Ann, Bobbyann, Bobby-Anne, Bobbyanne

Bobbi-Jo (American) a combination of Bobbi + Jo.
Bobbiejo, Bobbie-Jo, Bobbijo, Bobby-Jo, Bobijo

Bobbi-Lee (American) a combination of Bobbi + Lee.
Bobbilee, Bobbi-Lee, Bobbylee, Bobby-Leigh, Bobile

Bonita (Spanish) pretty.
Bonesha, Bonetta, Bonnetta

Bonnie, Bonny (English, Scottish) beautiful, pretty. (Spanish) familiar forms of Bonita.
Boni, Bonie, Bonne, Bonnee, Bonnell, Bonney, Bonni, Bonnin

Bonnie-Bell (American) a combination of Bonnie + Belle.
Bonnebell, Bonnebelle, Bonnibell, Bonnibelle, Bonniebell, Bonniebelle, Bonnybell, Bonnybelle

Bradley (English) broad meadow.
Bradlee, Bradleigh, Bradlie

Brady (Irish) spirited.
Bradee, Bradey, Bradi, Bradie, Braedi, Braidee, Braidi, Braidie, Braidy, Braydee

Braeden (English) broad hill.
Bradyn, Braedan, Braedean, Braedyn, Braedon, Braiden, Braidan, Braidon, Braidyn, Brayden, Braydon

Braelyn (American) a combination of Braeden + Lynn.
Braelen, Braelene, Braelin, Braelle, Braelenn, Braelon, Braelyne, Braelynn, Bralee, Brailen, Braylee, Braylen, Braylin, Braylon, Braylyn, Braylynn

Branda (Hebrew) blessing.

Brandee (Dutch) a form of Brandy.
Brande, Brandea, Brendee

Branden (English) beacon valley.
Branda, Brandon, Brendan, Brandyn, Brennan

Brandi, Brandie (Dutch) forms of Brandy.
Brandei, Brandice, Brandiee, Brandii, Brandily, Brandin, Brandis, Brandise, Brani, Branndie, Brendi

Brandy (Dutch) an after-dinner drink made from distilled wine.
Brand, Brandace, Brandaise, Brandala, Brandee, Brandeli, Brandell, Brandi, Brandye, Brandylee, Brandy-Lee, Brandy-Leigh, Brann, Brantley, Branyell, Brendy

Brandy-Lynn (American) a combination of Brandy + Lynn.
Brandalyn, Brandalynn, Brandelyn, Brandelynn, Brandelyne, Brandelynne, Brandilyn, Brandilynn, Brandilynne, Brandlin, Brandlyn, Brandolyn, Brandolynn, Brandolynne, Brandylyn, Brandy-Lyn, Brandylynne

Braxton (English) Brock's town.
Braxten, Braxtyn

Brea, Bria (Irish) short forms of Breana, Briana.
Breah, Breea, Briah, Brya

Breana, Breanna (Irish) forms of Briana.
Brea, Breanah, Breanda, Bre-Anna, Breannah, Breannea, Breannia, Breasha, Breauna, Breeanna, Breila

Breann, Breanne (Irish) short forms of Briana.
Breane, Bre-Ann, Bre-Anne, Breaunne, Bree, Breean, Breeann, Breeanne, Breelyn, Breeon, Breiann, Breighann, Breyenne, Brieann, Brion

Breasha (Russian) a familiar form of Breana.

Breauna, Breunna, Briauna (Irish) forms of Briana.
Breaunna, Breeauna, Breuna, Breuna, Briaunna

Breck (Irish) freckled.
Brecken

Bree (English) broth. (Irish) a short form of Breann. See also Brie.
Breay, Brei, Breigh

Breeana, Breeanna (Irish) forms of Briana.
Breeanah, Breeannah

Breena (Irish) fairy palace. A form of Brina.
Breenea, Breene, Breina, Brina

Breiana, Breianna (Irish) forms of Briana.
Breiane, Breiann, Breianne

Brenda (Irish) little raven. (English) sword.
Brendell, Brendelle, Brendette, Brendie, Brendyl, Brenna

Brenda-Lee (American) a combination of Brenda + Lee.
Brendalee, Brendaleigh, Brendali, Brendaly, Brendalys, Brenlee, Brenley

Brenna, Breanne (Irish) a form of Brenda.
Bren, Brenie, Brenin, Brenn, Brennah, Brennaugh, Brenne

Brennan (English) a form of Brendan (see Boys' Names).
Brennea, Brennen, Brennon, Brenryn

Breona, Breonna (Irish) forms of Briana.
Breeona, Breiona, Breionna, Breonah, Breonia, Breonie, Breonne

Brett (Irish) a short form of Brittany. See also Brita.
Bret, Brette, Brettin, Bretton

Breyana, Breyann, Breyanna (Irish) forms of Briana.
Breyan, Breyane, Breyannah, Breyanne

Breyona, Breyonna (Irish) forms of Briana.
Breyonia

Briana, Brianna (Irish) strong; virtuous, honorable.
Bhrianna, Brana, Brea, Breana, Breann, Breauna, Breeana, Breiana, Breona, Breyana, Breyona, Bria, Briahna, Brianah, Briand, Brianda, Briannah, Brianne, Brianni, Briannon, Brienna, Brina, Briona, Briyana, Bryana, Bryona

Brianne (Irish) a form of Briana.
Briane, Briann, Brienne, Bryanne

Briar (French) heather.
Brear, Brier, Bryar

Bridey (Irish) a familiar form of Bridget.
Bridi, Bridie, Brydie

Bridget (Irish) strong. See also Bedelia, Bryga, Gitta.
Berget, Birgitte, Bride, Bridey, Bridger, Bridgete, Bridgett, Bridgette, Bridgid, Bridgot, Brietta, Brigada, Briget, Brigid, Brigida, Brigitte, Brita

Bridgett, Bridgette (Irish) forms of Bridget.
Bridgitte, Brigette, Bridggett, Briggitte, Bridgitt, Brigitta

Brie (French) a type of cheese. Geography: a region in France known for its cheese. See also Bree.
Briea, Brielle, Briena, Brieon, Brietta, Briette

Brieana, Brieanna (American) combinations of Brie + Anna.
Brieannah

Brieann, Brieanne (American) combinations of Brie + Ann. See also Briana.
Brie-Ann, Brie-Anne

Brielle (French) a form of Brie.
Briel, Briele, Briell, Briella

Brienna, Brienne (Irish) forms of Briana.
Briene, Brieon, Brieona, Brieonna

Brienne (French) a form of Briana.
Briemn

Brigette (French) a form of Bridget.
Briget, Brigett, Brigetta, Brigettee, Brigget

Brigitte (French) a form of Bridget.
Briggitte, Brigit, Brigita

Brina (Latin) a short form of Sabrina. (Irish) a familiar form of Briana.
Bin, Brinan, Brinda, Brindy, Briney, Brinia, Brinlee, Brinly, Brinn, Brinna, Brinnan, Briona, Bryn, Bryna

Briona (Irish) a form of Briana.
Brione, Brionna, Brionne, Briony, Brionna, Bryony

Brisa (Spanish) beloved. Mythology: Briseis was the Greek name of Achilles's beloved.
Breezy, Breza, Brisha, Brisha, Brissa, Bryssa

Brita (Irish) a form of Bridget. (English) a short form of Britany.
Bretta, Brieta, Brietta, Brit, Britta
Britta

Britaney, Brittany, Brittaney (English) forms of Britany.
Britaney, Brittany.
Britanee, Britanny, Britenee, Briteny, Britianey, British, Britkeney, Britley, Britlyn, Britney, Briton

Britani, Brittani, Brittanie (English) forms of Britany.
Brit, Britania, Britanica, Britanie, Britanii, Britann, Britannia, Britatani, Britian, Britini, Britiane, Brittanee, Brittanni, Brittannia, Brittannie, Brittenie, Brittiani, Brittianni

Britany, Brittany (English) from Britain.
See also Brett.
Bria, Briana, Brianey, Briani, Brianna, Brillyn, Britney, Britt, Brittainny, Brittainy, Brittany, Brittena, Britteny, Brittani, Brittanica, Brittanny, Brittany-Ann, Brittanyne, Brittell, Britteny, Brittiny, Brittini, Brittlin, Brittlynn, Brittnee, Britton, Bryttany

Britin, Brittin (English) from Britain.
Britann, Brittan, Brittin, Brittina, Brittine, Brittini, Brittiny

Britney, Brittney, Brittny (English) forms of Britany.
Britney, Bridnee, Bridney, Britnay, Britne, Britnee, Britnei, Britni, Britny, Britnye, Brittnay, Brittnaye, Brynnea, Bryni

Britni, Brittni, Brittnie (English) forms of Britney, Britney.
Britnie

Britt, Britta (Latin) short forms of Britany, Brittany. (Swedish) strong.
Brett, Briet, Brit, Brita, Brite

Briton, Britin (English) forms of Britin, Britin.
Briton

Brittany (English) a form of Britany, Brittany.
Briten, Brittenay, Brittence, Britteney, Brittenie

Brittini, Brittiny (English) forms of Britany, Brittany.
Brittinee, Brittiney, Brittinie, Brittiny

Brittnee (English) a form of Britany, Brittany.
Britnea, Brittnei, Brittneigh

Briyana, Briyanna (Irish) forms of Briana.

Brodie (Irish) ditch; canal builder.
Brodee, Brodi, Brody

Bronnie (Welsh) a familiar form of Bronwyn.
Bron, Bronia, Bronney, Bronny, Bronya

Bronwyn (Welsh) white breasted.
Bonnie, Bronwen, Bronwin, Bronwynn, Bronwynne

Brook, Brooke (English) brook, stream.
Bhrooke, Brookelle, Brookie, Brooks, Brooky

Brooklyn, Brooklynn (American) combinations of Brook + Lynn.
Brookellen, Brookelyn, Brookelyne, Brookelynn, Brookelen, Brookelin, Brooklyne, Brooklynne

Bruna (German) a short form of Brunhilda.
Brona

Brunhilda (German) armored warrior.
Brinhilda, Brinhilde, Bruna, Brunhilde, Brünnhilde, Brynhild, Brynhilda, Brynhilde, Hilda

Bryce (Welsh) alert; ambitious.

Bryana, Bryanna, Bryanne (Irish) short forms of Bryana.
Bryann, Bryanni

Bryga (Polish) a form of Bridget.
Brigid, Brygida, Brygitka

Brylie (American) a combination of the letter B + Riley.
Brylee, Brylei, Bryley, Bryli

Bryn, Brynn (Latin) from the boundary line. (Welsh) mound.
Brinn, Brynee, Brynne

Bryna (Latin, Irish) a form of Brina.
Brynan, Brynna, Brynnan

Bryona, Bryonna (Irish) forms of Briana.
Bryonia, Bryony

Bryttani, Bryttany (English) forms of Britany.
Brytani, Brytanie, Brytanny, Brytany, Brytnee, Brytnie, Bryton, Bryttanee, Bryttanie, Bryttine, Bryttney, Bryttnie, Brytton

Buffy (American) buffalo; from the plains.
Buffee, Buffey, Buffie, Buffye

Bunny (Greek) a familiar form of Bernice. (English) little rabbit. See also Bonnie.
Bunni, Bunnie

Burgundy (French) Geography: a region of France known for its Burgundy wine.
Burgandi, Burgandie, Burgandy, Burgunde

Cachet (French) prestigious; desirous.
Cachae, Cache, Cachee, Cachée

Cadence (Latin) rhythm.
Cadena, Cadenza, Kadena

Cady (English) a form of Kady.
Cade, Cadee, Cadey, Cadi, Cadie, Cadine, Cadye

Caeley, Cailey, Cayley (American) forms of Kaylee, Kelly.
Caela, Caelee, Caeleigh, Caeley, Caeli, Caelie, Caelly, Caely, Caeley, Cailee, Caili, Caile, Cailley, Caillie, Caily, Caylee

Caelin, Caelyn (American) forms of Kaelyn.
Caelan, Caelinn, Caelynn, Cailan, Caylan

Cai (Vietnamese) feminine.
Cae, Cay, Caye

Cailida (Spanish) adoring.
Kailida

Cailin, Cailyn (American) forms of Caitlin.
Caileen, Cailene, Cailine, Cailynn, Cailynne, Calen, Cayleen, Caylen, Caylene, Caylin, Cayline, Caylyn, Caylyne, Caylynne

Caitlan (Irish) a form of Caitlin.
Caitland, Caitlandt

Caitlin (Irish) pure. See also Kaitlin, Katelin, Katelyn, Kaytlyn.
Caetlin, Cailin, Caitlan, Caitleen, Caitlenn, Caitlene, Caitlenn, Caitline, Caitlinn, Caitlon, Caitlyn, Catlee, Catleen, Catleene, Catlin

Caitlyn, Caitlynn (Irish) forms of Caitlin. See also Kaitlyn.
Caitlyne, Caitlynne, Catelyn, Catlyn, Catlynn, Catlynne

Cala (Arabic) castle, fortress. See also Callie, Kala.
Calah, Calan, Calla, Callah

Calandra (Greek) lark.
Calan, Calandrea, Calandria, Caleida, Calendra, Calendre, Kalandra, Kalandria

Caleigh, Caley (American) forms of Caley.
Caeley, Caileigh, Caleah

Cali, Calli (Greek) forms of Calie. See also Kali.
Calee

Calida (Spanish) warm; ardent.
Calina, Calinda, Callida, Callinda, Kalida

Callie (Greek, Arabic) a familiar form of Cala, Callista. See also Kalli.
Cal, Cali, Calie, Callee, Calley, Calli, Cally, Caly

Callista (Greek) most beautiful. See also Kallista.
Calesta, Calista, Callie, Calysta

Calvina (Latin) bald.
Calvine, Calvinetta, Calvinette

Calypso (Greek) concealer. Botany: a pink orchid native to northern regions. Mythology: the sea nymph who held Odysseus captive for seven years.
Caly, Lypsie, Lypsy

Cam (Vietnamese) sweet citrus.
Kam

Camara (American) a form of Cameron.
Camera, Cameri, Cameria, Camira, Camry

Camberly (American) a form of Kimberly.
Camber, Camberlee, Camberleigh

Cambria (Latin) from Wales. See also Kambria.
Cambery, Cambreia, Cambie, Cambrea, Cambree, Cambrie, Cambria, Cambry, Cambrya, Cami

Camden (Scottish) winding valley.
Camdyn

Camellia (Italian) Botany: a camellia is an evergreen tree or shrub with fragrant roselike flowers.
Camala, Camalia, Camallia, Camela, Camelia, Camelia, Camella, Camellita, Cami, Kamelia, Kamellia

Cameo (Latin) gem or shell on which a portrait is carved.
Cami, Kameo

Cameron (Scottish) crooked nose. See also Kameron, Kamryn.
Camara, Cameran, Cameren, Camira, Camiran, Camiron, Camryn

Cami (French) a short form of Camille. See also Kami.
Camey, Camie, Cammi, Cammie, Cammy, Cammye, Camy

Camila, Camilla (Italian) forms of Camille. See also Kamila, Mila.
Camilia, Camillia, Camilya, Camilla, Chamelea, Chamelia, Chamika, Chamila, Chamilia

Camille (French) young ceremonial attendant. See also Millie.
Cam, Cami, Camiel, Camielle, Camil, Camila, Camile, Camill, Cammille, Cammillie, Cammiyn, Cammyl, Cammyll, Camylle, Chamelle, Chamille, Kamille

Camri, Camrie (American) short forms of Camryn. See also Kamri.
Camrea, Camree, Camry, Camry

Camryn (American) a form of Cameron. See also Kamryn.
Camri, Camrin, Camron, Camryn

Camylle (French) a form of Camille.
Camylle, Camyll

Candace (Greek) glittering white; glowing. History: the title of the queens of ancient Ethiopia. See also Dacey, Kandace.
Cace, Canace, Canda, Candas, Candece, Candelle, Candi, Candiace, Candice, Candyce

Candi, Candy (American) familiar forms of Candace, Candice, Candida. See also Kandi.
Candee, Candi, Candia, Candide, Candita

Candice, Candis (Greek) forms of Candace.
Candes, Candi, Candias, Candis, Candise, Candiss, Candus

Candida (Latin) bright white.
Candeea, Candi, Candia, Candida, Candita

Candra (Latin) glowing. See also Kandra.
Candrea, Candria

Candyce (Greek) a form of Candace.
Candys, Candyse, Cyndyss

Canisha (American) a combination of Cami + Aisha.
Caneasha, Caneesha, Caneisha, Canesa, Canesha, Caneshaa, Canesha, Caniesha, Canyeshia

Cantara (Arabic) small crossing.
Cantarah

Cantrelle (French) song.
Cantrella

Capri (Italian) a short form of Caprice. Geography: an island off the west coast of Italy. See also Kapri.
Capria, Caprie, Capry

Caprice (Italian) fanciful.
Cappi, Caprece, Caprecia, Capresha, Capricia, Capriese, Caprina, Capris, Caprise, Caprisha, Capritta

Cara (Latin) dear. (Irish) friend. See also Karah.
Caira, Caragh, Carah, Caralee, Caranda, Carey, Carra

Caralee (Irish) a form of Cara.
Caralea, Caraleigh, Caralia, Caralie, Carely

Caralyn (English) a form of Caroline.
Caralin, Caraline, Caralynn, Caralynna, Caralynne

Caressa (French) a form of Carissa.
Caresa, Carese, Caresse, Carissa, Charessa, Charesse, Karessa

Carey (Welsh) a familiar form of Cara, Caroline, Karen, Katherine. See also Carrie, Kari.
Caree, Cari, Carey, Cary

Cari, Carie (Welsh) forms of Carey, Kari.

Carina (Italian) dear little one. (Swedish) a form of Karen. (Greek) a familiar form of Cora.
Carena, Carinah, Carine, Carinna

Carine (Italian) a form of Carina.
Carin, Carinn, Carinne

Carisa, Carrisa (Greek) forms of Carissa.
Carise, Carisha, Carisia, Charisa

Carissa (Greek) beloved. See also Karissa.
Caressa, Carisa, Carrissa, Charissa

Carita (Latin) charitable.
Caritta, Karita, Karitta

Carla (German) farmer. (English) strong. (Latin) a form of Carol, Caroline.
Carila, Carilla, Carleta, Catla, Carliqua, Carliyle, Carlonda, Carlyjo, Carlyle, Carlysle

Carlee, Carleigh, Carley (English) forms of Carly. See also Karlee.
Carle, Carlea, Carleah, Carleh

Carleen, Carlene (English) forms of Caroline. See also Karlene.
Carlaen, Carlaena, Carleena, Carlen, Carlena, Carlenna, Carline, Carlyn, Carlyne

Carli, Carlie (English) forms of Carly. See also Karli.

Carlin (Irish) little champion. (Latin) a short form of Caroline.
Carlan, Carlana, Carlandra, Carlina, Carlinda, Carline, Carling, Carllan, Carlyn, Carllen, Carllin

Carlisa (American) a form of Carlissa.
Carlis, Carlise, Carlyse, Carleesia, Carlesia, Carletha, Carlethe, Carlicia, Carlis, Carlise, Carlisha, Carlisia, Carlyse

Carlissa (American) a combination of Carla + Lissa.
Carleeza, Carlisa, Carliss, Carlissah, Carlisse, Carlissia, Carlista

Carlotta (Italian) a form of Charlotte.
Carletta, Carlita, Carlota

Carly (English) a familiar form of Caroline, Charlotte. See also Karli.
Carlee, Carli, Carlie, Carlye

Carlyn, Carlynn (Irish) forms of Carlin.
Carlyna, Carlynne

Carmela, Carmella (Hebrew) garden; vineyard. Bible: Mount Carmel in Israel is often thought of as paradise. See also Karmel.
Carma, Carmalla, Carmarit, Carmel, Carmeli, Carmelia, Carmelina, Carmelit, Carmelle, Carmellia, Carmellina, Carmesa, Carmesha, Carmi, Carmie, Carmiel, Carmil, Carmilla, Carmile, Carmilla, Carmille, Carmisha, Leeta, Lita

Carmelit (Hebrew) a form of Carmela.
Carmaletta, Carmalit, Carmalita, Carmalitha, Carmelitia, Carmelitha, Carmellit, Carmellita, Carmellitha, Carmellitia

Carmen (Latin) song. Religion: Nuestra Señora del Carmen—Our Lady of Mount Carmel—is one of the titles of the Virgin Mary. See also Karmen.
Carma, Carmaine, Carman, Carmelina, Carmencita, Carmene, Carmi, Carmia,

Carmin, Carmina, Carmine, Carmita, Carmon, Carmynn, Charmaine

Carol (German) farmer. (French) song of joy. (English) strong. See also Charlene, Kalle, Karoll.
Carel, Cariel, Caro, Carola, Carole, Carolenia, Carolinda, Caroline, Caroll, Carrie, Carrol, Carroll, Caryl

Carolane, Carolann, Carolanne (American) combinations of Carol + Ann. Forms of Caroline.
Carolan, Carol Ann, Carole-Anne

Carole (English) a form of Carol.
Carolee, Karole, Karrole

Carolina (Italian) a form of Caroline. See also Karolina.
Carilena, Carlena, Carlina, Caroleena, Caroleina, Carolena, Carrolena

Caroline (French) little and strong. See also Carla, Carleen, Carlin, Karolina.
Caralin, Caraline, Carileen, Carilene, Carilin, Carline, Carling, Carly, Caro, Carolann, Caroleen, Carolin, Carolina, Carolyn, Carrie, Carroleen, Carrolene, Carrolin, Caroline, Cary, Charlene

Carolyn (English) a form of Caroline. See also Karolyn.
Carilyn, Carilynn, Carilynne, Carlyn, Carlynn, Carlynne, Carolyne, Carolynn, Carolynne, Carrolyn, Carrolynn, Carrolyne

Caron (Welsh) loving, kindhearted, charitable.
Caronne, Carron, Carrone

Carra (Irish) a form of Cara.
Carrah

Carrie (English) a familiar form of Carol, Caroline. See also Carey, Kari, Karri.
Carree, Carrey, Carri, Carria, Carry

Carson (English) child of Carr.
Carsen, Carsyn

Carter (English) cart driver.

Caryl (Latin) a form of Carol.
Caryle, Caryll, Carylle

Caryn (Danish) a form of Karen.
Caren, Carren, Carrin, Carryn, Caryna, Caryne, Carynn

Carys (Welsh) love.
Caris, Caryse, Ceris, Cerys

Casandra (Greek) a form of Cassandra.
Casandera, Casandre, Casandrea, Casandrey, Casandri, Casandria, Casandra, Casaundra, Casaundre, Casondra, Casondri, Casondria

Casey (Irish) brave. (Greek) a familiar form of Acacia. See also Kasey.
Cacy, Casy, Casie, Casse, Cassee, Cassey, Cassye, Cayc, Cayce, Cayse, Caysee, Caysy

Casie (Irish) a form of Casey.
Caci, Caesi, Caisie, Casci, Casie, Casi, Cayci, Caysi, Caysie, Cazzi

Casidy (Irish) a form of Cassidy.
Casidee, Casidi

Cass (Greek) a short form of Cassandra.

Cassady (Irish) a form of Cassidy.
Casadee, Casadi, Casadie, Cassadee, Cassadey, Cassadi, Cassadie, Cassadina

Cassandra (Greek) helper of men. Mythology: a prophetess of ancient Greece whose prophesies were not believed. See also Kassandra, Sandra, Sandy, Zandra.
Casandra, Cass, Cassandre, Cassandri, Cassandry, Cassaundra, Cassie, Casondra

Cassaundra (Greek) a form of Cassandra.
Cassaundre, Cassaundra, Cassaundri, Cassaundria

Cassia (Greek) a cinnamon-like spice. See also Kasia.
Casia, Cass, Casya

Cassidy (Irish) clever. See also Kassidy.
Casidy, Cassidy, Casseday, Cassidy, Cassidee, Cassidie, Cassidie, Cassity

Cassie, Cassey, Cassi (Greek) familiar forms of Cassandra, Catherine. See also Kassie.
Cassee, Cassi, Cassy, Casy

Cassiopeia (Greek) clever. Mythology: the wife of the Ethiopian king Cepheus; the mother of Andromeda.
Cassio

Cassondra (Greek) a form of Cassandra.
Cassondre, Cassondri, Cassondria

Catalina (Spanish) a form of Catherine. See also Katalina.
Cataleen, Catalena, Catalene, Catalin, Catalyn, Catalyna, Cateline

Catarina (German) a form of Catherine.
Catarena, Catarin, Catarina, Caterin, Caterina, Caterine

Catelyn (Irish) a form of Caitlin.
Catelin, Cateline, Catelyne, Catelynn

Catharine (Greek) a form of Catherine.
Catharin, Catharina, Catharyn

Catherine (Greek) pure. (English) a form of Katherine.
Cat, Catalina, Catarina, Cate, Cathann, Catharine, Catherene, Catheria, Catherin, Catheren, Catherina, Catheryne, Cathi, Cathleen, Cathelyn, Cathline, Cathryn, Cathy, Catlaina, Catreeka, Catrelle, Catrice, Catrika, Catrina

Cathi, Cathy (Greek) familiar forms of Catherine, Cathleen. See also Kathy.
Catha, Cathe, Cathee, Cathey, Cathie

Cathleen (Irish) a form of Catherine. See also Caitlin, Kathleen.
Caithlyn, Cathaleen, Cathelin, Cathelina, Cathelyn, Cathi, Cathleana, Cathleene, Cathlene, Cathlin, Cathline

Cathrine (Greek) a form of Catherine.

Cathryn (Greek) a form of Catherine.
Cathryne, Cathrynn, Catryn

Catrina (Slavic) a form of Catherine, Katrina.
Catriona, Catrina, Catreen, Catreena, Catrene, Catreria, Catrin, Catrina, Catriona, Catroina

Cayla (Hebrew) a form of Kayla.
Caylea, Caylia

Caylee, Caylie (American) forms of Cayley.
Caeley, Cailey, Cayley, Cayle, Cayleigh, Cayli, Cayly

Ceara (Irish) a form of Ciara.
Ceaira, Ceairah, Ceairra, Cearaa, Cearie, Cearah, Cearra, Cera

Cecelia (Latin) a form of Cecilia. See also Sheila.
Caceli, Cacelia, Cece, Cecelia, Ceceli, Cecelia, Cecelie, Cecely, Cecelyn, Cecette, Cescelia, Cescelie

Cecilia (Latin) blind. See also Cicely, Cissy, Secilia, Selia, Sissy.
Cacilia, Caecilia, Cecelia, Cecil, Cecila, Cecile, Cecilea, Cecilija, Cecilla, Cecille, Cecillia, Cecily, Ceciliya, Cecilia, Cecylia, Cee, Ceil, Ceila, Ceilagh, Ceileh, Ceileigh, Ceilena, Celia, Cesilia, Cicelia

Cecily (Latin) a form of Cecilia.
Cacilie, Cecilee, Ceciley, Cecilie, Cecily, Cicely, Cilley

Ceil (Latin) a short form of Cecilia.
Ceel, Ciel

Ceira, Ceirra (Irish) forms of Ciara.
Cere

Celena (Greek) a form of Selena.
Celeena, Celene, Celenia, Celine, Cena

Celene (Greek) a form of Celena.
Celeen

Celeste (Latin) celestial, heavenly.
Cele, Celeeste, Celense, Celes, Celesia, Celesley, Celest, Celesta, Celestia, Celestial, Celestin, Celestina, Celestine,
Celestinia, Celestyn, Celestyna, Cellest, Celleste, Selestina

Celia (Latin) a short form of Cecilia.
Ceilia, Celie

Celina (Greek) a form of Celena. See also Selina.
Caleena, Calena, Calina, Celena, Celinda, Celinka, Celinna, Celka, Cellina

Celine (Greek) a form of Celena.
Caline, Celeen, Celene, Celine, Cellinn

Cera (French) a short form of Cerise.
Cerea, Ceri, Ceria, Cerra

Cerella (Latin) springtime.
Cerelisa, Ceres

Cerise (French) cherry; cherry red.
Cera, Cerese, Cerice, Cericia, Cerissa, Cerria, Cerrice, Cerrina, Cerrita, Cerryce, Ceryce, Cherise

Cesilia (Latin) a form of Cecilia.
Cesia, Cesya

Chablis (French) a dry, white wine. Geography: a region in France where wine grapes are grown.
Chabeli, Chabely, Chabely, Chablee, Chabley, Chabli

Chadee (French) from Chad, a country in north-central Africa. See also Sade.
Chaday, Chadday, Chade, Chadea, Chadi

Chai (Hebrew) life.
Chae, Chaela, Chaeli, Chaella, Chaena, Chaia

Chaka (Sanskrit) a form of Chakra. See also Shaka.
Chakai, Chakia, Chakka, Chakkah

Chakra (Sanskrit) circle of energy.
Chaka, Chakara, Chakaria, Chakena, Chakina, Chakira, Chakrah, Chakria, Chakeriya, Chakyra

Chalice (French) goblet.
Chalace, Chalcie, Chalece, Chalicea, Chalie, Chaliese, Chalis, Chalisa, Chalise, Chalisk, Chalissa, Chalisse, Challa, Challaine, Challis, Challisse, Challyse, Chalsey, Chalyce, Chalyn, Chalyse, Chalyssa, Chalyse

Chalina (Spanish) a form of Rose.
Chaline, Chalini

Chalonna (American) a combination of the prefix Cha + Lona.
Chalon, Chalona, Chalonda, Chalomn, Chalonn, Chalonte, Shalon

Chambray (French) a lightweight fabric.
Chambrae, Chambre, Chambree, Chambrée, Chambrey, Chambria, Chambrie

Chan (Cambodian) sweet-smelling tree.

Chana (Hebrew) a form of Hannah.
Chanae, Chanai, Chanay, Chanea, Chanie

Chancey (English) chancellor; church official.
Chance, Chancee, Chancie, Chancy

Chanda (Sanskrit) short tempered. Religion: the demon defeated by the Hindu goddess Chamunda. See also Shanda.
Chandae, Chandey, Chandi, Chandie, Chandin

Chandelle (French) candle.
Chandal, Chandel, Shandal, Shandel

Chandler (Hindi) moon. (Old English) candlemaker.
Chandlar, Chandlier, Chandlor, Chandlyr

Chandra (Sanskrit) moon. Religion: the Hindu god of the moon. See also Shandra.
Chandrae, Chandray, Chandre, Chandrea, Chandrelle, Chandria

Chanel (English) channel. See also Shanel.
Chanal, Chaneel, Chaneil, Chanele, Chanell, Channal, Channel, Chenelle

Chanell, Chanelle (English) forms of Chanel.
Channell, Shanell

Chanise (American) a form of Shanice.
Charisse, Chenise, Chenise

Channa (Hindi) chickpea.
Channah

Chantal (French) song.
Chantal, Chantael, Chantaela, Chantala, Chantale, Chantalla, Chantalle, Chantana, Chantara, Chantasia, Chantae, Chantiana, Chantel, Chantoya, Chantrill, Chantel

Chante (French) a short form of Chantal.
Chanta, Chantae, Chantai, Chantay,

Chantaye, Chanté, Chantéa, Chantee, Chanti, Chantia, Chaunte, Chauntea, Chauntéa, Chauntee

Chantel, Chantell, Chantelle (French) forms of Chantal. See also Shantel.
Chanteese, Chantela, Chantele, Chantella, Chanter, Chantey, Chantez, Chantrel, Chantrell, Chantrelle, Chatell

Chantilly (French) fine lace. See also Shantille.
Chantiel, Chantielle, Chantil, Chantila, Chantilée, Chantill, Chantille

Chantrea (Cambodian) moon; moonbeam.
Chantra, Chantrey, Chantri, Chantria

Chantrice (French) singer. See also Shantrice.
Chantreese, Chantress

Chardae, Charde (Punjabi) charitable. (French) short forms of Chardonnay. See also Shardae.
Charda, Chardai, Charday, Chardea, Chardee, Chardée, Chardese, Chardey, Chardie

Chardonnay (French) a dry white wine.
Char, Chardae, Chardnay, Chardney, Chardon, Chardonae, Chardonai, Chardonay, Chardonaye, Chardonae, Chardonna, Chardonee, Chardonnae, Chardonnée, Chardonnée, Chardonney, Shardonay, Shardonnay

Charis (Greek) grace; kindness.
Charece, Charece, Chareeze, Charese, Chari, Charice, Charie, Charish, Charisse

Charissa, Charisse (Greek) forms of Charity.
Charesa, Charese, Charessa, Charesse, Charis, Charisa, Charise, Charisha, Charissee, Charisa, Charyssa

Charity (Latin) charity, kindness.
Charery, Charis, Charissa, Charisse, Charista, Charita, Chariti, Charitie, Sharity

Charla (French, English) a short form of Charlene, Charlotte.
Char, Charlea

Charlaine (English) a form of Charlene.
Charlaina, Charlane, Charlanna, Charlayna, Charlayne

Charlee, Charley (German, English) forms of Charlie.
Charle, Charleigh

Charlene (English) a form of Caroline. See also Carol, Karla, Sharlene.
Charla, Charlaine, Charlean, Charleen, Charlene, Charleesa, Charlena, Charlenae, Charlesena, Charline, Charlyn, Charlyne, Charlynn, Charlyne, Charlzina, Charoline

Charlie (German, English) strong.
Charlee, Charley, Charli, Charyl, Chatty, Sharli, Sharlie

Charlotte (French) a form of Caroline. Literature: Charlotte Brontë was a British novelist and poet best known for her novel Jane Eyre. See also Karlotte, Lotte, Sharlotte, Tottie. Carlotta, Carly, Chara, Charl, Charl, Charlette, Charlet, Charletta, Charlette, Charlita, Charlotta, Charlott,

*Charlotta, Charlottie, Charlotty, Charlot,
Charolette, Charolot, Charolotte*

Charmaine (French) a form of
Carmen. See also Sharmaine.
*Charmy, Charma, Charmae,
Charmagne, Charmaigne, Charmain,
Charmaine, Charmalique, Charman,
Charmane, Charmar, Charmara,
Charmayane, Charmayne, Charmeen,
Charmeine, Charmene, Charmese,
Charmian, Charmin, Charmine,
Charmion, Charmisa, Charmon,
Charmyn, Charmyne, Charmynne*

Charnette (American) a combination
of Charo + Annette.
Charnetta, Charnita

Charnika (American) a combination
of Charo + Nika.
Charneka, Charniqua, Charnique

Charo (Spanish) a familiar form of
Rosa.
Charyanna (American) a combination
of the prefix Cha + Anna.
Charian, Charyian, Cheryn

Chasidy, Chassidy (Latin) forms of
Chastity.
*Chasa Dee, Chasadie, Chasady,
Chasidey, Chasidey, Chasidie, Chassedi,
Chassidi, Chasydi*

Chasity (Latin) a form of Chastity.
*Chasiti, Chasitie, Chasitty, Chassey,
Chassie, Chassiti, Chassity, Chassy*

Chastity (Latin) pure.
*Chasidy, Chasity, Chasta, Chastady,
Chastidy, Chastin, Chastitie, Chastney,
Chasty*

Chauntel (French) a form of Chantal.
*Chaunta, Chauntae, Chauntay,
Chaunte, Chauntell, Chauntelle,
Chauntiel, Chaunttell, Chawntelle,
Chontelle*

Chava (Hebrew) life. (Yiddish) bird.
Religion: the original name of Eve.
*Chabah, Chavae, Chavah, Chavalah,
Chavarra, Chavarria, Chave, Chavé,
Chavette, Chaviva, Chavis, Hava, Kaja*

Chavella (Spanish) a form of Isabel.
*Chavel, Chaveli, Chavell, Chavelle,
Chevelle, Chavely, Chevie*

Chavi (Gypsy) girl.
Chavali

Chavon (Hebrew) a form of Jane.
*Chavona, Chavonda, Chavonn,
Chavonne, Shavon*

Chavonne (Hebrew) a form of
Chavon. (American) a combination
of the prefix Cha + Yvonne.
*Chavondria, Chavonna, Chevon,
Chevonn, Chevonna*

Chaya (Hebrew) life; living.
*Chaike, Chaye, Chayka, Chayla,
Chaylah, Chaylea, Chaylee, Chaylene,
Chaya*

Chelci, Chelcie (English) forms of
Chelsea.
Chelce, Chelcee, Chelcey, Chelcy

Chelsea (English) seaport. See also
Kelsi, Shelsea.
*Chelci, Chelsee, Chelsia, Chelsa,
Chelsae, Chelsah, Chelse, Chelseah,
Chelsee, Chelsey, Chelsia, Chelsie,
Chesea, Cheslee, Chessea*

Chelsee (English) a form of Chelsea.
Chelsei, Chelseigh

Chelsey, Chelsy (English) forms of
Chelsea. See also Kelsey.
*Chelcy, Chelsay, Chelssy, Chelsey,
Chelsye, Chelsy*

Chelsie (English) a form of Chelsea.
*Chelli, Chellie, Chellise, Chellsie, Chelsi,
Chelsie, Cheslie, Chessie*

Chenelle (English) a form of Chanel.
Chenel, Chenell

Chenoa (Native American) white
dove.
*Chenee, Chenika, Chenita, Chenna,
Chenoah*

Cher (French) beloved, dearest.
(English) a short form of Cherilyn.
Chere, Cheri, Cherie, Sher

Cherelle, Cherrelle (French) forms of
Cheryl. See also Sherelle.
*Charell, Charelle, Cherell, Cherrel,
Cherrell*

Cherese (Greek) a form of Cherish.
Chereese, Cheresa, Cheresse, Cherice

Cheri, Cherie (French) familiar forms
of Cher.
Cheree, Chérie, Cheriee, Cherri, Cherrie

Cherilyn (English) a combination of
Cheryl + Lynn.
*Cher, Cheralyn, Chereen, Chereena,
Cherilynn, Cherlyn, Cherlynn, Cheralyn,
Cherrilyn, Cherrylyn, Cherylene, Cherylin,
Cheryline, Cheryl-Lyn, Cheryl-Lynn,
Cheryl-Lynne, Cherylyn, Cherylynn,
Cherylynne, Sherilyn*

Cherise (French) a form of Cherish. See also Sharice, Sherice.
Charisa, Charise, Cherece, Cherese, Cheresa, Cherice, Cheriss, Cherissa, Cherisse, Cherise

Cherish (English) dearly held, precious.
Charish, Charisha, Cheerish, Cherise, Cherishe, Cherrish, Sherish

Cherokee (Native American) a tribal name.
Cherika, Cherkita, Cherokee, Sherokee

Cherry (Latin) a familiar form of Charity. (French) cherry; cherry red.
Chere, Cheree, Cherey, Cherida, Cherita, Cherry, Cherrita, Cherry-Ann, Cherry-Anne, Cherye, Chery, Cherye

Cheryl (French) beloved. See also Sheryl.
Charel, Charil, Charyl, Cherelle, Cherrelle, Cheryl-Ann, Cheryl-Anne, Cheryle, Cherylee, Cheryll, Cherylle, Cheryl-Lee

Chesarey (American) a form of Desiree.
Chesarae, Chessa

Chesna (Slavic) peaceful.
Chesnee, Chesney, Chesnie, Chesny

Chessa (American) a short form of Chesarey.
Chessi, Chessie, Chessy

Cheyanne (Cheyenne) a form of Cheyenne.
Cheyan, Cheyana, Cheyane, Cheyann, Cheyanna, Cheyeana, Cheyeanna, Cheyeanne

Cheyenne (Cheyenne) a tribal name. See also Shaianne, Sheyenne, Shianne, Shyann.
Cheyanne, Cheyenne, Cheyenna, Cheyene, Cheyenna, Cheyna, Chi, Chi-Anna, Chie, Chyanne

Cheyla (American) a form of Sheila.
Cheylan, Cheyleigh, Cheylo

Cheyna (American) a short form of Cheyenne.
Chey, Cheye, Cheyne, Cheynee, Cheyney, Cheynna

Chiara (Italian) a form of Clara.
Cheara, Chiarra

Chika (Japanese) near and dear.
Chikako, Chikara, Chikeona

Chiku (Swahili) chatterer.

China (Chinese) fine porcelain. Geography: a country in eastern Asia. See also Ciana, Shina.
Chinaetta, Chinah, Chinasa, Chinda, Chinea, Chinesia, Chinna, Chinna, Chinna, Chyna, Chynna

Chinira (Swahili) God receives.
Chinara, Chinarah, Chinirah

Chinue (Ibo) God's own blessing.

Chiquita (Spanish) little one. See also Shiquita.
Chaqueta, Chaquita, Chica, Chickie, Chicky, Chikata, Chikita, Chiquera, Chiquila, Chiquite, Chiquitia, Chiquithe, Chiquitia, Chiquitta

Chiyo (Japanese) eternal.
Chiya

Chloe (Greek) blooming, verdant. Mythology: another name for Demeter, the goddess of agriculture.
Chloé, Chlöe, Chloee, Chlöie, Cloe, Kloe

Chloris (Greek) pale. Mythology: the only daughter of Niobe to escape the vengeful arrows of Apollo and Artemis. See also Loris.
Cloris, Clorissa

Cho (Korean) beautiful.
Choe

Cholena (Native American) bird.

Chris (Greek) a short form of Christina. See also Kris.
Chrys, Cris

Chriki (Swahili) blessing.

Chrissa (Greek) a short form of Christina. See also Khrissa.
Chryssa, Chryssa, Crissa, Cryssa

Chrissy (English) a familiar form of Christina.
Chrissie, Chrissey, Chrissie, Crissie

Christa (German) a short form of Christina. History: Christa McAuliffe, an American school teacher, was the first civilian on a U.S. space flight. See also Krista.
Chrysta, Crista, Crysta

Christabel (Latin, French) beautiful Christian.
Christabell, Christabella, Christabelle, Christable, Cristabel, Kristabel

Christain (Greek) a form of Christina.
Christiana, Christiann, Christianna

Christal (Latin) a form of Crystal. (Scottish) a form of Christina.
Christalene, Christalin, Christaline, Christall, Christalle, Christalyn, Christelle, Christle, Chrystal

Christelle (French) a form of Christal.
Christel, Christele, Christell, Chrystel, Chrystelle

Christen, Christin (Greek) forms of Christina. See also Kristen.
Christian, Christyn, Chrystan, Chrysten, Chrystyn, Crestienne

Christena, Christen (Greek) forms of Christina.

Christi, Christie (Greek) short forms of Christina, Christine. See also Kristi.
Christy, Chrysti, Chrystie, Chrysty, Kristi

Christian, Christiana, Christianna (Greek) forms of Christina. See also Kristian, Krystian.
Christiane, Christiann, Christi-Ann, Christianne, Christi-Anne, Christianni, Christiaun, Christiean, Christien, Christiena, Christienne, Christinan, Christy-Ann, Christy-Anne, Crystian, Chrystyann, Chrystyanne, Crystiann, Crystianne

Christin (Greek) a short form of Christina.
Christen, Chrystin

Christina (Greek) Christian; anointed. See also Khristina, Kristina, Stina, Tina.
Chris, Chrissa, Chrissy, Christa, Christain, Christal, Christeena, Christella, Christen, Christena, Christi, Christian,

Christie, Christin, Christinaa, Christine, Christinea, Christinia, Christinna, Christinnah, Christna, Christy, Christyn, Christyna, Christynna, Chrystina, Chrystyna, Cristeena, Cristena, Cristina, Crystina, Chrystena, Cristena

Christine (French, English) a form of Christina. See also Kirsten, Kristen, Kristine.
Chrisa, Christeen, Christen, Christene, Christi, Christie, Christy, Chrystine, Cristeen, Cristene, Cristine, Crystine

Christophe (Greek) Christ-bearer.

Christy (English) a short form of Christina, Christine.
Cristy

Christyn (Greek) a form of Christina.
Christyne

Chrys (English) a form of Chris.
Krys

Chrystal (Latin) a form of Christal.
Chrystale, Chrystalla, Chrystallina, Chrystallynn,

Chu Hua (Chinese) chrysanthemum.

Chumani (Lakota) dewdrops.
Chumany

Chun (Burmese) nature's renewal.

Chyanne, Chyenne (Cheyenne) forms of Cheyenne.
Chyan, Chyana, Chyane, Chyann, Chyanna, Chyeana, Chyenn, Chyenna, Cheyenne

Chyna, Chynna (Chinese) forms of China.

Ciana (Chinese) a form of China. (Italian) a form of Jane.
Cian, Ciandra, Ciann, Cianna

Ciara, Ciarra (Irish) black. See also Sierra.
Ceara, Chiairah, Ciaara, Ciaera, Ciaira, Ciarah, Ciaria, Ciarrah, Cieara, Ciearra, Ciearria, Ciera, Cierra, Cioria, Cyarra

Cicely (English) a form of Cecilia. See also Sissy.
Cicelia, Cicelie, Ciceley, Cicilia, Cicilie, Cicily, Cile, Cilka, Cilla, Cilli, Cillie, Cilly

Cidney (French) a form of Sydney.
Cidnee, Cidni, Cidnie

Ciera, Cierra (Irish) forms of Ciara.
Ceira, Cierah, Ciere, Cieria, Cierrah, Cierre, Cierria, Cierro

Cinderella (French, English) little cinder girl. Literature: a fairy tale heroine.
Cindella

Cindy (Greek) moon. (Latin) a familiar form of Cynthia. See also Sindy.
Cindee, Cindi, Cindie, Cyndi

Cinthia, Cinthya (Greek) forms of Cynthia.
Cinthiya, Cintia

Cira (Spanish) a form of Cyrilla.

Cissy (American) a familiar form of Cecelia, Cicely.
Cissey, Cissi, Cissie

Claire (French) a form of Clara.
Clair, Klaire, Klarye

Clairissa (Greek) a form of Clarissa.
Clairisa, Clairisse, Clarissa

Clara (Latin) clear; bright. Music: Clara Schumann was a famous nineteenth-century German composer. See also Chiara, Klara.
Claira, Claire, Clarabelle, Clare, Claresta, Clarette, Clarie, Clarina, Clarinda, Clarine, Clarissa, Claria

Clarabelle (Latin) bright and beautiful.
Clarabella, Claribel, Claribell

Clare (English) a form of Clara.
Clarey, Clari, Clary

Clarice (Latin) a familiar form of Clara.
Clarey, Clari, Clary

Clarice (Italian) a form of Clara.
Claris, Clarise, Clarisse, Claryce, Clerise, Klarice, Klarise

Clarisa (Greek) a form of Clarissa.
Claresa, Clarise, Clarisia

Clarissa (Greek) brilliant. (Italian) a form of Clara. See also Klarissa.
Clairissa, Claretia, Claressa, Claresta, Clarisa, Clarissia, Claritza, Clarizza, Clarrisa, Clarrissa, Clerissa

Clarita (Spanish) a form of Clara.
Clairette, Clareta, Claretta, Clarette, Claritza

Claudia (Latin) lame. See also Gladys, Klaudia.
Claudeen, Claudel, Claudelle, Claudette, Claudex, Claudiana, Claudiane, Claudie, Claudie-Anne, Claudina, Claudine

Claudette (French) a form of Claudia.
Claudetta

Claudie (Latin) a form of Claudia.
Claudee

Clea (Greek) a form of Cleo, Clio.

Clementine (Latin) merciful.
Clemence, Clemencia, Clemencie, Clemency, Clementia, Clementina, Clemenza, Clemette

Cleo (Greek) a short form of Cleopatra.
Chloe, Clea

Cleone (Greek) famous.
Cleonie, Cleonna, Cliona

Cleopatra (Greek) her father's fame. History: a great Egyptian queen.

Cleta (Greek) illustrious.

Clio (Greek) proclaimer; glorifier. Mythology: the Muse of history.
Clea

Cloe (Greek) a form of Chloe.
Clo, Cloei, Cloey, Cloie

Clotilda (German) heroine.

Coco (Spanish) coconut. See also Koko.

Codi, Cody (English) cushion. See also Kodi.
Coady, Codee, Codey, Codia, Codie

Colby (English) coal town. Geography: a region in England known for cheese-making. See also Kolby.
Cobi, Cobie, Colbi, Colbie

Colette (Greek, French) a familiar form of Nicole.
Coe, Coetta, Coletta, Collet, Collete,

Collett, Colletta, Collette, Kolette

Colleen (Irish) girl. See also Kolina.
Coe, Coel, Cole, Coleen, Colene, Coley, Coline, Collene, Collen, Collene, Collie, Collina, Colline, Colly

Collina (Irish) a form of Colleen.
Colena, Colina, Colinda

Concetta (Italian) pure.
Concettina, Conchetta

Conchita (Spanish) conception.
Chita, Concepita, Concha, Conciana

Concordia (Latin) harmonious. Mythology: the goddess governing the peace after war.
Con, Cordae, Cordaye

Connie (Latin) a familiar form of Constance.
Con, Connee, Conni, Conny, Konnie, Konny

Connor (Scottish) wise. (Irish) praised; exhaled.
Connar, Conner, Connery, Conor

Constance (Latin) constant; firm. History: Constance Motley was the first African-American woman to be appointed as a U.S. federal judge. See also Konstance, Kosta.
Connie, Constancia, Constancy, Constanta, Constantia, Constantina, Constantine, Constantina, Constanza, Constynse

Constanza (Spanish) a form of Constance.
Constanz, Constanze

Consuelo (Spanish) consolation.
Religion: Nuestra Señora del
Consuelo—Our Lady of
Consolation—is a name for the
Virgin Mary.
*Consolata, Consuela, Consuella,
Consula, Conzuelo, Konsuela, Konsuelo*

Cora (Greek) maiden. Mythology:
Kore is another name for
Persephone, the goddess of the
underworld. See also Kora.
*Corah, Coralee, Coretta, Corissa, Corey,
Corra*

Corabelle (American) a combination
of Cora + Belle.
Corabel, Corabella

Coral (Latin) coral. See also Koral.
Coraal, Corral

Coralee (American) a combination of
Cora + Lee.
*Coralea, Cora-Lee, Coralena, Coralene,
Coraley, Coralie, Coraline, Coraly,
Coralyn, Corella, Corilee, Koralie*

Coralie (American) a form of Coralee.
*Corali, Coralia, Coralina, Coralynn,
Coralynne*

Corazon (Spanish) heart.

Corbin (Latin) raven.
Corbe, Corbi, Corby, Corbyn, Corbynn

Cordasha (American) a combination
of Cora + Dasha.

Cordelia (Latin) warm-hearted.
(Welsh) sea jewel. See also Delia,
Della.
Cordae, Cordelie, Cordett, Cordette,

*Cordi, Cordilia, Cordilla, Cordula,
Kordelia, Kordula*

Cordi (Welsh) a short form of Cordelia.
Cordey, Cordia, Cordie, Cordy

Coretta (Greek) a familiar form of
Cora.
*Coreta, Corette, Correta, Corretta,
Corrette, Koretta, Korretta*

Corey, Cory (Irish) from the hollow.
(Greek) familiar forms of Cora. See
also Kori.
Coree, Cori, Correy, Correye, Corry

Coriann, Corianne (American) combi-
nations of Cori + Ann, Cori + Anne.
*Corian, Coriane, Cori-Ann, Corri,
Corri-Ann, Corrianne, Corrie-Anne*

Corina, Corinna (Greek) familiar
forms of Corinne. See also Korina.
*Coreena, Coriana, Corianna, Corinda,
Corrina, Corrinna, Coryna*

Corinne (Greek) maiden.
*Coreen, Coren, Corin, Corina, Corine,
Corinee, Corinn, Corinna, Corinna,
Coryn, Corynn, Coryne*

Corissa (Greek) a familiar form of Cora.
Coresa, Coressa, Corisa, Coryssa, Korissa

Corliss (English) cheerful; goodhearted.
Corlisa, Corlise, Corlissa, Corly, Korliss

Cornelia (Latin) horn colored. See also
Kornelia, Nelia, Nellie.
*Carna, Carniella, Corneilla, Cornela,
Cornelie, Cornella, Cornelle, Cornie,
Cornilear, Cornisha, Corry*

Corrina, Corrine (Greek) forms of
Corinne.
*Correen, Corren, Corrin, Corrinn,
Corrinna, Corrinne, Corrinne, Corryn*

Cortney (English) a form of Courtney.
*Cortnae, Cortnea, Cortnee, Cortneia,
Cortni, Cortnie, Cortny, Cortnye, Corttney*

Cosette (French) a familiar form of
Nicole.
Cosetta, Cossetta, Cossette, Cozette

Courtenay (English) a form of
Courtney.
Courtaney, Courtany, Courteney, Courteny

Courtnee, Courtnie (English) forms
of Courtney.
*Courtne, Courtnée, Courtnei,
Courtneigh, Courtni, Courtnii*

Courtney (English) from the court.
See also Kortney, Kourtney.
*Cortney, Courtena, Courtenay, Courtene,
Courtnae, Courtnay, Courtnee, Courtny,
Courtonie*

Crisbell (American) a combination of
Crista + Belle.
Crisbel, Cristabel

Crista, Crysta (Italian) forms of Christa.
Cristah

Cristal (Latin) a form of Crystal.
*Cristalie, Cristalina, Cristalle, Cristel,
Cristela, Cristelia, Cristella, Cristelle,
Cristhie, Cristle*

Cristen, Cristin (Irish) forms of
Christen, Christin. See also Kristin.
*Cristan, Cristyn, Crystan, Crysten,
Crystin, Crystyn*

Cristina, Cristine (Greek) forms of Christina. See also Kristina.
Cristiona, Cristy

Cristy (English) a familiar form of Cristina. A form of Chrissy. See also Kristy.
Cristey, Cristi, Cristie, Crysti, Crystie, Crysty

Crystal (Latin) clear, brilliant glass. See also Kristal, Krystal.
Christal, Chrystal, Chrystal-Lynn, Chrystel, Cristal, Crystala, Crystale, Crystalee, Crystalin, Crystall, Crystalle, Crystaly, Crystel, Crystela, Crystelia, Crystelle, Crysthelle, Crystl, Crystle, Crystol, Crystole, Crystyl

Crystalin (Latin) crystal pool.
Crystal-Ann, Cristalanna, Crystal-Anne, Cristalina, Cristallina, Crystalynn, Crystallynne, Cristilyn, Crystalina, Crystal-Lee, Crystal-Lynn, Crystalynn, Crystalynn

Crystina (Greek) a form of Christina.
Crystin, Crystine, Crystyn, Crystyna, Crystyne

Curran (Irish) heroine.
Cura, Curin, Curina, Currina

Cybele (Greek) a form of Sybil.
Cybel, Cybil, Cybill, Cybille

Cydney (French) a form of Sydney.
Cydne, Cydnee, Cydnei, Cydni, Cydnie

Cyerra (Irish) a form of Ciara.
Cyera, Cyerria

Cyndi (Greek) a form of Cindy.
Cynda, Cyndal, Cyndale, Cyndall, Cyndee, Cyndel, Cyndia, Cyndie, Cyndle, Cyndy

Cynthia (Greek) moon. Mythology: another name for Artemis, the moon goddess. See also Hyacinth, Kynthia.
Cindy, Cinthia, Cyneria, Cynethia, Cynithia, Cynthea, Cynthiana, Cynthiann, Cynthie, Cynthiana, Cynthya, Cyntia, Cynteria, Cythia, Synthia

Cyrilla (Greek) noble.
Cerelia, Cerella, Cira, Cirilla, Cyrella, Cyrille

D

Dacey (Irish) southerner. (Greek) a familiar form of Candace.
Dacee, Daci, Daci, Dacia, Dacie, Dacy, Daicee, Daici, Daicie, Daicy, Daycee, Daycie, Dayci, Daycy

Dacia (Irish) a form of Dacey.
Daciah

Dae (English) day. See also Dai.
Daiah

Daeja (French) a form of Déja.
Daejah, Daeja

Daelynn (American) a combination of Dae + Lynn.
Daeleen, Daelena, Daelin, Daelyn, Daelynne

Daeshandra (American) a combination of Dae + Shandra.
Daeshandria, Daeshaundra, Daeshaundria, Daeshaundra, Daeshaumdria, Daeshondria, Daeshondria, Daeshawndria,

Daeshawna (American) a combination of Dae + Shawna.
Daeshan, Daeshaun, Daeshauna, Daeshavon, Daeshawn, Daeshawnta, Daeshon, Daeshona

Daeshonda (American) a combination of Dae + Shonda.
Daeshanda, Daeshawnda

Dafny (American) a form of Daphne.
Dafany, Daffany, Daffie, Daffy, Dafna, Dafne, Dafney, Dafnie

Dagmar (German) glorious.
Dagmara

Dagny (Scandinavian) day.
Dagna, Dagnanna, Dagne, Dagney, Dagnie

Dahlia (Scandinavian) valley. Botany: a perennial flower. See also Daliah.
Dahliah, Dahlya, Dahlye

Dai (Japanese) great. See also Dae.
Day, Daye

Daija, Daijah (French) forms of Déja.
Daijah, Daijea, Daijha, Daijiah, Dajiah

Daisha (American) a form of Dasha.
Daesha, Daishae, Daishia, Daishya, Dasia

Daisy (English) day's eye. Botany: a white and yellow flower.
Daisee, Daisey, Daisi, Daisia, Daisie, Dasey, Dasi, Dasie, Dasy, Daysi, Deisy

Daja, Dajah (French) forms of Déja.
Dajae, Dajai, Daje, Dajha, Dajia

Dakayla (American) a combination of the prefix Da + Kayla.
Dakala, Dakeila

Dakira (American) a combination of the prefix Da + Kira.
Dakara, Dakaria, Dakarra, Dakirah, Dakyra

Dakota (Native American) a tribal name.
Dakkota, Dakoda, Dakotah, Dakotha, Dakotta, Dekoda, Dekota, Dekotah, Dekotha

Dale (English) valley.
Dael, Dahl, Daile, Daleleana, Dalena, Dalina, Dayle

Dalia, Daliah (Hebrew) branch. See also Dahlia.
Daelia, Dailia, Daleah, Daleia, Dalialah, Daliyah

Dalila (Swahili) gentle.
Dalela, Dalida, Dalilah, Dalila

Dalisha (American) a form of Dallas.
Dalisa, Dalishea, Dalishia, Dalishya, Dalisia, Dalissia

Dallas (Irish) wise.
Dalis, Dalise, Dalisha, Dalisse, Dallace, Dallis, Dallise, Dallus, Dallys, Dalyce, Dalys

Damaris (Greek) gentle girl. See also Maris.
Dama, Damar, Damara, Damarius, Damarys, Damarylis, Damarys, Dameress, Dameris, Damiris, Dammaris, Dammeris, Damris, Demaras, Demaris

Damiana (Greek) tamer, soother.
Daimenia, Daimiona, Damia, Damiann, Damianna, Damianne, Damien, Damienne, Damiona, Damon, Demion

Damica (French) friendly.
Damee, Dameeka, Dameka, Damekah, Damicah, Damicia, Damicka, Damie, Damieka, Damika, Damikah, Damyka, Demeeka, Demeka, Demekah, Demica, Demicah

Damita (Spanish) small noblewoman.
Damee, Damesha, Dameshia, Damesia, Dametia, Dametra, Dametrah

Damonica (American) a combination of the prefix Da + Monica.
Damonec, Damoneke, Damonik, Damonika, Damonique, Diamoniqua, Diamonique

Dana (English) from Denmark; bright as day.
Daina, Dainna, Danah, Danaia, Danan, Danarra, Dane, Danean, Danna, Dayna

Danae (Greek) Mythology: the mother of Perseus.
Danaë, Danay, Danayla, Danays, Danai, Danea, Danee, Dannae, Denae, Denee

Danalyn (American) a combination of Dana + Lynn.
Danalee, Donaleen

Daneil (Hebrew) a form of Danielle.
Daneal, Daneala, Daneale, Daneel, Daneela, Daneila

Danella (American) a form of Danielle.
Danayla, Danela, Danelia, Danelle, Danna, Donella, Donnella

Danelle (Hebrew) a form of Danielle.
Danael, Danalle, Danel, Danele, Danell, Danella, Donelle, Donnelle

Danesha, Danisha (American) forms of Danessa.
Daneisha, Daneshia, Daniesha, Danishia

Danessa (American) a combination of Danielle + Vanessa. See also Doneshia.
Danasia, Danesa, Daneshia, Danessia, Daniesa, Danisa, Danissa

Danessia (American) a form of Danessa.
Danesia, Danieshia, Danisia, Danissia

Danette (American) a form of Danielle.
Danetra, Danett, Danetta, Donnita

Dani (Hebrew) a familiar form of Danielle.
Danee, Danie, Danne, Dannee, Danni, Dannie, Danny, Dannye, Dany

Dania, Danya (Hebrew) short forms of Danielle.
Daniah, Danja, Dannia, Danyae

Danica, Danika (Slavic) morning star. (Hebrew) forms of Danielle.
Daneca, Daneeka, Daneekah, Danicah, Danicka, Danieka, Danikah, Danikla, Danneeka, Dannica, Dannika, Dannikah, Danryka, Denica, Donica, Donika, Donnaica, Donnica, Donnika

Danice (American) a combination of Danielle + Janice.
Donice

Daniela (Italian) a form of Danielle.
Daniellah, Dannilla, Danijela

Danielan (Spanish) a form of Danielle.

Daniella (English) a form of Dana.
Danka, Danniella, Danyella

Danielle (Hebrew, French) God is my judge.
Daneen, Danell, Danelle, Danelle, Dani, Danial, Danialle, Danica, Daniel, Daniela, Danielan, Daniele, Danielka, Daniell, Daniella, Danika, Danille, Danit, Dannielle, Danyel, Donniella

Danille (American) a form of Danielle.

Danit (Hebrew) a form of Danielle.
Danett, Danis, Danisha, Daniss, Danita, Danitra, Danitrea, Danitria, Danitza, Daniz

Danna (Hebrew) a short form of Danella.
Danella, Dannah

Dannielle (Hebrew, French) a form of Danielle.
Danniele, Danniell

Daphne (Greek) laurel tree.
Dafny, Daphane, Daphany, Dapheney, Daphna, Daphnee, Daphnique, Daphnit, Daphny

Daphnee (Greek) a form of Daphne.
Daphaney, Daphanie, Daphney, Daphni, Daphnie

Dara (Hebrew) compassionate.
Dahra, Daira, Dairah, Darah, Daraka, Daralea, Daralee, Daraleigh, Daralie, Davarie, Darda, Darice, Darisa, Darissa, Darja, Darra, Darrah

Darby (Irish) free. (Scandinavian) deer estate.
Darb, Darbe, Darbi, Darbie, Darby, Darbye

Darci, Darcy (Irish) dark. (French) fortress.
Darcee, Darcelle, Darcey, Darcie, Darsi, Darsie

Daria (Greek) wealthy.
Dari, Darya, Darria, Darya, Daryia

Darian, Darrian (Greek) forms of Daron.
Dariana, Dariane, Dariann, Darianna, Dariyan, Dariyanne, Dariana, Darianne, Dariann, Darrianna, Darrianne, Darrianne, Derrian, Driana

Darielle (French) a form of Daryl.
Dariel, Dariela, Dariell, Dariel, Darielle

Darien, Darrien (Greek) forms of Daron.
Dariene, Darienne, Dariene

Darilynn (American) a form of Darlene.
Darlene.

Daru (Hindi) pine tree.

Daryl (English) beloved. (French) a short form of Darlene.
Darelle, Darielle, Daril, Darilynn, Darel, Darell, Darielle, Darreshia, Darryl, Darryll, Daryll, Darylle

Darion, Darrion (Irish) forms of Daron.
Dariona, Darione, Darionne, Dariona, Darrionna

Darla (English) a short form of Darlene.
Darlecia, Darli, Darlice, Darlie, Darlis, Darly, Darlys

Darlene (French) little darling. See also Daryl.
Darilynn, Darla, Darlean, Darlee, Darleen, Darlene, Darlena, Darlena, Darlenia, Darlenne, Darletha, Darlin, Darline, Darling Darlyn, Darlynn, Darlyne

Darnee (Irish) a familiar form of Darnelle.

Darnelle (English) hidden place.
Darnee, Darnel, Darnell, Darnella, Darnelle, Darnetta, Darnette, Darniece, Darnita, Darnyell

Darnesha, Darnisha (American) forms of Darnelle.
Darneisha, Darneishia, Darneshea, Darneshia, Darnesia, Darnisisha, Darnisia, Darrenisha

Daron (Irish) great.
Darian, Darien, Darion, Daronica, Daronice, Darron, Daryn

Darselle (French) a form of Darcelle.
Darsel, Darsell, Darsella

Danyel, Danyell, Danyelle (American) forms of Danielle.
Danyel, Danyae, Danyail, Danyaile, Danyal, Danyea, Danyele, Danyiel, Danyielle, Danyle, Donnyale, Donnyell, Donyale, Doryell

Danna — [see above]

Darcelle (French) a form of Darci.
Darcel, Darcell, Darcella, Darselle

Daryn (Greek) gifts. (Irish) great.
Daron, Daryan, Daryne, Darynn, Darynne

Dasha, Dasia (Russian) forms of Dorothy.
Daisha, Dashae, Dashenka, Dashia, Dashiah, Dasiah, Daysha

Dashawna (American) a combination of the prefix Da + Shawna.
Dashaun, Dashaunna, Dashay, Dashell, Dayshana, Dayshawnna, Dayshona, Deshawna

Dashiki (Swahili) loose-fitting shirt worn in Africa.
Dashi, Dashika, Dashka, Desheka, Deshiki

Dashonda (American) a combination of the prefix Da + Shonda.
Dashaunda, Dishante

Davalinda (American) a combination of Davida + Linda.
Davalynda, Davelinda, Davilinda, Darylinda

Davalynda (American) a form of Davalinda.
Davelynda, Davilynda, Darylynda

Davalynn (American) a combination of Davida + Lynn.
Davalin, Davalyn, Davalynne, Davelin, Davelyn, Davelynn, Davelynne, Davilin, Davilyn, Davilynn, Davilynne, Dayleen, Devlyn

Davida (Hebrew) beloved. Bible: David was the second king of Israel. See also Vida.
Daveta, Davetta, Davette, Davika, Davita

Davina (Scottish) a form of Davida. See also Vina.
Dava, Davannah, Davean, Davee, Daveen, Daveena, Davene, Daveon, Davey, Davi, Daviana, Davie, Davin, Davinder, Davine, Davineen, Davinia, Davinna, Davonna, Davria, Devean, Deveen, Devene, Devina

Davisha (American) a combination of the prefix Da + Aisha.
Daveisha, Davesia, Davis, Davisa

Davonna (Scottish, English) a form of Davina, Devonna.
Davion, Daviona, Davionna, Davon, Davona, Davonda, Davone, Davonia, Davonne, Davonnia

Dawn (English) sunrise, dawn.
Dawana, Dawandrea, Dawanna, Dawin, Dawna, Dawne, Dawnee, Dawnetta, Dawnisha, Dawnlynn, Dawnn, Dawnrae

Dawna (English) a form of Dawn.
Dawnna, Dawnya

Dawnyelle (American) a combination of Dawn + Danielle.
Dawnele, Dawnell, Dawnelle, Dawnyel, Dawnyella

Dawnisha (American) a form of Dawn.
Dawnesha, Dawni, Dawniell, Dawnielle, Dawnisia, Dawniss, Dawnita, Dawnnisha, Dawnysha, Dawnysia

Dayana (Latin) a form of Diana.
Dayanara, Dayani, Dayanna, Dayanne, Dayanni, Deyanaira, Dyani, Dyanna, Dyia

Dayle (English) a form of Dale.
Dayla, Daylan, Daylea, Daylee

Dayna (Scandinavian) a form of Dana.
Daynah, Dayne, Daynna, Deyna

Daysha (American) a form of Dasha.
Daysa, Dayshalie, Daysia, Deisha

Daysi, Deysi (English) forms of Daisy.
Daysee, Daysia, Daysie, Daysy, Deysia, Deysy

Dayton, Daytona (English) day town; bright, sunny town.
Daytonia

Deana (Latin) divine. (English) valley.
Deanah, Deane, Deanielle, Deanisha, Deanna, Deeana, Deeann, Deeanna, Deena

Deandra (American) a combination of Dee + Andrea.
Dandrea, Deandre, Deandré, Deandrea, Deandree, Deandreia, Deandria, Deandra, Deaundra, Deaundria, Deeandra, Deyaneira, Deondra, Diandra, Diandre, Diandrea, Diondra, Dyandra

Deangela (Italian) a combination of the prefix De + Angela.
Deangala, Deangalique, Deangle

Deanna (Latin) a form of Deana, Diana.
Deaana, Deahana, Deandra, Deandre, Déanna, Deannia, Deeanna, Deena

Deanne (Latin) a form of Diane.
Deahanne, Deane, Deann, Déanne, Deeann, Dee-Ann, Deeanne

Debbie (Hebrew) a short form of Deborah.
Debbee, Debbey, Debbi, Debby, Debee, Debi, Debie

Deborah (Hebrew) bee. Bible: a great Hebrew prophetess.
Deb, Debbie, Debbra, Debborah, Debby, Debor, Debora, Deborah, Deborha, Deborrah, Debra, Debrena, Debrina, Debroah, Devora, Dobra

Debra (American) a form of Deborah.
Debbra, Debbrah, Debrah, Debra, Debria

Dedra (American) a form of Deidre.
Deeadra, Deedra, Deedrea, Deedrie

Dedriana (American) a combination of Dedra + Adriana.
Dedranae

Dee (Welsh) black, dark.
De, Dea, Deah, Dede, Dedie, Deea, Deedee, Dee Dee, Didi

Deena (American) a form of Deana, Dena, Dinah.

Deidra, Deidre (Irish) forms of Deirdre.
Deidrah, Deidrea, Deidrie, Dieda, Diedre, Dierdra

Deirdre (Irish) sorrowful; wanderer.
Dedra, Deerdre, Deidra, Deidre, Deirdree, Didi, Diedra, Dierdre, Dierdrie, Dierdrie

Deisy (English) a form of Daisy.
Deisi, Deissy

Deitra (Greek) a short form of Demetria.
Deetra, Detria

Déja (French) before.
Daeja, Daija, Deejay, Dejae, Dejai, Dejanae, Dejanelle, Dejon

Dejanae (French) a form of Déja.
Dajahnae, Dajona, Dejana, Dejanah, Dejanae, Dejanai, Dejanay, Dejane, Dejanea, Dejanee, Dejanna, Dejannaye, Dejna, Dejonae

Dejon (French) a form of Déja.
Daijon, Dajan, Dejone, Dejonee, Dejonelle, Dejonna

Deka (Somali) pleasing.
Dekah

Delacy (American) a combination of the prefix De + Lacy.
Delaceya

Delainey (Irish) a form of Delaney.
Delaine, Delainee, Delainni, Delainie, Delainy

Delana (German) noble protector.
Dalanna, Dalayna, Dalena, Dalena, Dalenna, Dalina, Dalinda, Dalinna, Delaina, Delania, Delanya, Delayna, Delena, Delenya, Delina, Dellaina

Delaney (Irish) descendant of the challenger. (English) a form of Adeline.
Dalaney, Dalania, Dalene, Dalenee, Datine, Del, Delainey, Delane, Delanee, Delanie, Delany, Delayne, Delayney, Delaynie, Deleani, Déline, Della, Dellaney

Delanie (Irish) a form of Delaney.
Delani

Delfina (Greek) a form of Delphine. (Spanish) dolphin.
Delfeena, Delfine

Delia (Greek) visible; from Delos, Greece. (German, Welsh) a short form of Adelaide, Cordelia.
Delhia, Delea, Deli, Deliah, Deliana, Delianne, Delinda, Dellia, Dellya, Delya

Delicia (English) delightful.
Delecia, Delesha, Delice, Delisa, Delise, Delisha, Delishia, Delisiah, Delya, Delys, Delyse, Delysia, Doleesha

Delilah (Hebrew) brooder; Bible: the companion of Samson. See also Lila.
Dalialah, Dalilah, Delia, Delilia

Della (English) a short form of Adelaide, Cordelia, Delaney.
Del, Dela, Dell, Delle, Delli, Dellis, Dells

Delores (Spanish) a form of Dolores.
Delora, Delore, Deloria, Delories, Deloris, Delorise, Delorita, Delsie

Delphine (Greek) from Delphi, Greece. See also Delfina.
Delpha, Delphe, Delphi, Delphia, Delphina, Delphinia, Delvina

Delsie (English) a familiar form of Delores.
Delsa, Delsey, Delza

Delta (Greek) door. Linguistics: the fourth letter in the Greek alphabet. Geography: a triangular land mass at the mouth of a river.
Delte, Deltora, Deltoria, Deltra

Demetria (Greek) cover of the earth. Mythology: Demeter was the Greek goddess of the harvest.
Deitra, Demeta, Demeteria, Demetra, Demetriana, Demetrianna, Demetris, Demetrice, Demetriona, Demetris, Demetrish, Demetrius, Demi, Demita, Demitra, Demitria, Dymitra

Demi (French) half. (Greek) a short form of Demetria.
Demia, Demiah, Demii, Demmi, Demmie, Demy

Dena (English, Native American) valley. (Hebrew) a form of Dinah. See also Deana.
Deane, Deena, Deeyn, Denae, Denah, Dene, Denea, Deney, Denna, Deonna

Denae (Hebrew) a form of Dena.
Denaé, Denay, Denee, Deneé

Deni (French) a short form of Denise.
Deney, Denie, Denni, Dennie, Denny, Dinnie, Dinny

Denica, Denika (Slavic) forms of Danica.
Denikah, Denikia

Denise (French) Mythology: follower of Dionysus, the god of wine.
Danice, Danise, Denese, Deni, Denice, Denicy, Deniece, Denisha, Denisse, Denize, Dennise, Dennys, Denyce, Denys, Denyse

Denisha (American) a form of Denise.
Deneesha, Deneichia, Deneisha, Deneishea, Denesha, Deneshia, Deniesha, Denishia

Denisse (French) a form of Denise.
Denesse, Denissa

Deonna (English) a form of Dena.
Deon, Deona, Deonah, Deondra, Deonne

Derika (German) ruler of the people.
Dereka, Derekia, Derica, Dericka, Derrica, Derricka, Derrika

Derry (Irish) redhead.
Deri, Derie

Deryn (Welsh) bird.
Derien, Derienne, Derion, Derin, Deron, Derren, Derrin, Derrine, Derrion, Derriona, Deryne

Desarae (French) a form of Desiree.
Desara, Desarai, Desaraie, Desaray, Desare, Desaré, Desarea, Desaree, Desarie, Dezarae

Deserae, Desirae (French) forms of Desiree.
Desera, Deserai, Deseray, Desere, Deseree, Deseret, Deseri, Deserie, Deserrae, Deserray, Deserré, Dessirae, Dezeray, Dezere, Dezerea, Dezrae, Dezyrae

Deshawna (American) a combination of the prefix De + Shawna.
Dashauna, Deshan, Deshane, Deshaun, Deshawn, Desheania, Deshona, Deshonna

Deshawnda (American) a combination of the prefix De + Shawnda.
Deshanda, Deshandra, Deshaundra, Deshaundra, Deshonda

Desi (French) a short form of Desiree.
Désir, Desira, Dezi, Dezia, Dezzia, Dezzie

Desiree (French) desired, longed for. See also Dessa.
Chesarey, Desarae, Deserae, Desi, Desirae, Desirah, Desirai, Desiray, Desire, Desirea, Desireah, Desireé, Désirée, Desirey, Desiri, Desray, Desree, Dessie, Dessire, Dezarae, Dezirae, Dezinee

Dessa (Greek) wanderer. (French) a form of Desiree.

Desta (Ethiopian) happy. (French) a short form of Destiny.
Desti, Destie, Desty

Destany (French) a form of Destiny.
Destanee, Destaney, Destani, Destanie, Destannee, Destannie

Destinee, Destini, Destinie (French) forms of Destiny.
Desteni, Destiana, Destine, Destinée, Destinie

Destiney (French) a form of Destiny.

Destiny (French) fate.
Desnine, Desta, Destany, Destenee, Destenie, Desteny, Destin, Destinee, Destiney, Destini, Destinie, Destonie, Destynee, Dezstany

Destynee, Destyni (French) forms of Destiny.
Desty, Destyn, Destyne, Destyne, Destynie

Deva (Hindi) divine.
Deeva

Devan (Irish) a form of Devin.
Devana, Devane, Devanee, Devaney,
Devani, Devanie, Devann, Devanna,
Devannae, Devanne, Devany

Devi (Hindi) goddess. Religion: the
Hindu goddess of power and
destruction.

Devin (Irish) poet.
Devan, Deven, Devena, Devenji,
Devine, Devinn, Devine, Deryn

Devon (English) a short form of
Devonna. (Irish) a form of Devin.
Devaen, Devion, Devione, Devionne,
Devone, Devoni, Devonne

Devonna (English) from Devonshire.
Davonna, Devon, Devona, Devonda,
Devondra, Devonia

Devora (Hebrew) a form of Deborah.
Deva, Devorah, Devra, Devrah

Deyn (Irish) a form of Devin.
Devyn, Deryne, Devynn, Derynne

Dextra (Latin) adroit, skillful.
Delextra, Dextria

Dezarae, Dezirae, Deziree (French)
forms of Desiree.
Dezaraee, Dezarai, Dezaray, Dezare,
Dezaree, Dezarey, Dezerie, Deziray,
Dezirea, Dezirée, Dezorae, Dezra

Di (Latin) a short form of Diana, Diane,
Dy

Dia (Latin) a short form of Diana,
Diane.

Diamond (Latin) precious gem.
Diamantina, Diamon, Diamonda,
Diamonde, Diamonia, Diamonique,
Diamonte, Diamontina, Dyamond

Diana (Latin) divine. Mythology: the
goddess of the hunt, the moon, and
fertility. See also Deanna, Deanne,
Dyan.
Daiana, Daianna, Dayana, Dayanna,
Di, Dia, Dianah, Dianalyn, Dianarose,
Dianatris, Dianca, Diandra, Diane,
Dianelis, Diania, Dianielle, Dianita,
Dianna, Diany's, Didi

Diane, Dianne (Latin) short forms of
Diana.
Deane, Deanne, Deeane, Deeanne, Di,
Dia, Diahann, Dian, Diani, Dianie,
Diann

Dianna (Latin) a form of Diana.
Diahanna, Diannah

Diantha (Greek) divine flower.
Diandre, Dianthe

Diedra (Irish) a form of Deidre.
Didra, Diedre

Dillan (Irish) loyal, faithful.
Dillon, Dillyn

Dilys (Welsh) perfect; true.

Dina (Hebrew) a form of Dinah.
Dinna, Dyna

Dinah (Hebrew) vindicated. Bible: a
daughter of Jacob and Leah.
Dina, Dinnah, Dynah

Dinka (Swahili) people.

Dionna (Greek) an alternative form of
Dionne.
Deona, Deondra, Deoria, Deonna,
Deonyia, Diona, Diondra, Diondrea

Dion (French) golden.
Diora, Dior, Diorra, Diorre

Divinia (Latin) divine.
Devina, Devinae, Devinia, Devinie,
Devirra, Diveena, Divina, Divine,
Divinita, Diviya

Dita (Spanish) a form of Edith.
Ditka, Ditta

Divina (Latin) divine.

Dixie (French) tenth. (English) wall;
dike. Geography: a nickname for the
American South.
Dix, Dixee, Dixi, Dixy

Diza (Hebrew) joyful.
Ditza, Ditzah, Dizah

Dodie (Hebrew) beloved. (Greek) a
familiar form of Dorothy.
Doda, Dode, Dodee, Dodi, Dody

Dolly (American) a short form of
Dolores, Dorothy.
Dol, Doll, Dollee, Dolley, Dolli, Dollie,
Dollina

Dolores (Spanish) sorrowful. Religion:
Nuestra Señora de los Dolores—Our
Lady of Sorrows—is a name for the
Virgin Mary. See also Lola.
Delores, Deloria, Dolly, Doloritas,
Doloria, Doloritas

Dionne (Greek) divine queen.
Mythology: Dione was the mother
of Aphrodite, the goddess of love.
Deonne, Dion, Dione, Dionee, Dioniz,
Dionna, Dione

Dominica, Dominika (Latin) belonging to the Lord. See also Mika.
*Domenica, Domenika, Domineca,
Domineka, Dominga, Domini,
Dominick, Dominicka, Dominique,
Dominixe, Domino, Dominyka,
Domka, Domnicka, Domonica,
Domonice, Domonika*

Dominique, Domonique (French) forms of Dominica, Dominika.
*Domanique, Domeneque, Domenique,
Domeneque, Dominiqua, Domino,
Dominoque, Dominique, Dominuque,
Domique, Domminique, Domoniqua*

Domino (English) a short form of Dominica, Dominique.

Dona (English) world leader; proud ruler. (Italian) a form of Donna.
*Donae, Donah, Donalda, Donaldina,
Donelda, Donellia, Doni*

Doña (Italian) a form of Donna.
*Donail, Donalea, Donalisa, Donay,
Doni, Doria, Dorie, Donise, Donitrae*

Donata (Latin) gift.
*Donatha, Donato, Donatta, Donetta,
Donette, Donita, Donnette, Donnita, Donte*

Dondi (American) a familiar form of Donna.
Dondra, Dondrea, Dondria

Doneshia, Donisha (American) forms of Danessa.
*Donasha, Donashay, Doneisha,
Doneishia, Donesha, Donisa, Donisha,
Donishia, Donnesha, Donnisha*

Donna (Italian) lady.
Doña, Dondi, Donnae, Donnalee,

*Donnalen, Donnay, Donne, Donnell,
Donni, Donnie, Donnise, Donny,
Dontia, Donya*

Donniella (American) a form of Danielle.
*Donella, Doniele, Doniell, Doniella,
Donielle, Donnella, Donnielle,
Donnyella, Donyelle*

Dora (Greek) gift. A short form of Adora, Eudora, Pandora, Theodora.
*Dorah, Doralia, Doralie, Doralisa,
Doraly, Doralynn, Doran, Dorchen,
Dore, Dorece, Doree, Dorece, Doreen,
Dorelia, Dorella, Dorelle, Doresha,
Doressa, Doretta, Dori, Dorielle, Dorika,
Doriley, Dorilis, Dorinda, Dorion,
Dorita, Doro, Dory*

Doralynn (English) a combination of Dora + Lynn.
Doralin, Doralyn, Doralynne, Dorlin

Doreen (Irish) moody, sullen. (French) golden. (Greek) a form of Dora.
*Doreena, Dorena, Dorene, Dorina,
Dorine*

Doretta (American) a form of Dora, Dorothy.
Doretha, Dorette, Dorettie

Dori, Dory (American) familiar forms of Dora, Doria, Doris, Dorothy.
*Dore, Dorey, Dorie, Dorree, Dorri,
Dorrie, Dorry*

Doria (Greek) a form of Dorian.
Dori

Dorian (Greek) from Doris, Greece.
Dorean, Doriana, Doriane, Doriann,

*Dorianna, Dorianne, Dorin, Dorina,
Dorri,
Dorriane*

Dorinda (Spanish) a form of Dora.

Doris (Greek) sea. Mythology: wife of Nereus and mother of the Nereids or sea nymphs.
*Dori, Dorice, Dorisa, Dorise, Dorris,
Dorrise, Dorrys, Dory, Dorys*

Dorothea (Greek) a form of Dorothy. See also Thea.
*Dorethea, Dorotea, Doroteya, Dorotha,
Dorothia, Dorotthea, Dorthea, Dorthia*

Dorothy (Greek) gift of God. See also Theodora.
*Dasha, Dodie, Lolotea, Theodora.
Dasya, Do, Doa, Doe, Dolly, Doortje,
Dorathy, Dordei, Dordi, Doretta, Dori,
Dorika, Doritha, Dorka, Dorle, Dorlisa,
Doro, Dorolice, Dorosia, Dorota,
Dorothea, Dorothee, Dorothi, Dorothie,
Dorottya, Dorte, Dortha, Dorthy, Dory,
Dosi, Dossie, Dosya, Dottie*

Dorrit (Greek) dwelling. (Hebrew) generation.
Dorit, Dorita, Doritt

Dottie, Dotty (Greek) familiar forms of Dorothy.
Dot, Dottee

Drew (Greek) courageous; strong. (Latin) a short form of Drusilla.
Dru, Drue

Drinka (Spanish) a form of Alexandria.
Dreena, Drena, Drina

Drusi (Latin) a short form of Drusilla.
*Drucey, Druci, Drucie, Drucy, Drusey,
Drusie, Drusy*

Drusilla (Latin) descendant of Drusus, the strong one. See also Drew.
Dreusila, Drucella, Drucill, Drucilla, Druscilla, Drusi

Dulce (Latin) sweet.
Delcina, Delcine, Douce, Doucie, Dulcea, Dulcey, Dulci, Dulcia, Dulciana, Dulcibel, Dulcibella, Dulcie, Dulcine, Dulcinea, Dulcy, Dulse, Dulsea

Dulcinea (Spanish) sweet. Literature: Don Quixote's love interest.

Duscha (Russian) soul; sweetheart; term of endearment.
Duschah, Dusha, Dushenka

Dusti, Dusty (English) familiar forms of Dustine.
Dustee, Dustie

Dustine (German) valiant fighter. (English) brown rock quarry.
Dusteena, Dusti, Dustin, Dustina, Dustyn

Dyamond, Dymond (Latin) forms of Diamond.
Dyamin, Dyamon, Dyamone, Dymin, Dymon, Dymonde, Dymone, Dymonn

Dyana (Latin) a form of Diana. (Native American) deer.
Dyan, Dyane, Dyani, Dyann, Dyanna, Dyanne

Dylan (Welsh) sea.
Dylaan, Dylaina, Dylana, Dylane, Dylanee, Dylanie, Dylann, Dylanna, Dylen, Dylin, Dyllan, Dylynn

Dyllis (Welsh) sincere.
Dilys, Dylis, Dyllis, Dylys

Dynasty (Latin) powerful ruler.
Dynastee, Dynasti, Dynastie

Dyshawna (American) a combination of the prefix Dy + Shawna.
Dyshanta, Dyshawn, Dyshonda, Dyshonna

Earlene (Irish) pledge. (English) noblewoman.
Earla, Earlean, Earlecia, Earleen, Earlena, Earlina, Earlinda, Earline, Erla, Erlana, Erlene, Erlenne, Erlina, Erlinda, Erline, Eritsha

Eartha (English) earthy.
Ertha

Easter (English) Easter time. History: a name for a child born on Easter.
Eastan, Eastlyn, Easton

Eboni, Ebonie (Greek) forms of Ebony.
Ebanie, Ebeni, Ebonni, Ebonnie

Ebone, Ebonee (Greek) forms of Ebony.
Abonee, Ebanee, Eboné, Ebonea, Ebonee, Ebonnee

Ebony (Greek) a hard, dark wood.
Abony, Eban, Ebanie, Ebany, Ebbony, Ebone, Eboney, Eboni, Ebonie, Ebonique, Ebonisha, Ebonye, Ebonyi

Echo (Greek) repeated sound. Mythology: the nymph who pined for the love of Narcissus until only her voice remained.
Echoe, Ecko, Ekko, Ekkoe

Eda (Irish, English) a short form of Edana, Edith.

Edana (Irish) ardent; flame.
Eda, Edan, Edanna

Edda (German) a form of Hedda.
Etta

Eddy (American) a familiar form of Edwina.
Eady, Eddi, Eddie, Edy

Edeline (English) noble; kind.
Adeline, Edelyne, Editine, Editlyne

Eden (Babylonian) a plain. (Hebrew) delightful. Bible: the earthly paradise.
Eaden, Ede, Edena, Edene, Edenia, Edin, Edyn

Edie (English) a familiar form of Edith.
Eadie, Edi, Edy, Edye, Eyde, Eydie

Edith (English) rich gift. See also Dita.
Eadith, Eda, Ede, Edetta, Edette, Edie, Edit, Edita, Edite, Editha, Edithe, Editta, Ediva, Edyta, Edyth, Edytha, Edythe

Edna (Hebrew) rejuvenation. Religion: the wife of Enoch, according to the Book of Enoch.
Adna, Adnisha, Ednah, Edneisha, Edneshia, Ednisha, Ednita, Edona

Edrianna (Greek) a form of Adrienne.
Edria, Edriana, Edrina

Edwina (English) prosperous friend. See also Winnie.
Eddy, Edina, Edweena, Edweena, Edwine, Edwinna, Edwyna, Edwynn

Effia (Ghanaian) born on Friday.

Effie (Greek) spoken well of. (English) a short form of Alfreda, Euphemia.
Effi, Effia, Effy, Ephie

Eileen (Irish) a form of Helen. See also Aileen, Ilene.
Eilean, Eileena, Eileene, Eilena, Eilene, Eiley, Eilie, Eilieh, Eilina, Eiline, Eilleen, Eillen, Eilyn, Eleen, Elene

Ekaterina (Russian) a form of Katherine.
Ekaterine, Ekaterini

Ela (Polish) a form of Adelaide.

Elaina (French) a form of Helen.
Elainea, Elainia, Elainna

Elaine (French) a form of Helen. See also Lainey, Laine.
Eilane, Elain, Elaina, Elaini, Elan, Elana, Elane, Elania, Elanie, Elanit, Elauna, Elayna, Ellaine

Elana (Greek) a short form of Eleanor. See also Ilana, Lana.
Elan, Elanee, Elaney, Elani, Elania, Elanie, Elanna, Elanni

Elayna (French) a form of Elaina.
Elayn, Elaynah, Elayne, Elayni

Elberta (English) a form of Alberta.
Elbertha, Elberthina, Elberthine, Elbertina, Elbertine

Eldora (Spanish) golden, gilded.
Eldoree, Eldorey, Eldori, Eldoria, Eldorie, Eldory

Eleanor (Greek) light. History: Anna Eleanor Roosevelt was a U.S. delegate to the United Nations, a writer, and the thirty-second First Lady of the United States. See also Elana, Ella, Ellen, Leanore, Lena, Lenore, Leonore, Leora, Nellie, Nora, Noreen.
Elana, Elanor, Elanore, Eleanora, Eleanore, Elena, Eleni, Elenor, Elenorah, Elenore, Eleonore, Eleanore, Elianore, Elinor, Elinore, Elladine, Ellenor, Ellie, Elliner, Ellinor, Ellinore, Elna, Elnore, Elynor, Elynore

Eleanora (Greek) a form of Eleanor. See also Lena.
Elenora, Eleonora, Elianora, Ellenora, Ellenorah, Elnora, Elynora

Electra (Greek) shining; brilliant. Mythology: the daughter of Agamemnon, leader of the Greeks in the Trojan War.
Elektra

Elena (Greek) a form of Eleanor. (Italian) a form of Helen.
Eleana, Eleen, Eleena, Elen, Elene, Elenitsa, Elenka, Elenna, Elenoa, Elenola, Elina, Elena, Lena

Eleni (Greek) a familiar form of Eleanor.
Elenie, Eleny

Eleora (Hebrew) the Lord is my light.
Eliona, Elina, Elora

Elexis (Greek) a form of Alexis.
Elexas, Elexes, Elexess, Elexeya, Elexia, Elexiah

Elexus (Greek) a form of Alexius, Alexus.
Elexius, Elexsus, Elexxus, Elexys

Elfrida (German) peaceful. See also Freda.
Elfrea, Elfreda, Elfredda, Elfreeda, Elfreyda, Elfrieda, Elfryda

Elga (Norwegian) pious. (German) a form of Helga.
Elgiva

Elia (Hebrew) a short form of Eliana.
Eliah

Eliana (Hebrew) my God has answered me. See also Iliana.
Elia, Eliane, Elianna, Ellianna, Liana, Liane

Eliane (Hebrew) a form of Eliana.
Elianne, Elliane, Ellianne

Elicia (Hebrew) a form of Elisha. See also Alicia.
Elecia, Elica, Elicea, Elicet, Elichia, Eliscia, Elisia, Elissia, Ellecia, Ellicia

Elida, Elide (Latin) forms of Alida.
Elidee, Elidia, Elidy

Elisa (Spanish, Italian, English) a short form of Elizabeth. See also Alisa, Ilisa.
Elecea, Eleesa, Elesa, Elesia, Elisa, Elisya, Ellisa, Ellisia, Ellissa, Ellissia, Ellisya, Ellisya, Elysa, Elysia, Elyssia, Elyssya, Lisa

Elisabeth (Hebrew) a form of Elizabeth.
Elisabet, Elisabeta, Elisabethe, Elisabetta, Elisabette, Elisabith, Elisebet, Elisheba, Elisheva

Elise (French, English) a short form of Elizabeth, Elysia. See also Ilise, Liese, Lisette, Lissie.
Eilis, Eilise, Elese, Élise, Elisee, Elisie, Elisse, Elizé, Ellice, Ellise, Ellyce, Ellyse, Elsey, Elsie, Elsy, Elyce, Elyci, Elyse, Elyze, Lisel, Lisl, Lison

Elisha (Hebrew) a form of Alisha. See also Ilisha, Lisha.
Eleacia, Eleasha, Eleesha, Elesha, Eleshia, Eletcia, Elicia, Elishah, Elishena, Elishua, Elishka, Ellesha, Ellecia, Ellisha, Elsha, Elysha, Elyshia

Elissa, Elyssa (Greek, English) forms of Elizabeth. Short forms of Melissa. See also Alissa, Alyssa, Lissa.
Elissah, Ellissa, Ellyssa, Ilissa, Ilyssa

Elita (Latin, French) chosen. See also Lida, Lita.
Elitia, Ellitia, Elitie, Ellitia, Ellitie, Ilida, Ilita, Litia

Eliza (Hebrew) a short form of Elizabeth. See also Aliza.
Eliz, Elizaida, Elizalina, Elize, Elizea

Elizabet (Hebrew) a form of Elizabeth.
Elizabete, Elizabette

Elizabeth (Hebrew) consecrated to God. Bible: the mother of John the Baptist. See also Bess, Beth, Betsy, Betty, Elsa, Ilse, Libby, Liese, Liesel, Lisa, Lisbeth, Lisette, Lissa, Lissie, Liz, Liza, Lizabeta, Lizabeth, Lizbeth, Lizina, Lizzy, Veta, Yelisabeta, Zizi.
Alizabeth, Eliabeth, Elisa, Elisabeth, Elise, Elissa, Eliza, Elizabee, Elizabet, Elizaveta, Elizabeth, Elka, Elsabeth, Elsbeta, Elschen, Elspeth, Elysabeth, Elzbieta, Elzsébet, Helsa, Ilizzabet, Lusa, Elzveta

Elizaveta (Polish, English) a form of Elizabeth.
Elisavet, Elisaveta, Elisavetta, Elisaveta, Elizavet, Elizavetta, Elizaveta, Elsveta

Elka (Polish) a form of Elizabeth.
Ellka, Ilka

Elke (German) a form of Adelaide, Alice.
Elkah, Ilki

Ella (English) elfin; beautiful fairy-woman. (Greek) a short form of Eleanor.
Ellah, Ellamae, Ellia, Ellie

Elle (Greek) a short form of Eleanor. (French) she.
El, Ele, Ell

Ellen (English) a form of Eleanor, Helen.
Elen, Elenee, Elery, Elin, Elina, Elinda, Ellan, Ellena, Ellene, Ellie, Ellin, Ellon, Ellyn, Ellynn, Ellynne, Elyn

Ellice (English) a form of Elise.
Ellecia, Ellyce, Elyce

Ellie, Elly (English) short forms of Eleanor, Ella, Ellen.
Ele, Elie, Ellee, Elleigh, Elli

Elma (Turkish) sweet fruit.

Elmira (Arabic, Spanish) a form of Almira.
Elmeera, Elmera, Elmeria, Elmyra

Elnora (American) a combination of Ella + Nora.

Elodie (American) a form of Melody. (English) a form of Alodie.
Elodee, Elodia, Elody

Eloise (French) a form of Louise.
Elois, Eloisa, Eloisia

Elora (American) a short form of Elnora.
Ellora, Elloree, Elorie

Elsa (German) noble. (Hebrew) a short form of Elizabeth. See also Ilse.
Ellsa, Ellse, Else, Elsja

Elsbeth (German) a form of Elizabeth.
Elsbet, Elzbet, Elzbeta

Elsie (German) a familiar form of Elsa, Helsa.
Ellsie, Ellsy, Elsi, Elsy

Elspeth (Scottish) a form of Elizabeth.
Elsper, Elspie

Elva (English) elfin. See also Alva, Alvina.
Elvia, Elvie

Elvina (English) a form of Alvina.
Elvenea, Elviniea, Elvinia, Elvinna

Elvira (Latin) white; blond. (German) closed up. (Spanish) elfin. Geography: the town in Spain that hosted a Catholic synod in 300 A.D.
Elva, Elvera, Elvire, Elvira, Vira

Elyse (Latin) a form of Elysia.
Ellysa, Ellyse, Elyce, Elys, Elysee, Elysse, Elysse

Elysia (Greek) sweet; blissful. Mythology: Elysium was the dwelling place of happy souls.
Elise, Elishia, Ellicia, Elycia, Elyssa, Ilysha, Ilysia

Elyssa (Latin) a form of Elysia.
Ellyssa

Emalee (Latin) a form of Emily.
Emaili, Emalea, Emaleigh, Emali, Emalia, Emalie

Emani (Arabic) a form of Iman.
Eman, Emane, Emaneé, Emanie, Emann

Emanuelle (Hebrew) a form of Emmanuelle.
Emanual, Emanuel, Emanuela, Emanuella

Ember (French) a form of Amber.
Emberlee, Emberly

Emelia, Emelie (Latin) forms of Emily.
Emellie

Emely (Latin) a form of Emily.
Emelly

Emerald (French) bright green gem-stone.
Emelda, Esmeralda

Emery (German) industrious leader.
Emeri, Emerie

Emilee, Emilie (English) forms of Emily.
Emile, Emilea, Emileigh, Émilie, Emiliee, Emillee, Emillie, Emmélie, Emmilee, Emylee

Emilia (Italian) a form of Amelia.
Emalia, Emelia, Emila

Emily (Latin) flatterer. (German) industrious. See also Amelia, Emma, Millie.
Eimile, Em, Emaily, Emalee, Emeli, Emelia, Emelie, Emelita, Emely, Emilee, Emiley, Emili, Emilia, Emilie, Émilie, Emilis, Emilka, Emillie, Emilly, Emmaline, Emmaly, Emmélie, Emmey, Emmi, Emmie, Emmilly, Emmily, Emmy, Emmye, Emyle

Emilyann (American) a combination of Emily + Ann.
Emileane, Emileann, Emileanna, Emileanne, Emiliana, Emiliann, Emilianna, Emilianne, Emillyann, Emillyanna, Emillyanne, Emiliana, Emiliann, Emilianna, Emilianne

Emma (German) a short form of Emily. See also Amy.
Em, Ema, Emmah, Emmy

Emmalee (American) a combination of Emma + Lee. A form of Emily.
Emalea, Emalee, Emilee, Emmalea, Emmalei, Emmaleigh, Emmaley, Emmali, Emmalia, Emmalie, Emmaliese, Emmalyse, Emylee

Emmaline (French) a form of Emily.
Emalina, Emaline, Emelina, Emeline, Emilina, Emilinia, Emiline, Emmalina, Emmalene, Emmeline, Emmiline

Emmalynn (American) a combination of Emma + Lynn.
Emelyn, Emelyne, Emelynne, Emilyn, Emilynn, Emilynne, Emlyn, Emlynn, Emlynne, Emmalyn, Emmalynne

Emmanuelle (Hebrew) God is with us.
Emanuelle, Emmanuela, Emmanuella

Emmy, Emy (German, French) a familiar form of Emma.
Emi, Emie, Emiy, Emmi, Emmie, Emmye

Emmylou (American) a combination of Emmy + Lou.
Emlon, Emmalou, Emmelou, Emmilou, Emylou

Ena (Irish) a form of Helen.
Enna

Enid (Welsh) life; spirit.

Enrica (Spanish) a form of Henrietta. See also Rica.
Enrieta, Enrietta, Enrika, Enriqua, Enriqueta, Enriquetta, Enriquette

Eppie (English) a familiar form of Euphemia.
Effie, Effy, Eppy

Erica, Erika (Scandinavian) ruler of all. (English) brave ruler. See also Arica, Rica, Ricki.
Erica, Ericha, Ericka, Errica

Ericka, Erika (Scandanavian) forms of Erica.
Erickah, Erikaa, Erikah, Erikka, Erricka, Errika, Eyka, Erykka, Eyrika

Erin (Irish) peace. History: another name for Ireland. See also Arin.
Earin, Earrin, Eran, Eren, Erena, Erene, Ereni, Eri, Erian, Erina, Erine, Erinetta, Erinn, Errin, Eryn

Erinn (Irish) a form of Erin.
Erinna, Erinne

Erma (Latin) a short form of Ermine, Hermina. See also Irma.
Ermelinda

Ermine (Latin) a form of Hermina.
Erma, Ermin, Ermina, Erminda, Erminia, Erminie

Erna (English) a short form of Ernestine.

Ernestine (English) earnest, sincere.
Erna, Ernaline, Ernesia, Ernesta, Ernestina, Ernesztina

Eryn (Irish) a form of Erin.
Eiryn, Eryne, Erynn, Erynne

Eshe (Swahili) life.
Eisha, Esha

Esmé (French) a familiar form of Esmeralda. A form of Amy.
Esma, Esme, Esmée

Esmeralda (Greek, Spanish) a form of Emerald.
Emelda, Esmé, Esmerelda, Esmerilda, Esmiralda, Ezmerelda, Ezmirilda

Esperanza (Spanish) hope. See also Speranza.
Esparanza, Epe, Esperance, Esperans, Esperansa, Esperanta, Esperanz, Esperanza

Essence (Latin) life; existence.
Essa, Essen, Esseence, Essences, Essense, Essynce

Essie (English) a short form of Estelle, Esther.
Essa, Essey, Essie, Essy

Estee (English) a short form of Estelle, Esther.
Esta, Estée, Esti

Estefani, Estefania, Estefany (Spanish) forms of Stephanie.
Estéfana, Estefania, Estefane, Estefanie, Estefany

Estelle (French) a form of Esther. See also Stella, Trella.
Essie, Estee, Estel, Estela, Estele, Esteley, Estelina, Estelita, Estell, Estella, Estellita, Estelia, Esthella

Estephanie (Spanish) a form of Stephanie.
Estephania, Estephani, Estephany

Esther (Persian) star. Bible: the Jewish captive whom Ahasuerus made his queen. See also Hester.
Essie, Estee, Ester, Esthur, Eszter, Eszti

Estrella (French) star.
Estrela, Estrelinha, Estrell, Estrelle, Estrellita

Ethana (Hebrew) strong; firm.

Ethel (English) noble.
Ethelda, Ethelin, Etheline, Ethelle, Ethelyn, Ethelynn, Ethelynne, Ethyl

Etta (German) little. (English) a short form of Henrietta.
Etka, Etke, Etti, Ettie, Etty, Itke, Itta

Étoile (French) star.

Eudora (Greek) honored gift. See also Dora.

Eugenia (Greek) born to nobility. See also Gina.
Eugenie, Eugenina, Euginia, Eugnia

Eugenie (Greek) a form of Eugenia.
Eugenee, Eugénie

Eulalia (Greek) well spoken. See also Ula.
Eula, Eulalee, Eulalie, Eulalya, Eulia

Eun (Korean) silver.

Eunice (Greek) happy; victorious. Bible: the mother of Saint Timothy.

See also Unice.

Euphemia (Greek) spoken well of; in good repute. History: a fourth-century Christian martyr.
Effam, Effie, Eppie, Eufemia, Euphan, Euphemie, Euphie

Eurydice (Greek) wide, broad. Mythology: the wife of Orpheus.
Euridice, Euridyce, Eurydyce

Eustacia (Greek) productive. (Latin) stable; calm. See also Stacey.
Eustasia

Eva (Greek) a short form of Evangelina. (Hebrew) a form of Eve. See also Ava, Chava.
Éva, Evah, Evalea, Evalee, Evike

Evaline (French) a form of Evelyn.
Evalin, Evalina, Evalyn, Evalynn, Eveleen, Evelene, Evelina, Eveline

Evangelina (Greek) bearer of good news.
Eva, Evangelene, Evangelia, Evangelica, Evangeline, Evangelique, Evangelyn, Evangelynn

Evania (Irish) young warrior.
Evan, Evana, Evanka, Evann, Evanna, Evanne, Evany, Eveania, Evvanne, Evvnnea, Evyan

Eve (Hebrew) life. Bible: the first woman created by God. (French) a short form of Evonne. See also Chava, Hava, Naeva, Vica, Yeva.
Eva, Evie, Evita, Evvaka, Evyn, Ewa, Yeva

Evelin (English) a form of Evelyn.
Evelina, Eveline

Evelyn (English) hazelnut.
Avalyn, Aveline, Evaleen, Evalene, Evaline, Evalyn, Evalynn, Evalynne, Eveleen, Evelin, Evelyna, Evelyne, Evelynn, Evelynne, Evline, Evalina

Everett (German) courageous as a boar.

Evette (French) a form of Yvette. A familiar form of Evonne. See also Ivette.
Evett

Evie (Hungarian) a form of Eve.
Evey, Evi, Evicka, Evike, Evka, Evuska, Evvie, Evvy, Evy, Ewa

Evita (Spanish) a form of Eve.

Evline (English) a form of Evelyn.
Evleen, Evlene, Evlin, Evlina, Evlyn, Evlynn, Evlynne

Evonne (French) a form of Yvonne. See also Ivonne.
Evanne, Eve, Evenie, Evenne, Eveny, Evette, Evin, Evon, Evona, Evone, Evoni, Evonna, Evonnie, Evony, Evyn, Evynn, Evyona, Eyvone

Ezri (Hebrew) helper; strong.
Ezra, Ezria

Fabia (Latin) bean grower.
Fabiana, Fabienne, Fabiola, Fabra, Fabria

Fabiana (Latin) a form of Fabia.
Fabyana

Fabienne (Latin) a form of Fabia.
Fabian, Fabiann, Fabianne, Fabiene, Fabreanne

Fabiola, Faviola (Latin) forms of Fabia.
Fabiole, Fabyola, Faviana, Faviolha

Faith (English) faithful; fidelity. See also Faye, Fidelity.
Fayth, Faythe

Faizah (Arabic) victorious.

Falda (Icelandic) folded wings.
Faida, Fayda

Faline (Latin) catlike.
Faleen, Falena, Falene, Falin, Falina, Fallyn, Fallyne, Faylina, Fayline, Faylyn, Faylynn, Faylynne, Feleria, Felina

Fallon (Irish) grandchild of the ruler.
Falan, Falen, Fallan, Fallen, Fallonne, Falon, Falyn, Falynn, Falynne, Phalon

Fancy (French) betrothed. (English) whimsical; decorative.
Fanchette, Fanchon, Fanci, Fancia, Fancie

Fannie, Fanny (American) familiar forms of Frances.
Fan, Fanette, Fani, Fania, Fannee, Fanney, Fanni, Fannia, Fanny, Fanya

Fantasia (Greek) imagination.
Fantasy, Fantasya, Fantaysia, Fantazia, Fiantasi

Farah, Farrah (English) beautiful; pleasant.
Fara, Farra, Fayre

Faren, Farren (English) wanderer.
Faran, Fare, Farin, Faron, Farrahn, Farran, Farrand, Farrin, Farron, Farryn, Farye, Faryn, Feran, Ferin, Feron, Ferran, Ferren, Ferrin, Ferron, Ferryn

Fatima (Arabic) daughter of the Prophet. History: the daughter of Muhammad.
Fatema, Fathma, Fatimah, Fatime, Fatma, Fatmah, Fatme, Fattim

Fawn (French) young deer.
Faun, Fawna, Fawne

Fawna (French) a form of Fawn.
Fauna, Faunia, Faunna

Faye (French) fairy; elf. (English) a form of Faith.
Fae, Fay, Fayann, Fayanna, Fayette, Fayina, Fey

Fayola (Nigerian) lucky.
Fayla, Feyla

Felecia (Latin) a form of Felicia.
Fleia

Felica (Spanish) a short form of Felicia.
Falisa, Felisa, Felisca, Feliza

Felice (Latin) a short form of Felicia.
Feleee, Felicie, Felise, Felize, Felyce, Felysse

Felicia (Latin) fortunate; happy. See also Lecia, Phylicia.
Falecia, Faleshia, Falicia, Fela, Felecia, Faleia, Felice, Felicidad, Feliciona, Felicity, Felicya, Felisea, Felisha, Felisia, Felisiana, Felissya, Felita, Felixia, Felixia, Felka, Fellia, Felycia, Felysia, Felyssia, Fleasia, Fleichia, Fleishia, Flichia

Felicity (English) a form of Felicia.
Falicity, Felicita, Felicitas, Félicité, Féliciti, Felisita, Felisity

Felisha (Latin) a form of Felicia.
Faleisha, Falesha, Falisha, Falleshia, Feleasha, Feleisha, Felesha, Felishia, Fellishia, Felysha, Flisha

Fern (English) fern. (German) a short form of Fernanda.
Ferne, Ferni, Fernlee, Fernleigh, Fernley, Fernly

Feodora (Greek) gift of God.
Fedora, Fedoria

Femi (French) woman. (Nigerian) love me.
Femie, Femmi, Femmie, Femy

Fernanda (German) daring, adventurous. See also Andee, Nan.
Ferdie, Ferdinanda, Ferdinande, Fern, Fernande, Fernandette, Fernandina, Nanda

Fiala (Czech) violet.

Fidelia (Latin) a form of Fidelity.
Fidela, Fidele, Fidelina

Fidelity (Latin) faithful, true. See also Faith.
Fidelia, Fidelita

Fifi (French) a familiar form of Josephine.
Feef, Feefee, Fifine

Filippa (Italian) a form of Philippa.
Felipa, Filipa, Filippina, Filipina

Filomena (Italian) a form of Philomena.
Fila, Filah, Filemon

Fiona (Irish) fair, white.
Fionna

Fionnula (Irish) white shouldered. See also Nola, Nuala.
Fenella, Fenula, Finella, Finola, Finula

Flair (English) style; verve.
Flaire, Flare

Flannery (Irish) redhead. Literature: Flannery O'Connor was a renowned American writer.
Flan, Flann, Flanna

Flavia (Latin) blond, golden haired.
Flavere, Flaviar, Flavie, Flavien, Flavienne, Flaviere, Flavio, Flavyere, Fulvia

Flavie (Latin) a form of Flavia.
Flavi

Flo (American) a short form of Florence.

Fleur (French) flower.
Fleure, Fleuree, Fleurette

Flora (Latin) flower. A short form of Florence. See also Lore.
Fiora, Fiore, Fiorenza, Flor, Florann, Florella, Florelle, Floren, Floria, Floriana, Florianna, Florica, Florinel

Florence (Latin) blooming; flowery; prosperous. History: Florence Nightingale, a British nurse, is considered the founder of modern nursing. See also Florida.
Fiorenza, Flo, Flora, Florance, Florencia, Florency, Florendra, Florentia, Florentina, Florentyna, Florenza, Floretta, Florentina, Florette, Florie, Florina, Florine, Floris, Flossie

Floria (Basque) a form of Flora.
Flori, Floria

Florida (Spanish) a form of Florence.
Floridia, Florinda, Florita

Florie (English) a familiar form of Florence.
Flore, Flori, Florri, Florrie, Florry, Flory

Floris (English) a form of Florence.
Florisa, Florise

Flossie (English) a familiar form of Florence.
Floss, Flossi, Flossy

Fola (Yoruba) honorable.

Fonda (Latin) foundation. (Spanish) inn.
Fondea, Fonta

Fontanna (French) fountain.
Fontaine, Fontana, Fontane, Fontanne, Fontayne

Fortuna (Latin) fortune; fortunate.
Fortoona, Fortune

Fran (Latin) a short form of Frances.
Frain, Frann

Frances (Latin) free; from France. See also Paquita.
Fanny, Fran, Franca, France, Francee, Francena, Francesca, Francess, Francesta, Franceta, Francetta, Francine, Francis, Francisca, Françoise, Frankie, Fannie, Franny

Francesca (Italian) a form of Frances.
Franceska, Francesca, Francesta, Franchesca, Franzetta

Franchesca (Italian) a form of
Francesca.
*Cheka, Chekka, Chesca, Cheska,
Francheca, Francheka, Franchelle,
Franchesa, Francheska, Francheskea,
Franchesska*

Franci (Hungarian) a familiar form of
Francine.
Francey, Francie, Francy

Francine (French) a form of Frances.
*Franceen, Franceine, Franceline, Francene,
Francenia, Franci, Francin, Francina,
Francyne*

Francis (Latin) a form of Frances.
Francise, Franncia, Francys

Francisca (Italian) a form of Frances.
*Franciska, Franciszka, Frantiska,
Franziska*

Françoise (French) a form of Frances.
Frankie (American) a familiar form of
Frances.
*Francka, Francki, Franka, Frankey,
Franki, Frankia, Franky, Frankye*

Frannie, Franny (English) familiar
forms of Frances.
Frani, Frania, Franney, Franni, Frany

Freda, Freida, Frida (German) short
forms of Alfreda, Elfrida, Frederica,
Sigfreda.
*Frayda, Fredda, Fredella, Fredia, Fredra,
Freeda, Freeha, Freia, Frida, Frideborg,
Frieda*

Freddi, Freddie (English) familiar
forms of Frederica, Winifred.
Fredda, Freddy, Fredi, Fredia, Fredy, Frici

Frederica (German) peaceful ruler.
See also Alfreda, Rica, Ricki.
*Farica, Federica, Freda, Fredalena,
Fredaline, Freddi, Freddie, Frederickeina,
Frederika, Frederike, Frederina,
Frederine, Frederique, Fredith, Fredora,
Fredrea, Fredrica, Fredricah, Fredricia,
Freida, Fritzi, Fryderica*

Frederika (German) a form of
Frederica.
*Fredericka, Fredreka, Fredricka, Fredrika,
Fryderyka*

Frederike (German) a form of
Frederica.
Fredericke, Friederike

Frederique (French) a form of
Frederica.
Frédérique, Rike

Freja (Scandinavian) a form of Freya.

Freya (Scandinavian) noblewoman.
Mythology: the Norse goddess of love.
Fraya, Freya

Fritzi (German) a familiar form of
Frederica.
*Friezi, Fritze, Fritzie, Fritzinn,
Fritzline, Fritzy*

G

Gabriel, Gabriele (French) forms of
Gabrielle.
*Gabbriel, Gabbryel, Gabreal, Gabreale,
Gabreil, Gabrial, Gabryel*

Gabriela, Gabriella (Italian) forms of
Gabrielle.
*Gabriala, Gabrialla, Gabriela,
Gabriellia, Gabrila, Gabrilla, Gabryella*

Gabrielle (French) devoted to God.
*Gabbrielle, Gabielle, Gabreale,
Gabrealle, Gabielle, Gabreale,
Gabriana, Gabriel, Gabriela, Gabriele,
Gabriell, Gabriella, Gabrielle, Gabrina,
Gabryelle, Gabryell, Gabryelle, Gaby,
Garriella*

Gaby (French) a familiar form of
Gabrielle.
*Gabbey, Gabbi, Gabbie, Gabby, Gabey,
Gabi, Gabie, Gavi, Gary*

Gada (Hebrew) lucky.
Gadah

Gaea (Greek) planet Earth.
Mythology: the Greek goddess of
Earth.
Gaia, Gaiea, Gaya

Gaetana (Italian) from Gaeta.
Geography: a city in southern Italy.
Gaetan, Gaétane, Gaetanne

Gagandeep (Sikh) sky's light.
Gagandip, Gagnadeep, Gagndeep

Gail (Hebrew) a short form of
Abigail.(English) merry, lively.
*Gael, Gaela, Gaelle, Gaila, Gaile, Gale,
Gayla, Gayle*

Gala (Norwegian) singer.
Galla

Galen (Greek) healer; calm. (Irish) lit-
tle and lively.
*Gaelen, Gaellen, Galyn, Gaylaine,
Gayleen, Gaylen, Gaylene, Gaylyn*

Galena (Greek) healer; calm.

Gali (Hebrew) hill; fountain; spring.
Galice, Galie

Galina (Russian) a form of Helen.
Gailya, Galayna, Galenka, Galia,
Galiana, Galiena, Galina, Galochka,
Galya, Galyna

Ganesa (Hindi) fortunate. Religion:
Ganesha was the Hindu god of wisdom.

Ganya (Hebrew) garden of the Lord.
(Zulu) clever.
Gana, Gani, Gania, Ganice, Ganit

Gardenia (English) Botany: a sweet-
smelling flower.
Deeni, Denia, Gardena, Gardinia

Garland (French) wreath of flowers.

Garnet (English) dark red gem.
Garnetta, Garnette

Garyn (English) spear carrier.
Garan, Garen, Garra, Garyn

Gasha (Russian) a familiar form of
Agatha.
Gashka

Gay (French) merry.
Gae, Gai, Gaye

Gayle (English) a form of Gail.
Gayla

Gayna (English) a familiar form of
Guinevere.
Gaynah, Gayner, Gaynor

Geela (Hebrew) joyful.
Gela, Gila

Geena (American) a form of Gena.
Geana, Geeana, Geeanna

Gelya (Russian) angelic.

Gema, Gemma (Latin, Italian) jewel,
precious stone. See also Jemma.
Gem, Gemmey, Gemmie, Gemmy

Gemini (Greek) twin.
Gemelle, Gemina, Geminine,
Geminna

Gen (Japanese) spring. A short form of
names beginning with "Gen."

Gena (French) a form of Gina. A short
form of Geneva, Genevieve, Iphigenia.
Geanna, Geena, Geenah, Gen, Genae,
Gendi, Genia, Genea, Geneja, Geni,
Genia, Genie

Geneen (Scottish) a form of Jeanine.
Geanine, Geannine, Gen, Genene,
Genine, Gineen, Ginene

Genell (American) a form of Jenelle.
Genovee, Genovee, Genovive

Genesis (Latin) origin; birth.
Genes, Genese, Genesha, Genesia,
Genesis, Genessa, Genesse, Genessie,
Genessis, Genicis, Genises, Genysis, Xenesis

Geneva (French) juniper tree. A short
form of Genevieve. Geography: a city
in Switzerland.
Geena, Gen, Gena, Genevieve, Geneva,
Geneve, Geneve, Ginneva, Janeva, Jeaneva,
Jeneva

Genevieve (German, French) a form
of Guinevere. See also Gwendolyn.
Gen, Gena, Genaveeve, Genaveve,
Genavie, Genavieve, Genavive, Geneva,
Genevee, Geneve, Genevieve,
Geneveeve, Genevie, Genevieve,
Genevieve, Ginette, Gineve, Ginevieve,
Ginevie, Guineviere, Guinivive,
Gwenevieve, Guenivive, Jennavieve

Genevra (French, Welsh) a form of
Guinevere.
Gen, Genever, Genevera, Ginevra

Genice (American) a form of Janice.
Gen, Genece, Genice, Genesa, Genesee,
Genessia, Genis, Genise

Genita (American) a form of Janita.
Gen, Genet, Geneta

Genna (English) a form of Jenna.
Gen, Gennae, Gennay, Genni, Gennie,
Genny

Genovieve (French) a form of
Genevieve.
Genovee, Genovee, Genovive

Georgeanna (English) a combination
of Georgia + Anna.
Georgana, Georganna, Georgeana,
Georgiana, Georgianna, Georgyana

Georgeanne (English) a combination
of Georgia + Anne.
Georgann, Georganne, Georgean,
Georgeann, Georgie, Georgyann,
Georgyanne

Jennifer (American) a form of
Jennifer.
Gen, Genifer, Ginnifer

Georgene (English) a familiar form of Georgia.
Georgeena, Georgeina, Georgena, Georgenia, Georgenia, Georgienne, Georgina, Georgine

Georgette (French) a form of Georgia.
Georgeta, Georgett, Georgetta, Georjetta

Georgia (Greek) farmer. Art: Georgia O'Keeffe was an American painter known especially for her paintings of flowers. Geography: a southern American state; a country in Eastern Europe. See also Jirina, Jorja.
Georgene, Georgette, Georgie, Giorgia

Georgianna (English) a form of Georgeanna.
Georgiana, Georgiann, Georgianne, Georgie, Georgieann, Georgionna

Georgie (English) a familiar form of Georgeanne, Georgia, Georgianna.
Geogi, Georgy, Giorgi

Georgina (English) a form of Georgia.
Georgena, Georgene, Georgine, Giorgina, Jorgina

Geraldine (German) mighty with a spear. See also Dena, Jeraldine.
Geralda, Geraldina, Geraldyna, Geraldyne, Gerhardine, Geri, Gerianna, Gerianne, Gerrilee, Giralda

Geralyn (American) a combination of Geraldine + Lynn.
Geralisha, Geralynn, Gerilyn, Gerrilyn

Gerardo (English) brave spearwoman.
Geraldine

Gerda (Norwegian) protector. (German) a familiar form of Gertrude.
Gerta

Geri (American) a familiar form of Geraldine. See also Jeri.
Gerri, Gerrie, Gerry

Germaine (French) from Germany. See also Jermaine.
Germain, Germana, Germanee, Germani, Germanie, Germaya, Germine

Gertie (German) a familiar form of Gertrude.
Geri, Gertey, Gerti, Gerty

Gertrude (German) beloved warrior. See also Trudy.
Gerda, Gerta, Gertie, Gertina, Gertraud, Gertrud, Gertruda

Gervaise (French) skilled with a spear.

Gessica (Italian) a form of Jessica.
Gesica, Gesika, Gess, Gesse, Gessy

Geva (Hebrew) hill.
Gevah

Ghada (Arabic) young; tender.
Gada

Ghita (Italian) pearly.
Gita

Gianna (Italian) a short form of Giovanna. See also Jianna, Johana.
Geona, Geonna, Giana, Gianella, Gianetta, Gianina, Gianinna, Gianne, Giannee, Giannella, Giannetta, Gianni, Giannie, Giannina, Gianny, Gianoula

Gigi (French) a familiar form of Gilberte.
Geegee, G. G., Giggi

Gilana (Hebrew) joyful.
Gila, Gilah

Gilberte (German) brilliant; pledge; trustworthy. See also Berti.
Gigi, Gilberta, Gilbertina, Gilbertine, Gill

Gilda (English) covered with gold.
Gilde, Gildi, Gildie, Gildy

Gill (Latin, German) a short form of Gilberte, Gillian.
Gili, Gilli, Gillie, Gilly

Gillian (Latin) a form of Jillian.
Gila, Gilana, Gilena, Gili, Gilian, Gill, Gilliana, Gilliane, Gilliann, Gillianna, Gillianne, Gillie, Gilly, Gillyan, Gillyane, Gillyann, Gillyanne, Gyllian, Lian

Gin (Japanese) silver. A short form of names beginning with "Gin."

Gina (Italian) a short form of Angelina, Eugenia, Regina, Virginia. See also Jina.
Gena, Gin, Ginah, Ginai, Ginna

Ginette (English) a form of Genevieve.
Gin, Ginata, Ginett, Ginetta, Ginnetta, Ginnette

Ginger (Latin) flower; spice. A familiar form of Virginia.
Gin, Ginja, Ginjer, Ginny

Gitana (Spanish) gypsy; wanderer.

Gita (Yiddish) good. (Polish) a short form of Margaret.
Gitka, Gitta, Gituska

Gissel, Gisselle (German) forms of Giselle.
Gissell

Gisela (German) a form of Giselle.
Gisella, Gissella

Gisele (German) pledge; hostage. See also Jizelle.
Ghisele, Gisel, Gisela, Gisele, Gesèle, Giseli, Gisell, Gissell, Gisselle, Gizela, Gysell

Giovanna (Italian) a form of Jane.
Geovana, Geovanna, Geovonna, Giavanna, Giavonna, Giovana, Giovanne, Giovanni, Giovannica, Giovonna, Givonnie, Jeveny

Giordana (Italian) a form of Jordana.

Giorgianna (English) a form of Georgeanna.
Giorgina

Ginny (English) a familiar form of Ginger, Virginia. See also Jin, Jinny.
Gin, Gini, Ginney, Ginni, Ginnie, Giny, Gionni, Gionny

Ginnifer (English) white; smooth; soft. (Welsh) a form of Jennifer.
Gin, Ginifer

Ginia (Latin) a familiar form of Virginia.
Gin

Gitta (Irish) a short form of Bridget.
Getta

Giulia (Italian) a form of Julia.
Giulana, Giuliana, Giulianna, Giulliana, Giula, Giuliana, Giulietta

Gizela (Czech) a form of Giselle.
Gizel, Gizele, Gizella, Gizelle, Gizi, Gizlei, Gizus

Gladis (Irish) a form of Gladys.
Gladi, Gladiz

Gladys (Latin) small sword. (Irish) princess. (Welsh) a form of Claudia.
Glad, Gladis, Gladness, Gladys, Glady, Guladys

Glenda (Welsh) a form of Glenna.
Glanda, Glennda, Glynda

Glenna (Irish) valley, glen. See also Glynnis.
Glenda, Glenetta, Glenina, Glenine, Glenn, Glenne, Glennesha, Glennia, Glennie, Glenora, Gleny, Glyn

Glennesha (American) a form of Glenna.
Glenesha, Glenisha, Glennisha, Glennishia

Gloria (Latin) glory. History: Gloria Steinem, a leading American feminist, founded *Ms.* magazine.
Gloresha, Gloriah, Gloribel, Gloriela, Gloriella, Gloriella, Gloris, Glorisha, Glorina, Glory

Glorianne (American) a combination of Gloria + Anne.
Gloriane, Gloriana, Gloriane, Gloriann, Glorianna

Glory (Latin) a form of Gloria.

Glynnis (Welsh) a form of Glenna.
Glenice, Glenis, Glenise, Glenyse, Glennis, Glennys, Glennys, Glenyss, Glinnis, Glinys, Glynesha, Glynice, Glynis, Glynisha, Glyniss, Glynitra, Glynys, Glynyss

Goma (Swahili) joyful dance.

Golda (English) gold. History: Golda Meir was a Russian-born politician who served as prime minister of Israel.
Goldarina, Golden, Goldie, Goldina

Goldie (English) a familiar form of Golda.
Goldi, Goldy

Grace (Latin) graceful.
Engracia, Graca, Gracia, Gracie, Graciela, Graciella, Gracinha, Graice, Grata, Gratia, Gray, Grayce, Grecia

Graceanne (English) a combination of Grace + Anne.
Gracann, Graceanna, Gracen, Graciana, Gracianna, Gracin, Gratiana

Gracia (Spanish) a form of Grace.
Gracea, Grecia

Gracie (English) a familiar form of Grace.
Gracee, Gracey, Graci, Gracy, Graciie, Graysie

Grant (English) great; giving.

Grayson (English) bailiff's child.
Graison, Graisyn, Grasien, Grasyn, Graysen

Grazia (Latin) a form of Grace.
Graziella, Grazielle, Graziosa, Grazyna

Grecia (Latin) a form of Grace.

Greer (Scottish) vigilant.
Grear, Grier

Greta (German) a short form of Gretchen, Margaret.
Greatal, Greatel, Greeta, Gretal, Grete, Gretel, Gretha, Grethal, Grethe, Grethel, Gretta, Grette, Grieta, Gryta, Grytta

Gretchen (German) a form of Margaret.
Greta, Gretchin, Gretchyn

Gricelda (German) a form of Griselda.
Gricelle

Grisel (German) a short form of Griselda.
Grisell, Griselle, Grissel, Grissele, Grissell, Grizel

Griselda (German) gray woman warrior. See also Selda, Zelda.
Gricelda, Grisel, Griseldis, Griseldys, Griselys, Grishilda, Grishilde, Grisselda, Grissely, Grizelda

Guadalupe (Arabic) river of black stones. See also Lupe.
Guadalup, Guadalupe, Guadlupe, Guadalupe, Gualalupe

Gudrun (Scandinavian) battler. See also Runa.
Gudren, Gudrin, Gudrinn, Gudruna

Guillerma (Spanish) a short form of Guillermina.
Guilla, Guillermina

Guinevere (French, Welsh) white wave; white phantom. Literature: the wife of King Arthur. See also Gayna, Genevieve, Genevra, Jennifer, Winifred, Wynne.
Generva, Genn, Ginette, Guenevere, Guenna, Guinivere, Guinna, Gwen, Gwenevere, Gwenivere, Guynnevere

Gunda (Norwegian) female warrior.
Gundala, Gunta

Gurit (Hebrew) innocent baby.

Gurleen (Sikh) follower of the guru.

Gurpreet (Punjabi) religion.
Gurprit

Gusta (Latin) a short form of Augusta.
Gus, Gussi, Gussie, Gussy, Gusti, Gustie, Gusty

Gwen (Welsh) a short form of Guinevere, Gwendolyn.
Gwenesha, Gweness, Gweneta, Gwenetta, Gwenette, Gweni, Gwenisha, Gwenita, Gwenn, Gwenna, Gwennie, Gwenny

Gwenda (Welsh) a familiar form of Gwendolyn.
Gwinda, Gwynda, Gwynedd

Gwendolyn (Welsh) white wave; white browed; new moon. Literature: Gwendoloena was the wife of Merlin, the magician. See also Genevieve, Gwyneth, Wendy.
Guendolen, Guen, Gwendalin, Gwenda, Gwendalee, Gwendaline, Gwendalyn, Gwendalynn, Gwendela, Gwendelyn, Gwendelynn, Gwendilyn, Gwendolen, Gwendolene, Gwendolin, Gwendoline, Gwendolyne, Gwendolynn, Gwendolynne, Gwendylan, Gwyndolyn, Gwyndolen

Gwyn (Welsh) a short form of Gwyneth.
Gwinn, Gwinne, Gwynn, Gwynne

Gwyneth (Welsh) a form of Gwendolyn. See also Winnie, Wynne.
Gweneth, Gwenith, Gwenneth, Gwenyth, Gwenyth, Gwyn, Gwynneth

Gypsy (English) wanderer.
Gipsy, Gypsie, Jipsi

H

Habiba (Arabic) beloved.
Habibah, Habibeh

Hachi (Japanese) eight; good luck.
Hachiko, Hachiyo

Hadara (Hebrew) adorned with beauty.
Hadarah

Hadassah (Hebrew) myrtle tree.
Hadas, Hadasah, Hadassa, Haddasa, Haddasah

Hadiya (Swahili) gift.
Hadaya, Hadia, Hadiyah, Hadiyyah

Hadley (English) field of heather.
Hadlea, Hadlee, Hadleigh, Hadli, Hadlie, Hadly

Hadriane (Greek, Latin) a form of Adrienne.
Hadriana, Hadrianna, Hadrianne, Hadriene, Hadrienne

Haeley (English) a form of Haley. Haelee, Haeleigh, Haeli, Haelie, Haelleigh, Haelli, Haellie, Haely

Hagar (Hebrew) forsaken; stranger. Bible: Sarah's handmaiden, the mother of Ishmael. *Hagar*

Haidee (Greek) modest. Hady, Haide, Haidi, Haidy, Haydee, Haydy

Haiden (English) heather-covered hill. Haden, Hadyn, Haeden, Haidn, Haidyn

Hailee (English) a form of Hayley. Haile, Hailei, Haileigh, Hailee

Hailey (English) a form of Hayley. Haeley, Haely, Hailea, Hailey, Haily, Haiy

Haili, Hailie (English) forms of Hayley. Hayley, Hailie, Hailli, Hailie

Haldana (Norwegian) half-Danish.

Halee (English) a form of Haley. Hale, Halea, Haleah, Haleh, Halei

Haleigh (English) a form of Haley.

Haley (Scandinavian) heroine. See also Hailey, Hayley. Halee, Haleigh, Hali, Halley, Hallie, Haly, Halye

Hali, Halie (English) forms of Haley. Haligh

Halia (Hawaiian) in loving memory. Halima, Halime

Halimah (Arabic) gentle; patient.

Halina (Hawaiian) likeness. (Russian) a form of Helen. Haleen, Haleena, Halena, Halinka

Halla (African) unexpected gift. Hala, Hallah, Halle

Hallie (Scandinavian) a form of Haley. Hallee, Hallei, Halleigh, Halli

Halley (English) a form of Haley. Hally, Halye

Halona (Native American) fortunate. Halonah, Haloona, Haona

Halsey (English) Hall's island. Halsea, Halsie

Hama (Japanese) shore.

Hana, Hanah (Japanese) flower. (Arabic) happiness. (Slavic) forms of Hannah. Hanae, Hanan, Haneen, Hanicka, Hanin, Hanita, Hanka

Hanako (Japanese) flower child.

Hania (Hebrew) resting place. Haniya, Hanja, Hannia, Hanniah, Harya

Hanna (Hebrew) a form of Hannah.

Hannah (Hebrew) gracious. Bible: the mother of Samuel. See also Anci, Anezka, Ania, Anka, Ann, Anna, Annalie, Anneka, Chana, Nina, Nusi. Hana, Hanna, Hanneke, Hannele, Hanni, Hannon, Honna

Happy (English) happy.

Hara (Hindi) tawny. Religion: another name for the Hindu god Shiva, the destroyer.

Harlee, Harleigh, Harlie (English) forms of Harley. Harlei, Harli

Harley (English) meadow of the hare. See also Arleigh. Harlee, Harleey, Harly

Harleyann (English) a combination of Harley + Ann. Harlann, Harlanna, Harlanne, Harleen, Harlene, Harleyanna, Harleyanne, Harliann, Harlianna, Harlianne, Harlina, Harline

Harmony (Latin) harmonious. Harmene, Harmeni, Harmon, Harmonee, Harmonei, Harmoni, Harmonia, Harmonie

Harpreet (Punjabi) devoted to God. Harpri

Harriet (French) ruler of the household. (English) a form of Henrietta. Literature: Harriet Beecher Stowe was an American writer noted for her novel *Uncle Tom's Cabin*. Harri, Harrie, Harriet, Harrietta, Harriette, Harriot, Harriott, Hattie

Haru (Japanese) spring.

Hasana (Swahili) she arrived first. Culture: a name used for the first-born female twin. See also Huseina. Hasanna, Hasna, Hassana, Hassna, Hassona

Hasina (Swahili) good.
Haseena, Hasena, Hassina

Hateya (Moquelumnan) footprints.

Hattie (English) familiar forms of Harriet, Henrietta.
Hatti, Hatty, Hetti, Hettie, Hetty

Hausu (Moquelumnan) like a bear yawning upon awakening.

Hava (Hebrew) a form of Chava. See also Eve.
Havah, Havvah

Haven (English) a form of Heaven.
Havan, Havana, Havanna, Havannah, Haryn

Haviva (Hebrew) beloved.
Havalee, Havelah, Havi, Hayah

Hayden (English) a form of Haiden.
Hayde, Haydin, Haydn, Haydon

Hayfa (Arabic) shapely.

Haylee, Hayleigh, Haylie (English) forms of Hayley.
Hayle, Haylea, Haylei, Hayli, Haylle, Hayllie

Hayley (English) hay meadow. See also Hailey, Haley.
Hailee, Haili, Haylee, Hayly

Hazel (English) hazelnut tree; commanding authority.
Hazal, Hazaline, Haze, Hazeline, Hazell, Hazelle, Hazen, Hazyl

Heather (English) flowering heather.
Heath, Heatherlee, Heatherly

Heaven (English) place of beauty and happiness. Bible: where God and

angels are said to dwell.
Haven, Heavan, Heavenly, Heavin, Heavon, Heavyn, Hevean, Heven, Hevin

Hedda (German) battler. See also Edda, Hedy.
Heda, Hedaya, Hedia, Hedvick, Hedvig, Hedvika, Hedwig, Hedwiga, Heida, Hetta

Hedy (Greek) delightful; sweet. (German) a familiar form of Hedda.
Hedey, Heddi, Heddie, Heddy, Hede, Hedi

Heidi, Heidy (German) short forms of Adelaide.
Heida, Heide, Heidee, Heidie, Heydy, Hidee, Hidi, Hidie, Hidy, Hiede, Hiedi, Hydi

Helen (Greek) light. See also Aileen, Aili, Alena, Eileen, Elaina, Elaine, Eleanor, Ellen, Galina, Ila, Ilene, Ilona, Jelena, Leanore, Leena, Lelya, Lenci, Lene, Liolya, Nellie, Nitsa, Olena, Onella, Yalena, Yelena.
Elana, Ena, Halina, Hela, Hele, Helena, Helene, Helle, Hellen, Helli, Hellin, Hellon, Hellyn, Helon

Helena (Greek) a form of Helen. See also Ilena.
Halena, Halina, Helaina, Helana, Helania, Helayna, Heleana, Heleena, Helenia, Helenka, Helenna, Helina, Hellanna, Hellena, Hellenna, Helona, Helonna

Helene (French) a form of Helen.
Helaine, Helanie, Helayne, Heleen, Heleine, Helène, Helenor, Heline, Hellenor

Helga (German) pious. (Scandinavian) a form of Olga. See also Elga.
Helkey, Helkie, Helky

Helki (Native American) touched.

Helma (German) a short form of Wilhelmina.
Halma, Helme, Helmi, Helmine, Hilma

Heloise (French) a form of Louise.
Héloïse, Hlois

Helsa (Danish) a form of Elizabeth.
Helse, Helsey, Helsi, Helsie, Helsy

Heltu (Moquelumnan) like a bear reaching out.

Henna (English) a familiar form of Henrietta.
Hena, Henaa, Henah, Heni, Henia, Henry, Henya

Henrietta (English) ruler of the household. See also Enrica, Etta, Yetta.
Harriet, Hattie, Hatty, Hendrika, Heneretta, Henka, Henna, Henrietta, Henriette, Henretta, Henrica, Henrie, Henrieta, Henriete, Henriette, Henrika, Henrique, Henriquetta, Henryetta, Hetta, Hettie

Hera (Greek) queen; jealous. Mythology: the queen of heaven and the wife of Zeus.

Hermia (Greek) messenger.

Hermina (Latin) noble. (German) soldier. See also Erma, Ermine, Irma.
Herma, Hermenia, Hermia, Herminna

Hermione (Greek) earthy. Hermalina, Hermia, Hermina, Hermine, Herminia

Hermosa (Spanish) beautiful.

Hertha (English) child of the earth. Heartha, Hirtha

Hester (Dutch) a form of Esther. Hessi, Hessie, Hessye, Hesther, Hettie

Hestia (Persian) star. Mythology: the Greek goddess of the hearth and home. Hestea, Hesti, Hestie, Hesty

Heta (Native American) racer.

Hetta (German) a form of Hedda. (English) a familiar form of Henrietta.

Hettie (German) a familiar form of Henrietta, Hester. Henrietta, Hester. Hetti, Hetty

Hilary, Hillary (Greek) cheerful, merry. See also Alair. Hilaree, Hilari, Hilaria, Hilarie, Hilery, Hillaree, Hillari, Hillarie, Hillary, Hilleree, Hilleri, Hillerie, Hillery, Hillianne, Hilliary, Hillory

Hilda (German) a short form of Brunhilda, Hildegarde. Helle, Hilde, Hildey, Hildie, Hildur, Hildy, Hulda, Hylda

Hildegarde (German) fortress. Hilda, Hildagard, Hildagarde, Hildegard, Hildred

Hinda (Hebrew) hind; doe. Hindey, Hindie, Hindy, Hynda

Hisa (Japanese) long lasting. Hisae, Hisako, Hisay

Hiti (Eskimo) hyena. Hitty

Hoa (Vietnamese) flower; peace. Ho, Hoai

Hola (Hopi) seed-filled club.

Holley (English) a form of Holly. Holleah, Hollee

Holli, Hollie (English) forms of Holly. Holeigh, Holleigh

Hollis (English) near the holly bushes. Hollie, Hollyce, Holyce

Holly (English) holly tree. Holley, Holli, Hollie, Hollye

Hollyann (English) a combination of Holly + Ann. Holliann, Hollianna, Hollianne, Hollyanne, Hollyn

Hollyn (English) a short form of Hollyann. Holin, Holena, Hollina, Hollyn

Honey (English) sweet. (Latin) a familiar form of Honora. Honalee, Hunney, Hunny

Hong (Vietnamese) pink.

Honora (Latin) honorable. See also Nora, Onora. Honey, Honner, Honnor, Honnour, Honor, Honorah, Honoria, Honoree, Honoria, Honorina, Honorine, Honour, Honoure

Hope (English) hope. Hopey, Hopi, Hopie

Hortense (Latin) gardener. See also Ortensia. Hortencia, Hortensia

Hoshi (Japanese) star. Hoshie, Hoshiko, Hoshiyo

Hua (Chinese) flower.

Huata (Moquelumnan) basket carrier.

Huong (Vietnamese) flower.

Hunter (English) hunter. Hunta, Huntar, Hunter

Huseina (Swahili) a form of Hasana.

Hyacinth (Greek) Botany: a plant with colorful, fragrant flowers. See also Cynthia, Jacinda. Giacinta, Hyacintha, Hyacinthe, Hyacinthia, Hyacinthie, Hycinth, Hycynth

Hydi, Hydeia (German) forms of Heidi. Hyde, Hydea, Hydee, Hydia, Hydie, Hydiea, Hydia

Hye (Korean) graceful.

I

Ian (Hebrew) God is gracious. Iain, Iain, Iana, Iann, Ianna, Iannel, Iyana

Ianthe (Greek) violet flower. Iantha, Ianthia, Ianthina

Icess (Egyptian) a form of Isis. Ices, Icess, Icesse, Icey, Icia, Icis, Icy

Ida (German) hard working. (English) prosperous.
Idah, Idaia, Idalia, Idalis, Idaly, Idamae, Idania, Idarina, Idarine, Idaya, Ide, Idelle, Idette, Idys

Idalina (English) a combination of Ida + Lina.
Idaleena, Idaleene, Idalena, Idalene, Idaline

Idalis (English) a form of Ida.
Idalesse, Idalise, Idaliz, Idallis, Idallis, Idelis, Idelys, Idialis

Ideashia (American) a combination of Ida + Iesha.
Idasha, Idaysha, Ideesha, Idesha

Idelle (Welsh) a form of Ida.
Idell, Idella, Idil

Iesha (American) a form of Aisha.
Ieachia, Ieaisha, Ieasha, Ieashe, Ieesha, Ieisha, Ieisha, Ieishia, Iescha, Ieshah, Ieshea, Iesheia, Ieshia, Iiesha, Iisha

Ignacia (Latin) fiery, ardent.
Ignacie, Ignasha, Ignashia, Ignatia, Ignatzia

Ikia (Hebrew) God is my salvation. (Hawaiian) a form of Isaiah (see Boys' Names).
Ikaisha, Ikea, Ikeea, Ikeia, Ikeisha, Ikeishi, Ikeishia, Ikesha, Ikeshia, Ikeya, Ikeyia, Ikiea, Ikiia

Ila (Hungarian) a form of Helen.

Ilana (Hebrew) tree.
Ilaina, Ilane, Ilani, Ilania, Ilainie, Illana, Illane, Illani, Ilania, Illanie, Ilanit

Ileana (Hebrew) a form of Iliana.
Ilea, Ileah, Ileane, Ileanna, Ileanne, Illeana

Ilena (Greek) a form of Helena.
Ileana, Ileena, Ileina, Ilina, Ilyna

Ilene (Irish) a form of Helen. See also Aileen, Eileen.
Ileen, Ileene, Iline, Ilyne

Iliana (Greek) from Troy.
Ileana, Ili, Ilia, Iliani, Illiana, Illiani, Illianna, Illyana, Illyanna

Ilima (Hawaiian) flower of Oahu.

Ilisa (Scottish, English) a form of Alisa, Elisa.
Ilicia, Ilissa, Iliza, Illisa, Illissa, Illysa, Illyssa, Ilycia, Ilysa, Ilysia, Ilyssa, Ilyza

Ilise (German) a form of Elise.
Ilese, Illytse, Ilyce, Ilyse

Ilisha (Hebrew) a form of Alisha, Elisha. See also Lisha.
Ileshia, Ilishia, Ilysha, Ilyshia

Ilka (Hungarian) a familiar form of Ilona.
Ilke, Milka, Milke

Ilona (Hungarian) a form of Helen.
Ilka, Illona, Illonia, Illonya, Ilonka, Ilyona

Ilse (German) a form of Elizabeth. See also Elsa.
Ilsa, Ilsey, Ilsie, Ilsy

Ima (Japanese) presently. (German) a familiar form of Amelia.

Imala (Native American) strong-minded.

Iman (Arabic) believer.
Aman, Imana, Imane, Imani

Imani (Arabic) a form of Iman.
Amani, Emani, Imahni, Imanie, Imanii, Imonee, Imoni

Imelda (German) warrior.
Imalda, Irmhilde, Melda

Imena (African) dream.
Imee, Imene

Imogene (Latin) image, likeness.
Emogene, Emogene, Imogenia, Imojean, Imojeen, Innogen, Innogene

Ina (Irish) a form of Agnes.
Ena, Inanna, Inanne

India (Hindi) from India.
Indea, Indeah, Indee, Indeia, Indeya, Indi, Indiah, Indian, Indiana, Indianna, Indie, Indieya, Indiya, Indy, Indya

Indigo (Latin) dark blue color.
Indiga, Indygo

Indira (Hindi) splendid. History: Indira Nehru Gandhi was an Indian politician and prime minister.
Indiana, Indra, Indre, Indria

Ines, Inez (Spanish) forms of Agnes. See also Ynez.
Inés, Inesa, Inesita, Ineßita, Inessa

Inga (Scandinavian) a short form of Ingrid.
Ingaberg, Ingaborg, Inge, Ingeberg, Ingeborg, Ingela

Ingrid (Scandinavian) hero's daughter; beautiful daughter.
Inga, Inger

Inoa (Hawaiian) name.

Ioana (Romanian) a form of Joan. *Ioani, Ioanna*

Iola (Greek) dawn; violet colored. (Welsh) worthy of the Lord. *Iole, Iolee, Iolia*

Iolana (Hawaiian) soaring like a hawk.

Iolanthe (English) a form of Yolanda. See also Jolanda. *Iolanda, Iolande*

Iona (Greek) violet flower. *Ione, Ioney, Ioni, Ionia, Iyona, Iyonna*

Iphigenia (Greek) sacrifice. Mythology: the daughter of the Greek leader Agamemnon. See also Gena.

Irene (Greek) peaceful. Mythology: the goddess of peace. See also Orina, Rena, Rene, Yarina. *Irén, Irien, Irina, Jereni*

Irina (Russian) a form of Irene. *Eirena, Erena, Ira, Irana, Iranda, Ireena, Irena, Irenea, Irenka, Iriana, Irin, Irinia, Irinka, Irona, Ironka, Irusya, Iryna, Irynka, Rina*

Iris (Greek) rainbow. Mythology: the goddess of the rainbow and messenger of the gods. *Irisa, Irisla, Irissa, Irita, Irys, Iryssa*

Irma (Latin) a form of Erma. *Irmina, Irminia*

Isabeau (French) a form of Isabel.

Isabel (Spanish) consecrated to God. See also Bel, Belle, Chavella, Ysabel. *Isbal, Isabeau, Isabeli, Isabelita, Isabella, Isabelle, Ishbel, Isobel, Issie, Izabel, Izabele, Izabella*

Isabella (Italian) a form of Isabel. *Isabela, Isabella, Izabella*

Isabelle (French) a form of Isabel. *Isabele, Isabell*

Isadora (Latin) gift of Isis. *Isidora*

Isela (Scottish) a form of Isla. *Isel*

Isha (American) a form of Aisha. *Ishae, Ishana, Ishanaa, Ishanda, Ishanee, Ishaney, Ishani, Ishanna, Ishaun, Ishawna, Ishaya, Ishenda, Ishia, Iysha*

Ishi (Japanese) rock. *Ishiko, Ishiyo, Shiiko, Shiiyo*

Isis (Egyptian) supreme goddess. Mythology: the goddess of nature and fertility. *Icess, Issis, Isys*

Isla (Scottish) Geography: the River Isla is in Scotland. *Isela*

Isobel (Spanish) a form of Isabel. *Isobell, Isobella, Isobelle*

Isoka (Benin) gift from god. *Soka*

Isolde (Welsh) fair lady. Literature: a princess in the Arthurian legends; a heroine in the medieval romance *Tristan and Isolde.* See also Yseult. *Isolda, Isolt, Izolde*

Issie (Spanish) a familiar form of Isabel. See also Isabel. *Isa, Issi, Issy, Iza*

Ita (Irish) thirsty.

Italia (Italian) from Italy. *Itali, Italie, Italy, Italya*

Itamar (Hebrew) palm island. *Isamar, Isamari, Isamaria, Ithamar, Itamar*

Itzel (Spanish) protected. *Itcel, Itchel, Itsel, Itssel, Itza, Itzalana, Itzayana, Itzell, Itzhel, Ixchel*

Iva (Slavic) a short form of Ivana. *Ivah*

Ivana (Slavic) God is gracious. See also Yvana. *Iva, Ivanah, Ivania, Ivanka, Ivanna, Ivania, Ivany*

Iverem (Tiv) good fortune; blessing.

Iverna (Latin) from Ireland. *Ivernah*

Ivette (French) a form of Yvette. See also Evette. *Ivet, Ivete, Iveth, Ivetha, Ivett, Ivetta*

Ivonne (French) a form of Yvonne. See also Evonne. *Ivon, Ivona, Ivone, Ivonna, Ivona, Ivonka, Ivonna, Ivonne*

Ivory (Latin) made of ivory. *Ivoory, Ivori, Ivorie, Ivorine, Ivree*

Ivria (Hebrew) from the land of Abraham. *Ivriah, Ivrit*

Ivy (English) ivy tree.
Ivey, Ivie

Iyabo (Yoruba) mother has returned.

Iyana, Iyanna (Hebrew) forms of Ian.
Iyanah, Iyannah, Iyannia

Izabella (Spanish) a form of Isabel.
Izabela, Izabell, Izabellah, Izabelle, Izobella

Izusa (Native American) white stone.

Jabrea, Jabria (American) combinations of the prefix Ja + Brea.
Jabreal, Jabree, Jabreea, Jabreena, Jabrelle, Jabreona, Jabri, Jabriah, Jabriana, Jabrie, Jabriel, Jabrielle, Jabrienna, Jabrina

Jacalyn (American) a form of Jacqueline.
Jacalynn, Jacolyn, Jacolyne, Jacolynn

Jacelyn (American) a form of Jocelyn.
Jaceline, Jacelyne, Jacelynn, Jacilyn, Jacilyne, Jacilynn, Jacylyn, Jacylyne, Jacylynn

Jacey, Jacy (Greek) familiar forms of Jacinda. (American) combinations of the initials J. + C.
Jace, Jac-E, Jacee, Jaci, Jacie, Jacylin, Jaice, Jaicee

Jaci, Jacie (Greek) forms of Jacey.
Jacci, Jacia, Jacie, Jaciel, Jaici, Jaicie

Jacinda, Jacinta (Greek) beautiful, attractive. (Spanish) forms of Hyacinth.
Jacenda, Jacenta, Jacey, Jacinthe, Jacintia, Jacynthe, Jakinda, Jaxine

Jacinthe (Spanish) a form of Jacinda.
Jainte, Jacinth, Jacintha

Jackalyn (American) a form of Jacqueline.
Jackalene, Jackalin, Jackaline, Jackalynn, Jackalynne, Jackelin, Jackeline, Jackelyn, Jackelynne, Jackelyn, Jackelin, Jackilyn, Jackilynn, Jackelynne, Jackolin, Jackoline, Jackolyn, Jackolynn, Jackolynne

Jackeline, Jackelyn (American) forms of Jacqueline.
Jackelin, Jackelline, Jackellyn, Jockeline

Jacki, Jackie (American) familiar forms of Jacqueline.
Jackee, Jackey, Jackia, Jackielee, Jacky, Jackye

Jacklyn (American) a form of Jacqueline.
Jacklin, Jackline, Jacklyne, Jacklynn, Jacklynne

Jackquel (French) a short form of Jacqueline.
Jackquenetta, Jackquiline, Jackquenetta, Jackquiline, Jackquilynn, Jackquilynne, Jackquilynne

Jaclyn (American) a short form of Jacqueline.
Jacleen, Jaclin, Jacline, Jaclyne, Jaclynn

Jacobi (Hebrew) supplanter, substitute. Bible: Jacob was the son of Isaac, brother of Esau.
Coby, Jacoba, Jacobee, Jacobette, Jacobia, Jacobina, Jacoby, Jacolbi, Jacolbia, Jacolby

Jacqualine (French) a form of Jacqueline.
Jacqualin, Jacqualine, Jacqualyn, Jacqualyne, Jacqualynn

Jacquelin (French) a form of Jacqueline.
Jacquelina

Jacqueline (French) supplanter, substitute; little Jacqui.
Jaclyn, Jacalyn, Jackeline, Jacki, Jacklyn, Jackquel, Jaclyn, Jacqueena, Jacqueine, Jacquel, Jacqueleen, Jacquelene, Jacquelin, Jacquelyn, Jacquelyna, Jacquelyne, Jacquenetta, Jacquenette, Jacqui, Jacquiline, Jacquine, Jakelin, Jaquelin, Jaquelyne, Jaquelyn, Jocqueline

Jacquelyn, Jacquelynn (French) forms of Jacqueline.
Jacquelyne, Jackequelynn, Jacquelyne, Jacquelynne

Jacqui (French) a short form of Jacqueline.
Jacquay, Jacqué, Jacquee, Jacqueta, Jacquete, Jacquetta, Jacquette, Jacquie, Jacquise, Jacquita, Jaquay, Jaqui, Jaquie, Jaquiese, Jaquina, Jaquita

Jacqulin, Jacqulyn (American) forms of Jacqueline.
Jacquilin, Jacqul, Jacqulin, Jacqulyne, Jacqulynn, Jacqulynne, Jacquoline

Jacquiline (French) a form of Jacqueline.
Jacquil, Jacquilin, Jacquilyn, Jacquilyne, Jacquilynn

Jacynthe (Spanish) a form of Jacinda.
Jacynda, Jacynta, Jacynth, Jacyntha

Jada (Spanish) a form of Jade.
Jadah, Jadda, Jadae, Jadziah,
Jaeda, Jaeda, Jayda

Jade (Spanish) jade.
Jada, Jadea, Jadeann, Jadee, Jaden, Jadera,
Jadi, Jadie, Jadrienne, Jady, Jadyn, Jaeda,
Jaida, Jaide, Jaiden, Jayde, Jayden

Jadelyn (American) a combination of
Jade + Lynn.
Jadalyn, Jadelaine, Jadeline, Jadelyne,
Jadelynn, Jadielyn

Jaden (Spanish) a form of Jade.
Jadeen, Jadena, Jadene, Jadeyn, Jadin,
Jadine, Jadyen, Jadine

Jadyn (Spanish) a form of Jade.
Jadyn, Jaedyn, Jaedynn

Jael (Hebrew) mountain goat; climber.
See also Yael.
Jaela, Jaelee, Jaeli, Jaelie, Jaelle, Jahla,
Jahlea

Jae (Latin) jaybird. (French) a familiar
form of Jacqueline.
Jaea, Jaey, Jaya

Jaelyn, Jaelynn (American) combina-
tions of Jae + Lynn.
Jaeleen, Jaelin, Jaelinn, Jaelyn, Jailyn,
Jalyn, Jalynn, Jayleen, Jaylyn, Jay'lynn,
Jaylynne

Jaffa (Hebrew) a form of Yaffa.
Jaffice, Jaffit, Jafit, Jafra

Jaha (Swahili) dignified.
Jahaida, Jahaira, Jahayra, Jahida,
Jahira, Jahitza

Jai (Tai) heart. (Latin) a form of Jaye.

Jaida, Jaide (Spanish) forms of Jade.
Jaidah, Jaidan

Jaiden, Jaidyn (Spanish) forms of Jade.
Jaidey, Jaidi, Jaidin, Jaidon

Jailyn (American) a form of Jaelyn.
Jaileen, Jailen, Jailene, Jailin, Jailine

Jaimee (French) a form of Jaime.

Jaimie (French) a form of Jaime.
Jaima, Jaimee, Jaimey, Jaimie, Jaimini,
Jaimi, Jaimmie

Jakeisha (American) a combination of
Jakki + Aisha.
Jakeisia, Jakesha, Jakisha

Jakelin (American) a form of
Jacqueline.
Jakeline, Jakelyn, Jakelynn, Jakelynne

Jakki (American) a form of Jacki.
Jakala, Jakea, Jakeela, Jakeida, Jakeira,
Jakela, Jakelia, Jakell, Jakena, Jaketta,
Jakevia, Jaki, Jakia, Jakiah, Jakira, Jakita,
Jakiya, Jakiyah, Jakke, Jakkia

Jaleesa (American) a form of Jalisa.
Jaleca, Jalece, Jaleeca, Jalesah, Jalese,
Jalesia, Jalesica, Jaleisha, Jaleisya

Jalena (American) a combination of
Jane + Lena.
Jalaina, Jalana, Jalani, Jalanie, Jalayna,
Jalean, Jaleen, Jaleena, Jaleene, Jalen,
Jalene, Jalina, Jaline, Jallena, Jalyna,
Jelayna, Jelena, Jelitsa, Jelyna

Jalesa, Jalessa (American) forms of
Jalisa.
Jalese, Jalesha, Jaleshia, Jalesia

Jalia, Jalea (American) combinations
of Jae + Leah.
Jaleah, Jalee, Jaleea, Jaleeya, Jaleia, Jaliza

Jalila (Arabic) great.

Jalisa, Jalissa (American) combinations of Jae + Lisa.
Jaleesa, Jalesa, Jalise, Jalisha, Jalysa

Jalyn, Jalynn (American) combinations
of Jae + Lynn. See also Jaylyn.
Jaelin, Jaeline, Jaelyn, Jaelyne, Jaelynn,
Jaelynne, Jalin, Jaline, Jalyne, Jalynne

Jalysa (American) a form of Jalisa.
Jalyse, Jalyssa, Jalysia

Jamaica (Spanish) Geography: an
island in the Caribbean.
Jameca, Jamecia, Jameica, Jameika,
Jameka, Jamica, Jamika, Jamoka, Jemaica,
Jemika, Jemyka

Jamani (American) a form of Jami.
Jamana

Jamaria (American) combinations of
Jae + Maria.
Jamar, Jamara, Jamarea, Jamaree, Jamari,
Jamarie, Jameria, Jamerial, Jamira

Jamecia (Spanish) a form of Jamaica.

Jamee (French) a form of Jaime.

Jameika, Jameka (Spanish) forms of
Jamaica.
Jamaika, Jamaka, Jamecka, Jamekia,
Jamekka

Jamesha (American) a form of Jami.
Jameisha, Jamese, Jameshia, Jameshyia,
Jamesia, Jamesika, Jamesina,
Jamessa, Jameta, Jametta, Janiesha,
Jamisha, Jammesha, Jammisha

Jamey (English) a form of Jami, Jamie.

Jami, Jamie (Hebrew, English)
supplanter, substitute.
Jama, Jamani, Jamay, Jamesha, Jamey,
Jamia, Jamii, Jamis, Jamise, Jammie, Jamy,
Jamye, Jayme, Jaymee, Jaymie

Jamia (English) a form of Jami, Jamie.
Jamea, Jamiah, Jamiea, Jamiya, Jamiyah,
Jamya, Jamyah

Jamica (Spanish) a form of Jamaica.
Jamika

Jamila (Arabic) beautiful. See also Yamila.
Jahmela, Jahmelia, Jahmil, Jahmila,
Jameela, Jameelah, Jameeliah, Jamela,
Jameela, Jamelia, Jameliah, Jamell, Jamella,
Jamelle, Jamely, Jamelya, Jamiela, Jamielee,
Jamilah, Jamilee, Jamilia, Jamiliah, Jamilla,
Jamillah, Jamille, Jamillia, Jamilya, Jamyla,
Jemeela, Jemela, Jemila, Jemilla

Jamilynn (English) a combination of
Jami + Lynn.
Jamielin, Jamieline, Jamielyn, Jamielyne,
Jamielynn, Jamielynne, Jamilin, Jamiline,
Jamilyn, Jamilyne, Janilynne

Jammie (American) a form of Jami.
Jammi, Jammice, Jammise

Jamonica (American) a combination
of Jami + Monica.
Jamoni

Jamylin (American) a form of
Jamilynn.
Jamylin, Jamyline, Jamylyn, Jamylyne,
Jamylynn, Jamylynne, Jaymylin,
Jaymyline, Jaymylyn, Jaymylyne,
Jaymylynn, Jaymylynne

Jan (English) a short form of Jane,
Janet, Janice.
Jania, Jandy

Jana (Hebrew) gracious, merciful.
(Slavic) a form of Jane. See also Yana.
Janalee, Janalisa, Janna, Janne

Janae, Janay (American) forms of
Jane.
Janaé, Janaea, Janaeh, Janah, Janai,
Janaya, Janaye, Janea, Janee, Janée,
Jannae, Jannay, Jenae, Jenay, Jenaya,
Jennae, Jennay, Jennaya, Jennaye

Janai (American) a form of Janae.
Janaiah, Janaira, Janaiya

Janalynn (American) a combination of
Jana + Lynn.
Janalin, Janaline, Janalyn, Janalyne,
Janalynne

Janan (Arabic) heart; soul.
Jananee, Janani, Jananie, Janann, Jananni

Jane (Hebrew) God is gracious. See
also Chavon, Jean, Joan, Juanita,
Seana, Shana, Shawna, Sheena,
Shona, Shunta, Sinead, Zaneta,
Zanna, Zhana.
Jaine, Jan, Jana, Janae, Janay, Janelle,
Janessa, Janet, Jania, Janice, Janie, Janika,
Janine, Janis, Janka, Jasia, Jayna,
Jayne, Jenica

Janel, Janell (French) forms of Janelle.
Janiel, Jannel, Jannell, Janyll, Jaynel,
Jaynell

Janelle (French) a form of Jane.
Janel, Janela, Janele, Janelis, Janell,
Janella, Janelli, Janellie, Janelly, Janely,
Janelys, Janielle, Janille, Jannelle,
Jannellies, Jaynelle

Janesha (American) a form of Janessa.
Janeisha, Janeshia, Janiesha, Janisha,
Janishia, Jannesha, Jannisha, Jarysha,
Jenesha, Jenisha, Jennisha

Janessa (American) a form of Jane.
Janeesa, Janesa, Janeesa, Janesha, Janesia,
Janeska, Janessi, Janessia, Janiesa, Janissa,
Jannesa, Jannessa, Jannisa, Jannissa,
Jaryssa, Jenesa, Jenessa, Jenissa, Jennissa,
Jennissa

Janet (English) a form of Jane. See also
Jessie, Yanet.
Jan, Janeta, Janete, Janeth, Janett, Janette,
Jannet, Janot, Jante, Janyte

Janeth (English) a form of Janet.
Janetha, Janith, Janneth

Janette, Jannette (French) forms of
Janet.
Janett, Janetta, Jannett, Jannetta

Janice (Hebrew) God is gracious.
(English) a familiar form of Jane. See
also Genice.
Jan, Janece, Janecia, Janeice, Janiece,
Janizzette, Jannice, Janniece, Janyce,
Jenice, Jhanice, Jynice

Janie (English) a familiar form of Jane.
Janey, Jani, Janyh, Jannie, Janny, Jany

Janika (Slavic) a form of Jane.
Janaca, Janeca, Janecka, Janeika, Janeka,
Janica, Janick, Janicka, Janieka, Janieka,
Janikke, Janique, Janka, Jankia, Jannica,
Jannicke, Jannika, Janyca, Jenica, Jenicka,
Jenika, Jeniqua, Jenique, Jennica, Jennika,
Jonika

Janine (French) a form of Jane.
Janeann, Janeanne, Janeen, Janenan,
Janene, Janina, Jannen, Jannina, Jannine,
Jannyne, Janyne, Jeannine, Jeneen, Jenine,
Jenis, Jennise, Jennisse

Janita (American) a form of Juanita.
See also Genita.
Janita, Janitza, Jaynita, Jenita,
Jennita

Janna (Arabic) harvest of fruit.
(Hebrew) a short form of Johana.
Janaya, Janaye, Jannae, Jannah, Jannai

Jannie (English) a familiar form of Jan,
Jane.
Janney, Janny

Janie (American) a combination of
Jacqueline + Anna.
Jaqua, Jaquai, Jaquanda, Jaquania,
Jaquanna

Jaquelen (American) a form of
Jacqueline.
Jaquala, Jaquera, Jaqulene, Jaquonna

Jaquelin, Jaqueline (French) forms of
Jacqueline.
Jaqualin, Jaqualine, Jaqualine, Jaquline,
Jaquella

Jaquelyn (French) a form of
Jacqueline.
Jaquelyne, Jaquelynn, Jaquelynne

Jardena (Hebrew) a form of Jordan.
(French, Spanish) garden.
Jardan, Jardana, Jardane, Jarden, Jardenia,
Jardin, Jardine, Jardyn, Jardyne

Jarian (American) a combination of
Jane + Marian.

Jarita (Arabic) earthen water jug.
Jara, Jaretta, Jari, Jaria, Jarica, Jarida,
Jarietta, Jarika, Jarina, Jaritta, Jaritza,
Jarixa, Jarrika, Jarrine

Jas (American) a short form of Jasmine.
Jase, Jass, Jaz, Jazz, Jazze, Jazzi

Jasia (Polish) a form of Jane.
Jaisha, Jasa, Jasea, Jasha, Jashae, Jashala,
Jashona, Jashonte, Jasie, Jassie, Jaysa

Jasmain (Persian) a short form of
Jasmine.
Jasmaine, Jasmane, Jassmain, Jassmaine

Jasmarie (American) a combination of
Jasmine + Marie.

Jasmin (Persian) a form of Jasmine.
Jasimin, Jasman, Jasmeen, Jasmen,
Jasmon, Jassmin, Jassmin

Jasmine (Persian) jasmine flower. See
also Jessamine, Yasmin.
Jas, Jasma, Jasmain, Jasme, Jasmeet,
Jasmene, Jasmin, Jasmina, Jasminne,
Jasmira, Jasmit, Jasmyn, Jassma, Jassmin,
Jasmine, Jassmit, Jassmon, Jassmyn,
Jazmin, Jazmyn, Jazzmin

Jasmyn, Jasmyne (Persian) forms of
Jasmine.
Jasmynn, Jasmynne, Jassmyn

Jaspreet (Punjabi) virtuous.
Jaspar, Jasparit, Jasparita, Jasper, Jasprit,
Jasprita, Jasprite

Jatara (American) a combination of
Jane + Tara.
Jataria, Jatarra, Jatori, Jatoria

Javana (Malayan) from Java.
Javanna, Javanne, Javona, Javonna,
Javana, Javanna, Javn

Javiera (Spanish) owner of a new
house. See also Xaviera.
Javeera, Viera

Javona, Javonna (Malayan) forms of
Javana.
Javon, Javonda, Javone, Javoni, Javonne,
Javonni, Javonya

Jaya (Hindi) victory.
Jaea, Jaia

Jaycee (American) a combination of
the initials J. + C.
Jacee, Jacey, Jaci, Jacie, Jacy, Jaye, Jaycey,
Jayci, Jaycie, Jaycy

Jayda (Spanish) a form of Jada.
Jaydah, Jeyda

Jayde (Spanish) a form of Jade.

Jaydee (American) a combination of
the initials J. + D.
Jadee, Jadey, Jadi, Jadie, Jady, Jaydey,
Jaydi, Jaydie, Jaydy

Jayden (Spanish) a form of Jade.
Jaydeen, Jaydene, Jaydin, Jaydn, Jaydon

Jaye (Latin) jaybird.
Jae, Jay

Jayla (American) a short form of Jaylene.
Jaylaa, Jaylah, Jayli, Jaylia, Jayliah, Jaylie

Jaylene (American) forms of Jaylyn.
Jaylene, Jayla, Jaylan, Jayleana, Jaylee, Jayleen, Jayleene, Jaylen, Jaylenne

Jaylin (American) a form of Jaylyn.
Jayline, Jaylinn

Jaylyn, Jaylynn (American) combinations of Jaye + Lynn. See also Jalyn.
Jaylene, Jaylin, Jaylyne, Jaylynne

Jayme, Jaymie (English) forms of Jami.
Jaymi, Jaymia, Jaymine, Jaymini

Jaymee, Jaymi (English) forms of Jami.

Jayna (Hebrew) a form of Jane.
Jaynae, Jaynah, Jaynna

Jayne (Hindi) victorious. (English) a form of Jane.
Jayn, Jaynie, Jaynne

Jaynie (English) a familiar form of Jayne.
Jaynee, Jayni

Jazlyn (American) a combination of Jazmin + Lynn.
Jasleen, Jazaline, Jazalyn, Jazleen, Jazlene, Jazlin, Jazline, Jazlon, Jazlynn, Jazlynne, Jazzalyn, Jazzleen, Jazzlene, Jazzlin, Jazzline, Jazzlyn, Jazzlynn, Jazzlynne

Jazmin, Jazmine (Persian) forms of Jasmine.
Jazmaine, Jazman, Jazmen, Jazminn, Jazmon, Jazzmit

Jazmyn, Jazmyne (Persian) forms of Jasmine.
Jazmynn, Jazmynne, Jazzmyn, Jazzmyne

Jazmin, Jazzmine (Persian) forms of Jasmine.
Jazzman, Jazzmeen, Jazzmen, Jazzmene, Jazzmenn, Jazzmon

Jean, Jeanne (Scottish) God is gracious. See also Kini.
Jeana, Jeanann, Jeancie, Jeane, Jeaneia, Jeanette, Jeaneva, Jeanice, Jeanie, Jeanine, Jeanmaria, Jeanmarie, Jeanna, Jeanné, Jeannie, Jeannita, Jeannot, Jeantelle

Jeana, Jeanna (Scottish) forms of Jean.
Jeanae, Jeannae, Jeannia

Jeanette, Jeannett (French) forms of Jean.
Jeanet, Jeanete, Jeanett, Jeanetta, Jeanetti, Jeanita, Jeannette, Jeannetta, Jeannita, Jenet, Jenett, Jenette, Jennet, Jennett, Jennetta, Jennette, Jennita, Jinetta, Jinette

Jeanie, Jeannie (Scottish) familiar forms of Jean.
Jeannee, Jeanney, Jeani, Jeanny, Jeany

Jeanine, Jenine (Scottish) forms of Jean. See also Geneen.
Jeaneane, Jeaneen, Jeanene, Jeanina, Jeannina, Jeannine, Jennine

Jelena (Russian) a form of Helen. See also Yelena.
Jalaine, Jalane, Jalani, Jalanna, Jalayna,

Jalayne, Jaleen, Jaleena, Jaleene, Jalena, Jalene, Jaleina, Jelaine, Jelana, Jelane, Jelani, Jelanni, Jelayna, Jelayne, Jelean, Jeleana, Jeleen, Jeleena, Jelene

Jelisa (American) a combination of Jean + Lisa.
Jalisa, Jelesha, Jelessa, Jelise, Jelissa, Jellisa, Jellice, Jellise, Jelysa, Jelysia, Jillisa, Jillissa, Julissa

Jem (Hebrew) a short form of Jemima.
Gem, Jemi, Jemia, Jemiah, Jemie, Jemm, Jemmi, Jemmy

Jemima (Hebrew) dove.
Jamin, Jamima, Jem, Jemimah, Jemma

Jemma (Hebrew) a short form of Jemima. (English) a form of Gemma.
Jemmia, Jemmiah, Jemmie, Jemmy

Jena, Jenae (Arabic) forms of Jenna.
Jenah, Jenai, Jenal, Jenay, Jenaya, Jenea

Jendaya (Zimbabwean) thankful.
Daya, Jenda, Jendayah

Jenelle (American) a combination of Jenny + Nell.
Genell, Jeanell, Jeanelle, Jenall, Jenalle, Jenel, Jenela, Jenele, Jenell, Jenella, Jenille, Jenmel, Jennell, Jennella, Jennelle, Jennielle, Jennille, Jinelle, Jinnell

Jenessa (American) a form of Jenisa.
Jenesa, Jenese, Jenesia, Jenessia, Jennesa, Jennese, Jennessa, Jinessa

Jenica (Romanian) a form of Jane.
Jenecca, Jenika, Jenikka, Jennica, Jennika

Jenifer, Jeniffer (Welsh) forms of Jennifer.
Jenefer

Jenilee (American) a combination of Jennifer + Lee.
Jenalea, Jenalee, Jenaleigh, Jenaly, Jenelea, Jenelee, Jeneleigh, Jenely, Jenely, Jenleigh, Jenly, Jennalee, Jennely, Jennielee, Jennilea, Jennilee, Jennilie

Jenisa (American) a combination of Jennifer + Nisa.
Jenessa, Jenisha, Jenissa, Jennisa, Jennise, Jennisha, Jennissa, Jennisse, Jennysa, Jennyssa, Jenysa, Jenyse, Jenyssa, Jenysse

Jenka (Czech) a form of Jane.

Jenna (Arabic) small bird. (Welsh) a short form of Jennifer. See also Gen.
Jena, Jennae, Jennah, Jennai, Jennat, Jennay, Jennaya, Jennaye, Jhenna

Jenni, Jennie (Welsh) familiar forms of Jennifer.
Jeni, Jenne, Jenné, Jennee, Jenney, Jennia, Jennie, Jennita, Jennora, Jensine

Jennifer (Welsh) white wave; white phantom. A form of Guinevere. See also Gennifer, Ginnifer, Yenifer.
Jen, Jenifer, Jeniffer, Jenipher, Jenna, Jennafer, Jenni, Jenniferanne, Jenniferlee, Jenniffer, Jennifier, Jenniffer, Jennilee, Jenniphe, Jennipher, Jenny, Jennyfer

Jennilee (American) a combination of Jenny + Lee.
Jennalea, Jennalee, Jennielee, Jennila, Jennilie, Jinnalee

Jennilyn, Jennilynn (American) combinations of Jenni + Lynn.
Jennalin, Jennalina, Jennalyn, Jennalynn, Jenneylin, Jennilyn, Jennalyne, Jennalynn, Jennalyne, Jennilin, Jennilina, Jennilyne, Jennilynne

Jenny (Welsh) a familiar form of Jennifer.
Jenney, Jenni, Jennie, Jeny, Jinny

Jennyfer (Welsh) a form of Jennifer.
Jenyfer

Jerica (American) a combination of Jeri + Erica.
Jereca, Jerecka, Jerice, Jericka, Jerika, Jerrica, Jerrice, Jeryka

Jeri, Jerri, Jerrie (American) short forms of Geraldine. See also Geri.
Jera, Jerae, JeRae, Jeree, Jeriel, Jerilee, Jerinda, Jerra, Jerrah, Jerrece, Jerree, Jerriann, Jerrilee, Jerrine, Jerry, Jerrylee, Jerrye, Jerzy

Jereni (Russian) a form of Irene.
Jerena, Jerenae, Jerina

Jeraldine (English) a form of Geraldine.
Jeraldeen, Jeraldene, Jeraldina, Jeraldyne, Jeralee, Jeri

Jermaine (French) a form of Germaine.
Jermain, Jerman, Jermanay, Jermanaye, Jermane, Jermanee, Jermani, Jermanique, Jermany, Jermayne, Jermecia, Jermia, Jermice, Jermicia, Jermika, Jermila

Jermaine, Jennilyn → see full entries

Jerilyn (American) a combination of Jeri + Lynn.
Jeralin, Jeraline, Jeralyn, Jeralyne, Jeralynn, Jeralynne, Jerelin, Jereline, Jerelyn, Jerelynn, Jerelyne, Jerelynne, Jerilin, Jeriline, Jerilyne, Jerilynn, Jerilynne, Jerrilyn, Jerrilynn, Jerrilyne, Jerrilynne, Jerrylea

Jerrica (American) a form of Jerica.
Jerreka, Jerricah, Jerrica, Jerricka, Jerrieka, Jerrika

Jerusha (Hebrew) inheritance.
Jerushah, Yerusha

Jesenia, Jessenia (Arabic) flower.
Jescenia, Jessennia, Jesserya

Jesica, Jesika (Hebrew) forms of Jessica.
Jesica, Jesicah, Jesikah

Jessa (American) a short form of Jessalyn, Jessamine, Jessica.
Jesa, Jesha, Jessah

Jessalyn (American) a combination of Jessica + Lynn.
Jesalin, Jesaline, Jesalyn, Jesalyne, Jesalynn, Jesalyne, Jeslin, Jesline, Jeslyn, Jeslyne, Jeslynn, Jeslynne, Jessaline, Jessalin, Jessaline, Jessalyne, Jessalynn, Jessalynne, Jesselin, Jesseline, Jesselyn, Jesselyne, Jesselynn, Jesselynne, Jesselyn

Jessamine (French) a form of Jasmine.
Jessa, Jessamin, Jessamon, Jessamy, Jessamyn, Jessemin, Jessemine, Jessimin, Jessimine, Jessmine, Jessmon, Jessmy, Jessmyn

Jesse, Jessi (Hebrew) forms of Jessie.
Jese, Jesi, Jesie

Jesseca (Hebrew) a form of Jessica.

Jessica (Hebrew) wealthy. Literature: a name perhaps invented by Shakespeare for a character in his play *The Merchant of Venice*. See also Gessica, Yessica.
Jesica, Jesika, Jessa, Jessaca, Jessaca, Jessca, Jesseca, Jessia, Jessicah, Jessicca, Jessicia, Jessika, Jessie, Jessika, Jessiqua, Jessy, Jessyca, Jessyka, Jezeca, Jezia, Jezika, Jezya

Jessie, Jessy (Hebrew) short forms of Jessica. (Scottish) forms of Janet.
Jescie, Jesey, Jess, Jesse, Jessé, Jessey, Jessi, Jessia, Jessiya, Jessye

Jessika (Hebrew) a form of Jessica.
Jessieka

Jesslyn (American) a short form of Jessalyn.
Jesslyn, Jessilynn, Jesslin, Jesslynn, Jesslynne

Jessyca, Jessyka (Hebrew) forms of Jessica.

Jésusa (Hebrew, Spanish) God is my salvation.

Jetta (English) jet black mineral. (American) a familiar form of Jevette.
Jeta, Jetia, Jetje, Jette, Jettie

Jevette (American) a combination of Jean + Yvette.
Jetta, Jeva, Jeveta, Jevetta

Jewel (French) precious gem.
Jewelann, Jewelia, Jeweliana, Jeweliann, Jewelie, Jewell, Jewelle, Jewellee, Jewellene, Jewellie, Juel, Jule

Jezebel (Hebrew) unexalted; impure. Bible: the wife of King Ahab.
Jesibel, Jessabel, Jessebel, Jez, Jezabel,

Jezabella, Jezabelle, Jezebell, Jezebella, Jezebelle

Jianna (Italian) a form of Giana.
Jiana, Jianina, Jianine, Jianni, Jiannini

Jibon (Hindi) life.

Jill (English) a short form of Jillian.
Jil, Jilli, Jillie, Jilly

Jillaine (Latin) a form of Jillian.
Jilaine, Jilane, Jilayne, Jillana, Jillane, Jillann, Jillanne, Jillayne

Jilleen (Irish) a form of Jillian.
Jileen, Jilene, Jiline, Jillene, Jillenne, Jilline, Jillyn

Jillian (Latin) youthful. See also Gillian.
Jilian, Jiliana, Jiliann, Jilianna, Jilianne, Jilienna, Jilienne, Jill, Jillaine, Jilliana, Jilliann, Jillianna, Jillianne, Jilleen, Jillien, Jillienne, Jillion, Jillyn

Jimi (Hebrew) supplanter, substitute.
Jimae, Jimaria, Jimee, Jimella, Jimena, Jimia, Jimiah, Jimie, Jimiyah, Jimmeka, Jimmet, Jimmi, Jimmia, Jimmie

Jimisha (American) a combination of Jimi + Aisha.
Jimica, Jimicia, Jimmicia, Jimysha

Jin (Japanese) tender. (American) a short form of Ginny, Jinny.

Jina (Swahili) baby with a name. (Italian) a form of Gina.
Jena, Jinae, Jinan, Jinda, Jinna, Jinnae

Jinny (Scottish) a familiar form of Jenny. (American) a familiar form of Virginia. See also Ginny.
Jin, Jinnee, Jinney, Jinni, Jinnie

Jirina (Czech) a form of Georgia.
Jirah, Jireh

Jizelle (American) a form of Giselle.
Jessel, Jezel, Jezell, Jezella, Jezelle, Jisel, Jisela, Jisell, Jisella, Jiselle, Jissel, Jissell, Jissella, Jisselle, Jizel, Jizella, Joselle

Jo (American) a short form of Joanna, Jolene, Josephine.
Joangie, Joetta, Joette, Joey

Joan (Hebrew) God is gracious. History: Joan of Arc was a fifteenth-century heroine and resistance fighter. See also Ioana, Jean, Juanita, Siobahn.
Joane, Joaneil, Joanel, Joanelle, Joanie, Joanmarie, Joann, Joannanette, Joanne, Joannel, Joanny, Jonni

Joana, Joanna (English) a form of Joan. See also Yoanna.
Janka, Jhoana, Jo-Ana, Joandra, Joanka, Joananna, Jo-Anie, Joanka, Jo-Anna, Joannah, Jo-Annie, Joeana, Joeanna, Johana, Johanna, Johannah

Joanie, Joannie (Hebrew) familiar forms of Joan.
Joanee, Joani, Joanni, Joenie, Johanie, Johnnie, Joni

Joanne (English) a form of Joan.
Joanann, Joananne, Joann, Jo-Ann, Jo-Anne, Joayn, Joeann, Joeanne

Joanny (Hebrew) a familiar form of Joan.
Joany

Joaquina (Hebrew) God will establish.
Joaquine

jobeth (English) a combination of Jo + Beth.
Joby

joby (Hebrew) afflicted. (English) a familiar form of Jobeth.
Joby, Jobi, Jobie, Jobina, Jobita, Johnna, Jobye, Jobyna

jocacia (American) a combination of Joy + Acacia.

jocelin, joceline (Latin) forms of Jocelyn.
Jocelina, Jocelin

jocelyn (Latin) joyous. See also Yocelin, Yoselin.
Jacelyn, Jasleen, Jocelin, Jocelle, Jocelyne, Jocelynn, Joci, Jocia, Jocilyn, Jocilynn, Jocinta, Joclyn, Joclynn, Josalyn, Joselin, Joselyn, Joselyn, Joshlyn, Joslin, Joslin, Josslyn, Joycelyn

jocelyne (Latin) a form of Jocelyn.
Joceline, Jocelynne, Jochyne

jodi, jodie, jody (American) familiar forms of Judith.
Jodee, Jodele, Jodell, Jodelle, Jodeva, Jodey, Jodia, Jodiee, Jodilee, Jodi-Lee, Jodilynn, Jodi-Lynn, Jodi, Jody

jodiann (American) a combination of Jodi + Ann.
Jodene, Jodi-Ann, Jodianna, Jodi-Anna, Jodianne, Jodi-Anne, Jodiann, Jody-Ann, Jodyanna, Jody-Anna, Jodyanne, Jody-Anne, Jodyne

joelle (Hebrew) God is willing.
Joela, Joele, Joelee, Joeli, Joelia, Joelie, Joell, Joella, Joelle, Joelli, Joelly, Joely, Joyelle

joelynn (American) a combination of Joelle + Lynn.
Joeleen, Joelene, Joeline, Joellen, Joellin, Joelyne

johana, johanna, johannah (German) forms of Joana.
Janna, Joahna, Johanah, Johanka, Johanne, Johnna, Johonna, Jonna, Joyhanna, Joyhannah

johanie, johannie (Hebrew) forms of Joanie.
Johani, Johanni, Johanny, Johany

johnna, jonna (American) forms of Johanna, Joanna.
Jahna, Jahnaya, Jhona, Jhonna, Johna, Johnda, Johnielynn, Johnnie-Lynn, Johnnquia, Joncie, Jonda, Jondrea, Jontel, Jutta

johnnessa (American) a combination of Johnna + Nessa.
Jahnessa, Johneatha, Johnecia, Johnesha, Johnetra, Johnisha, Johnrise, Joryssa

joi (Latin) a form of Joy.
Joia, Joie

jokla (Swahili) beautiful robe.

jolanda (Greek) a form of Yolanda. See also Iolanthe.
Jola, Jolan, Jolan, Jolande, Jolander, Jolanka, Jolanta, Jolantha, Jolanthe

joleen, joline (English) forms of Jolene.
Jolene, Joleena, Jolleen, Jollene

jolene (Hebrew) God will add, God will increase. (English) a form of Josephine.
Jo, Jolaine, Jolana, Jolane, Jolanna, Jolanne, Jolayne, Jole, Jolean, Jolena, Jolene, Jolina, Jolinda, Joline, Jolirm, Jolleane, Joleen, Joline

jolie (French) pretty.
Jole, Jolea, Jolee, Joleigh, Joley, Joli, Jolitieth, Jollee, Jollie, Jolly, Joly, Jolye

jolisa (American) a combination of Jo + Lisa.
Joleesa, Joleisha, Joleishia, Jolieasa, Jolise, Jolisha, Jolisia, Jolysa, Jolyssa, Julisa

jolynn (American) a combination of Jo + Lynn.
Jolyn, Jolyne, Jolynne

jonatha (Hebrew) gift of God.
Johnasha, Johnasia, Jonesha, Jonisha

jonelle (American) a combination of Joan + Elle.
Jahnell, Jahnelle, Johnel, Johnell, Johnella, Johnelle, Jonel, Jonell, Jonella, Joryelle, Jynell, Jynelle

jonesha, jonisha (American) forms of Jonatha.
Joneisha, Jonesa, Joneshia, Jonessa, Jonisa, Jonishia, Jonneisha, Jonneisha, Jonnessia

joni (American) a familiar form of Joan.
Jona, Jonae, Jonai, Jonann, Jonati, Joncey, Jonci, Joncie, Jonie, Jonilee, Joni-lee, Jonis, Jony

Jonika (American) a form of Janika.
Johnica, Johnique, Johnquia, Johnnica, Johnnika, Joneika, Jonica, Joniqua, Jonique

Jonina (Hebrew) dove. See also Yonina.
Jona, Jonita, Jonnina

Jonita (Hebrew) a form of Jonina. See also Yonita.
Johnetta, Johnette, Johnita, Johnittia, Jonati, Jonetia, Jonetta, Jonette, Jonit, Jonnita, Jonta, Jontae, Jontaé, Jontaya

Jonni, Jonnie (American) familiar forms of Joan.
Jonny

Jonquil (Latin, English) Botany: an ornamental plant with fragrant yellow flowers.
Jonquelle, Jonquie, Jonquill, Jonquille

Jontel (American) a form of Johna.
Jontaya, Jontell, Jontelle, Jontia, Jontila, Jontrice

Jora (Hebrew) autumn rain.
Jorah

Jordan (Hebrew) descending. See also Jardena.
Jordain, Jordaine, Jordana, Jordane, Jordann, Jordanna, Jordanne, Jordany, Jordea, Jordee, Jorden, Jordi, Jordian, Jordie, Jordin, Jordon, Jordyn, Jori, Jorie, Jourdan

Jordana, Jordanna (Hebrew) forms of Jordan. See also Giordana, Yordana.
Jordannah, Jordina, Jordonna, Jourdana, Jourdanna

Jorden, Jordin, Jordon (Hebrew) forms of Jordan.
Jordenne, Jordine

Jordyn (Hebrew) a form of Jordan.
Jordyne, Jordynn, Jordynne

Jori, Jorie (Hebrew) familiar forms of Jordan.
Jorai, Jorea, Joree, Jorée, Jorey, Jorian, Jorin, Jorina, Jorine, Joria, Jorre, Jorrey, Jorri, Jorrian, Jorrie, Jorry, Jory

Joriann (American) a combination of Jori + Ann.
Jori-Ann, Jorianna, Jori-Anna, Jorianne, Jori-Anne, Jorriann, Jorrianna, Jorrianne, Jorryann, Jorryanna, Jorryanne, Joryann, Joryanna, Joryanne

Jorja (American) a form of Georgia.
Jeorgi, Jeorgia, Jorgana, Jorgi, Jorgia, Jorgina, Jorjana, Jorji

Josalyn (Latin) a form of Jocelyn.
Josalene, Josalin, Josalind, Josaline, Josalynn, Joshalyne

Joscelin, Joscelyn (Latin) forms of Jocelyn.
Josceline, Joscelyne, Joscelynn, Joscelynne, Joselin, Joseline, Joselyn, Joselyne, Joselynn, Joselynne, Joshlyn

Josee, Josée (American) familiar forms of Josephine.
Joesee, Josey, Josi, Josina, Josy, Jozee

Josefina (Spanish) a form of Josephine.
Josefa, Josefena, Joseffa, Josefine

Joselin, Joseline (Latin) forms of Jocelyn.
Joselina, Joselinne, Joselina

Joselle (American) a form of Jizelle.
Joesell, Jozelle

Joselyn, Joslyn (Latin) forms of Jocelyn.
Joselene, Joselyne, Joselynn, Joshely, Josiline, Joslyn

Josephine (French) God will add, God will increase. See also Fifi, Pepita, Yosepha.
Fina, Jo, Joey, Josee, Josée, Josefina, Josepha, Josephe, Josephene, Josephin, Josephina, Josephyna, Josephyne, Josette, Josey, Josie, Jozephine, Jozié, Sefa

Josette (French) a familiar form of Josephine.
Joesette, Josetta, Joshetta, Jozette

Josey, Josie (Hebrew) familiar forms of Josephine.
Josi, Josse, Jossee, Jossie, Josy, Josye

Joshann (American) a combination of Joshlyn + Ann.
Joshana, Joshanna, Joshanne

Joshlyn (Latin) a form of Jocelyn. (Hebrew) God is my salvation.
Joshalin, Joshalyn, Joshalynn, Joshalynne, Joshelle, Joshleen, Joshlin, Joshline, Joshlyne, Joshlynn, Joshlynne

Josiane, Josianne (American) combinations of Josie + Anne.
Josian, Josie-Ann, Josieann

Josilin, Joslin (Latin) forms of Jocelyn.
Josielina, Josiline, Josilyn, Josilyne, Josilina, Josilynne, Joslin, Josline, Joslyn, Joslyne, Joslyn, Joslynne

Jossalin (Latin) a form of Jocelyn.
Jossaline, Jossalyn, Jossalynne, Josselyn, Josslin, Jossline

Josselyn (Latin) a form of Jocelyn.
Josselen, Josseline, Josselin, Jossellin, Jossellyn, Josselyne, Josselynn, Josselynne, Josslyn, Josslynne, Josslynn, Josslynne

Jovana (Latin) a form of Jovanna.
Jovana, Jovan, Jovanah, Jovena, Jovian, Jovan, Jovana

Jourdan (Hebrew) a form of Jordan.
Jourdain, Jourdann, Jourdanne, Jourden, Jourdian, Jourdon, Jourdyn

Jovanna (Latin) majestic. (Italian) a form of Giovanna. Mythology: Jove, also known as Jupiter, was the supreme Roman god.
Jeovanna, Jovado, Joval, Jovana, Jovann, Jovannie, Jovaughn, Jovena, Jovenia, Jovira, Jovon, Jovonda, Jovonna, Jovonnah, Jovonne, Jovonna

Jovanie (Italian) a familiar form of Jovanna.
Jovanee, Jovani, Jovanie, Jovanne, Jovanni, Jovanny, Jovonnie

Jovita (Latin) jovial.
Joveda, Joveta, Jovetta, Jovida, Jovita

Joy (Latin) joyous.
Joe, Joi, Joya, Joye, Joyetta, Joyella, Joyia, Joyous, Joyrina

Joyanne (American) a combination of Joy + Anne.
Joyan, Joyann, Joyanna,

Joyce (Latin) joyous. A short form of Jocelyn.
Joice, Joycy, Joycie, Joyous, Joysel

Joycelyn (American) a form of Jocelyn.
Joycelin, Joyceline, Joycelyne, Joycelynn, Joycelyne

Joylyn (American) a combination of Joy + Lynn.
Joyleen, Joylene, Joylin, Joyline, Joylyne, Joylynn, Joy-Lynn, Joylynne

Jozie (Hebrew) a familiar form of Josephine.
Jozee, Jozée, Jozi, Jozy

Juana (Spanish) a short form of Juanita.
Juanell, Juaney, Juanita, Juanit, Juanna, Juania

Juandalyn (Spanish) a form of Juanita.
Juatin, Juandalin, Juandaline, Juandalyne, Juandalynn, Juandalynne

Juanita (Spanish) a form of Jane, Joan. See also Kwanita, Nita, Waneta, Wanika.
Juana, Juandalyn, Juanetce, Juanequa, Juanesha, Juanice, Juanicia, Juaniqua, Juanisha, Juanishia

Juci (Hungarian) a form of Judy.
Jucika

Judith (Hebrew) praised. Mythology: the slayer of Holofernes, according to ancient Jewish legend. See also Yehudit, Yudita.
Giuditta, Ioudith, Jodi, Jodie, Jody, Jude, Judine, Judit, Judita, Judite, Juditha, Juditte, Judy, Judya, Jutka

Judy (Hebrew) a familiar form of Judith.
Juci, Judi, Judie, Judye

Judyann (American) a combination of Judy + Ann.
Judana, Judiann, Judianna, Judianne, Judyanne

Jula (Polish) a form of Julia.
Jula, Julca, Juliska, Julka

Julene (Basque) a form of Julia. See also Yulene.
Julena, Julina, Juline, Julinka, Juliska, Julleen, Jullena, Jullene, Julyne

Julia (Latin) youthful. See also Giulia, Jill, Jillian, Sulia, Yulia.
Iulia, Jula, Julea, Juleah, Julene, Juliah, Juliana, Juliann, Julica, Julie, Julieta, Juliet, Julija, Julina, Julisa, Julissa, Julita, Juliya, Julka, Julysa

Juliana, Julianna (Czech, Spanish, Hungarian) forms of Julia.
Julieana, Julieanna, Juliena, Juliana, Julianna, Julyanna, Juliana

Julie (English) a form of Julia.
Juel, Jule, Julee, Juli, Julie-Lynn, Julie-Mae, Julie, Julie, Julie, July, July

Juliann, Julianne (English) forms of Julia.
Julean, Julian, Juliane, Julieann, Julie-Ann, Julieanne, Julie-Anne, Julien, Juliene, Julienn, Julienne, Julian

Juliet, Juliette (French) forms of Julia.
Julet, Julieta, Juliett, Julietta, Juliet, Juliet, Julietta

Julisa, Julissa (Latin) forms of Julia.
Julis, Julisha, Julyssa, Julyssa

Julita (Spanish) a form of Julia.
Julitta, Julyta

Jumaris (American) a combination of Julie + Maris.

Jun (Chinese) truthful.

June (Latin) born in the sixth month.
Juna, Junea, Junel, Junell, Junella, Junelle, Junette, Juney, Junia, Junie, Juniet, Junieta, Junietta, Juniette, Junina, Junita

Juno (Latin) queen. Mythology: the supreme Roman goddess.

Justice (Latin) just, righteous.
Justis, Justise, Justiss, Justisse, Justus, Justyce, Justys

Justina (Italian) a form of Justine.
Jestena, Jestina, Justinna, Justyna

Justine (Latin) just, righteous.
Giustina, Jestine, Juste, Justi, Justi, Justice, Justie, Justina, Justinn, Justy, Justyn, Justyne, Justynn, Justynne

Kacey, Kacy (Irish) brave. (American) forms of Casey. Combinations of the initials K + C.
K. C., Kace, Kacee, Kaci, Kacie, Kaicee, Kaicey, Kasey, Kasie, Kaycee, Kayci, Kaycie

Kachina (Native American) sacred dancer.
Kachine

Kaci, Kacie (American) forms of Kacey, Kacy.
Kasci, Kaycie, Kaysie

Kacia (Greek) a short form of Acacia.
Kaycia, Kaysia

Kadedra (American) a combination of Kady + Dedra.
Kadeadra, Kadedrah, Kadedria, Kadeedra, Kadeidra, Kadeidre, Kadeidria

Kadejah (Arabic) a form of Kadijah.
Kadeija, Kadejiah, Kadejá, Kadejia

Kadelyn (American) a combination of Kady + Lynn.

Kadesha (American) a combination of Kady + Aisha.
Kadeesha, Kadeeshia, Kadeesia, Kadeesiah, Kadeezia, Kadesa, Kadeshia, Kadeshia, Kadesia, Kadessa, Kadezia

Kadie (English) a form of Kady.
Kadi, Kadia, Kadiah

Kadijah (Arabic) trustworthy.
Kadajah, Kadeeja, Kadeejah, Kadija

Kadisha (American) a form of Kadesha.
Kadiesha, Kadieshia, Kadishia, Kadisia, Kadysha, Kadyshia

Kady (English) a form of Katy. A combination of the initials K. + D. See also Cady.
K. D., Kade, Kadee, Kadey, Kadie, Kadya, Kadyn, Kaidi, Kaidy, Kayde, Kaydee, Kaydey, Kaydi, Kaydie, Kaydy

Kaedé (Japanese) maple leaf.

Kaela (Hebrew, Arabic) beloved, sweetheart. A short form of Kalila, Kelila.
Kaelah, Kaelea, Kaeleah, Kaelee, Kayla

Kaelee, Kaeli (American) forms of Kaela.
Kaeli, Kaeleigh, Kaeley, Kaelia, Kaelie, Kaelii, Kaelly, Kaely, Kaelye

Kaelin (American) a form of Kaelyn.
Kaeleen, Kaelene, Kaelina, Kaelinn, Kalan

Kaelyn (American) a combination of Kae + Lynn. See also Caelin, Kaylyn.
Kaelan, Kaelen, Kaelin, Kaelynn, Kaelynne

Kaetlyn (Irish) a form of Kaitlin.
Kaetlin, Kaetlynn

Kagami (Japanese) mirror.

Kahsha (Native American) fur robe.
Kasha, Kashae, Kashia

Kai (Hawaiian) sea. (Hopi, Navaho) willow tree.
Kae, Kaie

Kaia (Greek) earth. Mythology: Gaea was the earth goddess.
Kaiah, Kaija

Kaila (Hebrew) laurel; crown.
Kailah, Kailea, Kaileah, Kailee, Kailey, Kayla

Kailee, Kailey (American) familiar forms of Kaylee. Forms of Kaila.
Kaile, Kaileh, Kaileigh, Kaili, Kailia, Kailie, Kailli, Kaillie, Kaily, Kailya

Kailyn, Kailynn (American) forms of Kaitlin.
Kailan, Kaileen, Kailena, Kailen, Kailena, Kailene, Kaileyne, Kailin, Kailina, Kailon, Kailyne

Kairos (Greek) last, final, complete. Mythology: the last goddess born to Jupiter.

Kaishawn (American) a combination of Kai + Shawna.
Kaeshun, Kaisha, Kaishala, Kaishon

Kaishawn (American) a combination of Kai + Shawna.

Kaitlin (Irish) pure. See also Katelin.
Kaethyn, Kaitlyn, Kaitlynn, Kaitlan, Kaitland, Kaitleen, Kaitlen, Kaitlind, Kaitlinn, Kaitlinne, Kaiton, Kaytlin

Kaitlyn, Kaitlynn (Irish) forms of Caitlyn.
Kaitelynne, Kaitlynne

Kaiya (Japanese) forgiveness.
Kaiyah, Kaiyia

Kala (Arabic) a short form of Kalila. A form of Cala.
Kalah, Kalla, Kallah

Kalama (Hawaiian) torch.

Kalani (Hawaiian) chieftain; sky.
Kailani, Kalanie, Kaloni

Kalare (Latin, Basque) bright; clear.

Kalea (Hawaiian) bright; clear.
Kahlea, Kahleah, Kailea, Kaileah, Kaleah, Kaleeia, Kaleia, Kalia, Kallea, Kalleah, Kaylea, Kayleah, Khalea, Khaleah

Kalee, Kaleigh, Kaley, Kalie (American) forms of Caley, Kaylee, Kalei, Kaleigh, Kalley, Kaly, Kaley

Kalei (Hawaiian) flower wreath.
Kahlei, Kailei, Kalei, Kaylei, Khalei

Kalena (Hawaiian) pure. See also Kalina.
Kaleen, Kaleena, Kalene, Kalenea, Kalenna

Kalere (Swahili) short woman.

Kali (Hindi) the black one. (Hawaiian) hesitating. Religion: a form of the Hindu goddess Devi. See also Cali.
Kalee, Kaleigh, Kaley, Kalie, Kallee, Kalley, Kalli, Kallie, Kaly, Kallye, Kaly

Kalila (Arabic) beloved, sweetheart. See also Kaela.
Kahlila, Kala, Kaleela, Kalilla, Kaylil, Kaylila, Kelila, Khalia, Khalilah, Khalillah, Kylila, Kylilah, Kylilah

Kalia (Hawaiian) a form of Kalea.
Kaliah, Kaliea, Kalieya

Kalifa (Somali) chaste; holy.

Kalina (Slavic) flower. (Hawaiian) a form of Karen. See also Kalena.
Kalin, Kalinna, Kalyna, Kalynah, Kalyna

Kalinda (Hindi) sun.
Kaleenda, Kalindi, Kalynda, Kalyndi, Kalynn

Kalisa (American) a combination of Kate + Lisa.
Kalise, Kalissa, Kalysa, Kalyssa

Kalisha (American) a combination of Kali + Aisha.
Kaleesha, Kaleisha, Kalisha

Kaliska (Moquelumnan) coyote chasing deer.

Kallan (Slavic) stream, river.
Kalahn, Kalan, Kalen, Kallen, Kallon, Kalon

Kalle (Finnish) a form of Carol.
Kaille, Kaylle

Kalli, Kallie (Greek) forms of Callie. Familiar forms of Kalliope, Kallista, Kalliyan.
Kalle, Kallee, Kalley, Kallita, Kaly

Kalliope (Greek) a form of Calliope.
Kalli, Kallie, Kallyope

Kallista (Greek) a form of Callista.
Kalesta, Kalista, Kallesta, Kalli, Kallie, Kallysta, Kaysta

Kalliyan (Cambodian) best.

Kaltha (English) marigold, yellow flower.

Kaluwa (Swahili) forgotten one.
Kalua

Kalyca (Greek) rosebud.
Kalica, Kalika, Kaly

Kalyn, Kalynn (American) forms of Kaylyn.
Kalin, Kallen, Kallin, Kallon, Kaltyn, Kalyne, Kalynne

Kama (Sanskrit) loved one. Religion: the Hindu god of love.

Kamala (Hindi) lotus.
Kamalah, Kammala

Kamali (Mahona) spirit guide; protector.
Kamalie

Kamaria (Swahili) moonlight.
Kamar, Kamara, Kamarae, Kamaree, Kamari, Kamariah, Kamarie, Kamariya, Kamariyah, Kamarya

Kamata (Moquelumnan) gambler.

Kambria (Latin) a form of Cambria.
Kambra, Kambrie, Kambriea, Kambry

Kamea (Hawaiian) one and only; precious.
Kameah, Kameo, Kamiya

Kameke (Swahili) blind.

Kameko (Japanese) turtle child. Mythology: the turtle symbolizes longevity.

Kameron (American) a form of Cameron.
Kameran, Kamri

Kami (Japanese) divine aura. (Italian, North African) a short form of Kamila, Kamilah. See also Cami.
Kamie, Kammi, Kammie, Kammy, Kammye, Kamy

Kamila (Slavic) a form of Camila. See also Millie.
Kameela, Kamela, Kamelia, Kamella, Kami, Kamilah, Kamilia, Kamilka, Kamilla, Kamille, Kamma, Kammilla, Kamyla

Kamilah (North African) perfect.
Kameela, Kameelah, Kami, Kamillah, Kammilah

Kamiya (Hawaiian) a form of Kamea.
Kamia, Kamiah, Kamiyah

Kamri (American) a short form of Kameron. See also Camri.
Kamree, Kamrey, Kamrie, Kamry, Kamrye

Kamryn (American) a short form of Kameron. See also Camryn.
Kameryn, Kamren, Kamrin, Kamron, Kamrynn

Kanani (Hawaiian) beautiful.
Kana, Kanae, Kanan

Kanda (Native American) magical power.

Kandace, Kandice (Greek) glittering white; glowing. (American) forms of Candace, Candice.
Kandas, Kandess, Kandi, Kandis, Kandise, Kandiss, Kandus, Kandyce, Kandys, Kandyse

Kandi (American) a familiar form of Kandace, Kandice. See also Candi.
Kandhi, Kandia, Kandie, Kandy, Kendi, Kendie, Kendy, Kenndi, Kenndie, Kenndy

Kandra (American) a form of Kendra. See also Candra.
Kandrea, Kandree, Kandria

Kane (Japanese) two right hands.

Kaneisha, Kanisha (American) forms of Keneisha.
Kaneasha, Kanecia, Kaneesha, Kanesah, Kanesha, Kaneshea, Kaneshia, Kanessa, Kaneysha, Kanieee, Kanishia

Kanene (Swahili) a little important thing.

Kani (Hawaiian) sound.

Kanika (Mwera) black cloth.
Kanica, Kanicka

Kannitha (Cambodian) angel.

Kanoa (Hawaiian) free.

Kanya (Hindi) virgin. (Tai) young lady. Religion: a form of the Hindu goddess Devi.
Kanea, Kania, Kaniya, Kanyia

Kapri (American) a form of Capri.
Kapre, Kapree, Kapria, Kaprice, Kapricia, Kaprisha, Kaprisia

Kapua (Hawaiian) blossom.

Kapuki (Swahili) first-born daughter.

Kara (Greek, Danish) pure.
Kaira, Kairah, Karah, Karalea, Karaleah, Karalee, Karalie, Kari, Karra

Karah (Greek, Danish) a form of Kara. (Irish, Italian) a form of Cara.
Karrah

Karalynn (English) a combination of Kara + Lynn.
Karalin, Karaline, Karalyn, Karalyne, Karalynne

Karelle (American) a form of Carol.
Karel, Kareli, Karell, Karely

Karen (Greek) pure. See also Carey, Carina, Caryn.
Kaaren, Kalina, Karaina, Karan, Karena, Karin, Karina, Karine, Karna, Karon, Karren, Karyn, Kerron, Koren

Karena (Scandinavian) a form of Karen.
Kareen, Kareena, Kareina, Karenah, Karene, Kareena, Kareena, Karrene

Karessa (French) a form of Caressa.

Kari (Greek) pure. (Danish) a form of Caroline, Katherine. See also Carey, Karee, Karey, Karia, Kariah, Karie, Karrey, Karri, Karrie, Karry, Kary

Kariane, Karianne (American) combinations of Kari + Ann.
Karian, Kariana, Kariann, Karianna

Karida (Arabic) untouched, pure.
Kareeda, Karita

Karilynn (American) a combination of Kari + Lynn.
Kareelin, Kareeline, Kareelinn, Kareelyne, Kareelynn, Kareelynne, Karilin, Kariline, Karilinn, Karilyn, Karilyne, Karilynne, Karyline, Karylin, Karylinn, Karylyn, Karylyne, Karylynn, Karylynne

Karimah (Arabic) generous.
Kareema, Kareemah, Karima, Karime

Karin (Scandinavian) a form of Karen.
Kaarin, Kareen, Karina, Karine, Karinne, Karrin, Kerrin

Karina (Russian) a form of Karen.
Kaarina, Kaarina, Karinna, Karyna, Karynna

Karine (Russian) a form of Karen.
Karrine, Karryne, Karyne

Karis (Greek) graceful.
Karess, Karice, Karise, Karis, Karisse, Karys, Karyss

Karissa (Greek) a form of Carissa.
Karese, Karesse, Karisa, Karisha, Karisma, Karisma, Karissima, Kariza, Karrisa, Karrissa, Karysa, Karyssa, Kerisa

Karla (German) a form of Carla.
(Slavic) a short form of Karoline, Caroline. See also Carla.
Karila, Karilla, Karle, Karlena, Karlicka, Karline, Karleen, Karlena, Karlin, Karlina, Karlisha, Karlisia, Karlitha, Karla, Karlon, Karlyn

Karlee, Karleigh (American) forms of Carlee.
Karley, Karly. See also Carlee.
Karlea, Karleah, Karlei

Karlene, Karlyn (American) forms of Carlen.
Karleen, Karlen, Karlena, Karlign, Karlin, Karlina, Karlinna, Karlyan, Karlynn, Karlynne

Karley, Karly (Latin) little and strong. (American) forms of Carly.
Karlee, Karley, Karlie, Karlyan, Karlye

Karli, Karlie (American) forms of Karley, Karly. See also Carli.

Karlotte (American) a form of Charlotte.
Karlita, Karletta, Karlette, Karlotta

Karma (Hindi) fate, destiny; action.

Karmel (Hebrew) a form of Carmela.
Karmeita, Karmela, Karmelina, Karmella, Karmelle, Karmiella, Karmella, Karmyla

Karmen (Latin) song.
Karman, Karmencita, Karmin, Karmina, Karmine, Karmita, Karmon, Karmyn, Karmyne

Karolane (American) a combination of Karoll + Anne.
Karolan, Karolann, Karolanne, Karol-Anne

Karolina (Slavic) forms of Caroline. See also Carolina.
Karaleen, Karalena, Karalene, Karalin, Karaline, Karaleen, Karalena, Karaline, Karlen, Karlena, Karlene, Karleen, Karoleena, Karolena, Karolinka, Karoleen, Karolena, Karolene, Karolin, Karoline

Karoll (Slavic) a form of Carol.
Karel, Karilla, Karily, Karol, Karola, Karole, Karoly, Karol, Karyl, Kerril

Karolyn (American) a form of Carolyn.
Karalyn, Karalyna, Karalynn, Karalynne, Karlyn, Karilyna, Karilynn, Karilynne, Karlyn, Karlyna, Karlyne, Karlynne, Karolyn, Karolyne, Karolyn, Karolynn, Karolyna, Karolynn, Karrolynne

Karri, Karrie (American) forms of Carrie.
Kari, Karie, Karry, Kary

Karsen, Karsyn (English) child of Kar. Forms of Carson.
Karson

Karuna (Hindi) merciful.

Karyn (American) a form of Karen.
*Karyne, Karynn, Karynna, Kerrynne,
Kerrynne*

Kasa (Hopi) fur robe.

Kasandra (Greek) a form of Kassandra.
*Kasander, Kasandria, Kasandra,
Kasaundra, Kasoundra, Kasoundra*

Kasey, Kasie (Irish) brave. (American)
forms of Casey, Kacey.
*Kaisee, Kaisie, Kasci, Kascy, Kasee, Kasi,
Kassee, Kassey, Kasy, Kasya, Kaysci,
Kaysea, Kaysee, Kaysey, Kaysi, Kaysie,
Kaysy*

Kashawna (American) a combination
of Kate + Shawna.
*Kasha, Kashae, Kashana, Kashanna,
Kashawna, Kashawn, Kasheana,
Kasheanna, Kasheena, Kashena,
Kashonda, Kashonna*

Kashmir (Sanskrit) Geography: a
region located between India and
Pakistan.
*Cashmere, Kashmear, Kashmere,
Kashmia, Kashmira, Kasmir, Kasmira,
Kazmir, Kazmira*

Kasi (Hindi) from the holy city.

Kasia (Polish) a form of Cassia.
See also Cassia.
*Kashia, Kasiah, Kasian, Kasienka,
Kasja, Kaska, Kassa, Kassia, Kassya,
Kasya*

Kasinda (Umbundu) our last baby.

Kassandra (Greek) a form of
Cassandra.
*Kassandr, Kassandre, Kassandré,
Kassaundra, Kassi, Kassondra,*

*Kassondria, Kassoundra, Kazandra,
Khrisandra, Krisandra, Krissandra*

Kassi, Kassie (American) familiar forms
of Kassandra, Kassidy. See also Cassie.
Kassey, Kassia, Kassy

Kassidy (Irish) clever. (American) a
form of Cassidy.
*Kassadee, Kassadi, Kassadie, Kassadina,
Kassady, Kasseday, Kassedee, Kassi,
Kassiddy, Kassidee, Kassidi, Kassidie,
Kassity, Kassydi*

Katalina (Irish) a form of Caitlin. See
also Catalina.
*Kataleen, Kataleena, Katalena, Katalin,
Katalyn, Katalynn*

Katarina (Czech) a form of Katherine.
*Kata, Katareena, Katarena, Katarin,
Katarine, Katarinna, Katarinne,
Katarrina, Kataryna, Katarzyna,
Katinka, Katrika, Katrinka*

Kate (Greek) pure. (English) a short
form of Katherine.
*Kait, Kata, Katee, Kati, Katica, Katie,
Katka, Katy, Katya*

Katee, Katey (English) familiar forms
of Kate, Katherine.

Katelin (Irish) a form of Caitlin. See
also Kaitlin.
*Kaetlin, Katalin, Katelan, Kateland,
Katelen, Katelen, Katelene, Katelind,
Kateline, Katelinn, Katelun, Kaytlin*

Katelyn, Katelynn (Irish) forms of
Caitlin.
*Kaetlyn, Kaethynn, Kaethynne, Katelyne,
Katelynne, Kaytlyn, Kaytlynn,
Kaytlynne*

Katerina (Slavic) a form of Katherine.
Katenka, Katerine, Katerini, Katerinka

Katharine (Greek) a form of
Katherine.
*Katharaine, Katharin, Katharina,
Katharyn*

Katherine (Greek) pure. See also
Carey, Catherine, Ekaterina, Kara,
Karen, Kari, Kasia, Katerina,
Yekaterina.
*Ekaterina, Ekatrinna, Kasienka, Kasin,
Kat, Katarina, Katchen, Kate, Katee,
Katharn, Katharine, Katharine,
Kathereen, Katheren, Katherene,
Katherenne, Katherin, Katherina,
Katheryn, Katheryne, Kathi, Kathleen,
Kathrine, Kathryn, Kathy, Kathyrine,
Katia, Katina, Katlaina, Katoka,
Katreeka, Katrina, Kay, Kitty*

Kathi, Kathy (English) familiar forms
of Katherine, Kathleen. See also
Cathi.
*Kaethe, Katha, Kathe, Kathee, Kathey,
Kathi, Kathie, Katka, Katla, Kató*

Kathleen (Irish) a form of Katherine.
See also Cathleen.
*Katheleen, Kathelene, Kathi, Kathileen,
Kathlean, Kathleena, Kathleene,
Kathlene, Kathlin, Kathlina, Kathlyn,
Kathlyne, Kathlynn, Kathy, Katleen*

Kathrine (Greek) a form of Katherine.
*Kathreen, Kathreena, Kathrene, Kathrin,
Kathrina*

Kathryn (English) a form of
Katherine.
*Kathren, Kathryne, Kathrynn,
Kathrynne*

Kati (Estonian) a familiar form of Kate.
Kaija, Katya, Katye

Katia, Katya (Russian) forms of Katherine.
Cattiah, Katiya, Kattia, Kattiah, Katyah

Katie (English) a familiar form of Kate.
Katee, Kati, Kãtia, Katti, Kattie, Katy, Kayte, Kaytee, Kaytie

Katlyn (Irish) a form of Katlyn.
Katlin, Katlynn

Katlin (Irish) a form of Katlyn.
Katlina, Katline

Katlyn (Greek) pure. (Irish) a form of Katelin.
Kaatlain, Katilyn, Katland, Katlin, Kathynd, Kathyne, Katlynn, Katlynne

Katriel (Hebrew) God is my crown.
Katrelle, Katri, Katrie, Katry, Katryel

Katrina (German) a form of Katherine. See also Catrina, Trina.
Kareena, Katreena, Katrena, Katri, Katrica, Katricia, Katrien, Katrin, Katryna, Katrinia, Katriona, Katryn, Katryna, Kattrina, Kattryna, Katus, Katuska

Katy (English) a familiar form of Kate. See also Cady.
Kady, Katey, Katy, Kaye

Kaulana (Hawaiian) famous.
Kaula, Kauna, Kahuna

Kaveri (Hindi) Geography: a sacred river in India.

Kavindra (Hindi) poet.

Kawena (Hawaiian) glow.
Kawana, Kawona

Kay (Greek) rejoicer. (Teutonic) a fortified place. (Latin) merry. A short form of Katherine.
Caye, Kae, Kai, Kaye, Kayla

Kaya (Hopi) wise child. (Japanese) resting place.
Kaja, Kayah, Kayia

Kaycee (American) a combination of the initials K. + C.
Kayce, Kaysee, Kaysey, Kaysi, Kaysie, Kaysii

Kaydee (American) a combination of the initials K. + D.
Kayda, Kayde, Kayden, Kaydi, Kaydie

Kayla (Arabic, Hebrew) laurel; crown. A form of Kaela, Kaila. See also Cayla.
Kaylah, Kaylea, Kaylee, Kayleen, Kaylene, Kaylia, Kayline, Keyla

Kaylah (Arabic, Hebrew) a form of Kayla.
Kayleah, Kaylia, Keylah

Kaylan, Kaylen (Hebrew) forms of Kayleen.
Kaylana, Kayland, Kaylani, Kaylann, Kaylean, Kayleanna, Kayleanna, Kaylenn

Kaylee (American) a form of Kayla. See also Caeley, Kalee.
Kailee, Kayle, Kayleigh, Kayley, Kayli, Kaylie

Kayleen, Kaylene (Hebrew) beloved, sweetheart. Forms of Kayla.
Kaylan, Kayleena, Kayleene, Kaylen, Kaylena

Kayleigh (American) a form of Kaylee.
Kaylee, Kaylei

Kayley, Kayli, Kaylie (American) forms of Kaylee.

Kaylin (American) a form of Kaylyn.
Kaylon

Kaylyn, Kaylynn (American) combinations of Kay + Lynn. See also Kaelyn.
Kailyn, Kalynn, Kayleen, Kaylene, Kaylin, Kaylyna, Kaylyne, Kaylynne

Kaytlin, Kaytlyn (Irish) forms of Kaitlin.
Kaytlan, Kaytlann, Kaytlen, Kaytlinn, Kaytlyne, Kaytlynne

Keala (Hawaiian) path.

Keandra, Keondra (American) forms of Kenda.
Keandrah, Keandre, Keandrea, Keandria, Kedeana, Kedia, Keonda, Keondre, Keondria

Keana, Keanna (German) bold; sharp. (Irish) beautiful.
Keanah, Keanne, Keanu, Keenan, Keeyana, Keeyanah, Keeyanna, Keeyona, Keeyonna, Keiana, Keianna, Keona, Keonna

Keara (Irish) dark; black. Religion: an Irish saint.
Keaira, Kearah, Kearia, Kearra, Keera, Keerra, Keiara, Keiarah, Keiarra, Keiara, Keira, Kera

Keaira (Irish) a form of Keara.
Keair, Keairah, Keaira, Keaire, Keairea

Kearsten, Keirsten (Greek) forms of Kirstin.
Kearstin, Kearston, Kearstyn, Keirstan, Keirstein, Keirstin, Keirston, Keirstyn, Keirstynne

Keeley, Keely (Irish) forms of Kelly.
Kealee, Kealey, Keali, Kealie, Keallie, Kealy, Keela, Keelan, Keele, Keelee, Keeleigh, Keeli, Keelia, Keelie, Keellie, Keelye, Keighla, Keilee, Keileigh, Keiley, Keilly, Kiela, Kiele, Kieley, Kielly, Kiely

Keelyn (Irish) a form of Kellyn.
Kealyn, Keelin, Keilan, Kielyn

Keena (Irish) brave.
Keenya, Kina

Keesha (American) a form of Keisha.
Keesa, Keeshae, Keeshana, Keeshanne, Keeshawna, Keeshonna, Keeshya, Keiosha

Kei (Japanese) reverent.

Keiana, Keianna (Irish) forms of Keana. (American) forms of Kiana.
Keiann, Keiannah, Keionna

Keiki (Hawaiian) child.
Keikana, Keikann, Keikanna, Keikanne

Keiko (Japanese) happy child.

Keila (Arabic, Hebrew) a form of Kayla.
Keilah, Kela, Kelah

Keilani (Hawaiian) glorious chief.
Kaylani, Keilan, Keilana, Keilany, Kelana, Kelanah, Kelane, Kelani, Kelanie

Keira (Irish) a form of Keara.
Keiara, Keiarra, Keirra, Keirrah, Kera, Keyeira

Keisha (American) a short form of Keneisha.
Keasha, Keashia, Keesha, Keishaun, Keishauna, Keishawn, Kesha, Keysha, Kiesha, Kisha, Kishanda

Keita (Scottish) woods; enclosed place.
Keiti

Kekona (Hawaiian) second-born child.

Kelcey, Kelci, Kelcie (Scottish) forms of Kelsey.
Kelse, Kelcee, Kelcy

Kelila (Hebrew) crown, laurel. See also Kaela, Kayla, Kalila.
Kelilah, Kelula

Kelley (Irish) a form of Kelly.

Kelli, Kellie (Irish) familiar forms of Kelly.
Keleigh, Keli, Kelia, Keliah, Kelie, Kellee, Kelleigh, Kellia, Kellisa

Kelly (Irish) brave warrior. See also Caeley.
Keeley, Keely, Kelley, Kelli, Kellie, Kellye

Kellyanne (Irish) a combination of Kelly + Anne.
Kelliann, Kellianne, Kellyann

Kellyn (Irish) a combination of Kelly + Lyn.
Keelyn, Kelleen, Kellen, Kellene, Kellina, Kelline, Kellynn, Kellynne

Kelsea (Scottish) a form of Kelsey.
Kelcea, Keltia, Kelsa, Kelsae, Kelsay, Kelse

Kelsey (Scandinavian, Scottish) ship island. (English) a form of Chelsea.
Kelcey, Kelda, Kellsee, Kellsei, Kellsey, Kellsie, Kellsy, Kelsea, Kelsei, Kelsey, Kelsi, Kelsy, Kelsye

Kelsi, Kelsie, Kelsy (Scottish) forms of Chelsea.
Kalsie, Kelti, Keltie, Kellsi

Kenda (English) water baby. (Dakota) magical power.
Keandra, Kendra, Kennda

Kendal (English) a form of Kendall.
Kendahl, Kendale, Kendalie, Kendalin, Kendalyn, Kendalynn, Kendel, Kendele, Kendil, Kindal

Kendall (English) ruler of the valley.
Kendal, Kendalla, Kendalle, Kendell, Kendelle, Kendera, Kendia, Kendyl, Kinda, Kindall, Kindi, Kindle, Kynda, Kyndal, Kyndall, Kyndel

Kendra (English) a form of Kenda.
Kandra, Kendrah, Kendre, Kendrea, Kendreah, Kendria, Kenndra, Kentra, Kentrae, Kindra, Kyndra

Kendyl (English) a form of Kendall.
Kendyle, Kendyll

Keneisha (American) a combination of the prefix Ken + Aisha.
Kaneisha, Keisha, Keneesha, Kenesha, Keneshia, Kenisha, Kenneisha, Kennesha, Kenneshia, Keosha, Kineisha

Kenenza (English) a form of Kennice.
Kenza

Kenia (Hebrew) a form of Kenya.
Keniya, Kennia

Kenisha (American) a form of Keneisha.
Kenisa, Kenise, Kenishia, Kenissa, Kennisa, Kennisha, Kennysha

Kenna (Irish) a short form of Kennice.

Kennedy (Irish) helmeted chief. History: John F. Kennedy was the thirty-fifth U.S. president.
Kenedee, Kenedey, Kenedi, Kenedie, Kenedy, Kenidee, Kenidi, Kenidie, Kenidy, Kennadee, Kennadi, Kennadie, Kennedey, Kennedee, Kennedey, Kennedi, Kennedie, Kennidee, Kennidi, Kennidy, Kynnedi

Kennice (English) beautiful.
Kanice, Keneese, Kenenza, Kenese, Kennise

Kenya (Hebrew) animal horn. Geography: a country in Africa.
Keenya, Kenia, Kenja, Kenyah, Kenyana, Kenyatta, Kenyia

Kenyatta (American) a form of Kenya.
Kenyata, Kenyatah, Kenyatte, Kenyattia, Kenyatta, Kenyette

Kenzie (Scottish) light skinned. (Irish) a short form of Mackenzie.
Kenzea, Kenzee, Kenzey, Kenzi, Kenzia, Kenzy, Kinzie

Keona, Keonna (Irish) forms of Keana.
Keiona, Keionna, Keoana, Keoni, Keonia, Keonnah, Keonni, Keonnia

Keosha (American) a short form of Keneisha.
Keoshae, Keoshi, Keoshia, Keosia

Kerani (Hindi) sacred bells. See also Rani.
Kera, Kerah, Keran, Kerana

Kerensa (Cornish) a form of Karenza.
Karensa, Karenza, Kerenza

Keri, Kerri, Kerrie (Irish) forms of Kerry.
Keriann, Kerianne, Keriann, Kerrianne

Kerry (Irish) dark haired. Geography: a county in Ireland.
Keary, Keriy, Keree, Kerey, Keri, Kerri, Kerrie, Kerryann, Kerryanne, Kery, Kiera, Kiera

Kerstin (Scandinavian) a form of Kirsten.
Kerstan, Kerste, Kerstein, Kersten, Kerstie, Kerstien, Kerston, Kerstyn, Kerstynn

Kesare (Latin) long haired. (Russian) a form of Caesar (see Boys' Names).

Kesha (American) a form of Keisha.
Keshah, Keshal, Keshala, Keshan, Keshana, Keshara, Keshawn, Keshawna, Keshawnna

Keshia (American) a form of Keisha. A short form of Keneisha.
Kecia, Keishia, Keschia, Keshea, Kesia, Kesiah, Kessia, Kessiah

Kesi (Swahili) born during difficult times.

Kessie (Ashanti) chubby baby.
Kess, Kessa, Kesse, Kessey, Kessi

Kevyn (Irish) beautiful.
Keva, Kevan, Keven, Kevia, Keviana, Kevinna, Kevion, Kevion, Kevionna, Kevon, Kevona, Kevone, Kevonia, Kevonne, Kevonya, Kevynn

Keyana, Keyanna (American) forms of Kiana.
Keya, Keyanah, Keyanda, Keyannah

Keyara (Irish) a form of Kiara.
Keyarah, Keyari, Keyara, Keyera, Keyerah, Keyerra

Keyona, Keyonna (American) forms of Kiana.
Keyonda, Keyondra, Keyonnia, Keyonnie

Keysha (American) a form of Keisha.
Keyosha, Keyoshia, Keyshana, Keyshanna, Keyshawn, Keyshawna, Keyshia, Keyshla, Keyshona, Keyshonna

Keziah (Hebrew) cinnamon-like spice. Bible: one of the daughters of Job.
Kazia, Kaziah, Keizi, Keizia, Keiziah, Kezi, Kezia, Kizzy

Khadijah (Arabic) trustworthy. History: Muhammed's first wife.
Khadija, Khadijah, Khadeja, Khadeejah, Khadeja, Khadejah, Khadejha, Khadija, Khadije, Khadjia, Khadjiah

Khalida (Arabic) immortal, everlasting.
Khali, Khalia, Khaliah, Khalidda, Khalita

Khrissa (American) a form of Chrissa. (Czech) a form of Krista.
Khrishia, Khryssa, Krisha, Krisia, Krissa, Krysha, Kryssa

Khristina (Russian, Scandinavian) a form of Kristina, Christina.
Khristeen, Khristen, Khristin, Khristine, Khyristya, Khristyana, Khristyna, Khrystyne

Ki (Korean) arisen.

Kia (African) season's beginning. (American) a short form of Kiana.
Kiah

Kiana (American) a combination of the prefix Ki + Ana.
Keana, Keiana, Keyana, Keyona, Khiana, Khianah, Khianna, Ki, Kiahna, Kiane, Kiani, Kiania, Kianna, Kiauna, Kiandra, Kiandria, Kiauna, Kiaundra, Kiyana, Kyana

Kianna (American) a form of Kiana.
Kiannah, Kianne, Kianni

Kiara (Irish) little and dark.
Keyara, Kiarra, Kieara, Kiearah, Kiearra, Kyara

Kiaria, Kiarra, Kichi (Japanese) fortunate.

Kiele (Hawaiian) gardenia; fragrant blossom.
Kiela, Kieley, Kieli, Kielli, Kielly

Kiera, Kierra (Irish) forms of Kerry.
Kierana, Kieranna, Kierea

Kiersten, Kierstin (Scandinavian) forms of Kirsten.
Keirstan, Kerstin, Kierstan, Kierston, Kierstyn, Kierstynn

Kiki (Spanish) a familiar form of names ending in "queta."

Kiku (Japanese) chrysanthemum.
Kiko

Kiley (Irish) attractive; from the straits.
Kilea, Kilee, Kileigh, Kili, Kilie, Kylee, Kyli, Kylie

Kim (Vietnamese) needle. (English) a short form of Kimberly.
Kima, Kimette, Kym

Kimana (Shoshone) butterfly.
Kiman, Kimani

Kimber (English) a short form of Kimberly.
Kimbra

Kimberlee, Kimberley (English) forms of Kimberly.
Kimbalee, Kimberlea, Kimberlei, Kimberleigh, Kimbley

Kimberly (English) chief, ruler.
Cymberly, Cymbre, Kim, Kimba, Kimbely, Kimber, Kimbereley, Kimberely, Kimberlee, Kimberli, Kimberlie, Kimberlyn, Kimbery, Kimbria, Kimbrie, Kimbry, Kimmie, Kymberly

Kimberlyn (English) a form of Kimberly.
Kimberlin, Kimberlynn

Kimi (Japanese) righteous.
Kimia, Kimika, Kimiko, Kimiyo, Kimmi, Kimmie, Kimmy

Kimmie (English) a familiar form of Kimberly.
Kimee, Kimmie, Kimmee, Kimmi, Kimmy, Kimy

Kina (Hawaiian) from China.

Kineisha (American) a form of Keneisha.
Kineesha, Kinesha, Kineshia, Kinisha, Kinishia

Kineta (Greek) energetic.
Kinetta

Kini (Hawaiian) a form of Jean.
Kina

Kinsey (English) offspring; relative.
Kinsee, Kinsley, Kinza, Kinze, Kinzee, Kinzey, Kinzi, Kinzie, Kinzy

Kinsley (American) a form of Kinsey.
Kinslee, Kinslie, Kinslyn

Kioko (Japanese) happy child.
Kiyo, Kiyoko

Kiona (Native American) brown hills.
Kionah, Kioni, Kionna

Kira (Persian) sun. (Latin) light.
Kirah, Kiri, Kiria, Kiro, Kirra, Kirrah, Kirri

Kiran (Hindi) ray of light.

Kirby (Scandinavian) church village. (English) cottage by the water.
Kirbee, Kirbi

Kirima (Eskimo) hill.

Kirsi (Hindi) amaranth blossoms.
Kirsie

Kirsta (Scandinavian) a form of Kirsten.

Kirsten (Greek) Christian; anointed. (Scandinavian) a form of Christine. *Karsten, Kearsten, Keirstan, Kerstin, Kiersten, Kirsteni, Kirsta, Kirstan, Kirstene, Kirstie, Kirstin, Kirston, Kirsty, Kirstyn, Kjersten, Kursten, Kyersten, Kyrsten, Kyrstin*

Kirstin (Scandinavian) a form of Kirsten. *Karstin, Kirsteen, Kirstien, Kirstien, Kirstine*

Kirstie, Kirsty (Scandinavian) familiar forms of Kirsten. *Kerstie, Kirsta, Kirstie, Kirstee, Kirstey, Kirsti, Kjersti, Kyrsty*

Kirstyn (Greek) a form of Kirsten. *Kirstynn*

Kisa (Russian) kitten. *Kisha, Kiska, Kissa, Kiza*

Kishi (Japanese) long and happy life.

Kissa (Ugandan) born after twins.

Kita (Japanese) north.

Kitra (Hebrew) crowned.

Kitty (Greek) a familiar form of Katherine. *Ketter, Ketti, Ketty, Kit, Kittee, Kitteen, Kittey, Kitti, Kittie*

Kiwa (Japanese) borderline.

Kiyana (American) a form of Kiana. *Kiya, Kiyah, Kiyan, Kiyani, Kiyanna, Kiyenna*

Kizzy (American) a familiar form of Keziah. *Kezi, Kissie, Kizzi, Kizzie*

Klara (Hungarian) a form of Clara. *Klára, Klari, Klarika*

Klarise (German) a form of Klarissa. *Klarice, Kläris, Klarye*

Klarissa (German) clear, bright. (Italian) a form of Clarissa. *Klarisa, Klarise, Klarisa, Klarissa, Klarrissia, Klarrisza, Klarysa, Klaryssa, Kleresa*

Klaudia (American) a form of Claudia. *Klaudija*

Kloe (American) a form of Chloe. *Khloe, Kloee, Kloey, Klohe, Kloie*

Kodi (American) a form of Codi. *Kodee, Kodey, Kodie, Kody, Kodye, Koedi*

Koffi (Swahili) born on Friday. *Kaffe, Kaffi, Koffe, Koffie*

Koko (Japanese) stork. See also Coco.

Kolby (American) a form of Colby. *Kobie, Koby, Kolbee, Kolbey, Kolbi, Kolbie*

Kolina (Swedish) a form of Katherine. See also Colleen. *Koleen, Kolena, Kolene, Koli, Koleen, Kollena, Kollene, Kolyn, Kolyna*

Kona (Hawaiian) lady; (Hindi) angular. *Kori, Konia*

Konstance (Latin) a form of Constance. *Konstantina, Konstantine, Konstanza, Konstanze*

Kora (Greek) a form of Cora. *Korah, Kore, Koren, Koressa, Koretta, Korra*

Koral (American) a form of Coral. *Korel, Korele, Korella, Korilla, Koral, Korrel, Korrell, Korrelle*

Kori (American) a short form of Korina. See also Corey, Cori. *Koree, Korey, Koria, Korie, Kori, Korrie, Korry, Kory*

Korina (Greek) a form of Corina. *Koreena, Korena, Koriana, Korianna, Korine, Koritina, Korreena, Korrina, Koryna, Koryna*

Korine (Greek) a form of Korina. *Koreen, Korene, Koriane, Korianne, Korin, Korinn, Korinne, Korrin, Korrine, Korrine, Korryn, Korrynne, Koryn, Koryne, Korynn*

Kornelia (Latin) a form of Cornelia. *Karniella, Karniella, Karnis, Kornelija, Kornelis, Kornelya, Korny*

Kortney (English) a form of Courtney. *Kortnay, Kortnee, Kortni, Kortnie, Kortny*

Kosma (Greek) order; universe. *Cosma*

Kosta (Latin) a short form of Constance. *Kostia, Kostusha, Kostya*

Koto (Japanese) harp.

Kourtney (American) a form of Courtney.
Kourtnay, Kourtne, Kourtnee, Kourtnei, Kourtneigh, Kourtni, Kourtny, Kourtynie

Kris (American) a short form of Kristine. A form of Chris.
Khris, Krissy

Krissy (American) a familiar form of Kris.
Krissey, Krissi, Krissie

Krista (Czech) a form of Christina. See also Christa.
Khrista, Khrista, Khryssa, Khrysta, Krissa, Kryssa, Krysta

Kristal (Latin) a form of Crystal.
Kristale, Kristall, Kristill, Kristl, Kristle, Kristy

Kristan (Greek) a form of Kristen.
Kristana, Kristanna, Kristanne, Kriston, Krystan, Krystane

Kristen (Greek) Christian; anointed. (Scandinavian) a form of Christine.
Christen, Kristan, Kristene, Kristien, Kristin, Kristyn, Krysten

Kristi, Kristie (Scandinavian) short forms of Kristine.
Christi

Kristian, Kristiana (Greek) Christian; anointed. Forms of Christian.
Khristian, Kristian, Kristiane, Kristiann, Kristi-Ann, Kristianna, Kristianne, Kristi-Anne, Kristienne, Kristyan, Kristyana, Kristy-Ann, Kristy-Anne

Kristin (Scandinavian) a form of Kristen. See also Cristen.
Kristin, Krystin

Kristina (Greek) Christian; annointed. (Scandinavian) a form of Christina. See also Cristina.
Khristina, Kristena, Kristina, Kristeena, Kristena, Kristinka, Krystina

Kristine (Scandinavian) a form of Christine.
Kris, Kristeen, Kristene, Kristi, Kristie, Kristy, Krystine, Krystyne

Kristy (American) a familiar form of Kristine, Krystal. See also Cristy.
Kristi, Kristia, Kristie, Krysia, Krysti

Kristyn (Greek) a form of Kristen.
Kristyne, Kristynn

Krysta (Polish) a form of Krista.
Krystah, Krystka

Krystal (American) clear, brilliant glass.
Kristabel, Kristal, Krystalann, Krystalanne, Krystale, Krystall, Krystalle, Krystel, Krystil, Krystle, Krystol

Krystalee (American) a combination of Krystal + Lee.
Kristalea, Kristaleah, Kristalee, Krystalea, Krystaleah, Krystlea, Krystleah, Krystlee, Krystelea, Krystleleah, Krystelee

Krystalynn (American) a combination of Krystal + Lynn.
Kristaline, Kristalyn, Kristalynn, Kristaline, Kristalynn, Kristilyn, Kristlyn, Krystaleen, Krystalene, Krystalin, Krystalina, Krystallyn, Krystalyn, Krystalynne

Krystel (Latin) a form of Krystal.
Kristel, Kristell, Kristelle, Krystelle

Krysten (Greek) a form of Kristen.
Krystene, Krystyn, Krystyne

Krystian, Krystiana (Greek) forms of Christian.
Krystiana, Krystianna, Krystianne, Krysty-Ann, Krystyan, Kristyana, Krystyanna, Krystyanne, Krysty-Anne, Krystyen

Krystin (Czech) a form of Kristin.

Krystina (Greek) a form of Kristina.
Krysteena, Krystena, Krystyna, Krystynka

Krystle (American) a form of Krystal.
Krystl, Krystyl

Kudio (Swahili) born on Monday.

Kuma (Japanese) bear. (Tongan) mouse.

Kumiko (Japanese) girl with braids.
Kumi

Kumuda (Sanskrit) lotus flower.

Kuniko (Japanese) child from the country.

Kunto (Twi) third-born.

Kuri (Japanese) chestnut.

Kusa (Hindi) God's grass.

Kwanita (Zuni) a form of Juanita.

Kwashi (Swahili) born on Sunday.

Kwau (Swahili) born on Thursday.

Kyana (American) a form of Kiana.
Kyanah, Kyani, Kyann, Kyanna, Kyanne, Kyanni, Kyeanna, Kyeanna

Kyara (Irish) a form of Kiara.
Kyanna, Kyera, Kyerra, Kyarah, Kyaria, Kyarre, Kyarra, Kyera, Kyerra

Kyla (Irish) attractive. (Yiddish) crown; laurel.
Khyla, Kylah, Kylea, Kyleah, Kylia

Kyle (Irish) attractive.
Kial, Kiele, Kylee, Kyleigh, Kylene, Kylie

Kylee (Irish) a familiar form of Kyle.
Kylea, Kyleah, Kylie, Kyliee

Kyleigh (Irish) a form of Kyle.
Kyliegh

Kylene (Irish) a form of Kyle.
Kyleen, Kylen, Kylyn, Kylynn

Kylie (West Australian Aboriginal) curled stick; boomerang. (Irish) a familiar form of Kyle.
Keiley, Keilley, Keily, Keily, Kiley, Kye, Kyle, Kyley, Kyli, Kyllie

Kymberly (English) a form of Kimberly.
Kymber, Kymberlee, Kymberleigh, Kymberley, Kymberli, Kymberlie, Kymberlyn, Kymberlynn, Kymberlynne

Kyndal, Kyndall (English) forms of Kendall.
Kyndahl, Kyndalle, Kyndel, Kyndell, Kyndelle, Kyndle, Kyndol

Kynthia (Greek) a form of Cynthia.
Kyndi

Kyoko (Japanese) mirror.

Kyra (Greek) ladylike. A form of Cyrilla.
Keera, Keira, Kira, Kyrah, Kyrene, Kyria, Kyriah, Kyriann, Kyrie

L

Lacey, Lacy (Latin) cheerful. (Greek) familiar forms of Larissa.
Lacee, Laci, Lacie, Laye

Lachandra (American) a combination of the prefix La + Chandra.
Lachanda, Lachandice

Laci, Lacie (Latin) forms of Lacey.
Lacia, Laciann, Lacianne

Lacrecia (Latin) a form of Lucretia.
Lacrasha, Lacreash, Lacreasha, Lacreashia, Lacreisha, Lacresha, Lacreshia, Lacresia, Lacretia, Lacriticia, Lacreisha, Lacresia, Lacrisha, Lacrishia, Larissa

Lada (Russian) Mythology: the Slavic goddess of beauty.

Ladasha (American) a combination of the prefix La + Dasha.
Ladaesha, Ladaisa, Ladaisha, Ladaishea, Ladaishia, Ladaishiah, Ladashea, Ladashia, Ladasia, Ladassa, Ladaysha, Ladesha, Ladisha, Ladosha

Ladeidra (American) a combination of the prefix La + Deidra.
Ladedra, Ladiedra

Ladonna (American) a combination of the prefix La + Donna.
Ladan, Ladana, Ladon, Ladona, Ladonne, Ladonya

Laela (Arabic, Hebrew) a form of Leila.
Lael, Laele

Lahela (Hawaiian) a form of Rachel.

Laila (Arabic) a form of Leila.
Lailah, Laili, Lailie

Laine, Layne (French) short forms of Elaine.
Lain, Laina, Lainah, Lainee, Lainna, Layna

Lainey, Layney (French) familiar forms of Elaine.
Laini, Lainie, Laynee, Layni, Laynie

Lajila (Hindi) shy, coy.

Lajuana (American) a combination of the prefix La + Juana.
Lajianna, Lawana, Lawanza, Lawanze, Lawania

Laka (Hawaiian) attractive; seductive; tame. Mythology: the goddess of the hula.

Lakayla (American) a combination of the prefix La + Kayla.
Lakala, Lakaya, Lakeila, Lakela, Lakella

Lakeisha (American) a combination of the prefix La + Keisha. See also Lekasha.
Lakaesha, Lakaisha, Lakashia, Lakaysha, Lakaysia, Lakeasha, Lakecia, Lakeesh, Lakeesha, Lakeeshia, Lakesha, Lakeshia, Lakeysha, Lakeeshia, Lakezia, Lakicia, Lakieshia, Lakisha

Laken, Lakin, Lakyn (American) short forms of Lakendra.
Lakena, Lakyna, Lakynn

Lakendra (American) a combination of the prefix La + Kendra.
Lakanda, Lakedra, Laken, Lakenda

Lakenya (American) a combination of the prefix La + Kenya.
Lakeena, Lakeenna, Lakeenya, Lakena, Lakenia, Lakinja, Lakinya, Lakwanya, Lekenia, Lekenya

Lakesha, Lakeshia, Lakisha (American) forms of Lakeisha.
Lakecia, Lakeesha, Lakesa, Lakese, Lakesia, Lakeshya, Lakesi, Lakesia, Lakeyshia, Lakiesha

Laketa (American) a combination of the prefix La + Keita.
Lakeeta, Lakeetah, Lakeita, Lakeitha, Lakeithia, Laketha, Laketia, Laketta, Lakieta, Lakietha, Lakita, Lakitia, Lakitra, Lakitri, Lakitta

Lakia (Arabic) found treasure.
Lakiea, Lakkia

Lakota (Dakota) a tribal name.
Lakoda, Lakohta, Lakotah

Lakresha (American) a form of Lucretia.
Lacresha, Lacreshia, Lacresia, Lacretia, Lacrisha, Lakreshia, Lakrisha, Lekresha, Lekresia

Lakya (Hindi) born on Thursday.
Lakeya, Lakeyah, Lakieya, Lakiya, Lakyia

Lala (Slavic) tulip.
Lalah, Lalla

Lalasa (Hindi) love.

Laleh (Persian) tulip.
Lalah

Lali (Spanish) a form of Lulani.
Lalia, Lalli, Lally

Lalita (Greek) talkative. (Sanskrit) charming; candid.

Lallie (English) babbler.
Lalli, Lally

Lamesha (American) a combination of the prefix La + Mesha.
Lamees, Lameesha, Lameise, Lameisha, Lameshia, Lamisha, Lamishia, Lemisha

Lamia (German) bright land.
Lama, Lamiah

Lamis (Arabic) soft to the touch.
Lamese, Lamise

Lamonica (American) a combination of the prefix La + Monica.
Lamoni, Lamonika

Lamya (Arabic) dark lipped.
Lama

Lan (Vietnamese) flower.

Lana (Latin) woolly. (Irish) attractive, peaceful. A short form of Alana, Elana. (Hawaiian) floating; buoyant.
Lanae, Lanai, Lanata, Lanay, Laneah, Laneetra, Lanette, Lanna, Lannah

Landa (Basque) another name for the Virgin Mary.

Landon (English) open, grassy meadow.
Landan, Landen, Landin, Landyn, Landynne

Landra (German, Spanish) counselor.
Landrea

Lane (English) narrow road.
Laina, Laney, Layne

Laneisha (American) a combination of the prefix La + Keneisha.
Laneasha, Lanecia, Laneesha, Laneise, Laneishia, Lanesha, Laneshe, Laneshea, Laneshia, Lanesia, Lanessa, Lanesse, Lanisha, Lanishia

Laney (English) a familiar form of Lane.
Lanie, Lanni, Lanny, Lany

Lani (Hawaiian) sky; heaven. A short form of Atalanta, 'Aulani, Leilani.
Lanee, Lanei, Lania, Lanie, Lanita, Lanney, Lanni, Lannie

Laporsha (American) a combination of the prefix La + Porsha.
Laporcha, Laporche, Laporscha, Laporsche, Laporschia, Laporshe, Laporshia, Laportia

Laqueena (American) a combination of the prefix La + Queenie.
Laqueen, Laquena, Laquenetta, Laquinna

Laquinta (American) a combination of the prefix La + Quintana.
Laquanta, Laquenta, Laquenda, Laquineta, Laquinta, Laquinda

Laquisha (American) a combination of the prefix La + Queisha.
Laquasha, Laquaysha, Laqueisha, Laquesha, Laquiesha

Laquita (American) a combination of the prefix La + Queta.
Laqeita, Laqueta, Laquetta, Laquia, Laquiata, Laquieta, Laquitta, Lequita

Lara (Greek) cheerful. (Latin) shining; famous. Mythology: a Roman nymph. A short form of Laraine, Larissa, Laura. *Larae, Larah, Laretta, Larette*

Laraine (Latin) a form of Lorraine. *Lara, Laraene, Larain, Larane, Larayn, Larayne, Laraynna, Larein, Lareina, Lareine, Laren, Larenn, Larenya, Larraine, Laurraine*

Larina (Greek) seagull. *Larena, Larine*

Larisa (Greek) a form of Larissa. *Lareesa, Lareese, Laresa, Laris, Larise, Larisha, Larrisa, Larysa, Laurisa*

Larissa (Greek) cheerful. See also Lacey, Laura, Laressa, Larisa, Larissah, Larrissa, Larryssa, Larysa, Laurissa

Lark (English) skylark.

Lashae, Lashay (American) combinations of the prefix La + Shay. *Lasha, Lashai, Lashata, Lashaya, Lashaye, Lashea*

Lashana (American) a combination of the prefix La + Shana. *Lashanay, Lashane, Lashanna, Lashannon, Lashona, Lashonna*

Lashanda (American) a combination of the prefix La + Shanda. *Lashandra, Lashanta, Lashante*

Lashawna (American) a combination of the prefix La + Shawna. *Lashaun, Lashauna, Lashaune, Lashaunna, Lashaunta, Lashaunte, Lashaund, Lashawnda, Lashawn, Lashawne, Lashawnda, Lashawnia, Leshawn, Leshawna*

Lashonda (American) a combination of the prefix La + Shonda. *Lachonda, Lashaunda, Lashaundra, Lashon, Lashond, Lashonde, Lashondia, Lashondra, Lashonta, Lashunda, Lashunte, Leshande, Leshondra, Leshundra*

Latanya (American) a combination of the prefix La + Tanya. *Latana, Latandra, Latania, Latanja, Latanna, Latanna, Latonsha*

Latara (American) a combination of the prefix La + Tara.

Latasha (American) a combination of the prefix La + Tasha. *Latacha, Lataica, Latai, Lataisha, Latashia, Latasia, Lataysha, Letasha, Letashia, Letasiah*

Latavia (American) a combination of the prefix La + Tavia.

Lateefah (Arabic) pleasant. (Hebrew) pat, caress. *Lateefa, Latifa, Latifah, Latipha*

Latesha (American) a form of Leticia. *Lataeasha, Lateasha, Lateashia, Lateicia, Lateicia, Lateisha, Lateshia, Latesa, Lateysha, Latisa, Latissa, Leteisha, Leteshia*

Latia (American) a combination of the prefix La + Tia. *Latea, Lateia, Latijah*

Latika (Hindi) elegant. *Lateeka, Lateka*

Latisha (Latin) joy. (American) a combination of the prefix La + Tisha. *Laetitia, Laeticia, Latashia, Lateashia,*

Latona (Latin) Mythology: the powerful goddess who bore Apollo and Diana. *Latonna, Latonnah*

Latonia (American) a combination of the prefix La + Tonya. (Latin) a form of Latona. *Latoni, Latonia*

Latonya (American) a combination of the prefix La + Tonya. *Lateashia, Latecia, Lateesha, Latecia, Lateisha, Latice, Laticia, Latisha, Latishya, Latissha, Latitia, Latysha*

Latoria (American) a combination of the prefix La + Tori. *Latoia, Latoiya, Latoja, Latornay, Latoreia, Latory, Latoya, Latoyra, Latoyia*

Latosha (American) a combination of the prefix La + Tosha. *Latoshia, Latoshya, Latosia*

Latoya (American) a combination of the prefix La + Toya. *Latoia, Latoiya, LaToya, Latoyia, Latoye, Latoyia, Latoyita, Latoyo*

Latrice (American) a combination of the prefix La + Trice. *Latrece, Latreece, Latresa, Latrese, Latressa, Letreece, Letrice*

Latricia (American) a combination of the prefix La + Tricia. *Latrecia, Latresha, Latreshia, Latrica, Latrisha, Latrishia*

Laura (Latin) crowned with laurel. *Lara, Laurah, Lauralee, Laurel, Laurella, Lauren, Lauricia, Laurie, Laurka, Laury, Lauryn, Lavra, Lolly Lora, Loretta, Lori, Lorinda, Lorna, Lowa*

Laurel (Latin) laurel tree.
Laural, Laurell, Laurelle, Lorel, Lorelle

Lauren (English) a form of Laura.
Lauran, Laureen, Laurena, Laurene, Laurien, Laurin, Laurine, Lauryen, Loren, Lorena

Laurence (Latin) crowned with laurel.
Laurencia, Laurens, Laurent, Laurentana, Laurentina, Lawrencia

Laurianna (English) a combination of Laurie + Anna.
Laurana, Laurann, Laureana, Laureanne, Laureen, Laureena, Laurian, Lauriana, Lauriane, Laurianna, Laurie Ann, Laurie Anne, Laurina

Laurie (English) a familiar form of Laura.
Lari, Larilia, Laure, Lauré, Lauri, Laurie

Laury (English) a familiar form of Laura.

Lauryn (English) a familiar form of Laura.
Laurynn

Laveda (Latin) cleansed, purified.
Lavare, Lavetta, Lavette

Lavelle (Latin) cleansing.
Lavella

Lavena (Irish, French) joy. (Latin) a form of Lavina.

Laverne (Latin) springtime. (French) grove of alder trees. See also Verna.
Laverine, Lavern, Laverna, La Verne

Lavina (Latin) purified; woman of Rome. See also Vina.
Lavena, Lavenia, Lavinia, Lavinie,

Levenia, Levinia, Livinia, Lowinia, Lovina, Lovinia

Lavonna (American) a combination of the prefix La + Yvonne.
Lavon, Lavonda, Lavonder, Lavondria, Lavone, Lavonia, Lavonica, Lavonn, Lavonne, Lavonnie, Lavonya

Lawan (Tai) pretty.
Lawanne

Lawanda (American) a combination of the prefix La + Wanda.
Lawonda, Lawynda

Layce (American) a form of Lacey.
Laycee, Layci, Laycia, Laycie, Laysa, Laysea, Laysie

Layla (Hebrew, Arabic) a form of Leila.
Laylah, Layli, Laylie

Le (Vietnamese) pearl.

Lea (Hawaiian) Mythology: the goddess of canoe makers. (Hebrew) a form of Leah.

Leah (Hebrew) weary. Bible: the first wife of Jacob. See also Lia.
Lea, Léa, Lee, Leea, Leeah, Leia

Leala (French) faithful, loyal.
Lealia, Lealie, Leial

Lean, Leann, Leanne (English) forms of Leeann, Lian.
Leana, Leane, Leanna

Leandra (Latin) like a lioness.
Leanda, Leandre, Leandrea, Leandria, Leeandra, Leeandra

Leanna, Leeanna (English) forms of Liana.
Leana, Leeana, Leianna

Leanore (Greek) a form of Eleanor. (English) a form of Helen.
Leanora, Lenore

Lecia (Latin) a short form of Felecia.
Leasia, Leecia, Leesha, Leesia, Lesha, Leshia, Lesia

Leda (Greek) lady. Mythology: the queen of Sparta and the mother of Helen of Troy.
Ledah, Lyda, Lydah

Lee (Chinese) plum. (Irish) poetc. (English) meadow. A short form of Ashley, Leah.
Lea, Leigh

Leeann, Leeanne (English) combinations of Lee + Ann. Forms of Lian.
Leane, Leean, Leian, Leiann, Leianne

Leena (Estonian) a form of Helen. (Greek, Latin, Arabic) a form of Lina.

Leeza (Hebrew) a short form of Aleeza. (English) a form of Lisa, Liza.
Leesa

Lei (Hawaiian) a familiar form of Leilani.

Leigh, Leigha (English) forms of Leah.
Leighanna, Leighanne, Leighanne

Leiko (Japanese) arrogant.

Leila (Hebrew) dark beauty; night. (Arabic) born at night. See also Laela, Layla, Lila.
Laila, Lela, Leela, Leelah, Leilah, Lelia, Lela, Lelah, Leland, Lelia, Leyla

Leilani (Hawaiian) heavenly flower; heavenly child.
Lailanee, Lailani, Lailanie, Lailany, Lailoni, Lani, Lei, Leilany, Leiloni, Leilony, Lelani, Lelania

Lekasha (American) a form of Lakeisha.
Lekeesha, Lekeisha, Lekesha, Lekeshia, Lekesia, Lekicia, Lekisha

Leli (Swiss) a form of Magdalen.
Lelie

Lelia (Greek) fair speech. (Hebrew, Arabic) a form of Leila.
Leliah, Lelika, Lelita, Lellia

Lelya (Russian) a form of Helen.

Lena (Hebrew) dwelling or lodging. (Latin) temptress. (Norwegian) illustrious. (Greek) a short form of Eleanor. Music: Lena Horne, a well-known African American singer and actress.
Lenah, Lene, Lenee, Leni, Lenka, Lenna, Lennah, Lina, Linah

Leneisha (American) a combination of the prefix Le + Keneisha.
Lenece, Lenesha, Lenietsha, Leniestia, Leniescia, Lenisia, Lenise, Lenisha, Lennise, Lenniisha, Lynesha

Lene (German) a form of Helen.
Leni, Line

Lenci (Hungarian) a form of Helen.
Lency

Lenia (German) a form of Leona.
Lenayah, Lenda, Lenea, Leneen, Lenna, Lennah, Lennea, Leny

Lenita (Latin) gentle.
Leneta, Lenette, Lennette

Lenore (Greek, Russian) a form of Eleanor.
Lenni, Lenor, Lenora, Lenorah

Leona (German) brave as a lioness. See also Lona.
Leoia, Leoine, Leola, Leolah, Leonae, Leonah, Leondra, Leone, Leonelle, Leonia, Leonice, Leonicia, Leonie, Leonissa, Leonna, Leonne, Liona

Leonie (German) a familiar form of Leticia.
Leoni, Léonie, Leony

Leontine (Latin) like a lioness.
Leona, Leonine, Leontyne, Léontyne

Leora (Hebrew) light. (Greek) a familiar form of Eleanor. See also Liora.
Leorah, Leorit

Leotie (Native American) prairie flower.

Lera (Russian) a short form of Valera.
Lerka

Lesley (Scottish) gray fortress.
Leslea, Leslee, Leslie, Lesly, Lezlee, Lezley

Leslie (Scottish) a form of Lesley.
Leslei, Lesleigh, Lesli, Lesslie, Lezli

Lesly (Scottish) a form of Lesley.
Leslye, Lessly, Lezly

Leta (Latin) glad. (Swahili) bringer. (Greek) a short form of Aleta.
Lita, Lyta

Leticia (Latin) joy. See also Latisha, Tisha.
Laticia, Leisha, Let, Leta, Letesa, Letesha, Leteshia, Letha, Lethia, Letice, Letichia, Letisha, Letishia, Letisia, Letissa, Letita, Letitia, Letiticia, Letiza, Letizia, Letty, Letycia, Loutitia

Letty (English) a familiar form of Leticia.
Letta, Letti, Lettie

Levana (Hebrew) moon; white. (Latin) risen. Mythology: the goddess of newborn babies.
Lévana, Levania, Levanna, Levenia, Levana, Livona

Levia (Hebrew) joined, attached.
Leevya, Levi, Levie

Levina (Latin) flash of lightning.
Levene

Levani (Fijian) anointed with oil.

Levona (Hebrew) spice; incense.
Leavonia, Levonat, Levonna, Levonne, Livona

Lewana (Hebrew) a form of Levana.
Lébhanah, Lewanna

Lexandra (Greek) a short form of Alexandra.
Lisandra

Lexi, Lexie (Greek) familiar forms of Alexandra.
Leksi, Lexey, Lexy

Lexia (Greek) a familiar form of Alexandra.
Leska, Lesya, Lexa, Lexane, Lexina, Lexine

Lexis (Greek) a short form of Alexius, Alexus.
Laexis, Lexius, Lexsis, Lexxis

Lexus (Greek) a short form of Alexis.
Lexuss, Lexxus, Lexyss

Leya (Spanish) loyal. (Tamil) the constellation Leo.
Leyah, Leyla

Lia (Greek) bringer of good news. (Hebrew, Dutch, Italian) dependent. See also Leah.
Liah

Lian (Chinese) graceful willow. (Latin) a short form of Gillian, Lillian.
Lean, Leeann, Liann, Liann, Lianne

Liane, Lianne (Hebrew) short forms of Eliane. (English) forms of Lian.
Leeanne

Libby (Hebrew) a familiar form of Elizabeth.
Ibby, Lib, Libbee, Libbey, Libbie

Liberty (Latin) free.
Liberti, Libertie

Licia (Greek) a short form of Alicia.
Licha, Lishia, Lisia, Lycia

Lida (Greek) happy. (Slavic) loved by people. (Latin) a short form of Alida, Elita.
Leeda, Lidah, Lidochka, Lyda

Lide (Latin, Basque) life.

Lidia (Greek) a form of Lydia.
Lidea, Lidi, Lidija, Lidiya, Lidka, Lidya

Lien (Chinese) lotus.
Lienne

Liesabet (German) a short form of Elizabeth.
Liesbeth, Lisbete

Liese (German) a familiar form of Elise, Elizabeth.
Liesa, Lieschen, Lise

Liesel (German) a familiar form of Elizabeth.
Leesel, Leesl, Leezel, Leezl, Liesl, Liezel, Liezl, Lisel

Lila (Arabic) night. (Hindi) free will of God. (Persian) lilac. A short form of Dalila, Delilah, Lillian.
Lilah, Lilia, Lyla, Lylah

Lilac (Sanskrit) lilac; blue purple.

Lilia (Persian) a form of Lila.
Lili

Lilian (Latin) a form of Lillian.
Liliane, Liliann, Lilianne

Liliana (Latin) a form of Lillian.
Lileana, Lilliana, Lilianna, Lilliana, Lillianna

Lilibeth (English) a combination of Lilly + Beth.
Lilibet, Lillibeth, Lillybeth, Lilybet, Lilybeth

Lilith (Arabic) of the night; night demon. Mythology: the first wife of Adam, according to ancient Jewish legends.
Lillis, Lily

Lillian (Latin) lily flower.
Lian, Lil, Lila, Lilas, Lileane, Lilia, Lilian, Liliana, Lilias, Lilitha, Lilja, Lilla, Lilli, Lillia, Lilliane, Lilliann, Lillianne, Lillyann, Lis, Liuka

Lillyann (English) a combination of Lilly + Ann. (Latin) a form of Lillian.
Lillyan, Lillyanne, Lily, Lilyan, Lilyana, Lilyann, Lilyanna, Lilyanne

Lily (Latin, Arabic) a familiar form of Lilith, Lillian, Lillyann.
Lil, Lile, Lili, Lilie, Lilijana, Lilika, Lilike, Liliosa, Lilium, Lilka, Lille, Lilli, Lillie, Lilly

Limber (Tiv) joyful.

Lin (Chinese) beautiful jade. (English) a form of Lynn.
Linh, Linn

Lina (Greek) light. (Arabic) tender. (Latin) a form of Lena.

Linda (Spanish) pretty.
Lind, Lindy, Linita, Lynda

Lindsay (English) a form of Lindsey.
Lindsi, Linsay, Lyndsay

Lindsey (English) linden tree island; camp near the stream.
Lind, Lindsea, Lindsee, Lindsi, Linsey, Lyndsey, Lynsey

Lindsi (American) a familiar form of Lindsay, Lindsey. Lindsie, Lindsy, Lindzee, Lindzey, Lindzy

Lindy (Spanish) a familiar form of Linda. Linde, Lindee, Lindey, Lindi, Lindie

Linette (Welsh) idol. (French) bird. Lanette, Linet, Linnet, Linnetta, Linnette, Lyannette, Lynette

Ling (Chinese) delicate, dainty.

Linnea (Scandinavian) lime tree. Botany: the national flower of Sweden. Lin, Linae, Linea, Linnae, Linnaea, Linneah, Lynea, Lynnea

Linsey (English) a form of Lindsey. Linsea, Linsee, Linsi, Linsie, Linsy, Linzee, Linzey, Linzi, Linzie, Linzy, Linzzi, Lynsey

Liolya (Russian) a form of Helen.

Liora (Hebrew) light. See also Leora.

Lirit (Hebrew) poetic; lyrical, musical.

Liron (Hebrew) my song. Leron, Lerone, Lirone

Lisa (Hebrew) consecrated to God. (English) a short form of Elizabeth. Leeza, Liesa, Liisa, Lise, Lisenka, Lisette, Liszka, Litsa, Lysa

Lisbeth (English) a short form of Elizabeth. Lisbet

Lise (German) a form of Lisa.

Lisette, Lissette (French) forms of Lisa, Liseta, Lisete, Liseth, Lisett, Lisetta, Lisettina, Lisset, Lissete, Lizet, Lizette, Lysette

Lisha (Arabic) darkness before midnight. (Hebrew) a short form of Alisha, Elisha, Ilisha. Lishe

Lissa (Greek) honey bee. A short form of Elissa, Elizabeth, Melissa, Millicent. Lyssa

Lissie (American) a familiar form of Allison, Elise, Elizabeth. Lissee, Lissey, Lissi, Lissy, Lissye

Lita (Latin) a familiar form of names ending in "lita." Leta, Litah, Litta

Litonya (Moquelumnan) darting hummingbird.

Liv (Latin) a short form of Livia, Olivia.

Livana (Hebrew) a form of Levana. Livna, Livnat

Livia (Hebrew) crown. A familiar form of Olivia. (Latin) olive. Levia, Liv, Livie, Livy, Livya, Livye

Liviya (Hebrew) brave lioness; royal crown. Leviya, Levya, Livya

Livona (Hebrew) a form of Levona.

Liz (English) a short form of Elizabeth. Lizz

Liza (American) a short form of Elizabeth. Leeza, Lizela, Lizka, Lyza

Lizabeta (Russian) a form of Elizabeth. Lizabelah, Lizaveta, Lizonka

Lizabeth (English) a short form of Elizabeth. Lisabet, Lisabeth, Lisabette, Lizabethe, Lizbet, Lizbett

Lizbeth (English) a short form of Elizabeth. Lizbet, Lizbett

Lizet, Lizette (French) forms of Lisette. Lizet, Lizete, Lizeth, Lizett, Lizzette

Lizina (Latvian) a familiar form of Elizabeth.

Lizzy (American) a familiar form of Elizabeth. Lizzie, Lizy

Logan (Irish) meadow. Logann, Loganne, Logen, Logenn, Loghan, Logun, Logyn, Logynn

Lois (German) famous warrior.

Lola (Spanish) a familiar form of Carlota, Dolores, Louise. Lolah, Lolita

Lolita (Spanish) sorrowful. A familiar form of Lola. Lila, Lulita

Lolly (English) sweet; candy. A familiar form of Laura.

Lolotea (Zuni) a form of Dorothy.

Lomasi (Native American) pretty flower.

Lona (Latin) lioness. (English) solitary. (German) a short form of Leona.
Loni, Lonna

London (English) fortress of the moon. Geography: the capital of the United Kingdom.
Landyn, Londen, Londun, Londyn

Loni (American) a form of Lona.
Lonee, Lonie, Lonni, Lonnie

Lora (Latin) crowned with laurel. (American) a form of Laura.
Lorah, Lorane, Lorann, Lorra, Lorrah, Lorrane

Lore (Basque) flower. (Latin) a short form of Flora.
Lor

Lorelei (German) alluring. Mythology: the siren of the Rhine River who lured sailors to their deaths. See also Lurleen.
Loralee, Loralei, Lorali, Loralie, Loralyn, Loreal, Lorelea, Loreli, Lorilee, Lorilyn

Lorelle (American) a form of Laurel.

Loren (American) a form of Lauren.
Loreen, Lorena, Lorin, Lorne, Lorren, Lorrin, Lorryn, Loryn, Lorynne

Lorena (English) a form of Lauren.
Lorene, Lorenea, Lorenia, Lorenna, Lorina, Lorrina, Lorrine, Lurana

Lorenza (Latin) a form of Laura.
Laurencia, Laurentia, Laurentina

Loretta (English) a familiar form of Laura.
Larretta, Lauretta, Laurette, Loretah, Lorette, Lorita, Lorretta, Lorrette

Lori (Latin) crowned with laurel. (French) a short form of Lorraine. (American) a familiar form of Laura.
Loree, Lorey, Loria, Lorianna, Lorianne, Lorie, Loree, Lorri, Lorrie, Lory

Lorin (American) a form of Loren.
Lorine

Lorinda (Spanish) a form of Laura.

Loris (Latin) thong. (Dutch) clown. (Greek) a short form of Chloris.
Laurice, Laurys, Lorice

Lorna (Latin) crowned with laurel. Literature: probably coined by Richard Blackmore in his novel *Lorna Doone*.
Lorna

Lorraine (Latin) sorrowful. (French) from Lorraine, a former province of France. See also Rayna.
Laraine, Lorain, Loraine, Lorayne, Lorein, Loreine, Lori, Lorine, Lorrain, Lorraina, Lorrayne, Lorreine

Lotte (German) a short form of Charlotte.
Lotie, Lotta, Lottchen, Lottey, Lottie, Loty, Loty

Lotus (Greek) lotus.

Lou (American) a short form of Louise, Luella.
Lu

Louam (Ethiopian) sleep well.

Louisa (English) a familiar form of Louise. Literature: Louisa May Alcott was an American writer and reformer best known for her novel *Little Women*.
Aloisa, Eloisa, Heloisa, Lou, Louisah, Louisane, Louisina, Louiza, Lovisa, Luisa, Luiza, Lujziza, Lujzika

Louise (German) famous warrior. See also Alison, Eloise, Heloise, Lois, Lola, Ludovica, Luella, Lulu.
Loise, Lou, Louisa, Louisette, Louisiane, Louisine, Louise, Loyce, Loyise, Luise

Lourdes (French) from Lourdes, France. Religion: a place where the Virgin Mary was said to have appeared.

Love (English) love, kindness, charity.
Lovely, Lovewell, Lovey, Lovie, Lovy, Lu, Luvy

Lovisa (German) a form of Louisa.

Luann (Hebrew, German) graceful woman warrior. (Hawaiian) happy, relaxed. (American) a combination of Louise + Ann.
Louann, Louanne, Lu, Lua, Luan, Luane, Luanna, Luanne, Luanni, Luannie

Luana (German) a form of Luann
Levanna, Louanna, Luana, Luwana

Lubov (Russian) love.
Luba, Lubna, Lubochka, Lyuba, Lyubov

Lucerne (Latin) lamp; circle of light. Geography: the Lake of Lucerne is in Switzerland.
Lucerna, Lucero

Lucero (Latin) a form of Lucerne. Lucy.

Lucetta (English) a familiar form of Lucy.
Lucette

Lucia (Italian, Spanish) a form of Lucy.
Luciana, Lucianna

Lucie (French) a familiar form of Lucy.

Lucille (English) a familiar form of Lucy.
Lucila, Lucile, Lucilla

Lucinda (Latin) a form of Lucy. See also Cindy.

Lucine (Arabic) moon. (Basque) a form of Lucy.
Lucienne, Lucina, Lucyna, Lukene, Lusine, Luzine

Lucita (Spanish) a form of Lucy.
Lusita

Lucretia (Latin) rich; rewarded.
Larecia, Loucrecia, Lucrece, Lucrecia, Lucreecia, Lucrecsha, Lucreshia, Lucrezia, Lucrishia

Lucrezia (Italian) a form of Lucretia.
History: Lucrezia Borgia was the Duchess of Ferrara and a patron of learning and the arts.

Lucy (Latin) light; bringer of light.
Luca, Luce, Lucetta, Luci, Lucia, Lucida, Lucie, Lucija, Lucika, Lucille, Lucinda, Lucine, Lucita, Luciya, Lucya, Lucza, Luzi

Ludmilla (Slavic) loved by the people. See also Mila.
Ludie, Ludka, Ludmila, Lyuba, Lyudmila

Ludovica (German) a form of Louise.
Ludovika, Ludwiga

Luella (English) elf. (German) a familiar form of Louise.
Loella, Lou, Louella, Ludella, Luelle, Lula, Lulu

Luisa (Spanish) a form of Louisa.

Lulani (Polynesian) highest point of heaven.

Lulu (Arabic) pearl. (English) soothing, comforting. (Native American) hare. (German) a familiar form of Louise, Luella.
Loulou, Lula, Lulie

Luna (Latin) moon.
Lunetta, Lunette, Lunnea, Lunnete

Lupe (Latin) wolf. (Spanish) a short form of Guadalupe.
Lupi, Lupita, Luppi

Lupita (Latin) a form of Lupe.

Lurleen, Lurlene (Scandinavian) war horn. (German) forms of Lorelei.
Lura, Lurette, Lurline

Lusa (Finnish) a form of Elizabeth.

Lusela (Moquelumnan) like a bear swinging its foot when licking it.

Luvena (Latin, English) little; beloved.
Lovena, Lovina, Luvenia, Luvina

Luyu (Moquelumnan) like a pecking bird.

Luz (Spanish) light. Religion: Nuestra Señora de Luz—Our Lady of the Light—is another name for the Virgin Mary.
Luzi, Luzija

Lycoris (Greek) twilight.

Lyda (Greek) a short form of Lidia, Lydia.

Lydia (Greek) from Lydia, an ancient land in Asia. (Arabic) strife.
Lidia, Lidija, Lidiya, Lyda, Lydie, Lydië

Lyla (French) island. (English) a form of Lyle (see Boys' Names). (Arabic, Hindi, Persian) a form of Lila.
Lila, Lilah

Lynda (Spanish) pretty. (American) a form of Linda.
Lyndah, Lynde, Lyndi, Lynnda

Lyndell (English) a form of Lynelle.
Lyndall, Lyndel, Lyndella

Lyndi (Spanish) a familiar form of Lynda.
Lyndee, Lindie, Lyndy, Lynndie, Lynndy

Lyndsey (English) linden tree island; camp near the stream. (American) a form of Lindsey.
Lyndsea, Lyndsee, Lyndsi, Lyndsie, Lyndsy, Lyndzee, Lyndzey, Lyndzi, Lyndzie, Lyndzie

Lyndsay (American) a form of Lindsay.
Lyndsaye

Lynelle (English) pretty.
Linel, Linell, Linnell, Lynell, Lynel, Lynela, Lynell

Lynette (Welsh) idol. (English) a form of Linette.
Lynet, Lynetta, Lynnet, Lynnete

Lynn, Lynne (English) waterfall; pool below a waterfall.
Lin, Lina, Linley, Linn, Lyn, Lynlee, Lynley, Lynna, Lynnae, Lynnea

Lynnell (English) a form of Lynelle.
Linnell, Lynnelle

Lynsey (American) a form of Lyndsey.
Lynnsey, Lynnzey, Lynsie, Lynsy, Lynzee, Lynzey, Lynzi, Lynzie, Lynzy

Lyra (Greek) lyre player.
Lyre, Lyric, Lyrica, Lyrie, Lyris

Lysandra (Greek) liberator.
Lisandra, Lysandre, Lytle

Lysanne (American) a combination of Lysandra + Anne.
Lisanne, Lizanne

Mab (Irish) joyous. (Welsh) baby. Literature: queen of the fairies.
Mabry

Mabel (Latin) lovable. A short form of Amabel.
Mabelle, Mable, Mabyn, Maible, Maybel, Maybeline, Maybelle, Maybull

Macawi (Dakota) generous; motherly.

Macayla (American) a form of Michaela.
Macaela, Macaila, Macala, Macalah, Macaylah, Macayle, Macayli, Mackayla

Macey, Macie, Macy (Polish) familiar forms of Macia.
Macee, Maci, Macye

Machaela (Hebrew) a form of Michaela.
Machael, Machaelah, Machaelie, Machaila, Machala, Macheala

Machiko (Japanese) fortunate child.
Machi

Macia (Polish) a form of Miriam.
Macelia, Macey, Machia, Macie, Macy, Masha, Mashia

Mackenna (American) a form of Mackenzie.
Mackena, Makenna, Mckenna

Mackenzie (Irish) child of the wise leader. See also Kenzie.
Macenzie, Mackenna, Mackensi, Mackensie, Mackenze, Mackenzee, Mackenzi, Mackenzia, Mackenzy, Mackenzye, Mackinsey, Mackynze, Makenzie, McKenzie, Mckinzie, Mekenzie, Mykenzie

Mackinsey (Irish) a form of Mackenzie.
Mackinsie, Mackinze, Mackinzee, Mackinzey, Mackinzi, Mackinzie

Mada (English) a short form of Madaline, Magdalen.
Madda, Mahda

Madaline (English) a form of Madeline.
Mada, Madailein, Madaleen, Madaline, Madalene, Madalin, Madaline

Madalyn (Greek) a form of Madeline.
Madalyne, Madalynn, Madalynne

Maddie (English) a familiar form of Madeline.
Maddi, Maddy, Mady, Maidie, Maydey

Maddison (English) a form of Madison.
Maddisan, Maddisen, Maddisson, Maddisyn, Maddyson

Madelaine (French) a form of Madeline.
Madelane, Madelayne

Madeleine (French) a form of Madeline.
Madalaine, Madalayne, Madeleine, Madelein, Madeliene

Madelena (English) a form of Madeline.
Madalaina, Madalena, Madalina, Madalena, Madaleina, Madelaina, Madelyna

Madeline (Greek) high tower. See also Lena, Lina, Maud.
Madaline, Madalyn, Maddie, Madel, Madeline, Madelene, Madelena, Madelene, Madelia, Madella, Madelle, Madelon, Madelyn, Madge, Madilyn, Madlen, Madlin, Madline, Madlyn, Madolyn, Maida

Madelyn (Greek) a form of Madeline.
Madelyne, Madelynn, Madelynne, Madilyn, Madlyn, Madolyn

Madge (Greek) a familiar form of Madeline, Margaret.
Madgi, Madgie, Mady

Madilyn (Greek) a form of Madeline.
Madilen, Madiline, Madilyne, Madilynn

Madisen (English) a form of Madison. *Madisan, Madisin, Madissen, Madisun*

Madison (English) good; child of Maud. *Maddison, Madisen, Madisson, Madisyn, Madyson, Mattison*

Madisyn (English) a form of Madison. *Madisyyn, Madisynn, Madisynne*

Madolyn (Greek) a form of Madeline. *Madoline, Madolyne, Madolynn, Madolynne*

Madonna (Latin) my lady. *Madona*

Madrona (Spanish) mother. *Madre, Madrena*

Madyson (English) a form of Madison. *Madysen, Madysun*

Mae (English) a form of May. History: Mae Jemison was the first African American woman in space. *Maelea, Maeleah, Maelen, Maelle, Maona*

Maegan (Irish) a form of Megan. *Maegen, Maeghan, Maegin*

Maeko (Japanese) honest child. *Mae, Maemi*

Maeve (Irish) joyous. Mythology: a legendary Celtic queen. See also Mavis. *Maevi, Maevy, Maive, Mayve*

Magali, Magaly (Hebrew) from the high tower. *Magalie, Magally*

Magan, Magen (Greek) forms of Megan. *Maggen, Maggin*

Magda (Czech, Polish, Russian) a form of Magdalen. *Mahda, Makda*

Magdalen (Greek) high tower. Bible: Magdala was the home of Saint Mary Magdalen. See also Madeline, Malena, Marlene. *Mada, Magda, Magdala, Magdalen, Magdalena, Magdalena, Magdalene, Magdaline, Magdalyn, Magdalynn, Magdalene, Magdelene, Magdeline, Magdalyn, Magdlen, Magdolna, Maggie, Magola, Maighdlin, Mala, Malaine*

Magdalena (Greek) a form of Magdalen. *Magdalina, Magdalena, Magdelina*

Magena (Native American) coming moon.

Maggie (Greek) pearl. (English) a familiar form of Magdalen, Margaret. *Mag, Maggee, Maggey, Maggi, Maggia, Maggie, Maggiemae, Maggy, Magi, Magie, Mags*

Maggy, Meggy (English) forms of Maggie. *Maggey, Magy*

Magnolia (Latin) flowering tree. See also Nollie. *Nola*

Mahal (Filipino) love.

Mahala (Arabic) fat, marrow; tender. (Native American) powerful woman. *Mahalah, Mahalar, Mahalia, Mahala, Mahila, Mahlah, Mahlaha, Mehala, Mehalah*

Mahalia (American) a form of Mahala. *Mahala, Mahaley, Mahaliah, Mahalie, Mahayla, Mahaylah, Mahaylia, Mahelea, Maheleah, Mahelia, Mahilia, Mehalia*

Maharene (Ethiopian) forgive us.

Mahesa (Hindi) great lord. Religion: a name for the Hindu god Shiva. *Maheesa, Mahisa*

Mahina (Hawaiian) moon glow.

Mahila (Sanskrit) woman.

Mahira (Hebrew) energetic. *Mahri*

Mahogony (Spanish) rich, strong. *Mahogani, Mahoganey, Mahogani, Mahoganie, Mahoganny, Mahogeny, Mahogny, Mahogony, Mohogany*

Mai (Japanese) brightness. (Vietnamese) flower. (Navajo) coyote.

Maia (Greek) mother; nurse. Mythology: the loveliest of the Pleiades, the seven daughters of Atlas, and the mother of Hermes. See also Maya. *Maiah, Maie, Maiya*

Maida (English) maiden. (Greek) a short form of Madeline. *Maidel, Mayda, Maydena*

Maija (Finnish) a form of Mary. *Maji, Maiiki*

Maika (Hebrew) a familiar form of Michaela. *Maikala, Maikka, Maiko*

Maira, Maire (Irish) forms of Mary.
Maairah, Mair, Mairi, Mairin, Mairin, Mairona, Mairwen

Maisie (Scottish) familiar forms of Margaret.
Maisa, Maise, Maisey, Maisi, Maisy, Maizie, Maycee, Maysie, Mayzie, Mazey, Mazie, Mazzy, Mazzy, Mysie, Myzie

Maita (Spanish) a form of Martha.
Maite, Maitia

Maitlyn (American) a combination of Maita + Lynn.
Maitlan, Maitland, Maitlynn, Mattlyn

Maiya (Greek) a form of Maia.
Maiyah

Maja (Arabic) a short form of Majidah.
Majal, Majalisa, Majalyn, Majalynn

Majidah (Arabic) splendid.
Maja, Majida

Makaela, Makaila (American) forms of Michaela.
Makaelah, Makaelee, Makaella, Makaely, Makail, Makailah, Makailee, Makailla, Makaillah, Makaealah, Makaell

Makala (Hawaiian) myrtle. (Hebrew) a form of Michaela.
Makalae, Makalah, Makalai, Makalea, Makalee, Makaleah, Makaleigh, Makaley, Makalia, Makalie, Makalya, Makela, Makelah, Makell, Makella

Makana (Hawaiian) gift, present.

Makani (Hawaiian) wind.

Makara (Hindi) Astrology: another name for the zodiac sign Capricorn.

Makayla (American) a form of Michaela.
Macayla, Makaylah, Makaylee, Makayleigh, Makayli, Makaylia, Makaylla, Makell, Makyla, Makeylah, Mckayla, Mekayla, Mikayla

Makell (American) a short form of Makayla.
Makaela, Makala, Makayla. Makele, Makelle, Mckell, Mekel

Makenna (American) a form of Mackenna.
Makena, Makennah, Mikenna

Makenzie (Irish) a form of Mackenzie.
Makense, Makensey, Makensie, Makenze, Makenzee, Makenzey, Makenzi, Makenzy, Makenzye, Makinzey, Makynzey, Mekenzie, Mykenzie

Mala (Greek) a short form of Magdalen.
Malana, Malee, Mali

Malana (Hawaiian) bouyant, light.

Malaya (Filipino) free.
Malayaa, Malayah, Malayna, Malea, Maleah

Malena (Swedish) a familiar form of Magdalen.
Malen, Malenna, Malin, Malina, Maline, Malini, Malinna

Malha (Hebrew) queen.
Maliah, Malkah, Malkia, Malkiah, Malkie, Malkiya, Malkiyah, Miliah

Mali (Tai) jasmine flower. (Tongan) sweet. (Hungarian) a short form of Malika.
Malea, Malee, Maley

Malia (Hawaiian, Zuni) a form of Mary. (Spanish) a form of Maria.
Malea, Maleah, Maleeya, Maleeyah, Maleia, Maliah, Maliasha, Malie, Maliea, Maliya, Maliyah, Malli, Mally

Malika (Hungarian) industrious. (Arabic) queen.
Malak, Maleeka, Maleka, Mali, Maliaka, Malik, Malikah, Malikee, Maliki, Malikia, Malky

Malina (Hebrew) tower. (Native American) soothing. (Russian) raspberry.
Malin, Maline, Malina, Malinna, Mallie, Mallin

Malinda (Greek) a form of Melinda.
Malinde, Malinna, Malynda

Malini (Hindi) gardener.
Maliny

Malissa (Greek) a form of Melissa.
Malisa, Malisah, Malyssa

Mallalai (Pashto) beautiful.

Malley (American) a familiar form of Mallory.
Mallee, Malli, Mallie, Mally, Maly

Mallorie (French) a form of Mallory.
Malerie, Mallari, Mallerie, Malloreigh, Mallori

Mallory (German) army counselor. (French) unlucky.
Maliri, Mallary, Mallauri, Mallery, Malley, Malloree, Mallorey, Mallorie, Malorie, Malory, Malorym, Malree, Malrie, Mellory

Malorie, Malory (German) forms of Mallory.
Malarie, Maloree, Malori, Melorie, Melory

Malva (English) a form of Melba.
Malvi, Malvy

Malvina (Scottish) a form of Melvina. Literature: a name created by the eighteenth-century romantic poet James Macpherson.
Malvane, Malvi

Mamie (American) a familiar form of Margaret.
Mame, Mamee, Mami, Mammie, Mamy, Mamye

Mamo (Hawaiian) saffron flower; yellow bird.

Mana (Hawaiian) psychic; sensitive.
Manal, Manali, Manna, Mannah

Manar (Arabic) guiding light.
Manaya

Manda (Spanish) woman warrior. (Latin) a short form of Amanda.
Mandy

Mandara (Hindi) calm.

Mandeep (Punjabi) enlightened.

Mandisa (Xhosa) sweet.

Mandy (Latin) lovable. A familiar form of Amanda, Manda, Melinda.
Mandee, Mandi, Mandie

Manette (French) a form of Mary.

Mangena (Hebrew) song; melody.
Mangina

Mani (Chinese) a mantra repeated in Tibetan Buddhist prayer to impart understanding.
Manee

Manka (Polish, Russian) a form of Mary.

Manon (French) a familiar form of Marie.
Mannon

Manpreet (Punjabi) mind full of love.
Manprit

Mansi (Hopi) plucked flower.
Mancey, Manci, Mancie, Mansey, Mansie, Mansy

Manuela (Spanish) a form of Emmanuelle.
Manuela, Manuelita, Manuelia, Manuelle

Manya (Russian) a form of Mary.

Mara (Hebrew) melody. (Greek) a short form of Amara. (Slavic) a form of Mary.
Mahra, Marae, Marah, Maralina, Maraline, Marra

Marabel (English) a form of Mirabel.
Marabella, Marabelle

Maranda (Latin) a form of Miranda.

Maraya (Hebrew) a form of Mariah.
Mareya

Marcela (Latin) a form of Marcella.
Marcele, Marcelen, Marcelia, Marceline, Marcela

Marcelen (English) a form of Marcella.
Marcelen, Marcelin, Marcelina, Marceline,

Mani (Chinese) a mantra repeated in Tibetan Buddhist prayer to impart understanding.
Marcellin, Marcelline, Marcelyn, Marilen

Marcella (Latin) martial, warlike. Mythology: Mars was the god of war.
Marsil, Mara, Maree, Marcel, Marcela, Marcelen, Marcell, Marcelle, Marcella, Marcia, Marcie, Marciella, Marcile, Marcilla, Marcille, Marsella, Marselle, Marstella

Marcena (Latin) a form of Marcella, Marcia.
Macena, Marceen, Marcene, Marcenia, Marceyne, Marcina

Marci, Marcie (English) familiar forms of Marcella, Marcia.
Mara, Maree, Marcita, Marcy, Marsi, Marsie

Marcia (Latin) martial, warlike. See also Marquita.
Marcena, Marchia, Marci, Marciale, Marcie, Marcsa, Marsha, Martia

Marciann (American) a combination of Marci + Ann.
Mariane, Marianna, Marcianne, Marcyane, Marcyanna, Marcyanne

Marcilynn (American) a combination of Marci + Lynn.
Marcilen, Marcilin, Marciline, Marcilyn, Marcilyne, Marcilynne, Marcylen, Marcylin, Marcyline, Marcylyn, Marcylyne, Marcylynn, Marcylynne

Marcy (English) a form of Marci.
Marsey, Marsy

Mardi (French) born on Tuesday. (Aramaic) a familiar form of Martha.

Mare (Irish) a form of Mary.
Mair, Maire

Marelda (German) renowned warrior.
Marella, Marilda

Maren (Latin) sea. (Aramaic) a form of Mary. See also Marina.
Marin, Marine, Marinn, Miren

Maressa, Maressa (Latin) forms of Marisa.
Maresha, Meresa

Maretta (English) a familiar form of Margaret.
Maret, Marette

Margaret (Greek) pearl. History: Margaret Hilda Thatcher served as British prime minister. See also Gita, Greta, Gretchen, Marjorie, Markita, Meg, Megan, Peggy, Reet, Rita.
Madge, Maergrethe, Maggie, Maisie, Mamie, Maretta, Marga, Margalo, Marganit, Margara, Maretha, Margarett, Margarette, Margarida, Margarit, Margarita, Margaro, Margaux, Marge, Margeret, Margeretta, Margerette, Margery, Margetta, Margiad, Margie, Margisia, Margit, Margo, Margot, Magret, Marguerite, Meta

Margarit (Greek) a form of Margaret.
Margalide, Margalit, Margalith, Margarid, Margariit, Margerit

Margarita (Italian, Spanish) a form of Margaret.
Margareta, Margaretta, Margarida, Margaritis, Margaritta, Margeretta, Margharita, Margherita, Margrieta, Margrita, Marguarita, Marguerita, Margurita

Margaux (French) a form of Margaret.
Margeaux

Marge (English) a short form of Margaret, Marjorie.
Margie

Margery (English) a form of Margaret.
Margerie, Margorie

Margie (English) a familiar form of Marge, Margaret.
Margey, Margi, Margy

Margit (Hungarian) a form of Margaret.
Marget, Margette, Margita

Margo, Margot (French) forms of Margaret.
Mago, Margaro

Margret (German) a form of Margaret.
Magreta, Margrete, Margreth, Margrett, Margretta, Margrete, Margrieta, Magrita

Marguerite (French) a form of Margaret.
Margarete, Margaretha, Margarethe, Margarite, Margerite, Marguaretta, Marguarette, Marguarite, Marguerette, Margurite

Mari (Japanese) ball. (Spanish) a form of Mary.

Maria (Hebrew) bitter; sea of bitterness. (Italian, Spanish) a form of Mary.
Maie, Malia, Marea, Mareah, Mariabella, Mariae, Mariesa, Mariessa, Mariha, Marija, Mariya, Mariyah, Marja, Marya

Mariah (Hebrew) a form of Mary. See also Moriah.
Maraia, Manaya, Mariyah, Marriah, Meriah

Mariam (Hebrew) a form of Miriam.
Mariana, Mariame, Mariem, Meryam

Marian (English) a form of Maryann.
Mariana, Mariane, Mariann, Marianne, Mariene, Marion, Marrian, Marriann

Mariana, Marianna (Spanish) forms of Marian.
Marriana, Marrianna, Maryana, Maryanna

Mariane, Marianne (English) forms of Marian.
Marrianne, Maryanne

Maribel (French) beautiful. (English) a combination of Maria + Bell.
Marabel, Marbelle, Mariabella, Maribella, Maribelle, Maridel, Marybel, Marybella, Marybelle

Marice (Italian) a form of Mary. See also Maris.
Marica, Marise, Marisse

Maricela (Latin) a form of Marcella.
Maricel, Mariceli, Maricelia, Maricella, Maricely

Maridel (English) a form of Maribel.

Marie (French) a form of Mary.
Maree, Marietta, Marrie

Mariel, Marielle (German, Dutch) forms of Mary.
Marial, Marieke, Marielana, Mariele, Marieli, Marielle, Marieline, Mariell, Mariellen, Marielsie, Mariely, Marielys

Mariela, Mariella (German, Dutch) forms of Mary.

Marietta (Italian) a familiar form of Marie.
Maretta, Marette, Mariet, Mariette, Marrietta

Marieve (American) a combination of Mary + Eve.

Marigold (English) Mary's gold. Botany: a plant with yellow or orange flowers.
Marygold

Marika (Dutch, Slavic) a form of Mary.
Marica, Marieke, Marija, Marijke, Marikah, Marike, Marikia, Marikka, Mariska, Mariske, Marrika, Maryk, Maryka, Merica, Merika

Mariko (Japanese) circle.

Marilee (American) a combination of Mary + Lee.
Marili, Marilie, Marily, Marilee, Marylea, Marylee, Merrilee, Merrili, Merrily

Marilla (Hebrew, German) a form of Mary.
Marella, Marelle

Marilou (American) a form of Marylou.
Marilu, Mariluz

Marilyn (Hebrew) Mary's line of descendants. See also Merilyn.
Maralin, Maralyn, Maralynne, Maralynne, Marelyn, Maralin, Marilin, Marillyn, Marilyne, Marilynn, Marilynne, Marlyn, Marolyn, Maralynn, Marrilin, Marrilyn, Marrilynn, Marylin, Marylyn, Marylynn, Marylynn, Marylynne, Marylyne, Marylynne

Marina (Latin) sea. See also Maren.
Mareena, Marena, Marenka, Marinae, Marinah, Marinda, Marindi, Marina, Marinka, Marinna, Maryna, Merina, Mirena

Marini (Swahili) healthy; pretty.

Marion (French) a form of Mary.
Marrian, Marrion, Maryon, Maryonn

Maris (Latin) sea. (Greek) a short form of Amaris, Damaris. See also Marice.
Maries, Marise, Marris, Marys, Maryse, Meris

Marisa (Latin) sea.
Maresa, Mariesa, Mariessa, Marisela, Marissa, Marita, Mariza, Marrisa, Maryssa, Marysa, Maryse, Maryssa, Merisa

Marisela (Latin) a form of Marisa.
Mariseli, Marisella, Marishelle, Marissela

Marisha (Russian) a familiar form of Mary.
Mareshah, Marishenka, Marishka, Mariska

Marisol (Spanish) sunny sea.
Marise, Marizol, Marysol

Marissa (Latin) a form of Maris, Marisa.
Maressa, Marisa, Marisha, Marissah, Marisse, Marizza, Marrissa, Marrissia, Maryssa, Merissa, Morissa

Marit (Aramaic) lady.
Marita, Marite

Marita (Spanish) a form of Marisa. (Aramaic) a form of Marit.
Marité, Maritha

Maritza (Arabic) blessed.
Maritsa, Marittsa

Mariyan (Arabic) purity.
Mariya, Mariyah, Mariyana, Mariyanna

Marja (Finnish) a form of Mary.
Marjae, Marjatta, Marjie

Marjan (Persian) coral. (Polish) a form of Mary.
Marje, Marjey, Marji, Marjy

Marianne (Arabic) a form of Mary.

Marjie (Scottish) a familiar form of Marjorie.
Marje, Marjey, Marji, Marjy

Marjolaine (French) marjoram.

Marjorie (Greek) a familiar form of Margaret. (Scottish) a form of Mary.
Majorie, Marge, Margeree, Margery, Margerie, Margey, Margeree, Margery, Margerie, Margie, Margorie, Margory, Margerie, Marjarie, Marjary, Marjery, Marjori, Marjory

Markayla (American) a combination or Mary + Kayla.
Markea, Markaiah, Markaya, Markayel, Markeela, Markel

Markeisha (English) a combination of Mary + Keisha.
Markasha, Markeesa, Markeisia, Markesha, Markeshia, Markeisia, Markesha, Markeshia, Markisha, Markishia, Marquesha

Markita (Czech) a form of Margaret.
Markea, Markeah, Markeda, Markee, Markeeta, Marketa, Marketta, Marketi, Markie, Marketeia, Marketa, Markeitha, Marketta, Merkeate

Marla (English) a short form of Marlena, Marlene.
Marlah, Marlea, Marleah

Marlana (English) a form of Marlena.
Marlaena, Marlaina, Marlainna, Marlania, Marlanna, Marlayna, Marleana

Marlee (English) a form of Marlene.
Marlea, Marleah, Marleigh

Marlena (German) a form of Marlene.
Marla, Marlaina, Marlana, Marlanna, Marleena, Marlina, Marlinda, Marlyna, Marna

Marlene (Greek) high tower. (Slavic) a form of Magdalen.
Marla, Marlaine, Marlane, Marlayne, Marlee, Marleen, Marleene, Marlen, Marlena, Marlenne, Marley, Marlin, Marline, Marlyne

Marley (English) a familiar form of Marlene.
Marlee, Marli, Marlie, Marly

Marlis (English) a combination of Maria + Lisa.
Marles, Marlisa, Marlise, Marlys, Marlyse, Marlyssa

Marlo (English) a form of Mary.
Marlon, Marlow, Marlowe

Marlyn (Hebrew) a short form of Marilyn. (Greek, Slavic) a form of Marlene.
Marlynn, Marlynne

Marmara (Greek) sparkling, shining.
Marmee

Marni (Hebrew) a form of Marnie.
Marnia, Marnique

Marnie (Hebrew) a short form of Marnina.
Marna, Marnay, Marne, Marnee, Marney, Marni, Marnisha, Marnja, Marny, Marnya, Marnye

Marnina (Hebrew) rejoice.

Maroula (Greek) a form of Mary.

Marquise (French) noblewoman.
Markese, Marquees, Marquese, Marquice, Marquies, Marquiese, Marquis, Marquisa, Marquisee, Marquisha, Marquisse, Marquiste

Marquisha (American) a form of Marquise.
Marquiesha, Marquisia

Marquita (Spanish) a form of Marcia.
Marquatte, Marqueda, Marquedia, Marquee, Marqueita, Marquet, Marqueta, Marquetta, Marquette, Marquia, Marquida, Marquietta, Marquitra, Marquitia, Marquitta

Marrim (Chinese) tribal name in Manpur state.

Marsala (Italian) from Marseilles, France.
Marsali, Marseilles

Marsha (English) a form of Marcia.
Marcha, Marshae, Marshay, Marshel, Marshele, Marshell, Marshia, Marshiela

Marta (English) a short form of Martha, Martina.
Martá, Martä, Marte, Martia, Marttaha, Merta

Martha (Aramaic) lady; sorrowful. Bible: a friend of Jesus. See also Mardi.
Maita, Mara, Martaha, Marth,

Marthan, Marthe, Marthy, Marti, Martika, Martita, Mattie, Matty, Martus, Martuska, Masia

Marti (English) a familiar form of Martha, Martina.
Martie, Marty

Martina (Latin) martial, warlike. See also Tina.
Marta, Martel, Martella, Martelle, Martene, Marthena, Marthina, Marthine, Marti, Martine, Martinia, Martino, Martisha, Martosia, Martoya, Martricia, Martrina, Martyna, Martyne, Martynne

Martiza (Arabic) blessed.

Maru (Japanese) round.

Maruca (Spanish) a form of Mary.
Maruja, Maruska

Marvella (French) marvelous.
Marva, Marvel, Marvela, Marvele, Marvelle, Marvely, Marvetta, Marvette, Marvia, Marvina

Mary (Hebrew) bitter; sea of bitterness. Bible: the mother of Jesus. See also Maija, Malia, Maren, Mariah, Marjorie, Maura, Maureen, Miriam, Mitzi, Moira, Mollie, Muriel.
Maira, Maire, Manette, Manka, Manon, Manya, Mara, Mare, Maree, Maren, Marella, Marelle, Mari, Maria, Mariana, Marie, Marie, Mariel, Mariela, Marika, Marilla, Marilyn, Marion, Mariquilla, Mariquita, Marisha, Marja, Marjan, Marlo, Maroula, Marua, Marye, Maryla, Marynia, Masha, Mavra, Mendi, Mérane, Meridel, Mhairie, Mirja, Molara, Morag, Moya

Marya (Arabic) purity; bright white-ness.
Maryah

Maryam (Hebrew) a form of Miriam.
Maryama

Maryann, Maryanne (English) combinations of Mary + Ann.
Marian, Maryann, Maryan, Meryen

Marybeth (American) a combination of Mary + Beth.
Maribeth, Maribette

Maryellen (American) a combination of Mary + Ellen.
Mariellen

Maryjane (American) a combination of Mary + Jane.

Maryjo (American) a combination of Mary + Jo.
Marijo, Maryjoe

Marykate (American) a combination of Mary + Kate.
Mary-Kate

Marylou (American) a combination of Mary + Lou.
Marilou, Marylu

Maryssa (Latin) a form of Marissa.
Maryse, Marysia

Masago (Japanese) sands of time.

Masani (Luganda) gap toothed.

Masha (Russian) a form of Mary.
Mashka, Mashenka

Mashika (Swahili) born during the rainy season.
Masika

Matana (Hebrew) gift.
Matat

Mathena (Hebrew) gift of God.

Mathilde (German) a form of Matilda.
Mathilda

Matilda (German) powerful battler. See also Maud, Tilda, Tillie.
Máda, Mahaut, Matilde, Malkin, Mat, Matelda, Mathilde, Matilde, Mattie, Matty, Matusha, Matylda

Matrika (Hindi) mother. Religion: a name for the Hindu goddess Shakti in the form of the letters of the alphabet.
Matrica

Matsuko (Japanese) pine tree.

Matsusha (Spanish) a form of Matilda.
Matysia, Matuxa

Mattea (Hebrew) gift of God.
Matea, Mathea, Mathia, Matia, Matte, Matthea, Matthia, Mattia, Matya

Mattie, Matty (English) familiar forms of Martha, Matilda.
Matte, Mattey, Matti, Mattye

Maud, Maude (English) short forms of Madeline, Matilda. See also Madison.
Maudie, Maudine, Maudlin

Maura (Irish) dark. A form of Mary, Maureen. See also Moira.
Maurah, Maure, Maurette, Mauricette, Mauria

Maureen (French) dark. (Irish) a form of Mary.
Maura, Maurene, Mo, Moreen, Morena, Morene, Morine, Morreen, Moureen

Maurelle (French) dark; elfin.
Mauriel, Mauriell, Maurielle

Maurise (French) dark skinned; moor; marshland.
Maurisa, Maurissa, Maurita, Maurizia

Mausi (Native American) plucked flower.

Mauve (French) violet colored.

Mavis (French) thrush, songbird. See also Maeve.
Mavies, Mavin, Mavine, Mavon, Mavra

Maxie (English) a familiar form of Maxine.
Maxi, Maxy

Maxine (Latin) greatest.
Max, Maxa, Maxeen, Maxena, Maxene, Maxie, Maxima, Maxine, Maximiliane, Maxina, Maxina, Maxyne

May (Latin) great. (Arabic) discerning. (English) flower; month of May. See also Mae, Maia.
Maj, Mayberry, Maybeth, Mayday, Maydee, Maydena, Maye, Mayela, Mayella, Mayetta, Mayrene

Maya (Hindi) God's creative power. (Greek) mother; grandmother. (Latin) great. A form of Maia.
Mayam, Mya

Maybeline (Latin) a familiar form of Mabel.

Maygan, Maygen (Irish) forms of Megan.
Mayghan, Maygon

Maylyn (American) a combination of May + Lynn.
Mayelene, Mayleen, Maylen, Maylene, Maylin, Maylon, Maylynn, Maylynne

Mayoree (Tai) beautiful.
Mayra, Mayree, Mayariya

Mayra (Tai) a form of Mayoree.

Maysa (Arabic) walks with a proud stride.

Maysun (Arabic) beautiful.

Mazel (Hebrew) lucky.
Mazal, Mazala, Mazella

Mckayla (American) a form of Makayla.
Mckaela, Mckaila, Mckala, Mckaylah, Mckayle, Mckaylee, Mckayleh, Mckayleigh, Mckayli, Mckaylia, Mckaylie

Mckell (American) a form of Makell.
Mckelle

Mckenna (American) a form of Mackenna.
Mckena, Mckennah, Mckinna, Mckinnah

Mckenzie (Scottish) a form of Mackenzie.
Mckennzie, Mckensee, Mckensey, McKennzie, Mckensi, Mckensie, Mckensy, Mckenze, Mckenzee, Mckenzey, Mckenzi, Mckenzy, Mckenzye, Mckensie, Mckenzi, Mekenzie

Mckinley (Irish) daughter of the learned ruler.
Mckinlee, Mckinleigh, Mckinlie, Mckinnley

Mckinzie (American) a form of Mackenzie.
Mckinsey, Mckinzea, Mckinzea,

Mckinzee, Mckinzi, Mckinzy, Mckynze, Mckynzie

Mead, Meade (Greek) honey wine.

Meagan (Irish) a form of Megan.
Maegan, Meagain, Meagann, Meagen, Meagin, Meagnah, Meagon

Meaghan (Welsh) a form of Megan.
Maeghan, Meaghann, Meaghen, Mealgan

Meara (Irish) mirthful.

Meda (Native American) prophet; priestess.

Medea (Greek) ruling; (Latin) middle. Mythology: a sorceress who helped Jason get the Golden Fleece.
Medeia

Medina (Arabic) History: the site of Muhammed's tomb.
Medinah

Medora (Greek) mother's gift. Literature: a character in Lord Byron's poem *The Corsair.*

Meena (Hindi) blue semiprecious stone; bird. (Greek, German, Dutch) a form of Mena.

Meg (English) a short form of Margaret, Megan.

Megan (Greek) pearl; great. (Irish) a form of Margaret.
Maegan, Magan, Magen, Meagan, Meaghan, Magen, Maygan, Maygen, Meg, Megane, Megann, Megean, Megen, Meggan, Megger, Meghan, Megyn, Meygan

Megane (Irish) a form of Megan.
Magana, Meganna, Meganne

Megara (Greek) first. Mythology: Heracles's first wife.

Meggie (English) a familiar form of Margaret, Megan.
Meggi, Meggy

Meghan (Welsh) a form of Megan.
Meeghan, Meehan, Megha, Meghana, Meghane, Meghann, Meghanne, Meghean, Meghen, Mehgan, Mehgen

Mehadi (Hindi) flower.

Mehira (Hebrew) speedy; energetic.
Mahira

Mehitabel (Hebrew) benefited by trusting God.
Mehetabel, Mehitabelle, Hetty, Hitty

Mehri (Persian) kind; lovable; sunny.

Mei (Hawaiian) great. (Chinese) a short form of Meiying.
Meiko

Meira (Hebrew) light.
Meera

Meit (Burmese) affectionate.

Meiying (Chinese) beautiful flower.
Mei

Meka (Hebrew) a familiar form of Michaela.

Mekayla (American) a form of Michaela.
Mekaela, Mekaila, Mekayela, Mekaylia

Mel (Portuguese, Spanish) sweet as honey.

Mela (Hindi) religious service. (Polish) a form of Melanie.
Melanna, Melashka, Melenka, Milana

Melana (Russian) a form of Melanie.

Melanie (Greek) dark skinned.
Malania, Malanie, Meila, Melani, Melin, Melaine, Melanie, Melana, Melane, Melanee, Melaney, Melani, Melania, Mélanie, Melanka, Melanney, Melannie, Melany, Melanya, Melasya, Melonie, Melya, Milena, Milya

Melantha (Greek) dark flower.

Melba (Greek) soft; slender. (Latin) mallow flower.
Malva, Melva

Mele (Hawaiian) song; poem.

Melesse (Ethiopian) eternal.
Mellesse

Melia (German) a short form of Amelia.
Melea, Meleah, Meleia, Meleisha, Meli, Meliah, Melida, Melika, Mema

Melina (Latin) canary yellow. (Greek) a short form of Melinda.
Melaina, Meleana, Meleena, Melena, Meline, Melinia, Melinna, Melynna

Melinda (Greek) honey. See also Linda, Melina, Mindy.
Mallie, Malinda, Melinder, Mellinda, Melynda, Melyne, Milinda, Milynda, Mylenda, Mylinda, Mylynda

Meliora (Latin) better.
Melior, Meliori, Mellear, Melyor, Melyora

Melisa (Greek) a form of Melissa.
Melesa, Mélisa, Melise, Melisha, Melishia, Metisia, Meliza, Melizah, Melisa, Melosa, Mitisa, Mylisa, Myltisia

Melisande (French) a form of Melissa, Millicent.
Lisandra, Malisande, Malissande, Malyssandre, Melesande, Melisandra, Melisandre, Mélisandré, Melisenda, Melissande, Mélissandre, Mellisande, Melond, Melysande, Melyssandre

Melissa (Greek) honey bee. See also Elisa, Lissa, Melisande, Millicent.
Malissa, Mallissa, Melessa, Meleta, Melisa, Mélissa, Melisse, Melissia, Melitta, Melly, Melyssa, Milissa, Millie, Milly, Missy, Molissa, Mollissa, Mylissa, Mylissia

Melita (Greek) a form of Melissa. (Spanish) a short form of Carmelita.
Malita, Meleeta, Melitta, Melitza, Melletta, Molita

Melly (American) a familiar form of names beginning with "Mel." See also Millie.
Meli, Melie, Melli, Mellie

Melody (Greek) melody. See also Elodie.
Meladia, Melodee, Melodey, Melodi, Melodia, Melodie, Melodyann, Melodye

Melonie (American) a form of Melanie.
Mellony, Mellonie, Mellony, Melonee, Meloney, Meloni, Melonie, Melonnie, Melony

Melosa (Spanish) sweet; tender.

Melyne (Greek) a short form of Melinda.

Melvina (Irish) armored chief. See also Malvina.
Melvine, Melva, Melveen, Melvena, Melvene, Melvonna

Melyssa (Greek) a form of Melissa.
Melyn, Melynn, Melynne

Mena (German, Dutch) strong. (Greek) a short form of Philomena. History: Menes is believed to be the first king of Egypt.
Menah

Mendi (Basque) a form of Mary.
Menda, Mendy

Meranda (Latin) a form of Miranda.
Merana, Merandah, Merandia, Meranndda

Mérane (French) a form of Mary.
Meraine, Merane

Mercedes (Latin) reward, payment. (Spanish) merciful.
Mercades, Mercadez, Mercadie, Meceades, Merced, Mercede, Mercedees, Mercedez, Mercedies, Mercedis, Mersade, Mersades

Mercia (English) a form of Marcia. History: an ancient British kingdom.
Elodie.

Mercy (English) compassionate, merciful. See also Merry.
Mercey, Merci, Mercie, Mercille, Mersey Mercy, Merri, Mercie, Mercille, Mersey

Meredith (Welsh) protector of the sea.
Meredeth, Meredithe, Meredy, Meredyth, Meredythe, Meridath, Meridith, Merideth, Meridie, Meriditth, Merridith, Merry

Meri (Finnish) sea. (Irish) a short form of Meriel.

Meriel (Irish) shining sea.
Meri, Merial, Meriol, Meryl

Merilyn (English) a combination of Merry + Lynn. See also Marilyn.
Merelyn, Merlyn, Merralyn, Merrelyn, Merrilyn

Merissa (Latin) a form of Marissa.
Merisa, Merisha

Merle (Latin, French) blackbird.
Merl, Merla, Merlina, Merline, Merola, Murle, Myrle, Myrleen, Myrlene, Myrline

Merry (English) cheerful, happy. A familiar form of Mercy, Meredith.
Merree, Merree, Merri, Merrie, Merrielle, Merrile, Merrili, Merrilyn, Merris, Merrita

Meryl (German) famous. (Irish) shining sea. A form of Meriel, Muriel.
Meral, Merel, Merrall, Merrell, Merril, Merrile, Merrill, Merryl, Meryle, Meryll

Mesha (Hindi) another name for the zodiac sign Aries.
Meshal

Meta (German) a short form of Margaret.
Metta, Mette, Metti

Mhairie (Scottish) a form of Mary.
Mhaire, Mhairi, Mhari, Mhary

Mia (Italian) mine. A familiar form of Michelle.
Mea, Meah, Miah

Micaela (Hebrew) a form of Michaela.
Macaela, Micaella, Micaila, Micala, Micaela

Micah (Hebrew) a short form of Michaela. Bible: one of the Old Testament prophets.
Meecah, Mica, Micha, Mika, Myca, Mycah

Micayla, Michayla (Hebrew) forms of Michaela.
Micayle, Micaylee, Michaylah

Michaela (Hebrew) who is like God?
Machaela, Maika, Makaela, Makaila, Makala, Makayla, Mia, Micaela, Micayla, Michael, Michaelann, Michala, Michayla, Michealia, Michaelina, Michaeline, Michaell, Michaella, Michaelyn, Michaila, Michal, Michala, Micheal, Micheala, Michelia, Michelina, Michelle, Michely, Michelyn, Micheyla, Micheline, Micki, Miguela, Mikaela, Mikala, Misha, Mycala, Mychael, Mychal

Michala (Hebrew) a form of Michaela.
Michalann, Michale, Michalene, Michalin, Michalina, Michalisha, Michalla, Michalle, Michayla, Michayle, Michela

Michele (Italian) a form of Michaela.
Michaelle, Michal, Michela

Michelle (French) who is like God? See also Shelley.
Machealle, Machele, Machell, Machella, Machelle, Mechelle, Meichelle, Meschell, Meshell, Meshelle, Mia, Michel, Michéle, Michell, Michella, Michellene, Michellyn, Mischel, Mischelle, Mishael, Mishaela, Mishayla, Mishell, Mishella, Mitchele, Mitchell

Michi (Japanese) righteous way.
Miche, Michee, Michiko

Micki (American) a familiar form of Michaela.
Mickee, Mickeeya, Mickia, Mickie, Micky, Mickya, Miquia

Midori (Japanese) green.

Mieko (Japanese) prosperous.
Mieke

Mielikki (Finnish) pleasing.

Miette (French) small; sweet.

Migina (Omaha) new moon.

Mignon (French) dainty; petite; graceful.
Mignonette, Minnonette, Minnonette, Minyonette, Minyonne

Miguela (Spanish) a form of Michaela.
Miquel, Miguelina, Miguelita, Miquel, Miquela, Miquella

Mika (Japanese) new moon. (Russian) God's child. (Native American) wise racoon. (Hebrew) a form of Micah. (Latin) a form of Dominica.
Mikah, Mikka

Mikaela (Hebrew) a form of Michaela.
Mekaela, Mekala, Mickael, Mickaela, Mickala, Mickalla, Mickeel, Mickell, Mickelle, Mikael, Mikail, Mikaila, Mikal, Mikalene, Mikaloma, Mikalyn, Mikayla, Mikea, Mikeisha, Mikeita, Mikel, Mikela, Mikele, Mikell, Mikella, Mikesha, Mikeya, Mikhaela, Mikie, Mikiela, Mikkel, Mikyla, Mykaela

Mikala (Hebrew) a form of Michaela.
Mickala, Mikalah, Mikale, Mikalea, Mikalee, Mikaleh

Mikayla (American) a form of
Mikaela.
Mekayla, Mickayla, Mikala, Mikayle,
Mikeyla

Mikhaela (American) a form of
Mikaela.
Mikhail, Mikhaila, Mikhalea,
Mikhayla, Mikhelle

Miki (Japanese) flower stem.
Mikia, Mikkala, Mikie, Mikiea, Mikiyo,
Mikki, Mikkie, Mikkiya, Mikko, Miko

Milada (Czech) my love.
Mila, Milady

Mila (Russian) dear one. (Italian,
Slavic) a short form of Camila,
Ludmilla.
Milah, Milla

Milagros (Spanish) miracle.
Mila, Milagritos, Milagro, Milagrosa,
Mirari

Milana (Italian) from Milan, Italy.
(Russian) a form of Melana.
Milan, Milane, Milani, Milanka,
Milanna, Milanne

Milena (Greek, Hebrew, Russian) a
form of Ludmilla, Magdalen,
Melanie.
Mila, Milène, Milenia, Milenny, Milini,
Milini

Mildred (English) gentle counselor.
Mil, Mila, Mildrene, Mildrid, Millie,
Milly

Mieta (German) generous, merciful.

Minal (Native American) fruit.

Minda (Hindi) knowledge.

Milia (German) industrious. A short
form of Amelia, Emily.
Milah, Milka, Milla, Milya

Miliani (Hawaiian) caress.
Milanni, Miliary

Milissa (Greek) a form of Melissa.
Milessa, Milisa, Millisa, Millissa

Milka (Czech) a form of Amelia.
Milica, Milika

Millicent (English) industrious.
(Greek) a form of Melissa. See also
Lissa, Melisande.
Melicent, Meliscent, Mellicent, Mellisent,
Mely, Millicent, Millisent, Millie,
Milliestone, Millisent, Milly, Milzie,
Missy

Millie, Milly (English) familiar forms
of Amelia, Camille, Emily, Kamila,
Melissa, Mildred, Millicent.
Mili, Milla, Millee, Milley, Millie, Mylie

Mima (Burmese) woman.
Mimma

Mimi (French) a familiar form of
Miriam.

Mina (German) love. (Persian) blue
sky. (Arabic) harbor. (Japanese) south.
A short form of names ending in
"mina."
Meena, Mena, Min

Mindy (Greek) a familiar form of
Melinda.
Mindee, Mindi, Mindie, Mindyanne,
Mindylee, Myndy

Mine (Japanese) peak; mountain range.
Mineko

Minerva (Latin) wise. Mythology: the
goddess of wisdom.
Merva, Minivera, Minnie, Myna

Minette (French) faithful defender
Minnette, Minnita

Minka (Polish) a short form of
Wilhelmina.

Minna (German) a short form of
Wilhelmina.
Mina, Minka, Minnie, Minta

Minnie (American) a familiar form of
Mina, Minerva, Minna, Wilhelmina.
Mini, Minie, Minne, Minni, Minny

Minowa (Native American) singer.
Minowah

Minta (English) Literature: originally
coined by playwright Sir John
Vanbrugh in his comedy *The*
Confederacy.

Minya (Osage) older sister.

Mio (Japanese) three times as strong.

Mira (Latin) wonderful. (Spanish)
look, gaze. A short form of Almira,
Amira, Marabel, Mirabel, Miranda.
Mirae, Mirra, Mirah

Mirabel (Latin) beautiful.
Mira, Mirabell, Mirabella, Mirabelle, Mirable

Miracle (Latin) wonder, marvel.

Miranda (Latin) strange; wonderful; admirable. Literature: the heroine of Shakespeare's *The Tempest*. See also Randi.
Maranda, Marenda, Meranda, Mira, Miran, Miranada, Mirandia, Mirinda, Mirindé, Mironda, Mirranda, Muranda, Myranda

Mireille (Hebrew) God spoke. (Latin) wonderful.
Mirel, Mirel, Mirella, Mirelle, Mirelys, Mireya, Mireyda, Mirielle, Mirilla, Myrella, Myrilla

Mireya (Hebrew) a form of Mireille.
Mireea, Miriah, Miryah

Miri (Gypsy) a short form of Miriam.
Miria, Miriah

Miriam (Hebrew) bitter; sea of bitterness. Bible: the original form of Mary. See also Macia, Mimi, Mitzi.
Mairwen, Mariam, Maryam, Miriam, Mirham, Miri, Miriain, Miriama, Miriame, Mirian, Mirit, Mirjam, Mirjana, Mirriam, Mirrian, Miryam, Miryan, Myriam

Misha (Russian) a form of Michaela.
Mischa, Mishae

Missy (English) a familiar form of Melissa, Millicent.
Missi, Missie

Misty (English) shrouded by mist.
Missty, Mistee, Mistey, Misti, Mistie, Mistin, Mistina, Mistral, Mistylynn, Mystee, Mysti, Mystie

Mitra (Hindi) Religion: god of daylight. (Persian) angel.
Mita

Mituna (Moquelumnan) like a fish wrapped up in leaves.

Mitzi (German) a form of Mary, Miriam.
Mieze, Mitzee, Mitzie, Mitzy

Miwa (Japanese) wise eyes.
Miwako

Miya (Japanese) temple.
Miyah, Miyana, Miyanna

Miyo (Japanese) beautiful generation.
Miyoko, Miyuko

Miyuki (Japanese) snow.

Moana (Hawaiian) ocean; fragrance.

Mocha (Arabic) chocolate-flavored coffee.
Moka

Modesty (Latin) modest.
Modesta, Modeste, Modestia, Modestie, Modestina, Modestine, Modestus

Moesha (American) a short form of Monisha.
Myesha

Mohala (Hawaiian) flowers in bloom.
Moala

Moira (Irish) great. A form of Mary. See also Maura.
Moirae, Moirah, Moire, Moya, Moyra, Moyrah

Molara (Basque) a form of Mary.

Mollie, Molly (Irish) familiar forms of Mary.
Moli, Molie, Moll, Mollee, Molley, Molli, Mollissa

Mona (Irish) noble. (Greek) a short form of Monica, Ramona, Rimona.
Moina, Monah, Mone, Monea, Monna, Moyna

Monet (French) Art: Claude Monet was a leading French impressionist remembered for his paintings of water lilies.
Monae, Monay, Monee

Monica (Greek) solitary. (Latin) advisor.
Mona, Monca, Monee, Monia, Monic, Monice, Monicia, Monicka, Monika, Monique, Monise, Monn, Monnica, Monnie, Monya

Monifa (Yoruba) I have my luck.

Monika (German) a form of Monica.
Moneka, Monieka, Monike, Monnika

Monique (French) a form of Monica.
Moneeke, Moneik, Moniqua, Moniquea, Moniquie, Munique

Monisha (American) a combination of Monica + Aisha.
Moesha, Moneisha, Monishia

Montana (Spanish) mountain. Geography: a U.S. state.
Montanna

Mora (Spanish) blueberry.
Morae, Morea, Moria, Morita

Morela (Polish) apricot.
Morelia, Morelle

Morena (Irish) a form of Maureen.

Morgan (Welsh) seashore. Literature: Morgan le Fay was the half-sister of King Arthur.
Morgana, Morgance, Morgane, Morganetta, Morganette, Morganica, Morgann, Morganna, Morganne, Morgen, Morghan, Morgyn, Morrigan

Morghan (Welsh) a form of Morgan.
Morghen, Morghin, Morghyn

Moriah (Hebrew) God is my teacher. (French) dark skinned. Bible: the mountain on which the Temple of Solomon was built. See also Mariah.
Moria, Moriel, Morit, Morria, Morriah

Morie (Japanese) bay.

Morowa (Akan) queen.

Morrisa (Latin) dark skinned; moor; marshland.
Morisa, Morissa, Morrissa

Moselle (Hebrew) drawn from the water. (French) a white wine.
Mozelle

Mosi (Swahili) first-born.

Moswen (Tswana) white.

Mouna (Arabic) wish, desire.
Moona, Moonia, Mounia, Muna, Munia

Mrena (Slavic) white eyes.
Mren

Mumtaz (Arabic) distinguished.

Mura (Japanese) village.

Muriel (Arabic) myrrh. (Irish) shining sea. A form of Mary. See also Meryl.
Merial, Meriel, Meriol, Merrial, Merriel, Muire, Murial, Muriell, Murielle

Musetta (French) little bagpipe.
Musette

Muslimah (Arabic) devout believer.

Mya (Burmese) emerald. (Italian) a form of Mia.
My, Myah, Myia, Myiah

Myesha (American) a form of Moesha.
Myeisha, Myeshia, Myiesha, Myisha

Mykaela, Mykayla (American) forms of Mikaela.
Mykael, Mykaila, Mykal, Mykala, Mykaleen, Mykel, Mykela, Mykeyla

Myla (English) merciful.

Mylene (Greek) dark.
Mylaine, Mylana, Mylee, Myleen

Myra (Latin) fragrant ointment.
Maya, Myrena, Myria

Myranda (Latin) a form of Miranda.
Myrandah, Myrandia, Myrannda

Myriam (American) a form of Miriam.
Myriame, Myryam

Myrna (Irish) beloved.
Merna, Mirna, Moma, Muirna

Myrtle (Greek) dark green shrub.
Mertis, Mertle, Mirtle, Myrta, Myrtia, Myrtias, Myrtice, Myrtie, Myrtilla, Myrtis

N

Nabila (Arabic) born to nobility.
Nabeela, Nabiha, Nabilah

Nadda (Arabic) generous; dewy.
Nada

Nadette (French) a short form of Bernadette.

Nadia (French, Slavic) hopeful.
Nadea, Nadenka, Nadezhda, Nadiah, Nadie, Nadija, Nadijah, Nadine, Nadiya, Nadiyah, Nadja, Nadjae, Nadjah, Nadka, Nadsha, Nady, Nadya

Nadine (French, Slavic) a form of Nadia.
Nadean, Nadeana, Nadeen, Nadena, Nadene, Nadien, Nadin, Nadina, Nadyne, Naidene, Naidine

Nadira (Arabic) rare, precious.
Naadirah, Nadirah

Naeva (French) a form of Eve.
Nahvon

Nafuna (Luganda) born feet first.

Nagida (Hebrew) noble; prosperous.
Nagda, Ngeeda

Nahid (Persian) Mythology: another name for Venus, the goddess of love and beauty.

Nahimana (Dakota) mystic.

Naida (Greek) water nymph.
Naiad, Naiya, Nayad, Nyad

Naila (Arabic) successful.
Nailah

Nairi (Armenian) land of rivers. History: a name for ancient Armenia.
Naira, Naire, Nayra

Naiya (Greek) a form of Naida.
Naia, Naiyana, Naja, Najah, Naya

Najam (Arabic) star.
Naja, Najma

Najila (Arabic) brilliant eyes.
Naja, Najah, Najia, Najla, Najla

Nakeisha (American) a combination of the prefix Na + Keisha.
Nakeesha, Nakesha, Nakeshea, Nakeshia, Nakeysha, Nakiesha, Nakisha, Nekeisha

Nakeita (American) a form of Nikita.
Nakeeta, Nakeia, Nakeitha, Nakeitra, Nakeitress, Nakeitta, Nakeititia, Naketta, Nakieta, Nakitha, Nakitia, Nakitta, Nakyta

Nakia (Arabic) pure.
Nakea, Nakeia, Nakeya, Nakeyah, Nakeyia, Nakiah, Nakiaya, Nakiea, Nakiya, Nakiyah, Nekia

Nakita (American) a form of Nikita.
Nakkita, Naquita

Nalani (Hawaiian) calm as the heavens.
Nalanie, Nalany

Nami (Japanese) wave.
Namika, Namiko

Nan (German) a short form of Fernanda. (English) a form of Ann.
Nana, Nanice, Nanine, Nanna, Nanon

Nana (Hawaiian) spring.

Nanci (English) a form of Nancy.
Nancie, Nancsi, Nansi

Nancy (English) gracious. A familiar form of Nan.
Nainsi, Nance, Nancee, Nancey, Nanci, Nancine, Nancye, Nanette, Nanice, Nanncey, Nanncy, Nanouk, Nansee, Nansey, Nanuk

Nanette (French) a form of Nancy.
Nan, Nanete, Nannette, Nettie, Nineta, Ninete, Ninetta, Ninette, Nini, Ninita, Ninnetta, Ninnette, Nynette

Nani (Greek) charming. (Hawaiian) beautiful.
Nanni, Nannie, Nanny

Naomi (Hebrew) pleasant, beautiful. Bible: Ruth's mother-in-law.
Naoma, Naomia, Naomie, Naomy, Navit, Neoma, Neomi, Noami, Noemi, Noma, Nomi, Nyomi

Naomie (Hebrew) a form of Naomi.
Naome, Naomee, Noemie

Nara (Greek) happy. (English) north. (Japanese) oak.
Narah

Narcissa (Greek) daffodil. Mythology: Narcissus was the youth who fell in love with his own reflection.
Narcessa, Narcisa, Narcisse, Naryssa, Narissa, Narkissa

Narelle (Australian) woman from the sea.
Narel

Nari (Japanese) thunder.
Narie, Nariko

Narmada (Hindi) pleasure giver.

Nashawna (American) a combination of the prefix Na + Shawna.
Nashan, Nashana, Nashanda, Nashawn, Nashauna, Nashaunda, Nashaunna, Nashawn, Nasheena, Nashounda, Nashuana

Nashota (Native American) double; second-born twin.

Nastasia (Greek) a form of Anastasia.
Nastasha, Nastashia, Nastasja, Nastassa, Nastassia, Nastassiya, Nastassja, Nastassya, Nastasya, Nastazia, Nastisija, Nastka, Nastsya, Nastya

Nasya (Hebrew) miracle.
Nasia, Nasyah

Nata (Sanskrit) dancer. (Latin) swimmer. (Native American) speaker; creator. (Polish, Russian) a form of Natalie. See also Nadia.
Natia, Natka, Natya

Natacha (Russian) a form of Natasha.
Natachia, Natacia, Naticha

Natalee, Natali (Latin) forms of Natalie.
Natale, Nataleh, Nataleigh, Nattlee

Natalia (Russian) a form of Natalie. See also Talia.
Nacia, Natala, Natalea, Nataliia, Natalija, Natalina, Nataliya, Nataliyah, Natalja, Natalka, Natallea, Natallia, Natalya, Nathalia, Natka

Natalie (Latin) born on Christmas day. See also Nata, Natasha, Noel, Talia.
Nat, Natalee, Natali, Natalia, Nataliee, Nataline, Nathalie, Natalie, Nataly, Natilie, Natlie, Nattalie, Nattie

Nataline (Latin) a form of Natalie. Natalene, Natalene, Natalyn

Natalle (French) a form of Natalie. Natale

Nataly (Latin) a form of Natalie. Nathaly, Natally, Natalye

Natane (Arapaho) daughter. Natanne

Natara (Arabic) sacrifice. Natori, Natoria

Natania (Hebrew) gift of God. Natanya, Natee, Nathania, Nathenia, Netania, Nethania

Natasha (Russian) a form of Natalie. See also Stacey, Tasha.
Nahtasha, Natacha, Natasa, Natascha, Natashah, Natashea, Natashenea, Natashia, Natashiea, Natashiya, Natashka, Natasia, Natassia, Natassja, Natasza, Natawsha, Natausha, Natasja, Nateshia, Nathasha, Nathassha, Natisha, Natishia, Natosha, Netasha, Notosha

Natesa (Hindi) cosmic dancer. Religion: another name for the Hindu god Shiva.
Natisa, Natissa

Nathalie, Nathaly (Latin) forms of Natalie.
Nathalee, Nathali, Nathalia, Nathalya

Natie (English) a familiar form of Natalie.
Nati, Natti, Nattie, Natty

Natosha (Russian) a form of Natasha.
Natoshia, Natoshya, Netosha, Notosha

Nava (Hebrew) beautiful; pleasant.
Navah, Naveh, Navit

Nayely (Irish) a form of Neila.
Naeyli, Nayelia, Nayelli, Nayelly, Nayla

Neala (Irish) a form of Neila.
Nayela, Naylea, Naylia, Nealia, Neela, Neila, Neila

Necha (Spanish) a form of Agnes.
Necho

Neci (Hungarian) fiery, intense.
Necia, Necie

Neda (Slavic) born on Sunday.
Nedah, Nedi, Nedia, Neida

Nedda (English) prosperous guardian.
Neddi, Neddie, Neddy

Neely (Irish) a familiar form of Neila.
Nelia.
Nealee, Nealie, Nealy, Neelee, Neeley, Neeli, Neelie, Neeli, Neilie

Neema (Swahili) born during prosperous times.

Neena (Spanish) a form of Nina.
Neenah, Nena

Neila (Irish) champion. See also Neala, Neely.
Nayely, Neilah, Neile, Neile, Neilla, Neille

Nekeisha (American) a form of Nakeisha.
Nechesa, Neikeishia, Nekesha, Nekeshia, Nekeisha, Nekeishia, Nekeshia

Nekia (Arabic) a form of Nakia.
Nekeya, Nekiya, Nekiyah, Nekya, Nekiya

Nelle (Greek) stone.

Nellie, Nelly (English) familiar forms of Cornelia, Eleanor, Helen, Prunella.
Nel, Neli, Nell, Nella, Nelley, Nelli, Nelliamne, Nellice, Nellis, Nelma

Nenet (Egyptian) born near the sea. Mythology: Nunet was the goddess of the sea.

Neola (Greek) youthful.
Neolla

Neona (Greek) new moon.

Nereida (Greek) a form of Nerine.
Nereyda, Nereydia, Nerida

Nerine (Greek) sea nymph.
Nereida, Nerina, Nerita, Nerline

Nerissa (Greek) sea nymph. See also Rissa.
Narice, Narissa, Nerice, Nerisa, Nerisse, Nerrisa, Nerys, Neryssa

Nessa (Scandinavian) promontory. (Greek) a short form of Agnes. See also Nessie.
Nesa, Nesha, Neshia, Nesiah, Nessia, Nesta, Nessa, Neysa, Neysha, Neyshia

Nessie (Greek) a familiar form of Agnes, Nessa, Vanessa.
Nese, Neshie, Nesho, Nesi, Ness, Nessi, Nessy, Nest, Neys

Neta (Hebrew) plant, shrub. See also Nettie.
Netia, Netta, Nettia

Netis (Native American) trustworthy.

Nettie (French) a familiar form of Annette, Nanette, Antoinette.
Neti, Netie, Netta, Netti, Netty, Nety

Neva (Spanish) snow. (English) new. Geography: a river in Russia.
Neiva, Neve, Nevia, Neyva, Nieve, Niva, Nivea, Nivia

Nevada (Spanish) snow. Geography: a western U. S. state.
Neiva, Neva

Nevina (Irish) worshipper of the saint.
Neveen, Nevein, Nevena, Neveyan, Nevin, Nivena

Neylan (Turkish) fulfilled wish.
Neya, Neyla

Neza (Slavic) a form of Agnes.

Nia (Irish) a familiar form of Neila. Mythology: Nia Ben Aur was a legendary Welsh woman.
Neya, Niah, Niajia, Niya, Nya

Niabi (Osage) fawn.

Nichelle (American) a combination of Nicole + Michelle. Culture: Nichelle Nichols was the first African American woman featured in a television drama (*Star Trek*).
Nichele, Nichell, Nishelle

Nichole (French) a form of Nicole.
Nichol, Nichola, Nicholas, Nicholle

Nicki (French) a familiar form of Nicole.
Nicci, Nickey, Nickeya, Nickia, Nickie, Nickiya, Nicky, Niki

Nickole (French) a form of Nicole.
Nickol

Nicola (Italian) a form of Nicole.
Nacola, Necola, Nichola, Nickola, Nicolea, Nicolla, Nikekola, Nikola, Nikolia, Nykola

Nicole (French) a form of Nicholas. See also Colette, Cosette, Nikita.
Nacole, Necole, Nica, Nichole, Nicia, Nicki, Nickole, Nicol, Nicola, Nicolette, Nicoli, Nicolie, Nicoline, Nicolle, Nikayla, Nikelle, Nikki, Niquole, Nocole, Nycole

Nicolette (French) a form of Nicole.
Nicholette, Nicoletta, Nicollette, Nicollette, Nikoletta, Nikoletta, Nikoletta, Nikolette

Nicoline (French) a familiar form of Nicole.
Nicholine, Nicholyn, Nicoleen, Nicolene, Nicolina, Nicolyn, Nicolyne, Nicolynn, Nicolynne, Nikolene, Nikolina, Nikoline

Nicolle (French) a form of Nicole.
Nicholle

Nida (Omaha) Mythology: an elflike creature.
Nidda

Nidia (Latin) nest.
Nidi, Nidya

Niesha (American) pure. (Scandinavian) a form of Nissa.
Neisha, Neishia, Neissia, Nesha, Neshia, Nesia, Nessia, Niessia, Nisha, Nyesha

Nige (Latin) dark night.
Nigea, Nigela, Nija, Nijac, Nijah

Nika (Russian) belonging to God.
Nikka

Nikayla, Nikelle (American) forms of Nicole.
Nikeille, Nikel, Nikela, Nikelie

Nike (Greek) victorious. Mythology: the goddess of victory.

Niki (Russian) a short form of Nikita. (American) a familiar form of Nicole.
Nikia, Nikiah

Nikita (Russian) victorious people.
Nakeita, Nakita, Niki, Nikitah, Nikitia, Nikitta, Nikki, Nikkita, Niquita, Niquitta

Nikki (American) a familiar form of Nicole, Nikita.
Nicki, Nikia, Nikkea, Nikkey, Nikkia, Nikkiah, Nikkie, Nikko, Nikky

Nikole (French) a form of Nicole.
Nikkole, Nikkolie, Nikola, Nikole, Nikolena, Nicolia, Nikolina, Nikolle

Nila (Latin) Geography: the Nile River is in Africa. (Irish) a form of Neila.
Nilah, Nilesia, Nyla

Nili (Hebrew) Botany: a pea plant that yields indigo.

Nima (Hebrew) thread. (Arabic) blessing.
Nema, Niama, Nimali

Nina (Hebrew) a familiar form of Hannah. (Spanish) girl. (Native American) mighty. (Hebrew) a familiar form of Hannah.
Neena, Ninah, Ninaska, Ninja, Ninna, Ninon, Ninosca, Ninoshka.

Ninon (French) a form of Nina.

Nirel (Hebrew) light of God.
Nirali, Nirelle

Nirveli (Hindi) water child.

Nisa (Arabic) woman.

Nisha (American) a form of Niesha, Nissa.
Niasha, Nishay

Nishi (Japanese) west.

Nissa (Hebrew) sign, emblem. (Scandinavian) friendly elf; brownie. See also Nyssa.
Nisha, Nisse, Nissie, Nissy

Nita (Hebrew) planter. (Choctaw) bear. (Spanish) a short form of Anita, Juanita.
Nitai, Nitha, Nithai, Nitika

Nitara (Hindi) deeply rooted.

Nitasha (American) a form of Natasha.
Niiasha, Niteisha, Nitisha, Nitishia

Nitsa (Greek) a form of Helen.

Nituna (Native American) daughter.

Nitza (Hebrew) flower bud.
Nitzah, Nitzana, Nitzanit, Niza, Nizah

Nixie (German) water sprite.

Niya (Irish) a form of Nia.
Niyah, Niyana, Niyia, Nyia

Nizana (Hebrew) a form of Nitza.
Nitzana, Nitzania, Zana

Noel (Latin) Christmas. See also Natalie.
Noël, Noela, Noelani, Noele, Noeleen, Noelene, Noelia, Noeline, Noelle, Noelyn, Noelynn, Nohely, Noleen, Novelenn, Novelia, Novel, Noweleen, Nowell

Noelani (Hawaiian) beautiful one from heaven.
Nola

Noelle (French) Christmas.
Noell, Noella, Noelleen, Noelly, Noellyn

Noemi (Hebrew) a form of Naomi.
Noam, Noemie, Noemy, Nohemi, Nomi

Noemie (Hebrew) a form of Noemi.

Noemy (Hebrew) a form of Noemi.

Noga (Hebrew) morning light.

Nohely (Latin) a form of Noel.
Noeli, Noelie, Noely, Nohal, Noheli

Nokomis (Dakota) moon daughter.

Nola (Latin) small bell. (Irish) famous; noble. A short form of Fionnula.
Nuala

Noleta (Latin) unwilling.
Nolita

Nollie (English) a familiar form of Magnolia.
Nolia, Nolle, Nolley, Nolli, Nolly

Noma (Hawaiian) a form of Norma.

Nona (Latin) ninth.
Nonah, Noni, Nonia, Nonie, Nonna, Nonnah, Norya

Noor (Aramaic) a form of Nura.
Noorie, Nour, Nur

Nora (Greek) light. A familiar form of Eleanor, Honora, Leonore.
Norah, Noreen

Noreen (Irish) a form of Eleanor, Nora. (Latin) a familiar form of Norma.
Noorin, Noreena, Noreene, Noren, Norena, Norene, Norina, Norine, Nureen

Norell (Scandinavian) from the north.
Narell, Narelle, Norela, Norelle, Norely

Nori (Japanese) law, tradition.
Noria, Norica, Noriko, Noria

Norma (Latin) rule, precept.
Norina, Noreen, Normi, Normie

Nova (Latin) new. A short form of Novella, Novia. (Hopi) butterfly chaser. Astronomy: a star that releases bright bursts of energy.

Novella (Latin) newcomer.
Nova, Novela

Novia (Spanish) sweetheart.
Nova, Novka, Navia

Nu (Burmese) tender. (Vietnamese) girl.
Nue

Nuala (Irish) a short form of Fionnula.
Nola, Nula

Nuela (Spanish) a form of Amelia.

Nuna (Native American) land.

Nunciata (Latin) messenger.
Nunzia

Nura (Aramaic) light.
Noor, Noora, Noorah, Noura, Nurah

Nuria (Aramaic) the Lord's light.
Nuri, Nuriel, Nurin

Nurita (Hebrew) Botany: a flower with red and yellow blossoms.
Nurit

Nuru (Swahili) daylight.

Nusi (Hungarian) a form of Hannah.

Nuwa (Chinese) mother goddess. Mythology: another name for Nügua, the creator of mankind.

Nya (Irish) a form of Nia.
Nyaa, Nyah, Nyia

Nycole (French) a form of Nicole.
Nychelle, Nyolette, Nycolle

Nydia (Latin) nest.
Nyda

Nyesha (American) a form of Niesha.
Nyeisha, Nyeshia

Nyla (Latin, Irish) a form of Nila.
Nylah

Nyoko (Japanese) gem, treasure.

Nyomi (Hebrew) a form of Naomi.
Nyome, Nyomee, Nyomie

Nyree (Maori) sea.
Nyra, Nyrie

Nyssa (Greek) beginning. See also Nissa.
Nisha, Nissi, Nissy, Nyasia, Nysa

Nyusha (Russian) a form of Agnes.
Nyushenka, Nyushka

Oba (Yoruba) chief, ruler.

Obelia (Greek) needle.

Oceana (Greek) ocean. Mythology: Oceanus was the god of the ocean.
Ocean, Oceananna, Oceane, Oceania, Oceanna, Oceanne, Oceaonna, Oceon

Oceane (French) a form of Oceana.

Octavia (Latin) eighth. See also Tavia.
Octabia, Octaviah, Octaviais, Octavice, Octavie, Octavienne, Octavio, Octavious, Octavise, Octavya, Octivia, Otavia, Ottavia

Odele (Greek) melody, song.
Odelet, Odelette, Odell, Odelle

Odelia (Greek) ode; melodic. (Hebrew) I will praise God. (French) wealthy. See also Odetta.
Oda, Odeelia, Odeleya, Odelina, Odelinda, Odelyn, Odila, Odile, Odilia

Odella (English) wood hill.
Odela, Odelle, Odelyn

Odera (Hebrew) plough.

Odessa (Greek) odyssey, long voyage.
Adesha, Adeshia, Adessa, Adessia, Odessia

Odetta (German, French) a form of Odelia.
Oddetta, Odette

Odina (Algonquin) mountain.

Ofelia (Greek) a form of Ophelia.
Ofeelia, Ofilia

Ofira (Hebrew) gold.
Ofarrah, Ophira

Ofra (Hebrew) a form of Aphra.
Ofrat

Ogin (Native American) wild rose.

Ohanna (Hebrew) God's gracious gift.

Okalani (Hawaiian) heaven.
Okilani

Oki (Japanese) middle of the ocean.
Okie

Oksana (Latin) a form of Osanna.
Oksanna

Ola (Greek) a short form of Olesia.(Scandinavian) ancestor.

Olathe (Native American) beautiful.
Olathia

Oleda (Spanish) a form of Alida. See also Leda.
Oleta, Olida, Olita

Olena (Russian) a form of Helen.
Olena, Olenka, Olenna, Olenya, Olya

Olesia (Greek) a form of Alexandra.
Cesya, Ola, Olecia, Oleesha, Oleishia, Olesha, Olesya, Olexa, Olice, Olicia, Olisha, Olishia, Ollicia

Olethea (Latin) truthful. See also Alethea.
Oleta

Oletha (Scandinavian) nimble.
Oleta, Yaletha

Olga (Scandinavian) holy. See also Helga, Olivia.
Olenka, Olia, Olja, Ollya, Olya

Oliana (Polynesian) oleander.

Olina (Hawaiian) filled with happiness.

Olinda (Latin) scented. (Spanish) protector of property. (Greek) a form of Yolanda.

Olisa (Ibo) God.

Olive (Latin) olive tree.
Oliff, Oliffe, Olivet, Olivette

Olivia (Latin) a form of Olive. (English) a form of Olga. See also Liv, Livia.
Alivia, Alyvia, Oleva, Oliva, Olivea, Oliveia, Alyvia, Oliva, Olivea, Oliveia, Olivetta, Olivi, Olivianne, Olivya, Olivia, Ollie, Olva, Olyvia

Ollie (English) a familiar form of Olivia.
Olla, Olly, Ollye

Olwen (Welsh) white footprint.
Olwenn, Olwin, Olwyn, Olwyne

Olympia (Greek) heavenly.
Olimpia, Olympe, Olympie

Olyvia (Latin) a form of Olivia.

Oma (Hebrew) reverent. (German) grandmother. (Arabic) highest.

Omaira (Arabic) red.
Omar, Omara, Omarah, Omari, Omaria, Omara

Omega (Greek) last, final, end. Linguistics: the last letter in the Greek alphabet.

Ona (Latin, Irish) a form of Oona, Una. (English) river.

Onatah (Iroquois) daughter of the earth and the corn spirit.

Onawa (Native American) wide awake.
Onaja, Onajah

Ondine (Latin) a form of Undine.
Ondene, Ondina, Ondyne

Ondrea (Czech) a form of Andrea.
Ohndrea, Ohndreea, Ohndreya, Ohndria, Ondraya, Ondreana, Ondreea, Ondreya, Ondria, Ondrianna, Ondrea

Oneida (Native American) eagerly awaited.
Onida, Onyda

Onesha (American) a combination of Ondrea + Aisha.
Oneshia, Onessa, Onessia, Onethia, Oniesha, Onisha

Onella (Hungarian) a form of Helen.

Oni (Yoruba) born on holy ground.
Onnie

Onora (Latin) a form of Honora.
Onoria, Onorine, Onnora

Oona (Latin, Irish) a form of Una.
Oma, Onna, Onnie, Oonagh, Oonie

Opa (Choctaw) owl. (German) grandfather.

Opal (Hindi) precious stone.
Opale, Opalina, Opaline

Ophelia (Greek) helper. Literature: Hamlet's love interest in the Shakespearean play Hamlet.
Filia, Ofelia, Ophélie, Ophilia, Phelia

Oprah (Hebrew) a form of Orpah.
Ophra, Ophrah, Opra

Ora (Latin) prayer. (Spanish) gold. (English) seacoast. (Greek) a form of Aura.
Orah, Orlee, Orra

Oralee (Hebrew) the Lord is my light. See also Yareli.
Areli, Orali, Oralit, Orelle, Orlee, Orli, Orly

Oralia (French) a form of Aurelia. See also Oriana.
Oralis, Oriel, Orielda, Orielle, Oriena, Oriena, Orlene

Orazia — *(not present)*

Orea (Greek) mountains.
Oreal, Oria, Oriah

Orela (Latin) announcement from the gods; oracle.
Oreal, Orella, Orelle, Oriel, Orielle

Orabella (Latin) a form of Arabella.
Orabel, Orabela, Orabelle

Orenda (Iroquois) magical power.

Oretha (Greek) a form of Aretha.
Oreta, Oretta, Orette

Oriana (Latin) dawn, sunrise. (Irish) golden.
Onane, Orania, Orelda, Orelle, Ori, Oria, Orian, Oriane, Orianna, Orieana, Oryan

Orina (Russian) a form of Irene.
Orya, Oryna

Orinda (Hebrew) pine tree. (Irish) light skinned, white.
Orenda

Orino (Japanese) worker's field.
Ori

Oriole (Latin) golden; black-and-orange bird.
Auriel, Oriel, Oriell, Oriella, Oriola

Orla (Irish) golden woman.
Orlagh, Orlie, Orly

Orlanda (German) famous throughout the land.
Orlandia, Orlantha, Orlenda, Orlinda

Orlenda (Russian) eagle.

Orli (Hebrew) light.
Orlice, Orlie, Orly

Ormanda (Latin) noble. (German) mariner.
Orma

Ornice (Hebrew) cedar tree. (Irish) pale; olive colored.
Orna, Ornah, Ornat, Ornette, Ornit

Orpah (Hebrew) runaway. See also Oprah.
Orpa, Orpha, Orphie

Orquidea (Spanish) orchid.
Orquidia

Orsa (Latin) a short form of Orseline. See also Ursa.
Orsaline, Orse, Orsel, Orselina, Orseline, Orsola

Ortensia (Italian) a form of Hortense.

Orva (French) golden; worthy. (English) brave friend.

Osanna (Latin) praise the Lord.
Oksana, Osana

Osen (Japanese) one thousand.

Oseye (Benin) merry.

Osma (English) divine protector.
Ozma

Otilie (Czech) lucky heroine.
Otila, Otilia, Orka, Ottili, Orylia

Ovia (Latin, Danish) egg.

Owena (Welsh) born to nobility; young warrior.

Oya (Moquelumnan) called forth.

Oz (Hebrew) strength.

Ozara (Hebrew) treasure, wealth.

P

Padget (French) a short form of Page.
Padget, Paget, Pagett

Padma (Hindi) lotus.

Page (French) young assistant.
Padget, Pagen, Pagi, Page

Paige (English) young child.
Payge

Paisley (Scottish) patterned fabric first made in Paisley, Scotland.
Paislay, Paislee, Paisleyann, Paisleyanne, Paizlei, Paizleigh, Paizley, Paisley, Pazley

Paiton (English) warrior's town.
Paiten, Paityn, Paityne, Paiyton, Paten, Patton

Paka (Swahili) kitten. See also Paca.

Pakuna (Moquelumnan) deer bounding while running downhill.

Palila (Polynesian) bird.

Pallas (Greek) wise. Mythology: another name for Athena, the goddess of wisdom.

Palma (Latin) palm tree.
Pallma, Palmira

Palmira (Spanish) a form of Palma.
Palmirah, Pallmyra, Palmer, Palmyra

Paloma (Spanish) dove. See also Aloma.
Palloma, Palometa, Palomita, Paluma, Peloma

Pamela (Greek) honey.
Pam, Pama, Pamala, Pamalla, Pamelia, Pamelina, Pamella, Pamila, Pamilla, Pammela, Pammi, Pammie, Pammy, Pamula

Pancha (Spanish) free; from France.
Paca, Panchita

Paca (Spanish) a short form of Pancha. See also Paka.

Pandita (Hindi) scholar.

Pandora (Greek) all-gifted. Mythology: a woman who opened a box out of curiosity and released evil into the world. See also Dora.
Pandi, Pandorah, Pandora, Pandorah, Pandy, Panndora, Panndorah, Panndorrah

Pansy (Greek) flower; fragrant. (French) thoughtful.
Pansey, Pansie

Panthea (Greek) all the gods.
Pantheia, Pantheya

Panya (Swahili) mouse; tiny baby. (Russian) a familiar form of Stephanie.
Panyia

Panyin (Fante) older twin.

Paola (Italian) a form of Paula.
Paoli, Paolina

Papina (Moquelumnan) vine growing on an oak tree.

Paquita (Spanish) a form of Frances.
Paqua

Pari (Persian) fairy eagle.

Paris (French) Geography: the capital of France. Mythology: the Trojan prince who started the Trojan War by abducting Helen.
Parice, Paries, Parisa, Parise, Parish, Parisha, Pariss, Parisse, Parris, Parys, Parysse

Parker (English) park keeper.
Park, Parke

Parris (French) a form of Paris.
Parrise, Parrish, Parrisha, Parrys, Parrysh

Parthenia (Greek) virginal.
Parthenia, Parthenie, Parthinia, Pathina

Parveneh (Persian) butterfly.

Pascale (French) born on Easter or Passover.
Pascalette, Pascaline, Pascalle, Paschale, Paskel

Pasha (Greek) sea.
Palasha, Pascha, Pasche, Pashae, Pashe, Pashel, Pashka, Pasia, Passia

Passion (Latin) passion.
Pashion, Pashonne, Pasion, Passionaé, Passionate, Passionette

Pasua (Swahili) born by cesarean section.

Pat (Latin) a short form of Patricia, Patsy.

Pati (Moquelumnan) fish baskets made of willow branches.

Patia (Gypsy, Spanish) leaf. (Latin, English) a familiar form of Patience, Patricia.

Patience (English) patient.
Paciencia, Patia, Patiance, Patient, Patince, Patisha

Patra (Greek, Latin) a form of Petra.

Patrice (French) a form of Patricia.
Patrease, Patreece, Patreese, Patreice, Patrece, Patryce, Patrice

Patricia (Latin) noblewoman. See also Payton, Peyton, Tricia, Trisha, Trissa.
Pat, Patia, Patresa, Patrica, Patrice,

Patrica, Patriccia, Patrichea, Patriciana, Patricianna, Patricja, Patrichea, Patrickia, Patrisha, Patrisia, Patrisia, Patrissa, Patrizia, Patrizzia, Patricia, Patrycja, Patsy, Patty

Patsy (Latin) a familiar form of Patricia.
Pat, Patsey, Patsi

Patty (English) a familiar form of Patricia.
Patte, Pattee, Patti, Pattie

Paula (Latin) small. See also Pavla, Polly.
Palikei, Paola, Paulane, Paulann, Paule, Paulette, Paulina, Pauline, Paulla, Paria

Paulette (Latin) a familiar form of Paula.
Paulet, Paulett, Pauleta, Paulita, Paullett, Paulletta, Paullette

Paulina (Slavic) a form of Paula.
Paulena, Paulene, Paulenia, Paulina, Pauliianne, Paullena, Paulyna, Pauviina, Polena, Polina, Polinia

Pauline (French) a form of Paula.
Pauleen, Paulene, Paulien, Paulin, Paulyne, Paulynn, Pouline

Pausha (Hindi) lunar month of Capricorn.

Pavla (Czech, Russian) a form of Paula.
Pavlina, Pavlinka

Paxton (Latin) peaceful town.
Paxtin, Paxtynn

Payge (English) a form of Paige.

Payton (Irish) a form of Patricia.
Paydon, Paytan, Payten, Paytin, Paytn, Payton

Paz (Spanish) peace.

Pazi (Ponca) yellow bird.

Pazia (Hebrew) golden.
Paz, Paza, Pazice, Pazit

Peace (English) peaceful.

Pearl (Latin) jewel.
Pearle, Pearleen, Pearlena, Pearlene, Pearlette, Pearlina, Pearline, Pearlisha, Pearlyn, Perl, Perla, Perle, Perlette, Perlie, Perline, Perlline

Peggy (Greek) a familiar form of Margaret.
Peg, Pegeen, Pegg, Peggey, Peggi, Peggie, Pegi

Peke (Hawaiian) a form of Bertha.

Pela (Polish) a short form of Penelope.
Pele

Pelagia (Greek) sea.
Pelage, Pelageia, Pelagie, Pelga, Pelgia, Pellagia

Pelipa (Zuni) a form of Philippa.

Pemba (Bambara) the power that controls all life.

Penda (Swahili) loved.

Penelope (Greek) weaver. Mythology: the clever and loyal wife of Odysseus, a Greek hero.
Pela, Pen, Penelopa, Penna, Pennelope, Penny, Pinelopi

Peni (Carrier) mind.

Peninah (Hebrew) pearl.
Penina, Peninit, Peninnah, Penny

Penny (Greek) a familiar form of Penelope, Peninah.
Penee, Peni, Penney, Penni, Pennie

Peony (Greek) flower.
Peonie

Pepita (Spanish) a familiar form of Josephine.
Pepa, Pepi, Peppy, Peta

Pepper (Latin) condiment from the pepper plant.

Perah (Hebrew) flower.

Perdita (Latin) lost. Literature: a character in Shakespeare's play *The Winter's Tale*.
Perdida, Perdy

Perfecta (Spanish) flawless.

Peri (Greek) mountain dweller. (Persian) fairy or elf.
Perita

Perla (Latin) a form of Pearl.
Pearla

Perlie (Latin) a familiar form of Pearl.
Pearley, Pearlie, Pearly, Perley, Perli, Perly, Purley, Purly

Pernella (Greek, French) rock. (Latin) a short form of Petronella.
Parnella, Pernel, Pernell, Pernelle

Perri (Greek, Latin) small rock; traveler. (French) pear tree. (Welsh) child of Harry. (English) a form of Perry.
Perre, Perrey, Perriann, Perrie, Perrin, Perrine, Perry

Persephone (Greek) Mythology: the goddess of the underworld.
Persephanie, Persephany, Persephonie

Persis (Latin) from Persia.
Perssis, Persy

Peta (Blackfoot) golden eagle.

Petra (Greek, Latin) small rock. A short form of Petronella.
Patra, Pet, Peta, Petena, Peterina, Petraann, Petrice, Petrina, Petrine, Petrova, Petrovna, Pier, Pierce, Pietra

Petronella (Greek) small rock. (Latin) of the Roman clan Petronius.
Pernella, Peternella, Petra, Petrona, Petronela, Petronella, Petronelle, Petronia, Petronija, Petronilla, Petronille

Petula (Latin) seeker.
Petulah

Petunia (Native American) flower.

Peyton (Irish) a form of Patricia.
Peyden, Peydon, Peyten, Peytyn

Phaedra (Greek) bright.
Faydra, Phae, Phaidra, Phe, Phedre

Phallon (Irish) a form of Fallon.
Phalaine, Phalen, Phallan, Phallie, Phalon, Phalyn

Phebe (Greek) a form of Phoebe.
Pheba, Pheby

Pheodora (Greek, Russian) a form of Feodora.
Phedora, Phedorah, Pheodorah, Pheydora, Pheydorah

Philana (Greek) lover of mankind.
Phila, Philanna, Philene, Philiane, Philina, Philine

Philantha (Greek) lover of flowers.

Philicia (Latin) a form of Phylicia.
Philicia, Philesha, Philia, Philicha, Philyda

Philippa (Greek) lover of horses. See also Filippa.
Phil, Philipa, Philippe, Phillipina, Phillippine, Phillie, Philly, Pippa, Pippy

Philomena (Greek) love song; loved one. Bible: a first-century saint. See also Filomena, Mena.
Philoméne, Philomina

Phoebe (Greek) shining.
Phaebe, Phebe, Pheobe, Phoebey

Phylicia (Latin) fortunate; happy. (Greek) a form of Felicia.
Philicia, Phylecia, Phylesha, Phylesia, Phylicia, Phylisha, Phylisia, Phylissa, Phyllecia, Phyllicia, Phyllisha, Phyllisia, Phyllissa, Phyllyza

Phyllida (Greek) a form of Phyllis.
Fillida, Philida, Philidda, Philyda

Phyllis (Greek) green bough.
Filise, Fillys, Fyllis, Philis, Philis, Philliss, Philys, Philyss, Phylis, Phyllida, Phyllis, Phylliss, Phylys

Pia (Italian) devout.

Piedad (Spanish) devoted; pious.

Pier (French) a form of Petra.
Pierette, Pierrette, Pierra, Pierre

Pierce (English) a form of Petra.

Pilar (Spanish) pillar, column.
Peelar, Pilár, Pillar

Ping (Chinese) duckweed.

Pinga (Eskimo) Mythology: the goddess of game and the hunt.

Piper (English) pipe player.

Pippa (English) a short form of Phillipa.

Pippi (French) rosy cheeked.
Pippen, Pippie, Pippin, Pippy

Pita (African) fourth daughter.

Placidia (Latin) serene.
Placida

Pleasance (French) pleasant.
Pleasence

Polla (Arabic) poppy.
Pola

Polly (Latin) a familiar form of Paula.
Paili, Pali, Pauli, Paulie, Pauly, Poll, Pollee, Polley, Polli, Pollie

Pollyam (Hindi) goddess of the plague. Religion: the Hindu name invoked to ward off bad spirits.

Pollyanna (English) a combination of Polly + Anna. Literature: an overly optimistic heroine created by Eleanor Porter.

Poloma (Choctaw) bow.

Pomona (Latin) apple. Mythology: the goddess of fruit and fruit trees.

Poni (African) second daughter.

Poppy (Latin) poppy flower.
Popi, Poppey, Poppi, Poppie

Pora, Poria (Hebrew) fruitful.

Porcha (Latin) a form of Portia.
Porchae, Porchai, Porche, Porchia, Poria

Porscha, Porsche (German) forms of Portia.
Porsha, Porsche, Porschah, Porsché, Porschea, Porschia, Pourche

Porsha (Latin) a form of Portia.
Porshai, Porshay, Porshe, Porshea, Porshia

Portia (Latin) offering. Literature: the heroine of Shakespeare's play *The Merchant of Venice*.
Porcha, Porscha, Porsche, Porsha, Portiea

Precious (French) precious; dear.
Pracious, Preciose, Precisha, Prescious, Presious

Presley (English) priest's meadow.
Preslea, Preslee, Presli, Presli, Preslie, Presly, Preslye, Pressley, Presslie, Pressly

Prima (Latin) first, beginning first child.
Prema, Primalia, Primetta, Priminia

Primavera (Italian, Spanish) spring.

Primrose (English) primrose flower.
Primula

Princess (English) daughter of royalty.
Princess, Princes, Princesa, Princessa, Princetta, Princie, Princilla

Priscilla (Latin) ancient.
*Cilla, Piri, Precila, Precilla, Prescilla,
Pressilla, Pressilla, Pricila, Pricilla, Pris,
Prisca, Priscela, Priscella, Priscila,
Priscilla, Priscill, Priscille, Priscillia,
Prisella, Prisila, Prisilla, Prissila, Prissilla,
Prissy, Pryscylla, Prysilla*

Prissy (Latin) a familiar form of Priscilla.
Prisi, Priss, Prissi, Prissie

Priya (Hindi) beloved; sweet natured.
Pria

Procopia (Latin) declared leader.

Promise (Latin) promise, pledge.
Promis, Promiss, Promys, Promyse

Pru (Latin) a short form of Prudence.
Prue

Prudence (Latin) cautious; discreet.
Pru, Prudencia, Prudens, Prudy

Prudy (Latin) a familiar form of
Prudence.
Prudee, Prudi, Prudie

Prunella (Latin) brown; little plum.
See also Nellie.
Prunela

Psyche (Greek) soul. Mythology: a
beautiful mortal loved by Eros, the
Greek god of love.

Pua (Hawaiian) flower.

Pualani (Hawaiian) heavenly flower.
Puni

Purity (English) purity.
Pura, Pureza, Purisima

Pyralis (Greek) fire.
Pyrene

Qadira (Arabic) powerful.
Kadira

Qamra (Arabic) moon.
Kamra

Qitarah (Arabic) fragrant.

Quaashie (Ewe) born on Sunday.

Quadeisha (American) a combination
of Qadira + Aisha.
*Qudaisha, Quadaishia, Quadajah,
Quadasha, Quadasia, Quadayshia,
Quadaza, Quadejah, Quadesha,
Quadeshia, Quadiasha, Quaesha*

Quaneisha (American) a combination
of the prefix Qu + Niesha.
*Quaneasa, Quanece, Quanecia,
Quaneice, Quanesha, Quanisha,
Quansha, Quarnisha, Queisha,
Quanisha, Qynisha*

Quanesha (American) a form of
Quaneisha.
*Quanesha, Quaneesha, Quaneshia,
Quanesia, Quaness, Quanessia,
Quannesha, Quanneshia, Quannezia,
Quaynesha, Quinesha*

Quanika (American) a combination of
the prefix Qu + Nika.
*Quanikka, Quanikki, Quaniqua,
Quanique, Quantenique, Quavanica,
Queenika, Queenique*

Quanisha (American) a form of
Quaneisha.
*Quaniesha, Quanishia, Quaynisha,
Queenisha, Quenisha, Quenisha*

Quartilla (Latin) fourth.
Quantilla

Qubilah (Arabic) agreeable.

Queen (English) queen. See also
Quinn.
Queena, Queenie, Quenna

Queenie (English) a form of Queen.
Queenation, Queeneste, Queeny

Queisha (American) a short form of
Quaneisha.
Qeysha, Queshia, Queysha

Quenby (Scandinavian) feminine.

Quenisha (American) a combination
of Queen + Aisha.
*Queneesha, Queneisha, Quennisha,
Quensha, Quinesha, Quinisha*

Quenna (English) a form of Queen.
Quenell, Quenessa

Querida (Spanish) dear; beloved.

Questa (French) searcher.

Queta (Spanish) a short form of
names ending in "queta" or "quetta."
Quenetta, Quetta

Quiana (American) a combination of
the prefix Qu + Anna.
*Quian, Quianah, Quianda, Quiane,
Quiani, Quianita, Quianna, Quianne,
Quionna*

Quinby (Scandinavian) queen's estate.

Quincy (Irish) fifth.
Quincee, Quincey, Quinci, Quincia, Quincie

Quinella (Latin) a form of Quintana.

Quinesha, Quinisha (American) forms of Quenisha.
Quinesha, Quinessa, Quinessia, Quinisa, Quinishia, Quinnisha, Quineasha, Quonesha, Quonisha

Quinetta (Latin) a form of Quintana.
Queenetta, Queenette, Quinette, Quinnette

Quinn (German, English) queen. See also Queen.
Quin, Quinna, Quinne, Quyn

Quinshawna (American) a combination of Quinn + Shauna.
Quinshea

Quintana (Latin) fifth. (English) queen's lawn. See also Quinella, Quinetta.
Quintanna, Quinta, Quintanna, Quintara, Quintarah, Quintia, Quintilla, Quintina, Quintona, Quintonice

Quintessa (Latin) essence. See also Tess.
Quintaysha, Quintesa, Quintesha, Quintessia, Quintice, Quinticia, Quintisha, Quintosha

Quintrell (American) a combination of Quinn + Trella.
Quintela, Quintella, Quintrelle

Quiterie (Latin, French) tranquil.
Quita

Qwanisha (American) a form of people.
Quaneisha, Quanechia, Quanesha, Quanessia, Quantasha

R

Rabecca (Hebrew) a form of Rebecca.
Rabecka, Rabeca, Rabekah

Rabi (Arabic) breeze.
Rabia, Rabiah

Rachael (Hebrew) a form of Rachel.
Rachaele, Rachaell, Rachail, Rachalle

Racheal (Hebrew) a form of Rachel.

Rachel (Hebrew) female sheep. Bible: the second wife of Jacob. See also Lahela, Rae, Rochelle.
Racha, Rachael, Rachal, Racheal, Rachela, Rachelann, Rachele, Rachelle, Rahel, Rahela, Rahil, Rayene, Raychel, Raychelle, Rey, Ruchel

Rachelle (French) a form of Rachel. See also Shelley.
Rachalle, Rachell, Rachella, Rachelle, Raechelle, Rashel, Rashele, Rashell, Rashelle, Raychell, Rayshell, Rochelle

Racquel (French) a form of Rachel.
Rackel, Racquell, Racquella, Racquelle

Radella (German) counselor.

Radeyah (Arabic) content, satisfied.
Radeyah, Radhiya, Radiah, Radiyah

Radinka (Slavic) full of life; happy, glad.

Radmilla (Slavic) worker for the people.

Rae (English) doe. (Hebrew) a short form of Rachel.
Raeh, Raenice, Raeneisha, Raesha, Ray, Raye, Rayetta, Rayette, Rayma, Rey

Raeann (American) a combination of Rae + Ann. See also Rayanne.
Raea, Raean, Raeanna, Raeannah, Raeona, Reanna, Raeanne

Raechel (Hebrew) a form of Rachel.
Raechael, Raechal, Raechele, Raechell, Raechyl

Raeden (Japanese) Mythology: Raiden was the god of thunder and lightning.
Raeda, Raeden

Raegan (Irish) a form of Reagan.
Raegen, Raegene, Raegine, Raegyn

Raelene (American) a combination of Rae + Lee.
Rael, Raela, Raelani, Raele, Raeleah, Raelee, Raeleen, Raeleia, Raeleigh, Raeleigha, Raelein, Raelene, Raelennia, Raelesha, Raelin, Raelina, Raelle, Raelyn, Raelynn

Raelyn, Raelynn (American) forms of Raelene.
Raelene, Raelynda, Raelyne, Raelynne

Raena (German) a form of Raina.
*Raenah, Raenia, Raenie, Raenna,
Raeonna, Raeyauna, Raeyn, Raeyonna*

Raeven (English) a form of Raven.
*Raevin, Raevion, Raevon, Raevonna,
Raevyn, Raevynne, Raevwyn, Raewynne,
Raivan, Raiven, Raivin, Raivyn*

Rafa (Arabic) happy; prosperous.

Rafaela (Hebrew) a form of
Raphaela.
Rafaelia, Rafaella

Ragan (Irish) a form of Reagan.
*Ragean, Rageane, Rageen, Ragen,
Ragene, Rageni, Ragenna, Raggan,
Raygan, Raygen, Raygene, Rayghan,
Raygin*

Ragine (English) a form of Regina.
Raegina, Ragin, Ragina, Raginee

Ragnild (Scandinavian) battle counsel.
*Ragna, Ragnell, Ragnhild, Rainell,
Renilda, Renilde*

Raheem (Punjabi) compassionate
God.
Raheema, Rahima

Ráidah (Arabic) leader.

Raina (German) mighty. (English) a
short form of Regina. See also Rayna.
*Raeima, Raena, Raheena, Rain, Raindh,
Rainai, Raine, Rainea, Rainma, Reanna*

Rainbow (English) rainbow.
Rainbeau, Rainbeaux, Rainbo, Raynbow

Raine (Latin) a short form of Regina.
A form of Raina, Rane.
*Raina, Rainey, Raini, Rainie, Rainy,
Reyne*

Randall (English) protected.
*Randa, Randah, Randal, Randalee,
Randel, Randell, Randelle, Randi,
Randilee, Randilyn, Randlyn, Randy,
Randyl*

Randi, Randy (English) familiar forms
of Miranda, Randall.
*Rande, Randee, Randeen, Randene,
Randey, Randie, Randii*

Rane (Scandinavian) queen.
Raine

Rani (Sanskrit) queen. (Hebrew) joy-
ful. A short form of Kerani.
*Rahni, Ranee, Raney, Rania, Ranie,
Ranice, Ranique, Ranni, Rannie*

Ranita (Hebrew) song; joyful.
*Ranata, Ranice, Ranit, Ranite, Ranitta,
Romita*

Raniyah (Arabic) gazing.
Ranya, Ranyah

Rapa (Hawaiian) moonbeam.

Raphaela (Hebrew) healed by God.
Rafaella, Raphaella, Raphaelle

Raphaelle (French) a form of
Raphaela.
Rafaelle, Raphael, Raphaele

Raquel (French) a form of Rachel.
*Rakel, Rakhil, Rakhila, Raqueal,
Raquela, Raquella, Raquelle, Rickelle,
Rickquel, Ricquel, Ricquelle, Rikell,
Rikelle, Rockell*

Rasha (Arabic) young gazelle.
*Rahshea, Rahshia, Rashae, Rashai,
Rashea, Rashi, Rashia*

Raisa (Russian) a form of Rose.
*Raisah, Raissa, Raiza, Raysa, Rayza,
Razia*

Raizel (Yiddish) a form of Rose.
Rayzil, Razil, Reizel, Resel

Raja (Arabic) hopeful.
Raia, Rajaah, Rajae, Rajah, Rajai

Raku (Japanese) pleasure.

Raleigh (Irish) a form of Riley.
Ralea, Raleiah, Raley

Rama (Hebrew) lofty, exalted. (Hindi)
godlike. Religion: an incarnation of
the Hindu god Vishnu.
Ramah

Raman (Spanish) a form of Ramona.

Ramandeep (Sikh) covered by the
light of the Lord's love.

Ramla (Swahili) fortuneteller.
Ramlah

Ramona (Spanish) mighty; wise pro-
tector. See also Mona.
*Raman, Ramonda, Raymona, Romona,
Romonda*

Ramsey (English) ram's island.
Ramsha, Ramsi, Ramsie, Ramza

Ran (Japanese) water lily.
(Scandinavian) destroyer. Mythology:
the Norse sea goddess who destroys.

Rana (Sanskrit) royal. (Arabic) gaze,
look.
Rahna, Rahni, Rani

Ranait (Irish) graceful; prosperous.
Rane, Renny

Rashawna (American) a combination of the prefix Ra + Shawna.
Rashana, Rashanae, Rashanah, Rashanda, Rashane, Rashani, Rashanna, Rashanta, Rashaun, Rashauna, Rashaunda, Rashaundra, Rashaune, Rashawn, Rashawnda, Rashawnna, Rashon, Rashona, Rashonda, Rashunda

Rashel, Rashelle (American) forms of Rachel.
Rashele, Rashell, Rashella

Rashida (Swahili, Turkish) righteous.
Rahshea, Rahsheda, Rahsheita, Rashdah, Rasheda, Rashedah, Rasheeda, Rasheedah, Rasheeta, Rasheida, Rashidah, Rashidi

Rashieka (Arabic) descended from royalty.
Rasheeka, Rasheika, Rasheka, Rashika, Rasika

Rasia (Greek) rose.

Ratana (Tai) crystal.
Ratania, Ratanya, Ratna, Rattan, Rattana

Ratri (Hindi) night. Religion: the goddess of the night.

Raula (French) wolf counselor.
Raoula, Raulla, Raulle

Raven (English) blackbird.
Raeven, Raveen, Raveena, Raveenn, Ravena, Ravene, Ravenn, Ravenna, Ravennah, Ravenne, Raveon, Ravin, Ravon, Ravyn, Rayven, Revena

Ravin (English) forms of Raven.
Ravi, Ravina, Ravine, Ravinne, Ravion

Ravyn (English) a form of Raven.
Ravynn

Rawnie (Gypsy) fine lady.
Rawan, Rawna, Rhawnie

Raya (Hebrew) friend.
Raia, Raiah, Raiya, Ray, Rayah

Rayanne (American) a form of Raeann.
Rayane, Ray-Ann, Rayan, Rayana, Rayann, Rayanna, Rayeanna, Rayona, Rayonna, Reyan, Reyana, Reyann, Reyanna, Reyanne

Raychel, Raychelle (Hebrew) forms of Rachel.
Raychael, Raychele, Raychell, Raychil

Raylene (American) forms of Raylyn.
Ralina, Rayel, Rayele, Rayelle, Rayleana, Raylee, Rayleen, Rayleigh, Raylena, Raylin, Raylinn, Raylona, Raylyn, Raylynn, Raylynne

Raymonde (German) wise protector.
Rayma, Raymae, Raymie

Rayna (Scandinavian) mighty. (Yiddish) pure, clean. (English) king's advisor. (French) a familiar form of Lorraine. See also Raina.
Raynah, Rayne, Raynell, Raynelle, Raynette, Rayona, Rayonna, Reyna

Rayven (English) a form of Raven.
Rayvan, Rayvana, Rayvein, Rayvenne, Rayveona, Rayvin, Rayvon, Rayvonia

Rayya (Arabic) thirsty no longer.

Razi (Aramaic) secretive.
Rayzil, Rayzilee, Raz, Razia, Raziah, Raziela, Razilee, Razili

Raziya (Swahili) agreeable.

Rea (Greek) poppy flower.
Reah

Reagan (Irish) little ruler.
Reagen, Reaghan, Reagine

Reanna (German, English) a form of Raina. (American) a form of Raeann.
Reannah

Reanne (American) a form of Raeann, Reanna.
Reana, Reane, Reann, Reannan, Reanne, Reannen, Reannon, Reeana

Reba (Hebrew) fourth-born child. A short form of Rebecca. See also Reva, Riva.
Rabah, Reeba, Rheba

Rebeca (Hebrew) an alernate form of Rebecca.
Rebbeca, Rebecah

Rebecca (Hebrew) tied, bound. Bible: the wife of Isaac. See also Becca, Becky.
Rabecca, Reba, Rebbecca, Rebeca, Rebeccah, Rebeccea, Rebeccka, Rebecha, Rebecka, Rebeckah, Rebeckia, Rebecky, Rebekah, Rebeque, Rebi, Reveca, Riva, Rivka

Rebekah (Hebrew) a form of Rebecca.
Rebeka, Rebekha, Rebekka, Rebekkah, Rebekke, Revecca, Reveka, Revekka, Rifka

Rebi (Hebrew) a familiar form of Rebecca.
Rebbie, Rebe, Rebie, Reby, Ree, Reebie

Reena (Greek) peaceful. (English) a form of Rina. (Hebrew) a form of Rinah.
Reen, Reenie, Rena, Reyna

Reet (Estonian) a form of Margaret.
Reatha, Reta, Retha

Regan (Irish) a form of Reagan.
Regane, Reghan

Reganne (Irish) a form of Reagan.
Raagan, Ragan, Reagan, Regin

Reggie (English) a familiar form of Regina.
Reggi, Reggy, Regi, Regia, Regie

Regina (Latin) queen. (English) king's advisor. Geography: the capital of Saskatchewan. See also Gina.
Ragine, Raina, Raine, Rega, Regena, Regennia, Reggie, Regiena, Regine, Reginia, Regis, Reina, Rena

Regine (Latin) a form of Regina.
Regin

Rei (Japanese) polite, well behaved.
Reiko

Reilly (Irish) a form of Riley.
Reilee, Reileigh, Reiley, Reili, Reilley, Reily

Reina (Spanish) a short form of Regina. See also Reyna.
Reinah, Reine, Reinette, Reinie, Reinna, Reiny, Reiona, Renia, Rina

Rekha (Hindi) thin line.
Reka, Rekia, Rekiah, Rekiya

Remedios (Spanish) remedy.

Remi (French) from Rheims, France.
Raymi, Remee, Remie, Remy

Remington (English) raven estate.
Remmington

Ren (Japanese) arranger; water lily; lotus.

Rena (Hebrew) song; joy. A familiar form of Irene, Regina, Renata, Sabrina, Serena.
Reena, Rina, Rinna, Rinnah

Renae (French) a form of Renée.
Renay

Renata (French) a form of Renée.
Ranata, Rena, Renada, Renatta, Renita, Rennie, Renyatta, Rinada, Rinata

Rene (Greek) a short form of Irene, Renée.
Reen, Reenie, Reney, Rennie

Renée (French) born again.
Renae, Renata, Renay, Rene, Renea, Reneigh, Renell, Renelle, Renne

Renita (French) a form of Renata.
Reneeta, Renetta, Renitza

Rennie (English) a familiar form of Renata.
Reni, Renie, Renni

Reseda (Spanish) fragrant mignonette blossom.

Reshawna (American) a combination of the prefix Re + Shawna.
Resaunna, Reshana, Reshaunda, Reshaunda, Reshawnna, Reshonda, Reshonn, Reshonta

Resi (German) a familiar form of Theresa.
Resia, Ressa, Resse, Ressie, Reza, Rezka, Rezi

Reta (African) shaken.
Reeta, Retta, Rheta, Rhetta

Reubena (Hebrew) behold a child.
Reubina, Reuvena, Rubena, Rubenia, Rubine, Rubina, Rubyna

Reva (Latin) revived. (Hebrew) rain; one-fourth. A form of Reba, Riva.
Ree, Reeva, Revia, Revida

Reveca, Reveka (Slavic) forms of Rebecca, Rebekah.
Reve, Revecca, Revekka, Rivka

Rexanne (American) queen.
Rexan, Rexana, Rexann, Rexanna

Reyhan (Turkish) sweet-smelling flower.

Reyna (Greek) peaceful. (English) a form of Reina.
Reyana, Reyanna, Reyni, Reynna

Reynalda (German) king's advisor.

Réz (Latin, Hungarian) copper-colored hair.

Reza (Czech) a form of Theresa.
Rezi, Rezka

Rhea (Greek) brook, stream. Mythology: the mother of Zeus.
Rheá, Rhéa, Rhealyn, Rheanna, Rhia, Rhianna

Rheanna, Rhianna (Greek) forms of Rhea.
Rheana, Rheann, Rheanne, Rhiana, Rhianna

Rhian (Welsh) a short form of Rhiannon.
Rhiane, Rhyan, Rhyann, Rhyanne, Rian, Riane, Riann, Rianne, Riayn

Rhiannon (Welsh) witch; nymph; goddess.
Rheannan, Rheannin, Rheannon, Rheanon, Rhian, Rhianen, Rhianna, Rhiannan, Rhiannen, Rhianon, Rhianwen, Rhinnon, Rhyanna, Riana, Riannon, Rianon

Rhoda (Greek) from Rhodes, Greece.
Rhode, Rhodeia, Rhodie, Rhody, Roda, Rodi, Rodie, Rodina

Rhona (Scottish) powerful, mighty. (English) king's advisor.
Rhoae, Rhonnie

Rhonda (Welsh) grand.
Rhondene, Rhondiesha, Ronda, Ronelle, Ronnette

Ria (Spanish) river.
Riah

Riana, Rianna (Irish) short forms of Briana. (Arabic) forms of Rihana.
Reana, Reanna, Rhianna, Rhyanna, Riana, Rianah

Rica (Spanish) a short form of Erica, Frederica, Ricarda. See also Enrica, Sandrica, Terrica, Ulrica.
Ricca, Rieca, Rieka, Rikka, Riqua, Ryca

Ricarda (Spanish) rich and powerful ruler.
Rica, Richarda, Richarda, Richi, Ricki

Richael (Irish) saint.

Richelle (German, French) a form of Ricarda.
Richel, Richela, Richele, Richell, Richela, Richia

Rickelle (American) a form of Raquel.
Rickel, Rickela, Rickell

Ricki, Rikki (American) familiar forms of Erica, Frederica, Ricarda.
Rita, Ricci, Riccy, Rici, Rickee, Rickia, Rickie, Rickiee, Rickina, Rickita, Ricky, Ricquie, Riki, Rikia, Rikita, Rikka, Rikee, Rikkia, Rikkie, Rikky, Riko

Ricquel (American) a form of Raquel.
Ricquell, Ricquelle, Rikell, Rikelle

Rida (Arabic) favored by God.

Rihana (Arabic) sweet basil.
Rhiana, Rhianna, Riana, Rianna

Rika (Swedish) ruler.
Ricka

Riley (Irish) valiant.
Raleigh, Reilly, Rieley, Rielly, Riely, Rilee, Rileigh, Rilie

Rilla (German) small brook.

Rimona (Hebrew) pomegranate. See also Mona.

Rima (Arabic) white antelope.
Reem, Reema, Reemah, Rema, Remah, Rhymia, Rim, Ryma

Rin (Japanese) park. Geography: a Japanese village.
Riri, Rynn

Rina (English) a short form of names ending in "rina." (Hebrew) a form of Rena, Rinah.
Reena, Rena

Rinah (Hebrew) joyful.

Riona (Irish) saint.

Risa (Latin) laughter.
Reesa, Resa

Risha (Hindi) born during the lunar month of Taurus.
Rishah, Rishay

Rishona (Hebrew) first.
Rishina, Rishon

Rissa (Greek) a short form of Nerissa.
Risa, Rissah, Ryssa, Ryssah

Rita (Sanskrit) brave; honest. (Greek) a short form of Margarita.
Reatha, Reda, Reeta, Reida, Reitha, Rheta, Riet, Ritah, Ritamae, Ritamarie

Ritsa (Greek) a familiar form of Alexandra.
Ritsah, Ritsi, Ritsie, Ritsy

Riva (French) river bank. (Hebrew) a short form of Rebecca. See also Reba, Reva.
Rivalee, Rivi, Rivvy

River (Latin, French) stream, water.
Rivana, Rivanna, Rivers, Riviane

Rivka (Hebrew) a short form of Rebecca.
Riva, Rivah, Rivkah

Riza (Greek) a form of Theresa.
Riesa, Rizus, Rizza

Roanna (American) a form of Rosana.
Ranna, Roana, Roanda, Roanne

Robbi, Robbie (English) familiar forms of Roberta.
Robby, Robbye, Robey, Robi, Robia, Roby

Roberta (English) famous brilliance.
Roba, Robbi, Robbie, Robena, Robertena, Robertina

Robin (English) robin. A form of Roberta.
Robann, Robbin, Robeen, Roben, Robena, Robian, Robina, Robine, Robinette, Robinia, Robinn, Robinta, Robyn

Robinette (English) a familiar form of Robin.
Robernetta, Robinet, Robinett, Robinita

Robyn (English) a form of Robin.
Robyn, Robbynn, Robyne, Robynn, Robynne

Rochelle (French) large stone. (Hebrew) a form of Rachel. See also Shelley.
Reshelle, Roch, Rocheal, Rochealle, Rochel, Rochele, Rochell, Rochella, Rochette, Rockelle, Roshele, Roshell, Roshelle

Rocio (Spanish) dewdrops.
Roció

Roderica (German) famous ruler.
Rica, Rika, Rodericka, Roderika, Rodreicka, Rodricka, Rodrika

Rodnae (English) island clearing.
Rodna, Rodnetta, Rodnicka

Rodneisha (American) a combination of Rodnae + Aisha.
Rodesha, Rodisha, Rodishah, Rodnecia, Rodnesha, Rodneshia, Rodneycia, Rodneysha, Rodnisha

Rohana (Hindi) sandalwood. (American) a combination of Rose + Hannah.
Rochana, Rohena

Rohini (Hindi) woman.

Rolanda (German) famous throughout the land.
Ralna, Rolande, Rolando, Rolaunda, Roleesha, Rolene, Rolinda, Rollande, Rolonda

Rolene (German) a form of Rolanda.
Rolaine, Rolena, Rolleen, Rollene

Roma (Latin) from Rome.
Romai, Rome, Romeise, Romeka, Romelle, Romesha, Rometta, Romia, Romilda, Romilla, Romina, Romini, Romna, Romonia

Romaine (French) from Rome.
Romana, Romanda, Romanelle, Romania, Romanique, Romany, Romayne, Romona, Romy

Romy (French) a familiar form of Romaine. (English) a familiar form of Rosemary.
Romi, Romie

Rona (Scandinavian) short forms of Ronalda.
Rhona, Roana, Ronalda, Ronna, Ronnae, Ronnay, Ronne, Ronni, Ronsy

Ronaele (Greek) the name Eleanor spelled backwards.
Ronalee, Ronni, Ronnie, Ronny

Ronda (Welsh) a form of Rhonda.
Rondai, Rondesia, Rondi, Rondie, Ronelle, Ronnette, Ronni, Ronnie, Ronny

Rondelle (French) short poem.
Rhondelle, Rondel, Ronndelle

Roneisha (American) a combination of Rhonda + Aisha.
Roneasha, Ronecia, Ronee, Roneeka, Roneesha, Roneice, Ronese, Ronesha, Roneshia, Ronesia, Ronessa, Ronessia, Ronichia, Ronicia, Roniesha, Ronisha, Ronneisha, Ronnesa, Ronnesha, Ronneshia, Ronni, Ronnie, Ronniesha, Ronny

Ronelle (Welsh) a form of Rhonda, Ronda.
Ranell, Ranelle, Ronel, Ronella, Ronelle, Ronnella, Ronnelle

Ronisha (American) a form of Roneisha.
Ronise, Ronnise, Ronnisha, Ronnishia

Ronli (Hebrew) joyful.
Ronia, Ronice, Ronit, Ronlee, Ronlie, Ronni, Ronnie, Ronny

Ronnette (Welsh) a familiar form of Rhonda, Ronda.
Ronetta, Ronette, Ronit, Ronita, Ronnetta, Ronni, Ronnie, Ronny

Ronni, Ronnie, Ronny (American) familiar forms of Veronica and names beginning with "Ron."
Rone, Ronee, Roni, Ronnee, Ronney

Rori, Rory (Irish) famous brilliance; famous ruler.
Rorie

Ros, Roz (English) short forms of Rosalind, Rosalyn.
Rozz, Rozzey, Rozzi, Rozzie, Rozzy

Rosa (Italian, Spanish) a form of Rose. History: Rosa Parks inspired the American Civil Rights movement by refusing to give up her bus seat to a white man in Montgomery, Alabama. See also Charo, Roza.

Rosabel (French) beautiful rose.
Rosabela, Rosabelle, Rosabelle

Rosalba (Latin) white rose.
Rosalva, Roselba

Rosalie (English) a form of Rosalind.
Rosalee, Rosalee, Rosaleen, Rosaleigh, Rosalene, Rosalia, Rosalee, Rosaleie, Roselee, Roseli, Roselia, Roselie, Roseley, Rosely, Roselee, Rosali, Rozalia, Rozalie, Rozele

Rosalind (Spanish) fair rose.
Ros, Rosalie, Rosalinda, Rosalinde, Rosalyn, Rosalynd, Rosalynde, Roselind, Roselyn, Rosie, Roz, Rozalind, Rozland

Rosalinda (Spanish) a form of Rosalind.
Rosalina

Rosalyn (Spanish) a form of Rosalind.
Ros, Rosaleen, Rosalin, Rosaline, Rosalyne, Rosalynn, Rosalynne, Roslyn, Roslin, Roslyn, Roslyne, Roslynn, Roz, Rozalyn, Rozlyn

Rosamond (German) famous guardian.
Rosamunda, Rosamunnda, Rosemonde, Rozamond

Rosanna, Roseanna (English) combinations of Rose + Anna.
Ranna, Roanna, Rosana, Rosannah, Roseana, Roseannah, Rosehannah, Rosehannah, Rosie, Rossana, Rossanna, Rozana, Rozanna

Rosanne, Roseanne (English) combinations of Rose + Ann.
Roanne, Rosan, Rosann, Roseann, Rose Ann, Rose Anne, Rossann, Rossanne, Rozann, Rozanne

Rosario (Filipino, Spanish) rosary.
Rosarah, Rosaria, Rosarie, Rosary, Rosaura

Rose (Latin) rose. See also Chalina, Raisa, Raizel, Roza.
Rada, Rasia, Rasine, Rois, Róise, Rosa, Rosea, Rosella, Roselle, Roses, Rosetta, Rosie, Rosina, Rosita, Rosse

Roselani (Hawaiian) heavenly rose.

Roselyn (Spanish) a form of Rosalind.
Roseleen, Roselene, Roselin, Roseline, Roselyne, Roselynn, Roselynne

Rosemarie (English) a combination of Rose + Marie.
Rosamaria, Rosamarie, Rosemari, Rose Marie

Rosemary (English) a combination of Rose + Mary.
Romi, Romy

Rosetta (Italian) a form of Rose.
Roseta, Rosette

Roshan (Sanskrit) shining light.

Roshawna (American) a combination of Rose + Shawna.
Roshan, Roshana, Roshanda, Roshani, Roshann, Roshanna, Roshanta, Roshaun, Roshauna, Roshaunda, Roshaun, Roshaunda, Roshawnna, Roshona, Roshonda, Roshowna, Roshunda

Rosie (English) a familiar form of Rosalind, Rosanna, Rose.
Rosey, Rosi, Rosio, Rosse, Rosy, Rozsi, Rozy

Rosina (English) a familiar form of Rose.
Rosena, Rosenah, Rosene, Rosheen, Rozena, Rozina

Rosita (Spanish) a familiar form of Rose.
Roseeta, Roseta, Rozeta, Rozita, Rozyte

Roslyn (Scottish) a form of Rosalyn.
Roslin, Roslynn, Rosslyn, Rosslynn

Rossalyn (Scottish) cape; promontory.
Roslyn, Rosselyn, Rosylin, Roszalyn

Rowan (English) tree with red berries. (Welsh) a form of Rowena.
Rowana

Rowena (Welsh) fair-haired. (English) famous friend. Literature: Ivanhoe's love interest in Sir Walter Scott's novel *Ivanhoe*.
Ranna, Ronni, Row, Rowan, Rowe, Roweena, Rowen, Rowina

Roxana, Roxanna (Persian) forms of Roxann.
Roxana, Roxannah

Roxann, Roxanne (Persian) sunrise.
Literature: Roxanne is the heroine of
Edmond Rostand's play *Cyrano de
Bergerac*.
*Rocxann, Roxan, Roxana, Roxane,
Roxanna, Roxianne, Roxy*

Roxy (Persian) a familiar form of
Roxann.
Roxi, Roxie

Royale (English) royal.
*Royal, Royalene, Royalle, Roylee,
Roylene, Ryal, Ryale*

Royanna (English) queenly, royal.
Roya

Roza (Slavic) a form of Rosa.
*Roz, Rozalia, Roze, Rozel, Rozele,
Rozell, Rozella, Rozelli, Rozia, Rozsa,
Rozsi, Rozyte, Rozzca, Rozzie*

Rozene (Native American) rose blossom.
Rozena, Rozina, Rozine, Ruzena

Ruana (Hindi) stringed musical instrument.
Ruan, Ruon

Rubena (Hebrew) a form of
Reubena.
*Rubenia, Rubina, Rubine, Rubinia,
Rubyn, Rubyna*

Rubi (French) a form of Ruby.
Ruba, Rubbie, Rubee, Rubia, Rubie

Ruby (French) precious stone.
*Rubby, Rubetta, Rubette, Rubey, Rubi,
Rubiann, Rubyann, Rubye*

Ruchi (Hindi) one who wishes to
please.

Rudee (German) famous wolf.
*Rudeline, Rudell, Rudella, Rudi, Rudie,
Rudina, Rudy*

Rudra (Hindi) seeds of the rudraksha
plant.

Rue (German) famous. (French) street.
(English) regretful; strong-scented
herbs.
Ru, Ruey

Ruffina (Italian) redhead.
Rufeena, Rufeine, Rufina, Ruphyna

Rui (Japanese) affectionate.

Rukan (Arabic) steady; confident.

Rula (Latin, English) ruler.

Runa (Norwegian) secret; flowing.
Runna

Ruperta (Spanish) a form of Roberta.

Rupinder (Sanskrit) beautiful.

Ruri (Japanese) emerald.
Ruriko

Rusalka (Czech) wood nymph.
(Russian) mermaid.

Russhell (French) redhead; fox
colored.
Rushell, Rushelle, Russellynn, Russhelle

Rusti (English) redhead.
Russet, Rustie, Rusty

Ruth (Hebrew) friendship. Bible: daugh-
ter-in-law of Naomi.
*Rutha, Ruthalma, Ruthe, Ruthella,
Ruthetta, Ruthie, Ruthven*

Ruthann (American) a combination of
Ruth + Ann.
*Ruthan, Ruthanna, Ruthannah,
Ruthanne, Ruthina, Ruthine*

Ruthie (Hebrew) a familiar form of
Ruth.
Ruthey, Ruthi, Ruthy

Ruza (Czech) rose.
Ruzena, Ruzenka, Ruzha, Ruzsa

Ryan, Ryann (Irish) little ruler.
*Raiann, Raianne, Rhyann, Riana,
Riane, Ryana, Ryane, Ryanna, Ryanne,
Rye, Ryen, Ryenne*

Ryba (Czech) fish.

Rylee (Irish) valiant.
*Rye, Ryelee, Rylea, Ryleigh, Ryley,
Rylie, Rylina, Rylyn*

Ryleigh, Rylie (Irish) forms of Rylee.
Ryelie, Ryli, Rylleigh, Ryllie

Ryley (Irish) a form of Rylee.
Ryeley, Rylly, Ryly

Ryo (Japanese) dragon.
Ryoko

S

Saarah (Arabic) princess.

Saba (Arabic) morning. (Greek) a
form of Sheba.
Sabaah, Sabah, Sabba, Sabbah

Sabi (Arabic) young girl.

Sabina (Latin) History: the Sabine were a tribe in ancient Italy. See also Bina.
Sabeen, Sabena, Sabienne, Sabine, Sabinka, Sabinna, Sabiry, Saby, Sabyne, Savina, Sebina, Sebinah

Sabiya (Arabic) morning; eastern wind.
Saba, Sabaya, Sabiyah

Sable (English) sable; sleek.
Sabel, Sabela, Sabella

Sabra (Hebrew) thorny cactus fruit. (Arabic) resting. History: a name for native-born Israelis, who were said to be hard on the outside and soft and sweet on the inside.
Sabera, Sabira, Sabrah, Sabre, Sabrea, Sabreah, Sabree, Sabreea, Sabri, Sabria, Sabriah, Sabriya, Sebra

Sabreena (English) a form of Sabrina.
Sabreen, Sabrena, Sabrene

Sabrina (Latin) boundary line. (English) princess. (Hebrew) a familiar form of Sabra. See also Bree, Brina, Rena, Zabrina.
Sabre, Sabreena, Sabrinas, Sabrinah, Sabrine, Sabrinia, Sabrinna, Sabryna, Sebree, Sebrina, Sebrina

Sabryna (English) a form of Sabrina.
Sabrynna

Sacha (Russian) a form of Sasha.
Sache, Sachia

Sachi (Japanese) blessed; lucky.
Saatchi, Sachie, Sachiko

Sada (Japanese) chaste. (English) a form of Sadie.
Sadá, Sadah, Sadako

Sade (Hebrew) a form of Chadee, Sarah, Shardae, Sharday.
Sáde, Sadé, Sadea, Sadee, Shaday

Sadella (American) a combination of Sade + Ella.
Sadelle, Sydel, Sydella, Sydelle

Sadhana (Hindi) devoted.

Sadie (Hebrew) a familiar form of Sarah. See also Sada.
Saddie, Sadee, Sadey, Sadi, Sadiey, Sady, Sadye, Saide, Saidee, Saidey, Saidi, Saidie, Saidy, Sayde, Saydee, Saydie

Sadira (Persian) lotus tree. (Arabic) star.
Sadra

Sadiya (Arabic) lucky; fortunate.
Sadi, Sadia, Sadiah, Sadiyah, Sadiyyah, Sadya

Sadzi (Carrier) sunny disposition.

Saffron (English) Botany: a plant with purple or white flowers whose orange stigmas are used as a spice.
Sifron

Safiya (Arabic) pure; serene; best friend.
Safa, Safeya, Saffa, Safia, Safiyah

Sagara (Hindi) ocean.

Sage (English) wise. Botany: an herb used as a seasoning.
Sagia, Saige, Salvia

Sahara (Arabic) desert; wilderness.
Sahar, Saharah, Sahari, Saheer, Saher, Sahira, Sahra, Sahrah

Sai (Japanese) talented.
Saiko

Saida (Hebrew) a form of Sarah. (Arabic) happy; fortunate.
Saidah

Saige (English) a form of Sage.

Saira (Hebrew) a form of Sara.
Sairah, Sairi

Sakaë (Japanese) prosperous.

Sakari (Hindi) sweet.
Sakkara

Saki (Japanese) cloak; rice wine.

Sakti (Hindi) energy; power.

Sakuna (Native American) bird.

Sakura (Japanese) cherry blossom; wealthy; prosperous.

Sala (Hindi) sala tree. Religion: the sacred tree under which Buddha died.

Salali (Cherokee) squirrel.

Salama (Arabic) peaceful. See also Zulima.

Salena (French) a form of Salina.
Saleana, Saleen, Saleena, Salene, Salenna, Sallene

Salima (Arabic) safe and sound; healthy.
Saleema, Salema, Salim, Salimah, Salma

Salina (French) solemn, dignified.
Salena, Salin, Salinah, Salinda, Saline

Salliann (English) a combination of Sally + Ann.
Sallian, Sallianne, Sallyann, Sally-Ann, Sallyanne, Sally-Anne

Sally (English) princess. History: Sally Ride, an American astronaut, became the first U. S. woman in space.
Sal, Salaid, Sallee, Salletta, Sallette, Salley, Salli, Sallie

Salome (Hebrew) peaceful. History: Salome Alexandra was a ruler of ancient Judea. Bible: the niece of King Herod.
Saloma, Salomé, Salomey, Salomi

Salvadora (Spanish) savior.

Salvia (Spanish) healthy; saved. (Latin) a form of Sage.
Salvia, Salviana, Salviane, Salvina, Salvine

Samala (Hebrew) asked of God.
Samale, Sammala

Samanta (Hebrew) a form of Samantha.
Samantah, Smanta

Samantha (Aramaic) listener. (Hebrew) told by God.
Sam, Samana, Samanath, Samanatha, Samantha, Samanitha, Samanta, Samanth, Samanthe, Samanthi, Samanthia, Samatha, Sami, Sammanth, Sammantha, Semantha, Simantha, Smantha, Symantha

Samara (Latin) elm-tree seed.
Saimara, Samaira, Samar, Samarah, Samari, Samaria, Samariah, Samarie, Samarra, Samarea, Samary, Samera, Sameria, Samira, Sammar, Sammara, Samora

Samatha (Hebrew) a form of Samantha.
Sammatha

Sameh (Hebrew) listener. (Arabic) forgiving.
Samaiya, Samaya

Sami (Arabic) praised. (Hebrew) a short form of Samantha, Samuela.
Samia, Samiah, Samiha, Samina, Sammey, Sammi, Sammie, Sammijo, Sammy, Sammyjo, Samya, Samye

Samira (Arabic) entertaining.
Samirah, Samire, Samiria, Samirra, Samyra

Samone (Hebrew) a form of Simone.
Samoan, Samoane, Samon, Samona, Samoné, Samonia

Samuela (Hebrew) heard God, asked of God.
Samala, Samella, Samella, Sami, Samielle, Samille, Sammile, Samuelle

Samuelle (Hebrew) a form of Samuela.
Samuella

Sana (Arabic) mountaintop; splendid; brilliant.
Sanaa, Sanáa, Sanaah, Sane, Sanah

Sancia (Spanish) holy, sacred.
Sanceska, Sancha, Sancharia, Sanchia, Sancie, Santsia, Sanzia

Sandeep (Punjabi) enlightened.
Sandip

Sandi (Greek) a familiar form of Sandra.
Sandee, Sandia, Sandie, Sandiey, Sandine, Sanndie

Sandra (Greek) defender of mankind. A short form of Cassandra. History: Sandra Day O'Connor was the first woman appointed to the U.S. Supreme Court. See also Zandra.
Sahndra, Sandi, Sandira, Sandrea, Sandria, Sandrica, Sandy, Sanndra, Saundra

Sandrea (Greek) a form of Sandra.
Sandreea, Sandreia, Sandrell, Sandria, Sandria

Sandrica (Greek) a form of Sandra. See also Rica.
Sandricka, Sandrika

Sandrine (Greek) a form of Alexandra.
Sandreana, Sandrene, Sandrenna, Sandrianna, Sandrina

Sandy (Greek) a familiar form of Cassandra, Sandra.
Sandya, Sandye

Sanne (Hebrew, Dutch) lily.
Sanea, Saneh, Sanna, Sanneen

Santana (Spanish) saint.
Santa, Santaniata, Santanna, Santanne, Santena, Santenna, Shantana

Santina (Spanish) little saint.
Santinia

Sanura (Swahili) kitten.
Sanora

Sanuye (Moquelumnan) red clouds at sunset.

Sanya (Sanskrit) born on Saturday.
Saneiya, Sania, Sanyia

Sanyu (Luganda) happiness.

Sapata (Native American) dancing bear.

Sapphira (Hebrew) a form of Sapphire.
Safira, Sapheria, Saphira, Saphyra, Sephira

Sapphire (Greek) blue gemstone.
Saffire, Saphire, Saphyre, Sapphira

Sara (Hebrew) a form of Sarah.
Saira, Sarae, Saralee, Sarra, Sera

Sarah (Hebrew) princess. Bible: the wife of Abraham and mother of Isaac. See also Sadie, Saida, Sally, Saree, Sharai, Shari, Zara, Zarita.
Sahra, Sara, Saraha, Sarahann, Sarahi, Sarai, Sarann, Saray, Sarha, Sariah, Sarina, Sarita, Sarolta, Sarote, Sarrah, Sasa, Sayra, Sorcha

Sarai, Saray (Hebrew) forms of Sarah.
Saraya

Saralyn (American) Sarah + Lynn.
Saralena, Saralyn, Saralynn

Saree (Arabic) noble. (Hebrew) a familiar form of Sarah.
Sareeka, Sareka, Sari, Sarika, Sarka, Sarri, Sarrie, Sary

Sariah (Hebrew) forms of Sarah.
Saria, Sarie

Sarila (Turkish) waterfall.

Sarina (Hebrew) a familiar form of Sarah.
Sareen, Sareena, Saren, Sarena, Sarene, Sarenna, Sarin, Sarine, Sarinna, Sarine

Sarita (Hebrew) a familiar form of Sarah.
Saretta, Sarette, Sarit, Saritia, Saritta

Sarolta (Hungarian) a form of Sarah.

Sarotte (French) a form of Sarah.

Sarrah (Hebrew) a form of Sarah.
Sara

Sasa (Japanese) assistant. (Hungarian) a form of Sarah, Sasha.

Sasha (Russian) defender of mankind. See also Zasha.
Sacha, Sahsha, Sasa, Sascha, Saschae, Sashae, Sashah, Sashana, Sashe, Sashea, Sashel, Sashenka, Sashey, Sashi, Sashia, Sashira, Sashsha, Sashya, Sasjara, Sauscha, Sausha, Shasha, Shashi, Shashia

Sass (Irish) Saxon.
Sassie, Sassoon, Sassy

Satara (American) a combination of Sarah + Tara.
Sataria, Satarra, Sateriaa, Saterra, Sateria

Satin (French) smooth, shiny.
Satinder

Satinka (Native American) sacred dancer.

Sato (Japanese) sugar.
Satu

Saundra (English) a form of Sandra, Sondra.
Saundee, Saundi, Saundie, Saundy

Saura (Hindi) sun worshiper.

Savana, Savanna (Spanish) forms of Savannah.
Savena, Savhana, Savhanna, Savina, Savine, Savona, Savonna

Savannah (Spanish) treeless plain.
Sahvannah, Savana, Savanah, Savanha, Savanna, Savannha, Savanna, Savonnah, Savann, Savanna, Sevanh, Sevann, Sevanna, Svannah

Sawa (Japanese) swamp. (Moquelumnan) stone.

Sawyer (English) wood worker.
Sawyar, Sawyor

Sayde, Saydee (Hebrew) forms of Sadie.
Saydi, Saydia, Saydie, Saydy

Sayo (Japanese) born at night.

Sayra (Hebrew) a form of Sarah.
Sayrah, Sayre, Sayri

Scarlett (English) bright red. Literature: Scarlett O'Hara is the heroine of Margaret Mitchell's novel *Gone with the Wind*.
Scarlet, Scarlette, Scarlotte, Skarlette

Schyler (Dutch) sheltering.
Schuyla, Schuyler, Schuylia, Schylar

Scotti (Scottish) from Scotland.
Scota, Scotia, Scottie, Scotty

Seana, Seanna (Irish) forms of Jane.
See also Shauna, Shawna.
Seaana, Sean, Seane, Seann, Seannae, Seannah, Seannalisa, Seanté, Sianna, Sina

Sebastiane (Greek) venerable. (Latin) revered. (French) a form of Sebastian (see Boys' Names).
Sebastene, Sebastia, Sebastian, Sebastiana, Sebastien, Sebastienne

Seble (Ethiopian) autumn.

Sebrina (English) a form of Sabrina.
Sebrena, Sebrenna, Sebria, Sebriana

Secilia (Latin) a form of Cecilia.
Saselia, Sasilia, Sesilia, Sileas

Secunda (Latin) second.

Seda (Armenian) forest voices.

Sedna (Eskimo) well-fed. Mythology: the goddess of sea animals.

Seelia (English) a form of Sheila.

Seema (Greek) sprout. (Afghan) sky; profile.
Seemah, Sima, Simah

Sefa (Swiss) a familiar form of Josefina.

Seirra (Irish) a form of Sierra.
Seiara, Seiarra, Seira, Seirria

Seki (Japanese) wonderful.
Seka

Sela (English) a short form of Selena.
Seeley, Selah

Selam (Ethiopian) peaceful.

Selda (German) a short form of Griselda. (Yiddish) a form of Zelda.
Seldah, Selde, Sellda, Selldah

Selena (Greek) moon. Mythology: Selene was the goddess of the moon. See also Celena.
Saleena, Sela, Selana, Seleana, Seleena, Selen, Selenah, Selene, Sélené, Selenia, Selenna, Selina, Sena, Syleena, Sylena

Selene (Greek) a form of Selena.
Seleni, Selenie, Seleny

Selia (Latin) a short form of Cecilia.
Seel, Seil, Sela, Silia

Selima (Hebrew) peaceful.
Selema, Selemah, Selimah

Selina (Greek) a form of Celina, Selena.
Selie, Selin, Selinda, Seline, Selinia, Selinka, Sellina, Selyna, Selyne, Selynne, Sylina

Selma (German) devine protector. (Irish) fair, just. (Scandinavian) divinely protected. (Arabic) secure. See also Zelma.
Sellma, Sellmah, Selmah

Sema (Turkish) heaven; divine omen.
Semaj

Sen (Japanese) Mythology: a magical forest elf that lives for thousands of years.

Senalda (Spanish) sign.
Sena, Senda, Senna

Seneca (Iroquoian) a tribal name.
Senaka, Seneka, Senequa, Senequae, Senequai, Seneque

Septima (Latin) seventh.

Sequoia (Cherokee) giant redwood tree.
Segoiyia, Seqouyia, Seqoya, Sequoi, Sequoiah, Sequora, Sequoya, Sequoyah, Sikoya

Serafina (Hebrew) burning; ardent. Bible: seraphim are an order of angels.
Sarafina, Serafine, Seraphe, Seraphin, Seraphina, Seraphine, Seraphita, Serapia, Serofina

Serena (Latin) peaceful. See also Rena.
Sarina, Saryna, Seraina, Serana, Sereen, Sereina, Seren, Serenah, Serena, Serenea, Serenia, Serenna, Serina, Serreana, Serrena, Serrenna

Serenity (Latin) peaceful.
Serenidy, Serenitee, Serenitey, Sereniti, Serenitie, Serenity, Serrenity

Serilda (Greek) armed warrior woman.

Serina (Latin) a form of Serena.
Sereena, Serin, Serine, Serreena, Serrin, Serrina, Seryna

Sevilla (Spanish) from Seville.
Seville

Shaba (Spanish) rose.
Shabana, Shabina

Shada (Native American) pelican.
Shadae, Shadea, Shadeana, Shadee, Shadi, Shadia, Shadiah, Shadie, Shadiya, Shaida

Shaday (American) a form of Sade. Shadai, Shadaia, Shadaya, Shadayna, Shadei, Shadeziah, Shaday

Shadrika (American) a combination of the prefix Sha + Rika. Shadreeka, Shadreka, Shadrica, Shadricka, Shadrieka

Shae (Irish) a form of Shea. Shaenel, Shaeya, Shai, Shaia

Shaelee (Irish) a form of Shea. Shaeleigh, Shaeley, Shaelie, Shaely

Shaelyn (Irish) a form of Shea. Shael, Shaelaine, Shaelan, Shaelanie, Shaelanna, Shaeleen, Shaelene, Shaelin, Shaeline, Shaelyne, Shaelynn, Shae-Lynn, Shaelynne

Shafira (Swahili) distinguished. Shaffira

Shahar (Arabic) moonlit. Shahara

Shahina (Arabic) falcon. Shaheen, Shaheena, Shahi, Shahin

Shahla (Afghani) beautiful eyes. Shaila, Shailah, Shalah

Shaianne (Cheyenne) a form of Cheyanne. Shaeen, Shaeine, Shaian, Shaiana, Shaianda, Shaiane, Shaiann, Shaianna

Shaila (Latin) a form of Sheila. Shaela, Shaelea, Shaeyla, Shaiah, Shailee, Shailey, Shaili, Shailie, Shailla, Shaily, Shailyn, Shailynn

Shaina (Yiddish) beautiful. Shaena, Shainah, Shaine, Shainna, Shayna, Shanie, Shayna, Shayndel, Sheina, Sheindel

Shajuana (American) a combination of the prefix Sha + Juanita. See also Shawanna. Shajuan, Shajuanda, Shajuanita, Shajuanza

Shaka (Hindi) a form of Shakti. A short form of names beginning with "Shak." See also Chaka. Shakah, Shakha

Shakarah (American) a combination of the prefix Sha + Kara. Shacara, Shacara, Shaka, Shakari, Shakara, Shikara

Shakayla (Arabic) a form of Shakila. Shakaela, Shakaila, Shakala

Shakeena (American) a combination of the prefix Sha + Keena. Shaka, Shakeina, Shakeyna, Shakina, Shakyna

Shakeita (American) a combination of the prefix Sha + Keita. See also Shaqueita. Shaka, Shakeeta, Shakeitha, Shaketa, Shaketha, Shaketia, Shaketta, Sheketa, Shekeeta, Shekita, Shikitha

Shakera (Arabic) a form of Shakira. Chakeria, Shakeira, Shakeirra, Shakerah, Shakeria, Shakeriah, Shakeriay, Shakerra, Shakerri, Shakerria, Shakerya, Shakeryia, Shakeyra

Shakia (American) a combination of the prefix Sha + Kia. Shakeea, Shakeeyah, Shakeia, Shakeya, Shakya, Shekeia, Shekia, Shekiah, Shikia

Shakila (Arabic) pretty. Chakila, Shaka, Shakayla, Shakeela, Shakeena, Shakela, Shakelah, Shakilah, Shakyla, Shekila, Shekilla, Shikeela

Shakira (Arabic) thankful. Shakeira, Shacora, Shaka, Shakeera, Shakeerah, Shakeeria, Shakeir, Shakeirah, Shakeirat, Shakira, Shakeiria, Shakora, Shakyra, Shaquira, Shekiera, Shekira, Shkiera

Shakti (Hindi) energy, power. Religion: a form of the Hindu goddess Devi. Sakti, Shaka, Sita

Shakyra (Arabic) a form of Shakira. Shakyria

Shalana (American) a combination of the prefix Sha + Lana. Shalaana, Shalain, Shalaina, Shalaine, Shaland, Shalanda, Shalane, Shalann, Shalaun, Shalauna, Shalayna, Shalayne, Shallan, Shelan, Shelanda

Shaleisha (American) a combination of the prefix Sha + Aisha. Shalesha, Shalesia, Shalicia, Shalisha

Shaleah (American) a combination of the prefix Sha + Leah. Shalea, Shalee, Shaleea, Shalia, Shaliah

Shalena (American) a combination of the prefix Sha + Lena. Shalaena, Shaleen, Shaleena, Shalen, Shalena, Shalene, Shalené, Shalenna, Shalina, Shalinda, Shaline, Shaliri, Shalayna, Shelayne, Shelena

Shalisa (American) a combination of the prefix Sha + Lisa.
Shalesa, Shalese, Shalessa, Shalice, Shalicia, Shaliece, Shalise, Shalisha, Shalishea, Shalisia, Shalissa, Shalisse, Shalyce, Shalys, Shalyse

Shalita (American) a combination of the prefix Sha + Lita.
Shaleta, Shaletta, Shalida, Shalitta

Shalona (American) a combination of the prefix Sha + Lona.
Shalon, Shalone, Shalonna, Shalonne

Shalonda (American) a combination of the prefix Sha + Ondine.
Shalonde, Shalondine, Shalondra, Shalondria

Shalyn (American) a combination of the prefix Sha + Lynn.
Shalin, Shalina, Shalinda, Shaline, Shalyna, Shalynda, Shalyne, Shalynn, Shalynne

Shamara (Arabic) ready for battle.
Shamar, Shamarah, Shamare, Shamarea, Shamaree, Shamari, Shamaria, Shamariah, Shamarra, Shamarri, Shammara, Shamora, Shamori, Shamorra, Shamorria, Shamorriah

Shameka (American) a combination of the prefix Sha + Meka.
Shameeca, Shameeka, Shamica, Shamicia, Shamicka, Shamieka, Shamikia

Shamika (American) a combination of the prefix Sha + Mika.
Shameeca, Shameeka, Shamica, Shamieka, Shamicka, Shamieka, Shamikia

Shamira (Hebrew) precious stone.
Shamir, Shamiran, Shamiria, Shamyra

Shamiya (American) a combination of the prefix Sha + Mia.
Shamea, Shamia, Shamiah, Shamiyah, Shamyia, Shamyiah, Shamyne

Shana (Hebrew) God is gracious. (Irish) a form of Jane.
Shaana, Shan, Shanae, Shanda, Shandi, Shane, Shania, Shanna, Shannah, Shauna, Shawna

Shanae (Irish) a form of Shana.
Shanay, Shanea

Shanda (American) a form of Chanda, Shana.
Shandae, Shandah, Shandra, Shannda

Shandi (English) a familiar form of Shana.
Shandee, Shandeigh, Shandey, Shandice, Shandie

Shandra (American) a form of Chandra. See also Shanda.
Shandrea, Shandreka, Shandri, Shandria, Shandriah, Shandrice, Shandrie, Shandry

Shane (Irish) a form of Shana.
Shanea, Shaneah, Shanee, Shanée, Shanie

Shaneisha (American) a combination of the prefix Sha + Aisha.
Shanesha, Shaneshia, Shanessa, Shanisha, Shanissha

Shaneka (American) a form of Shanika.
Shanecka, Shaneeka, Shaneekah, Shaneequa, Shaneeque, Shaneika, Shaneikah, Shanekia, Shanequa, Shaneyka, Shonneka

Shanel, Shanell, Shanelle (American) forms of Chanel.
Schanel, Schanell, Shanella, Shanelly, Shannel, Shannell, Shannelle, Sherel, Shenela, Shenell, Shenelle, Shenelly, Shinelle, Shonelle, Shynelle

Shaneta (American) a combination of the prefix Sha + Neta.
Seanette, Shaneeta, Shanetha, Shanethis, Shanetta, Shanette, Shineta, Shonetta

Shani (Swahili) a form of Shany.

Shania (American) a form of Shana.
Shanasia, Shanaya, Shaniah, Shaniya, Sharya, Sheria

Shanice (American) a form of Janice. See also Chanise.
Chenise, Shanece, Shaneese, Shaneice, Shanese, Shanicea, Shanicee, Shanise, Shaneice, Shannice, Shanyce, Sheneice

Shanida (American) a combination of the prefix Sha + Ida.
Shaneeda, Shannida

Shanika (American) a combination of the prefix Sha + Nika.
Shaneka, Shanica, Shanicca, Shanicka, Shanieka, Shanike, Shanikia, Shanikka, Shanikqua, Shanikwa, Shaniqua, Shenika, Shineeca, Shonnika

Shaniqua (American) a form of Shanika.
Shaniqa, Shaniquah, Shanique, Shaniquia, Shaniquwa, Shaniqwa, Shenequa, Sheniqua, Shineqna, Shiniqua

Shanise (American) a form of Shanice.
Shanisa, Shanisha, Shanissa, Shanisse, Shineese

Shanita (American) a combination of the prefix Sha + Nita.
Shanitha, Shanita, Shanitta, Shinita

Shanley (Irish) hero's child.
Shanlee, Shanleigh, Shanlie, Shanly

Shanna (Irish) a form of Shana, Shannon.
Shanea, Shannah, Shannea

Shannen (Irish) a form of Shannon.
Shanena, Shanena, Shanene

Shannon (Irish) small and wise.
Shanan, Shanadoah, Shann, Shanna, Shannan, Shanneen, Shannen, Shannie, Shannin, Shannyn, Shanon

Shanta, Shantae, Shante (French) forms of Chantal.
Shantai, Shantay, Shantaya, Shantaye, Shanté, Shantea, Shantee, Shantée, Shanteia

Shantal (American) a form of Shantel.
Shantall, Shontal

Shantana (American) a form of Santana.
Shantan, Shantanae, Shantanell, Shantanicka, Shantanika, Shantanna

Shantara (American) a combination of the prefix Sha + Tara.
Shantaria, Shantarra, Shantera, Shanteria, Shanterra, Shantira, Shantora, Shantara

Shanteca (American) a combination of the prefix Sha + Teca.
Shanteca, Shanteka, Shantika, Shantikia

Shantel, Shantell (American) song.
Seantelle, Shantell, Shantia, Shantial, Shantiale, Shantie, Shantiel, Shanteal,

Shanteria (American) a form of Shantara.
Shanteria, Shanterria, Shanterrie, Shantieria, Shantirea, Shonteria

Shantesa (American) a combination of the prefix Sha + Tess.
Shantese, Shantise, Shantisha, Shonteca, Shontessa

Shantia (American) a combination of the prefix Sha + Tia.
Shanteya, Shanti, Shantida, Shantie, Shantteya, Shauntia, Shontia

Shantille (American) a form of Chantilly.
Shantel, Shantill, Shantillie, Shantillye, Shantyl, Shantyle

Shantina (American) a combination of the prefix Sha + Tina.
Shanteena, Shontina

Shantora (American) a combination of the prefix Sha + Tory.
Shantori, Shantoria, Shantory, Shantoya, Shantoria

Shantrice (American) a combination of the prefix Sha + Trice. See also Chantrice.
Shantrece, Shantrecia, Shantreece, Shantreese, Shantrese, Shantress, Shantrezia, Shantricia, Shantriece, Shantris, Shantrisse, Shontrice

Shany (Swahili) marvelous, wonderful.
Shaney, Shannai, Shannea, Shanni, Shannia, Shannie, Shanny, Sharya

Shappa (Native American) red thunder.

Shaquanda (American) a combination of the prefix Sha + Wanda.
Shaquan, Shaquana, Shaquand, Shaquandey, Shaquandra, Shaquandria, Shaquanera, Shaquani, Shaquanna, Shaquantay, Shaquante, Shaquantia, Shaquantae, Shaquona, Shaquonda, Shaquondria

Shaqueita, Shaquita (American) forms of Shakeita.
Shaqueta, Shaquetta, Shaquette, Shaquitta, Shaquita, Shaquittia

Shaquila, Shaquilla (American) forms of Shakila.
Shaquail, Shaquia, Shaquil, Shaquilah, Shaquile, Shaquill, Shaquillah, Shaquille, Shaquilia, Shaquela, Shaquele, Shaquila, Shaquiyla

Shaquira (American) a form of Shakira.
Shaquirah, Shaquira, Shaquira, Shaquri

Shara (Hebrew) a short form of Sharon.
Shaara, Sharah, Sharal, Sharala, Sharalee, Sharilyn, Sharlynn, Sharra, Sharrah

Sharai (Hebrew) princess. See also Sharon.
Sharae, Sharaé, Sharah, Sharaiah, Sharay, Sharaya, Sharayah

Sharan (Hindi) protector.
Sharaine, Sharanda, Sharanjeet

Shardae, Sharday (Punjabi) charity. (Yoruba) honored by royalty. (Arabic) runaway. A form of Chardae.
Sade, Shadae, Shanda, Shar-Dae, Shardai, Shar-Day, Sharde, Shardea, Shardee, Shardée, Shardei, Shardeia, Shardey

Sharee (English) a form of Shari.
Shareen, Shareena, Sharine

Shari (French) beloved, dearest. (Hungarian) a form of Sarah. See also Sharita, Sheree, Sherry.
Shara, Share, Sharee, Sharia, Shariah, Sharian, Shariann, Sharianne, Sharie, Sharra, Sharree, Sharri, Sharrie, Sharry, Shary

Sharice (French) a form of Cherice.
Shareese, Sharese, Sharese, Sharica, Sharicka, Shariece, Sharis, Sharise, Sharish, Shariss, Sharissa, Sharisse, Sharyse

Sharik (African) child of God.

Sharissa (American) a form of Sharice.
Sharesa, Sharessia, Sharisa, Sharisha, Shereeza, Shericia, Sherisa, Sherissa

Sharita (French) a familiar form of Shari. (American) a form of Charity. See also Sherita.
Shareeta, Sharita

Sharla (French) a short form of Sharlene, Sharlotte.

Sharlene (French) little and strong.
Scharlane, Scharlene, Shar, Sharla, Sharlaina, Sharlaine, Sharlane,

Sharlanna, Sharlee, Sharleen, Sharleine, Sharlena, Sharleyne, Sharline, Sharlyn, Sharlyne, Sharlynn, Sharlynne, Sherlean, Sherleen, Sherlene, Sherline

Sharlotte (American) a form of Charlotte.
Sharlet, Sharlett, Sharlott, Sharlotta

Sharna (American) a short form of Sharmaine.
Sharmae, Sharne

Sharmaine (American) a form of Charmaine.
Sharma, Sharmain, Sharman, Sharmane, Sharmanta, Sharmayne, Sharmeen, Sharmene, Sharmese, Sharmin, Sharmine, Sharmon, Sharmyn

Sharna (Hebrew) a form of Sharon.
Sharnae, Sharnay, Sharne, Sharnea, Sharnease, Sharnee, Sharneese, Sharnell, Sharnelle, Sharnese, Sharnett, Sharnetta, Sharnise

Sharon (Hebrew) desert plain. A form of Sharai.
Shaaron, Shara, Sharai, Sharan, Shareen, Sharen, Shari, Sharin, Sharna, Sharonda, Sharone, Sharran, Sharren, Sharrin, Sharron, Sharrona, Sharyn, Sharyon, Sheren, Sheron, Sherryn

Sharonda (Hebrew) a form of Sharon.
Sharronda, Sheronda, Sherrhonda

Sharrona (Hebrew) a form of Sharon.
Sharona, Sharone, Sharonia, Sharonna, Sharony, Sharronne, Sheron, Sherona, Sheronna, Sheron, Sherronna, Shirona

Shatara (Hindi) umbrella. (Arabic) good; industrious. (American) a combination of Sharon + Tara.
Shatarea, Shatari, Shataria, Shatarra, Shataura, Shateira, Shatera, Shaterah, Shateria, Shaterra, Shaterri, Shaterria, Shatherian, Shatierra, Shattiria

Shatoria (American) a combination of the prefix Sha + Tory.
Shatora, Shatorea, Shatori, Shatorri, Shatorria, Shatory, Shatorya, Shatoya

Shauna (Hebrew) God is gracious. (Irish) a form of Shana. See also Seana, Shona.
Shaun, Shaunah, Shaunda, Shaune, Shaunee, Shauneen, Shaunelle, Shaunette, Shauni, Shaunice, Shaunicy, Shaunie, Shaunika, Shaunisha, Shaunna, Shaunnea, Shaunta, Shaunua, Shaunya

Shaunda (Irish) a form of Shauna. See also Shanda, Shawnda, Shonda.
Shaundal, Shaundala, Shaundel, Shaundela, Shaundell, Shaundelle, Shaundra, Shaundrea, Shaundree, Shaundria, Shaundrice

Shaunta (Irish) a form of Shauna. See also Shawnta, Shonta.
Schunta, Shauntae, Shauntay, Shaunte, Shauntea, Shauntee, Shauntée, Shaunteena, Shauntei, Shauntia, Shauntier, Shauntrel, Shauntrell, Shauntrella

Shavon (American) a form of Shavonne.
Schavon, Schevon, Shavan, Shavana, Shavaun, Shavona, Shavonda, Shavone, Shavonia, Shivon

Shavonne (American) a combination of the prefix Sha +Yvonne. See also Siobhan.
Shavanna, Shavon, Shavonda, Shavonn, Shavonnie, Shavonni, Shavonna, Shavontae, Shavonte, Shavonté, Shavoun, Shivaun, Shivawn, Shivonne, Shyon, Shyvonne

Shawanna (American) a combination of the prefix Sha + Wanda. See also Shajuana, Shawna.
Shawan, Shawana, Shawanda, Shawante, Shiwani

Shawna (Hebrew) God is gracious. (Irish) a form of Jane. A form of Shana, Shauna. See also Seana, Shona.
Sauna, Shaw, Shawn, Shawna, Shawnai, Shawnea, Shawnee, Shawneen, Shawneena, Shawnell, Shawnette, Shawna, Shawnta, Sheona, Sián, Siana, Sianna

Shawnda (Irish) a form of Shawna. See also Shanda, Shaunda, Shonda.
Shawndal, Shawndala, Shawndan, Shawndel, Shawndra, Shawndrea, Shawndree, Shawndrell, Shawndria

Shawnee (Irish) a form of Shawna.
Shawne, Shawneea, Shawney, Shawni, Shawnie

Shawnika (American) a combination of Shawna + Nika.
Shawnaka, Shawnequa, Shawneika, Shawnicka

Shawnta (Irish) a form of Shawna. See also Shaunta, Shonta.
Shawntae, Shawntay, Shawnte, Shawnté, Shawntee, Shawntel, Shawntelle, Shawnteria, Shawntia, Shawntil, Shawntille, Shawntina, Shawntish, Shawntrice

Shay, Shaye (Irish) forms of Shea.
Shaya, Shayah, Shayda, Shayla, Shayia, Shayla, Shey, Sheye

Shayla (Irish) a form of Shay.
Shaylagh, Shaylah, Shaylain, Shaylan, Shaylea, Shayleah, Shaylla, Shaylyn, Sheyla

Shaylee (Irish) a form of Shea.
Shaylei, Shayleigh, Shayley, Shayli, Shaylie, Shayly, Shealy

Shaylyn (Irish) a form of Shea.
Shaylin, Shaylinn, Shaylan, Shaylynne, Shealyn, Sheylyn

Shayna (Hebrew) beautiful.
Shaynae, Shaynah, Shayne, Shaynee, Shayney, Shayni, Shaynie, Shaynna, Shaynne, Shayny, Sheana, Sheanna

Shea (Irish) fairy palace.
Shae, Shay, Shaylee, Shaylyn, Sheah, Shaelee, Shay, Shaelyn, Sheann, Sheanon, Sheara, Sheanna, Sheatara, Sheanna, Sheavon

Sheba (Hebrew) a short form of Bathsheba. Geography: an ancient country of south Arabia.
Saba, Sabah, Shebah, Sheeba

Sheena (Hebrew) God is gracious. (Irish) a form of Jane.
Sheenagh, Sheenah, Sheenan, Sheenead, Sheenika, Sheenna, Sheina, Shena, Shiona

Sheila (Latin) blind. (Irish) a form of Cecelia. See also Cheyla, Zelizi.
Seelia, Seila, Selia, Shaila, Sheela, Sheelagh, Sheelah, Sheilagh, Sheilah, Sheileen, Sheiletta, Sheilia, Sheillynn, Sheilya, Shela, Shelagh, Shelah, Shelia, Shila, Shiela, Shilah, Shilea, Shyla

Shelby, Shelbie (English) forms of Shelby.
Shelbe, Shellbi, Shellbie

Shelby (English) ledge estate.
Chelby, Schelby, Shel, Shelbe, Shelbee, Shelbey, Shelbi, Shelbie, Shelbye, Shelby

Sheldon (English) farm on the ledge.
Sheldina, Sheldine, Sheldrina, Sheldyn, Shelon

Shelisa (American) a combination of Shelley + Lisa.
Sheleza, Shelica, Shelicia, Shelise, Shelisse, Sheliza

Shelee (English) a form of Shelley.
Shelee, Shelena, Shelena, Sheley, Sheli, Shelia, Shelina, Shelinda, Shelita

Shelley, Shelly (English) meadow on the ledge. (French) familiar forms of Michelle. See also Rochelle.
Shelee, Shell, Shella, Shellaine, Shellany, Shellee, Shellene, Shelli, Shelliann, Shellian, Shellie, Shellina

Shelsea (American) a form of Chelsea.
Shellsea, Shellsey, Shelsey, Shelsie, Shelsy

Shena (Irish) a form of Sheena.
Shenada, Shenae, Shenah, Shenay, Shenda, Shene, Shenea, Sheneda, Shenee, Sheneena, Shenica, Shenika, Shenina, Sheniqua, Shenita, Shenna, Shennae, Shennah, Shenoa

Shera (Aramaic) light.
Sheera, Sheerah, Sherae, Sherah, Sheralee, Sheralle, Sheralyn, Sheralynn, Sheralynne, Sheray, Sheraya

Sheree (French) beloved, dearest.
Scherie, Sheeree, Shere, Shereé, Sherelle, Shereen, Shereena

Sherelle (French) a form of Cherelle, Sheryl.
Sherel, Sherell, Sheriel, Sherrel, Sherrell, Sherrelle, Shirelle

Sheri, Sherri (French) forms of Sherry.
Sheria, Sheriah, Sherie, Sherrie

Sherian (American) a combination of Sheri + Ann.
Sherianne, Sherrina

Sherice (French) a form of Cherice.
Scherise, Shereece, Shereece, Sherees, Shereese, Shericia, Sherise, Sherisse, Sherrish, Sherryse, Sheryce

Sheridan (Irish) wild.
Sherida, Sheridane, Sherideen, Sheriden, Sheridian, Sheridon, Sheridan, Sherridon

Sherika (Punjabi) relative. (Arabic) easterner.
Shereka, Sherica, Shericka, Sherria, Sherricka, Sherrika

Sherissa (French) a form of Sherry, Sheryl.
Shereeza, Sheresa, Shericia, Sherrish

Sherita (French) a form of Sherry, Sheryl. See also Sharita.
Shereta, Sheretta, Sherette, Sherrita

Sherleen (French, English) a form of Sheryl, Shirley.
Sherileen, Sherlene, Sherlin, Sherlina, Sherline, Sherlyn, Sherlyne, Sherlynne, Sherlena, Shirlene, Shirlina, Shirlyn

Sherry (French) beloved, dearest. A familiar form of Sheryl. See also Sheree.
Sherey, Sheri, Sherissa, Sherrey, Sherri, Sherria, Sherriah, Sherrie, Sherye, Sherry

Sheryl (French) beloved. A familiar form of Shirley. See also Sherry.
Sharel, Sharil, Sharilyn, Sharyl, Sharyll, Sheral, Sherell, Sheriel, Sheril, Sherill, Sherily, Sherilyn, Sherissa, Sherita, Sherleen, Sherral, Sherrelle, Sherril, Sherrill, Sherryl, Sherylly

Sherylyn (American) a combination of Sheryl + Lynn. See also Cherilyn.
Sharolin, Sharolyn, Sharyl-Lynn, Sheralyn, Sherilyn, Sherilynn, Sherilynne, Sherralyn, Sherralynn, Sherrilyn, Sherrilynn, Sherrilynne, Sherrylyn, Sherryn, Sherylanne

Shevonne (American) a combination of the prefix She + Yvonne.
Shevaun, Shevon, Shevonda, Shevone

Sheyenne (Cheyenne) a form of Cheyenne. See also Shyann, Shyanne.
Shayhan, Sheyan, Sheyane, Sheyann, Sheyanna, Sheyannah, Sheyanne, Sheyen, Sheyene, Shiante, Shyanne

Shianne (Cheyenne) a form of Cheyenne.
She, Shian, Shiana, Shianah, Shianda, Shiane, Shiann, Shianna, Shiannah, Shiary, Shieana, Shieann, Shieanne, Shiena, Shiene, Shienna

Shifra (Hebrew) beautiful.
Schifra, Shifrah

Shika (Japanese) gentle deer.
Shi, Shikah, Shikha

Shilo (Hebrew) God's gift. Bible: a sanctuary for the Israelites where the Ark of the Covenant was kept.
Shiloh

Shina (Japanese) virtuous, good; wealthy. (Chinese) a form of China.
Shinae, Shinay, Shine, Shinna

Shino (Japanese) bamboo stalk.

Shiquita (American) a form of Chiquita.
Shiquata, Shiquitta

Shira (Hebrew) song.
Shirah, Shiray, Shire, Shiree, Shiri, Shirit, Shyra

Shirlene (English) a form of Shirley.
Shirleen, Shirline, Shirlynn

Shirley (English) bright meadow. See also Sheryl.
Sherlee, Sherleen, Sherley, Sherli, Sherlie, Shir, Shirl, Shirlee, Shirlie, Shirly, Shirlly, Shurlee, Shurley

Shivani (Hindi) life and death.
Shiva, Shivana, Shivanie, Shivanna

Shizu (Japanese) silent.
Shizue, Shizuka, Shizuko, Shizuyo

Shona (Irish) a form of Jane. A form of Shana, Shauna, Shawna.
Shiona, Shonagh, Shonah, Shonalee, Shonda, Shone, Shonee, Shonette, Shoni, Shonie, Shonna, Shonnah, Shonta

Shonda (Irish) a form of Shona. See also Shanda, Shaunda, Shawnda.
Shondalette, Shondalyn, Shondel, Shondelle, Shondi, Shondia, Shondie, Shondra, Shondreka, Shounda

Shonta (Irish) a form of Shona. See also Shaunta, Shawnta.
Shonté, Shontae, Shontai, Shontalea, Shontasia, Shontavia, Shontaviea, Shontay, Shontaya, Shonte, Shonté, Shontedra, Shontee, Shonteral, Shonti, Shontol, Shontoy, Shontrail, Shountáe

Shoshana (Hebrew) a form of Susan. also Shauna, Shawnta.
Shosha, Shoshan, Shoshanah, Shoshane, Shoshanha, Shoshann, Shoshanna, Shoshannah, Shoshanna, Shoshannah, Shoshauna, Shoshana, Shoshone, Shoshonee, Shoshony, Shoshoni, Shoshana, Shushana, Sosha, Soshana

Shu (Chinese) kind, gentle.

Shug (American) a short form of Sugar.

Shula (Arabic) flaming, bright.
Shulah

Shulamith (Hebrew) peaceful. See also Sula.
Shulamit, Sulamith

Shunta (Irish) a form of Shonta.
Shuntae, Shunté, Shuntel, Shuntell, Shuntelle, Shuntia

Shura (Russian) a form of Alexandra.
Schura, Shurah, Shuree, Shureen, Shurelle, Shurita, Shurka, Shurlana

Shyann, Shyanne (Cheyenne) forms of Cheyenne. See also Sheyenne.
Shyan, Shyana, Shyandra, Shyane, Shyanna, Shyannah, Shye, Shyene, Shyenna, Shyenne

Shyla (English) a form of Sheila.
Shya, Shyah, Shylah, Shylan, Shylayah, Shylana, Shylane, Shyle, Shyleah, Shylee, Shyley, Shyli, Shylia, Shylie, Shylo, Shyloe, Shyloh, Shylon, Shylyn

Shyra (Hebrew) a form of Shira.
Shyrah, Shyrai, Shyrie, Shyro

Siara (Irish) a form of Sierra.
Siarah, Siarra, Siarrah, Siara

Sianna (Irish) a form of Seana.
Sian, Siana, Sianae, Sianai, Sianey, Siannah, Sianne, Sianni, Sianny, Siany

Sibeta (Moquelumnan) finding a fish under a rock.

Sibley (English) sibling; friendly. (Greek) a form of Sybil.
Sybley

Sidney (French) a form of Sydney.
Sidne, Sidnee, Sidnei, Sidneya, Sidni, Sidnie, Sidny, Sidnye

Sidonia (Hebrew) enticing.
Sydania, Syndonia

Sidonie (French) from Saint-Denis, France. See also Sydney.
Sedona, Sidaine, Sidanni, Sidelle, Sidoine, Sidona, Sidonae, Sidonia, Sidony

Sidra (Latin) star child.
Sidrah, Sidras

Sienna (American) a form of Ciana.
Seiri, Siena

Siera (Irish) a form of Sierra.
Sierah, Sieria

Sierra (Irish) black. (Spanish) saw toothed. Geography: any rugged range of mountains that, when viewed from a distance, has a jagged profile. See also Ciara.
Seara, Searria, Seera, Siara, Sieara, Siera, Sierah, Sierre, Sierrea, Sierriah, Syerra

Sigfreda (German) victorious peace. See also Freda.
Sigfreida, Sigfrida, Sigfrieda, Sigfryda

Sigmunda (German) victorious protector.

Signe (Latin) sign, signal. (Scandinavian) a short form of Sigourney.
Signa, Signe, Signy, Singna, Sinne

Signe (Latin) sign, signal.
Siegrid, Siegrida, Sigritt

Sigourney (English) victorious conquerer.
Signe, Sigourney, Sigourney

Sigrid (Scandinavian) victorious counselor.
Siegrid, Siegrida, Sigritt

Sihu (Native American) flower; bush.

Siko (African) crying baby.

Silvia (Latin) a form of Sylvia.
Silivia, Silva, Silvya

Simcha (Hebrew) joyful.

Simone (Hebrew) she heard. (French) a form of Simon (see Boys' Names).
Samone, Siminie, Simmi, Simmie, Simmona, Simmone, Simoane, Simona, Simonetta, Simonette, Simonia, Simonina, Simone, Somone, Symone

Simran (Sikh) absorbed in God.
Simren, Simrin, Simrun

Sina (Irish) a form of Seana.
Seena, Sinai, Sinaia, Sinan, Sinay

Sinclaire (French) prayer.
Sinclair

Sindy (American) a form of Cindy.
Sinda, Sindal, Sindee, Sindi, Sindia, Sindie, Sinnedy, Synda, Syndal, Syndee, Syndey, Syndi, Syndia, Syndie, Syndy

Sinead (Irish) a form of Jane.
Seonaid, Sine, Sinéad

Siobhan (Irish) a form of Joan. See also Shavonne.
Shibahn, Shibani, Shibhan, Shioban, Shobana, Shobha, Shobhana, Siobahn, Siobhana, Siobhann, Siobhon, Siovaun, Siovhan

Sirena (Greek) enchanter. Mythology: Sirens were sea nymphs whose singing enchanted sailors and made them crash their ships into nearby rocks.
Sireena, Sirene, Sirine, Syrena, Syrenia, Syrenna, Syrina

Sisika (Native American) songbird.

Sissy (American) a familiar form of Cecelia.
Sisi, Sisie, Sissey, Sissie

Sita (Hindi) a form of Shakti.
Sitah, Sitarah, Sitha, Sithara

Siti (Swahili) respected woman.

Skye (Arabic) water giver. (Dutch) a short form of Skyler. Geography: an island in the Hebrides, Scotland.
Ski, Skie, Skii, Skky, Sky, Skya, Skyy

Skylar (Dutch) a form of Skyler.
Skeyla, Skeyelar, Skyla, Skylair, Skylar

Skyler (Dutch) sheltering.
Skila, Skeilah, Skye, Skyeler, Skyelur, Skyla, Skylar, Skylee, Skylena, Skyli, Skylia, Skylie, Skylin, Skyllar, Skylor, Skylyn, Skylynn, Skylyr, Skyra

Sloane (Irish) warrior.
Sloan, Sloanne

Socorro (Spanish) helper.

Sofia (Greek) a form of Sophia. See also Zofia, Zsofia.
Sofeea, Sofeeia, Soffi, Sofi, Soficita, Sofie, Sofija, Sofiya, Sofka, Sofya

Solada (Tai) listener.

Solana (Spanish) sunshine.
Solande, Solanna, Soleil, Solena, Soley, Solina, Solinda

Solange (French) dignified.

Soledad (Spanish) solitary.
Sole, Soleda

Solenne (French) solemn, dignified.
Solaine, Solene, Soléne, Solenna, Solina, Soline, Solonez, Souline, Soulle

Soma (Hindi) lunar.

Sommer (English) summer; summoner. (Arabic) black. See also Summer.
Somara, Somer, Sommar, Sommara, Sommers

Sondra (Greek) defender of mankind.
Saundra, Sondre, Sonndra, Sonndre

Sonia (Russian, Slavic) a form of Sonya.
Sonica, Sonida, Sonita, Sonna, Sonni, Sonnia, Sonnie, Sonny

Sonja (Scandinavian) a form of Sonya.
Sonjae, Sonjia

Sonya (Greek) wise. (Russian, Slavic) a form of Sophia.
Sonia, Sonja, Sonnya, Sonyae, Sunya

Sook (Korean) pure.

Sopheary (Cambodian) beautiful girl.

✓**Sophia** (Greek) wise. See also Sonya, Zofia.
Sofia, Sophie

✓**Sophie** (Greek) a familiar form of Sophia. See also Zocha.
Sophey, Sophi, Sophy

Sophronia (Greek) wise; sensible.
Saffrona, Sofronia

Sora (Native American) chirping songbird.

Soraya (Persian) princess.
Suraya

Sorrel (French) reddish brown. Botany: a plant whose leaves are used as salad greens.

Soso (Native American) tree squirrel dining on pine nuts; chubby-cheeked baby.

Souzan (Persian) burning fire. *Sousan, Souzanne*

Spencer (English) dispenser of provisions. *Spenser*

Speranza (Italian) a form of Esperanza. *Speranca*

Spring (English) springtime. *Spryng*

Stacey, Stacy (Greek) resurrection. (Irish) a short form of Anastasia, Eustacia, Natasha. *Stace, Stacee, Staceyan, Staceyann, Staicy, Stacey, Stasya, Stayce, Staycee, Staci, Steacy*

Staci, Stacie (Greek) forms of Stacey. *Staci, Stacia, Stayci*

Stacia (English) a short form of Anastasia. *Stasia, Staysha*

Starla (English) a form of Starr. *Starria*

Starley (English) a familiar form of Starr. *Starle, Starlee, Starly*

Starleen (English) a form of Starr. *Starleena, Starlena, Starlene, Starlin, Starlyn, Starlynn, Starlen*

Starling (English) bird.

Starr (English) star. *Star, Staria, Starisha, Starla, Starleen, Starlet, Starlette, Starley, Starlight, Starre, Starrsha, Starsha, Starshanna, Startish*

Stasya (Greek) a familiar form of Anastasia. (Russian) a form of Stacey. *Stasa, Stasha, Stashia, Stasia, Stasya, Siaska*

Stefani, Steffani (Greek) forms of Stephanie. *Stafani, Stefanni, Stefane, Stefani, Stefni, Stefoni*

Stefanie (Greek) a form of Stephanie. *Stafanie, Staffany, Stefanie, Stefanee, Stefaney, Stefania, Stefanie, Stefanija, Stefannie, Stefcia, Stefenie, Stefianie, Steffi, Stefinie, Stefka*

Stefany, Steffany (Greek) forms of Stephanie. *Stefanny, Stefanya, Steffaney*

Steffi (Greek) a familiar form of Stefanie, Stephanie. *Stefa, Stefcia, Steffe, Steffie, Steffy, Steff, Stefka, Stefy, Stepha, Stephi, Stephie, Stephy*

Stella (Latin) star. (French) a familiar form of Estelle. *Stelle, Stellina*

Stepania (Russian) a form of Stephanie. *Stepa, Stepahny, Stepanida, Stepanie, Stepanyda, Stepfanie, Stephana*

Stephani (Greek) a form of Stephanie. *Stephania, Stephanni*

Stephanie (Greek) crowned. See also Estefani, Estephanie, Panya, Stevie, Zephania. *Stamatios, Stefani, Stefanie, Stefany, Steffie, Stepania, Stephaia, Stephaine, Stephana, Stephane, Stephanee, Stephani, Stephanida, Stephanie, Stephannie, Stephann, Stephanni, Stephany, Stephene, Stephenie, Stephanie, Stephney, Stesha, Steshka, Stevanee*

Stephany (Greek) a form of Stephanie. *Stephaney, Stepharye*

Stephene (Greek) a form of Stephanie. *Stephina, Stephine, Stephyne*

Stephenie (Greek) a form of Stephanie. *Stephena, Stephenee, Stepheney, Stepheni, Stephenny, Stepheny, Stephine, Stephinie*

Stephney (Greek) a form of Stephanie. *Stephenie, Stephine, Stephni, Stephnie, Stephny*

Sterling (English) valuable; silver penny.

Stevie (Greek) a familiar form of Stephanie. *Steva, Stevana, Stevanee, Stevee, Stevena, Stevey, Stevi, Stevy, Stevye*

Stina (German) a short form of Christina. *Steena, Stena, Stine, Stinna*

Stockard (English) stockyard.

Stormie (English) a form of Stormy.
Stormee, Stormi, Stormii

Stormy (English) impetuous by nature.
Storm, Storme, Stormey, Stormie, Stormm

Suchin (Tai) beautiful thought.

Sue (Hebrew) a short form of Susan, Susanna.

Sueann, Sueanna (American) combinations of Sue + Ann, Sue + Anna.
Suann, Suanna, Suannah, Suanne, Sueanne

Suela (Spanish) consolation.
Suelita

Sugar (American) sweet as sugar.
Shug

Sugi (Japanese) cedar tree.

Suke (Hawaiian) a form of Susan.

Sukey (Hawaiian) a familiar form of Susan.
Suka, Sukee, Suki, Sukie, Suky

Sukhdeep (Sikh) light of peace and bliss.
Sukhdip

Suki (Japanese) loved one. (Moquelumnan) eagle-eyed.
Sukie

Sula (Icelandic) large sea bird. (Greek, Hebrew) a short form of Shulamith, Ursula. Suletu (Moquelumnan) soaring bird.

Sulia (Latin) a form of Julia.
Suliana

Sulwen (Welsh) bright as the sun.

Sumalee (Tai) beautiful flower.

Sumati (Hindi) unity.

Sumaya (American) a combination of Sue + Maya.
Sumayah, Sumayya, Sumayyah

Sumi (Japanese) elegant, refined.
Sumiko

Summer (English) summertime. See also Sommer.
Sumer, Summar, Summerann, Summerbreeze, Summerhaze, Summerine, Summerlee, Summerlin, Summerlyn, Summerlynn, Summers, Sumrah, Summyr, Sumyr

Sun (Korean) obedient.
Suncance, Sundee, Sundeep, Sundi, Sundip, Sundrenea, Sunta, Sunya

Sunee (Tai) good.
Suni

Sun-Hi (Korean) good; joyful.

Suni (Zuni) native; member of our tribe.
Sunita, Sunitha, Suniti, Sunne, Sunni, Sunnie, Sunnilei

Sunki (Hopi) swift.
Sunkia

Sunny (English) bright, cheerful.
Sunni, Sunnie

Sunshine (English) sunshine.
Sunshyn, Sunshyne

Surata (Pakistani) blessed joy.

Suri (Todas) pointy nose.
Suree, Surena, Surenia

Surya (Sanskrit) Mythology: a sun god.
Suria, Suriya, Surra

Susammi (French) a combination of Susan + Aimee.
Suzami, Suzamie, Suzamy

Susan (Hebrew) lily. See also Shoshana, Sukey, Zsa Zsa, Zusa.
Sawsan, Siusan, Sosan, Sosana, Sue, Suesan, Sueva, Suisan, Suke, Susana, Susann, Susanna, Suse, Susen, Susette, Susie, Suson, Suzan, Suzanna, Suzannah, Suzanne, Suzette

Susana (Hebrew) a form of Susan.
Susanah, Susane

Susanna, Susannah (Hebrew) forms of Susan. See also Xuxa, Zanna, Zsuzsanna.
Sonel, Sosana, Sue, Suesanna, Susana, Susanah, Susanka, Susette, Susie, Suzanna

Suse (Hawaiian) a form of Susan.

Susette (French) a familiar form of Susan, Susanna.
Susetta

Susie, Suzie (American) familiar forms of Susan, Susanna.
Suse, Susey, Susi, Sussi, Sussy, Susy, Suze, Suzi, Suzy, Suzzie

Suzanna, Suzannah (Hebrew) forms of Susan.
Suzana, Suzenna, Suzzanna

Suzanne (English) a form of Susan.
Susanne, Suszanne, Suzane, Suzann, Suzzann, Suzzanne

Suzette (French) a form of Susan.
Suzetta, Suzzette

Suzu (Japanese) little bell.
Suzue, Suzuko

Suzuki (Japanese) bell tree.

Svetlana (Russian) bright light.
Sveta, Svetochka

Syá (Chinese) summer.

Sybella (English) a form of Sybil.
Sebila, Sibbella, Sibeal, Sibel, Sibell, Sibella, Sibelle, Sibilla, Sibylla, Sybel, Sybelle, Sybila, Sybilla

Sybil (Greek) prophet. Mythology:
sibyls were oracles who relayed the
messages of the gods. See also
Cybele, Sibley.
Sib, Sibbel, Sibbie, Sibbill, Sibby, Sibeal,
Sibel, Sibyl, Sibylle, Sibylline, Sybella,
Sybille, Syble

Sydnee (French) a form of Sydney.
Sydne, Sydnea, Sydnei

Sydney (French) from Saint-Denis,
France. See also Sidonie.
Cidney, Cydney, Sidney, Sy, Syd, Sydel,
Sydelle, Sydna, Sydnee, Sydni, Sydnie,
Sydny, Sydnye, Syndona, Syndonah

Sydni, Sydnie (French) forms of
Sydney.

Sying (Chinese) star.

Sylvana (Latin) forest.
Silvaine, Silvana, Silvanna, Silviane,

Sylvia (Latin) forest. Literature: Sylvia
Plath was a well-known American
poet. See also Silvia, Xylia.
Sylva, Sylvaine, Sylvanah, Sylvania,
Sylvanna, Sylvie, Sylviia, Sylvinnia,
Sylvonah, Sylvonia, Sylvonna

Sylvianne (American) a combination
of Sylvia + Anne.
Sylvian

Sylvie (Latin) a familiar form of
Sylvia.
Silvi, Silvie, Silvy, Sylvi

Symone (Hebrew) a form of Simone.
Symmeon, Symmone, Symona, Symoné,
Symonne

Symphony (Greek) symphony, har-
monious sound.
Symfoni, Symphanie, Symphany,
Symphanée, Symphoni, Symphoni

Syreeta (Hindi) good traditions.
(Arabic) companion.
Syreta, Syrita

<big>**T**</big>

Tabatha (Greek, Aramaic) a form of
Tabitha.
Tabathe, Tabathia, Tabbatha

Tabby (English) a familiar form of
Tabitha.
Tabbi

Tabia (Swahili) talented.
Tabea

Tabina (Arabic) follower of
Muhammad.

Tabitha (Greek, Aramaic) gazelle.
Tabatha, Tabbee, Tabbetha, Tabbey, Tabbi,
Tabbie, Tabbitha, Tabby, Tabetha, Tabiatha,
Tabita, Tabitha, Tabotha, Tabtha, Tabytha

Tabytha (Greek, Aramaic) a form of
Tabitha.
Tabbytha

Tacey (English) a familiar form of
Tacita.
Tace, Tacee, Taci, Tacy, Tacye

Taci (Zuni) washtub. (English) a form
of Lacey.
Tacia, Taciana, Tacie

Tacita (Latin) silent.
Tacy

Tadita (Omaha) runner.
Tadea, Tadra

Taelor (English) a form of Taylor.
Taelar, Taelee, Taelor, Taelore, Taelyr

Taesha (Latin) a form of Tisha.
(American) a combination of the
prefix Ta + Aisha.
Tadasha, Taeshayla, Taeshia, Takeisha,
Tahisha, Taiesha, Taisha, Taishae, Taisha,
Teashia, Teisha, Tesha

Taffy (Welsh) beloved.
Taffia, Taffine, Taffye, Tafia, Tafisa, Tafoya

Tahira (Arabic) virginal, pure.
Taheera, Taheerah, Tahera, Tahere, Taheria,
Taherri, Tahiara, Tahirah, Tahireh

Tahlia (Greek, Hebrew) a form of Talia.
Tahleah, Tahleia

Tailor (English) a form of Taylor.
Tailar, Tailer, Taillor, Tailyr

Taima (Native American) clash of thunder.
Taimi, Taimia, Taimy

Taipa (Moquelumnan) flying quail.
Taite (English) cheerful.
Tate, Tayte, Tayten

Taja (Hindi) crown.
Taiajána, Taija, Tajae, Tajah, Tahai, Tehya, Teja, Tejah, Tejal

Taka (Japanese) honored.

Takala (Hopi) corn tassel.

Takara (Japanese) treasure.
Takarah, Takaria, Takarra, Takra

Takayla (American) a combination of the prefix Ta + Kayla.
Takayler, Takeyli

Takeisha (American) a combination of the prefix Ta + Keisha.
Takecia, Takesha, Takeshia, Takeesia, Takeisha, Takishea, Takishia, Takeesha, Takeeisha, Tekeeshi, Tekeypsia, Tekisha, Tikesha, Tikeisha, Tokeesia, Tykeisha

Takenya (Hebrew) animal horn. (Moquelumnan) falcon. (American) a combination of the prefix Ta + Kenya.
Takenia, Takenja

Takeria (American) a form of Takira.
Takera, Takeri, Takerian, Takerra, Takierra, Takierria, Takoria

Taki (Japanese) waterfall.
Tiki

Takia (Arabic) worshiper.
Takeia, Takeiyah, Takeya, Takeyah, Takhiya, Takiah, Takija, Takiya, Takeiyah, Takeia, Takya, Takyah, Takyia, Taqiyya, Taquaia, Taquaya, Taquiia, Tekeiya, Tekeiyah, Tekeeyia, Tekeiya, Tekeiyah, Tikeia, Tykeia, Tykia

Takila (American) a form of Tequila.
Takayla, Takeila, Takela, Takella, Takeyla, Takiela, Takilah, Takeilla, Takeilya, Takeyla, Takylia, Tatakyla, Tehilla, Tekeila, Tekela, Tekelia, Tekelia, Tekilia, Tekilla, Tekilyah, Tekla

Takira (American) a combination of the prefix Ta + Kira.
Takara, Takarra, Takeara, Takeera, Takeira, Takeira, Takeana, Takeira, Takeirah, Takeirra, Takeira, Takirah, Takeirra, Takiria, Takirna, Takeora, Takyra, Takyrra, Taquera, Taquira, Tekeria, Tikara, Tikira, Tykera

Tala (Native American) stalking wolf.

Talasi (Hopi) corn tassel.
Talasea, Talasia

Taleah (American) a form of Talia.
Talaya, Talayah, Talaiya, Talea, Taleana, Taleea, Taleé, Talei, Taleia, Taleiya, Tylea, Tyleah, Tylee

Taleisha (American) a combination of Talia + Aisha.
Taileisha, Taleise, Talesha, Talicia, Taliesha, Talisa, Talisha, Talysha, Telisha, Titisha, Tyleasha, Tyleisha, Tylicia, Tylisha, Tylishia

Talena (American) a combination of the prefix Ta + Lena.
Talayna, Talihna, Taline, Tallenia, Talná, Tilena, Tilene, Tylena

Talesha (American) a form of Taleisha.
Taleesha, Talesa, Talese, Taleshia, Talesia, Tallese, Tallesia, Tylesha, Tyleshia, Tylysia

Talia (Greek) blooming. (Hebrew) dew from heaven. (Latin, French) birthday. A short form of Natalie. See also Thalia.
Tahlia, Taleah, Taliah, Taliatha, Taliea, Taliyah, Talley, Tallia, Tallya, Talya, Tylia

Talina (American) a combination of Talia + Lina.
Talin, Talinda, Taline, Tallyn, Talyn, Talynn, Tylina, Tyline

Talisa (English) a form of Tallis.
Talisha, Talishia, Talisita, Talissa, Talysa, Talysha, Talysia, Talyssa

Talitha (Arabic) young girl.
Taleetha, Taletha, Talethia, Taliatha, Talita, Talitiha, Taliya, Telita, Tiletha

Taliyah (Greek) a form of Talia.
Taleya, Taleyah, Taiieya, Talliyah, Talya, Talyah, Talyia

Talley (French) a familiar form of Talia.
Tali, Talle, Tallie, Tally, Taly, Talye

Tallis (French, English) forest.
Talice, Talisa, Talise, Tallys

Tallulah (Choctaw) leaping water.
Tallou, Talula

Tam (Vietnamese) heart.

Tama (Japanese) jewel. Tama, Tamah, Tamaiah, Tamala, Tema

Tamaka (Japanese) bracelet. Tamaki, Tamako, Timaka

Tamar (Hebrew) a short form of Tamara. (Russian) History: a twelfth-century Georgian queen. (Hebrew) a short form of Tamara. Tamer, Tamor, Tamour

Tamara (Hebrew) palm tree. See also Tammy. Tamar, Tamará, Tamarae, Tamarah, Tamarin, Tamará, Tamara, Tamaria, Tamarian, Tamarsha, Tamary, Tamera, Tamra, Tammara, Tamara, Tamora, Tamoya, Thama, Thamar, Thamara, Thamara, Timara, Tomara, Tymara

Tamassa (Hebrew) a form of Thomasina. Tamasin, Tamasine, Tamsen, Tamsin, Tamzen, Tamzin

Tameka (Aramaic) twin. Tameca, Tamecia, Tameeka, Tameeka, Tamekia, Tamieka, Tamiecka, Temeeka, Timeeka, Timeka, Tomekia, Tymeka, Tymmeeka

Tamera (Hebrew) a form of Tamara. Tamer, Tamerai, Tameran, Tameria, Tamera, Tammera, Thamer, Timera

Tamesha (American) a combination of the prefix Ta + Mesha. Tameesha, Tameisha, Tameshia, Tameshika, Tameshya, Tameshia, Tamisha, Tamishia, Temesha, Temisha, Timisha, Tomesha, Tomiese, Tomise, Tomisha, Tramisha, Tymesha

Tamika (Japanese) a form of Tamiko. Tamica, Tamicka, Tamikah, Tamikia, Tamikea, Tamiika, Tamyka, Timika, Tomika, Tymika, Tymmicka

Tamiko (Japanese) child of the people. Tami, Tamika, Tamike, Tamiqua, Tamiyo, Tamiko

Tamila (American) a combination of the prefix Ta + Mila. Tamela, Tamela, Tamilla, Tamille, Tamillia, Tamilya

Tamira (Hebrew) a form of Tamara. Tamir, Tamirae, Tamirah, Tamira, Tamirra, Tamryra, Tamyria, Tamyra

Tammi, Tammie (English) forms of Tammy. Tameia, Tami, Tania, Tamiah, Tamie, Tammja, Tamiya

Tammy (English) twin. (Hebrew) a familiar form of Tamara. Tamilyn, Tamlyn, Tammee, Tammey, Tammi, Tammie, Tamy Tanya

Tamra (Hebrew) a short form of Tamara. Tamra, Tamrah

Tamsin (English) a short form of Thomasina.

Tana (Slavic) a short form of Tanya. Taina, Tanae, Tanaeah, Tanah, Tanairi, Tanairy, Tanalia, Tanan, Tanana, Tanaya, Tanaz, Tanna, Tannah

Tandy (English) team. Tanda, Tandalaya, Tandi, Tandie, Tandis, Tandra, Tandrea, Tandria

Taneisha, Tanesha (American) combinations of the prefix Ta + Nesha. Tahniesha, Tainiesha, Tanaesha, Tanaysia, Taneasha, Taneesha, Taneshea, Taneshia, Taneshya, Tanesia, Tanessa, Tanessia, Taniesha, Tanesian, Tanniesha, Tannisha, Tannesha,

Taneya (Russian, Slavic) a form of Tanya. Tanea, Taneah, Tanee, Taneé, Taneia

Tani (Japanese) valley. (Slavic) stand of glory. A familiar form of Tania. Tahnee, Tahni, Tahnie, Tanee, Taney, Tanie, Tany

Tangia (American) a combination of the prefix Ta + Angela. Tangela, Tangi, Tangie, Tanji, Tanjia, Tanjie

Tania (Russian, Slavic) fairy queen. Taneea, Tani, Taniah, Tanija, Tanika, Tanis, Taniya, Tanna, Tannis, Tanniya, Tannya, Tarnia

Taniel (American) a combination of Tania + Danielle. Taniele, Tanielle, Teniel, Teniele, Tenielle

Tanika (American) a form of Tania. Tanikka, Tanikqua, Taniqua, Tanique, Tannica, Tanneka, Tanika

Tanis, Tannis (Slavic) forms of Tania, Tanya. Tanas, Tanese, Tanise, Tanise, Tanisia, Tanka, Tannese, Tanniece, Tanniese, Tannis, Tannyce, Tenice, Tenise, Tenyse, Tiannis, Tonise, Tranice, Tranise, Tynice, Tyniece, Tynise

Tanisha (American) a combination of the prefix Ta + Nisha.
Tahniscia, Tahnisha, Tannasha, Tanashea, Tanicha, Taniesha, Tanish, Tanishah, Tanishia, Taniitia, Tannicia, Tannisha, Tenisha, Tenishka, Tinisha, Tonisha, Tonnisha, Tynisha

Tanissa (American) a combination of the prefix Tania + Nissa.
Tanesa, Tanisa, Tannesa, Tannisa, Tennessa, Tranissa

Tanita (American) a combination of the prefix Ta + Nita.
Taneta, Tanetta, Tanitra, Tanitta, Teneta, Tenetta, Tenita, Tenitta, Tyneta, Tynetta, Tynette, Tynita, Tynitra, Tynitta

Tanith (Phoenician) Mythology: Tanit is the goddess of love.
Tänitha

Tanner (English) leather worker, tanner.
Tannor

Tansy (Greek) immortal. (Latin) tenacious, persistent.
Tancy, Tansee, Tansey, Tanshay, Tanzey

Tanya (Russian, Slavic) fairy queen.
Tahnee, Tahnya, Tana, Tanaya, Taneya, Tania, Tanis, Taniya, Tanka, Tannis, Tannya, Tanoya, Tany, Tanyia, Taunya, Taunya, Tharya

Tao (Chinese, Vietnamese) peach.

Tara (Aramaic) throw; carry. (Irish) rocky hill. (Arabic) a measurement.
Taira, Táirra, Taraea, Tarah, Taráh, Tarai, Taralee, Tarali, Tarasa, Tarasha, Taraya, Tarha, Tari, Tarra, Taryn, Tayra, Tehra

Taraneh (Persian) melody.

Taree (Japanese) arching branch.
Tarea, Tareya, Tari, Taria

Tari (Irish) a familiar form of Tara.
Taria, Tarika, Tarila, Tarilyn, Tarin, Tarina, Tarita

Tarissa (American) a combination of Tara + Rissa.
Taris, Tarisa, Tarise, Tarisha

Tarra (Irish) a form of Tara.
Tarrah

Taryn (Irish) a form of Tara.
Taran, Tareen, Tareena, Taren, Tarene, Tarin, Tarina, Tarren, Tarrena, Tarrin, Tarrina, Tarron, Tarryn, Taryna

Tasarla (Gypsy) dawn.

Tasha (Greek) born on Christmas day. (Russian) a short form of Natasha. See also Tashi, Tosha.
Tacha, Tachiana, Tahsha, Tasenka, Tashae, Tashana, Tashay, Tashe, Tashee, Tasheka, Tashka, Tasia, Taska, Taysha, Thasha, Tiaisha, Tysha

Tashana (American) a combination of the prefix Ta + Shana.
Tashan, Tashanda, Tashani, Tashanika, Tashanna, Tashiana, Tashianna, Tashina, Tshana, Tshiani, Tshianna, Tshianne, Toshanna, Toshani, Tyshana

Tashara (American) a combination of the prefix Ta + Shara.
Tashar, Tasharah, Tasharia, Tasharna, Tasharra, Tashera, Tasherey, Tasheri, Tasherra, Tashira, Tashirah

Tashawna (American) a combination of the prefix Ta + Shawna.
Tashauna, Tashauni, Tashaunie, Tashaunna, Tashaum, Tashaunda, Tashawma, Tashawmia, Tashonda, Tashondra, Tiashauna, Tishawn, Tishunda, Tishunta, Toshauna, Toshauna, Tyshauna, Tyshawna

Tasheena (American) a combination of the prefix Ta + Sheena.
Tasheana, Tasheeana, Tasheeni, Tashena, Tashenna, Tashennia, Tasheona, Tashina, Tisheena, Tosheena, Tysheana, Tysheena, Tyshyna

Tashelle (American) a combination of the prefix Ta + Shelley.
Tachell, Tashell, Techell, Techelle, Teshell, Teshelle, Tochell, Tochelle, Toshelle, Tychell, Tychelle, Tyshell, Tyshelle

Tashi (Hausa) a bird in flight. (Slavic) a form of Tasha.
Tashia, Tashie, Tashika, Tashima, Tashiya

Tasia (Slavic) a familiar form of Tasha.
Tachia, Tashea, Tasiya, Tassi, Tassia, Tassiana, Tassie, Tasya

Tassos (Greek) a form of Theresa.

Tata (Russian) a familiar form of Tatiana.
Tate, Tatia

Tate (English) a short form of Tatum. A form of Taite, Tata.

Tatiana (Slavic) fairy queen. See also Tanya, Tiana.
Tata, Tatania, Tatanya, Tateana, Tati, Tatia, Tatianna, Tatie, Tatihana, Tatiyana, Tatjana, Tatyana, Tiatiana

Tatianna (Slavic) a form of Tatiana.
Tatiiana, Tatitianna, Tateanna, Tationna

Tatiyana (Slavic) a form of Tatiana.
Tatiyana, Tatiyana, Tatiyanna, Tatiyonna,
Tatiyonna

Tatum (English) cheerful.
Tate, Tatumn

Tatyana (Slavic) a form of Tatiana.
Tatyanah, Tatyani, Tatyanna, Tatyannah,
Tatyona, Tatyonna

Taura (Latin) bull. Astrology: Taurus is
a sign of the zodiac.
Taurae, Tauria, Taurina

Tauri (English) a form of Tory.
Taure, Taurie, Taury

Tavia (Latin) a short form of Octavia.
See also Tawia.
Taiva, Tavia, Tava, Tavah, Tavita

Tavie (Scottish) twin.
Tavey, Tavi

Tawanna (American) a combination of
the prefix Ta + Wanda.
Taiivana, Taiiwana, Taquana, Taquanna,
Tavan, Tawana, Tawanda, Tawanne,
Tequana, Tequanna, Tequuanna, Tewanna,
Tewanna, Tiquana, Tiwanna, Tiwena,
Towanda, Towanna, Tywanna, Tywanna

Tawia (African) born after twins.
(Polish) a form of Tavia.

Tawni (English) a form of Tawny.
Tawni, Tawnia, Tawnia, Tawnie, Tawnnie,
Tiawni

Tawny (Gypsy) little one. (English)
brownish yellow, tan.
Tahnee, Tawj, Tauna, Tauné, Taunisha,
Tawnee, Tawnesha, Tawney, Tawni,
Tawryell, Tiauna

Tawnya (American) a combination of
Tawny + Tonya.
Tauna

Taya, Taye (English) short forms of
Taylor.
Taj, Tayah, Tayana, Tayiah, Tayma, Taya,
Taysha, Taysia, Tayva, Tayvonne, Teya,
Teyanna, Teyona, Teyuna, Tiaya, Tiya,
Tiyah, Tiyana, Tye

Tayla (English) a form of Taylor.
Talar, Tayla, Taylah, Taylee, Taylleigh, Taylie,
Teila

Tayler (English) a form of Taylor.
Tayller

Taylor (English) tailor.
Taelor, Tailor, Tairylor, Talor, Talora, Taya,
Taye, Tayla, Taylar, Tayler, Tayllor, Tayllore,
Tayloir, Taylorann, Taylore, Taylori,
Taylour, Taylur, Teylor

Tazu (Japanese) stork; longevity.
Taz, Tazi, Tazia

Teagan (Welsh) beautiful, attractive.
Taegen, Teage, Teagen, Teaghan,
Teaghanne, Teaghen, Teagin, Teague,
Tegan, Teeghan, Tegan, Teguen, Teigan,
Tejan, Tiegan, Tigan, Tijan, Tijana

Teal (English) river duck; blue green.
Teala, Teale, Tealia, Tealisha

Teaira (Latin) a form of Tiara.
Teaira, Teaire, Teairria, Teara, Tearah,
Teareya, Teari, Tearia, Teariea, Tearra,
Tearria

Teanna (American) a combination of
the prefix Te + Anna. A form of
Tiana.
Tean, Teana, Teanah, Teann, Teannah,
Teanne, Teaunna, Teena, Tenana

Teca (Hungarian) a form of Theresa.
Techa, Teka, Tica, Tika

Tecla (Greek) God's fame.
Tekla, Thecla

Teddi (Greek) a familiar form of
Theodora.
Tedde, Teddey, Teddie, Teddy, Tedi, Tediah,
Tedy

Tedra (Greek) a short form of
Theodora.
Tedra, Teddreya, Tedera, Teedra, Teidra

Tegan (Welsh) a form of Teagan.
Tega, Tegen, Teggan, Teghan, Tegin, Tegyn,
Teigen

Telisha (American) a form of Taleisha.
Teleesha, Teleisia, Telesa, Telesha, Teleshia,
Telesia, Telicia, Telisa, Telishia, Telisia,
Telissa, Telisse, Tellisha, Tellisha, Telsa,
Telysa

Temira (Hebrew) tall.
Temora, Timora

Tempest (French) stormy.
Tempesta, Tempeste, Tempestt, Tempist,
Tempistt, Tempress, Tempteste

Tenesha, Tenisha (American) combinations of the prefix Te + Niesha.
Tenecia, Teneesha, Teneisha, Teneshia, Tenesia, Tenessa, Teneusa, Teniesha, Tenishia

Tennille (American) a combination of the prefix Te + Nellie.
Taniel, Tanille, Tenead, Teneil, Teneille, Teniel, Tenille, Tenneal, Tenneill, Tenneille, Tennia, Tennie, Tennielle, Tennile, Tineal, Tiniel, Tonielle, Tonille

Teodora (Czech) a form of Theodora.
Teadora

Teona, Teonna (Greek) forms of Tiana, Tianna.
Teon, Teoni, Teonia, Teonie, Teonney, Teonnia, Teonnie

Tequila (Spanish) a kind of liquor. See also Takila.
Taquela, Taquella, Taquila, Taquilla, Tequilia, Tequilla, Tiquila, Tiquilia

Tera, Terra (Latin) earth. (Japanese) swift arrow. (American) forms of Tara.
Terah, Terai, Teria, Terrae, Terrah, Terria, Tierra

Teralyn (American) a combination of Terri + Lynn.
Taralyn, Teralyn, Teralynn, Teralin, Teralyn

Teresa (Greek) a form of Theresa. See also Tressa.
Taresa, Taressa, Tarissa, Terasa, Tercza, Tereasa, Tereatha, Terese, Teresea, Teresha, Teresia, Teresita, Tereska, Tereson, Teressa, Teretha, Tereza, Terezia, Terezie, Terezinha, Terezinha, Terezka, Terezsa, Terisa, Teriza, Terrasa, Teresa,

Teresha, Teresia, Teressa, Terrosina, Tersa, Tersea, Tenuska, Terza, Teté, Tyresa, Tyresia

Terese (Greek) a form of Teresa.
Tarese, Taress, Iaris, Tarise, Tereece, Tereese, Teress, Terez, Teris, Terrise

Teri (Greek) reaper. A familiar form of Theresa.
Terie

Terrelle (Greek) a form of Theresa.
Tarrell, Teral, Terall, Terel, Terell, Teriel, Terral, Terrall, Terrell, Terrella, Terriel, Terriell, Terrielle, Terrill, Terryelle, Terryl, Terryll, Terrylle, Teryl, Tyrell, Tyrelle

Terrene (Latin) smooth.
Tareena, Tarena, Teran, Teranee, Tereena, Terena, Terencia, Terene, Terenia, Terentia, Terina, Teran, Terren, Terrena, Terrin, Terrina, Terron, Terrosina, Terryn, Terun, Teryn, Teryna, Terynn, Tyreen, Tyrene

Terri (Greek) reaper. A familiar form of Theresa.
Terree, Terria, Terrie

Terriann (American) a combination of Terri + Ann.
Teran, Terian, Teriann, Terianne, Teriyan, Terrian, Terrian, Terrianne, Terryann

Terrianna (American) a combination of Terri + Anna.
Teriana, Terianna, Terriana, Terrianna, Terrina, Terriona, Terrionna, Terriyana, Terriyanna, Terryauna, Terryauna, Tyrina

Terrica (American) a combination of Terri + Erica. See also Rica.
Tereka, Terica, Tericka, Terika, Tereka, Terricka, Terrika, Tyria, Tyrica, Tyrika, Tyrikka, Tyronica

Terry (Greek) a short form of Theresa.
Tere, Teree, Terelle, Terene, Teri, Terie, Terrey, Terri, Terrie, Terrye, Tery

Terry-Lynn (American) a combination of Terry + Lynn.
Terelyn, Terelynn, Terri-Lynn, Terrilynn, Terrylynn

Tertia (Latin) third.
Tercia, Tercina, Tercine, Terecena, Tersia, Terza

Tess (Greek) a short form of Quintessa, Theresa.
Tes, Tese

Tessa (Greek) reaper.
Tesa, Tesah, Tesha, Tesia, Tessah, Tessia, Tezia

Tessie (Greek) a familiar form of Theresa.
Tesi, Tessey, Tessi, Tessy, Tezi

Tetsu (Japanese) strong as iron.

Tetty (English) a familiar form of Elizabeth.

Tevy (Cambodian) angel.
Teva

Teylor (English) a form of Taylor.
Teighlor, Teylar

Thaddea (Greek) courageous. (Latin) praiser.
Thada, Thadda

Thalassa (Greek) sea, ocean.

Thalia (Greek) a form of Talia. Mythology: the Muse of comedy.
Thaleia, Thalie, Thalya

Thana (Arabic) happy occasion.
Thaina, Thania, Thanie

Thanh (Vietnamese) bright blue.
(Punjabi) good place.
Thantra, Thanya

Thao (Vietnamese) respectful of parents.

Thea (Greek) goddess. A short form of Althea.
Theo

Thelma (Greek) willful.
Thelmatina

Thema (African) queen.

Theodora (Greek) gift of God. See also Dora, Dorothy, Feodora. *Taedra, Teddi, Tedra, Teodora, Teodory, Teodosia, Theda, Thedorsha, Thedrica, Theo, Theodore, Theodoria, Theodorian, Theodosia, Theodra*

Theone (Greek) gift of God.
Theondra, Theoni, Theonie

Theophania (Greek) God's appearance. See also Tiffany.
Theo, Theophanie

Theophila (Greek) loved by God.
Theo

Theresa (Greek) reaper. See also Resi, Reza, Riza, Tassos, Teca, Terrelle, Tracey, Tracy, Zilya. *Teresa, Teri, Terri, Terry, Tersea, Tess, Tessa, Tessie, Theresia, Theresina, Theresia, Theressa, Thereza, Therisa, Therissie, Thersa, Thersea, Tresha, Tressa, Trice*

Therese (Greek) a form of Theresa.
Terese, Thérèse, Theresia, Theressa, Thera, Theressa, Thersa

Theta (Greek) Linguistics: a letter in the Greek alphabet.

Thetis (Greek) disposed. Mythology: the mother of Achilles.

Thi (Vietnamese) poem.
Tiia, Thy, Thya

Thirza (Hebrew) pleasant.
Therza, Thirsa, Thirzah, Thursa, Thyrza, Tirshka, Tirza

Thomasina (Hebrew) twin. See also Tamassa. *Tamsin, Thomasa, Thomasia, Thomasin, Thomasine, Thomazine, Thomencia, Thomethia, Thomisha, Thomsina, Toma, Tomasa, Tomasina, Tomasine, Tomina, Tommie, Tommina*

Thora (Scandinavian) thunder.
Thordia, Thoris, Thorri, Thyra, Tyra

Thuy (Vietnamese) gentle.

Tia (Greek) princess. (Spanish) aunt. *Téa, Teah, Teeya, Teia, Ti, Tiakeisha, Tialeigh, Tiamarie, Tianda, Tiandria, Tiante, Tiia, Tiye, Tyia*

Tiana, Tianna (Greek) princess. (Latin) short forms of Tatiana. *Teana, Teanna, Tiahna, Tianah, Tiane, Tianea, Tianee, Tiani, Tiann, Tiannah, Tianne, Tianni, Tiaon, Tianna, Tiena, Tiona, Tionna, Tiyana*

Tiara (Latin) crowned.
Teair, Teaira, Teara, Teare, Tearia, Tearria, Teira, Tiera, Tiaira, Tiari, Tiaria, Tiarra, Tiera, Tyara

Tiarra (Latin) a form of Tiara.
Tiarra, Tiarrah, Tyarra

Tiauna (Greek) a form of Tiana.
Tiaunah, Tiaunia, Tiaunna

Tiberia (Latin) Geography: the Tiber River in Italy.
Tib, Tibbie, Tibby

Tichina (American) a combination of the prefix Ti + China.
Tichian, Tichin, Tichina

Tida (Tai) daughter.

Tiera, Tierra (Latin) forms of Tiara. *Tieana, Tiéra, Tierah, Tierre, Tierrea, Tieria*

Tierney (Irish) noble.
Tieranae, Tierani, Tieranie, Tieranni, Tierany Tiernan, Tiernee, Tierny

Tiff (Latin) a short form of Tiffani, Tiffanie, Tiffany.

Tiffani, Tiffanie (Latin) forms of Tiffany. *Tephanie, Tifanee, Tifani, Tifanie, Tiff, Tiffanee, Tiffayne, Tiffeni, Tiffenie, Tiffennie, Tiffiani, Tiffiane, Tiffine, Tiffni, Tiffnie, Tiffni, Tiffy, Tiffynie, Tifni*

Tiffany (Latin) trinity. (Greek) a short form of Theophania. See also Tyfany. *Taffanay, Taffany, Tifaney, Tifany, Tiff, Tiffanay, Tiffaney, Tiffani, Tiffanie, Tiffanny, Tiffeney, Tiffiney, Tiffney, Tiffony, Tiffnay, Tiffney, Tiffny, Tiffy, Tiphanie, Tiphany*

Tiffy (Latin) a familiar form of Tiffani, Tiffany.
Tiffey, Tiffi, Tiffie

Tijuana (Spanish) Geography: a border town in Mexico.
Tajuana, Tajuanna, Thejuana, Tiajuana, Tiajuanna, Tiawanna

Tilda (German) a short form of Matilda.
Tilde, Tildie, Tildy, Tylda, Tyldy

Tillie (German) a familiar form of Matilda.
Tilia, Tilley, Tilli, Tillia, Tilly, Tillye

Timi (English) a familiar form of Timothea.
Timia, Timie, Timmi, Timmie

Timothea (English) honoring God.
Thea, Timi

Tina (Spanish, American) a short form of Augustine, Martina, Christina, Valentina.
Teanna, Teena, Teina, Tena, Tenae, Tinai, Tine, Tinea, Tinia, Tiniah, Tinna, Tinnia, Tyna, Tynka

Tinble (English) sound bells make.
Tynble

Tinesha (American) a combination of the prefix Ti + Niesha.
Timnesha, Tinecia, Tineisha, Tinesa, Tineshia, Tinessa, Tinisha, Tinsia

Tinisha (American) a form of Tenisha.
Tiniesha, Tinieshia, Tinishia, Tinishya

Tiona, Tionna (American) forms of Tiana.
Teona, Teonna, Tionda, Tiondra, Tiondre,

Tioné, Tionette, Tioni, Tionia, Tionie, Tionja, Tionnah, Tionne, Tionya, Tyonna

Tiphanie (Latin) a form of Tiffany.
Tiphanee, Tiphani, Tiphany

Tiponya (Native American) great horned owl.
Tipper

Tipper (Irish) water pourer. (Native American) a short form of Tiponya.

Tira (Hindi) arrow.
Tirah, Tirea, Tirena

Tirtha (Hindi) ford.

Tirza (Hebrew) pleasant.
Thersa, Thirza, Tierza, Tirsa, Tirzah, Tirzha, Tyrzah

Tisa (Swahili) ninth-born.
Tisah, Tysa, Tyssa

Tish (Latin) a short form of Tisha.

Tisha (Latin) joy. A short form of Leticia.
Taesha, Tesha, Teisha, Tiesha, Tieshia, Tish, Tishal, Tishia, Tysha, Tyshia

Tita (Greek) giant. (Spanish) a short form of names ending in "tita." A form of Titus (see Boys' Names).

Titania (Greek) giant. Mythology: the Titans were a race of giants.
Tania, Teata, Titanna, Titanya, Titiana, Tiziana, Tytan, Tytania, Tytiana

Titiana (Greek) a form of Titania.
Titianay, Titiania, Titianna, Titiayana, Titionia, Titiyana, Titiyanna, Tityana

Tivona (Hebrew) nature lover.

Tiwa (Zuni) onion.

Tiyana (Greek) a form of Tiana.
Tiyani, Tiyani, Tiyania, Tiyanna, Tiyonna

Tobi (Hebrew) God is good.
Tobe, Tobee, Tobey, Tobie, Tobit, Toby, Tobye, Tova, Tovah, Tove, Tovi, Tybi, Tybie

Tocarra (American) a combination of the prefix To + Cara.
Tocana, Tocana

Toinette (French) a short form of Antoinette.
Toinetta, Tola, Tonetta, Tonette, Toni, Toniette, Twanette

Toki (Japanese) hopeful.
Toko, Tokoya, Tokyo

Tola (Polish) a form of Toinette.
Tolsia

Tomi (Japanese) rich.
Tomie, Tomiju

Tommie (Hebrew) a short form of Thomasina.
Tomme, Tommi, Tommia, Tommy

Tomo (Japanese) intelligent.
Tomoko

Tonesha (American) a combination of the prefix To + Niesha.
Toneisha, Toneisheia, Toneshia, Tonesia, Toniece, Tonisha, Tonneshia

Toni (Greek) flourishing. (Latin) praise-worthy.
Tonee, Toney, Tonia, Tonie, Toniee, Tonni, Tonnie, Tony, Tonye

Tonia (Latin, Slavic) a form of Toni. Tonya.
Tonea, Toniah, Toniea, Tonja, Tonje, Tonna, Tonni, Tonnia, Tonnie, Tonnja

Tonisha (American) a form of Toneisha.
Toniesha, Tonisa, Tonise, Tonisia, Tonnisha

Tonya (Slavic) fairy queen.
Tonia, Tonnya, Tonyea, Tonyetta, Tonyia

Topaz (Latin) golden yellow gem.

Topsy (English) on top. Literature: a slave in Harriet Beecher Stowe's novel *Uncle Tom's Cabin*.
Topsey, Topsey, Topsie

Tora (Japanese) tiger.

Tori (Japanese) bird. (English) a form of Tory.
Toria, Toriana, Torie, Torri, Torrie, Torrita, Tory, Toriah, Torria

Toria (English) a form of Tori, Tory. Toriah, Torria

Toriana (English) a form of Tori.
Toriani, Toriane, Toriann, Torianna, Torianne, Torianna, Torin, Torina, Torine, Torion, Torionna, Torionne, Toriyana, Torrina

Torie, Torrie (English) forms of Tori.
Tore, Toree, Torei, Tore, Torree

Torilyn (English) a combination of Tori + Lynn.
Torilyn, Torrilyn, Torrilynn

Torri (English) a form of Tori.

Tory (English) victorious. (Latin) a short form of Victoria.
Tauri, Torey, Tori, Torrey, Torreya, Torry, Torye, Torya, Torye, Toya

Tosha (Punjabi) armaments. (Polish) a familiar form of Antonia. (Russian) a form of Tasha.
Toshea, Toshia, Toshiea, Toshke, Tosia, Toska

Toshi (Japanese) mirror image. Toshie, Toshiko, Toshikyo

Toski (Hopi) squashed bug.

Totsi (Hopi) moccasins.

Tottie (English) a familiar form of Charlotte.
Tota, Totti, Toty

Tovah (Hebrew) good. Tova, Tovia

Toya (Spanish) a form of Tory.
Toia, Toyanika, Toyanna, Toyea, Toylea, Toyleah, Toylenn, Toylin, Toylyn

Tracey (Greek) a familiar form of Theresa. (Latin) warrior.
Trace, Tracee, Tracell, Traci, Tracie, Tracy, Traice, Tracey, Treesy

Traci, Tracie (Latin) forms of Tracey.
Tracia, Tracilee, Tracilyn, Traclynn, Tracina, Traici

Tralena (Latin) a combination of Tracy + Lena.
Traleen, Tralene, Tralin, Tralinda, Tralyn, Tralynn, Tralynne

Tranesha (American) a combination of the prefix Tra + Niesha.
Tranece, Traneis, Traneise, Traneisha, Tranese, Traneshia, Tranice, Traniece, Tranisha, Tranishia

Trashawn (American) a combination of the prefix Tra + Shawn.
Trashan, Trashana, Trashauna, Trashon, Trayshauna

Trava (Czech) spring grasses.

Treasure (Latin) treasure, wealth; valuable.
Treasa, Treasur, Treasuré, Treasury

Trella (Spanish) a familiar form of Estelle.

Tresha (Greek) a form of Theresa.
Trescha, Trescia, Treshana, Treshia

Tressa (Greek) a short form of Theresa. See also Teresa.
Treaser, Tresa, Tresca, Trese, Treska, Tressie, Trez, Treza, Trisa

Trevina (Irish) prudent. (Welsh) homestead.
Treva, Trevana, Trevena, Trevenia, Treveon, Trevia, Treviana, Trevien, Trevin, Trevona

Trevona (Irish) a form of Trevina.
Trevon, Trevonia, Trevonna, Trevonne, Trevorye

Triana (Latin) third. (Greek) a form of Trina.
Tria, Triann, Trianna, Trianne

Tricia (Latin) a form of Trisha.
Trica, Tricha, Trichelle, Tricina, Trickia, Trickia

Trice (Greek) a short form of Theresa.
Treece

Trilby (English) soft hat.
Tribi, Trilbie, Trilby

Trina (Greek) pure.
Treena, Treina, Trenna, Triana, Trinia, Trinchen, Trind, Trinda, Trine, Trinette, Trini, Trinica, Trinice, Triniece, Trinika, Trinique, Trinisa, Tryna

Trini (Greek) a form of Trina.
Trinia, Trinie

Trinity (Latin) triad. Religion: the Father, the Son, and the Holy Spirit.
Trinita, Trinite, Trinitee, Triniti, Trinnette, Trinty

Trish (Latin) a short form of Beatrice, Trisha.
Trishell, Trishelle

Trisha (Latin) noblewoman. (Hindi) thirsty. See also Tricia.
Treasha, Trish, Trishann, Trishanna, Trishanne, Trishara, Trishia, Trishna, Trissha, Trycia

Trissa (Latin) a familiar form of Patricia.
Trisa, Trisanne, Trisia, Trisina, Trissi, Trissie, Trissy, Tryssa

Trista (Latin) a short form of Tristen.
Trisatal, Tristess, Tristia, Trysta, Trystia

Tristan (Latin) bold.
Trista, Tristane, Tristanni, Tristany, Tristen, Tristian, Tristiana, Tristin, Triston, Trystan, Trystyn

Tristen (Latin) a form of Tristan.
Tristene, Trysten

Tristin (Latin) a form of Tristan.
Tristina, Tristine, Tristinye, Tristn, Trystin

Triston, Trystyn (Latin) forms of Tristan.
Tristony, Trystyn

Trixie (American) a familiar form of Beatrice.
Tris, Trissie, Trissina, Trix, Trixi, Trixy

Troya (Irish) foot soldier.
Troi, Troia, Troiana, Troiya, Troy

Trudel (Dutch) a form of Trudy.

Trudy (German) a familiar form of Gertrude.
Truda, Trude, Trudel, Trudessa, Trudey, Trudi, Trudie

Trycia (Latin) a form of Trisha.

Tryna (Greek) a form of Trina.
Tryane, Tryanna, Trynee

Tryne (Dutch) pure.
Trine

Tsigana (Hungarian) a form of Zigana.
Tsigane, Tzigana, Tzigane

Tu (Chinese) jade.

Tuesday (English) born on the third day of the week.
Tuesdae, Tuesdea, Tuesdee, Tuesdey, Tusdai

Tula (Hindi) born in the lunar month of Capricorn.
Tulah, Tulla, Tullah, Tuula

Tullia (Irish) peaceful, quiet.
Tulia, Tulliah

Tulsi (Hindi) basil, a sacred Hindi herb.
Tulsia

Turquoise (French) blue-green semi-precious stone.
Turkois, Turkoise, Turkoys, Turkoyse

Tusa (Zuni) prairie dog.

Tuyen (Vietnamese) angel.

Tuyet (Vietnamese) snow.

Twyla (English) woven of double thread.
Twila, Twilla

Tyanna (American) a combination of the prefix Ty + Anna.
Tya, Tyana, Tyann, Tyannah, Tyanne, Tyannia

Tyeisha (American) a form of Tyesha.
Tyeesha, Tyeishia, Tyiesha, Tyisha, Tyishea, Tyishia

Tyesha (American) a combination of Ty + Aisha.
Tyasha, Tyashia, Tyasia, Tyasiah, Tyeisha, Tyesha, Tyeyshia, Tyisha

Tyfany (American) a short form of Tiffany.
Tyfani, Tyfanny, Tyffani, Tyffanni, Tyffany, Tyffni, Typhanie, Typhany

Tykeisha (American) a form of Takeisha.
Tkeesha, Tykeisa, Tykeishia, Tykesha, Tykeshia, Tykeysha, Tykeza, Tykisha

Tykera (American) a form of Takira.
Tykeira, Tykeirah, Tykereiah, Tykeria, Tykeriah, Tykerria, Tykiera, Tykierra, Tykira, Tykiria, Tykirra

Tyler (English) tailor.
Tyller, Tylor

Tyna (Czech) a short form of Kristina.
Tynaa, Tynea, Tynia

Tyne (English) river.
Tine, Tyna, Tynelle, Tynessa, Tynetta

Tynesha (American) a combination of Ty + Niesha.
Tynaise, Tynece, Tyneicia, Tynesa, Tynesha, Tyneshia, Tynessia, Tyniesha, Tynisha, Tyseisha

Tynisha (American) a form of Tynesha.
Tyneisia, Tyneisia, Tynisa, Tynise, Tynishi

Tyra (Scandinavian) battler. Mythology: Tyr was the god of war. A form of Thora. (Hindi) a form of Tira.
Tyraa, Tyrah, Tyran, Tyree, Tyria

Tyshanna (American) a combination of Ty + Shawna.
Tyshana, Tyshanae, Tyshane, Tyshaun, Tyshaunda, Tyshawn, Tyshawna, Tyshawnah, Tyshawnda, Tyshawnna, Tysheana, Tysheanna, Tyshonia, Tyshonna, Tyshonya

Tytiana (Greek) a form of Titania.
Tytana, Tytanna, Tyteana, Tyteanna, Tytianna, Tytianni, Tytionna, Tytiyana, Tytiyanna, Tytyana, Tytyanna

U

U (Korean) gentle.

Udele (English) prosperous.
Uda, Udella, Udelle, Yudelle

Ula (Irish) sea jewel. (Scandinavian) wealthy. (Spanish) a short form of Eulalia.
Uli, Ulla

Ulani (Polynesian) cheerful.
Ulana, Ulane

Ulima (Arabic) astute; wise.
Ullima

Ulla (German, Swedish) willful. (Latin) a short form of Ursula. Ulli

Ulrica (German) wolf ruler; ruler of all. See also Rica.
Ulea, Ulrica, Ulricka, Ulrika, Ulrike

Ultima (Latin) last, endmost, farthest.

Ululani (Hawaiian) heavenly inspiration.

Ulva (German) wolf.

Uma (Hindi) mother. Religion: another name for the Hindu goddess Devi.

Umay (Turkish) hopeful.
Umai

Umeko (Japanese) plum-blossom child; patient.
Ume, Umeyo

Una (Latin) one; united. (Hopi) good memory. (Irish) a form of Agnes. See also Oona.
Unna, Uny

Undine (Latin) little wave. Mythology: the undines were water spirits. See also Ondine.
Undeen, Undene

Unice (English) a form of Eunice.
Unica, Uniika, Unik, Unikqua, Unikue

Unika (American) a form of Unique.
Unica, Uniika, Unikqua, Uniqua, Uniquia

Unique (Latin) only one.
Unika, Uniqia, Uniqua, Uniquia

Unity (English) unity.
Unita, Unita, Unitee

Unn (Norwegian) she who is loved.

Unna (German) woman.

Urania (Greek) heavenly. Mythology: the Muse of astronomy.
Uraina, Uranie, Uranya, Uranya

Urbana (Latin) city dweller.

Urika (Omaha) useful to everyone.
Ureka

Urit (Hebrew) bright.
Urice

Ursa (Greek) a short form of Ursula. (Latin) a form of Orsa.
Ursey, Ursi, Ursie, Ursy

Ursula (Greek) little bear. See also Sula, Ulla, Vorsila.
Irsaline, Ursa, Ursala, Ursel, Ursela, Ursella, Ursely, Ursilla, Ursilane, Ursola, Ursule, Ursulina, Ursuline, Urszula, Urszuli, Urzula

Usha (Hindi) sunrise.

Ushi (Chinese) ox. Astrology: a sign of the Chinese zodiac.

Uta (German) rich. (Japanese) poem.
Utako

Urika (German) a short form of Ursula. Ulli

Utina (Native American) woman of my country.
Utahna, Utona, Utonna

Vail (English) valley.
Vale, Vayle

Val (Latin) a short form of Valerie, Valerie.

Vala (German) singled out.
Valla

Valarie (Latin) a form of Valerie.
Valaree, Valaree, Valarey, Valari, Valaria, Vallarie

Valda (German) famous ruler.
Valida, Velda

Valencia (Spanish) strong. Geography: a region in eastern Spain.
Valecia, Valence, Valenica, Valentia, Valenzia

Valene (Latin) a short form of Valentina.
Valaine, Valean, Valeda, Valeen, Valen, Valena, Valeney, Valien, Valina, Valine, Vallan, Vallen

Valentina (Latin) strong. History: Valentina Tereshkova, a Soviet cosmonaut, was the first woman in space. See also Tina, Valene, Valli.
Val, Valantina, Vale, Valenteen, Valentena, Valentijn, Valentin, Valentine, Valiaka, Valtina, Valyn, Valynn

Valera (Russian) a form of Valerie. See also Lera.

Valeria (Latin) a form of Valerie.
Valaria, Valeriana, Valeriane, Valeria

Valerie (Latin) strong.
Vairy, Val, Valarie, Vale, Valera, Valeree, Valeri, Valeria, Valerie, Valery, Valka, Valleree, Valleri, Vallerie, Valli, Vallirie, Valona, Valorie, Valry, Valya, Valerie, Waleria

Valery (Latin) a form of Valerie.
Valerye, Vallary, Vallery

Valeska (Slavic) glorious ruler.
Valesca, Valese, Valeshia, Valeshka, Valezka, Valisha

Valli (Latin) a familiar form of Valentina, Valerie. Botany: a plant native to India.
Vallie, Vally

Valma (Finnish) loyal defender.

Valonia (Latin) shadow valley.
Vallon, Valona

Valora (Latin) a form of Valerie.
Valoria, Valorya, Velora

Valorie (Latin) a form of Valerie.
Vallori, Vallory, Valori, Valory

Vanda (German) a form of Wanda.
Vandana, Vandella, Vandetta, Vandi, Vannda

Vanesa (Greek) a form of Vanessa.
Vanesha, Vaneshah, Vanesia, Vanisa

Vanessa (Greek) butterfly. Literature: a name invented by Jonathan Swift as a nickname for Esther Vanhomrigh. See also Nessie.
Van, Vanassa, Vanesa, Vaneshia, Vanesse, Vanessia, Vanessica, Vanetta, Vaneza, Vaniece, Vaniessa, Vanija, Vanika, Vanissa,

Vania, Vanna, Vannessa, Vannessa, Vanni, Vannie, Vanny, Varnessa, Venessa

Vanetta (English) a form of Vanessa.
Vaneta, Vanita, Vannetta, Vannetta, Vannita, Venetta

Vania, Vanya (Russian) familiar forms of Anna.
Vanija, Vanina, Vaniya, Vanja, Vanka, Vannia

Vanity (English) vain.
Vaniti, Vanity

Vanna (Cambodian) golden. (Greek) a short form of Vanessa.
Vana, Vanae, Vanelly, Vannah, Vannalee, Vannaleigh, Vannie, Vanny

Vannessa, Vannessa (Greek) forms of Vanessa.
Vannesha, Vanneza

Vanora (Welsh) white wave.
Vannora

Vantrice (American) a combination of the prefix Van + Trice.
Vantrece, Vantricia, Vantrisa, Vantrissa

Varda (Hebrew) rose.
Vadit, Vardia, Vardice, Vardina, Vardis, Vardit

Varvara (Slavic) a form of Barbara.
Vara, Varenka, Varina, Varinka, Varya, Varyusha, Vava, Vavka

Vashti (Persian) lovely. Bible: the wife of Ahasuerus, king of Persia.
Vashtee, Vashtie, Vashty

Veanna (American) a combination of the prefix Ve + Anna.
Veeana, Veena, Veenaya, Veeona

Veda (Sanskrit) sacred lore; knowledge. Religion: the Vedas are the sacred writings of Hinduism.
Vedad, Vedis, Veeda, Veida, Veleda, Vida

Vedette (Italian) sentry; scout. (French) movie star.
Vedetta

Vega (Arabic) falling star.

Velda (German) a form of Valda.

Velika (Slavic) great, wondrous.

Velma (German) a familiar form of Vilhelmina.
Valma, Vellma, Vilma, Vilna

Velvet (English) velvety.

Venecia (Italian) from Venice, Italy.
Vanecia, Vanetia, Veneise, Venesa, Veneshia, Venesher, Venesse, Venessia, Venetia, Venette, Venezia, Venica, Veniece, Venise, Venisha, Venishia, Venita, Venitia, Venize, Vennesa, Vennice, Vennisa, Vennise, Vonitia, Vonizia

Venessa (Latin) a form of Vanessa.
Venesse, Venesa, Venese, Veneshia, Venesia, Venisa, Venissa, Vennessa

Venus (Latin) love. Mythology: the goddess of love and beauty.
Venis, Venusa, Venusina, Vinny

Vera (Latin) true. (Slavic) faith. A short form of Elvera, Veronica. See also Verena, Wera.
Vara, Veera, Veira, Veradis, Vere, Verka, Verla, Viera, Vira

Verbena (Latin) sacred plants.
Verbeena, Verbina

Verda (Latin) young, fresh.
Verdi, Verdie, Viridiana, Viridis

Verdad (Spanish) truthful.

Verena (Latin) truthful. A familiar form of Vera, Verna.
Verene, Verenis, Vereniz, Verina, Verine, Vernika, Veroshka, Verunka, Verusya, Virna

Verenice (Latin) a form of Veronica.
Verenis, Verenise, Vereniz

Verity (Latin) truthful.
Verita, Veritie

Verlene (Latin) a combination of Veronica + Lena.
Verleen, Verlena, Verlin, Verlinda, Verline, Verlyn

Verna (Latin) springtime. (French) a familiar form of Laverne. See also Verena, Wera.
Verasha, Verla, Verne, Vernetia, Vernetta, Vernette, Vernia, Vernice, Vernita, Verusya, Viera, Virida, Virna, Virnell

Vernice (Latin) a form of Bernice, Verna.
Vernese, Verneshia, Vernessa, Vernica, Vernice, Verniece, Vernika, Vernique, Vernis, Vernise, Vernisha, Vernisheia, Vernissia

Veronica (Latin) true image. See also Ronni, Weronika.
Varonica, Vera, Veranique, Veronice, Verhonica, Veronia, Verohnica, Veron, Verona, Verone, Veronic, Veronic, Veronica, Veronika, Veronique, Véronique, Veronne, Veronnica, Veruszhka, Vironica, Vron, Vronica

Veronika (Latin) a form of Veronica.
Varonika, Veronick, Veronik, Veronike, Veronka, Veronkia, Veruka

Veronique, Véronique (French) forms of Veronica.
Véspera (Latin) evening star.

Vesta (Latin) keeper of the house. Mythology: the goddess of the home.
Vessy, Vest, Vesteria

Veta (Slavic) a familiar form of Elizabeth.
Veeta, Vita

Vi (Latin, French) a short form of Viola, Violet.
Vye

Vianca (Spanish) a form of Bianca.
Vianeca, Vianica

Vianey (American) a familiar form of Viana.
Vianney, Viany

Vianna (American) a combination of Vi + Anna.
Viana, Vianey, Viann, Vianne

Vica (Hungarian) a form of Eve.

Vicki, Vickie (Latin) familiar forms of Victoria.
Vi, Vici, Vicke, Vickee, Vickiana, Vickilyn, Vickki, Vicky, Vika, Viki, Vikie, Vikki, Vikky

Vicky (Latin) a familiar form of Victoria.
Vicy, Vickey, Viky, Vikkey, Vikky

Victoria (Latin) victorious. See also
Tory, Wicktoria, Wisia.
*Vicki, Vicky, Victoire, Victoriana,
Victorianna, Victorie, Victorina, Victorine,
Victoriya, Victorria, Victorriah, Victory,
Victorya, Viktoria, Vitoria, Vyctoria*

Vida (Sanskrit) a form of Veda.
(Hebrew) a short form of Davida.
Vidamarie

Vidonia (Portuguese) branch of a vine.
Vedonia, Vidonya

Vienna (Latin) Geography: the capital
of Austria.
*Veena, Vena, Venna, Vienette, Vienne,
Vina*

Viktoria (Latin) a form of Victoria.
*Viktorie, Viktorija, Viktorina, Viktorine,
Viktorka*

Vilhelmina (German) a form of
Wilhelmina.
Velma, Vilhelmine, Vilma

Villette (French) small town.
Vietta

Vilma (German) a short form of
Vilhelmina.

Vina (Hindi) Mythology: a musical
instrument played by the Hindu
goddess of wisdom. (Spanish) vine-
yard. (Hebrew) a short form of
Davina. See also Lavina.
*Veena, Vena, Viña, Vinesha, Vinessa,
Vinia, Viniece, Vinique, Vinisha, Viñita,
Vinna, Vinni, Vinnie, Vinny, Vinora,
Vyna*

Vincentia (Latin) victor, conqueror.
*Vicenta, Vincenta, Vincentena, Vincentina,
Vincentine, Vincenza, Vincy, Vinnie*

Viñita (Spanish) a form of Vina.
*Vineeta, Viñeeta, Vinetta, Viñette, Viñitha,
Viñita, Viñiti, Viñitia, Vyñetta, Vyñette*

Viola (Latin) violet; stringed
instrument in the violin family.
Literature: the heroine of
Shakespeare's play *Twelfth Night*.
*Vi, Violaine, Violanta, Violante, Viole,
Violeine*

Violet (French) Botany: a plant with
purplish blue flowers.
*Vi, Violeta, Violette, Vyolet, Vyoletta,
Vyolette*

Violeta (French) a form of Violet.
Violetta

Virgilia (Latin) rod bearer, staff bearer.
Virgillia

Virginia (Latin) pure, virginal.
Literature: Virginia Woolf was a well-
known British writer. See also Gina,
Ginger, Ginny, Jinny.
*Verginia, Verginya, Virge, Virgen, Virgenia,
Virgenya, Virgie, Virgine, Virginie,
Virginië, Virginio, Virginnia, Virgy,
Virjeana*

Virginie (French) a form of Virginia.

Viridiana (Latin) a form of Viridis.

Viridis (Latin) green.
Viridis, Virida, Viridia, Viridiana

Virtue (Latin) virtuous.

Vita (Latin) life.
*Veeta, Veta, Vitaliana, Vitalina, Vitel,
Vitella, Vitia, Vika, Vitke*

Vitoria (Spanish) a form of Victoria.
Vittoria

Viv (Latin) a short form of Vivian.

Viva (Latin) a short form of Aviva,
Vivian.
Vica, Vivan, Vivva

Viveca (Scandinavian) a form of
Vivian.
*Viu, Viveca, Viveeka, Viveka, Vivica,
Vivica, Vyveca*

Vivian (Latin) full of life.
*Vevay, Vevey, Viv, Viva, Viveca, Vivee,
Vivi, Vivia, Viviana, Viviane, Viviann,
Vivianne, Vivie, Vivien, Vivienne, Vivina,
Vivion, Vivyan, Vivyann, Vivyanne,
Vyvyan, Vyvyann, Vyvyanne*

Viviana (Latin) a form of Vivian.
Viu, Vivianna, Vivyana, Vyvyana

Vondra (Czech) loving woman.
Vonda, Vondrea

Voneisha (American) a combination
of Yvonne + Aisha.
Voneishia, Vonesha, Voneshia

Vonna (French) a form of Yvonne.
Vona

Vonny (French) a familiar form of
Yvonne.
Vonney, Vonni, Vonnie

Vontricia (American) a combination
of Yvonne + Tricia.
Vontrece, Vontrese, Vontrice, Vontriece

Vorsila (Greek) a form of Ursula.
Vorsilla, Vorsula, Vorsulla, Vorsyla

Wadd (Arabic) beloved.

Waheeda (Arabic) one and only.

Wainani (Hawaiian) beautiful water.

Wakana (Japanese) plant.

Wakanda (Dakota) magical power.
Wakenda

Wakeisha (American) a combination of the prefix Wa + Keisha.
Wakeishia, Wakesha, Wakeshia, Wakesia

Walad (Arabic) newborn.
Waladah, Walidah

Walda (German) powerful; famous.
Waldira, Waldine, Walida, Wallda, Welda

Waleria (Polish) a form of Valerie.
Wala

Walker (English) cloth; walker.
Walker

Wallis (English) from Wales.
Wallie, Walliss, Wally, Wallys

Wanda (German) wanderer. See also Wendy.
Vanda, Wahnda, Wandah, Wandely, Wandie, Wandis, Wandja, Wandzia, Wannda, Wonda, Wonnda

Wandie (German) a familiar form of Wanda.
Wandi, Wandy

Waneta (Native American) charger. See also Juanita.
Waneeta, Wanita, Wanite, Wanneta, Wannita, Wonnita, Wynita

Wanetta (English) pale face.
Wanette, Wannetta, Wannette

Wanika (Hawaiian) a form of Juanita.
Wanicka

Warda (German) guardian.
Wardah, Wardeh, Wardena, Wardenia, Wardia, Wardine

Washi (Japanese) eagle.

Wattan (Japanese) homeland.

Wauna (Moquelumnan) snow geese honking.
Waunakee

Wava (Slavic) a form of Barbara.

Waverly (English) quaking aspen-tree meadow.
Waverley, Waverli, Wavierlee

Waynesha (American) a combination of Waynette + Niesha.
Wayneesha, Wayneisha, Waynie, Waynisha

Waynette (English) wagon maker.
Waynel, Waynelle, Waynetta, Waynlyn

Weeko (Dakota) pretty girl.

Wehilani (Hawaiian) heavenly adornment.

Wenda (Welsh) a form of Wendy.
Wendaine, Wendayne

Wendelle (English) wanderer.
Wendaline, Wendall, Wendalyn, Wendeline, Wendella, Wendeline, Wendelly

Wendi (Welsh) a form of Wendy.
Wendie

Wendy (Welsh) white; light skinned. A familiar form of Gwendolyn, Wanda.
Wenda, Wende, Wendee, Wendey, Wendi, Wendye, Wendy

Wera (Polish) a form of Vera. See also Verna.
Wiera, Wiercia, Wierka

Weronika (Polish) a form of Veronica.
Weronikia

Wesisa (Musoga) foolish.

Weslee (English) western meadow.
Weslea, Wesleigh, Weslene, Wesley, Wesli, Wesia, Weslie, Weslyn

Whitley (English) white field.
Whitely, Whitlee, Whitlegh, Whitlie, Whitley

Whitnie (English) a form of Whitney.
Whitani, Whitnei, Whitni, Whytni, Whytnie

Whitney (English) white island.
Whiteny, Whitne, Whitné, Whitnee, Whitneigh, Whitnie, Whitny, Whittnye, Whytne, Whytney, Witney

Whittney (English) a form of Whitney.
Whittani, Whittanie, Whittany, Whitteny, Whittnee, Whittney, Whittni, Whittnie

Whoopi (English) happy; excited.
Whoopie, Whoopy

Wicktoria (Polish) a form of Victoria.
Wicktorja, Wiktoria, Wiktorja

Wilda (German) untamed. (English) willow.
Willda, Wylda

Wileen (English) a short form of Wilhelmina.
Wilene, Wileen, Willene

Wilhelmina (German) a form of Wilhelm (see Boys' Names). See also Billie, Guillerma, Helma, Minka, Minna, Minnie.
Vilhelmina, Wileen, Wilhelmine, Willa, Wilmina, Willamine, Willemina, Willette, Williamina, Willie, Willmina, Willmine, Wilma, Wimina

Wiikinia (Hawaiian) a form of Virginia.

Willa (German) a short form of Wilhelmina.
Willabella, Willette, Williabelle

Willette (English) a familiar form of Wilhelmina, Willa.
Wiletta, Wilette, Willetta, Willette

Willie (English) a familiar form of Wilhelmina.
Willi, Willina, Willisha, Willishia, Willy

Willow (English) willow tree.
Willough

Wilma (German) a short form of Wilhelmina.
Williemae, Wilmanie, Wilmayra, Wilmetta, Wilmette, Wilmina, Wilmyne, Wylma

Wilona (English) desired.
Willona, Willone, Wilone

Win (German) a short form of Winifred. See also Edwina.
Wyn

Winda (Swahili) hunter.

Windy (English) windy.
Windee, Windey, Windi, Windie, Wyndee, Wyndy

Winema (Moquelumnan) woman chief.

Winifred (German) peaceful friend. (Welsh) a form of Guinevere. See also Freddi, Una, Winnie.
Win, Winafred, Winefred, Winefride, Winifreda, Winifrieda, Winiefrida, Winifrid, Winifryd, Winnafred, Winnefred, Winniefred, Winnifred, Winnifrid, Wynafred, Wynifred, Wynnifred

Winna (African) friend.
Winnah

Winnie (English) a familiar form of Edwina, Gwyneth, Winnifred, Winona, Wynne. History: Winnie Mandela kept the anti-apartheid movement alive in South Africa while her then-husband, Nelson Mandela, was imprisoned. Literature: the lovable bear in A. A. Milne's children's story *Winnie-the-Pooh*.
Wina, Winne, Winney, Winni, Winny, Wynnie

Winola (German) charming friend.
Wynola

Winona (Lakota) oldest daughter.
Wanona, Wenona, Wenonah, Winnie, Winonah, Wynonna

Winter (English) winter.
Wintr, Wynter

Wira (Polish) a form of Elvira.
Wiria, Wirke

Wisia (Polish) a form of Victoria.
Wicia, Wikta

Wren (English) wren, songbird.

Wyanet (Native American) legendary beauty.
Wyaneta, Wyanita, Wynette

Wynne (Welsh) white, light skinned. A short form of Blodwyn, Guinivere, Gwyneth.
Winnie, Wyn, Wynn

Wynnonna (Lakota) a form of Winona.
Wynnona, Wynona

Wynter (English) a form of Winter.
Wynteria

Wyoming (Native American) Geography: a western U. S. state.
Wy, Wye, Wyoh, Wyomia

Xandra (Greek) a form of Zandra. (Spanish) a short form of Alexandra.
Xander, Xandrea, Xandria

Xanthe (Greek) yellow, blond. See also Zanthe.
Xanne, Xantha, Xanthia, Xanthippe

Xanthippe (Greek) a form of Xanthe. History: Socrates's wife. Xantippie

Xaviera (Basque) owner of the new house. (Arabic) bright. See also Javiera, Zaviera. Xavia, Xavière, Xavyera, Xiveria

Xela (Quiché) my mountain home.

Xena (Greek) a form of Xenia.

Xenia (Greek) hospitable. See also Zena, Zina. Xeenia, Xena, Xenea, Xenya, Xinia

Xiang (Chinese) fragrant.

Xiomara (Teutonic) glorious forest. Xiomaris, Xiomayra

Xiu Mei (Chinese) beautiful plum.

Xochitl (Aztec) place of many flowers. Xochil, Xochilt, Xochilth, Xochiti

Xuan (Vietnamese) spring.

Xuxa (Portuguese) a familiar form of Susanna.

Xylia (Greek) a form of Sylvia. Xylina, Xylona

Yachne (Hebrew) hospitable.

Yadira (Hebrew) friend. Yadirah, Yadirha, Yadya

Yael (Hebrew) strength of God. See also Jael. Yaeli, Yaella, Yeala

Yaffa (Hebrew) beautiful. See also Jaffa. Yafeal, Yaffit, Yafit

Yahaira (Hebrew) a form of Yakira. Yahara, Yahayra, Yahira

Yajaira (Hebrew) a form of Yakira. Yahaira, Yajaira, Yajayra, Yajhaira

Yakira (Hebrew) precious; dear.

Yalanda (Greek) a form of Yolanda. Yalanda, Yalonda, Ylana, Ylanda

Yalena (Greek, Russian) a form of Helen. See also Lena, Yelena.

Yaletha (American) a form of Oletha. Yelitsa

Yamary (American) a combination of the prefix Ya + Mary. Yamairy, Yamarie, Yamaris, Yamaya

Yamelia (American) a form of Amelia. Yamelij, Yamelya, Yamelys

Yamila (Arabic) a form of Jamila. Yamela, Yamely, Yamil, Yamile, Yamilet, Yamilej, Yamilla, Yamille

Yaminah (Arabic) right, proper. Yamina, Yamini, Yemina, Yeminah, Yemini

Yamka (Hopi) blossom.

Yamuna (Hindi) sacred river.

Yana (Slavic) a form of Jana. Yanae, Yanah, Yanay, Yanaye, Yanesi, Yanet, Yaneth, Yaney, Yani, Yanik, Yanina, Yanis, Yanisla, Yanitza, Yanixia, Yanna, Yannah, Yanni, Yannica, Yannice, Yannina

Yanaba (Navajo) brave.

Yaneli (American) a combination of the prefix Ya + Nellie. Yanela, Yanelis, Yaneliz, Yanelle, Yanelli, Yanely, Yanelys

Yanet (American) a form of Janet. Yanete, Yaneth, Yanethe, Yanette, Yannet, Yanneth, Yannette

Yáng (Chinese) sun.

Yareli (American) a form of Oralee. Yarely, Yaresly

Yarina (Slavic) a form of Irene. Yaryna

Yaritza (American) a combination of Yana + Ritsa. Yaritsa, Yarisa

Yarkona (Hebrew) green.

Yarmilla (Slavic) market trader.

Yashira (Afghan) humble; takes it easy. (Arabic) wealthy.

Yasmeen (Persian) a form of Yasmin. Yasemeen, Yasemin, Yasmeena, Yasmen, Yasmene, Yasmeni, Yasmenne, Yasmeen

Yasmin, Yasmine (Persian) jasmine flower. Yashmine, Yasiman, Yasimine, Yasma, Yasmaira, Yasmaine, Yasminia, Yasmon, Yasmyn, Yazmin, Yesmean, Yesmeen, Yesmin, Yesmina, Yesmine, Yesmyn

Yasu (Japanese) resting, calm.
Yasuko, Yasuyo

Yazmin (Persian) a form of Yasmin.
Yazmeen, Yazmen, Yazmene, Yazmina, Yazmine, Yazmyn, Yazmyne, Yazzmien, Yazzmine, Yazzmyn

Yecenia (Arabic) a form of Yesenia.

Yehudit (Hebrew) a form of Judith.
Yudit, Yudita, Yuta

Yei (Japanese) flourishing.

Yeira (Hebrew) light.

Yekaterina (Russian) a form of Katherine.

Yelena (Russian) a form of Helen, Jelena. See also Lena, Yalena.
Yeleana, Yelen, Yelenna, Yelenne, Yelina, Ylena, Ylenia, Ylenna

Yelisabeta (Russian) a form of Elizabeth.
Yelizaveta

Yemena (Arabic) from Yemen.
Yemina

Yen (Chinese) yearning; desirous.
Yeni, Yenih, Yenny

Yenene (Native American) shaman.

Yenifer (Welsh) a form of Jennifer.
Yenefer, Yennifer

Yeo (Korean) mild.
Yee

Yepa (Native American) snow girl.

Yesenia (Arabic) flower.
Yasenya, Yecenia, Yesinia, Yesnia, Yessenia

Yesica (Hebrew) a form of Jessica.
Yesika, Yesiko

Yessenia (Arabic) a form of Yesenia.
Yessena, Yessenya, Yissenia

Yessica (Hebrew) a form of Jessica.
Yessika, Yesyka

Yetta (English) a short form of Henrietta.
Yette, Yitta, Yitty

Yeva (Ukrainian) a form of Eve.

Yiesha (Arabic, Swahili) a form of Aisha.
Yiasha

Yin (Chinese) silver.

Ynez (Spanish) a form of Agnes. See also Inez.
Ynes, Ynesita

Yoanna (Hebrew) a form of Joanna.
Yoana, Yohana, Yohanka, Yohanna, Yohannah

Yocelin, Yocelyn (Latin) forms of Jocelyn.
Yoceline, Yocelyne, Yuceli

Yoi (Japanese) born in the evening.

Yoki (Hopi) bluebird.
Yokie

Yoko (Japanese) good girl.
Yo

Yolie (Greek) a familiar form of Yolanda.
Yola, Yoley, Yoli, Yoly

Yolanda (Greek) violet flower. See also Iolanthe, Jolanda, Olinda.
Yalanda, Yolie, Yolaine, Yolana, Yoland,

Yolande, Yolane, Yolanna, Yolantha, Yolanthe, Yolette, Yolonda, Yorlanda, Youlanda, Yulanda, Yulonda

Yoluta (Native American) summer flower.

Yomara (American) a combination of Yolanda + Tamara.
Yomaira, Yomarie, Yomira

Yon (Burmese) rabbit. (Korean) lotus blossom.
Yona, Yonna

Yoné (Japanese) wealth; rice.

Yonina (Hebrew) a form of Jonina.
Yona, Yonah

Yonita (Hebrew) a form of Jonita.
Yonat, Yonati, Yonit

Yoomee (Coos) star.
Yoome

Yordana (Basque) descendant. See also Jordana.

Yori (Japanese) reliable.
Yoriko, Yoriyo

Yoselin (Latin) a form of Jocelyn.
Yoseline, Yoselyn, Yosselin, Yosseline, Yosselyn

Yosepha (Hebrew) a form of Josephine.
Yosefa, Yosifa, Yuseffa

Yoshi (Japanese) good; respectful.
Yoshie, Yoshiko, Yoshiyo

Yovela (Hebrew) joyful heart; rejoicer.

Ysabel (Spanish) a form of Isabel. Ysabel, Ysabella, Ysabelle, Ysbel, Ysbella, Ysobel

Ysanne (American) a combination of Ysabel + Ann. Ysande, Ysann, Ysanna

Yseult (German) ice rule. (Irish) fair; light skinned. (Welsh) a form of Isolde. Yseulte, Ysolt

Yuana (Spanish) a form of Juana. Yuan, Yuanna

Yudelle (English) a form of Udele. Yudela, Yudell, Yudella

Yudita (Russian) a form of Judith. Yudit, Yudith, Yudit

Yuki (Japanese) snow. Yukie, Yukiko, Yukiyo

Yulene (Basque) a form of Julia. Yuleen

Yulia (Russian) a form of Julia. Yula, Yulenka, Yulinka, Yulka, Yulya

Yuliana (Spanish) a form of Juliana. Yulenia, Yuliani

Yuri (Japanese) lily. Yuree, Yuriko, Yuriyo

Yvanna (Slavic) a form of Ivana. Yvan, Yvana, Yvannia

Yvette (French) a familiar form of Yvonne. See also Evette, Ivette. Yavette, Yevett, Yevetta, Yvett, Yveta, Yvett, Yvetta

Yvonne (French) young archer. (Scandinavian) yew wood; bow wood. See also Evonne, Ivonne, Vonna, Vonny, Yvette. Yavanda, Yavanna, Yavonne, Yavonda, Yvonna, Yveline, Yvon, Yvone, Yvonnia, Yvonny

Z

Zabrina (American) a form of Sabrina. Zabreena, Zabrinia, Zabrinna, Zabryna

Zacharie (Hebrew) God remembered. Zacari, Zaccaus, Zacchaea, Zachary, Zachoia, Zackaria, Zackerisha, Zackeria, Zakaria, Zakarya, Zakeshia, Zakeiah, Zakiria, Zakiyah, Zakiyah, Zechari

Zachary (Hebrew) a form of Zacharie. Zacharie, Zackery, Zakary

Zada (Arabic) fortunate, prosperous. Zaida, Zayda, Zayeda

Zafina (Arabic) victorious.

Zafirah (Arabic) successful; victorious. Zafeerah, Zeeherah

Zahar (Hebrew) daybreak; dawn. Zahara, Zahara, Zahera, Zahira

Zahavah (Hebrew) golden. Zachava, Zahava, Zechavah, Zehavi, Zehavit, Zeheva, Zehuva

Zahra (Swahili) flower. (Arabic) white. Zahara, Zahraa, Zahrah, Zahreh, Zahria

Zaira (Hebrew) a form of Zara. Zaire, Zairea, Zirrea

Zakia (Swahili) smart. (Arabic) chaste. Zakea, Zakeia, Zakiah, Zakiya

Zakira (Hebrew) a form of Zacharie. Zakiera, Zakierra, Zakit, Zakirah, Zakiriya, Zykarah, Zykera, Zykeria, Zykerria, Zykira, Zykeira

Zakiya (Arabic) a form of Zakia. Zakeya, Zakeyia, Zakiya, Zakiyah, Zakiyya, Zakiyyah, Zakkiyah

Zalika (Swahili) born to royalty. Zuleika

Zaltana (Native American) high mountain.

Zandra (Greek) a form of Sandra. Zahndra, Zandrea, Zandria, Zandy, Zanndra, Zondra

Zaneta (Spanish) a form of Jane. Zaneta, Zanita, Zanitra

Zanna (Spanish) a form of Jane. (English) a short form of Susanna. Zaina, Zainah, Zainna, Zana, Zanae, Zanah, Zanella, Zanette, Zannah, Zannette, Zannia, Zannie

Zanthe (Greek) a form of Xanthe. Zanth, Zantha

Zara (Hebrew) a form of Sarah, Zora. Zaira, Zarah, Zarea, Zaree, Zareea, Zareen, Zareena, Zareh, Zareya, Zari, Zaria, Zariya, Zarria

Zarifa (Arabic) successful.

Zarita (Spanish) a form of Sarah.

Zasha (Russian) a form of Sasha.
Zascha, Zashenka, Zashka, Zasho

Zaviera (Spanish) a form of Xaviera.
Zavera, Zavirah

Zawati (Swahili) gift.

Zayit (Hebrew) olive.

Zaynah (Arabic) beautiful.
Zayn, Zayna

Zea (Latin) grain.

Zelda (Yiddish) gray haired. (German) a short form of Griselda. See also Selda.
Zelde, Zella, Zellda

Zelene (English) sunshine.
Zeleen, Zelena, Zeline

Zelia (Spanish) sunshine.
Zele, Zelene, Zelie, Zélie, Zelina

Zelizi (Basque) a form of Sheila.

Zelma (German) a form of Selma.

Zemirah (Hebrew) song of joy.

Zena (Greek) a form of Xenia. (Ethiopian) news. (Persian) woman. See also Zina.
Zanae, Zanah, Zeena, Zeenat, Zeenet, Zeenya, Zein, Zeina, Zenah, Zenana, Zenea, Zenia, Zenna, Zennah, Zennia, Zenya

Zenaida (Greek) white-winged dove.
Zenaide, Zenaïde, Zenayda, Zenochka

Zenda (Persian) sacred; feminine.

Zenobia (Greek) sign, symbol. History: a queen who ruled the city of Palmyra in ancient Syria.
Zeba, Zeeba, Zenobie, Zenovia

Zephania, Zephanie (Greek) forms of Stephanie.
Zepania, Zephanas, Zephany

Zephyr (Greek) west wind.
Zefryn, Zephra, Zephria, Zephyer, Zephyrine

Zera (Hebrew) seeds.
Zerah, Zeriah

Zerdali (Turkish) wild apricot.

Zerlina (Latin, Spanish) beautiful dawn. Music: a character in Mozart's opera *Don Giovanni*.
Zerla, Zerlinda

Zerrin (Turkish) golden.
Zerren

Zeta (English) rose. Linguistics: a letter in the Greek alphabet.
Zayit, Zetana, Zetta

Zetta (Portuguese) rose.

Zhana, Zhane (Slavic) forms of Jane.
Zhanae, Zhanay, Zhanaya, Zhané, Zhanea, Zhanee, Zhaney, Zhani, Zhaniah, Zhanna

Zhen (Chinese) chaste.

Zia (Latin) grain. (Arabic) light.
Zea

Zigana (Hungarian) gypsy girl. See also Tsigana.
Zigane

Zihna (Hopi) one who spins tops.

Zilla (Hebrew) shadow.
Zila, Zillah, Zylla

Zilpah (Hebrew) dignified. Bible: Jacob's wife.

Zilpha (Hebrew) dignified. Bible: Jacob's wife.
Zilpha, Zylpha

Zilya (Russian) a form of Theresa.

Zimra (Hebrew) song of praise.
Zamora, Zemira, Zemora, Zimria

Zina (African) secret spirit. (English) hospitable. (Greek) a form of Zena.
Zinah, Zine

Zinnia (Latin) Botany: a plant with beautiful, rayed, colorful flowers.
Zinia, Zinny, Zinnya, Zinya

Zipporah (Hebrew) bird. Bible: Moses' wife.
Zipora, Ziporah, Zipporia, Ziproh

Zita (Spanish) rose. (Arabic) mistress. A short form of names ending in "sita" or "zita."
Zeeta, Zyta, Zytka

Ziva (Hebrew) bright; radiant.
Zeeva, Ziv, Zivanka, Zivi, Zivit

Zizi (Hungarian) a familiar form of Elizabeth.
Zsi Zsi

Zocha (Polish) a form of Sophie.

Zoe (Greek) life.
Zoé, Zoë, Zoee, Zoelie, Zoeline, Zoelle, Zoey, Zoi, Zoie, Zowe, Zowey, Zowie, Zoya

Zoey (Greek) a form of Zoe.
Zooey

Zofia (Slavic) a form of Sophia. See also Sofia.
Zofka, Zsofia

Zohar (Hebrew) shining, brilliant.
Zoheret

Zohra (Hebrew) blossom.

Zohreh (Persian) happy.
Zahreh, Zohrah

Zola (Italian) piece of earth.
Zoela, Zoila

Zona (Latin) belt, sash.
Zonia

Zondra (Greek) a form of Zandra.
Zohndra

Zora (Slavic) aurora; dawn. See also Zara.
Zorah, Zorana, Zoreen, Zoreena, Zorna, Zorra, Zorrah, Zorya

Zorina (Slavic) golden.
Zorana, Zori, Zorie, Zorine, Zorna, Zory

Zoya (Slavic) a form of Zoe.
Zoia, Zoyara, Zoyechka, Zoyenka, Zoyya

Zsa Zsa (Hungarian) a familiar form of Susan.
Zhazha

Zsofia (Hungarian) a form of Sofia.
Zofia, Zsofi, Zsofka

Zsuzsanna (Hungarian) a form of Susanna.
Zsuska, Zsuzsa, Zsuzsi, Zsuzsika, Zsuzska

Zudora (Sanskrit) laborer.

Zuleika (Arabic) brilliant.
Zeleeka, Zul, Zulay, Zulekha, Zuleyka

Zulima (Arabic) a form of Salama.
Zuleima, Zulema, Zulemah, Zulimah

Zurafa (Arabic) lovely.
Ziraf, Zuruf

Zuri (Basque) white; light skinned.
(Swahili) beautiful.
Zuria, Zurie, Zurisha, Zury

Zusa (Czech, Polish) a form of Susan.
Zuzana, Zuzanka, Zuzia, Zuzka, Zuzu

Zuwena (Swahili) good.
Zwena

Zytka (Polish) rose.

Boys

Aakash (Hindi) a form of Akash.

Aaron (Hebrew) enlightened. (Arabic) messenger. Bible: the brother of Moses and the first high priest. See also Ron.
Aahron, Aaran, Aaren, Aareon, Aarin, Aaron, Aarron, Aaryn, Aaron, Aarin, Ahran, Ahren, Aranne, Arek, Aren, Ari, Arin, Aron, Aronek, Aronne, Aronos, Arran, Arron

Abasi (Swahili) stern.

Abban (Persian) Mythology: a figure associated with water and the arts.

Abbey (Hebrew) a familiar form of Abe.
Abey, Abbie, Abby

Abbott (Hebrew) father; abbot.
Ab, Abba, Abbah, Abban, Abbé, Abbot, Abott

Abbud (Arabic) devoted.

Abdirahman (Arabic) a form of Abdulrahman.
Abdirehman

Abdul (Arabic) servant.
Abdal, Abdeel, Abdel, Abdoul, Abdual, Abdull, Abul

Abdulaziz (Arabic) servant of the Mighty.
Abdelaziz, Abdelaziz, Abdulazaz, Abdulazeez

Abdullah (Arabic) servant of Allah.
Abdalah, Abdalla, Abdallah, Abdula, Abdulla, Abdulllah, Abdulah, Abdulla, Abdullahi

Abdulrahman (Arabic) servant of the Merciful.
Abdelrahim, Abdelrahman, Abdolrahem, Abdulrahman, Abdulrahaman, Abdurahman, Abdurahman, Abdurram

Abe (Hebrew) a short form of Abel, Abraham.

Abel (Hebrew) breath. (Assyrian) meadow. (German) a short form of Abelard. Bible: Adam and Eve's second son.
Abe, Abele, Abell, Able, Adal, Avel

Abelard (German) noble; resolute.
Ab, Abalard, Abel, Abelardo, Abelhard, Abilard, Addard, Adelard

Abi (Turkish) older brother.

Abiah (Hebrew) God is my father.
Abia, Abiel, Abija, Abijah, Abisha, Abishai, Aviya, Aviyah

Abie (Hebrew) a familiar form of Abraham.

Abiel (Hebrew) a form of Abiah.

Abir (Hebrew) strong.

Abisha (Hebrew) gift of God.
Abijah, Abishai

Abner (Hebrew) father of light. Bible: the commander of Saul's army.
Ab, Avner, Ebner

Abraham (Hebrew) father of many nations. Bible: the first Hebrew patriarch. See also Avram, Bram, Ibrahim.
Abarran, Abe, Aberham, Abey, Abhiram, Abie, Abrahaim, Abrahamo, Abraham, Abrahan, Abraharem, Abrahem, Abrahim, Abraham, Abram, Abramo, Abrao, Aram, Avram, Avram

Abrahan (Spanish) a form of Abraham.
Abrahon

Abram (Hebrew) a short form of Abraham. See also Bram.
Abramo, Abrams, Avram

Absalom (Hebrew) father of peace. Bible: the rebellious third son of King David. See also Avshalom, Axel.
Absalaam, Absalon, Abselon, Absolum

Acar (Turkish) bright.

Ace (Latin) unity.
Acer, Acey, Acie

Achilles (Greek) Mythology: a hero of the Trojan War. Literature: the hero of Homer's epic poem *Iliad*.
Achill, Achille, Achillea, Achillios, Akil, Akilles

Ackerley (English) meadow of oak trees.
Acerley, Ackerlea, Ackerleigh, Ackersley, Acklea, Ackleigh, Ackley, Aeklie

Acton (English) oak-tree settlement.

Adahy (Cherokee) in the woods.

Adair (Scottish) oak-tree ford.
Adaire, Adare

Adam (Phoenician) man; mankind. (Hebrew) earth; man of the red earth. Bible: the first man created by God. See also Adamson, Addison, Damek, Keddy, Macadam.
Ad, Adama, Adamec, Adamo, Adão, Adas, Addam, Addams, Addis, Addy, Adem, Adham, Adhamh, Adné, Adok, Adomas

Adamec (Czech) a form of Adam.
Adamek, Adamik, Adamka, Adamko, Adamok

Adamson (Hebrew) son of Adam.
Adams, Adamsson, Addamson

Adan (Irish) a form of Aidan.
Aden, Adian, Adin

Adar (Syrian) ruler; prince. (Hebrew) noble; exalted.
Addar

Adarius (American) a combination of Adam + Darius.
Adareus, Adarius, Adarrius, Adaro, Adarrus, Adaruis, Adauris

Addison (English) son of Adam.
Addis, Addisen, Addisun, Addyson, Adison, Adisson, Adyson

Addy (Hebrew) a familiar form of Adam, Adlai. (German) a familiar form of Adelard.
Addey, Addi, Addie, Ade, Adi

Ade (Yoruba) royal.

Adelard (German) noble; courageous.
Adal, Adalar, Adalard, Addy, Adel, Adél, Adelar

Aden (Arabic) Geography: a region in southern Yemen. (Irish) a form of Aidan, Aiden.

Adham (Arabic) black.

Adil (Arabic) just; wise.
Adeel, Adeele

Adin (Hebrew) pleasant.

Adir (Hebrew) majestic; noble.
Adeer

Adiv (Hebrew) pleasant; gentle.
Adeev

Adlai (Hebrew) my ornament.
Ad, Addy, Adley

Adler (German) eagle.
Ad, Addler, Adlar

Adli (Turkish) just; wise.

Admon (Hebrew) peony.

Adnan (Arabic) pleasant.
Adnaan

Adney (English) noble's island.
Adny

Adolf (German) noble wolf. History: Adolf Hitler's German army was defeated in World War II. See also Dolf.
Ad, Adolfo, Adolfus, Adolph

Adolfo (Spanish) a form of Adolf.
Adolpho

Adolph (German) a form of Adolf.
Adolphe, Adolpho, Adolphus, Adulphus

Adom (Akan) help from God.

Adon (Hebrew) Lord. (Greek) a short form of Adonis.

Adonis (Greek) highly attractive. Mythology: the attractive youth loved by Aphrodite.
Adon, Adonnis, Adonys

Adri (Indo-Pakistani) rock.
Adrey

Adrian (Greek) rich. (Latin) dark. (Swedish) a short form of Hadrian.
Adarian, Ade, Adorjan, Adrain, Adreian, Adreyan, Adri, Adriaan, Adriane, Adriann, Adrianne, Adriano, Adriaen, Adrien, Adrik, Adrion, Adrionn, Adrionne, Adron, Adryan, Adryn, Adryon

Adriano (Italian) a form of Adrian.
Adrianno

Adriel (Hebrew) member of God's flock.
Adrial

Adrien (French) a form of Adrian.
Adriene, Adrienne

Adrik (Russian) a form of Adrian.
Adric

Aeneas (Greek) praised. (Scottish) a form of Angus. Literature: the Trojan hero of Vergil's epic poem *Aeneid*. See also Eneas.

Afram (African) Geography: a river in Ghana, Africa.

Afton (English) from Afton, England.
Affton

Agamemnon (Greek) resolute. Mythology: the king of Mycenae who led the Greeks in the Trojan War.

Agni (Hindi) Religion: the Hindu fire god.

Agu (Ibo) leopard.

Agustin (Latin) a form of Augustine.
Agostino, Agoston, Aguistin, Agustine, Agustis, Agusto, Agustus

Ahab (Hebrew) father's brother. Literature: the captain of the Pequod in Herman Melville's novel *Moby-Dick*.

Ahanu (Native American) laughter.

Ahdik (Native American) caribou; reindeer.

Ahearn (Scottish) lord of the horses. (English) heron.
Ahearne, Aherin, Ahern, Aherne, Hearn

Ahir (Turkish) last.

Ahmad (Arabic) most highly praised. See also Muhammad.
Achmad, Achmed, Ahamad, Ahamada, Ahamed, Ahmaad, Ahmaud, Amad, Amahd, Amed

Ahmed (Swahili) praiseworthy.

Ahsan (Arabic) charitable.

Aidan (Irish) fiery.
Adan, Aden, Aiden, Aydan, Ayden, Aydin

Aiden, Ayden (Irish) a form of Aidan.
Aden, Aidon, Aidyn, Aydean

Aiken (English) made of oak.
Aicken, Aikin, Ayken, Aykin

Aimery (French) a form of Emery.
Aime, Aimerey, Aimeric, Aymeric, Aymery

Aimon (French) house. (Irish) a form of Eamon.

Aindrea (Irish) a form of Andrew.
Aindreas

Ainsley (Scottish) my own meadow.
Ainsleigh, Ainslie, Ansley, Aynslee, Aynsley, Aynslie

Aizik (Russian) a form of Isaac.

Ajala (Yoruba) potter.

Ajay (Punjabi) victorious; undefeatable. (American) a combination of the initials A. + J.
Aj, Aja, Ajae, Ajai, Ajaye, Ajaz, Aje, Ajee, Ajit

Ajit (Sanskrit) unconquerable.
Ajeet, Ajith

Akar (Turkish) flowing stream.
Akara

Akash (Hindi) sky.
Aakash, Akasha, Akshay

Akbar (Arabic) great.

Akecheta (Sioux) warrior.

Akeem, Akim (Hebrew) short forms of Joachim.
Achim, Akeeem, Ackim, Ahkieme, Akeam, Akee, Akeim, Akima, Arkeem

Akemi (Japanese) dawn.

Akil (Arabic) intelligent. (Greek) a form of Achilles.
Ahkeel, Akeel, Akeil, Akeyla, Akhil, Akiel, Akila, Akilah, Akile, Akili

Akins (Yoruba) brave.

Akira (Japanese) intelligent.
Akihito, Akio, Akiyo

Akiva (Hebrew) a form of Jacob.
Akiba, Kiva

Akmal (Arabic) perfect.

Aksel (Norwegian) father of peace.
Akseil

Akshay (American) a form of Akash.
Akshaj, Akshaya

Akshat (Sanskrit) uninjurable.

Akule (Native American) he looks up.

Al (Irish) a short form of Alan, Albert, Alexander.

Aladdin (Arabic) height of faith. Literature: the hero of a story in the *Arabian Nights*.
Ala, Alaa, Alaaddin, Aladean, Aladin, Aladino

Alain (French) a form of Alan.
Alaen, Alainn, Alayn, Allain

Alaire (French) joyful.

Alam (Arabic) universe.

Alan (Irish) handsome; peaceful.
Ailan, Ailin, Al, Alaan, Alain, Alair, Aland, Alande, Alando, Alani, Alann, Alano, Alanson, Alante, Alao, Allan, Allen, Alon, Alun

Alaric (German) ruler of all. See also Ulrich.
Alarick, Alarico, Alarik, Aleric, Allaric, Allarick, Alric, Alrick, Alrik

Alastair (Scottish) a form of Alexander.
Alaisdair, Alaistair, Alaister, Alasdair, Alaster, Alaster, Alastor, Aleister, Alester, Alistair, Allaistair, Allastair, Allaster, Allastir, Allysdair, Alystair

Alban (Latin) from Alba, Italy.
Albain, Albany, Albean, Albein, Alby, Auban, Auben

Albern (German) noble; courageous.

Albert (German, French) noble and bright. See also Elbert, Ulbrecht.
Adelbert, Ailbert, Al, Albertik, Alberto, Alberts, Albie, Albrecht, Alby, Alvertos, Aubert

Alberto (Italian) a form of Albert.
Berto

Albie, Alby (German, French) familiar forms of Albert.
Albee, Albi

Albin (Latin) a form of Alvin.
Alben, Albeno, Albinek, Albino, Albins, Albinson, Alby, Auben

Albion (Latin) white cliffs. Geography: a reference to the white cliffs in Dover, England.

Alcandor (Greek) manly; strong.

Alcott (English) old cottage.
Alcot, Alkot, Alkott, Allcott, Allcott, Allkot, Allkott

Aldair (German, English) a form of Alder.
Aldahir, Aldayr

Alden (English) old; wise protector.
Aldan, Aldean, Aldin, Aldous, Elden

Alder (German, English) alder tree.
Aldair

Aldo (Italian) old; elder. (German) a short form of Aldous.

Aldous (German) a form of Alden.
Aldis, Aldo, Aldon, Aldus, Elden

Aldred (English) old; wise counselor.
Alldred, Eldred

Aldrich (English) wise.
Aldric, Aldrick, Aldridge, Aldrige, Aldritch, Alldric, Alldrich, Alldrick, Alldridge, Eldridge

Aldwin (English) old friend.
Aldwyn, Eldwin

Alec, Alek (Greek) short forms of Alexander.
Aleck, Alekko, Elek

Alejándro (Spanish) a form of Alexander.
Alejándra, Aléjo, Alexjándro

Aleksandar, Aleksander (Greek) forms of Alexander.
Aleksandor, Aleksandr, Aleksandras, Aleksandur

Aleksei (Russian) a short form of Alexander.
Aleks, Aleksey, Aleksi, Aleksis, Aleksy, Alexei, Alexey

Alekzander, Alexzander (Greek) forms of Alexander.
Aleksander, Alekxzander, Alexkzandr, Alexzandr, Alexzandyr

Alem (Arabic) wise.

Aleric (German) a form of Alaric.
Alerick, Alleric, Allerick

Aleron (Latin) winged.

Alessandro (Italian) a form of Alexander.
Alessand, Allessandro

Alex (Greek) a short form of Alexander.
Alax, Alix, Allax, Allex, Elek

Alexander (Greek) defender of mankind. History: Alexander the Great was the conqueror of the civilized world. See also Alastair, Alistair, Iskander, Jando, Leks, Lex, Lexus, Macallister, Oleksandr, Olés, Sander, Sándor, Sandro, Sandy, Sasha, Xan, Xander, Zander, Zindel.
Al, Alec, Alesandar, Alejándro, Alek, Alekos, Aleksandar, Aleksander, Aleksei, Alekzander, Alessandro, Alex, Alexandar, Alexander, Alexandr, Alexandre, Alexandro, Alexandros, Alexi, Alexis, Alexxander, Alexzander, Alic, Alick, Alisander, Alixander

Alexandre (French) a form of Alexander.

Alexandro (Greek) a form of Alexander.
Alexandras, Alexandros, Alexandru

Alexi (Russian) a form of Aleksei. (Greek) a short form of Alexander. *Alexy*

Alexis (Greek) a short form of Alexander. *Alexei, Alexes, Alexey, Alexios, Alexius, Alexiz, Alexsis, Alexsus, Alexus*

Affie (English) a familiar form of Alfred. *Alfy*

Alfonso (Italian, Spanish) a form of Alphonse. *Affonso, Alfons, Alfonse, Alfonsus, Alfonza, Alfonzo, Alfonzus*

Alford (English) old river ford.

Alfred (English) elf counselor; wise counselor. See also Fred. *Ailfrid, Ailfryd, Alf, Alfeo, Alfie, Alfred, Alvred*

Alfredo (Italian, Spanish) a form of Alfred. *Alfrido*

Alger (German) noble spearman. (English) a short form of Algernon. See also Elger. *Algar, Allgar*

Algernon (English) bearded, wearing a moustache. *Algernon, Alger, Algie, Algin, Algon*

Algie (English) a familiar form of Algernon. *Algee, Algia, Algy*

Algis (German) spear.

Ali (Arabic) greatest. (Swahili) exalted. *Aly*

Alic (Greek) a short form of Alexander. *Alick, Alik, Alike, Aliko*

Alim (Arabic) scholar. (Arabic) a form of Alem.

Alisander (Greek) a form of Alexander. *Alissander, Alissandre, Alsandair, Alsandare, Alsander*

Alistair (English) a form of Alexander. *Alisdair, Alistaire, Alistar, Alister, Alistair, Allistair, Allister, Allistir, Alstair*

Alixander (Greek) a form of Alexander. *Alixandre, Alixzander*

Allan (Irish) a form of Alan. *Allane*

Allard (English) noble, brave. *Alard, Ellard*

Allen (Irish) a form of Alan. *Alen, Alley, Alleyn, Alleyne, Allie, Allin, Allon, Allyn*

Almon (Hebrew) widower.

Alois (German) a short form of Aloysius. *Aloys*

Alok (Sanskrit) victorious cry.

Alon (Hebrew) oak.

Aloisio (Spanish) a form of Louis.

Alonso, Alonzo (Spanish) forms of Alphonse. *Alano, Alanzo, Alon, Alonza, Elonzo, Lon, Lonnie, Lonso, Lonzo*

Aloysius (German) a form of Louis. *Alois, Alois, Aloisius, Aloisio*

Alphonse (German) noble and eager. *Alf, Alfie, Alfonso, Alonzo, Alphons, Alphonsa, Alphonso, Alphonsus, Fonzie*

Alphonso (Italian) a form of Alphonse. *Alphanso, Alphonzo, Fonso*

Alpin (Irish) attractive.

Alroy (Spanish) king.

Alston (English) noble's settlement. *Allston, Alstun*

Altair (Greek) star. (Arabic) flying.

Altman (German) old man. *Altmann, Atman*

Alton (English) old town.

Alva (Hebrew) sublime. *Alvah*

Alvan (German) a form of Alvin. *Alvand*

Alvar (English) army of elves. *Alvara*

Alvaro (Spanish) just; wise.

Alvern (Latin) spring. *Elvern*

Alvin (Latin) white; light skinned. (German) friend to all; noble friend; friend of elves. See also Albin, Elvin. *Aloin, Aluin, Aluino, Alvan, Alven, Alvie, Alvino, Alvy, Alwyn, Alwin, Elvin*

Alvis (Scandinavian) all-knowing.

Alwin (German) a form of Alvin.
Ailuyn, Aluyn, Alwyn, Aylwin

Amadeo (Italian) a form of Amadeus.

Amadeus (Latin) loves God. Music: Wolfgang Amadeus Mozart was a famous eighteenth-century Austrian composer.
Amad, Amadeaus, Amadée, Amadeo, Amadei, Amadio, Amadis, Amado, Amador, Amadou, Amando, Amedeo, Amodaos

Amal (Hebrew) worker. (Arabic) hopeful.

Amandeep (Punjabi) light of peace.
Amandip, Amanjit, Amanjot, Amanpreet

Amando (French) a form of Amadeus.
Amand, Amandio, Amaniel, Amato

Amani (Arabic) believer. (Yoruba) strength; builder.
Amanee

Amato (French) loved.
Amatto

Ambar (Sanskrit) sky.
Amber

Ambrose (Greek) immortal.
Ambie, Ambroise, Ambros, Ambrosi, Ambrosio, Ambrosius, Ambrus, Amby

Ameer (Hebrew) a form of Amir.
Ameir, Amer, Amere

Amerigo (Teutonic) industrious. History: Amerigo Vespucci was the Italian explorer for whom America is named.
Americo, Americus

Ames (French) friend.

Amicus (English, Latin) beloved friend.
Amico

Amiel (Hebrew) God of my people.
Ammiel

Amin (Hebrew, Arabic) trustworthy; honest. (Hindi) faithful.
Amine

Amir (Hebrew) proclaimed. (Punjabi) wealthy; king's minister. (Arabic) prince.
Aamer, Aamir, Ameer, Amire, Amiri

Amish (Sanskrit) honest.

Amit (Punjabi) unfriendly. (Arabic) highly praised.
Amitan, Amreet

Ammon (Egyptian) hidden. Mythology: the ancient god associated with reproduction.
Amman

Amol (Hindi) priceless, valuable.
Amul

Amon (Hebrew) trustworthy; faithful.

Amory (German) a form of Emory.
Amery, Amor

Amos (Hebrew) burdened, troubled. Bible: an Old Testament prophet.
Amose

Amram (Hebrew) mighty nation.
Amarien, Amran, Amren

Amrit (Sanskrit) nectar. (Punjabi, Arabic) a form of Amit.

An (Chinese, Vietnamese) peaceful.
Ana

Anand (Hindi) blissful.
Ananda, Anant, Ananth

Anastasius (Greek) resurrection.
Anas, Anastacio, Anastacios, Anastagio, Anastas, Anastase, Anastasi, Anastasio, Anastasios, Anastice, Anastisis, Anaztáz, Athanasius

Anatole (Greek) east.
Anatol, Anatoley, Anatoli, Anatolijus, Anatolio, Anatoliy, Anatoly, Anitoly

Anchali (Taos) painter.

Anders (Swedish) a form of Andrew.
Ander

Anderson (Swedish) son of Andrew.
Andersen

Andonios (Greek) a form of Anthony.
Andoni, Andonis, Andonny

Andor (Hungarian) a form of Andrew.

András (Hungarian) a form of Andrew.
Andraes, Andri, Andris, Andrius, Andriy, Andras, Aundras

André, André (French) forms of Andrew.
Andra, Andrae, Andrecito, Andree, Andrei, Aundre, Aundré

Andrea (Greek) a form of Andrew.
Andreas, Andries

Andreas (Greek) a form of Andrew.
Andreian, Andrej, Andrey, Andreyan, Andric, Aundrei

Andrei (Bulgarian, Romanian, Russian) a form of Andrew.

Andres (Spanish) a form of Andrew.
Andras, Andrés, Andrez

Andrew (Greek) strong; manly; courageous. Bible: one of the Twelve Apostles. See also Bandi, Drew, Endre, Evangelos, Kendrew, Ondro.
Aindrea, Anders, Andery, Andonis, Andor, András, Andre, André, Andrea, Andreas, Andrei, Andres, Andrews, Andru, Andrue, Andrus, Andy, Anker, Anndra, Antal, Audrew

Andros (Polish) sea. Mythology: the god of the sea.
Andris, Andrus, Andrus

Andy (Greek) a short form of Andrew.
Andino, Andis, Andje

Aneurin (Welsh) honorable; gold. See also Nye.
Aneirin

Anfernee (Greek) a form of Anthony.
Anferney, Anfernie, Anfurney, Anfranee, Anfrene, Anfrenee, Anpherne

Angel (Greek) angel. (Latin) messenger. See also Gotzon.
Ange, Angell, Angelo, Angie, Angy

Angelo (Italian) a form of Angel.
Angelo, Angelito, Angella, Angelos, Anglo

Angus (Scottish) exceptional; outstanding. Mythology: Angus Og was the Celtic god of youth, love, and beauty. See also Ennis, Gus.

Anh (Vietnamese) peace; safety.

Anibal (Phoenician) a form of Hannibal.

Anil (Hindi) wind god.
Aneel, Anel, Aniel, Aniello

Anka (Turkish) phoenix.

Anker (Danish) a form of Andrew.
Ankur

Annan (Scottish) brook. (Swahili) fourth-born son.

Annas (Greek) gift from God.
Anis, Anish, Anna, Annas

Anno (German) a familiar form of Johann.

Anoki (Native American) actor.

Ansel (French) follower of a nobleman.
Ancell, Ansa, Ansell

Anselm (German) divine protector. See also Elmo.
Anse, Anselme, Anselmi, Anselmo

Ansis (Latvian) a form of Janis.

Ansley (Scottish) a form of Ainsley.
Anslea, Anslee, Ansleigh, Anslie, Ansly, Ansy

Anson (German) divine. (English) Anne's son.

Antal (Hungarian) a form of Anthony.
Antek, Anti, Antos

Antares (Greek) giant, red star. Astronomy: the brightest star in the constellation Scorpio.
Antar, Antario, Antarious, Antarius, Antarr, Antars

Antavas (Lithuanian) a form of Anthony.
Antavious, Anthoni, Anthonia

Antavas (Lithuanian) a form of Anthony.
Antae, Antaeus, Antavious, Antavius, Ante, Anteo

Anthany (Latin, Greek) a form of Anthony.
Antaee, Antarie, Antenee, Anthan, Anthery, Anthine, Anthney

Anthonie (Latin, Greek) a form of Anthony.
Anthone, Anthonee, Anthoni, Anthonia

Anthony (Latin) praiseworthy. (Greek) flourishing. See also Tony.
Anathony, Andonios, Andor, András, Anothony, Antal, Antavas, Anfernee, Anthany, Anthaun, Anthey, Anthian, Antiino, Antione, Anthoney, Anthonio, Anthonia, Anthomia, Anthonny, Anthonio, Anthyoine, Anthyonny, Antione, Antijuan, Antoine, Anton, Antonio, Antory, Antuan, Antwon

Antione (French) a form of Anthony.
Antion, Antiono, Antionne, Antiono

Antjuan (Spanish) a form of Anthony.
Antajuan, Anthjuan, Antuan, Antuane

Antoan (Vietnamese) safe, secure.

Antoine (French) a form of Anthony.
*Anntoin, Anthoine, Antoiné, Antoinne,
Atoine*

Anton (Slavic) a form of Anthony.
*Anthon, Antone, Antonn, Antonne,
Antons, Antos*

Antonio (Italian) a form of Anthony.
See also Tino, Tonio.
*Anthonio, Antinio, Antoinio, Antonio,
Antonello, Antoneo, Antonin, Antonin,
Antonino, Antonnio, Antonios, Antonius,
Antonyia, Antonyio, Antonyo*

Antony (Latin) a form of Anthony.
*Antin, Antini, Antius, Antoney, Antoni,
Antonie, Antonin, Antonios, Antonius,
Antonyia, Antonyio, Antonyo, Anty*

Antti (Finnish) manly.
Anthey, Anthi, Anti

Antwan (Arabic) a form of Anthony.
*Antau, Antawan, Antawn, Anthawn,
Antowan, Antowaun, Antowine,
Antowne, Antowyn, Antuwan, Antuvain,
Antvaina, Antvaine, Antvainn,
Antvaion, Antvane, Antwann,
Antvanne, Antwarn, Antwaun, Antwen,
Antwian, Antwine, Antwuan, Antwun,
Antwyné*

Antwon (Arabic) a form of Anthony.
*Antowon, Antuwuon, Antuwion, Antuwione, Antuvione,
Antvoan, Antvoin, Antuvoin, Antvoone,
Antwonn, Antwonne, Antuvoun,*

*Antvyon, Antuwyone, Antyon, Antwyone,
Antyvon*

Anwar (Arabic) luminous.
Anour, Anouar, Anwi

Apiatan (Kiowa) wooden lance.

Apollo (Greek) manly. Mythology: the
god of prophecy, healing, music,
poetry, and light. See also Polo.
*Apolinar, Apolinario, Apollos, Apolo,
Apolonio, Appollo*

Aquila (Latin, Spanish) eagle.
*Acquilla, Aquil, Aquilas, Aquileo, Aquiles,
Aquilino, Aquilla, Aquille, Aquillino*

Araldo (Spanish) a form of Harold.
Aralado, Aralt, Aroldo, Arry

Aram (Syrian) high, exalted.
Ara, Aramia, Arra, Arram

Aramis (French) Literature: one of the
title characters in Alexandre Dumas's
novel *The Three Musketeers*.
Airamis, Aramith, Aramys

Aran (Tai) forest. (Danish) a form of
Aren. (Hebrew, Scottish) a form of
Arran.

Archer (English) bowman.
Archie

Archibald (German) bold. See also
Arkady.
*Arch, Archaimbaud, Archambault,
Archibaldo, Archibold, Archie*

Archie (German, English) a familiar
form of Archer, Archibald.
Archy

Ardal (Irish) a form of Arnold.
Ardale

Ardell (Latin) eager; industrious.
Ardel

Arden (Latin) ardent; fiery.
*Ard, Ardan, Ardene, Ardian, Ardie,
Ardin, Ardn, Arduino*

Ardon (Hebrew) bronzed.

Aren (Danish) eagle; ruler. (Hebrew,
Arabic) a form of Aaron.

Aretino (Greek, Italian) victorious.

Argus (Danish) watchful, vigilant.
Agos

Ari (Hebrew) a short form of Ariel.
(Greek) a short form of Aristotle.
*Aria, Arias, Arie, Arieh, Arih, Arij, Ario,
Arri, Ary, Arye*

Arian (Greek) a form of Arion.
*Ariana, Ariane, Ariann, Arianne, Arrian,
Aryan*

Aric (German) a form of Richard.
(Scandinavian) a form of Eric.
*Aaric, Arec, Areck, Arich, Arick, Ariek,
Arik, Arek, Arric, Arrick, Arrik, Aryk*

Ariel (Hebrew) lion of God. Bible:
another name for Jerusalem.
Literature: the name of a sprite in the
Shakespearean play *The Tempest*.
*Airel, Arel, Areli, Ari, Ariell, Ariya,
Ariyel, Arrial, Arriel*

Aries (Latin) ram. Astrology: the first
sign of the zodiac.
Ares, Arie, Ariez

Arif (Arabic) knowledgeable.
Aref

Arion (Greek) enchanted. (Hebrew) melodious.
Arian, Arien, Ario, Arione, Aryon

Aristides (Greek) son of the best.
Aris, Aristedes, Aristeed, Aristide, Aristides, Aristidis

Aristotle (Greek) best; wise. History: a third-century B.C. philosopher who tutored Alexander the Great.
Ari, Aris, Aristio, Aristo, Aristoles, Aristotelis

Arjun (Hindi) white; milk colored.
Arjen, Arjin, Arju, Arjuna, Arjune

Arkady (Russian) a form of Archibald.
Arcadio, Arkadi, Arkadij, Arkadiy

Arkin (Norwegian) son of the eternal king.
Aricin, Arkeen, Arkyn

Arledge (English) lake with the hares.
Arlidge, Arledge

Arlen (Irish) pledge.
Arlan, Arland, Arlend, Arlin, Arlinn, Arlyn, Arlynn

Arley (English) a short form of Harley.
Arleigh, Arlie, Arly

Arlo (Spanish) barberry. (English) fortified hill. A form of Harlow. (German) a form of Charles.

Arman (Persian) desire, goal.
Armaan, Armahn, Armaine

Armand (Latin, German) a form of Herman. See also Mandek.
Ardal, Arman, Armanda, Armando, Armands, Armanno, Armaud, Armande, Armond

Armando (Spanish) a form of Armand.
Armondo

Armani (Hungarian) sly; (Hebrew) a form of Armon.
Arman, Armann, Armoni, Armonie, Armonio, Armonni, Armony

Armon (Hebrew) high fortress, strong-hold.
Armani, Armen, Armin, Armino, Armond, Armons

Armstrong (English) strong arm. History: astronaut Neil Armstrong was the commander of Apollo 11 and the first person to walk on the moon.

Arnaud (French) a form of Arnold.
Arnauld, Arnault, Arnoll

Arne (German) a form of Arnold.
Arna, Arnay, Arnel, Arnele, Arnell, Arnelle

Arnette (English) little eagle.
Arnat, Arnet, Arnett, Arnetta, Arnot, Arnott

Arnie (German) a familiar form of Arnold.
Arney, Arni, Arnny, Arny

Arno (German) a short form of Arnold. (Czech) a short form of Ernest.
Arnou, Arnoux

Arnold (German) eagle ruler.
Ardal, Armald, Arnaldo, Arnaud, Arne, Arnie, Arnol, Arno, Arnoldas, Arnolde, Arnoll, Arndt, Arnulfo

Arnulfo (German) a form of Arnold.

Arnon (Hebrew) rushing river.
Arnan

Aron, Arron (Hebrew) forms of Aaron. (Danish) forms of Aren.
Arion

Aroon (Tai) dawn.

Arran (Scottish) island dweller. Geography: an island off the west coast of Scotland. (Hebrew) a form of Aaron.
Aren, Arrin, Arryn, Aryn

Arrigo (Italian) a form of Harry.
Arigo, Arrighetto

Arrio (Spanish) warlike.
Ario, Arrow, Arryo, Aryo

Arsenio (Greek) masculine; virile. History: Saint Arsenius was a teacher in the Roman Empire.
Arsen, Arsène, Arsenius, Arseny, Arsinio

Arsha (Persian) venerable.

Art (English) a short form of Arthur.

Artemus (Greek) gift of Artemis. Mythology: Artemis was the goddess of the hunt and the moon.
Artemas, Artemio, Artemis, Artemus, Artimis, Artimus

Arthur (Irish) noble; lofty hill. (Scottish) bear. (English) rock. (Icelandic) follower of Thor. See also Turi.
Art, Artair, Artek, Arth, Arther, Arthor, Artie, Artor, Arturo, Artus, Aurthar, Aurther, Aurthur

Artie (English) a familiar form of Arthur.
Arte, Artian, Artis, Arty, Atty

Arturo (Italian) a form of Arthur.
Arthuro, Artur

Arun (Cambodian, Hindi) sun.
Aruns

Arundel (English) eagle valley.

Arve (Norwegian) heir, inheritor.

Arvel (Welsh) wept over.
Arval, Arvell, Arvelle

Arvid (Hebrew) wanderer. (Norwegian) eagle tree. See also Ravid.
Arv, Arvad, Arve, Arvie, Arvind, Arvinder, Arvydas

Arvin (German) friend of the people; friend of the army.
Arv, Arvie, Arvind, Arvinder, Arvon, Arvy

Aryeh (Hebrew) lion.

Asa (Hebrew) physician, healer. (Yoruba) falcon.
Asaa, Ase

Asád (Arabic) lion.
Asaad, Asad, Asid, Assad, Azad

Asadel (Arabic) prosperous.
Asadoun, Asadul, Asael

Ascot (English) eastern cottage; style of necktie. Geography: a village near London and the site of the Royal Ascot horseraces.

Asgard (Scandinavian) court of the gods.

Ash (Hebrew) ash tree.
Ashby

Ashanti (Swahili) from a tribe in West Africa.
Ashan, Ashani, Ashante, Ashantee, Ashaunte

Ashby (Scandinavian) ash-tree farm. (Hebrew) a form of Ash.
Ashbey

Asher (Hebrew) happy; blessed.
Ashar, Ashor, Ashur

Ashford (English) ash-tree ford.
Ash, Ashtin

Ashley (English) ash-tree meadow.
Ash, Asheley, Ashelie, Ashely, Ashlan, Ashlee, Ashleigh, Ashlen, Ashlie, Ashlin, Ashling, Ashlinn, Ashlone, Ashly, Ashlyn, Ashlynn, Aslan

Ashon (Swahili) seventh-born son.

Ashton (English) ash-tree settlement.
Ashtan, Ashten, Ashtian, Ashtin, Ashtion, Ashtonn, Ashtun, Ashtyn

Ashur (Swahili) Mythology: the principal Assyrian deity.

Ashwani (Hindi) first. Religion: the first of the twenty-seven galaxies revolving around the moon
Ashwan

Ashwin (Hindi) star.

Asiel (Hebrew) created by God.

Asker (Turkish) soldier.

Aspen (English) aspen tree.

Aston (English) eastern town.
Asten, Astin

Aswad (Arabic) dark skinned, black.

Ata (Fante) twin.

Atek (Polish) a form of Tanek.

Athan (Greek) immortal.

Atherton (English) town by a spring.

Atid (Tai) sun.

Atif (Arabic) caring.
Ateef, Atef

Atlas (Greek) lifted; carried. Mythology: Atlas was forced by Zeus to carry the heavens on his shoulders as a punishment for his share of the war of the Titans.

Atley (English) meadow.
Atlea, Atlee, Atleigh, Atli, Attley

Attila (Gothic) little father. History: the Hun leader who invaded the Roman Empire.
Atalik, Atila, Atilio, Atilla, Atiya, Attal, Attila, Attilio

Atwater (English) at the water's edge.

Atwell (English) at the well.

Atwood (English) at the forest.

Atworth (English) at the farmstead.

Auberon (German) a form of
Oberon.
Auberon, Aubrey

Aubrey (German) noble; bearlike.
(French) a familiar form of Auberon.
See also Avery.
*Aubary, Aube, Aubery, Aubie, Aubré,
Aubree, Aubreii, Aubric, Aubry, Aubury*

Auburn (Latin) reddish brown.

Auden (English) old friend.

Audie (German) noble; strong.
(English) a familiar form of Edward.
Audi, Audiel, Audley, Audy

Audon (French) old; rich.
Audolon

Audric (English) wise ruler.
Audrik, Audrik

Audrey (English) noble strength.
Audra, Audre, Audrea, Audrius, Audry

Audun (Scandinavian) deserted, deso-
late.

Augie (Latin) a familiar form of
August.
Auggie, Augy

August (Latin) a short form of
Augustine, Augustus.
Agosto, Augie, Auguste, Augusto

Augustine (Latin) majestic. Religion:
Saint Augustine was the first arch-
bishop of Canterbury. See also
Austin, Gus, Tino.
*August, Agustin, Augustin, Augustinas,
Augustine, Austen, Auston,
Austyn*

Augustus (Latin) majestic; venerable.
History: an honorary title given to
the first Roman emperor, Octavius
Caesar.
August

Aukai (Hawaiian) seafarer.

Aundre (Greek) a form of Andre.
*Aundrae, Aundray, Aundrea, Aundrey,
Aundry*

Aurek (Polish) golden haired.

Aurelio (Latin) a short form of
Aurelius.
Aurel, Aurele, Aureli, Aurellio

Aurelius (Latin) golden. History:
Marcus Aurelius was a second-cen-
tury A.D. philosopher and emperor of
Rome.
*Arelian, Areliano, Aurèle, Aureliano,
Aurelien, Aurelien, Aurelio, Aurey, Auriel,
Aury*

Aurick (German) protecting ruler.
Auric

Austen, Auston, Austyn (Latin) short
forms of Augustine.
Austan, Austun, Austyne

Austin (Latin) a short form of
Augustine.
Astin, Austine, Oistin, Ostin

Avel (Greek) breath.

Avent (French) born during Advent.
Aventin, Aventino

Averill (French) born in April.
*Ave, Averel, Averell, Averiel, Averil,
Averyl, Averyll, Avrel, Avrell, Avrill,
Avryll*

Avery (English) a form of Aubrey.
*Avary, Aveary, Avere, Averee, Averey,
Averi, Averie, Avery, Avry*

Avi (Hebrew) God is my father.
Avian, Avidan, Avidor, Aviel, Avion

Aviv (Hebrew) youth; springtime.

Avner (Hebrew) a form of Abner.
Avneet, Avniel

Avram (Hebrew) a form of Abraham,
Abram.
*Avram, Avraam, Avraham, Avrahom,
Avrohom, Avrom, Avrum*

Avshalom (Hebrew) father of peace.
See also Absalom.
Avsalom

Awan (Native American) somebody.

Axel (Latin) axe. (German) small oak
tree; source of life. (Scandinavian) a
form of Absalom.
*Aksel, Ax, Axe, Axell, Axil, Axill, Axl,
Axle, Axyle*

Aydin (Turkish) intelligent.

Ayers (English) heir to a fortune.

Ayinde (Yoruba) we gave praise and
he came.

Aylmer (English) a form of Elmer.
Aillmer, Ailmer, Allmer, Ayllmer

Aymil (Greek) a form of Emil.

Aymon (French) a form of Raymond.

Ayo (Yoruba) happiness.

Azad (Turkish) free.

Azeem (Arabic) a form of Azim.
Aseem, Asim

Azi (Nigerian) youth.

Azim (Arabic) defender.
Azeem

Aziz (Arabic) strong.

Azizi (Swahili) precious.

Azriel (Hebrew) God is my aid.

Azuriah (Hebrew) aided by God.
Azaria, Azariah, Azuria

B

Baden (German) bather.
Baeden, Bayden, Baydon

Bahir (Arabic) brilliant, dazzling.

Bahram (Persian) ancient king.

Bailey (French) bailiff, steward.
Bail, Bailee, Bailie, Bailio, Baillie, Baily, Bailye, Baley, Bayley

Bain (Irish) a short form of Bainbridge.
Baine, Bayne, Baynn

Bainbridge (Irish) fair bridge.
Bain, Baynbridge, Bayne, Baynebridge

Baird (Irish) traveling minstrel, bard; poet.
Bairde, Bard

Bakari (Swahili) noble promise.
Bacari, Baccari, Bakarie

Baker (English) baker. See also Baxter.
Bakir, Bakory, Bakr

Bal (Sanskrit) child born with lots of hair.

Balasi (Basque) flat footed.

Balbo (Latin) stammerer.
Bailby, Balbi, Ballbo

Baldemar (German) bold; famous.
Baldemero, Baldomero, Baumar, Baumer

Balder (Scandinavian) bald. Mythology: the Norse god of light, summer, purity, and innocence.
Baldier, Baldur, Baudier

Baldric (German) brave ruler.
Baldrick, Baudric

Baldwin (German) bold friend.
Bald, Baldovino, Balduin, Balduinn, Baldwyn, Baldwynn, Balldwin, Baudoin

Balfour (Scottish) pastureland.
Balfor, Balfore

Balin (Hindi) mighty soldier.
Bali, Baylen, Baylin, Baylon, Valin

Ballard (German) brave; strong.
Balard

Balraj (Hindi) strongest.

Baltazar (Greek) a form of Balthasar.
Baltasar

Balthasar (Greek) God save the king. Bible: one of the three wise men who bore gifts for the infant Jesus.
Badassare, Baldassare, Baltazar, Balthasaar, Balthazar, Balthazzar, Baltsaros, Belshazar, Belshazzar, Boldizsár

Bancroft (English) bean field.
Ban, Bancrofft, Bank, Bankroft, Banky, Binky

Bandi (Hungarian) a form of Andrew.
Bandit

Bane (Hawaiian) a form of Bartholomew.

Banner (Scottish, English) flag bearer.
Bannor, Banny

Banning (Irish) small and fair.
Bannie, Banny

Barak (Hebrew) lightning bolt. Bible: the valiant warrior who helped Deborah.
Barrak

Baran (Russian) ram.
Baren

Barasa (Kikuyu) meeting place.

Barclay (Scottish, English) birch-tree meadow.
Bar, Barcley, Barklay, Barkley, Barklie, Barrclay, Berkeley

Bard (Irish) a form of Baird.
Bar, Barde, Bardia, Bardiya, Barr

Bardolf (German) bright wolf.
Bardo, Bardolph, Bardou, Bardoul, Bardulf, Bardulph

Bardrick (Teutonic) axe ruler.
Bardric, Bardrik

Baris (Turkish) peaceful.

Barker (English) lumberjack; advertiser at a carnival.

Barlow (English) bare hillside.
Barlowe, Barlow, Barlowe

Barnabas (Greek, Hebrew, Aramaic, Latin) son of the missionary. Bible: Christian apostle and companion of Paul on his first missionary journey.
Bane, Barna, Barnaba, Barnabus, Barnaby, Barnebas, Barnebus, Barney

Barnaby (English) a form of Barnabas.
Barnabe, Barnabé, Barnabee, Barnabey, Barnabi, Barnabie, Barnabé, Barnaby

Barnard (French) a form of Bernard.
Barn, Barnard, Barnhard, Barnhardo

Barnes (English) bear; son of Barnett.

Barnett (English) nobleman; leader.
Barn, Barnet, Barney, Baronet, Baronett, Barrie, Baron, Barry

Barney (English) a familiar form of Barnabas, Barnett.
Barnie, Barry

Barnum (German) barn; storage place. (English) baron's home.
Barnham

Baron (German, English) nobleman, baron.
Baaron, Barion, Baronie, Barrin, Barrion, Barron, Baryn, Bayron, Beron

Barrett (German) strong as a bear.
Bar, Baret, Barrat, Barret, Barretta, Barrette, Barry, Berrett, Berrit

Barric (English) grain farm.
Barrick, Beric, Berric, Berrick, Berrik

Barrington (English) fenced town. Geography: a town in England.

Barry (Welsh) son of Harry. (Irish) spear, marksman. (French) gate, fence.
Baris, Barri, Barrie, Barris, Bary

Bartholomew (Hebrew) son of Talmaí. Bible: one of the Twelve Apostles. See also Jernej, Parlan, Parthalán.
Balta, Bane, Bart, Bartek, Barth, Barthel, Barthelemy, Barthélémy, Barthélmy, Bartho, Bartholo, Bartholomaus, Bartholome, Bartholomeo, Bartholomeus, Bartholomieu, Bartholomieux, Bartlet, Barto, Bartolome, Bartolomé, Bartolome, Bartolomeé, Bartolomeo, Bartz, Bat

Barto (Spanish) a form of Bartholomew.
Bardo, Bardol, Bartol, Bartoli, Bartolo, Bartos

Barton (English) barley town; Bart's town.
Barrton, Bart

Bartram (English) a form of Bertram.
Barthram

Baruch (Hebrew) blessed.
Boruch

Basam (Arabic) smiling.
Basem, Basim, Bassam

Basil (Greek, Latin) royal, kingly. Religion: a saint and founder of

monasteries. Botany: an herb often used in cooking. See also Vasili, Wasili.
Bas, Basal, Base, Baseal, Basil, Basile, Basilio, Basilios, Basilius, Bassel, Bazeek, Bazel, Bazil, Bazyli

Basir (Turkish) intelligent, discerning.
Bashar, Basheer, Bashir, Bashiyr, Bechir, Bhasheer

Bassett (English) little person.
Basett, Basit, Basset, Bassit

Bastien (German) a short form of Sebastian.
Baste, Bastiaan, Bastian, Bastien, Bastion

Bat (English) a short form of Bartholomew.

Baul (Gypsy) snail.

Bavol (Gypsy) wind; air.

Baxter (English) a form of Baker.
Bax, Baxie, Baxty, Baxy

Bay (Vietnamese) seventh son. (French) chestnut brown color; evergreen tree. (English) howler.

Bayard (English) reddish brown hair.
Baiardo, Bay, Bayardo, Bayard, Bayrd

Bayley (French) a form of Bailey.
Baylee, Bayleigh, Baylie, Bayly

Baxter

Beacan (Irish) small.
Beacin, Bean

Beacher (English) beech trees.
Beach, Beachy, Beech, Beecher, Beechy

Beagan (Irish) small.
Beagen, Begin

Beale (French) a form of Beau.
Beal, Beall, Bealle, Beals

Beaman (English) beekeeper.
Beamann, Beamen, Beeman, Beman

Beamer (English) trumpet player.

Beasley (English) field of peas.

Beattie (Latin) blessed; happy; bringer of joy.
Beatie, Beatty, Beaty

Beau (French) handsome.
Beale, Beaux, Bo

Beaufort (French) beautiful fort.

Beaumont (French) beautiful mountain.

Beauregard (French) handsome; beautiful; well regarded.

Beaver (English) beaver.
Beav, Beavo, Beve, Bevo

Bebe (Spanish) baby.

Beck (English, Scandinavian) brook.
Beckett

Bede (English) prayer. Religion: the patron saint of lectors.

Bela (Czech) white. (Hungarian) bright.
Béla, Belaal, Belal, Belall, Belay, Bellal

Belden (French, English) pretty valley.
Beldin, Beldon, Bellden, Belldon

Belen (Greek) arrow.

Bell (French) handsome. (English) bell ringer.

Bellamy (French) beautiful friend.
Belamy, Bell, Bellamey, Bellamie

Bello (African) helper or promoter of Islam.

Belmiro (Portuguese) good-looking; attractive.

Bem (Tiv) peace.
Behm

Ben (Hebrew) a short form of Benjamin.
Behn, Benio, Benn, Benne, Benno

Ben-ami (Hebrew) son of my people.
Barani, Barami

Benedict (Latin) blessed. See also Venedictos, Venya.
Benci, Bendick, Bendict, Bendino, Bendix, Bendrick, Benedetto, Benedick, Benedicto, Benedictus, Benediket, Bengt, Benito, Benoit

Benedikt (German, Slavic) a form of Benedict.
Bendek, Bendik, Benedek, Benedik

Bengt (Scandinavian) a form of Benedict.
Beng, Benke, Bent

Beniam (Ethiopian) a form of Benjamin.
Beneyam, Beniamin, Beniamino

Benito (Italian) a form of Benedict. History: Benito Mussolini led Italy during World War II.
Benedo, Benino, Benno, Beno, Betto, Beto

Benjamen (Hebrew) a form of Benjamin.
Benejamen, Benjermen, Benjimen

Benjamin (Hebrew) son of my right hand. See also Peniamina, Veniamin.
Behnjamin, Bejamin, Benjiman, Ben, Benjaminas, Bengamin, Beniam, Benja, Benjahmin, Benjaim, Benjam, Benjamain, Benjaman, Benjamen, Benjamine, Benjaminn, Benjaminno, Benjamon, Benjamyn, Benjamynn, Benjernin, Benjermain, Benjermin, Benji, Benjie, Benjiman, Benjy, Benkamin, Bennjamin, Benny, Benyamin, Benyamino, Binyamin, Mincho

Benjiman (Hebrew) a form of Benjamin.
Benjimen, Benjimin, Benjimon, Benjimain

Benjiro (Japanese) enjoys peace.

Bennett (Latin) little blessed one.
Benet, Benett, Bennet, Benette, Bennete, Bennette

Benny (Hebrew) a familiar form of Benjamin.
Bennie

Beno (Hebrew) son. (Mwera) band member.

Benoit (French) a form of Benedict.
Benott

Benoni (Hebrew) son of my sorrow. Bible: Ben-oni was the son of Jacob and Rachel.
Ben-Oni

Benson (Hebrew) son of Ben. A short form of Ben Zion.
Bensan, Bensen, Benssen, Bensson

Bentley (English) moor; coarse grass meadow. *Bent*

Benton (English) Ben's town; town on the moors. *Bent*

Benzi (Hebrew) a familiar form of Ben Zion.

Ben Zion (Hebrew) son of Zion. *Benson, Benzi*

Beppe (Italian) a form of Joseph. *Beppy*

Ber (English) boundary. (Yiddish) bear.

Beredei (Russian) a form of Hubert. *Berdy, Berdj, Beredej, Beredy*

Berg (German) mountain. *Bergi, Berge, Bergh, Berje*

Bergen (German, Scandinavian) hill dweller. *Bergin, Birgin*

Berger (French) shepherd.

Bergren (Scandinavian) mountain stream. *Berg*

Berk (Turkish) solid, rugged.

Berkeley (English) a form of Barclay. *Berk, Berkeley, Berkie, Berkley, Berkly*

Berl (German) a form of Burl. *Berle, Berlie, Berlin, Berlyn*

Berlyn (German) boundary line. See also Burl. *Berlin, Burlin*

Bern (German) a short form of Bernard. *Berne*

Bernal (German) strong as a bear. *Bernald, Bernaldo, Bernel, Bernhald, Bernhold, Bernold*

Bernard (German) brave as a bear. See also Bjorn. *Barnard, Bear, Bearnard, Benek, Ber, Berend, Bern, Bernabé, Bernadas, Bernardel, Bernardin, Bernardo, Bernardus, Bernardyn, Bernart, Bernat, Bernek, Bernd, Bernel, Bernerd, Berngards, Bernhard, Bernhards, Bernhardt, Bernie, Bjorn, Burnard, Burnardo, Nardo*

Bernardo (Spanish) a form of Bernard. *Barnardino, Barnardo, Barnhardo, Benardo, Bernardino, Bernhardo, Berno, Burnardo, Nardo*

Bernie (German) a familiar form of Bernard. *Berney, Berni, Berny, Birney, Birnie, Birny, Burney*

Berry (English) berry; grape. *Berrie*

Bersh (Gypsy) one year.

Bert (German, English) bright, shining. A short form of Berthold, Berton, Bertram, Bertrand, Egbert, Filbert. *Bertie, Bertus, Birt, Burt*

Berthold (German) bright; illustrious; brilliant ruler. *Bert, Berthoud, Bertold, Bertolde*

Bertie (English) a familiar form of Bert, Egbert. *Berty, Birt, Birtie, Birty*

Bertin (Spanish) distinguished friend. *Berti*

Berto (Spanish) a short form of Alberto.

Berton (English) bright settlement; fortified town. *Bert*

Bertram (German) bright, illustrious. (English) bright raven. See also Bartram. *Beltran, Beltrán, Beltrano, Bert, Berton, Bertrae, Bertraim, Bertram, Bertron*

Bertrand (German) bright shield. *Bert, Bertran, Bertrando, Bertranno*

Berwyn (Welsh) white head. *Berwin, Berwynn, Berwynne*

Bevan (Welsh) son of Evan. *Beavan, Beaven, Beavin, Bev, Beve, Beven, Bevin, Bevo, Bevon*

Beverly (English) beaver meadow. *Beverlea, Beverleigh, Beverley, Beverlie*

Bevis (French) from Beauvais, France; bull. *Beauvais, Berys*

Bhagwandas (Hindi) servant of God.

Bickford (English) axe-man's ford.

Bienvenido (Filipino) welcome.

Bijan (Persian) ancient hero. *Biljan, Bijann, Bijhan, Bijhon, Bijon*

Bilal (Arabic) chosen.
Bila, Bilaal, Bilale, Bile, Bilel, Billaal, Bilall

Bill (German) a short form of William.
Bil, Billee, Billijo, Billye, Byll, Will

Billy (German) a familiar form of Bill, William.
Bille, Billey, Billie, Billy, Bily, Willie

Binah (Hebrew) understanding; wise.
Bina

Bing (German) kettle-shaped hollow.

Binh (Vietnamese) peaceful.

Binkentios (Greek) a form of Vincent.

Binky (English) a familiar form of Bancroft, Vincent.
Bink, Binkentios, Binkie

Birch (English) white; shining; birch tree.
Birk, Burch

Birger (Norwegian) rescued.

Birkey (English) island with birch trees.
Birk, Birkie, Birky

Birkitt (English) birch-tree coast.
Birk, Birket, Birkit, Burket, Burkett, Burkitt

Birley (English) meadow with the cow barn.
Birlee, Birlie, Birly

Birney (English) island with a brook.
Birne, Birnie, Birny, Burney, Burnie, Burny

Birtle (English) hill with birds.

Bishop (Greek) overseer. (English) bishop.
Bish, Bishup

Bjorn (Scandinavian) a form of Bernard.
Bjarne

Blackburn (Scottish) black brook.

Blade (English) knife, sword.
Bladen, Bladon, Bladyn, Blae, Blaed, Blayde

Bladimir (Russian) a form of Vladimir.
Bladimer

Blaine (Irish) thin, lean. (English) river source.
Blain, Blane, Blayne

Blair (Irish) plain, field. (Welsh) place.
Blaire, Blare, Blayr, Blayre

Blaise, Blaize (French) forms of Blaze.
Ballas, Balyse, Blais, Blaisot, Blas, Blase, Blasi, Blasien, Blasius, Blass, Blaz, Blaze, Blayz, Blayze, Blayzz

Blake (English) attractive; dark.
Blaik, Blaike, Blakely, Blakeman, Blakey, Blayke

Blakely (English) dark meadow.
Blakelee, Blakeleigh, Blakeley, Blakelie, Blakelin, Blakelyn, Blakery, Blakley, Blakney

Blanco (Spanish) light skinned; white; blond.

Blane (Irish) a form of Blaine.
Blaney, Blanne

Blayne (Irish) a form of Blaine.
Blayn, Blayney

Blaze (Latin) stammerer. (English) flame; trail mark made on a tree.
Balázs, Biaggio, Biagio, Blaise, Blaize, Blazen, Blazer

Bliss (English) blissful; joyful.

Bly (Native American) high.

Blythe (English) carefree; merry; joyful.
Blithe, Blyth

Bo (English) a form of Beau, Beauregard. (German) a form of Bogart.
Boe

Boaz (Hebrew) swift; strong.
Bo, Boas, Booz, Bos, Boz

Bob (English) a short form of Robert.
Bobb, Bobby, Bobek, Rob

Bobby (English) a familiar form of Bob, Robert.
Bobbey, Bobbi, Bobbie, Bobbye, Boby

Bobek (Czech) a form of Bob, Robert.

Boden (Scandinavian) sheltered. (French) messenger, herald.
Bodie, Bodin, Bodine, Bodyne, Boe

Bodie (Scandinavian) a familiar form of Boden.
Boddie, Bode, Bodee, Bodey, Bodhi, Bodi, Boedee, Boedi, Boedy

Bodil (Norwegian) mighty ruler.

Bodua (Akan) animal's tail.

Bogart (German) strong as a bow. (Irish, Welsh) bog, marshland.
Bo, Bogey, Bogie, Bogy

Bohdan (Ukrainian) a form of Donald. *Bogdan, Bogdashka, Bogdon, Bohden, Bohdon*

Bonaro (Italian, Spanish) friend. *Bona, Bonar*

Bonaventure (Italian) good luck.

Bond (English) tiller of the soil. *Bondie, Bondon, Bonds, Bondy*

Boniface (Latin) do-gooder. *Bonifacio, Bonifacius, Bonifacy*

Booker (English) bookmaker; book lover; Bible lover. *Bookie, Books, Booky*

Boone (Latin, French) good. History: Daniel Boone was an American pioneer. *Bon, Bone, Bonne, Boonie, Boony*

Booth (English) hut. (Scandinavian) temporary dwelling. *Boot, Boote, Boothe*

Borak (Arabic) lightning. Mythology: the horse that carried Muhammed to seventh heaven.

Borden (French) cottage. (English) valley of the boar; boar's den. *Bord, Bordie, Bordy*

Borg (Scandinavian) castle.

Boris (Slavic) battler, warrior. Religion: the patron saint of Moscow, princes, and Russia. *Boriss, Borja, Borris, Borya, Boryenka, Borys*

Borka (Russian) fighter. *Borkinka*

Boseda (Tiv) born on Saturday.

Bosley (English) grove of trees.

Botan (Japanese) blossom, bud.

Bourey (Cambodian) country.

Bourne (Latin, French) boundary. (English) brook, stream.

Boutros (Arabic) a form of Peter.

Bowen (Welsh) son of Owen. *Bow, Bowe, Bowie*

Bowie (Irish) yellow haired. History: James Bowie was an American-born Mexican colonist who died during the defense of the Alamo. *Bow, Bowen*

Boyce (French) woods, forest. *Boice, Boise, Boy, Boycey, Boycie*

Boyd (Scottish) yellow haired. *Boid, Boyde*

Brad (English) a short form of Bradford, Bradley. *Bradd, Brade*

Bradburn (English) broad stream.

Braden (English) broad valley. *Bradan, Bradden, Bradeon, Bradin, Bradine, Bradyn, Braeden, Braiden, Brayden, Bredan, Bredon*

Bradford (English) broad river crossing. *Brad, Bradford, Ford*

Bradlee (English) a form of Bradley. *Bradlea, Bradleigh, Bradlie*

Bradley (English) broad meadow. *Brad, Braddly, Bradlay, Bradlee, Bradly, Bradney*

Bradly (English) a form of Bradley.

Bradon (English) broad hill. *Braeden, Braidon, Braydon*

Bradshaw (English) broad forest.

Bradyn (English) a form of Braden. *Bradynne, Breidyn*

Brady (Irish) spirited. (English) broad island. *Bradey, Bradi, Bradie, Bradye, Braidy*

Braeden, Braiden (English) forms of Braden. *Braedan, Braedin, Braedyn, Braidyn*

Braedon (English) a form of Bradon. *Breadon*

Bragi (Scandinavian) poet. Mythology: the god of poetry, eloquence, and song. *Brage*

Braham (Hindi) creator. *Braheem, Braheim, Brahiem, Brahima, Brahm*

Brainard (English) bold raven; prince. *Brainerd*

Bram (Scottish) bramble, brushwood. (Hebrew) a short form of Abraham, Abram.
Brame, Bramm, Brandon

Bramwell (English) bramble spring.
Brammel, Brammell, Bramwel, Bramwyll

Branch (English) paw; claw; tree branch.

Brand (English) firebrand; sword. A short form of Brandon.
Brandall, Brande, Brandel, Brandell, Brander, Brandley, Brandol, Brandt, Brandy, Brann

Brandeis (Czech) dweller on a burned clearing.
Brandis

Branden (English) beacon valley.
Brandden, Brandene, Brandin, Brandine, Brandyn, Breandan

Brandon (English) beacon hill.
Bran, Brand, Brandan, Branddon, Brandone, Brandonn, Brandyn, Branndan, Branndon, Brannon, Breandon, Brendon

Brandt (English) a form of Brant.

Brandy (Dutch) brandy. (English) a familiar form of Brand.
Branddy, Brandey, Brandi, Brandie

Brandyn (English) a form of Branden, Brandon.
Brandynn

Brannon (Irish) a form of Brandon.
Branen, Brannan, Brannen, Branon

Branson (English) son of Brandon, Brant. A form of Bronson.
Bransen, Bransin, Branison

Brant (English) proud.
Brandt, Brannt, Brante, Brantley, Branton

Brantley (English) a form of Brant.
Brantlie, Brantly, Brentlee, Brentley, Brently

Braulio (Italian) a form of Brawley.
Brauli, Braulino

Brawley (English) meadow on the hillside.
Braulio, Brawlee, Brawly

Braxton (English) Brock's town.
Brax, Braxdon, Braxston, Braxten, Braxtin, Braxxton

Brayan (Irish, Scottish) a form of Brian.
Brayn, Brayon

Brayden (English) a form of Braden.
Braydan, Braydin, Bradyn, Breydan, Breyden, Brydan, Bryden

Braydon (English) a form of Bradon.
Braydoon, Brydon, Breydon

Breck (Irish) freckled.
Brec, Breckan, Brecken, Breckie, Breckin, Breckke, Breckyn, Brek, Brexton

Brede (Scandinavian) iceberg; glacier.

Brencis (Latvian) a form of Lawrence.
Brence

Brendan (Irish) little raven. (English) sword.
Breandan, Bren, Brenden, Brendis, Brendon, Brendyn, Brenn, Brennan, Brennen, Brenndan, Brenyan, Bryn

Brenden (Irish) a form of Brendan.
Bren, Brendene, Brendin, Brendine, Brennden

Brendon (English) a form of Brandon. (Irish, English) a form of Brendan.
Brenndon

Brennan, Brennen (English, Irish) forms of Brendan.
Bren, Brenan, Brenen, Brenin, Brenn, Brenna, Brennann, Brenner, Brennin, Brennon, Brennor, Brennyn, Brenon

Brent (English) a short form of Brenton.
Brendt, Brente, Brenton, Brentt

Brenton (English) steep hill.
Brent, Brentan, Brenten, Brentin, Brentten, Brentton, Brentyn

Bret, Brett (Scottish) from Great Britain. See also Britton.
Bhrett, Braten, Braton, Brayton, Bretin, Bretley, Bretlin, Breton, Brettan, Brette, Bretten, Bretton, Bret, Britt

Brewster (English) brewer.
Brew, Brewer, Bruwster

Breyon (Irish, Scottish) a form of Brian.
Breon, Breyan

Brian (Irish, Scottish) strong; virtuous; honorable. History: Brian Boru was an eleventh-century Irish king and national hero. See also Palaina.
Brayan, Breyon, Briana, Briann, Brianna, Brianne, Briano, Briant, Briante, Briaun, Briayan, Brien, Brience, Brient, Brin, Briny, Brion, Bryan, Bryen

Briar (French) heather.
Brier, Brierly, Bryar, Bryer, Bryor

Brice (Welsh) alert; ambitious. (English) son of Rice.
Bricen, Brienon, Bryce

Brick (English) bridge.
Bricker, Bricklen, Brickman, Brik

Bridger (English) bridge builder.
Bridd, Bridge, Bridgeley, Bridgely

Brigham (English) covered bridge. (French) troops, brigade.
Brig, Brigg, Briggs, Brighton

Brighton (English) bright town.
Breighton, Bright, Brightin, Bryton

Brion (Irish, Scottish) a form of Brian.
Brien, Brione, Briorn, Brionne

Brit, Britt (Scottish) forms of Bret, Brett. See also Briton.
Brit, Brittye

Briton (Scottish) from Great Britain. See also Bret, Brett, Brit, Britt.
Britain, Briten, Britian, Britt, Brittain, Brittan, Britten, Brition, Brittian, Britton

Brock (English) badger.
Broc, Brocke, Brockett, Brockie, Brockley, Brockton, Brocky, Brok, Broque

Brod (English) a short form of Broderick.
Brode, Broden

Broderick (Welsh) son of the famous ruler. (English) broad ridge. See also Roderick.
Brod, Broddie, Brodderick, Brodderick, Broderic, Broderrick, Brodrick

Brodie (Irish) a form of Brody.
Brodi, Broedi

Brodrick (Welsh, English) a form of Broderick.
Broddrick, Brodric, Brodrycke

Brody (Irish) ditch; canal builder.
Brodee, Broden, Brodey, Brodie, Broedy

Brogan (Irish) a heavy work shoe.
Brogen, Broghan, Broghen

Bromley (English) brushwood meadow.

Bron (Afrikaans) source.

Bronislaw (Polish) weapon of glory.
Bronisław

Bronson (English) son of Brown.
Bransen, Branstin, Branson, Bron, Bronnie, Bronnson, Bronny, Bronsan, Bronsen, Bronsin, Bronsonn, Bronsson, Bronsun, Bronsyn, Brunson

Brook (English) brook, stream.
Brooke, Brooker, Brookin, Brooklyn

Brooks (English) son of Brook.
Brookes, Broox

Brown (English) brown; bear.

Bruce (French) brushwood thicket; woods.
Brucy, Bruey, Brue, Bruis

Bruno (German, Italian) brown haired; brown skinned.
Brunon, Bruns

Bryan (Irish) a form of Brian.
Brayan, Bryann, Bryant, Bryen

Bryant (Irish) a form of Bryan.
Bryent

Bryce (Welsh) a form of Brice.
Brycen, Bryceton, Bryson, Bryston

Bryon (German) cottage. (English)
Bryeon, Bryn, Bryne, Brynn, Brynne, Bryone

Bryson (Welsh) son of Brice.
Brysan, Brysen, Brysun, Brysyn

Bryton (English) a form of Brighton.
Brayten, Brayton, Breyton, Bryan, Bryten, Brytin, Bryten, Brytton

Bubba (German) a boy.
Babba, Babe, Bebba

Buck (German, English) male deer.
Buckie, Buckley, Buckner, Bucko, Bucky

Buckley (English) deer meadow.
Bucklea, Bucklee

Buckminster (English) preacher.

Bud (English) herald, messenger.
Budd, Buddy

Buddy (American) a familiar form of Bud.
Budde, Buddey, Buddie

Buell (German) hill dweller. (English) bull.

Buford (English) ford near the castle.
Burford

Burgess (English) town dweller; shop-keeper.
Burg, Burges, Burgh, Burgiss, Burr

Burian (Ukrainian) lives near weeds.

Burke (German, French) fortress, castle.
Berk, Berke, Birk, Bourke, Burk, Burkey, Burkley

Burl (English) cup bearer; wine servant; knot in a tree. (German) a short form of Berlyn.
Berl, Burley, Burlie, Byrle

Burleigh (English) meadow with knotted tree trunks.
Burlee, Burley, Burlie, Byrleigh, Byrlee

Burne (English) brook.
Beirne, Burn, Burnell, Burnett, Burney, Byrn, Byrne

Burney (English) island with a brook. A familiar form of Rayburn.

Burr (Swedish) youth. (English) prickly plant.

Burris (English) town dweller.

Burt (English) a form of Bert. A short form of Burton.
Burtt, Burtt, Burty

Burton (English) fortified town.
Berton, Burt

Busby (Scottish) village in the thicket; tall military hat made of fur.
Busbee, Busbey, Buzz

Buster (American) hitter; puncher.

Butch (American) a short form of Butcher.

Butcher (English) butcher.
Butch

Buz (Scottish) a short form of Busby.
Buzzy

Byford (English) by the ford.

Byram (English) cattle yard.

Byrd (English) birdlike.
Bird, Birdie, Byrdie

Byrne (English) a form of Burne.
Byrn, Byrnes

Byron (French) cottage. (English) barn.
Beyren, Beyron, Biren, Biron, Buiron, Byram, Byran, Byrann, Byren, Byrom, Byrone

Cable (French, English) rope maker.
Cabell

Cadao (Vietnamese) folksong.

Cadby (English) warrior's settlement.

Caddock (Welsh) eager for war.

Cade (Welsh) a short form of Cadell.
Cady

Cadell (Welsh) battler.
Cade, Cadel, Cedell

Caden (American) a form of Kadin.
Cadan, Caddon, Cadian, Cadien, Cadin, Cadon, Cadyn, Caeden, Caedon, Caid, Caiden, Cayden

Cadmus (Greek) from the east. Mythology: a Phoenician prince who founded Thebes and introduced writing to the Greeks.

Caelan (Scottish) a form of Nicholas.
Cael, Caelon, Caelyn, Cailan, Cailean, Caillan, Cailun, Cailyn, Calan, Calen,

Caleon, Caley, Calin, Callan, Callon, Callyn, Calon, Calyn, Caylan, Cayley

Caesar (Latin) long-haired. History: a title for Roman emperors. See also Kaiser, Kesar, Sarito.
Caesare, Caesaer, Caeser, Caezar, Caezare, Ceasar, Cesar, Ceser, Cezar, Cézar, Czar, Seasar

Cahil (Turkish) young, naive.

Cai (Welsh) a form of Gaius.
Caio, Caius, Caw

Cain (Hebrew) spear; gatherer. Bible: Adam and Eve's oldest son. See also Kabil, Kane, Kayne.
Cainan, Cainan, Caine, Cainen, Caineth, Cayn, Cayne

Cairn (Welsh) landmark made of a mound of stones.
Cairne, Carr, Carne

Cairo (Arabic) Geography: the capital of Egypt.
Kairo

Cal (Latin) a short form of Calvert, Calvin.

Calder (Welsh, English) brook, stream.

Caldwell (English) cold well.

Cale (Hebrew) a short form of Caleb.

Caleb (Hebrew) dog; faithful. (Arabic) bold, brave. Bible: one of the twelve spies sent by Moses. See also Kaleb, Kayleb.
Caeleb, Calab, Calabe, Cale, Caley, Calib, Calieb, Callob, Calob, Calyb, Cayleb, Caylebb, Caylib, Caylob

Calen, Calin (Scottish) forms of Caelan.
Caelen, Caelin, Caellin, Cailen, Cailin, Caillin, Calean, Callen, Caylin

Caley (Irish) a familiar form of Caleb.
Calee, Caleigh

Calhoun (Irish) narrow woods. (Scottish) warrior.
Colhoun, Colhoune, Colquhoun

Callahan (Irish) descendant of Ceallachan.
Ceallachan, Calahan, Callaghan

Callum (Irish) dove.
Callam, Calum, Calym

Calvert (English) calf herder.
Cal, Calbert, Calvirt

Calvin (Latin) bald. See also Kalvin, Vinny.
Cal, Calv, Calvien, Calvon, Calvyn

Cam (Gypsy) beloved. (Scottish) a short form of Cameron. (Latin, French, Scottish) a short form of Campbell.
Camm, Cammie, Cammy, Camy

Cameron (Scottish) crooked nose. See also Kameron.
Cam, Camaron, Cameran, Cameren, Camerin, Cameron, Cameroun, Cameron, Cameron, Cameron, Cameryn, Camiren, Camiron, Cammeron, Cannon

Camille (French) young ceremonial attendant.
Camile

Camilo (Latin) child born to freedom; noble.
Camillo, Camillo, Camillus

Camron (Scottish) a short form of Cameron.
Cameron, Cammrin, Cammron, Camren, Camrin, Camryn, Camrynn

Canaan (French) a form of Cannon. History: an ancient region between the Jordan River and the Mediterranean.
Canan, Canen, Caynan

Candide (Latin) pure; sincere.
Candid, Candido, Candonino

Cannon (French) church official; large gun. See also Kannon.
Canaan, Cannan, Cannen, Cannin, Canning, Canon

Canute (Latin) white haired. (Scandinavian) knot. History: a Danish king who became king of England after 1016. See also Knute.
Cnut, Cnute

Cappi (Gypsy) good fortune.

Car (Irish) a short form of Carney.

Carey (Greek) pure. (Welsh) castle; rocky island. See also Karey.
Care, Caree, Cari, Carre, Carree, Carrie, Cary

Campbell (Latin, French) beautiful field. (Scottish) crooked mouth.
Cam, Camp, Campy

Carl (German, English) a short form of Carlton. A form of Charles. See also Carroll, Kale, Kalle, Karl, Karlen, Karol.
Carle, Carles, Carless, Carlis, Carll, Carlo, Carlos, Carlson, Carltos, Carlus

Carlin (Irish) little champion.
Carlan, Carlen, Carley Carlie, Carlino, Carly

Carlisle (English) Carl's island.
Carlyle, Carlysle

Carlito (Spanish) a familiar form of Carlos.
Carlitos

Carlo (Italian) a form of Carl, Charles.
Carolo

Carlos (Spanish) a form of Carl, Charles.
Carito

Carlton (English) Carl's town.
Carl, Carleton, Carlton, Carlston, Carltonn, Carltton, Charlton

Carmel (Hebrew) vineyard, garden. See also Carmine.
Carmello, Carmelo, Karmel

Carmichael (Scottish) follower of Michael.

Carmine (Latin) song; crimson. (Italian) a form of Carmel.
Carmain, Carmaine, Carman, Carmen, Carmon

Carnelius (Greek, Latin) a form of Cornelius.
Carnealius, Carnelius, Carnellius

Carnell (English) defender of the castle. (French) a form of Cornell.

Carney (Irish) victorious. (Scottish) fighter. See also Kearney.
Car, Carny, Karney

Carr (Scandinavian) marsh. See also Kerr.
Karr

Carrick (Irish) rock.
Caroog, Carricko

Carrington (Welsh) rocky town.

Carroll (Irish) champion. (German) a form of Carl.
Carel, Carell, Cariel, Cariell, Carol, Carole, Carolo, Carols, Carollan, Carolus, Carrol, Caryl, Caryl

Carson (English) son of Carr.
Carsen, Carsino, Carrson, Karson

Carsten (Greek) a form of Karsten.
Carston

Carter (English) cart driver.
Cart

Cartwright (English) cart builder.

Carvell (French, English) village on the marsh.
Carvel, Carvelle, Carvellius

Carver (English) wood-carver; sculptor.

Cary (Welsh) a form of Carey. (German, Irish) a form of Carroll.
Carray, Carry

Case (Irish) a short form of Casey. (English) a short form of Casimir.

Casey (Irish) brave.
Case, Casie, Casy, Cayse, Caysey, Kaey, Kasey

Cash (Latin) vain. (Slavic) a short form of Casimir.
Cashe

Casimir (Slavic) peacemaker.
Cachi, Cas, Case, Cash, Cashemere, Cashi, Cashmeire, Cashmere, Casimere, Casimire, Casimiro, Castimer, Kasimir, Kazio

Casper (Persian) treasurer. (German) imperial. See also Gaspar, Jasper, Kasper.
Caspar, Cass

Cass (Irish, Persian) a short form of Casper, Cassidy.

Cassidy (Irish) clever; curly haired. See also Kazio.
Casidy, Cass, Cassady, Cassie, Kassidy

Cassie (Irish) a familiar form of Cassidy.

Cassius (Latin, French) box; protective cover.
Cassia, Cassio, Cazzie

Castle (Latin) castle.
Cassle, Castel

Castor (Greek) beaver. Astrology: one of the twins in the constellation Gemini. Mythology: one of the patron saints of mariners.
Caster, Caston

Cater (English) caterer.

Cato (Latin) knowledgeable, wise.
Caton, Catón

Cavan (Irish) handsome. See also Kevin.
Caven, Cavin, Cavan, Cavoun

Cayden (American) a form of Caden.
Cayde, Caydin

Caylan (Scottish) a form of Caelan.
Caylans, Caylen, Caylon

Cazzie (American) a familiar form of Cassius.
Caz, Cazz, Cazzy

Ceasar (Latin) a form of Caesar.
Ceaser

Cecil (Latin) blind.
Cece, Cecile, Cecilio, Cecilius, Cecill, Celio, Siseal

Cedric (English) battle chieftain. See also Kedrick, Rick.
Cad, Caddaric, Ced, Cederic, Cedrec, Cédric, Cedrick, Cedryche, Sedric

Cedrick (English) a form of Cedric.
Ceddrik, Cederick, Cederrick, Cedirick, Cedrik

Ceejay (American) a combination of the initials C. + J.
Cejay, C.J.

Cemal (Arabic) attractive.

Cephas (Latin) small rock. Bible: the term used by Jesus to describe Peter.
Cepheus, Cephus

Cerdic (Welsh) beloved.
Canadoc, Canadog, Ceredig, Ceretic

Cerek (Polish) lordly; (Greek) a form of Cyril.

Cesar (Spanish) a form of Caesar. *Casar, César, Cesare, Cesaro, Cesaro, Cessar*

Cestmir (Czech) fortress.

Cezar (Slavic) a form of Caesar. *Cézar, Cezary, Cezek, Chezrae, Sezar*

Chace (French) a form of Chase. *Chaye*

Chad (English) warrior. A short form of Chadwick. Geography: a country in north-central Africa. *Ceadd, Chaad, Chadd, Chaddie, Chaddy, Chade, Chadleigh, Chaddie, Chadley, Chadlin, Chadlyn, Chadmen, Chado, Chadron, Chady*

Chadrick (German) mighty warrior. *Chaddrick, Chaderic, Chaderick, Chadrack, Chadric*

Chadwick (English) warrior's town. *Chad, Chadwicke, Chadvic, Chadwyck*

Chago (Spanish) a form of Jacob. *Chango, Chanti*

Chaim (Hebrew) life. See also Hyman. *Chai, Chaimek, Haim, Khaim*

Chaise (French) a form of Chase. *Chais, Chaisen, Chaison*

Chal (Gypsy) boy; son. *Chalie, Chalin*

Chalmers (Scottish) son of the lord. *Chalmer, Chalms, Chamar, Chamarr*

Cham (Vietnamese) hard worker. *Chams*

Chan (Sanskrit) shining; (English) a form of Chauncey; (Spanish) a form of Juan. *Chann, Chano, Chayo*

Chanan (Hebrew) cloud.

Chance (English) a short form of Chancellor, Chauncey. *Chane, Chancee, Chancey, Chancie, Chancy, Chanse, Chansy, Chants, Chantz, Chanze, Chanz, Chayce*

Chancellor (English) record keeper. *Chance, Chancelar, Chancelen, Chancelor, Chanceler, Chanceller, Chancelor, Chanselor, Chanslor*

Chander (Hindi) moon. *Chand, Chandan, Chandara, Chandary, Chandon*

Chandler (English) candle maker. *Chandelar, Chandlan, Chandlar, Chandlier, Chandlor, Chandlyr*

Chane (Swahili) dependable.

Chaney (French) oak. *Chayne, Cheaney, Cheney, Cheyn, Cheyne, Cheyney*

Channing (English) wise. (French) canon; church official. *Chane, Chann*

Chanse (English) a form of Chance. *Chans, Chansey*

Chankrisna (Cambodian) sweet smelling tree.

Chante (French) singer. *Chant, Chantha, Chanthar, Chantra, Chantry, Shantae*

Chapman (English) merchant. *Chap, Chappie, Chappy*

Charles (German) farmer. (English) strong and manly. See also Carl, Searlas, Tearlach, Xarles. *Arlo, Charales, Charels, Charlese, Carlo, Carlos, Charl, Charle, Charlen, Charlie, Charlot, Charlz, Charlzell, Chaz, Chick, Chip, Chuck*

Charlie (German, English) a familiar form of Charles. *Charle, Charlee, Charley, Charli, Charly*

Charlton (English) a form of Carlton. *Charlesten, Charleston, Charleton, Charlotin*

Charro (Spanish) cowboy.

Chase (French) hunter. *Chace, Chaise, Chasen, Chason, Chass, Chasse, Chastan, Chasten, Chastin, Chastinn, Chaston, Chasyn, Chayse*

Chaska (Sioux) first-born son.

Chauncey (English) chancellor; church official. *Chan, Chance, Chancey, Chaunce, Chauncei, Chauncy, Chauncey, Chaunszi*

Chavez (Hispanic) a surname used as a first name. *Chavaz, Chaves, Chaveze, Chavies, Chavis, Chavius, Chevez, Cheveze, Cheviez, Chevious, Chevis, Chivass, Chivez*

Chayse (French) a form of Chase. *Chaysea, Chaysen, Chayson, Chaysten*

Chayton (Lakota) falcon.

Chaz (English) a familiar form of Charles.
Chas, Chasz, Chaze, Chazwick, Chazy, Chazz, Chez

Ché (Spanish) a familiar form of José. History: Ernesto "Che" Guevara was a revolutionary who fought at Fidel Castro's side in Cuba.
Chay

Checha (Spanish) a familiar form of Jacob.

Cheche (Spanish) a familiar form of Joseph.

Chen (Chinese) great, tremendous.

Chencho (Spanish) a familiar form of Lawrence.

Chepe (Spanish) a familiar form of Joseph.
Cepito

Cherokee (Cherokee) people of a different speech.
Cherrakee

Chesmu (Native American) gritty.

Chester (English) a short form of Rochester.
Ches, Cheslav, Cheston, Chet

Chet (English) a short form of Chester.
Chett, Chette

Cheung (Chinese) good luck.

Chevalier (French) horseman, knight.
Chev, Chevy

Chevy (French) a familiar form of Chevalier. Geography: Chevy Chase is a town in Maryland. Culture: a short form of Chevrolet, an American automobile company.
Chev, Chevey, Chevi, Chevie, Chevvy, Chewy

Cheyenne (Cheyenne) a tribal name.
Chayan, Chayanne, Cheyeenne, Cheyene, Cheyne, Shayan

Chi (Chinese) younger generation. (Nigerian) personal guardian angel.

Chick (English) a familiar form of Charles.
Chic, Chickie, Chicky

Chico (Spanish) boy.

Chik (Gypsy) earth.

Chike (Ibo) God's power.

Chiko (Japanese) arrow; pledge.

Chilo (Spanish) a familiar form of Francisco.

Chilton (English) farm by the spring.
Chil, Chill, Chillton, Chilt

Chim (Vietnamese) bird.

Chinua (Ibo) God's blessing.
Chino, Chinou

Chioke (Ibo) gift of God.

Chip (English) a familiar form of Charles.
Chipman, Chipper

Chiram (Hebrew) exalted; noble.

Chris (Greek) a short form of Christian, Christopher. See also Kris.
Chriss, Christ, Chrys, Cris, Crist

Christain (Greek) a form of Christian.
Christai, Christan, Christane, Christaun, Christein

Christian (Greek) follower of Christ; anointed. See also Jaan, Kerstan, Khristian, Kit, Krister, Kristian, Krystian.
Chretien, Chris, Christa, Christain, Christé, Christen, Christensen, Christiaan, Christiana, Christiane, Christiann, Christianna, Christianno, Christiano, Christianos, Christien, Christin, Christino, Christion, Christon, Christos, Christyan, Christyon, Chritian, Chrystian, Cristian, Crystek

Christien (Greek) a form of Christian.
Christienne, Christinne, Chrystien

Christofer (Greek) a form of Christopher.
Christafer, Christafur, Christefor, Christerfer, Christiffer, Christoffer, Christoffher, Christofpher, Chrystofer

Christoff (Russian) a form of Christopher.
Chrisof, Christif, Christof, Cristofe

Christophe (French) a form of Christopher.
Christoph

Christopher (Greek) Christ-bearer. Religion: the patron saint of travelers. See also Cristopher, Kester, Kit, Kristopher, Risto, Stoffel, Tobal, Topher.
Chris, Chrisopherson, Christapher, Christepher, Christerpher, Christipher, Christobal, Christofer, Christoff, Christoforo, Christoher, Christoper, Christophe, Christophen, Christopher, Christophor, Christophore, Christophyr, Christopher, Christos, Christova, Christpher, Christphere, Christphor, Christpor, Christpher, Chrystophe, Cristobal

Christophoros (Greek) a form of Christopher.
Christoforo, Christoforos, Christophor, Christophoros, Christphor, Cristoforo, Cristopher

Christos (Greek) a form of Christopher. See also Khristos.
Cyd

Chucho (Hebrew) a familiar form of Jesus.

Chuck (American) a familiar form of Charles.
Chuckey, Chuckie, Chucky

Chui (Swahili) leopard.

Chul (Korean) firm.

Chuma (Ibo) having many beads, wealthy; (Swahili) iron.

Chuminga (Spanish) a familiar form of Dominic.
Chumin

Chumo (Spanish) a familiar form of Thomas.

Chun (Chinese) spring.

Chung (Chinese) intelligent.
Chungo, Chuong

Churchill (English) church on the hill. History: Sir Winston Churchill served as British prime minister and won a Nobel Prize for literature.

Cian (Irish) ancient.
Céin, Cianán, Kian

Cicero (Latin) chickpea. History: a famous Roman orator, philosopher, and statesman.
Cicerón

Cid (Spanish) lord. History: title for Rodrigo Díaz de Vivar, an eleventh-century Spanish soldier and national hero.
Cyd

Cirillo (Italian) a form of Cyril.
Cirilo, Cirillo, Cirilo, Ciro

Ciqala (Dakota) little.

Clancy (Irish) redheaded fighter.
Clancey, Clancy

Cisco (Spanish) a short form of Francisco.

Clare (Latin) a short form of Clarence.
Clair, Clarey, Clary

Cleary (Irish) learned.

Clarence (Latin) clear; victorious.
Clarance, Clare, Clarrance, Clarrence, Clearence

Clark (French) cleric; scholar.
Clarke, Clerc, Clerk

Claude (Latin, French) lame.
Claud, Claudan, Claudel, Claudell, Claudey, Claudi, Claudian, Claudianus, Claudie, Claudien, Claudin, Claudio, Claudis, Claudius, Claudy

Claudio (Italian) a form of Claude.

Claus (German) a short form of Nicholas. See also Klaus.
Claas, Claes, Clause

Clay (English) clay pit. A short form of Clayborne, Clayton.
Klay

Clayborne (English) brook near the clay pit.
Claibern, Claiborne, Claibourne, Clay, Clayborn, Clayborn, Claybourn, Clayburn, Clayburn, Cleborn

Clayton (English) town built on clay.
Clay, Clayten, Cleighton, Cleyton, Clyton, Klayton

Cleavon (English) cliff.
Clavin, Clavon, Clavone, Clayvon, Clayvon, Clévon, Clevon, Clevonn, Clyon

Clem (Latin) a short form of Clement.
Cleme, Clemmy, Clim

Clement (Latin) merciful. Bible: a coworker of Paul. See also Klement, Menz.
Clem, Clemens, Clément, Clemente, Clementius, Clemmons

Clemente (Italian, Spanish) a form of Clement.
Clemento, Clemenza

Cleon (Greek) famous.
Kleon

Cletus (Greek) illustrious. History: a Roman pope and martyr.
Cleatus, Cledis, Cleotis, Clete, Cletis

Cleveland (English) land of cliffs.
Cleaveland, Cleavland, Cleavon, Cleve, Clevelend, Clevelynn, Clevey, Clevie, Clevon

Cliff (English) a short form of Clifford, Clifton.
Clif, Cliff, Clive, Clyff, Clyph, Kliff

Clifford (English) cliff at the river crossing.
Cliff, Cliford, Chyfford, Klifford

Clifton (English) cliff town.
Cliff, Cliffton, Clift, Cliften, Chyfton

Clint (English) a short form of Clinton.
Klint

Clinton (English) hill town.
Clenten, Clint, Clinten, Clintion, Clinton, Clynton, Klinton

Clive (English) a form of Cliff.
Cleve, Clivans, Clivens, Clyve, Klyve

Clovis (German) famous soldier. See also Louis.

Cluny (Irish) meadow.

Clyde (Welsh) warm. (Scottish) Geography: a river in Scotland.
Cly, Clyud, Klyde

Coby (Hebrew) a familiar form of Jacob.
Cob, Cobby, Cobe, Cobey, Cobi, Cobia, Cobie

Cochise (Apache) hardwood. History: a famous Chiricahua Apache leader.

Coco (French) a familiar form of Jacques.
Coko, Koko

Codey (English) a form of Cody.
Coday

Codi, Codie (English) forms of Cody.
Coadi, Codea

Cody (English) cushion. History: William "Buffalo Bill" Cody was an American frontier scout who toured America and Europe with his Wild West show. See also Kody.
Coady, Coddy, Code, Codee, Codell, Codey, Codi, Codiak, Codie, Coedy

Coffie (Ewe) born on Friday.

Cola (Italian) a familiar form of Nicholas, Nicola.
Colas

Colar (French) a form of Nicholas.

Colbert (English) famous seafarer.
Cole, Colt, Colvert, Culbert

Colby (English) dark; dark haired.
Colbey, Colbi, Colbie, Colbin, Colebee, Coleby, Collby, Kolby

Cole (Latin) cabbage farmer. (English) a short form of Coleman.
Colet, Coley, Colie, Kole

Coleman (Latin) cabbage farmer. (English) coal miner.
Cole, Colemann, Colm, Colman, Koleman

Colin (Irish) young cub. (Greek) a short form of Nicholas.
Cailean, Colan, Cole, Colen, Coleon, Colinn, Collin, Colyn, Kolin

Colley (English) black haired; swarthy.
Colee, Collie, Collis

Collier (English) miner.
Colier, Collayer, Collie, Collyer, Colyer

Collin (Scottish) a form of Colin, Collins.
Collan, Collen, Collian, Collon, Collyn

Collins (Greek) son of Colin. (Irish) holly.
Collin, Collis

Colson (Greek, English) son of Nicholas.
Colsen, Coulson

Colt (English) young horse; frisky. A short form of Colter, Colton.
Cole

Colten (English) a form of Colton.

Colter (English) herd of colts.
Colt

Colton (English) coal town.
Colt, Coltan, Colten, Coltin, Coltinn, Coltn, Coltrane, Colttan, Coltton, Coltun, Coltyn, Coltyne, Kolton

Columba (Latin) dove.
Coim, Colum, Columbia, Columbus

Colwyn (Welsh) Geography: a river in Wales.
Colvin, Colvinn

Coman (Arabic) noble. (Irish) bent.
Comán

Conall (Irish) high, mighty.
Conal, Connall, Connel, Connell, Connelly, Connolly

Conan (Irish) praised, exalted. (Scottish) wise.
Conant, Conary, Connen, Connie, Connon, Connor, Conon

Conary (Irish) a form of Conan.
Conaire

Conlan (Irish) hero.
Conlen, Conley, Conlin, Conlyn

Conner (Irish) a form of Connor.
Connar, Connary, Conneer, Connery, Konner

Connie (English, Irish) a familiar form of Conan, Conrad, Constantine, Conway.
Con, Conn, Conney, Conny

Connor (Scottish) wise. (Irish) a form of Conan.
Conner, Connner, Connory, Connyr, Conor, Konner, Konnor

Conor (Irish) a form of Connor.
Conar, Coner, Conour, Konner

Conrad (German) brave counselor.
Connie, Conrade, Conrado, Corrado, Konrad

Conroy (Irish) wise.
Conry, Roy

Constant (Latin) a short form of Constantine.

Constantine (Latin) firm, constant. History: Constantine the Great was the Roman emperor who adopted the Christian faith. See also Dinos, Konstantin, Stancio.
Connie, Constantín, Constantijn, Constantin, Constantine, Constantino, Constantinos, Constantios, Costa

Conway (Irish) hound of the plain.
Connie, Conwy

Cook (English) cook.
Cooke

Cooper (English) barrel maker. See also Keiffer.
Coop, Couper

Corbett (Latin) raven.
Corbitt, Corbet, Corbette, Corbit, Corbitt

Corbin (Latin) raven.
Corban, Corben, Corbey, Corbie, Corbon, Corby, Corbyn, Korbin

Corcoran (Irish) ruddy.

Cordaro (Spanish) a form of Cordero.
Coradaro, Cordairo, Cordara, Cordarel, Cordarell, Cordarelle, Cordareo, Cordarin, Cordario, Cordarion, Cordarius, Cordarrius, Cordarius, Cordarel, Cordarell, Cordarris, Cordarrius, Cordarro, Cordarrus, Cordarryl, Cordaryal, Cordarryo, Cordarl

Cordell (French) rope maker.
Cord, Cordae, Cordale, Corday, Cordeal,

Cordero (Spanish) little lamb.
Cordaro, Cordeal, Cordeara, Cordearo, Cordeiro, Cordelro, Corder, Cordera, Cordeall, Corderio, Corderios, Cordernal, Corderro, Corderryn, Cordernn, Corderus, Cordiaro, Cordierre, Cordy, Corderio

Corey (Irish) hollow. See also Korey, Kory.
Core, Coreaa, Coree, Cori, Corian, Corie, Corio, Correy, Corria, Corrie, Corry, Corrye, Cory

Cormac (Irish) raven's son. History: a third-century king of Ireland who was a great lawmaker.
Cormack, Cormik

Cornelius (Greek) cornel tree. (Latin) horn colored. See also Kornel, Kornelius, Nelek.
Carnelius, Conny, Cornealous, Corneli, Cornelious, Cornelas, Cornelious, Cornelious, Cornelis, Corneliu, Cornell, Cornellious, Cornellis, Cornellius, Cornelous, Cornelus, Cornelys, Corney, Cornie, Cornelius, Corneilus, Corny, Cournelius, Cournelyous, Neilius, Nellie

Cornell (French) a form of Cornelius.
Carnell, Cornall, Cornel, Corneil, Cornelle, Corney, Cornie, Corny, Nellie

Cornwallis (English) from Cornwall.

Corrado (Italian) a form of Conrad.
Carrado

Corrigan (Irish) spearman.
Carrigan, Carrigen, Corrigon, Corrigun, Korrigan

Corrin (Irish) spear carrier.
Corin, Corion

Corry (Latin) a form of Corey.

Cort (German) bold. (Scandinavian) short. (English) a short form of Courtney.
Corte, Cortie, Corty, Kort

Cortez (Spanish) conqueror. History: Hernando Cortés was a Spanish conquistador who conquered Aztec Mexico.
Cartez, Cortes, Cortis, Cortize, Courtes, Courtez, Curtez, Kortez

Corwin (English) heart's companion; heart's delight.
Corwinn, Corwyn, Corwynn, Corwynne

Cory (Latin) a form of Corey. (French) a familiar form of Cornell. (Greek) a short form of Corydon.
Corye

Corydon (Greek) helmet, crest.
Coridon, Corradino, Cory, Coryden, Coryell

Cosgrove (Irish) victor, champion.

Cosmo (Greek) orderly; harmonious; universe.
Cos, Cosimo, Cosme, Cosmé, Cozmo, Kosmo

Costa (Greek) a short form of Constantine.
Costandinos, Costantinos, Costas, Costes

Coty (French) slope, hillside.
Cote, Cotee, Cotey, Coti, Cotie, Cotty, Cotye

Courtland (English) court's land.
Court, Courtlan, Courtlana, Courtlandt, Courtlin, Courtlind, Courtlon, Courtlyn, Kourtland

Courtney (English) court.
Cort, Cortnay, Cortne, Cortney, Court, Courten, Courtenay, Courteney, Courtnay, Courtnee, Curt, Kortney

Cowan (Irish) hillside hollow.
Coe, Coven, Covin, Cowen, Cowey, Cowie

Coy (English) woods.
Coye, Coyie, Coyt

Coyle (Irish) leader in battle.

Coyne (French) modest.
Coyan

Craddock (Welsh) love.
Caradoc, Caradog

Craig (Irish, Scottish) crag; steep rock.
Crag, Craige, Craigen, Craigery, Craigh, Craigon, Creag, Creg, Cregan, Cregg, Creig, Creigh, Criag, Kraig

Crandall (English) crane's valley.
Cran, Crandal, Crandel, Crandell, Crendal

Crawford (English) ford where crows fly.
Craw, Crow, Ford

Creed (Latin) belief.
Creedon

Creighton (English) town near the rocks.
Cray, Crayton, Creighm, Creight, Creighto, Crichton

Crepin (French) a form of Crispin.

Crispin (Latin) curly haired.
Crepin, Cris, Crispian, Crispien, Crispino, Crispo, Krispin

Cristian (Greek) a form of Christian.
Crétien, Cristean, Cristhian, Cristiano, Cristien, Cristino, Cristle, Criston, Cristos, Cristy, Cristyan, Crystek, Crystian

Cristobal (Greek) a form of Christopher.
Cristóbal, Cristoval, Cristovao

Cristoforo (Italian) a form of Christopher.
Cristofor

Cristopher (Greek) a form of Christopher.
Cristaph, Cristhofer, Cristifer, Cristofer, Cristoph, Cristophe, Crystapher, Crystifer

Crofton (Irish) town with cottages.

Cromwell (English) crooked spring, winding spring.

Crosby (Scandinavian) shrine of the cross.
Crosbey, Crosbie, Cross

Crosley (English) meadow of the cross.
Cross

Crowther (English) fiddler.

Cruz (Portuguese, Spanish) cross. *Cruze, Kruz*

Crystek (Polish) a form of Christian.

Cullen (Irish) handsome. *Cull, Cullan, Cullie, Cullin*

Culley (Irish) woods. *Cullie, Cully*

Culver (English) dove. *Colver, Cull, Cullie, Cully*

Cunningham (Irish) village of the milk pail.

Curran (Irish) hero. *Caran, Curon, Curr, Curren, Currey, Curri, Currie, Currin, Curry*

Currito (Spanish) a form of Curtis. *Curcio*

Curt (Latin) a short form of Courtney, Curtis. See also Kurt.

Curtis (Latin) enclosure. (French) courteous. See also Kurtis. *Curio, Currito, Curt, Curtice, Curtiss, Curtus*

Cuthbert (English) brilliant.

Cutler (English) knife maker. *Cut, Cuttie, Cutty*

Cy (Persian) a short form of Cyrus.

Cyle (Irish) a form of Kyle.

Cyprian (Latin) from the island of Cyprus. *Ciprian, Cipriano, Ciprien, Cyprien*

Cyrano (Greek) from Cyrene, an ancient city in North Africa. Literature: *Cyrano de Bergerac* is a play by Edmond Rostand about a great guardsman and poet whose large nose prevented him from pursuing the woman he loved. *Daquane, Daequon, Daequone, Daequan*

Cyril (Greek) lordly. See also Kiril. *Cerek, Cerel, Cyrell, Ceril, Ciril, Cirillo, Cyra, Cyrel, Cyrell, Cyrelle, Cyrill, Cyrille, Cyrillus, Syrell, Syril*

Cyrus (Persian) sun. Historical: Cyrus the Great was a king in ancient Persia. See also Kir. *Ciro, Cy, Cyress, Cyris, Cyriss, Cyruss, Syris, Syrus*

D

Dabi (Basque) a form of David.

Dabir (Arabic) tutor.

Dacey (Latin) from Dacia, an area now in Romania. (Irish) southerner. *Dace, Dache, Dacian, Dacias, Dacio, Dacy, Daicey, Daicy*

Dada (Yoruba) curly haired. *Dadi*

Daegel (English) from Daegel, England.

Daelen (English) a form of Dale. *Daelan, Daelin, Daelon, Daelyn, Daelyne*

Daemon (Greek, Latin) a form of Damon. *Daemean, Daemeon, Daemien, Daemin, Daemion, Daemon, Daemyen*

Daequan (American) a form of Daquan. *Daequane, Daequon, Daequone, Daequan*

Daeshawn (American) a combination of the prefix Da + Shawn. *Daesean, Daeshaun, Daeshon, Daeshun, Daisean, Daishawn, Daishaun, Daishon,*

Daevon (American) a form of Davon. *Daevion, Daevohn, Daevonne, Daevontey*

Dafydd (Welsh) a form of David. *Dafyd*

Dag (Scandinavian) day; bright. *Daeg, Daegan, Dagen, Dagny, Deegan*

Dagan (Hebrew) corn; grain. *Daegan, Daegon, Dagen, Dagon, Dgon*

Dagwood (English) shining forest.

Dai (Japanese) big. *Daimone*

Daimian (Greek) a form of Damian. *Daiman, Daimen, Daimeon, Daimian, Daimin, Daimon, Daimyan*

Daimon (Greek, Latin) a form of Damon.

Daiquan (American) a form of Dajuan. *Daekwann, Daekwon, Daiqone, Daiqua, Daiquane, Daiquann, Daiquaun, Daiquon, Daiquvon*

Daivon (American) a form of Davon.
Daivain, Daivion, Daivonn, Daivonte, Daiwan

Dajon (American) a form of Dajuan.
Dajean, Dajiawn, Dajin, Dajion, Dajn, Dajohn, Dajonae

Dajuan (American) a combination of the prefix Da + Juan. See also Dejuan.
Daejon, Daejuan, Daiquan, Dajon, Da Jon, Da-Juan, Dajwan, Dajwaun, Dakuan, Dakwan, Dawan, Dawaun, Dawawn, Dawon, Dawoyan, Dijuan, Diuan, Dujuan, D'Juan, D'juan, Dwaun

Dakarai (Shona) happy.
Dakairi, Dakar, Dakaraia, Dakari, Dakarri

Dakoda (Dakota) a form of Dakota.
Dacoda, Dacodah, Dakodah, Dakodas

Dakota (Dakota) friend; partner; tribal name.
Dac, Dack, Dackota, Dacota, DaCota, Dak, Dakota, Dakkota, Dakoata, Dakoda, Dakotah, Dakotha, Dakotta, Dekota

Dakotah (Dakota) a form of Dakota.
Dakottah

Daksh (Hindi) efficient.

Dalal (Sanskrit) broker.

Dalbert (English) bright, shining. See also Delbert.

Dale (English) dale, valley.
Dael, Daelen, Dal, Dalen, Daley, Dalibor, Dallan, Dallin, Dallyn, Daly, Dayl, Dayle

Dalen (English) a form of Dale.
Dailin, Dalaan, Dalan, Dalane, Daleon, Dalian, Dalibor, Dalione, Dallan, Dalon, Daylan, Daylen, Daylin, Daylon

Daley (Irish) assembly. (English) a familiar form of Dale.
Daily, Daly, Dawley

Dallan (English) a form of Dale.
Dallen, Dallon

Dallas (Scottish) valley of the water; resting place. Geography: a town in Scotland; a city in Texas.
Dal, Dalieass, Dall, Dalles, Dallis, Dalys, Dellis

Dallin, Dallyn (English) pride's people.
Dalin, Dalyn

Dalston (English) Daegel's place.
Dalis, Dallon

Dalton (English) town in the valley.
Dal, Dalaton, Dallton, Dalt, Daltan, Dalten, Daltin, Daltyn, Daulton, Delton

Dalvin (English) a form of Delvin.
Dalven, Dalvon, Dalvyn

Dalziel (Scottish) small field.

Damar (American) a short form of Damarcus, Damario.
Damare, Damari, Damarre, Damauri

Damarcus (American) a combination of the prefix Da + Marcus.
Damacus, Damar, Damarco, Damarcue, Damarick, Damark, Damarkco, Damarkis, Damarko, Damarkus, Damarques, Damarquez, Damarquis, Damarrco

Damario (Greek) gentle. (American) a combination of the prefix Da + Mario.
Damar, Damarea, Damareus, Damaria, Damarie, Damarino, Damarion, Damarious, Damaris, Damarius, Damarrea, Damarrion, Damarrious, Damarrius, Damaryo, Dameris, Damerius

Damek (Slavic) a form of Adam.
Damick, Damicke

Dameon (Greek) a form of Damian.
Damein, Dameion, Dameone

Dametrius (Greek) a form of Demetrius.
Dametri, Dametries, Dametrious, Damitri, Damitric, Damitrie, Damitrious, Damitrius

Damian (Greek) tamer; soother.
Daemon, Daimian, Damaiaon, Damaian, Damaien, Damain, Damaine, Damaion, Damani, Damanni, Damaun, Damayon, Dame, Damean, Dameon, Damian, Damiane, Damiann, Damiano, Damianos, Damien, Damion, Damiyan, Damjan, Damyan, Daymian, Dema, Demyan

Damien (Greek) a form of Damian. Religion: Father Damien ministered to the leper colony on the Hawaiian island Molokai.
Daemien, Daimien, Damie, Damienne, Damyen

Damion (Greek) a form of Damian.
Damieon, Damiion, Damin, Damine, Damionne, Damiyon, Dammion, Damyon

Damon (Greek) constant, loyal. (Latin) spirit, demon.
Daemen, Daemon, Daemond, Daimon, Daman, Damen, Damond, Damone, Damoni, Damonn, Damonni, Damontae, Damonte, Damontez, Damontis, Damyn, Daymon, Daymond

Dan (Vietnamese) yes. (Hebrew) a short form of Daniel.
Dahn, Danh, Danne

Dana (Scandinavian) from Denmark.
Dain, Daina, Dayna

Dandin (Hindi) holy man.

Dandré (French) a combination of the prefix De + André.
D'André, Dandrae, D'andrea, Dandras, Dandray, Dandre, Dondrea

Dane (English) from Denmark. See also Halden.
Dain, Daine, Darie, Dayne, Dhane

Danek (Polish) a form of Daniel.

Danforth (English) a form of Daniel.

Danial (Hebrew) a form of Daniel.
Danal, Daneal, Danial, Daniyal, Danile, Dannye

Danick, Dannick (Slavic) familiar forms of Daniel.
Danek, Danicka, Danik, Danika, Daryck

Daniel (Hebrew) God is my judge. Bible: a Hebrew prophet. See also Danno, Kanaiela.
Dacso, Dainel, Dan, Daneel, Daneil, Danek, Danel, Danforth, Danial, Danicke, Daniel, Daniël, Daniele,
Danielius, Daniell, Daniels, Danielson, Danilo, Daniyal, Dan'l, Dannel, Dannicke, Danniel, Dannil, Danno, Danny, Dano, Danukas, Dany, Danyel, Danyell, Daoud, Dasco, Dayne, Deniel, Doneal, Doniel, Donois, Dusan, Nelo

Daniele (Hebrew) a form of Daniel.
Danile, Danièle

Danilo (Slavic) a form of Daniel.
Daniele, Danil, Danila, Danilka, Darylo

Danior (Gypsy) born with teeth.

Danladi (Hausa) born on Sunday.

Danno (Hebrew) a familiar form of Daniel. (Japanese) gathering in the meadow. (Hebrew) a familiar form of Daniel.
Dannon, Dano.

Dannon (American) a form of Danno.
Daenen, Daenen, Dairon, Danaan, Danen, Danon

Danny, Dany (Hebrew) familiar forms of Daniel.
Dancy, Dani, Dannee, Danney, Danni, Dannie, Dannye

Dano (Czech) a form of Daniel.
Danko, Danno

Dante, Danté (Latin) lasting, enduring.
Danatay, Danaté, Dant, Dantae, Dantay, Dantee, Dauntay, Dauntaye, Daunté, Dauntrae, Deante, Dontae, Donté

Dantrell (American) a combination of Dante + Darell.
Dante + Darell, Dantre, Dantrey, Dantril, Dantyrell, Dontrell

Danyel (Hebrew) a form of Daniel.
Danya, Danyal, Danyale, Danyele, Danyell, Danyiel, Danyl, Danyle, Danylets, Danylo, Donyell

Daoud (Arabic) a form of David.
Daudi, Daudy, Dawud, Dawid

Daquan (American) a combination of the prefix Da + Quan.
Daequan, Dagon, Daquain, Daquaine, Da'quan, Daquandre, Daquandrey, Daquane, Daquann, Daquantae, Daquante, Daquarius, Daquaun, Daquin, Daquon, Daquone, Daquavon, Daquavin, Daquan, Daquawn, Daquawn, Daquan, Daquone, Dayquan, Dequain, Dequan, Dequann, Dequane, Dequann

Dar (Hebrew) pearl.

Dara (Cambodian) stars.

Daran (Irish) a form of Darren.
Darann, Daraun, Darian, Daran, Dayan, Deran

Darby (Irish) free. (English) deer park.
Dar, Darb, Darbee, Darbey, Darbie, Derby

Darcy (Irish) dark. (French) from Arcy, France.
Dar, Daray, D'Arcy, Darce, Darcee, Darcel, Darcey, Darcio, D'Arcy, Darsey, Darsy

Dareh (Persian) wealthy.

Darell (English) a form of Darrell.
Darall, Daralle, Dareal, Darel, Darelle, Darral, Darrall

Daren (Hausa) born at night. (Irish, English) a form of Darren.
Dare, Dayren, Dheren

Darian, Darrian (Irish) forms of Darren.
Daryan

Darick (German) a form of Derek.
Darek, Daric, Darico, Darieck, Dariek, Darik, Daryk

Darien, Darrien (Irish) forms of Darren.

Darin (Irish) a form of Darren.
Daryn, Darynn, Daytrin, Dearin, Dharin

Dario (Spanish) affluent.

Darion Darrion (Irish) forms of Darren.
Daryeon, Daryon

Darius (Greek) wealthy.
Dairus, Dare, Darieus, Darioush, Dariuse, Dariush, Dariuss, Dariusz, Darrius

Darnell (English) hidden place.
Dar, Darn, Darnall, Darneal, Darneil, Darnel, Darnelle, Darnyell, Darnyll

Daron (Irish) a form of Darren.
Daeron, Dairon, Darone, Daronn, Darroun, Dayron, Dearon, Dharon, Diron

Darrell (French) darling, beloved; grove of oak trees.
Dare, Darel, Darell, Daral, Darrel, Darrill, Darol, Darryl, Derrell

Darren (Irish) great. (English) small; rocky hill.
Davan, Dare, Daren, Darian, Darien,
Darin, Darion, Daron, Daran, Darrian,
Darrien, Darrience, Darrin, Darrion,
Daron, Darryn, Darun, Daryn,
Dearon, Deren, Dereon, Derren, Derron

Darrick (German) a form of Derek.
Darrec, Darrek, Darric, Darrik, Darryk

Darrin (Irish) a form of Darren.

Darrion (Irish) a form of Darren.
Dairean, Dairion, Darian, Darien,
Darion, Darrian, Darrien, Darrione,
Darriyun, Derrian, Derrion

Darrius (Greek) a form of Darius.
Darreus, Darrias, Darrious, Darris,
Darriuss, Darrus, Darryus, Derrious,
Derris, Derrius

Darron (Irish) a form of Darren.
Darrian, Daroun

Darryl (French) darling, beloved; grove of oak trees. A form of Darrell.
Dahrll, Darryle, Darryll, Daryl, Daryle,
Daryll, Derryl

Darshan (Hindi) god; godlike. Religion: another name for the Hindu god Shiva.
Darshaun, Darshon

Darton (English) deer town.
Darel, Dartrel

Darwin (English) dear friend. History: Charles Darwin was the British naturalist who established the theory of evolution.
Darvin, Darvon, Darwyn, Derwin,
Derwynn, Durwin

Daryl (French) a form of Darryl.
Darel, Daril, Darl, Darly, Daryll,
Daryle, Daryll, Darylle, Daroyl

Dasan (Pomo) leader of the bird clan.
Dassan

Dashawn (American) a combination of the prefix Da + Shawn.
Dasean, Dashan, Dashaane, Dashante,
Dashaun, Dashaunte, Dashean, Dashon,
Dashawn, Dashonnie, Dashonte, Dashuan,
Dashun, Dashwan, Dayshawn

Dauid (Swahili) a form of David.

Daulton (English) a form of Dalton.

Davante (American) a form of Davonte.
Davanta, Davantay, Davinte

Davaris (American) a combination of Dave + Darius.
Davario, Davarious, Davarius, Davarrius,
Davarus

Dave (Hebrew) a short form of David, Davis.

Davey (Hebrew) a familiar form of David.
Davee, Davi, Davie, Davy

David (Hebrew) beloved. Bible: the second king of Israel. See also Dov, Havika, Kawika, Taaveti, Taffy, Tevel.
Dabi, Daevid, Dafydd, Dai, Daivid,
Daoud, Dauid, Dav, Dave, Daved,
Daveed, Daveen, Davey, Davidde,
Davide, Davidek, Davido, Davon,
Davoud, Dayvid, Davit,
Davud, Dayvid, Dodya, Dov

Davin (Scandinavian) brilliant Finn.
Daevin, Davion, Davon, Davyn, Davan, Davin, Davine, Davyn, Deavan, Deaven

Davis (Welsh) son of David.
Dave, Davidson, Davies, Davison

Davion (American) a form of Davin.
Daquan, Dayquain, Dayquawane, Dayquin, Dayquan

Davon (American) a form of Davin.
Daevon, Daivon, Davon, Davone, Davonn, Davonne, Deavon, Devon

Davonte (American) a combination of Davon + the suffix Te.
Davante, Davonnte, Davonta, Davontae, Davontah, Davontai, Davontay, Davontaye, Davontea, Davontee, Davonti

Dawan (American) a form of Davin.
Dawann, Dawante, Dawaun, Dawayne, Dawon, Dawone, Dawoon, Dawyne, Dawyun

Dawit (Ethiopian) a form of David.

Dawson (English) son of David.
Dawsyn

Dax (French, English) water.
Daxton

Daymian (Greek) a form of Damian.
Daymayne, Daymen, Daymeon, Daymiane, Daymien, Daymiin, Daymirin, Daymion, Daymn

---

Dayne (Scandinavian) a form of Dane.
Dayn

Dayquan (American) a form of Daquan.

Dayshawn (American) a form of Dashawn.
Daysean, Daysen, Dayshaun, Dayshon, Dayson

Dayton (English) day town; bright, sunny town.
Daeton, Daion, Daython, Daython, Daytona, Daytonn, Deyton

Dayvon (American) a form of Davin.
Dayveon, Dayveon, Dayvin, Dayvion, Dayvonn

De (Chinese) virtuous.

Deacon (Greek) one who serves.
Deke

Dean (French) leader. (English) valley.
See also Dino.
Deane, Deen, Dene, Deyn, Deyne

Deandre (French) a combination of the prefix De + André.
D'andre, D'andré, D'André, D'andrea, Deandra, Deandrae, Déandre, Deandré, De André, De Andrea, Deandres, Deandrey, Deandrea, Deaundra, Deaundray, Deaundre, De Aundre, Deaundrej, Deaundry, Deondre, Diandre, Dondre

Deangelo (Italian) a combination of the prefix De + Angelo.
Dang, Dangelo, D'Angelo, Danglo, Deaengelo, Deangelio, Deangella,

---

Deangelo, De Angelo, Deangilo, Deanglea, Deanglo, Deangulo, Diangelo, Di'angelo

Deante (Latin) a form of Dante.
Deanta, Deantai, Deantay, Deanté, De Anté, Deanteé, Deaunta, Diante, Diantey

Deanthony (American) a combination of the prefix De + Anthony.
D'anthony, Danton, Dianthony

Dearborn (English) deer brook.
Dearbourn, Dearburne, Dearburn, Deerborn

Decarlos (Spanish) a combination of the prefix De + Carlos.
Dacarlos, Decarlo, Di'carlos

Decha (Tai) strong.

Decimus (Latin) tenth.

Dedrick (German) ruler of the people. See also Derek, Theodoric.
Deadrick, Deddrick, Dedericke, Dedrek, Dedreko, Dedric, Dedrix, Dedrrick, Deedrick, Diedrick, Diedrich, Dietrich, Detrick

Deems (English) judge's child.

Deion (Greek) a form of Dion.
Deione, Deionta, Deionte

Dejuan (American) a combination of the prefix De + Juan. See also Dajuan.
Dejan, Dejon, Dejuane, Dejun, Dewan, Dewaun, Devon, Dijaun, Djuan, D'Juan, Dujuan, Dujuane, D'Won

Dekel (Hebrew, Arabic) palm tree, date tree.

Dekota (Dakota) a form of Dakota.
Decoda, Dekoda, Dekodda, Dekotes

Del (English) a short form of Delbert, Delvin, Delwin.

Delaney (Irish) descendant of the challenger.
Delaine, Delainey, Delainy, Delan, Delane, Delanny, Delany

Delano (French) nut tree. (Irish) dark.
Delanio, Delayno, Dellano

Delbert (English) bright as day. See also Dalbert.
Bert, Del, Dilbert

Delfino (Latin) dolphin.
Delfine

Déli (Chinese) virtuous.

Dell (English) small valley. A short form of Udell.

Delling (Scandinavian) scintillating.

Delmar (Latin) sea.
Dalmar, Dalmer, Delmare, Delmario, Delmarr, Delmer, Delmor, Delmore

Delon (American) a form of Dillon.
Deloin, Delone, Deloni, Delonne

Delroy (French) belonging to the king. See also Elroy, Leroy.
Delray, Delree, Delroi

Delshawn (American) a combination of Del + Shawn.
Delsean, Delshon, Delsin, Delson

Delsin (Native American) he is so.
Delsy

Delton (English) a form of Dalton.
Delten, Deltyn

Delvin (English) proud friend; friend from the valley.
Dalvin, Del, Delavan, Delvian, Delvon, Delvyn, Delwin

Delwin (English) a form of Delvin.
Dalwin, Dalwyn, Del, Dellwin, Dellwyn, Delwyn, Delwynn

Deman (Dutch) man.

Demarco (Italian) a combination of the prefix De + Marco.
Damarco, Demarcco, Demarceo, Demarcio, Demarkeo, Demarkeo, Demarko, Demarquo, D'Marco

Demarcus (American) a combination of the prefix De + Marcus.
Damarcus, Damarcus, Demarces, Demarcis, Demarcius, Demarcos, Demarcuse, Demarkes, Demarkeis, Demarkos, Demarkus, Demarqus, D'Marcus

Demario (Italian) a combination of the prefix De + Mario.
Demarea, Demaree, Demareo, Demari, Demaria, Demariea, Demarion, Demarreio, Demariez, Demarious,

Demaris, Demariuz, Demarrio, Demerio, Demerrio

Demarius (American) a combination of the prefix De + Marius.

Demarquis (American) a combination of the prefix De + Marquis.
Demarques, Demarquez, Demarqui

Dembe (Luganda) peaceful.
Damba

Demetri, Demitri (Greek) short forms of Demetrius.
Dametri, Damitré, Demeter, Demetre, Demetrea, Demetriel, Demitre, Demitrie, Domotor

Demetris (Greek) a short form of Demetrius.
Demeatric, Demeatrice, Demeatris, Demetres, Demetress, Demetric, Demetrice, Demetrick, Demetrics, Demetrios, Demetrik, Demitrez, Demitries, Demitris

Demetrius (Greek) lover of the earth. Mythology: a follower of Demeter, the goddess of the harvest. See also Dimitri, Mimis, Mitsos.
Dametrius, Demeitrius, Demeterious, Demetrious, Demetri, Demetrias, Demetrio, Demetrios, Demetrious, Demetris, Demetriu, Demetrium, Demetrois, Demetruis, Demetrus, Demitrius, Demitri, Demitrias, Demitriu, Demitrius, Demitrus, Demtrus, Dimitri, Dimitrios, Dimitrius, Dmetrius, Dynek

Demichael (American) a combination of the prefix De + Michael.
Dumichael

Demond (Irish) a short form of Desmond.
Demonde, Demonds, Demone, Dumonde

Demont (French) mountain.
Démont, Demonta, Demontae, Demontay, Demontiaz, Demonte, Demontez, Demontre

Demorris (American) a combination of the prefix De + Morris.
Demoris, DeMorris, Demorris

Demos (Greek) people.
Demas, Demosthenes

Demothi (Native American) talks while walking.

Dempsey (Irish) proud.
Demp, Demps, Dempsie, Dempsy

Dempster (English) one who judges.
Demster

Denby (Scandinavian) Geography: a Danish village.
Danby, Den, Denbey, Denney, Dennie, Denny

Denham (English) village in the valley.

Denholm (Scottish) Geography: a town in Scotland.

Denis (Greek) a form of Dennis.
Denise, Deniz

Denley (English) meadow; valley.
Denlie, Denly

Denman (English) man from the valley.

Dennis (Greek) Mythology: a follower of Dionysus, the god of wine. See also Dion, Nicho.
Den, Dénes, Denies, Denis, Deniz, Dennes, Dennet, Dennez, Denny, Dennys, Denya, Denys, Deon, Dinis

Dennison (English) son of Dennis. See also Dyson, Tennyson.
Den, Denison, Denisson, Dennyson

Denny (Greek) a familiar form of Dennis.
Den, Denney, Dennie, Dery

Denton (English) happy home.
Dent, Denten, Dentin

Denver (English) green valley. Geography: the capital of Colorado.

Denzel (Cornish) a form of Denzil.
Danzel, Danzell, Dennzel, Denzal, Denzale, Denzall, Denzell, Denzelle, Denzle, Denzsel

Denzell (Cornish) Geography: a location in Cornwall, England.
Dennzil, Dennzyl, Denzel, Denziel, Denzil, Denzill, Denzyel, Denzyl, Donzell

Deon (Greek) a form of Dennis. See also Dion.
Deion, Deone, Deonn, Deonno

Deontae (American) a combination of the prefix De + Dontae.
Deonta, Deontai, Deontay, Deontaye, Deonte, Deonté, Deontea, Deonteya, Deontia, Deontre, Dionte

Deonte, Deonté (American) forms of Deontae.
D'Ante, Deante, Deontée, Deontie

Deontre (American) forms of Deonte.
Deontrae, Deontrais, Deontray, Deontre, Deontrez, Deontreze, Deontrus

Dequan (American) a combination of the prefix De + Quan.
Dequain, Dequane, Dequann, Dequante, Dequantez, Dequantis, Dequaun, Dequavius, Dequawn, Dequian, Dequin, Dequine, Dequinn, Dequion, Dequoin, Dequon, Dequan, Dequone

Dereck, Derick (German) forms of Derek.
Dereke, Dericka, Derico, Deriek, Derique, Deryck, Deryk, Deryke, Detrek

Derek (German) a short form of Theodoric. See also Dedrick, Dirk.
Darek, Darick, Darrick, Derak, Dereck, Derele, Deric, Derick, Derk, Derke, Derrek, Derrick, Deryek

Dermot (Irish) free from envy. (English) free. (Hebrew) a short form of Jeremiah. See also Kermit.
Der, Dermod, Dermott, Diarmid, Diarmuid

Deron (Hebrew) bird; freedom. (American) a combination of the prefix De + Ron.
Daaron, Daron, Da-Ron, Darone, Darron, Dayron, Deron, Deronn, Deronne, Derrin, Derrion, Derron,

Deronn, Derronne, Derryn, Diron, Duron, Durron, Dyron

Deror (Hebrew) lover of freedom.
Derori, Derorie

Derek (German) a form of Derek.
Derec, Derreck

Derrell (French) a form of Darrell.
Derel, Derele, Derell, Derelle, Derrel, Dérrell, Derriel, Derril, Derrill, Deryl, Deryll

Derren (Irish, English) a form of Darren.
Deren, Derran, Derraun, Derreon, Derrian, Derrien, Derrin, Derrion, Derron, Derryn, Deryan, Deryn, Deryon

Derrick (German) ruler of the people. A form of Derek.
Derric, Derrik, Derryck, Derryk

Derry (Irish) redhead. Geography: a city in Northern Ireland.
Darrie, Darry, Derri, Derrie, Derrye, Dery

Derryl (French) a form of Darryl.
Deryl, Deryll

Derward (English) deer keeper.

Derwin (English) a form of Darwin.
Derwyn

Desean (American) a combination of the prefix De + Sean.
Dasean, D'Sean, Dusean

Deshane (American) a combination of the prefix De + Shane.
Deshan, Deshayne

Deshaun (American) a combination of the prefix De + Shaun.
Deshan, Deshane, Desharn, Deshaon, Deshaune, Dshaun, D'Shaun, Dushaun

Deshawn (American) a combination of the prefix De + Shawn.
Dashawn, Dashaun, Deshauwn, Deshavan, Deshawon, Deshon, D'Shawn, D'Shaun, Dushan, Dushawn

Deshea (American) a combination of the prefix De + Shea.
Deshay

Déshi (Chinese) virtuous.

Deshon (American) a form of Deshawn.
Deshondre, Deshone, Deshonn, Deshonte, Deshun, Deshunn

Desiderio (Spanish) desired.

Desmond (Irish) from south Munster.
Demond, Des, Desi, Desimon, Desman, Desmand, Desmane, Desmen, Desmine, Desmon, Desmound, Desmund, Desmyn, Dezmon, Dezmond

Destin (French) destiny, fate.
Destan, Desten, Destine, Deston, Destry, Destyn

Destry (American) a form of Destin.
Destrey, Destrie

Detrick (German) a form of Dedrick.
Detric, Detri, Detrich, Detrik, Detrix

Devan (Irish) a form of Devin.
Devaan, Devain, Devane, Devann, Devean, Devnn, Divan

Devante (American) a combination of Devan + the suffix Te.
Devanta, Devantae, Devantay, Devanté, Devantée, Devantez, Devanty, Devaughnae, Devaughnte, Devaunte, Deventae, Deventay, Devente, Divante

Devaughn (American) a form of Devin.
Devaugh, Devaun

Devayne (American) a form of Dewayne.
Devain, Devaine, Devan, Devane, Devayn, Devein, Deveion

Deven (Hindi) for God. (Irish) a form of Devin.
Deaven, Deiven, Devein, Deveon, Deven, Diven

Deverell (English) riverbank.

Devin (Irish) poet.
Deavin, Deivin, Dev, Devan, Devaughn, Deven, Devlyn, Devon, Devvin, Devy, Devyn, Dyvon

Devine (Latin) divine. (Irish) ox.
Davon, Deviin, Devon, Devyn, Devyne, Dewine

Devlin (Irish) brave, fierce.
Dev, Devlan, Devland, Devlen, Devlon, Devlyn

Devon (Irish) a form of Devin.
Deavon, Deivon, Deivone, Deivonne, Deveon, Deveone, Devion, Deveon, Devohn, Devonae, Devone, Devoni, Devonio, Devonn, Devonne, Devontaine, Devonn, Devonne, Devon, Dewone, Divon, Diuon

Devonta (American) a combination of Devon + the suffix Ta.
Deveonta, Devonnta, Devonntae, Devontae, Devontai, Devontay, Devontaye

Devonte (American) a combination of Devon + the suffix Te.
Deveonte, Devionte, Devonté, Devontae, Devonti, Devontia, Devontre

Devyn (Irish) a form of Devin.
Deryin, Derynn, Deryyne

Dewayne (Irish) a combination of the prefix De + Wayne.
(American) a combination of Dwayne.
Dewwayne, Dewayne, Dewain, Dewaine, Dewan, Dewane, Dewaun, Dewaune, Dewayen, Dewean, Dewon, Dewune

Dewei (Chinese) highly virtuous.

Dewey (Welsh) prized.
Deu, Dewi, Dewie

DeWitt (Flemish) blond.
Dewitt, Dwight, Wit

Dexter (Latin) dexterous, adroit.
(English) fabric dyer.
Daxter, Decca, Deck, Decka, Dekka, Dex, Dextar, Dextor, Dextrel, Dextron

Dezmon, Dezmond (Irish) forms of Desmond.
Dezman, Dezmand, Dezmen, Dezmin

Diamond (English) brilliant gem; bright guardian.
Diaman, Diamanta, Diamante, Diamend, Diamenn, Diamont, Diamonta, Diamonte, Diamund, Dimond, Dimonta, Diamonte, Dimonte

Dick (German) a short form of Frederick, Richard.
Dic, Dicken, Dickens, Dicky, Dik

Dickson (English) son of Dick.
Dickenson, Dickerson, Dikerson, Dikson

Dickran (Armenian) History: an ancient Armenian king.
Dicran, Dikran

Didi (Hebrew) a familiar form of Jedidiah, Yedidyah.

Diedrich (German) a form of Dedrick, Dietrich.
Didrich, Didrick, Didrik, Diederick

Didier (French) desired, longed for.

Diego (Spanish) a form of Jacob, James.
Iago, Diaz, Jago

Dieter (German) army of the people.
Deiter

Dietbald (German) a form of Theobald.
Dietbalt, Dietbolt

Dietrich (German) a form of Dedrick.
Dietirick, Deitrick, Deke, Diedrich, Dietrick, Dierck, Dieter, Dieterich, Dieterick, Dietz

Digby (Irish) ditch town; dike town.

Dillan (Irish) a form of Dillon.
Dilan, Dillian, Dilun, Dilyan

Dillon (Irish) loyal, faithful. See also Dylan.
Daylon, Delon, Dil, Dill, Dillan, Dillen,

Dillie, Dillin, Dillion, Dilly, Dillyn, Dilon, Dilyn, Dilynn

Dilwyn (Welsh) shady place.
Dillwyn

Dima (Russian) a familiar form of Vladimir.
Dimka

Dimitri (Russian) a form of Demetrius.
Dimetra, Dimetri, Dimetric, Dimetrie, Dimitr, Dimitric, Dimitrie, Dimitrik, Dimitris, Dimitry, Dimmy, Dmitri, Dymitr, Dymitry

Dimitrios (Greek) a form of Demetrius.
Dhimitrios, Dimitrius, Dimos, Dmitrios

Dimitrius (Greek) a form of Demetrius.
Dimetrius, Dimitrias, Dimitrios, Dimitrious, Dmitrius

Dinh (Vietnamese) calm, peaceful.
Din

Dingbang (Chinese) protector of the country.

Dino (German) little sword. (Italian) a form of Dean.
Deano

Dinos (Greek) a familiar form of Constantine, Konstantin.

Dinsmore (Irish) fortified hill.
Dinnie, Dinny, Dinse

Diogenes (Greek) honest. History: an ancient philosopher who searched with a lantern in daylight for an honest man.
Diogenese

Dion (Greek) a short form of Dennis, Dionysus.
Deion, Deon, Dio, Dione, Dionigi, Dionis, Dionn, Dionne, Diontae, Dionte, Diontray

Dionte (American) a form of Deontae.
Diante, Dionta, Diontae, Diontay, Diontaye, Dionté, Diontea

Dionysus (Greek) celebration. Mythology: the god of wine.
Dion, Dionesios, Dioricio, Dionisio, Dionisios, Dionusios, Dionysios, Dionysius, Dunixi

Diquan (American) a combination of the prefix Di + Quan.
Diqawan, Diqawn, Diquane

Dirk (German) a short form of Derek, Theodoric.
Derk, Dirck, Dirke, Durc, Durk, Dyrk

Dixon (English) son of Dick.
Dickson, Dix

Doane (English) low, rolling hills.
Doan

Dob (English) a familiar form of Robert.
Dobie

Dobry (Polish) good.

Doherty (Irish) harmful.
Docherty, Dougherty, Douherty

Dolan (Irish) dark haired.
Dolin, Dolyn

Dolf, Dolph (German) short forms of Adolf, Adolph, Rudolf, Rudolph.
Dolfe, Dolfi, Dolphe, Dolphus

Dom (Latin) a short form of Dominic.
Dome, Domó

Domenic (Latin) an alternate form of Dominic.
Domanick, Domenick

Domenico (Italian) a form of Dominic.
Domenic, Domicio, Dominico, Menico

Domingo (Spanish) born on Sunday. See also Mingo.
Demingo, Domingos

Dominic (Latin) belonging to the Lord. See also Chuminga.
Deco, Demenico, Dom, Domanic, Domeka, Domenic, Domenico, Domini, Domini, Dominik, Dominique, Dominitric, Dominy, Domminic, Domnenique, Domokos, Domonic, Nick

Dominick (Latin) a form of Dominic.
Domiku, Domineck, Dominick, Dominicke, Dominiek, Dominik, Dominnick, Dominyck, Domminick, Dommonick, Domnick, Domokos, Domonick, Donek, Dumin

Dominik (Latin) an alternate form of Dominic.
Domenik, Dominiko, Dominyk, Dominik

Dominique (French) a form of Dominic.
Domeniq, Domeniqu, Domenique, Domenqe, Dominiqu, Dominque, Dominiqueia, Dominenique, Dominique, Domoniqu, Domonique, Domonique

Domokos (Hungarian) a form of Dominic.
Dedo, Dome, Domek, Domok, Domonkos

Don (Scottish) a short form of Donald. See also Kona.
Donn

Donahue (Irish) dark warrior.
Donohoe, Donohue

Donal (Irish) a form of Donald.

Donald (Scottish) world leader; proud ruler. See also Bohdan, Tauno.
Don, Donal, Dónal, Donaldo, Donall, Donalt, Donát, Donaugh, Donnie

Donatien (French) gift.
Donathan, Donathon

Donato (Italian) gift.
Dodek, Donatello, Donati, Donatien, Donatus

Donavan (Irish) a form of Donovan.
Donaven, Donavin, Donavon, Donavyn

Dondre (French) a form of Deandre.
Dondra, Dondrae, Dondray, Dondré, Dondrea

Dong (Vietnamese) easterner.
Duong

Donkor (Akan) humble.

Dmitri (Russian) a form of Dimitri.
Dmetriy, Dmitiri, Dmitri, Dmitrik, Dmitriy

Donnell (Irish) brave; dark.
Doneal, Donel, Donele, Donell, Donelle, Donnel, Donnele, Donnelly, Doniel, Donyel, Donyell

Donnelly (Irish) a form of Donnell.
Donelly, Donlee, Donley

Donnie, Donny (Irish) familiar forms of Donald.

Donovan (Irish) dark warrior.
Dohnovan, Donavan, Donavan, Donevon, Donivan, Donnivan, Donnovan, Donnoven, Donoven, Donovin, Donovon, Donvan

Dontae, Donté (American) forms of Dante.
Donta, Dontai, Dontao, Dontate, Dontavius, Dontavius, Dontay, Dontaye, Dontea, Dontee, Dontez

Dontrell (American) a form of Dantrell.
Dontral, Dontrall, Dontray, Dontre, Dontreal, Dontrel, Dontrelle, Dontriel, Dontriell

Donzell (Cornish) a form of Denzell.
Donzeil, Donzel, Donzelle, Donzello

Dooley (Irish) dark hero.
Dooly

Dor (Hebrew) generation.

Doran (Greek, Hebrew) gift. (Irish) stranger; exile.
Dore, Dorin, Dorran, Doren, Dorn, Dory

Dorian (Greek) from Doris, Greece. See also Isidore.
Dore, Dorey, Dorie, Dorien, Dorin, Dorion, Doryan, Doron, Dorrian,

Dorrien, Dorrin, Dorrion, Dorron, Dorryen, Dory

Dotan (Hebrew) law.
Dothan

Doug (Scottish) a short form of Dougal, Douglas.
Dougie, Dougy; Dugey; Dugie, Dugy

Dougal (Scottish) dark stranger. See also Doyle.
Doug, Dougall, Dugal, Dugald, Dugall, Dughall

Douglas (Scottish) dark river, dark stream. See also Koukalaka.
Doug, Douglass, Dougles; Dugald, Dughlas

Dov (Yiddish) bear. (Hebrew) a familiar form of David.
David, Dovidas, Dovid

Dovev (Hebrew) whisper.

Dow (Irish) dark haired.

Doyle (Irish) a form of Dougal.
Doy, Doyal, Doyel

Drago (Italian) a form of Drake.

Drake (English) dragon; owner of the inn with the dragon trademark.
Drago

Draper (English) fabric maker.
Dray, Drapyr

Draven (American) a combination of the letter D + Raven.
Dravian, Dravin, Dravion, Dravon, Dravone, Dravyn, Drayven, Drevon

Dreng (Norwegian) hired hand; brave.

Dreshawn (American) a combination of Drew + Shawn.
Dreshaun, Dreshon, Dreshown

Drevon (American) a form of Draven.
Drevan, Drevaun, Dreven, Drevin, Drevion, Drevone

Drew (Welsh) wise. (English) a short form of Andrew.
Drewe, Dru

Dru (English) a form of Drew.
Druan, Drud, Drue, Drugi, Drui

Drummond (Scottish) druid's mountain.
Drummund, Drumond, Drumund

Drury (French) loving. Geography: Drury Lane is a street in London's theater district.

Dryden (English) dry valley.
Dry

Duane (Irish) a form of Dwayne.
Denne, Duain, Duaine, Duana

Duarte (Portuguese) rich guard. See also Edward.

Duc (Vietnamese) moral.
Duoc, Duy

Dudd (English) a short form of Dudley.
Dud, Dudde, Duddy

Dudley (English) common field.
Dudd, Dudly

Duer (Scottish) heroic.

Duff (Scottish) dark.
Duffey, Duffie, Duffy

Dugan (Irish) dark.
Doogan, Dougan, Douggan, Duggan

Duke (French) leader; duke.
Dukey, Dukie, Duky

Dukker (Gypsy) fortuneteller.

Dulani (Ngumi) cutting.

Dumaka (Ibo) helping hand.

Duman (Turkish) misty, smoky.

Duncan (Scottish) brown warrior. Literature: King Duncan was Macbeth's victim in Shakespeare's play *Macbeth*.
Dunc, Dunn

Dunham (Scottish) brown.

Dunixi (Basque) a form of Dionysus.

Dunley (English) hilly meadow.

Dunlop (Scottish) muddy hill.

Dunmore (Scottish) fortress on the hill.

Dunn (Scottish) a short form of Duncan.
Dun, Dune, Dunne

Dunstan (English) brownstone fortress.
Dun, Dunston

Dunton (English) hill town.

Dur (Hebrew) stacked up. (English) a short form of Durwin.

Durand (Latin) a form of Durant.

Durant (Latin) enduring.
Duran, Durance, Durand, Durante, Durontae, Durrant

Durell (Scottish, English) king's doorkeeper. See also Dorrell.
Durel, Durial, Durrel, Durrell, Durrelle

Durko (Czech) a form of George.

Durriken (Gypsy) fortuneteller.

Durril (Gypsy) gooseberry.
Durrel, Durrell

Durward (English) gatekeeper.
Du, Ward

Durwin (English) a form of Darwin.

Dushawn (American) a combination of the prefix Du + Shawn.
Dusan, Dusean, Dushan, Dushane, Dushaun, Dushon, Dushun

Dustin (German) valiant fighter. (English) brown rock quarry.
Dust, Dustain, Dustan, Dusten, Dustie, Dustine, Dustion, Duston, Dusty, Dustyn, Dustynn

Dusty (English) a familiar form of Dustin.
Dustyn (English) a form of Dustin.

Dutch (Dutch) from the Netherlands; from Germany.

Duval (French) a combination of the prefix Du + Val.
Duvall, Duveuil

Dwaun (American) a form of Dajuan.
Dwan, Dwaun, Dwaunn, Dwon, Dwunn

Dwayne (Irish) dark. See also Dewayne.
Dawayne, Dawyne, Duane, Duwain, Duvan, Duwane, Duwayn, Duwayne, Dwain, Dwaine, Dwan, Dwane, Dwyane, Dywan, Dywane, Dywayne, Dywone

Dwight (English) a form of DeWitt.

Dyami (Native American) soaring eagle.

Dyer (English) fabric dyer.

Dyke (English) dike; ditch.
Dike

Dylan (Welsh) sea. See also Dillon.
Dylane, Dylann, Dylen, Dylian, Dylin, Dyllan, Dyllen, Dyllian, Dyllin, Dyllyn, Dylon, Dylyn

Dylon (Welsh) a form of Dylan.
Dyllion, Dyllon

Dyre (Norwegian) dear heart.

Dyson (English) a short form of Dennison.
Dysen, Dysonn

Ea (Irish) a form of Hugh.

Eachan (Irish) horseman.

Eagan (Irish) very mighty.
Egan, Egon

Eamon (Irish) a form of Edmond,
Edmund.
Aimon, Eammon, Eamonn

Ean (English) a form of Ian.
*Eaen, Eann, Eayon, Eion, Eyan,
Eyon*

Earl (Irish) pledge. (English)
nobleman.
*Airle, Earld, Earle, Earlie, Early,
Eorl, Erl, Erle, Errol*

Earnest (English) a form of Ernest.
Earn, Earnesto, Earnie, Ernest

Easton (English) eastern town.
Eason, Easten, Eastin, Eastton

Eaton (English) estate on the river.
Eatton, Eiton, Eyton

Eb (Hebrew) a short form of
Ebenezer.
Ebb, Ebbie, Ebby

Eben (Hebrew) rock.
Eban, Ebin, Ebon

Ebenezer (Hebrew) foundation stone.
Literature: Ebenezer Scrooge is a
miserly character in Charles
Dickens's *A Christmas Carol*.
*Eb, Ebbaneza, Eben, Ebeneezer,
Ebeneezer, Ebenezar, Eveneser*

Eberhard (German) courageous as a
boar. See also Everett.
*Eber, Ebere, Eberardo, Eberhardt, Evard,
Everard, Everardo, Everhardt, Everhart*

Ebner (English) a form of Abner.

Ebo (Fante) born on Tuesday.

Ed (English) a short form of Edgar,
Edmund, Edsel, Edward.
Edd

Edan (Scottish) fire.

Edbert (English) wealthy; bright.
Ediberto

Eddie (English) a familiar form of
Edgar, Edsel, Edward.
Eddee, Eddy Edi, Edie

Eddy (English) a form of Eddie.
Eddye, Edy

Edel (German) noble.
Adel, Edell, Edelmar, Edelweiss

Eden (Hebrew) delightful. Bible: the
garden that was first home to Adam
and Eve.
*Eaden, Eadin, Edan, Edenson, Edin,
Edyn, Eiden*

Eder (Hebrew) flock.
Ederick, Edir

Edgar (English) successful spearman.
See also Garek, Gerik, Medgar.
Ed, Eddie, Edek, Edgard, Edgardo, Edgars

Edgardo (Spanish) a form of Edgar.

Edison (English) son of Edward.
Edisen, Edisen, Edson

Edmond (English) a form of Edmund.
*Eamon, Edmon, Edmonde, Edmondo,
Edmondson, Esmond*

Edmund (English) prosperous protec-
tor.
*Eadmund, Eamon, Edmand, Edmaund,
Edmond, Edmun, Edmunds*

Edmundo (Spanish) a form of
Edmund.
Edmando, Mundo

Edo (Czech) a form of Edward.

Edoardo (Italian) a form of Edward.

Edorta (Basque) a form of Edward.

Edouard (French) a form of Edward.
Édoard, Édoard

Edric (English) prosperous ruler.
*Eddric, Eddrick, Ederick, Edrek, Edrice,
Edrick, Edrico*

Edsel (English) rich man's house.
Ed, Eddie, Edsell

Edson (English) a short form of
Edison.
Eddson, Edsen

Eduardo (Spanish) a form of Edward.
Estuardo, Estuardo

Edur (Basque) snow.

Edward (English) prosperous guardian.
See also Audie, Duarte, Ekewaka,
Ned, Ted, Teddy.
*Ed, Eddie, Edik, Edko, Edo, Edoardo,
Edorta, Edouard, Eduard, Eduardo,
Edus, Edvard, Edvardo, Edvardo,
Edwards, Edwy, Edzio, Ekewaka, Elzio,
Ewart*

Edwin (English) prosperous friend. See
also Ned, Ted.
*Eadwinn, Edik, Edlin, Edwino, Edwan,
Edwen, Edwon, Edwyn*

Efrain (Hebrew) fruitful.
*Efran, Efrane, Efrayin, Efren, Efrian,
Eifraine*

Efrat (Hebrew) honored.

Efrem (Hebrew) a short form of Ephraim.
Efe, Efraim, Efrim, Efrum

Efren (Hebrew) a form of Efrain, Ephraim.

Egan (Irish) ardent, fiery.
Egann, Egen, Egon

Egbert (English) bright sword. See also Bert, Bertie.

Egerton (English) Edgar's town.
Edgarton, Edgartown, Edgerton, Egeton

Egil (Norwegian) awe inspiring.
Eigil

Eginhard (German) power of the sword.
Eginhardt, Einhard, Einhardt, Enno

Egon (German) formidable.

Egor (Russian) a form of George. See also Igor, Yegor.

Ehren (German) honorable.

Eikki (Finnish) ever powerful.

Einar (Scandinavian) individualist.
Ejnar, Inar

Eion (Irish) a form of Ean, Ian.
Eann, Eian, Ein, Eine, Einn

Eitan (Hebrew) a form of Ethan.
Eita, Eithan, Eiton

Ejau (Ateso) we have received.

Ekewaka (Hawaiian) a form of Edward.

Ekon (Nigerian) strong.

Elam (Hebrew) highlands.

Elan (Hebrew) tree. (Native American) friendly.
Elann

Elbert (English) a form of Albert.
Elberto

Elchanan (Hebrew) a form of John.
Elchan, Elchonon, Elhanan, Elhannan

Elden (English) a form of Alden, Aldous.
Eldan, Eldin

Elder (English) dweller near the elder trees.

Eldon (English) holy hill.

Eldred (English) a form of Aldred.
Eldrid

Eldridge (English) a form of Aldrich.
El, Eldred, Eldredge, Eldrege, Eldrid, Eldrige, Elric

Eldwin (English) a form of Aldwin.
Eldvinn, Eldwynn, Elduynn

Eleazar (Hebrew) God has helped. See also Lazarus.
Elazar, Elazaro, Eleasar, Eléazar, Eliazar, Eliezer

Elek (Hungarian) a form of Alec, Alex.
Elec, Elic, Elik

Elger (German) a form of Alger.
Elger, Ellgar, Ellger

Elgin (English) noble; white.
Elgan, Elgen

Eli (Hebrew) uplifted. A short form of Elijah, Elisha. Bible: the high priest

who trained the prophet Samuel. See also Elliot.
Elie, Elier, Ellie, Eloi, Eloy, Ely

Elia (Zuni) a short form of Elijah.
Eliah, Elio, Eliya, Elya

Elian (English) a form of Elijah. See also Trevelyan.
Elion

Elias (Greek) a form of Elijah.
Elia, Eliasz, Elice, Eliyas, Ellias, Ellie, Ellis, Elyas, Elyes

Eliazar (Hebrew) a form of Eleazar.
Eliasar, Eliazer, Elizar, Elizardo

Elie (Hebrew) a form of Eli.

Eliezer (Hebrew) a form of Eleazar.
Elieser

Elihu (Hebrew) a short form of Eliyahu.
Elih, Eliu, Ellihu

Elijah (Hebrew) a form of Eliyahu. Bible: a Hebrew prophet. See also Eli, Elisha, Elliot, Ilias, Ilya.
El, Elia, Elian, Elias, Elija, Elijha, Elijiah, Elijio, Elijuah, Elijuo, Elisjsha, Eliya, Eliyah, Ellis

Elika (Hawaiian) a form of Eric.

Eliseo (Hebrew) a form of Elisha.
Elisee, Elisée, Elisei, Elisiah, Elisio

Elisha (Hebrew) God is my salvation. Bible: a Hebrew prophet, successor to Elijah. See also Eli, Elijah.
Elijsha, Eliseo, Elish, Elishah, Elisher, Elishia, Elishua, Elysha, Lisha

Eliyahu (Hebrew) the Lord is my God.
Eliyahou, Elihu

Elkan (Hebrew) God is jealous.
Elkana, Elkanah, Elkin, Elkins

Elki (Moquelumnan) hanging over the top.

Elard (German) sacred; brave.
Allard, Ellerd

Ellery (English) from a surname derived from the name Hilary.
Ellarj, Ellerey

Elliot, Elliott (English) forms of Eli, Elijah.
Eliot, Eliott, Elliott, Eliud, Eliut, Elyot, Elyott

Ellis (English) a form of Elias.
Elis

Ellison (English) son of Ellis.
Elison, Ellson, Ellyson, Elson

Ellsworth (English) nobleman's estate.
Ellsworth, Elsworth

Elman (German) like an elm tree.
Ellman

Elmer (English) noble; famous.
Aylmer, Elemér, Ellmer, Elmir, Elmo

Elmo (Greek) lovable, friendly. (Latin) a familiar form of Anselm. (English) a form of Elmer.

Elmore (English) moor where the elm trees grow.

Elonzo (Spanish) a form of Alonzo.
Elon, Elon, Elonso

Eloy (Latin) chosen.
Eloi

Elroy (French) a form of Delroy, Leroy.
Elroi

Elrad (Hebrew) God rules.
Rad, Radd

Elsdon (English) nobleman's hill.

Elston (English) noble's town.
Ellston

Elsu (Native American) swooping, soaring falcon.

Elsworth (English) noble's estate.

Elton (English) old town.
Alton, Eldon, Ellton, Elthon, Eltonia

Elvern (Latin) a form of Alvern.
Elver, Elverne

Elvin (English) a form of Alvin.
El, Elvyn, Elwin, Elwyn, Elwynn

Elvio (Spanish) light skinned; blond.

Elvis (Scandinavian) wise.
El, Elviz, Elvys

Elvy (English) elfin warrior.

Elwell (English) old well.

Elwood (English) old forest. See also Wood.
Wood, Woody.

Ely (Hebrew) a form of Eli. Geography: a region of England with extensive drained fens.
Elya, Elyie

Eman (Czech) a form of Emmanuel.
Emaney, Emani

Emanuel (Hebrew) a form of Emmanuel.
Emaniel, Emannual, Emannuel, Emanual, Emanuale, Emmanuael, Emanuell, Emanuele, Emanuelle

Emerson (German, English) son of Emery.
Emmerson, Emreson

Emery (German) industrious leader.
Aimery, Emari, Emarri, Emeri, Emerich, Emerio, Emmerich, Emmeric, Emmery, Emmo, Emory, Emrik, Emry, Imre, Imrich

Emil (Latin) flatterer. (German) industrious. See also Milko, Milo.
Aymil, Emiel, Emile, Emilek, Emiliano, Emilio, Emill, Emils, Emilyan, Emlyn

Émile, Emile (French) a form of Emil.
Emiel, Emile, Emile

Emiliano (Italian) a form of Emil.
Emilian, Emilion

Emilien (Latin) friendly; industrious.

Emilio (Italian, Spanish) a form of Emil.
Emielio, Emileo, Emilio, Emilios, Emillio

Emlyn (Welsh) waterfall.
Emelen, Emlen, Emlin

Emmanuel (Hebrew) God is with us. See also Immanuel, Maco, Mango, Manuel.
Eman, Emanuel, Emanuell, Emek, Emmahnuel, Emmaniel, Emmanuael, Emmanuele, Emmanual, Emmanuele, Emmannuel, Emmanuil, Emmanuell, Emmanule, Emmanuele, Emmanuele, Emmanuil, Emmanuwel

Emmett (German) industrious; strong. (English) ant. History: Robert Emmett was an Irish patriot. *Em, Emet, Emett, Emitt, Emmet, Emmette, Emmitt, Emmot, Emmott, Emmy*

Emmitt (German, English) a form of Emmett. *Emmit*

Emory (German) a form of Emery. *Amory, Emmory, Emorye*

Emre (Turkish) brother.

Emrick (German) a form of Emery. *Emeric, Emerick, Emric, Emrique, Emryk*

Enapay (Sioux) brave appearance; he appears.

Endre (Hungarian) a form of Andrew. *Ender*

Eneas (Greek) a form of Aeneas. *Eneias, Enné*

Engelbert (German) bright as an angel. See also Ingelbert. *Bert, Englebert*

Enli (Dene) that dog over there.

Ennis (Greek) mine. (Scottish) a form of Angus. *Eni, Enni*

Enoch (Hebrew) dedicated, consecrated. Bible: the father of Methuselah. *Enoc, Enock, Enok*

Enos (Hebrew) man. *Enosh*

Enric (Romanian) a form of Henry. *Enrica*

Enrick (Spanish) a form of Henry. *Enricky*

Enrico (Italian) a form of Henry. *Enzio, Enzo, Rico*

Enrikos (Greek) a form of Henry.

Enrique (Spanish) a form of Henry. See also Quiqui. *Enrigué, Enriqué, Enriquez, Enrique*

Enver (Turkish) bright; handsome.

Enyeto (Native American) walks like a bear.

Enzi (Swahili) powerful.

Eoin (Welsh) a form of Evan.

Ephraim (Hebrew) fruitful. Bible: the second son of Joseph. *Efraim, Efrayim, Efrem, Efren, Ephraen, Ephrain, Ephram, Ephrem, Ephriam*

Erasmus (Greek) lovable. *Erasme, Erasmo, Rasmus*

Erastus (Greek) beloved. *Eraste, Erastious, Ras, Rastus*

Erbert (German) a short form of Herbert. *Ebert, Erberto*

Ercole (Italian) splendid gift.

Erek (Scandinavian) a form of Eric. *Erec*

Erhard (German) strong; resolute. *Erhardt, Erhart*

Eriberto (Italian) a form of Herbert. *Erberto, Heriberto*

Eric (Scandinavian) ruler of all. (English) brave ruler. (German) a short form of Frederick. History: Eric the Red was a Norwegian explorer who founded Greenland's first colony. *Aric, Ehrich, Eilka, Erek, Éric, Erica, Erica, Erich, Erick, Erico, Erik, Erikur, Eric, Eryc, Rick*

Erich (Czech, German) a form of Eric.

Erick (English) a form of Eric. *Errick, Eryk*

Erickson (English) son of Eric. *Erickzon, Erics, Ericson, Ericsson, Erikson, Erikzzon, Erigson*

Erik (Scandinavian) a form of Eric. *Erek, Erike, Erikeur, Errick, Errik, Eric, Erike, Eriks, Eryk*

Erikur (Icelandic) a form of Eric, Erik.

Erin (Irish) peaceful. History: an ancient name for Ireland. *Erine, Erinn, Erino, Eron, Errin, Eryn, Erym*

Erland (English) nobleman's land. *Erlend*

Erling (English) nobleman's son.

Ermanno (Italian) a form of Herman. *Erman*

Ermano (Spanish) a form of Herman. *Ermin, Ermine, Erminio, Ermon*

Ernest (English) earnest, sincere. See also Arno.
Earnest, Ernestino, Ernesto, Ernestus, Ernie, Erno, Ernst

Ernesto (Spanish) a form of Ernest.
Ernester, Neto

Ernie (English) a familiar form of Ernest.
Earnie, Erney, Erny

Erno (Hungarian) a form of Ernest.
Ernö

Ernst (German) a form of Ernest.
Erns

Erol (Turkish) strong, courageous.
Eroll

Eron (Irish) a form of Erin.
Erran, Erren, Errion, Erron

Errando (Basque) bold.

Errol (Latin) wanderer. (English) a form of Earl.
Erol, Erold, Eroll, Eryl

Erroman (Basque) from Rome.

Erskine (Scottish) high cliff. (English) from Ireland.
Ersin, Erskin, Kinny

Ervine (English) a form of Irving.
Erv, Ervin, Ervince, Erving, Ervins

Ervin, Erwin (English) sea friend. Forms of Irving, Irwin.
Earvin, Erv, Erven, Ervyn, Erwan, Erwinek, Erwinn, Erwyn, Erwynn

Esau (Hebrew) rough; hairy; Bible: Jacob's twin brother.
Esaw

Esequiel (Hebrew) a form of Ezekiel.

Eshkol (Hebrew) grape clusters.

Eskil (Norwegian) god vessel.

Esmond (English) rich protector.

Espen (Danish) bear of the gods.

Essien (Ochi) sixth-born son.

Este (Italian) east.
Estes

Estéban (Spanish) a form of Stephen.
Estabon, Esteben, Estefan, Estefano, Estefen, Estephan, Estephen

Estebe (Basque) a form of Stephen.

Estevan (Spanish) a form of Stephen.
Esteven, Estevon, Estiven

Estevao (Spanish) a form of Stephen.
Estevez

Ethan (Hebrew) strong; firm.
Eathan, Eathen, Eathon, Eeathen, Eitan, Etan, Ethaen, Ethe, Ethen, Ethian

Étienne (French) a form of Stephen.
Eitan, Etien, Étienn, Ettien

Ettore (Italian) steadfast.
Etor, Etore

Etu (Native American) sunny.

Euclid (Greek) intelligent. History: the founder of Euclidean geometry.

Eugen (German) a form of Eugene.

Eugene (Greek) born to nobility. See also Ewan, Gene, Gino, Iukini, Jenö, Yevgenyi, Zenda.
Eoghan, Eugen, Eugéne, Eugeni, Eugenio, Eugenius, Evgeny, Ezven

Eugenio (Spanish) a form of Eugene.

Eulises (Latin) a form of Ulysses.

Eustace (Greek) productive. (Latin) stable, calm. See also Stacey.
Eustache, Eustachius, Eustachy, Eustashe, Eustasius, Eustatius, Eustazio, Eustis, Eustiss

Evan (Irish) young warrior. (English) a form of John. See also Bevan, Owen.
Eavan, Eoin, Ev, Evaine, Evann, Evans, Even, Evens, Evin, Evon, Evyn, Ewan, Ewen

Evangelos (Greek) a form of Andrew.
Evagelos, Evaggelos, Evangelo

Evelyn (English) hazelnut.
Evelin

Everardo (German) strong as a boar.
Everado

Everett (English) a form of Eberhard.
Ev, Evered, Everet, Everette, Everhett, Everit, Everitt, Everrett, Evert, Evrett

Everley (English) boar meadow.
Everlea, Everlee

Everton (English) boar town.

Evgeny (Russian) a form of Eugene. See also Zhek.
Evgeni, Evgenij, Evgenyi

Evin (Irish) a form of Evan.
Evian, Evinn, Evins

Ewald (German) always powerful. (English) powerful lawman.

Ewan (Scottish) a form of Eugene, Evan. See also Keon.
Ewann, Euann, Ewen, Ewhen

Ewert (English) ewe herder, shepherd.
Ewart

Ewing (English) friend of the law.
Ewin, Ewynn

Exavier (Basque) a form of Xavier.
Exaviar, Exavior, Ezavier

Eyota (Native American) great.

Ezekiel (Hebrew) strength of God.
Bible: a Hebrew prophet. See also
Haskel, Zeke.
*Esequiel, Ezakeil, Ezechiel, Ezeck,
Ezekiel, Ezeckel, Ezekeial, Ezekiel,
Ezekeyial, Ezekial, Ezekielle, Ezell,
Ezequiel, Ezkiakah, Eziechiele*

Ezequiel (Hebrew) a form of Ezekiel.
Esequiel, Eziequel

Ezer (Hebrew) a form of Ezra.

Ezra (Hebrew) helper; strong. Bible: a
Jewish priest who led the Jews back
to Jerusalem.
*Esdras, Esra, Ezer, Ezera, Ezrah, Ezri,
Ezry*

Ezven (Czech) a form of Eugene.
Esven, Esvin, Ezavin, Ezavine

Faber (German) a form of Fabian.

Fabian (Latin) bean grower.
*Fabain, Fabayan, Fabe, Fabein, Fabek,
Fabeon, Faber, Fabert, Fabi, Fabiano,
Fabien, Fabin, Fabio, Fabion, Fabius,*

Fabiyan, *Fabiyus, Fabyan, Fabyen,
Fabyian, Faybien*

Fabiano (Italian) a form of Fabian.
Fabianno, Fabio

Fabio (Latin) a form of Fabian.
(Italian) a short form of Fabiano.
Fabbio

Fabrizio (Italian) craftsman.
Fabrice, Fabricio, Fabrizius

Fabron (French) little blacksmith;
apprentice.
Fabre, Fabroni

Fadey (Ukrainian) a form of
Thaddeus.
*Faday, Faddei, Faddey, Faddy, Fade,
Fadeyka, Fadie, Fady*

Fadi (Arabic) redeemer.
Fadhi

Fadil (Arabic) generous.
Fadeel, Fadel

Fagan (Irish) little fiery one.
Fagin

Fahd (Arabic) lynx.
Fahaad, Fahad

Fai (Chinese) beginning.

Fairfax (English) blond.
Fair, Fax

Faisal (Arabic) decisive.
*Faisel, Faisil, Faisl, Faiyaz, Faiz, Faizal,
Faize, Faizel, Faizi, Fasel, Fasil, Faysal,
Fayzal, Fayzel*

Fakhir (Arabic) excellent.
Falhkry, Fakher

Fakih (Arabic) thinker; reader of the
Koran.

Falco (Latin) falconer.
Falcon, Falk, Falke, Falken

Falito (Italian) a familiar form of
Rafael, Raphael.

Falkner (English) trainer of falcons.
See also Falco.
*Falconer, Falconner, Faulconer, Faulconner,
Faulkner*

Fane (English) joyful, glad.
Fanes, Faniel

Faraji (Swahili) consolation.

Farid (Arabic) unique.

Faris (Arabic) horseman.
*Faraz, Fares, Farhaz, Farice, Fariez,
Farris*

Farley (English) bull meadow; sheep
meadow. See also Lee.
*Fairlay, Fairlee, Fairleigh, Fairley, Fairlie,
Far, Farlay, Farlee, Farleigh, Farlie, Farly,
Farrleigh, Farrley*

Farnell (English) fern-covered hill.
Farnall, Fernald, Fernall, Furnald

Farnham (English) field of ferns.
Farnam, Farnum, Fernham

Farnley (English) fern meadow.
*Farnlea, Farnlee, Farnleigh, Farnly,
Fernlea, Fernlee, Fernleigh, Fernley*

Faroh (Latin) a form of Pharaoh.

Farold (English) mighty traveler.

Farquhar (Scottish) dear.
Fark, Farq, Farquar, Farquarson, Farque, Farquharson, Farquy, Farqy

Farr (English) traveler.
Faer, Farran, Farren, Farrin, Farrington, Farron

Farrell (Irish) heroic; courageous.
Farrel, Farrill, Farryll, Ferrell

Farrow (English) piglet.

Farruco (Spanish) a form of Francis, Francisco.
Frascuelo

Faruq (Arabic) honest.
Farook, Farooq, Faroque, Farouk, Faruqh

Faste (Norwegian) firm.

Fath (Arabic) victor.

Fatin (Arabic) clever.

Faust (Latin) lucky, fortunate. History: the sixteenth-century German necromancer who inspired many legends.
Fausting, Faustis, Fausto, Faustus

Faustino (Italian) a form of Faust.
Feri, Ferke, Ferko

Fausto (Italian) a form of Faust.

Faustino (Italian) a form of Faust.

Favian (Latin) understanding.
Favain, Favio, Favyen

Faxon (German) long-haired.

Federico (Italian, Spanish) a form of Frederick.
Federic, Federigo, Federquito

Feivel (Yiddish) God aids.

Feliks (Russian) a form of Felix.

Felipe (Spanish) a form of Philip.
Feeleep, Felipino, Felo, Filip, Filippo, Filips, Fillp, Flip

Felippo (Italian) a form of Philip.
Felip, Filippo, Lipp, Lippo, Pip, Pippo

Felix (Latin) fortunate; happy. See also Pitin.
Fee, Felic, Félice, Feliciano, Felicio, Felike, Feliks, Felo, Félix, Felizio, Phelix

Felton (English) field town.
Felten, Feltin

Fenton (English) marshland farm.
Fen, Fennie, Fenny, Fintan, Finton

Feodor (Slavic) a form of Theodore.
Dorek, Fedar, Fedinka, Fedor, Fedya, Fyodor

Feoras (Greek) smooth rock.

Ferdinand (German) daring, adventurous. See also Hernando.
Fernando, Ferd, Ferda, Ferdie, Ferdinand, Ferdy, Ferdynand, Fernando, Nando

Ferenc (Hungarian) a form of Francis.
Feri, Ferke, Ferko

Fergus (Irish) strong; manly.
Fearghas, Fearghus, Feargus, Ferghus, Fergie, Ferguson, Fergusson

Fermin (French, Spanish) firm, strong.
Ferman, Firmin, Furman

Fernando (Spanish) a form of Ferdinand.
Ferando, Ferdinando, Ferdinand, Ferdo, Fernand, Fernandez, Fernendo

Feroz (Persian) fortunate.

Ferran (Arabic) baker.
Feran, Feron, Ferrin, Ferron

Ferrand (French) iron gray hair.
Farand, Farrand, Farrant, Fernant

Ferrell (Irish) a form of Farrell.
Ferrel, Ferrill, Ferryl

Ferris (Irish) a form of Peter.
Fares, Faris, Fariz, Farris, Farrish, Feris, Ferriss

Fico (Spanish) a familiar form of Frederick.

Fidel (Latin) faithful. History: Fidel Castro was the Cuban revolutionary who overthrew a dictatorship in 1959 and established a communist regime in Cuba.
Fidèle, Fidèle, Fidelio, Fidelis, Fidell, Fido

Field (English) a short form of Fielding.
Fields

Fielding (English) field; field worker.
Field

Fife (Scottish) from Fife, Scotland.
Fyfe

Fifi (Fante) born on Friday.
Fifis

Fil (Polish) a form of Phil.
Filipek

Filbert (English) brilliant. See also Bert.
Filberte, Filberto, Filiberto, Philbert

Filiberto (Spanish) a form of Filbert.

Filip (Greek) a form of Philip.
Filip, Filippo

Fillipp (Russian) a form of Philip.
Filip, Filipe, Filipek, Filips, Fill, Fillip, Filya

Filmore (English) famous.
Fillmore, Filmer, Fylmer, Fylmer, Philmore

Filya (Russian) a form of Philip.

Fineas (Irish) a form of Phineas.
Finneas`

Finian (Irish) light skinned; white.
Finnen, Finnian, Fionan, Fionn, Phinean

Finlay (Irish) blond-haired soldier.
Findlay, Findley, Finlea, Finlee, Finley, Finn, Finnlea, Finnley

Finn (German) from Finland. (Irish) blond haired; light skinned. A short form of Finlay. (Norwegian) from the Lapland.
Fin, Finnie, Finnis, Finny

Finnegan (Irish) light skinned; white.
Finegan

Fiorello (Italian) little flower.
Fiore

Firas (Arabic) persistent.

Firman (French) firm; strong.
Ferman, Firmin

Firth (English) woodland.

Fischel (Yiddish) a form of Phillip.

Fiske (English) fisherman.

Fitch (English) weasel, ermine.
Fitche

Fitz (English) son.
Filz

Fitzgerald (English) son of Gerald.

Fitzhugh (English) son of Hugh.
Hugh

Fitzpatrick (English) son of Patrick.

Fitzroy (Irish) son of Roy.

Flaminio (Spanish) Religion: Marcantonio Flaminio coauthored one of the most important texts of the Italian Reformation.

Flann (Irish) redhead.
Flainn, Flannan, Flannery

Flavian (Latin) blond, yellow haired.
Flavel, Flavelle, Flavien, Flavio, Flaviusz

Flavio (Italian) a form of Flavian.
Flabio, Flavious, Flavius

Fleming (English) from Denmark; from Flanders.
Flemming, Flemmyng, Flemyng

Fletcher (English) arrow featherer, arrow maker.
Flecher, Fletch

Flint (English) stream; flint stone.
Flynt

Flip (Spanish) a short form of Felipe. (American) a short form of Philip.

Florencio (Italian) a form of Florent.

Florent (French) flowering.
Florenci, Florencio, Florentin, Florentino, Florentyn, Florentz, Florinio, Florino

Florian (Latin) flowering, blooming.
Florien, Florrian, Flory, Floryan

Floyd (English) a form of Lloyd.

Flurry (English) flourishing, blooming.

Flynn (Irish) son of the red-haired man.
Flin, Flinn, Flyn

Folke (German) a form of Volker.
Folker

Foluke (Yoruba) given to God.

Foma (Bulgarian, Russian) a form of Thomas.
Fomka

Fonso (German, Italian) a short form of Alphonso.
Fonzo

Fontaine (French) fountain.

Fonzie (German) a familiar form of Alphonse.
Fons, Fonsie, Fonsy, Fonz

Forbes (Irish) prosperous.
Forbe

Ford (English) a short form of names ending in "ford."

Fordel (Gypsy) forgiving.

Forest (French) a form of Forrest.
Forestt, Foryst

Forester (English) forest guardian.
Forrester, Forrie, Forry, Forster, Foss, Foster

Forrest (French) forest; woodsman.
Forest, Forester, Forrestar, Forrester, Forrestt, Forrie

Fortino (Italian) fortunate, lucky.

Fortune (French) fortunate, lucky.
Fortun, Fortunato, Fortuné, Fortunio

Foster (Latin) a short form of Forester.

Fowler (English) trapper of wildfowl.

Fran (Latin) a short form of Francis.
Frahn

Francesco (Italian) a form of Francis.
Franta

Franchot (French) a form of Francis.

Francis (Latin) free; from France.
Religion: Saint Francis of Assisi was
the founder of the Franciscan order.
See also Farruco, Ferenc.
*Fran, France, Frances, Francesco,
Franchot, Francisco, Franciskus, Franco,
François, Frang, Frank, Franke,
Frans, Francis, Fransis, Franta, Franny,
Frants, Frantz, Frantisek, Franz, Frencis*

Francisco (Portuguese, Spanish) a
form of Francis. See also Chilo,
Cisco, Farruco, Paco, Pancho.
Franco, Fransisco, Fransysco, Frisco

Franco (Latin) a short form of Francis.
Franko

François (French) a form of Francis.
Françoise

Frank (English) a short form of Francis,
Franklin. See also Palani, Pancho.
*Franc, Franck, Franek, Frang, Franio,
Franke, Frankie, Franko*

Frankie (English) a familiar form of
Frank.
*Franckey, Franke, Frankey, Franki,
Frankly, Franqui*

Franklin (English) free landowner.
*Fran, Francklen, Francklin, Francklyn,
Françylen, Franke, Franklen,
Franklinn, Franklyn, Franquelin*

Franklyn (English) a form of Franklin.
Franklynn

Frans (Swedish) a form of Francis.
Frants

Frantisek (Czech) a form of Francis.
Franta

Franz (German) a form of Francis.
*Fransz, Frantz, Franzen, Franzie,
Franzin, Franzl, Franzy*

Fraser (French) strawberry. (English)
curly haired.
Fraizer, Frasier, Fraze, Frazer, Frazier

Frayne (French) dweller at the ash
tree. (English) stranger.
Fraine, Frayn, Frean, Freen, Freyne

Fred (German) a short form of Alfred,
Frederick, Manfred.
Fredd, Fredde, Freddo, Fredson

Freddie, **Freddy** (German) familiar
forms of Frederick.
Freddi, Freddy, Fredi, Fredy

Freddie (German) a familiar form of
Frederick.
Freddi, Freddy, Fredi, Fredy

Frederic (German) a form of Frederick.
*Frédéric, Frederik, Frederric, Fredric,
Fredrich*

Frederick (German) peaceful ruler.
See also Dick, Eric, Fico, Peleke,
Rick.
*Federico, Fico, Fred, Fredderick, Freddie,
Fredrick, Fredy, Fredek, Frederic,
Frederick, Frédérick, Frederik, Frederique,
Frederric, Fredo, Fredrick, Fredwick,
Fredryck, Fredy, Friedrich, Fritz*

Frederico (Spanish) a form of
Frederick.
Fredrico, Frederigo

Frederik (German) a form of
Frederick.
Frédérik, Frederik, Fredrik

Frederique (French) a form of
Frederick.

Fredo (Spanish) a form of Fred.

Fredrick (German) a form of
Frederick.
Fredric, Fredricka, Fredricks

Free (English) free.
*Free, Freedman, Freemin, Freemon,
Freeman, Friedman, Friedmann*

Freeman (English) free.
*Free, Freedman, Freemin, Freemon,
Freeman, Friedman, Friedmann*

Freeborn (English) child of freedom.
Free

Fremont (German) free; noble protector.

Frewin (English) free; noble friend.
Frewen

Frey (English) lord. (Scandinavian)
Mythology: the Norse god who dispenses peace and prosperity.

Frick (English) bold.

Fridolf (English) peaceful wolf.
Freydolf, Freydulf, Fridulf

Friedrich (German) a form of
Frederick.
*Fried, Friedel, Friedrich, Fridrich,
Friedrike, Friedryk, Fryderyk*

Frisco (Spanish) a short form of Francisco.

Fritz (German) a familiar form of Frederick.
Fritson, Fritts, Fritzchen, Fritzl

Frode (Norwegian) wise.

Fulbright (German) very bright.
Fulbert

Fuller (English) cloth thickener.

Fulton (English) field near town.

Funsoni (Nguni) requested.

Fyfe (Scottish) a form of Fife.
Fyffe

Fynn (Ghanaian) Geography: another name for the Offin River in Ghana.

Fyodor (Russian) a form of Theodore.

Gabby (American) a familiar form of Gabriel.
Gabbi, Gabbie, Gabi, Gabie, Gaby

Gabe (Hebrew) a short form of Gabriel.

Gabino (American) a form of Gabriel.
Gabin, Gabrino

Gábor (Hungarian) God is my strength.
Gabbo, Gabko, Gabo

Gabrial (Hebrew) a form of Gabriel.
Gabriael, Gabraiel, Gabrail, Gabreal, Gabrieal, Gabryalle

Gabriel (Hebrew) devoted to God. Bible: the angel of the Annunciation.
Gab, Gabe, Gabby, Gabino, Gabis, Gábor, Gabrell, Gabrel, Gabriell, Gabrial, Gabriell, Gabriele, Gabrielle, Gabrielli, Gabrile, Gabris, Gabryel, Gabys, Gavril, Gebereal, Ghabriel, Riel

Gabrielli (Italian) a form of Gabriel.
Gabriello

Gadi (Arabic) God is my fortune.
Gad, Gaddy, Gadiel

Gaetan (Italian) from Gaeta, a region in southern Italy.
Gaetano, Gaetono

Gage (French) pledge.
Gager, Gaige, Gaje

Gaige (French) a form of Gage.

Gair (Irish) small.
Gaer, Gear, Geir

Gaius (Latin) rejoicer. See also Cai.

Galbraith (Irish) Scotsman in Ireland.
Galbrait, Galbreath

Gale (Greek) a short form of Galen.
Gael, Gail, Gaile, Gayle

Galen (Greek) healer; calm. (Irish) little and lively.
Gaelan, Gaelen, Galin, Gaelyn, Gailen, Galan, Gale, Galeno, Galin, Galyn, Gaylen

Galeno (Spanish) illuminated child. (Greek, Irish) a form of Galen.

Gallagher (Irish) eager helper.

Galloway (Irish) Scotsman in Ireland.
Galluay, Galway

Galt (Norwegian) high ground.

Galton (English) owner of a rented estate.
Gallton

Galvin (Irish) sparrow.
Gal, Gall, Gallven, Gallvin, Galvan, Galven

Gamal (Arabic) camel. See also Jamal.
Gamall, Gamel, Gamil

Gamble (Scandinavian) old.

Gan (Chinese) daring, adventurous. (Vietnamese) near.

Gannon (Irish) light skinned, white.
Gannan, Gannen, Gannie, Ganny

Ganya (Zulu) clever.

Gar (English) a short form of Gareth, Garnett, Garrett, Garvin.
Garr

Garcia (Spanish) mighty with a spear.

Gardner (English) gardener.
Gard, Gardener, Gardie, Gardiner, Gardy

Garek (Polish) a form of Edgar.

Garen (English) a form of Garry.
Garan, Garen, Garin, Garion, Garon, Garyn, Garyon

Gareth (Welsh) gentle.
Gar, Garith, Gareth, Garrith, Garth, Garyth

Garett (Irish) a form of Garrett. Gared, Garet, Garette, Garhett, Garit, Garitt

Garfield (English) field of spears; battlefield.

Garland (French) wreath of flowers; prize. (English) land of spears; battleground. Garlan, Garlen, Garlan, Garlund, Garlyn

Garman (English) spearman. Garmann, Garman

Garner (French) army guard, sentry. Garnier

Garnett (Latin) pomegranate seed; garnet stone. (English) armed with a spear. Gar, Garnet, Garrie, Garnett

Garnock (Welsh) dweller by the alder river.

Garrad (English) a form of Garrett. Gared, Garrad, Garrod, Gerred, Gerrid, Gerrod, Garrode, Jared

Garret (Irish) a form of Garrett. Garrit, Garyt, Geret, Garrid, Gerrit, Gerrot

Garrett (Irish) brave spearman. See also Jarrett. Gar, Gareth, Garett, Garrad, Garret, Garrette, Gerrit, Gerrott

Garrick (English) oak spear. Gaerick, Garek, Garick, Garik, Garreck, Garrick, Garrik, Garryck, Garryk, Gerreck, Gerrick

Garren, Garrin (English) forms of Garry. Garran, Garrion, Garron, Garryn, Gerren, Gerron, Gerryn

Garrison (French) troops stationed at a fort; garrison. Garison, Garisson, Garris

Garroway (English) spear fighter. Garraway

Garry (English) a form of Gary. Garen, Garrey, Garri, Garrie, Garren, Garrin

Garson (English) son of Gar.

Garth (Scandinavian) garden, gardener. (Welsh) a short form of Gareth.

Garvey (Irish) rough peace. Garbhán, Garrey, Garvie, Gary, Garvan, Garvie, Gary

Garvin (English) comrade in battle. Gar, Garvan, Garven, Garvyn, Garwen, Garvin, Garvyn, Garvynn

Garwood (English) evergreen forest. See also Wood, Woody. Garwood

Gary (German) mighty spearman. (English) a familiar form of Gerald. See also Kali. Gare, Garey, Gari, Garry

Gaspar (French) a form of Casper. Gáspár, Gaspard, Gaspare, Gasparo, Gasper, Gazsi

Gaston (French) from Gascony, France. Gascon, Gastaun

Gaute (Norwegian) great.

Gautier (French) a form of Walter. Galtero, Gaultiero, Gualtier, Gualtiero, Gauthier

Gavin (Welsh) white hawk. Gav, Gavan, Gaven, Gavin, Gavino, Gavn, Gavohn, Gavon, Gavyn, Gavynn, Gawain

Gavriel (Hebrew) man of God. Gav, Gavi, Gavrel, Gavril, Gavy

Gavril (Russian) a form of Gavriel. Ganya, Gavrilo, Gavrilushka

Gawain (Welsh) a form of Gavin. Gawaine, Gawayn, Gawayne, Gawen, Gwayne

Gaylen (Greek) a form of Galen. Gaylin, Gaylinn, Gaylon, Gaylyn

Gaylord (French) merry lord; jailer. Gaillard, Gallard, Gay, Gayelord, Gaylor

Gaynor (Irish) son of the fair-skinned man. Gainer, Gainor, Gay, Gayner, Gaynnor

Geary (English) variable, changeable. Geary, Gery

Gedeon (Bulgarian, French) a form of Gideon.

Geffrey (English) a form of Geoffrey. See also Jeffrey. Gefery, Geff, Geffery, Geffard

Gellert (Hungarian) a form of Gerald.

Gena (Russian) a short form of Yevgenyi. Genka, Genya, Gine

Genaro (Latin) consecrated to God.
Genero, Genero, Gennaro

Gene (Greek) a short form of Eugene.
Genek

Genek (Polish) a form of Gene.

Geno (Italian) a form of John. A short form of Genovese.
Genio, Jeno

Genovese (Italian) from Genoa, Italy.
Geno, Genovis

Gent (English) gentleman.
Gentle, Gentry

Genty (Irish, English) snow.

Geoff (English) a short form of Geoffrey.

Geoffery (English) a form of Geoffrey.
Geofery

Geoffrey (English) a form of Jeffrey. See also Giotto, Godfrey, Gottfried, Jeff.
Geffrey, Geoff, Geoffery, Geoffre, Geoffrie, Geoffroi, Geoffroy, Geofrey, Geofri, Gofery

Geordan (Scottish) a form of Gordon.
Geordann, Geordian, Geordin, Geordon

Geordie (Scottish) a form of George.
Geordi, Geordy

Georg (Scandinavian) a form of George.

George (Greek) farmer. See also Durko, Egor, Iorgos, Jerzy, Jiri, Joji, Jörg, Jorge, Jorgen, Joris, Jorrín, Jur, Jurgis, Keoki, Mahiái, Semer, Yegor, Yorgos, Yoyi, Yrjo, Yuri, Zhora.
Geordie, Georg, Georgas, Georges, Georget, Georgi, Georgii, Georgio,
Georgios, Georgiy, Georgy, Geork, Gheorghe, Giorgio, Giorgos, Goerge, Goran, Gordios, Gorge, Gorje, Gorya, Grzegorz, Gyorgy

Georges (French) a form of George.
Geórges

Georgio (Italian) a form of George.

Georgios (Greek) a form of George.
Georgious, Georgius

Georgy (Greek) a familiar form of George.
Georgie

Geovanni, Geovanny (Italian) forms of Giovanni.
Geovan, Geovani, Geovanne, Geovannee, Geovannhi, Geovany

Geraint (English) old.

Gerald (German) mighty spearman. See also Fitzgerald, Jarell, Jarrell, Jerald, Jerry, Kharald.
Garald, Garold, Garolds, Gary, Gearalt, Gellert, Gérald, Geralde, Geraldo, Gerale, Geraud, Gerek, Gerick, Gerik, Gerold, Gerrald, Gerrell, Gérrick, Gerrild, Gerrin, Gerrit, Gerrold, Gerry, Geryld, Giraldo, Giraud, Girauld

Geraldo (Italian, Spanish) a form of Gerald.

Gerard (English) brave spearman. See also Jerard, Jerry.
Garrard, Garrat, Garratt, Gearard, Gerard, Gerar, Gérard, Gerardo, Geraro, Géraud, Gerd, Gerek, Gerhard, Gerrard, Gerrit, Gerry, Girard

Gerardo (Spanish) a form of Gerard.
Gherardo

Géraud (French) a form of Gerard.
Gerad, Gerraud

Gerek (Polish) a form of Gerard.

Geremia (Hebrew) exalted by God. (Italian) a form of Jeremiah.

Geremiah (Italian) a form of Jeremiah.
Geremia, Gerimiah, Geromiah

Gerhard (German) a form of Gerard.
Garhard, Gerhardi, Gerhardt, Gerhart, Gerhort

Gerik (Polish) a form of Edgar.
Geric, Gerik

Germain (French) from Germany. (English) sprout, bud. See also Jermaine.
Germaine, German, Germane, Germano, Germayn, Germayne

Gerome (English) a form of Jerome.

Geronimo (Greek, Italian) a form of Jerome. History: a famous Apache chief.
Geronemo

Gerrit (Dutch) a form of Gerald.

Gerry (English) a familiar form of Gerald, Gerard. See also Jerry.
Geri, Gerre, Gerri, Gerrie, Gerryson

Gershom (Hebrew) exiled. (Yiddish) stranger in exile.
Gersham, Gersho, Gershon, Gerson, Geurson, Gurshiam, Gurshan

Gerson (English) son of Gar.
Gersan, Gershawn

Gert (German, Danish) fighter.

Gervaise (French) honorable. See also Jervis.
Garvais, Garvaise, Garvey, Gervais, Gervase, Gervasio, Gervaso, Gervayse, Gervis, Gervazy.

Gerwin (Welsh) fair love.

Gethin (Welsh) dusky.
Geth.

Ghazi (Arabic) conqueror.

Ghilchrist (Irish) servant of Christ. See also Gil.
Gilchrist, Gilcrist, Gilie, Gill, Gilley, Gilly.

Chislain (French) pledge.

Gi (Korean) brave.

Gia (Vietnamese) family.

Giacinto (Portuguese, Spanish) a form of Jacinto.
Giacintho.

Giacomo (Italian) a form of Jacob.
Gaimo, Giacamo, Giaco, Giacobbe, Giacobo, Giacopo.

Gian (Italian) a form of Giovanni, John.
Gianetto, Giann, Gianne, Giannes, Gianni, Giannis, Giannos, Ghian.

Giancarlo (Italian) a combination of John + Charles.
Giancarlos, Gianncarlo.

Gianluca (Italian) a combination of John + Lucas.

Gianni (Italian) a form of Johnny.
Giani, Gionni.

Gianpaolo (Italian) a combination of John + Paul.

Gib (English) a short form of Gilbert.
Gibb, Gibbie, Gibby.

Gibor (Hebrew) powerful.

Gibson (English) son of Gilbert.
Gibbon, Gibbons, Gibbs, Gibson, Gilson.

Gidon (Hebrew) a form of Gideon.

Gideon (Hebrew) tree cutter. Bible: the judge who defeated the Midianites.
Gedeon, Gideone, Gidon, Hedeon.

Gifford (English) bold giver.
Giff, Giffard, Gifferd, Giffie, Giffy.

Gig (English) horse-drawn carriage.

Gil (Greek) shield bearer. (Hebrew) happy. (English) a short form of Ghilchrist, Gilbert.
Gili, Gill, Gilli, Gillie, Gillis, Gilly.

Gilad (Arabic) camel hump; from Giladi, Saudi Arabia.
Giladi, Gilead.

Gilamu (Basque) a form of William.
Gillen.

Gilbert (English) brilliant pledge; trustworthy. See also Gil, Gillett.
Gib, Gilberto, Gilburt, Giselbert, Giselberto, Giselbertus, Guilbert.

Gilberto (Spanish) a form of Gilbert.

Gilby (Scandinavian) hostage's estate. (Irish) blond boy.
Gilbey, Gillbey, Gillbie, Gillby.

Gilchrist (Irish) a form of Ghilchrist.

Gilen (Basque, German) illustrious pledge.

Giles (French) goatskin shield.
Gide, Gilles, Gyles.

Gillean (Irish) Bible: Saint John's servant.
Gillan, Gillen, Gillian.

Gillespie (Irish) son of the bishop's servant.
Gillis.

Gillett (French) young Gilbert.
Gelett, Gelette, Gillette.

Gilmer (English) famous hostage.

Gilmore (Irish) devoted to the Virgin Mary.
Gillmore, Gilmour, Gilmour.

Gilon (Hebrew) circle.

Gilroy (Irish) devoted to the king.
Gilderoy, Gildray, Gildroy, Gillroy, Roy.

Gino (Greek) a familiar form of Eugene. (Italian) a short form of names ending in "gene," "gino."
Ghrio.

Giona (Italian) a form of Jonah.

Giordano (Italian) a form of Jordan.
Giordan, Giordana, Giordin, Guordan.

Giorgio (Italian) a form of George.

Giorgos (Greek) a form of George.
Georgos, Giorgios

Giosia (Italian) a form of Joshua.

Giotto (Italian) a form of Geoffrey.

Giovani (Italian) a form of Giovanni.
Giavani, Giovan, Giovane, Giovanie, Giovon

Giovanni (Italian) a form of John. See also Jeovanni, Jiovanni.
Geovanni, Geovanny, Gian, Gianni, Giannino, Giovani, Giovann, Giovannie, Giovanno, Giovanny, Giovonathon, Giovonni, Giovonnia, Giovonnie, Givonni

Giovanny (Italian) a form of Giovanni.
Giovany

Gipsy (English) wanderer.
Gipson, Gypsy

Girvin (Irish) small; tough.
Girvan, Girven, Girvon

Gitano (Spanish) gypsy.

Giuliano (Italian) a form of Julius.
Giulano, Giulino, Giulliano

Giulio (Italian) a form of Julius.
Guilano

Giuseppe (Italian) a form of Joseph.
Giuseppi, Giuseppino, Giusseppe, Guiseppe, Guiseppi, Guiseppie, Guisseppe

Giustino (Italian) a form of Justin.
Giusto

Givon (Hebrew) hill; heights.
Givan, Givaun, Givyn

Gladwin (English) cheerful. See also Win.
Glad, Gladdie, Gladdy, Gladwinn, Gladwyn, Gladwynne

Glanville (English) village with oak trees.

Glen (Irish) a form of Glenn.
Glyn

Glendon (Scottish) fortress in the glen.
Glenden, Glendin, Glenn, Glennden, Glennton, Glenton

Glendower (Welsh) from Glyndwr, Wales.

Glenn (Irish) a short form of Glendon.
Gleann, Glen, Glennie, Glennis, Glennon, Glenry, Glynn

Glentworth (English) from Glenton, England.

Glenville (Irish) village in the glen.

Glyn (Welsh) a form of Glen.
Glin, Glynn

Goddard (German) divinely firm.
Godard, Godart, Goddart, Godhardt, Godhart, Gothard, Gothardt, Gotthard, Gotthart

Godfrey (Irish) God's peace. (German) a form of Jeffrey. See also Geoffrey, Gottfried.
Giotto, Godefroi, Godfree, Godfry, Godofredo, Godoired, Godrey, Goffredo, Gofraidh, Gofredo, Gorry

Godwin (English) friend of God. See also Win.
Godewyn, Godwinn, Goduyn,

Goodwin (English) golden friend. See also Win.
Goodwyn, Goodwynn, Gooduynne

Goel (Hebrew) redeemer.

Goldwin (English) golden friend. See also Win.
Golden, Goldewin, Goldewinn, Goldewyn, Goldwyn, Golduyn

Goliath (Hebrew) exiled. Bible: the giant Philistine whom David slew with a slingshot.
Golliath

Gomda (Kiowa) wind.

Gomer (Hebrew) completed, finished. (English) famous battle.

Gonza (Rutooro) love.

Gonzalo (Spanish) wolf.
Goncalve, Gonsalo, Gonsalve, Gonzales, Gonzalee, Gonzolo

Gordon (English) triangular-shaped hill.
Geordan, Gord, Gordain, Gordan, Gorden, Gordonn, Gordy

Gordy (English) a familiar form of Gordon.
Gordie

Gore (English) triangular-shaped land; wedge-shaped land.

Gorman (Irish) small; blue eyed.

Goro (Japanese) fifth.

Gosheven (Native American) great leaper.

Gottfried (German) a form of Geoffrey, Godfrey.
Goffrid, Goffrids, Gotffrid

Gotzon (German) a form of Angel.

Covert (Dutch) heavenly peace.

Gower (Welsh) pure.

Gowon (Tiv) rainmaker.
Gowan

Gozol (Hebrew) soaring bird.
Gozal

Grady (Irish) noble; illustrious.
Gradea, Gradee, Gradey, Gradleigh, Graidey, Graidy

Graeme (Scottish) a form of Graham.
Graem

Graham (English) grand home.
Graeham, Graehame, Graehme, Graeme, Grahamme, Grahm, Grahame, Grahme, Gram, Grame, Gramm, Grayeme, Grayham

Granger (French) farmer.
Grainger, Grange

Grant (English) a short form of Grantland.
Grand, Grantham, Granthem, Grantley

Grantland (English) great plains.
Grant

Granville (French) large village.
Gran, Granvel, Granvil, Granvile, Granvill, Grenville, Grevile

Gray (English) gray haired.
Graye, Grey, Greye

Grayden (English) gray haired.
Graden, Graydan, Graydyn, Greyden

Graydon (English) gray hill.
Gradon, Grayton, Greydon

Grayson (English) bailiff's son. See also Sonny.
Graysen, Greyson

Greeley (English) gray meadow.
Greelea, Greeleigh, Greely

Greenwood (English) green forest.
Green, Greener

Greg, Gregg (Latin) short forms of Gregory.
Craig, Greig, Gregson

Gregor (Scottish) a form of Gregory.
Gregoor, Grégor, Gregore

Gregorio (Italian, Portuguese) a form of Gregory.
Gregorios

Greggory (Latin) a form of Gregory.
Greggery

Gregory (Latin) vigilant watchman. See also Jörn, Krikor.
Gergely, Gergo, Gregoir, Gregory, Greer, Greg, Gregary, Greger, Gregery, Greggory, Grégoire, Gregor, Gregory, Gregori, Gregorie, Gregorio, Gregorius, Gregors, Gregos, Gregrey, Gregroy, Gregry, Gries, Grisha, Grzegorz

Gresham (English) village in the pasture.

Greyson (English) a form of Grayson.
Greysen, Greysten, Greyston

Griffin (Latin) hooked nose.
Griff, Griffen, Griffie, Griffon, Griffy, Gryphon

Griffith (Welsh) fierce chief; ruddy.
Griffen, Griff, Griffeth, Griffie, Griffi, Griffyn, Griffynn, Gryphon

Grigori (Bulgarian) a form of Gregory.
Grigor, Grigori, Grigor, Grigore, Grigorios, Grigory

Grimshaw (English) dark woods.

Grisha (Russian) a form of Gregory.

Griswold (German, French) gray forest.
Gris, Griz, Grizwald

Grosvener (French) big hunter.

Grover (English) grove.
Grove

Gualberto (Spanish) a form of Walter.
Gualerio

Guadalupe (Arabic) river of black stones.
Guadalope

Gualtiero (Italian) a form of Walter.
Gualterio

Guglielmo (Italian) a form of William.

Guido (Italian) a form of Guy.

Guilford (English) ford with yellow flowers.
Guildford

Guilherme (Portuguese) a form of William.

Guillaume (French) a form of William.
Guillaums, Guilleaume, Guilem, Guyllaume

Guillermo (Spanish) a form of William.
Guillermo

Gunnar (Scandinavian) a form of Gunther.
Guner, Gunner

Gunther (Scandinavian) battle army; warrior.
Guenter, Guenther, Gun, Gunnar, Guntar, Gunter, Guntero, Gunthar, Günther

Guotin (Chinese) polite; strong leader.

Gurion (Hebrew) young lion.
Gur, Guri, Guriel

Gurpreet (Sikh) devoted to the guru; devoted to the Prophet.
Gurjeet, Gurmeet, Guruprit

Gurvir (Sikh) guru's warrior.
Gurveer

Gus (Scandinavian) a short form of Angus, Augustine, Gustave.
Guss, Gussie, Gussy, Gusti, Gustry, Gusty

Gustaf (Swedish) a form of Gustave.
Gustaaf, Gustaff

Gustave (Scandinavian) staff of the Goths. History: Gustavus Adolphus was a king of Sweden. See also Kosti, Tabo, Tavo.
Gus, Gustaf, Gustaff, Gustaof, Gustav, Gustár, Gustava, Gustaves, Gustavo, Gustavs, Gustavus, Gustik, Gustus, Gusztav

Gustavo (Italian, Spanish) a form of Gustave.
Gustabo

Guthrie (German) war hero. (Irish) windy place.
Guthrey, Guthry

Gutierre (Spanish) a form of Walter.

Guy (Hebrew) valley. (German) warrior. (French) guide. See also Guido.
Guyon

Guyapi (Native American) candid.

Gwayne (Welsh) a form of Gawain.
Gwaine, Gwayn

Gwidon (Polish) life.

Gwilym (Welsh) a form of William.
Guillym

Gwyn (Welsh) fair; blessed.
Gwynn, Gwynne

Gyasi (Akan) marvelous baby.

Gyorgy (Russian) a form of George.
Gyoergy, Gyõrgy, Gyuri, Gyurka

Gyula (Hungarian) youth.
Gyala, Gyuszi

Habib (Arabic) beloved.

Hackett (German, French) little wood cutter.
Hacket, Hackit, Hackitt

Hackman (German, French) wood cutter.

Hadar (Hebrew) glory.

Haddad (Arabic) blacksmith.

Hadden (English) heather-covered hill.
Haddan, Haddon, Haden

Haden (English) a form of Hadden.
Hadin, Hadon, Hadyn, Haeden

Hadi (Arabic) guiding to the right.
Hadee, Hady

Hadley (English) heather-covered meadow.
Had, Hadlea, Hadlee, Hadleigh, Hadly, Lee, Leigh

Hadrian (Latin, Swedish) dark.
Adrian, Hadrien

Hadwin (English) friend in a time of war.
Hadwinn, Hadwyn, Hadwynn, Hadwynne

Hagan (German) strong defense.
Haggan

Hagen (Irish) young, youthful.

Hagley (English) enclosed meadow.

Hagos (Ethiopian) happy.

Hahnee (Native American) beggar.

Hai (Vietnamese) sea.

Haidar (Arabic) lion.
Haider

Haiden (English) a form of Hayden.
Haidyn

Haig (English) enclosed with hedges.

Hailey (Irish) a form of Haley.
Haile, Hailie, Haily, Hale

Haji (Swahili) born during the pilgrimage to Mecca.

Hakan (Native American) fiery.

Hakeem (Arabic) a form of Hakim.
Hakeam, Hakiem

Hakim (Arabic) wise. (Ethiopian) doctor.
Hakeem, Hakiem

Hakon (Scandinavian) of Nordic ancestry.
Haaken, Haakin, Haakon, Haeo, Hak, Hakan, Hako

Hal (English) a short form of Halden, Hall, Harold.

Halbert (English) shining hero.
Bert, Halburt

Halden (Scandinavian) half-Danish. See also Dane.
Hal, Haldan, Haldane, Halfdan, Halvdan

Hale (English) a short form of Haley. (Hawaiian) a form of Harry.
Hayle, Heall

Halen (Swedish) hall.

Haley (Irish) ingenious.
Hailey, Hale, Haleigh, Halley, Hayley, Hayleigh, Hayli

Halford (English) valley ford.

Hali (Greek) sea.

Halian (Zuni) young.

Halil (Turkish) dear friend.
Halill

Halim (Arabic) mild, gentle.
Haleem

Hall (English) manor, hall.
Hal, Halstead, Halsted

Hallam (English) valley.

Hallan (English) dweller at the hall; dweller at the manor.
Halin, Hallene, Hallin

Halley (English) meadow near the hall; holy.
Hallie

Halliwell (English) holy well.
Hallewell, Hellewell, Helliwell

Hallward (English) hall guard.

Halsey (English) Hal's island.

Halstead (English) manor grounds.
Halsted

Halton (English) estate on the hill.

Halvor (Norwegian) rock; protector.
Halvard

Ham (Hebrew) hot. Bible: one of Noah's sons.

Hamal (Arabic) lamb. Astronomy: a bright star in the constellation of Aries.

Hamar (Scandinavian) hammer.

Hamid (Arabic) praised. See also Muhammad.
Haamid, Hamaad, Hamadi, Hamd, Hamdrem, Hamed, Hameed, Hamidi, Hammad, Hammed, Humayd

Hamill (English) scarred.
Hamel, Hamell, Hammill

Hamilton (English) proud estate.
Hamel, Hamelton, Hamil, Hamill, Tony

Hamish (Scottish) a form of Jacob, James.

Hamisi (Swahili) born on Thursday.

Hamlet (German, French) little village; home. Literature: one of Shakespeare's tragic heroes.

Hamlin (German, French) loves his home.
Hamblin, Hamlen, Hamelin, Hamlen, Hamlyn, Lin

Hammet (English, Scandinavian) village.
Hammett, Hamnet, Hamnett

Hammond (English) village.
Hammond

Hampton (English) Geography: a town in England.
Hamp

Hamza (Arabic) powerful.
Hamzah, Hamze, Hamzeh, Hamzia

Hanale (Hawaiian) a form of Henry.
Haneke

Hanan (Hebrew) grace.
Hananel, Hananiah, Johanan

Hanbal (Arabic) pure. History: Ahmad Ibn Hanbal founded an Islamic school of thought.

Handel (German, English) a form of John. Music: George Frideric Handel was a German composer whose works include *Messiah* and *Water Music.*

Hanford (English) high ford.

Hanif (Arabic) true believer.
Haneef, Hanef

Hank (American) a familiar form of Henry.

Hanley (English) high meadow.
Handlea, Handleigh, Handley, Hanlea, Hanlee, Hanleigh, Hanly, Henlea, Henlee, Henleigh, Henley

Hannes (Finnish) a form of John.

Hannibal (Phoenician) grace of God. History: a famous Carthaginian general who fought the Romans.
Anibal

Hanno (German) a short form of Johan.
Hanna, Hannah, Hannon, Hannu, Hanon

Hans (Scandinavian) a form of John.
Hanschen, Hansel, Hants, Hanz

Hansel (Scandinavian) a form of Hans.
Haensel, Hansell, Hansl, Hanzel

Hansen (Scandinavian) son of Hans.
Hanson

Hansh (Hindi) god; godlike.

Hanson (Scandinavian) a form of Hansen.
Hansen, Hanssen, Hansson

Hanus (Czech) a form of John.

Haoa (Hawaiian) a form of Howard.

Hara (Hindi) seizer. Religion: another name for the Hindu god Shiva.

Harald (Scandinavian) a form of Harold.
Haraldo, Haralds, Haralpos

Harb (Arabic) warrior.

Harbin (German, French) little bright warrior.
Harben, Harbyn

Harcourt (French) fortified dwelling.
Court, Harcort

Hardeep (Punjabi) a form of Harpreet.

Harden (English) valley of the hares.
Hardian, Hardin

Harding (English) brave; hardy.
Hardin

Hardwin (English) brave friend.

Hardy (German) bold, daring.
Hardie

Harel (Hebrew) mountain of God.
Harell, Hariel, Harrell

Harford (English) ford of the hares.

Hargrove (English) grove of the hares.
Hargreave, Hargreaves

Hari (Hindi) tawny.
Hariel, Harin

Harith (Arabic) cultivator.

Harjot (Sikh) light of God.
Harjeet, Harjit, Harjodh

Harkin (Irish) dark red.
Harkan, Harken

Harlan (English) hare's land; army land.
Harland, Harlen, Harlenn, Harlin, Harlon, Harlyn, Harlynn

Harland (English) a form of Harlan.
Harlend

Harley (English) hare's meadow; army meadow.
Arley, Harlea, Harlee, Harleigh, Harly

Harlow (English) hare's hill; army hill. See also Arlo.

Harman, Harmon (English) forms of Herman.
Harm, Harmen, Harmond, Harms

Harold (Scandinavian) army ruler. See also Jindra.
Araldo, Garald, Garold, Hal, Harald, Haraldas, Haraldo, Haralds, Harry, Heraldo, Herold, Heronim, Herrick, Herryck

Haroun (Arabic) lofty; exalted.
Haarun, Harin, Haron, Haroon, Harron, Harun

Harper (English) harp player.
Harp, Harpo

Harpreet (Punjabi) loves God, devoted to God.
Hardeep

Harris (English) a short form of Harrison.
Haris, Hariss

Harrison (English) son of Harry.
Harrison, Harreson, Harris, Harrisen, Harrisson

Harrod (Hebrew) hero; conqueror.

Harry (English) a familiar form of Harold. See also Arrigo, Hale, Parry.
Harm, Harray, Harrey, Harri, Harrie

Hart (English) a short form of Hartley.

Hartley (English) deer meadow.
Hart, Hartlea, Hartlee, Hartleigh, Hartly

Hartman (German) hard; strong.

Hartwell (English) deer well.
Harwell, Harwill

Hartwig (German) strong advisor.

Hartwood (English) deer forest.
Harwood

Harvey (German) army warrior.
Harv, Hervé, Hervey, Hervie, Hervy

Harvir (Sikh) God's warrior.
Harvier

Hasad (Turkish) reaper, harvester.

Hasan (Arabic) a form of Hassan.
Hasaan, Hasain, Hasaun, Hashaan, Hason

Hasani (Swahili) handsome.
Hasan, Hasanni, Hassani, Heseny, Hassen, Hassian, Hussani, Husani

Hashim (Arabic) destroyer of evil.
Haashim, Hasham, Hasheem, Hashem

Hasin (Hindi) laughing.
Hasen, Hasen, Hassin, Hazen, Hesen

Haskel (Hebrew) a form of Ezekiel.
Haskell

Haslett (English) hazel-tree land.
Haze, Hazel, Hazlett, Hazlitt

Hassan (Arabic) handsome.
Hasan, Hassen, Hasson

Hassel (German, English) witches' corner.
Hassal, Hassall, Hassell, Hazael, Hazell

Hastin (Hindi) elephant.

Hastings (Latin) spear. (English) house council.
Hastie, Hasty

Hatim (Arabic) judge.
Hatem, Hatim

Hauk (Norwegian) hawk.
Hawkeye

Havelock (Norwegian) sea battler.

Haven (Dutch, English) harbor, port; safe place.
Haeven, Havin, Hevin, Hevon, Hovan

Havika (Hawaiian) a form of David.

Hawk (English) hawk.
Hawke, Hawkin, Hawkins

Hawley (English) hedged meadow.
Hawleigh, Hawly

Hawthorne (English) hawthorn tree.

Hayden (English) hedged valley.
Haiden, Haydan, Haydenn, Haydn, Haydon

Hayes (English) hedged valley.
Haydon

Hayward (English) guardian of the hedged area.
Haward, Heyward, Heyward

Haywood (English) hedged forest.
Heywood, Woody

Hearn (Scottish, English) a short form of Ahearn.
Hearne, Herin, Hern

Heath (English) heath.
Heathe, Heith

Heathcliff (English) cliff near the heath. Literature: the hero of Emily Brontë's novel *Wuthering Heights*.

Heaton (English) high place.

Heber (Hebrew) ally, partner.

Hector (Greek) steadfast. Mythology: the greatest hero of the Trojan War in Homer's epic poem *Iliad*.

Hedley (English) heather-filled meadow.
Headley, Headly, Hedly

Heinrich (German) a form of Henry.
Heindrick, Heiner, Heinreich, Heinrik, Hinrich

Heinz (German) a familiar form of Henry.

Helaku (Native American) sunny day.

Helge (Russian) holy.

Helki (Moquelumnan) touching.

Helmer (German) warrior's wrath.

Helmut (German) courageous.
Helmuth

Heman (Hebrew) faithful.

Henderson (Scottish, English) son of Henry.
Hendrie, Hendries, Hendron, Henryson

Hendrick (Dutch) a form of Henry.
Hendricks, Hendrickson, Hendrik, Hendriks, Hendrikus, Hendrix, Henning

Heniek (Polish) a form of Henry.
Henier

Henley (English) high meadow.

Henning (German) a form of Hendrick, Henry.

Henoch (Yiddish) initiator.
Enoch, Henock, Henok

Henri (French) a form of Henry.
Henrico, Henrri

Henrick (Dutch) a form of Henry.
Heinrik, Henerik, Henrich, Henrik, Henryk

Henrique (Portuguese) a form of Henry.

Henry (German) ruler of the household. See also Arrigo, Enric, Enrick, Enrico, Enrik, Enrikos, Enrique, Hanale, Honok, Kiki.
Hagan, Hank, Harro, Harry, Heike, Heinrich, Heinz, Hendrick, Henery, Heniek, Henning, Henraoi, Henri, Henrick, Henrim, Henrique, Henry, Heromin, Hersz

Heraldo (Spanish) a form of Harold.
Herald, Hiraldo

Herb (German) a short form of Herbert.
Herbie, Herby

Herbert (German) glorious soldier.
Bert, Erbert, Eriberto, Harbert, Hebert, Hébert, Heberto, Herb, Heriberto, Hurbert

Hercules (Latin) glorious gift. Mythology: a Greek hero of fabulous strength, renowned for his twelve labors.
Herakles, Herc, Hercule, Herculie

Heriberto (Spanish) a form of Herbert.
Heribert

Herman (Latin) noble. (German) soldier. See also Armand, Ermanno, Ermano, Mandek.
Harmon, Hermann, Hermaan, Hermie, Herminio, Hermino, Hermon, Hermy, Heromin

Hermes (Greek) messenger. Mythology: the divine herald of Greek mythology.

Hernan (German) peacemaker.

Hernando (Spanish) a form of Ferdinand.
Hernandes, Hernandez

Herrick (German) war ruler.
Herrik, Herryk

Herschel (Hebrew) a form of Hershel.
Herchel, Hersch, Herschel, Herschell

Hersh (Hebrew) a short form of Hershel.
Hersch, Hirsh

Hershel (Hebrew) deer.
Herschel, Hersh, Hershal, Hershall, Hershell, Herzl, Hirschel, Hirshel

Hertz (Yiddish) my strife.
Herzel

Hervé (French) a form of Harvey.

Hesperos (Greek) evening star.
Hespero

Hesutu (Moquelumnan) picking up a yellow jacket's nest.

Hew (Welsh) a form of Hugh.
Hewe, Huw

Hewitt (German, French) little smart one.
Hewe, Hewet, Hewett, Hewie, Hewit, Hewlett, Hewlitt, Hugh

Hewson (English) son of Hugh.

Hezekiah (Hebrew) God gives strength.
Hezekyah, Hazikiah, Hezikyah

Hiamovi (Cheyenne) high chief.

Hibah (Arabic) gift.

Hideaki (Japanese) smart, clever.
Hideo

Hieremias (Greek) God will uplift.

Hieronymos (Greek) a form of Jerome. Art: Hieronymus Bosch was a fifteenth-century Dutch painter.
Hierome, Hieronim, Hieronimo, Hieronimos, Hieronymo, Hieronymus

Hieu (Vietnamese) respectful.

Hilario (Spanish) a form of Hilary.

Hilary (Latin) cheerful. See also Ilari.
Hi, Hilair, Hilare, Hilarie, Hilario, Hilarion, Hilarius, Hil, Hill, Hillary, Hillery, Hilliary, Hillie, Hilly

Hildebrand (German) battle sword.
Hildebrando, Hildo

Hilel (Arabic) new moon.

Hillel (Hebrew) greatly praised. Religion: Rabbi Hillel originated the Talmud.

Hilliard (German) brave warrior.
Hillard, Hiller, Hilliar, Hillierd, Hillyard, Hillyer, Hillyerd

Hilmar (Swedish) famous noble.

Hilton (English) town on a hill.
Hylton

Hinto (Dakota) blue.

Hinun (Native American) spirit of the storm.

Hippolyte (Greek) horseman.
Hippolito, Hippolit, Hippolitos, Hippolytus, Ippolito

Hiram (Hebrew) noblest; exalted.
Hi, Hirom, Huram, Hyrum

Hiromasa (Japanese) fair, just.

Hiroshi (Japanese) generous.

Hisoka (Japanese) secretive, reserved.

Hiu (Hawaiian) a form of Hugh.

Ho (Chinese) good.

Hoang (Vietnamese) finished.

Hobart (German) Bart's hill.
Hobard, Hobbie, Hobby, Hobie, Hoebart

Hobert (German) Bert's hill.
Hobey

Hobson (English) son of Robert.
Hobbs, Hobs

Hoc (Vietnamese) studious.

Hod (Hebrew) a short form of Hodgson.

Hodgson (English) son of Roger.
Hod

Hogan (Irish) youth.
Hogin

Holbrook (English) brook in the hollow.
Brook, Holbrooke

Holden (English) hollow in the valley.
Holdan, Holdin, Holdon, Holdun, Holdyn

Holic (Czech) barber.

Holland (French) Geography: a former province of the Netherlands.

Holleb (Polish) dove.
Hollub, Holub

Hollis (English) grove of holly trees.
Hollie, Holly

Holmes (English) river islands.

Holt (English) forest.
Holten, Holton

Homer (Greek) hostage; pledge; security. Literature: a renowned Greek epic poet.
Homar, Homere, Homère, Homero, Homeros, Homerus

Hondo (Shona) warrior.

Honesto (Filipino) honest.

Honi (Hebrew) gracious.
Choni

Honok (Polish) a form of Henry.

Honon (Moquelumnan) bear.

Honorato (Spanish) honorable.

Honoré (Latin) honored.
Honor, Honoratus, Honoray, Honorio, Honorius

Honovi (Native American) strong.

Honza (Czech) a form of John.

Hop (Chinese) agreeable.

Horace (Latin) keeper of the hours. Literature: a famous Roman lyric poet and satirist.
Horacio, Horaz

Horacio (Latin) a form of Horace.

Horatio (Latin) clan name. See also Orris.
Horatius, Oratio

Horst (German) dense grove; thicket.
Hurst

Horton (English) garden estate.
Hort, Horten, Orton

Hosa (Arapaho) young crow.

Hosea (Hebrew) salvation. Bible: a Hebrew prophet.
Hose, Hoseia, Hoshea, Hosheah

Hotah (Lakota) white.

Hototo (Native American) whistler.

Houghton (English) settlement on the headland.

Houston (English) hill town. Geography: a city in Texas.
Housten, Houstin, Hustin, Huston

Howard (English) watchman. See also Haoa.
Howie, Ward

Howe (German) high.
Howey, Howie

Howell (Welsh) remarkable.
Howel

Howi (Moquelumnan) turtledove.

Howie (English) a familiar form of Howard, Howland.
Howey

Howin (Chinese) loyal swallow.

Howland (English) hilly land.
Howie, Howlan, Howlen

Hoyt (Irish) mind; spirit.

Hu (Chinese) tiger.

Hubbard (German) a form of Hubert.

Hubert (German) bright mind; bright spirit. See also Beredei, Uberto.
Bert, Hobart, Hubbard, Hubbert, Huber, Hubertek, Huberto, Hubertson, Hubie, Huey, Hugh, Hugibert, Huibert, Humberto

Huberto (Spanish) a form of Hubert.
Humberto

Hubie (English) a familiar form of Hubert.
Hube, Hubi

Hud (Arabic) Religion: a Muslim prophet.

Hudson (English) son of Hud.

Huey (English) a familiar form of Hugh.
Hughey, Hughie, Hughy, Hui

Hugh (English) a short form of Hubert. See also Ea, Hewitt, Huxley, Maccoy, Ugo.
Fitzhugh, Hew, Hiu, Hue, Huey, Hughes, Hugo, Hugues

Hugo (Latin) a form of Hugh.
Ugo

Hulbert (German) brilliant grace.
Bert, Hulbard, Hulburd, Hulburt, Hull

Humbert (German) brilliant strength. See also Umberto.
Hum, Humberto

Humberto (Portuguese) a form of Humbert.

Humphrey (German) peaceful strength. See also Onofrio, Onufry.
Hum, Humfredo, Humfrey, Humfrid, Humfried, Humfry, Hump, Humph, Humphery, Humphry, Humphrys, Hunfredo

Hung (Vietnamese) brave.

Hunt (English) a short form of names beginning with "Hunt."

Hunter (English) hunter.
Hunt, Huntar

Huntington (English) hunting estate.
Hunt, Huntingdon

Huntley (English) hunter's meadow.
Hunt, Huntlea, Huntlee, Huntleigh, Huntly

Hurley (Irish) sea tide.
Hurlee, Hurleigh

Hurst (English) a form of Horst.
Hearst, Hirst

Husam (Arabic) sword.

Husamettin (Turkish) sharp sword.

Huslu (Native American) hairy bear.

Husain (Arabic) a form of Hussein.
Hossain, Husain, Husani, Husayn, Hussan, Hussayn

Hussein (Arabic) little; handsome.
Hossein, Houssein, Houssin, Huissien, Huossein, Husein, Husien, Hussain, Hussien

Hussien (Arabic) a form of Hussein.
Husian, Hussin

Hutchinson (English) son of the hutch dweller.
Hutcheson

Hute (Native American) star.

Hutton (English) house on the jutting ledge.
Hut, Hutt, Huttan

Huxley (English) Hugh's meadow.
Hux, Huxlea, Huxlee, Huxleigh, Lee

Huy (Vietnamese) glorious.

Hy (Vietnamese) hopeful. (English) a short form of Hyman.

Hyacinthe (French) hyacinth.

Hyatt (English) high gate.
Hyat

Hyde (English) cache; measure of land equal to 120 acres; animal hide.

Hyder (English) tanner, preparer of animal hides for tanning.

Hyman (English) a form of Chaim.
Haim, Hayim, Hayyim, Hayyim, Hy, Hyam, Hymie

Hyun-Ki (Korean) wise.

Hyun-Shik (Korean) clever.

I

Iago (Spanish, Welsh) a form of Jacob, James. Literature: the villain in Shakespeare's *Othello*.
Jago

Iain (Scottish) a form of Ian.

Iakobos (Greek) a form of Jacob.
Iakov, Iakovos, Iakvs

Ian (Scottish) a form of John. See also Ean, Eion.
Iain, Iane, Iann

Ianos (Czech) a form of John.
Iannis

Ib (Phoenician, Danish) oath of Baal.

Iban (Basque) a form of John.

Ibon (Basque) a form of Ivor.

Ibrahim (Hausa) my father is exalted.
Ibraham, Ibrahaim, Ibraheem, Ibrahem, Ibrahiem, Ibrahiim, Ibrahmin

Ichabod (Hebrew) glory is gone. Literature: Ichabod Crane is the main character of Washington Irving's story "The Legend of Sleepy Hollow."

Idi (Swahili) born during the Idd festival.

Idris (Welsh) eager lord. (Arabic) Religion: a Muslim prophet.
Idreas, Idres, Idres, Idress, Idress, Idriece, Idriss, Idrissa, Idrisys

Iestyn (Welsh) a form of Justin.

Igashu (Native American) wanderer; seeker.
Igasho

Iggy (Latin) a familiar form of Ignatius.
Igasho

Ignacio (Italian) a form of Ignatius.
Ignazio

Ignatius (Latin) fiery, ardent. Religion: Saint Ignatius of Loyola founded the Jesuit order. See also Inigo, Neci.
Iggie, Iggy, Ignac, Ignác, Ignace, Ignacio, Ignacius, Ignatios, Ignatious, Ignatz, Ignaz, Ignazio

Igor (Russian) a form of Inger, Ingvar. See also Egor, Yegor.
Igoryok

Ihsan (Turkish) compassionate.

Ike (Hebrew) a familiar form of Isaac. History: the nickname of the thirty-fourth U.S. president Dwight D. Eisenhower.
Ikee, Ikey

Iker (Basque) visitation.

Ilan (Hebrew) tree. (Basque) youth.

Ilari (Basque) a form of Hilary.
Ilario

Ilias (Greek) a form of Elijah.
Illias, Illyas, Ilyas, Ilyes

Illan (Basque, Latin) youth.

Ilom (Ibo) my enemies are many.

Ilya (Russian) a form of Elijah.
Ilia, Ilie, Ilija, Iliya, Ilja, Illia, Illya

Imad (Arabic) supportive; mainstay.

Iman (Hebrew) a short form of Immanuel.
Imani, Imanni

Immanuel (Hebrew) a form of Emmanuel.
Iman, Imanol, Imanuel, Immanuele, Immanuel

Imran (Arabic) host.

Imre (Hungarian) a form of Emery.
Imri

Imrich (Czech) a form of Emery.

Inay (Hindi) god; godlike.

Ince (Hungarian) innocent.

Inder (Hindi) god; godlike.
Inderbir, Inderdeep, Inderjeet, Inderjit, Inderpal, Inderpreet, Inderveer, Indervir, Indra, Indrajit

Indiana (Hindi) from India.
Indi, Indy

Inek (Welsh) a form of Irvin.

Ing (Scandinavian) a short form of Ingmar.
Inge

Ingelbert (German) a form of Engelbert.
Inglebert

Inger (Scandinavian) son's army.
Igor, Ingemar, Ingmar

Ingmar (Scandinavian) famous son.
Ing, Ingamar, Ingamur, Ingemar

Ingram (English) angel.
Inglis, Ingra, Ingraham, Ingrim

Ingvar (Scandinavian) Ing's soldier.
Igor, Ingevar

Inigo (Basque) a form of Ignatius.
Iñaki, Iniego, Iñigo

Iniko (Ibo) born during bad times.

Innis (Irish) island.
Innes, Inness, Inniss

Innocenzio (Italian) innocent.
Innocenty, Inocenci, Inocencio, Inocente, Inosente

Inteus (Native American) proud; unashamed.

Ioakim (Russian) a form of Joachim.
Ioachime, Ioakimo, Iov

Ioan (Greek, Bulgarian, Romanian) a form of John.
Ioane, Ioann, Ioannes, Ioannikios, Ioannis, Ionel

Iokepa (Hawaiian) a form of Joseph.
Keo

Iolo (Welsh) a form of Irvin.
Iorwerth

Ionakana (Hawaiian) a form of Jonathan.

Iorgos (Greek) a form of George.

Iosif (Greek, Russian) a form of Joseph.

Iosua (Romanian) a form of Joshua.

Ipyana (Nyakyusa) graceful.

Ira (Hebrew) watchful.

Iram (English) bright.

Irumba (Rutooro) born after twins.

Irv (Irish, Welsh, English) a short form of Irvin, Irving.

Irvin (Irish, Welsh, English) a short form of Irving. See also Ervine.
Inek, Irv, Irven, Irvine, Irvinn, Irvon

Irving (Irish) handsome. (Welsh) white river. (English) sea friend. See also Ervin, Ervine.
Irv, Irvin, Irvington, Irvin, Irwing

Irwin (English) a form of Irving. See also Ervin.
Irvinn, Irvyn

Isa (Arabic) a form of Jesus.
Isaah

Isaac (Hebrew) he will laugh. Bible: the son of Abraham and Sarah. See also Itzak, Izak, Yitzchak.
Aizik, Icek, Ike, Ikey, Ikie, Isaak, Isaakios, Isiac, Isiac, Isacco, Isack, Isaic, Ishaq, Isiac, Isiaic, Issa, Issca, Izaak, Izak, Izzy

Isaak (Hebrew) a form of Isaac.
Isack, Isak, Isik, Issak

Isaiah (Hebrew) God is my salvation. Bible: a Hebrew prophet.
Isa, Isai, Isaia, Isaias, Isaid, Isaih, Isaiah, Ishaq, Isia, Isiah, Isiash, Issia, Issiah, Izaiah, Izaiha, Izaya, Izayah, Izayaih, Izayiah, Izeyah, Izeyha

Isaias (Hebrew) a form of Isaiah.
Isaiahs, Isais, Izayus

Isam (Arabic) safeguard.

Isas (Japanese) meritorious.

Isekemu (Native American) slow-moving creek.

Isham (English) home of the iron one.

Ishan (Hindi) direction.
Ishaan, Ishaun

Ishaq (Arabic) a form of Isaac.
Ishaac, Ishak

Ishmael (Hebrew) God will hear. Literature: the narrator of Herman Melville's novel *Moby-Dick*.
Ismael, Isamail, Ishma, Ishmail, Ismale, Ishmeal, Ishmeil, Ishmel, Ishmil, Ismael, Ismail

Isidore (Greek) gift of Isis. See also Dorian, Ysidro.
Isidor, Isadore, Isadorios, Isidor, Isidro, Issy, Ixidor, Izadore, Izidor, Izidore, Izydor, Izzy

Isidro (Greek) a form of Isidore.
Isidoro, Isidoros

Iskander (Afghan) a form of Alexander.

Ismael (Arabic) a form of Ishmael.

Ismail (Arabic) a form of Ishmael.
Ismeil, Ismiel

Israel (Hebrew) prince of God; wrestled with God. History: the nation of Israel took its name from the name given Jacob after he wrestled with the angel of the Lord. See also Yisrael.
Iser, Isreal, Israhel, Isrell, Israel, Isser, Izrael, Izzy, Yisrael

isreal (Hebrew) a form of Israel.
Isrial

Issa (Swahili) God is our salvation.

Issac (Hebrew) a form of Isaac.
Issac, Issaic, Issic

Issiah (Hebrew) a form of Isaiah.
Issaiah, Issia

Istu (Native American) sugar pine.

István (Hungarian) a form of Stephen.
Isti, Istvan, Pista

Ithel (Welsh) generous lord.

Ittamar (Hebrew) island of palms.
Itamar

Itzak (Hebrew) a form of Isaac,
Yitzchak.
Itzik

lukini (Hawaiian) a form of Eugene.
Kini

lustin (Bulgarian, Russian) a form of Justin.

Ivan (Russian) a form of John.
Iván, Ivanchik, Ivanichek, Ivann, Ivano, Ivas, Iven, Ivin, Ivon, Ivyn, Varya

Ivar (Scandinavian) a form of Ivor. See also Yves, Yvon.
Iv, Iva

Ives (English) young archer.
Ive, Iven, Ivey, Yves

Ivo (German) yew wood; bow wood.
Ibon, Ifor, Ivar, Ives, Ivon, Ivonnie, Ivor, Yvo

Ivor (Scandinavian) a form of Ivo.
Ibon, Ivar, Ives, Ivor, Ivory, Ivry

Iwan (Polish) a form of John.

Iye (Native American) smoke.

Iyapo (Yoruba) many trials; many obstacles.

Izzy (Hebrew) a familiar form of Isaac, Isidore, Israel.
Issy

Izak (Czech) a form of Isaac.
Itzhak, Ixaka, Izaac, Izaak, Izac, Izaic, Izak, Izec, Izeeke, Izick, Izik, Izsak, Izsák, Izzak

Jaan (Estonian) a form of Christian.

Jaap (Dutch) a form of Jim.

Jabari (Swahili) fearless, brave.
Jabar, Jabahri, Jabar, Jabarae, Jabare, Jabaree, Jabarei, Jabarie, Jabarri, Jabari, Jabary, Jabbar, Jabbaree, Jabbari, Jaber, Jabiari, Jabier, Jabori, Jaborie

Jabez (Hebrew) born in pain.
Jabe, Jabes, Jabesh

Jabin (Hebrew) God has created.
Jabain, Jabien, Jabon

Jabir (Arabic) consoler, comforter.
Jabiri, Jabori

Jabril (Arabic) a form of Jibril.
Jabrail, Jabree, Jabreel, Jabrel, Jabrell, Jabrelle, Jabri, Jabrial, Jabrie, Jabriel, Jabrielle, Jabrille

Jabulani (Shona) happy.

Jacan (Hebrew) trouble.
Jachin

Jacen (Greek) a form of Jason.
Jacon

Jacari (American) a form of Jacorey.
Jacarey, Jacaris, Jacarius, Jacarre, Jacarri, Jacarris, Jacarus, Jacary, Jacaure, Jacaurri, Jaccar, Jaccari

Jace (American) a combination of the initials J. + C.
JC, J.C., Jacee, Jacek, Jacey, Jacie, Jaice, Jaice, Jaicee

Jacinto (Portuguese, Spanish) hyacinth. See also Giacinto.
Jacindo, Jacint, Jacinta

J

J (American) an initial used as a first name.
J.

Ja (Korean) attractive, magnetic.

Jaali (Swahili) powerful.

Jack (American) a familiar form of Jacob, John. See also Keaka.
Jackie, Jacko, Jackub, Jak, Jax, Jock, Jocko

Jackie, Jacky (American) familiar forms of Jack.
Jackey

Jackson (English) son of Jack.
Jacksen, Jacksin, Jacson, Jakson, Jaxon

Jaco (Portuguese) a form of Jacob.

Jacob (Hebrew) supplanter, substitute. Bible: son of Isaac, brother of Esau. See also Akiva, Chago, Checha, Coby, Diego, Giacomo, Hamish, Iago, Iakobos, James, Kiva, Koby, Kuba, Tiago, Yakov, Yasha, Yoakim.
Jaap, Jachob, Jack, Jackob, Jackub, Jaco, Jacobb, Jacobe, Jacobi, Jacobo, Jacoby, Jacolbi, Jacolby, Jacque, Jacques, Jacub, Jacob, Jago, Jaicob, Jaime, Jake, Jakob, Jalu, Jasha, Jaycob, Jecis, Jeks, Jeska, Jim, Jocek, Jock, Jocob, Jocobb, Jocoby, Jocolby, Jokubas

Jacobi, Jacoby (Hebrew) forms of Jacob.
Jachobi, Jacobbe, Jacobee, Jacobey, Jacobie, Jacobii, Jacobis

Jacobo (Hebrew) a form of Jacob.

Jacobson (English) son of Jacob.
Jacobs, Jacobsen, Jacobsin, Jacobus

Jacorey (American) a combination of Jacob + Corey.
Jacari, Jacori, Jacoria, Jacorie, Jacoris, Jacorius, Jacorrey, Jacorrien, Jacorry, Jacory, Jacouri, Jacourie, Jakari

Jacque (French) a form of Jacob.
Jacquay, Jacqui, Jocque, Jocqui

Jacques (French) a form of Jacob, James. See also Coco.
Jackque, Jackques, Jackquise, Jacot, Jacquan, Jacquees, Jacquese, Jacquess, Jacquet, Jacquett, Jacquez, Jacquis, Jacquise, Jacquez, Jarques, Jarquis

Jacquez, Jaquez (French) forms of Jacques.
Jaques, Jaquese, Jaqueus, Jaqueze, Jaquis, Jaquise, Jaquze, Jocquez

Jacy (Tupi-Guarani) moon.
Jaicy, Jaycee

Jade (Spanish) jade, precious stone.
Jacid, Jaid, Jaide

Jaden (Hebrew) a form of Jadon.
Jadee, Jadeen, Jadenn, Jadeon, Jadin, Jaeden

Jadon (Hebrew) God has heard.
Jaden, Jadyn, Jaedon, Jaiden, Jaydon

Jadrien (American) a combination of Jay + Adrien.
Jad, Jada, Jadd, Jader, Jadrian

Jadyn (Hebrew) a form of Jadon.
Jadyne, Jaelyn

Jaegar (German) hunter.
Jaager, Jaeger, Jagur

Jael (Hebrew) mountain goat.
Yael

Jaelen (American) a form of Jalen.
Jaelan, Jaelaun, Jaelin, Jaelon, Jaelyn

Ja'far (Sanskrit) little stream.
Jafar, Jafari, Jaffar, Jaffer, Jafur

Jagger (English) carter.
Jagar, Jager, Jaggar

Jago (English) a form of James.

Jaguar (Spanish) jaguar.
Jagguar

Jahi (Swahili) dignified.

Jahlil (Hindi) a form of Jalil.
Jahlal, Jahlee, Jahleel, Jahliel

Jahmar (American) a form of Jamar.
Jahmare, Jahmari, Jahmarr, Jahmer

Jahvon (Hebrew) a form of Javan.
Jahvan, Jahvine, Jahwaan, Jahwon

Jai (Tai) heart.
Jaie, Jaii

Jaiden (Hebrew) a form of Jadon.
Jaidan, Jaidon, Jaidyn

Jailen (American) a form of Jalen.
Jailan, Jailani, Jaileen, Jailen, Jailon, Jailyn, Jailynn

Jaime (Spanish) a form of Jacob, James.
Jaimee, Jaimey, Jaimie, Jaimito, Jaimy, Jayme, Jaymie

Jairo (Spanish) God enlightens.
Jair, Jairay, Jaire, Jairus, Jarius

Jaison (Greek) a form of Jason.
Jaisan, Jaisen, Jaishon, Jaishun

Jaivon (Hebrew) a form of Javan.
Jaiven, Jaivion, Jaiwon

Jaja (Ibo) honored.

Jajuan (American) a combination of the prefix Ja + Juan.
Ja Juan, Jauan, Jawaun, Jejuan, Jujuan, Juwan

Jakari (American) a form
of Jacorey.
Jakaire, Jakar, Jakaray, Jakaree,
Jakarius, Jakarre, Jakarri, Jakaris

Jake (Hebrew) a short form of Jacob.
Jakie, Jayk, Jayke

Jakeem (Arabic) uplifted.

Jakob (Hebrew) a form of Jacob.
Jakeob, Jaikab, Jaikob, Jakeb, Jakeob,
Jakeub, Jakib, Jakin, Jakobe, Jakobi,
Jakobus, Jakoby, Jakor, Jakovian, Jakub,
Jakeubek, Jekebs

Jakome (Basque) a form of James.
Xanti

Jal (Gypsy) wanderer.

Jalan (American) a form of Jalen.
Jalaan, Jalaen, Jalain, Jaland, Jalane,
Jalani, Jalanie, Jalaun, Jalaun, Jalan,
Jalian

Jaleel (Hindi) a form of Jalil.
Jaleell, Jaleil, Jalel

Jalen (American) a combination of the
prefix Ja + Len.
Jaelen, Jailen, Jalan, Jaleen, Jalend, Jalene,
Jalin, Jallen, Jalon, Jalyn

Jalil (Hindi) revered.
Jahlil, Jalaal, Jalal

Jalin, Jalyn (American) forms of Jalen.
Jalian, Jaline, Jalynn, Jalynne

Jalon (American) a form of Jalen.
Jalone, Jaloni, Jalun

Jam (American) a short form of Jamal.
Jamar.
Jama

Jamaal (Arabic) a form of Jamal.

Jamaine (Arabic) a form of Germain.

Jamal (Arabic) handsome. See also
Gamal.
Jahmal, Jahmall, Jahmalle, Jahmeal,
Jahmeel, Jahmeil, Jahmel, Jahmelle,
Jahmil, Jahmile, Jaimal, Jam, Jamaad,
Jamael, Jamahl, Jamalle, Jamar, Jamad,
Jamal, Jamall, Jamalle, Jamar, Jamaral,
Jamel, Jamil, Jammal, Jamor, Jaumal,
Jarmal, Jaumal, Jemal, Jermal, Jomal,
Jomall

Jamar (American) a form of Jamal.
Jam, Jamaar, Jamaari, Jamahrae, Jamair,
Jamara, Jamaras, Jamaraus, Jamarl, Jamarr,
Jamare, Jamarea, Jamaree, Jamari,
Jamaris, Jamaur, Jamaree, Jamari,
Jammar, Jarmar, Jarmar, Jaumar, Jemar,
Jemar, Jimar, Jomar

Jamarcus (American) a combination
of the prefix Ja + Marcus.
Jamarco, Jamarkes, Jemarcus, Jimarcus

Jamari (American) a form of Jamario.
Jamare, Jamarea, Jamaree, Jamareh,
Jamaria, Jamarie, Jamaul

Jamario (American) a combination of
the prefix Ja + Mario.
Jamareo, Jamari, Jamariel, Jamarious,
Jamaris, Jamariya, Jemario,
Jemaris

Jamarquis (American) a combination
of the prefix Ja + Marquis.
Jamarkees, Jamarkens, Jamarkeis,
Jamarese, Jamarquese, Jamarques,
Jamarquez, Jamarquies, Jamarquis

Jamel (Arabic) a form of Jamal.
Jameel, Jamele, Jamell, Jamelle, Jammel,
Jamnel, Jamnul, Jarmel, Jaumal, Jaumell,
Je-Mell, Jimell

James (Hebrew) supplanter, substitute.
(English) a form of Jacob. Bible:
James the Great and James the Less
were two of the Twelve Apostles. See
also Diego, Hamish, Iago, Kimo,
Santiago, Seamus, Seumas, Yago,
Yasha.
Jacques, Jago, Jaime, Jaimes, Jakome,
Jamesie, Jamesy, Jamez, Jameze, Jamie,
Jamies, Jamse, Jamyes, Jamze, Jas, Jasha,
Jay, Jaymes, Jem, Jemes, Jim

Jameson (English) son of James.
Jamerson, Jamesian, Jamison, Jaymeson

Jamie (English) a familiar form of
James.
Jaime, Jaimey, Jaimie, Jame, Jamee, Jamey,
Jameyel, Jami, Jamia, Jamiah, Jamian,
Jamie, Jamiee, Jamiee, Jammy, Jamy
Jamye, Jayme, Jaymee, Jaymie

Jamil (Arabic) a form of Jamal.
Jamiel, Jamiell, Jamielle, Jamill,
Jamille, Jamyl, Jarmil

Jamin (Hebrew) favored.
Jamen, Jamian, Jamien, Jamion, Jamionn,
Jamon, Jaman, Jamyn, Jarmin, Jarmon,
Jaymin

Jamison (English) son of James.
Jamiesen, Jamieson, Jamis, Jamisen,
Jamyson, Jaymison

Jamon (Hebrew) a form of Jamin.
Jamohn, Jamone, Jamoni

Jamond (American) a combination of James + Raymond.
Jamod, Jamont, Jamonta, Jamontae, Jamontay, Jamonte, Jarmond

Jamor (American) a form of Jamal.
Jamoree, Jamori, Jamorie, Jamories, Jamorrio, Jamorris, Jamory, Jamour

Jamsheed (Persian) from Persia.
Jamshaid, Jamshed

Jan (Dutch, Slavic) a form of John.
Jaan, Jana, Janae, Jann, Janne, Jano, Janson, Jenda, Yan

Janco (Czech) a form of John.
Jancsi, Janke, Janko

Jando (Spanish) a form of Alexander.
Jandino

Janeil (American) a combination of the prefix Ja + Neil.
Janal, Janel, Janell, Janelle, Janiel, Janielle, Janile, Janille, Jarnail, Jarneil, Jarnell

Janek (Polish) a form of John.
Janak, Janik, Janika, Janka, Jankiel, Janko

Janis (Latvian) a form of John.
Ansis, Jancis, Zanis

Janne (Finnish) a form of John.
Jann, Jannes

János (Hungarian) a form of John.
Jancsi, Jani, Jankia, Jano

Janson (Scandinavian) son of Jan.
Janse, Jansen, Jansin, Janssen, Jansun, Jantzen, Janzen, Jensen, Jenson

Jantzen (Scandinavian) a form of Janson.
Janten, Jantsen, Jantson

Janus (Latin) gate, passageway; born in January. Mythology: the Roman god of beginnings and endings.
Jannse, Jannus, Januario, Janusz

Japheth (Hebrew) handsome. (Arabic) abundant. Bible: a son of Noah. See also Yaphet.
Japeth, Japhet

Jaquan (American) a combination of the prefix Ja + Quan.
Jaequan, Jaiqaun, Jaiqiuan, Jaqaun, Jaqawan, Jaquaan, Jaquain, Ja'quan, Jaquane, Jaquann, Jaquanne, Jaquavius, Jaquaun, Jaquin, Jaquon, Jaqwan

Jaquarius (American) a combination of Jaquan + Darius.
Jaquari, Jaquarious, Jaquaris

Jaquavius (American) a form of Jaquan.
Jaquavas, Jaquaveis, Jaquaveius, Jaquaveon, Jaquaveous, Jaquavias, Jaquavious, Jaquavis, Jaquavus

Jaquon (American) a form of Jaquan.
Jaeqvon, Jaqoun, Jaquinn, Jaqune, Jaquoin, Jaquone, Jaqvon

Jarad (Hebrew) a form of Jared.
Jaraad, Jaraed

Jarah (Hebrew) sweet as honey.
Jerah

Jardan (Hebrew) a form of Jordan.
Jarden, Jardin, Jardon

Jareb (Hebrew) contending.
Jarib

Jared (Hebrew) a form of Jordan.
Jahred, Jaired, Jarad, Jaredd, Jareid, Jarid, Jarod, Jarrad, Jarrett, Jarrod, Jarryd, Jerad, Jered, Jerod, Jerrad, Jerred, Jerrod, Jerryd, Jordan

Jarek (Slavic) born in January.
Janiuszck, Jannarius, Jannisz, Jare, Jarrek, Jarric, Jarrick

Jarell (Scandinavian) a form of Gerald.
Jairell, Jarael, Jareil, Jarel, Jarelle, Jariel, Jarrell, Jarryl, Jayryl, Jerel, Jerell, Jerrell, Jharell

Jaren (Hebrew) a form of Jaron.
Jarian, Jarien, Jarin, Jarion

Jareth (American) a combination of Jared + Gareth.
Jarreth, Jereth, Jarreth

Jarett (English) a form of Jarrett.
Jaret, Jarette

Jarl (Scandinavian) earl, nobleman.

Jarlath (Latin) in control.
Jarl, Jarlen

Jarman (German) from Germany.
Jerman

Jarod (Hebrew) a form of Jared.
Jarodd, Jaroid

Jaron (Hebrew) he will sing; he will cry out.
Jaaron, Jairon, Jaron, Jarone, Jaren, Jarron, Jaryn, Jayron, Jayronn, Je Ronn, J'ron

Jaroslav (Czech) glory of spring.
Jarda

Jarred (Hebrew) a form of Jared.
Ja'red, Jarrad, Jarrayd, Jarrod,
Jarryd, Jerrid

Jarrell (English) a form of Gerald.
Jarel, Jarell, Jarrel, Jerall, Jerel, Jerell

Jarren (Hebrew) a form of Jaron.
Jarrin, Jarran, Jarrian, Jarrin

Jarrett (English) a form of Garrett,
Jared.
Jairett, Jareth, Jarett, Jarette, Jarhett,
Jarratt, Jarret, Jarrette, Jarrot, Jarrott, Jerrett

Jarrod (Hebrew) a form of Jared.
Jarod, Jerod, Jerrod

Jarryd (Hebrew) a form of Jared.
Jarrayd, Jaryd

Jarvis (German) skilled with a spear.
Jarvaris, Jarv, Jarvaris, Jarvas, Jarvaska,
Jarvey, Jarvez, Jarvie, Jarvios, Jarvious,
Jarvis, Jarvorice, Jarvoris, Jarvous, Jarvus,
Javaris, Jervey, Jervis

Jas (Polish) a form of John. (English) a
familiar form of James.
Jasio

Jasha (Russian) a familiar form of
Jacob, James.
Jascha

Jashawn (American) a combination of
the prefix Ja + Shawn.
Jasean, Jashan, Jashaun, Jashion, Jashon

Jaskaran (Sikh) sings praises to the
Lord.
Jaskaren, Jaskarn, Jaskiran

Jasmin (Persian) jasmine flower.
Jasman, Jasmarie, Jasmine, Jasmon,
Jasmond

Jason (Greek) healer. Mythology: the
hero who led the Argonauts in
search of the Golden Fleece.
Jacen, Jacson, Jahson, Jaison, Jasan,
Jasaun, Jase, Jasen, Jasin, Jasson, Jasten,
Jasun, Jasyn, Jathan, Jaxon, Jay, Jayson

Jasper (French) brown, red, or yellow
ornamental stone. (English) a form of
Casper. See also Kasper.
Jaspar, Jazper, Jespat, Jesper

Jaspal (Punjabi) living a virtuous
lifestyle.

Jasson (Greek) a form of Jason.
Jassen, Jassin

Jatinra (Hindi) great Brahmin sage.

Javan (Hebrew) Bible: son of Japheth.
Jaevan, Jahvaughan, Jahvon, Jaivon,
Javaunte, Javaon, JaVaughn, Javen, Javian,
Javien, Javin, Javine, Javaanta, Javon,
Javona, Javone, Javonte, Jayvin, Jayvion,
Jayvon, Jevan, Jevon

Javante (American) a form of Javan.
Javantae, Javantai, Javantée, Javanti

Javaris (English) a form of Jarvis.
Javaor, Javar, Javarias, Javare, Javares,
Javari, Javarias, Javario, Javaris,
Javaro, Javarous, Javarre, Javarreis,
Javarri, Javarrious, Javarris, Javarro,
Javarous, Javarre, Javarus, Javorious,
Javoris, Javorius

Javas (Sanskrit) quick, swift.
Javvas, Jayvis

Javier (Spanish) owner of a new
house. See also Xavier.
Jabier, Javer, Javere, Javiar

Javon (Hebrew) a form of Javan.
Jaavon, Jaevin, Jaevon, Jaevon, Javeon,
Javoney, Javionne, Javohn, Javona, Javone,
Javonnie, Javonnte, Javonn, Javonni,
Javonté, Javontee, Javonteh,
Javontey

Javonte (American) a form of Javan.
Javona, Javontae, Javontai, Javontay,
Javontaye, Javonté, Javontee, Javonteh,
Javontey

Jawaun (American) a form of Jajuan.
Jawaan, Jawaun, Jawn, Jawon,
Jawuan

Jawhar (Arabic) jewel; essence.

Jaxon (English) a form of Jackson.
Jaxen, Jaxsen, Jaxson, Jaxsun, Jaxun

Jay (French) blue jay. (English) a short
form of James, Jason.
Jae, Jai, Jaye, Jeays, Jeyes

Jayce (American) a combination of
the initials J. + C.
JC, J.C., Jaye, Jaycee, Jay Cee, Jaycey,
Jecie

Jaycob (Hebrew) a form of Jacob.
Jaycub, Jaykob

Jayde (American) a combination of
the initials J. + D.
JD, J.D., Jayd, Jaydee, Jayden

Jayden (American) a form of Jayde.
Jaydan, Jaydin, Jaydn, Jaydon

Jaylee (American) a combination of Jay + Lee.
Jayla, Jayle, Jaylen

Jaylen (American) a combination of Jay + Len.
Jaylaan, Jaylan, Jayland, Jayleen, Jaylend, Jaylin, Jayln, Jaylon, Jaylun, Jaylund, Jaylyn

Jaylin (American) a form of Jaylen.
Jaylian, Jayline

Jaylon (American) a form of Jaylen.
Jayleon

Jaylyn (American) a form of Jaylen.
Jaylynd, Jaylynn, Jaylynne

Jayme (English) a form of Jamie.
Jaymie

Jaymes (English) a form of James.
Jaymis, Jayms, Jaymz

Jayquan (American) a combination of Jay + Quan.
Jaykuan, Jaykwon, Jayqon, Jayquawn, Jayqunn

Jayson (Greek) a form of Jason.
Jaycent, Jaysean, Jaysen, Jayshaun, Jayshawn, Jayshon, Jayshun, Jaysin, Jaysn, Jayssen, Jaysson, Jaysun

Jayvon (American) a form of Javon.
Jayvion, Jayvohn, Jayvone, Jayvonn, Jayvontay, Jayvonte, Jayvuan, Jayvuann, Jayvin

Jazz (American) jazz.
Jaz, Jazze, Jazzlee, Jazzman, Jazzmen, Jazzmin, Jazzmon, Jazztin, Jazzton, Jazzy

Jean (French) a form of John.
Jéan, Jeane, Jeannah, Jeannie, Jeannot, Jeano, Jeanot, Jeanty, Jene

Jeb (Hebrew) a short form of Jebediah.
Jebb, Jebi, Jeby

Jebediah (Hebrew) a form of Jedidiah.
Jeb, Jebadia, Jebadiah, Jebadieh, Jebidiah

Jed (Hebrew) a short form of Jedidiah. (Arabic) hand.
Jedd, Jeddy, Jedi

Jediah (Hebrew) hand of God.
Jedaia, Jedaiah, Jedeiah, Jedi, Yedaya

Jedidiah (Hebrew) friend of God, beloved of God. See also Didi.
Jebediah, Jed, Jedadiah, Jedadediah, Jedediah, Jedediha, Jedidia, Jedidiah, Jedidiyah, Yedidya

Jedrek (Polish) strong; manly.
Jedric, Jedrik, Jedrus

Jeff (English) a short form of Jefferson, Jeffrey. A familiar form of Geoffrey.
Jef, Jefe, Jeffe, Jeffey, Jeffie, Jeffy, Jhef

Jefferson (English) son of Jeff.
History: Thomas Jefferson was the third U.S. president.
Jeferson, Jeff, Jeffers

Jeffery (English) a form of Jeffrey.
Jefery, Jeffari, Jeffary, Jeffeory, Jefferay, Jeffereoy, Jefferey, Jefferie, Jeffory

Jefford (English) Jeff's ford.

Jeffrey (English) divinely peaceful. See also Geffrey, Geoffrey, Godfrey.
Jeff, Jefferies, Jeffery, Jeffie, Jeffree, Jeffrie,

Jeffrey, Jeffrie, Jeffries, Jeffry, Jefre, Jefri, Jefry, Jeoffroi, Joffre, Joffrey

Jeffry (English) a form of Jeffrey.

Jehan (French) a form of John.
Jehann

Jehu (Hebrew) God lives. Bible: a military commander and king of Israel.
Yehu

Jelani (Swahili) mighty.
Jel, Jelan, Jelanie, Jelaun

Jem (English) a short form of James, Jeremiah.
Jemmie, Jemmy

Jemal (Arabic) a form of Jamal.
Jemaal, Jemael, Jemale, Jemel

Jemel (Arabic) a form of Jemal.
Jemeal, Jemehl, Jemehyl, Jemell, Jemelle, Jemello, Jemeyle, Jemile, Jemmy

Jemond (French) worldly.
Jemon, Jémond, Jemonde, Jemone

Jenkin (Flemish) little John.
Jenkins, Jenkyn, Jenkyns, Jennings

Jenõ (Hungarian) a form of Eugene.
Jenci, Jency, Jenoe, Jensi, Jensy

Jens (Danish) a form of John.
Jense, Jensen, Jenson, Jenssen, Jensy, Jentz

Jeovanni (Italian) a form of Giovanni.
Jeovahny, Jeovan, Jeovani, Jeovany

Jequan (American) a combination of the prefix Je + Quan.
Jequan, Jequann, Jequon

Jerad, Jerrad (Hebrew) forms of Jared.
Jeread, Jeredd

Jerahmy (Hebrew) a form of Jeremy:
Jerahmeel, Jerahmeil, Jerahmey

Jerald (English) a form of Gerald.
Jeraldo, Jerold, Jerrald, Jerrold, Jerry

Jerall (English) a form of Jarrell.
Jerael, Jerai, Jerail, Jeraile, Jeral, Jerale,
Jerall, Jerrail, Jerral, Jerrel, Jerrell, Jerrelle

Jeramie, Jeramy (Hebrew) forms of
Jeremy.
Jerame, Jeramee, Jeramey, Jerami, Jerammie

Jerard (French) a form of Gerard.
Jarard, Jarrard, Jerardo, Jeraude, Jerrard

jere (Hebrew) a short form of
Jeremiah, Jeremy.
Jeré, Jeree

Jered, Jerred (Hebrew) forms of
Jared.
Jereed, Jerid, Jeryd, Jeryd

Jerel, Jerell, jerell (English) forms of
Jarell.
Jerelle, Jeriel, Jeril, Jerrail, Jerrel, Jerrall,
Jerrel, Jerrill, Jerriol, Jerroll, Jerryl, Jerryll,
Jeryl, Jeryle

Jereme, Jeremey (Hebrew) forms of
Jeremy.
Jarame

Jeremiah (Hebrew) God will uplift.
Bible: a Hebrew prophet. See also
Dermot, Yeremey, Yirmaya.
Geremiah, Jaramia, Jem, Jemeriah,
Jermiah, Jeramiah, Jeramiia, Jere, Jereias,
Jeremaya, Jeremi, Jeremia, Jeremiad,
Jeremias, Jeremijia, Jeremy, Jerimiah,
Jerimiha, Jerimya, Jermiah, Jermijia, Jerry

Jeremie, Jérémie (Hebrew) forms of
Jeremy.
Jeremi, Jérémie, Jeremii

Jeremy (English) a form of Jeremiah.
Jaremay, Jaremi, Jaremy, Jem, Jemmy,
Jerahmy, Jeramie, Jeramy, Jere, Jereamy,
Jereme, Jeremee, Jeremey, Jeremie, Jérémie,
Jeremy, Jéremy, Jeremye, Jereomy, Jeriemy,
Jerime, Jerimy, Jermey, Jeromy, Jeremy

Jeriah (Hebrew) Jehovah has seen.

Jericho (Arabic) city of the moon.
Bible: a city conquered by Joshua.
Jeric, Jericke, Jerico, Jerike, Jerick,
Jerrico, Jerricoh, Jeryco

Jermaine (French) a form of Germain.
(English) sprout, bud.
Jaman, Jeremaine, Jeremane, Jeremane,
Jermain, Jerman, Jermane, Jermanie,
Jermanny, Jermany, Jermayn, Jermayne,
Jermiane, Jermine, Jer-Mon, Jermone,
Jermoney, Jurmaine

Jermal (Arabic) a form of Jamal.
Jermael, Jermail, Jermaul, Jermel,
Jermell, Jermil, Jermol, Jermyll

Jermey (English) a form of Jeremy.
Jerme, Jermee, Jermere, Jermery, Jermie,
Jermy, Jhermie

Jermiah (Hebrew) a form of Jeremiah.
Jermiha, Jermiya

Jerney (Slavic) a form of
Bartholomew.

Jerod, Jerrod (Hebrew) forms of
Jarrod.
Jerode, Jeroid

Jerolin (Basque, Latin) holy.

Jerome, Jérôme (Latin) holy. See also
Geronimo, Hieronymos.
Gerome, Jere, Jeroen, Jerom, Jérome,
Jérôme, Jeromo, Jeromy, Jeron, Jerónimo,
Jerome, Jeromy

Jeron (English) a form of Jerome.
Jeromee, Jeromey, Jeromie
Jéron, Jerone, Jeronime, Jerrin, Jerrion,
Jerron, Jerrone, J'ron

Jeromy (Latin) a form of Jerome.
Jeron, Jerome, Jeronimo, Jerrin, Jerrion,
Jerron, Jerrone, J'ron

Jerrett (Hebrew) a form of Jarrett.
Jeret, Jerett, Jeritt, Jerret, Jerrette, Jerriot,
Jerritt, Jerrot, Jerrott

Jerrick (American) a combination of
Jerry + Derrick.
Jaric, Jarrick, Jerick, Jerrik

Jerry (German) mighty spearman.
(English) a familiar form of Gerald,
Gerard. See also Gerry, Kele.
Jehri, Jere, Jeree, Jeris, Jerison, Jeri, Jerric,
Jery

Jervis (English) a form of Gervaise,
Jarvis.

Jerzy (Polish) a form of George.
Jersey, Jerzey, Jurek

Jess (Hebrew) a short form of Jesse.
Jeshuah

Jesse (Hebrew) wealthy. Bible: the
father of David. See also Yishai.
Jese, Jesee, Jesi, Jess, Jessé, Jessee, Jessie,
Jessy

Jessie (Hebrew) a form of Jesse.
Jessie, Jessi, Jessi

Jerall ...

Jerel ...

Jeremiah

Jerod, Jerrod

Jermiah (Hebrew) a form of Jeremiah.
Jermiha, Jermiya

Jeshua (Hebrew) a form of Joshua.

Jessy (Hebrew) a form of Jesse.
Jescey, Jessey, Jessye, Jessyie, Jesy

Jestin (Welsh) a form of Justin.
Jessten, Jesten, Jeston, Jesstin, Jesston

Jesus (Hebrew) a form of Joshua.
Bible: son of Mary and Joseph,
believed by Christians to be the Son
of God. See also Chucho, Isa, Yosu.
Jecho, Jessus, Jesu, Jesú, Jesús, Josu

Jesús (Hispanic) a form of Jesus.

Jethro (Hebrew) abundant. Bible: the
father-in-law of Moses. See also
Yitro.
Jeth, Jethroe, Jetro, Jett

Jett (English) hard, black mineral.
(Hebrew) a short form of Jethro.
Jet, Jetson, Jetter, Jetty

Jevan (Hebrew) a form of Javan.
Jevaun, Jeven, Jevin

Jevon (Hebrew) a form of Javan.
*Jevion, Jevohn, Jevone, Jevonn, Jevonne,
Jevonnie*

Jevonte (American) a form of Jevon.
Jevonta, Jevontae, Jevontaye, Jevonté

Jibade (Yoruba) born close to royalty.

Jibben (Gypsy) life.
Jibin

Jibril (Arabic) archangel of Allah.
Jabril, Jibreel, Jibriel

Jilt (Dutch) money.

Jim (Hebrew, English) a short form of
James. See also Jaap.
Jimbo, Jimm, Jimmy

Jimbo (American) a familiar form of
Jim.
Jimboo

Jimell (Arabic) a form of Jamel.
*Jimel, Jimelle, Jimill, Jimmell, Jimmelle,
Jimmiel, Jimmil*

Jimiyu (Abaluhya) born in the dry season.

Jimmie (English) a form of Jimmy.
Jimi, Jimie, Jimmee, Jimmi

Jimmy (English) a familiar form of
Jim.
Jimmey, Jimmie, Jimmye, Jimmyjo, Jimy

Jimoh (Swahili) born on Friday.

Jin (Chinese) gold.
Jinn

Jindra (Czech) a form of Harold.

Jing-Quo (Chinese) ruler of the country.

Jiovanni (Italian) a form of Giovanni.
*Jio, Jiovani, Jiovanie, Jiovannie,
Jiovanny, Jiovany, Jiovoni, Jivan*

Jirair (Armenian) strong; hard working.

Jiri (Czech) a form of George.
Jirka

Jiro (Japanese) second son.

Jivin (Hindi) life giver.
Jivanta

Jo (Hebrew, Japanese) a form of Joe.

Joab (Hebrew) God is father. See also
Yoav.
Joabe, Joaby

Joachim (Hebrew) God will establish.
See also Akeem, Ioakim, Yehoyakem.
*Joacheim, Joakim, Joaquim, Joaquin,
Jokin, Jov*

João (Portuguese) a form of John.

Joaquim (Portuguese) a form of
Joachim.

Joaquín (Spanish) a form of Joachim,
Yehoyakem.
*Jehoichin, Joaquin, Joaquin, Jocquinn,
Joquin, Juaquin*

Job (Hebrew) afflicted. Bible: a righteous man whose faith in God sur-
vived the test of many afflictions.
Jobe, Jobert, Jobey, Jobie, Joby

Joben (Japanese) enjoys cleanliness.
Joban, Jobin

Jobo (Spanish) a familiar form of
Joseph.

Joby (Hebrew) a familiar form of Job.
Jobie

Jock (American) a familiar form of
Jacob.
Jocko, Joco, Jocoby, Jocolby

Jocquez (French) a form of Jacquez.
Jocques, Jocquis, Jocquise

Jodan (Hebrew) a combination of Jo
+ Dan.
*Jodahn, Joden, Jodhan, Jodian, Jodin,
Jodon, Jodonnis*

Jody (Hebrew) a familiar form of
Joseph.
Jodey, Jodi, Jodie, Jodiha, Joedy

Joe (Hebrew) a short form of Joseph.
Jo, Joey, Joey

Joel (Hebrew) God is willing. Bible: an Old Testament Hebrew prophet.
Jóel, joel, Joell, Joelle, Joely, Jole, Yoel

Joey (Hebrew) a familiar form of Joe, Joseph.

Joeseph (Hebrew) a form of Joseph.
Joesph

Johan, Johann (German) forms of John. See also Anno, Hanno, Yoan, Yohan.
Joahan, Joan, Joannes, Johahn, Johan, Johanan, Johane, Johannan, Johannes, Johanthan, Johathan, Johation, Johian, Johon

Johannes (German) a form of Johan, Johann.
Johannes, Johannus, Johansen, Johanson, Johonson

John (Hebrew) God is gracious. Bible: the name honoring John the Baptist and John the Evangelist. See also Eilchanan, Evan, Geno, Gian, Giovanni, Handel, Hannes, Hans, Hanus, Honza, Ian, Ianos, Iban, Ioan, Ivan, Iwan, Keoni, Kwam, Ohannes, Sean, Ugutz, Yan, Yanka, Yanni, Yochanan, Yohance, Zane.
Jack, Jacsi, Jaenda, Jahn, Jan, Janak, Janco, Janek, Janis, Janne, Jánes, Jansen, Janoe, Jantzen, Jas, Jean, Jehan, Jen, Jenkin, Jenkyn, Jens, Jhan, Jhanick, Jhon, Jian, João, João, Jock, Joen, Johan, Johann, Johne, Johni, Johniee, Johnnie, Johnny, Johnson, Jon, Jonam, Jonas, Jone, Jones, Jonny, Jonté, Jovan, Juan, Juliana

Johnathan (Hebrew) a form of Jonathan.
Jhonathan, Johathe, Johnaten, Johnathann, Johnathaon, Johnathen, Johnathyne, Johnatten, Johniathin, Johnothan, Johnthan

Johnathon (Hebrew) a form of Jonathon. See also Yanton.
Johnathon

Johnnie (Hebrew) a familiar form of John.
Johnie, Johnie, Johnni, Johnsie, Jonni, Jonnie

Johnny (Hebrew) a familiar form of John. See also Gianni.
Jantje, Jhonny, Johney, Johnney, Johnny

Johnson (English) son of John.
Johnston, Jonson

Joji (Japanese) a form of George.

Jojo (Fante) born on Monday.

Jokim (Basque) a form of Joachim.

Jolon (Native American) valley of the dead oaks.

Jomar (American) a form of Jamar.
Jomari, Jomarie, Jomari

Jomei (Japanese) spreads light.

Jon (Hebrew) a form of John. A short form of Jonathan.
J'on, Jori, Jonn, Jonnie, Jonny, Jory

Jonah (Hebrew) dove. Bible: an Old Testament prophet who was swal-

lowed by a large fish.
Giona, Jona, Yonah, Yunus

Jonas (Hebrew) he accomplishes. (Lithuanian) a form of John.
Jonahs, Jonass, Jonaus, Jonelis, Jonukas, Jonas, Jonutis, Joonas

Jonatan (Hebrew) a form of Jonathan.
Jonatane, Jonate, Jonattan, Jonnattan

Jonathan (Hebrew) gift of God. Bible: the son of King Saul who became a loyal friend of David. See also Ionakana, Yanton, Yonatan.
Janathan, Johnathan, Johnathon, Jon, Jonatan, Jonatha, Johnathan, Jonathin, Jonathon, Jonathyn, Jonethen, Jonotham, Jonnathan

Jonathon (Hebrew) a form of Jonathan.
Joanathon, Johnathon, Jonnathon, Jonothon, Jonition, Jonnathon, Yanaton

Jones (Welsh) son of John.
Joenns, Joness, Jonesy

Jonny (Hebrew) a familiar form of John.
Jonhy, Joni, Jonnee, Jory

Jontae (French) a combination of Jon + the suffix Tae.
Johntae, Jontay, Jontea, Jonteau, Jontez

Jontay (American) a form of Jontae.
Johntay, Johnte, Johntez, Jontai, Jonté, Jontez

Joop (Dutch) a familiar form of Joseph.
Jopie

Joost (Dutch) just.

Joquin (Spanish) a form of Joaquin.
Joquan, Joquawn, Joqunn, Joquon

Jora (Hebrew) teacher.
Yora, Jorah

Joram (Hebrew) Jehovah is exalted.
Joran, Jorim

Jordan (Hebrew) descending. See also
Giordano, Yarden.
*Jardan, Jared, Jordaan, Jordae, Jordain,
Jordaine, Jordane, Jordani, Jordanio,
Jordann, Jordanny, Jordano, Jordany,
Jordao, Jordayne, Jorden, Jordian, Jordin,
Jordon, Jordun, Jordy, Jordyn, Jorrdan,
Jory, Jourdan*

Jorden (Hebrew) a form of Jordan.
Jordenn

Jordon (Hebrew) a form of Jordan.
Jeordon, Johordan

Jordy (Hebrew) a familiar form of
Jordan.
Jordi, Jordie

Jordyn (Hebrew) a form of Jordan.

Jorell (American) he saves. Literature: a
name inspired by the fictional character Jor-El, Superman's father.
Jorel, Jor-El, Jorelle, Jorl, Jorrel, Jorrell

Jörg (German) a form of George.
Jeorg, Juergen, Jungen, Jürgen

Jorge (Spanish) a form of George.
Jorrin

Jorgen (Danish) a form of George.
Joergen, Jorgan, Jörgen

Joris (Dutch) a form of George.

Jörn (German) a familiar form of
Gregory.

Jorrin (Spanish) a form of George.
Jorian, Jorje

Jory (Hebrew) a familiar form of
Jordan.
Joar, Joary, Jorey, Jori, Jorie, Jorrie

José (Spanish) a form of Joseph. See
also Ché, Pepe.
*Josean, Joseito, Josee, Joseito, Joselito,
Josey*

Josef (German, Portuguese, Czech,
Scandinavian) a form of Joseph.
Joosef, Joseff, Josif, Jozef, József, Juzef

Joseluis (Spanish) a combination of
Jose + Luis.

Joseph (Hebrew) God will add, God
will increase. Bible: in the Old
Testament, the son of Jacob who
came to rule Egypt; in the New
Testament, the husband of Mary. See
also Beppe, Cheche, Chepe,
Giuseppe, Iokepa, Iosif, Osip, Pepa,
Peppe, Pino, Sepp, Yeska, Yosef,
Yousef, Youssel, Yusif, Yusuf, Zeusef.
*Jazeps, Jo, Jobo, Jody, Joe, Joeseph, Joey,
Jojo, Joop, Joos, Jooseppi, Jopie, José,
Joseba, Josef, Josep, Josephat, Josephe,
Josephie, Josephis, Josheph, Josip, Jóska,
Joza, Joze, Jozef, Jozeph, Jozhe, Jozio,
Jozka, Jozsi, Jozzepi, Jupp, Juziu*

Josh (Hebrew) a short form of Joshua.
Joshe

Josha (Hindi) satisfied.

Joshi (Swahili) galloping.

Joshua (Hebrew) God is my salvation.
Bible: led the Israelites into the
Promised Land. See also Giosia,
Iosua, Jesus, Yehoshua.
*Jeshua, Johsua, Johusa, Josh, Joshau,
Joshaua, Joshauh, Joshawa, Joshawah,
Joshia, Joshu, Joshuaa, Joshuah, Joshuea,
Joshuia, Joshula, Joshus, Joshusa,
Joshuwa, Joshwa, Josue, Jousha, Jozshua,
Jozsua, Jozua, Jushua*

Josiah (Hebrew) fire of the Lord. See
also Yoshiyahu.
Joshiah, Josia, Josiahs, Josian, Josias, Josie

Joss (Chinese) luck; fate.
Josse, Jossy

Josue (Hebrew) a form of Joshua.
Joshue, Jossue, Josu, Josua, Josuha, Jozus

Jotham (Hebrew) may God complete.
Bible: a king of Judah.

Jourdan (Hebrew) a form of Jordan.
*Jourdain, Jourden, Jourdin, Jourdon,
Jourdyn*

Jovan (Latin) Jove-like, majestic.
(Slavic) a form of John. Mythology:
Jove, also known as Jupiter, was the
supreme Roman deity.
*Johvan, Johvon, Jovaan, Jovane, Jovani,
Jovanic, Jovann, Jovanni, Jovannis,
Jovanny, Jovany, Jovaughn, Jovaun, Joven,
Jovenel, Jovenel, Jovi, Jovian, Jovin,
Jovito, Jovoan, Jovon, Jovone, Jovonn,
Jovonne, Jovoun, Jowaun, Yovan, Yovani*

Jovani, Jovanni (Latin) forms of Jovan.
Jovanie, Jovannie, Jovoni, Jovonie, Jovonni

Jovanny, Jovany (Latin) forms of Jovan.
Jovony

Jr (Latin) a short form of Junior.
Jr.

Juan (Spanish) a form of John. See also Chan.
Juanch, Juanchito, Juane, Juanito, Juann, Juann

Juancarlos (Spanish) a combination of Juan + Carlos.

Juaquin (Spanish) a form of Joaquin.
Juaqin, Juaqine, Juaquan, Juaquine

Jubal (Hebrew) ram's horn. Bible: a musician and a descendant of Cain.

Judah (Hebrew) praised. Bible: the fourth of Jacob's sons. See also Yehudi.
Juda, Judas, Judd, Jude

Judas (Latin) a form of Judah. Bible: Judas Iscariot was the disciple who betrayed Jesus.
Jude

Judd (Hebrew) a short form of Judah.
Jud, Judson

Jude (Latin) a short form of Judah, Judas. Bible: one of the Twelve Apostles, author of "The Epistle of Jude."

Judson (English) son of Judd.

Juhana (Finnish) a form of John.
Juha, Juho

Juku (Estonian) a form of Richard.
Jukka

Jules (French) a form of Julius.
Joles, Jule

Julian (Greek, Latin) a form of Julius.
Jolyon, Julean, Juliaan, Julianne, Juliano, Julien, Juliusn, Jullian, Julyan

Julien (Latin) a form of Julian.
Juliene, Julienn, Julienne, Jullien, Jullin

Julio (Hispanic) a form of Julius.

Julius (Greek, Latin) youthful, downy bearded. History: Julius Caesar was a great Roman dictator. See also Giuliano.
Jolyon, Julas, Jule, Jules, Julen, Jules, Julian, Julias, Julie, Julio, Juliusz, Julius

Jumaane (Swahili) born on Tuesday.

Jumah (Arabic, Swahili) born on Friday; a holy day in the Islamic religion.
Jimoh, Juma

Jumoke (Yoruba) loved by everyone.

Jun (Chinese) truthful. (Japanese) obedient; pure.
Junnie

Junior (Latin) young.
Jr, Junios, Junius, Junor

Jupp (German) a form of Joseph.

Jur (Czech) a form of George.
Juraz, Jurek, Jurik, Jurko, Juro

Jurgis (Lithuanian) a form of George.
Jurgi, Juri

Juro (Japanese) best wishes; long life.

Jurrien (Dutch) God will uplift.
Jore, Jurian, Jurre

Justen (Latin) a form of Justin.
Jasten

Justice (Latin) a form of Justis.

Justin (Latin) just, righteous. See also Giustino, Iestyn, Iustin, Tutu, Ustin, Yustyn.
Jastin, Jaston, Jestin, Jobst, Joost, Jost, Jusa, Just, Justain, Justan, Justas, Justek, Justen, Justian, Justinas, Justine, Justinian, Justinus, Justo, Juston, Justino, Justins, Justinn, Justyn

Justis (French) just.
Justice, Justs, Justus, Justyse

Justyn (Latin) a form of Justin.
Justn, Justyne, Justynn

Juvenal (Latin) young. Literature: a Roman satirist.
Juvon, Juvone

Juwan (American) a form of Jajuan.
Juvon, Juvone, Juvaan, Juvaain, Juwaine, Juwann, Juvaann, Juwon, Juwonn, Juwann, Juwane, Juwann, Juwan, Jwon

Kabiito (Rutooro) born while foreigners are visiting.

Kabil (Turkish) a form of Cain.
Kabel

Kabir (Hindi) History: an Indian mystic poet.
Kabar, Kabeer, Kabier

Kabonero (Runyankore) sign.

Kabonesa (Rutooro) difficult birth.

Kacey (Irish) a form of Casey. (American) a combination of the initials K. + C. See also KC.
Kace, Kacee, Kaci, Kacy, Kaesy, Kase, Kasey, Kasie, Kasy, Kaycee

Kadar (Arabic) powerful.
Kader

Kadarius (American) a combination of Kade + Darius.
Kadairious, Kadarious, Kadaris, Kadarrius, Kadarris, Kaddarrius, Kaderious, Kaderius

Kade (Scottish) wetlands. (American) a combination of the initials K. + D.
Kadee, Kady, Kaid, Kaide, Kaydee

Kadeem (Arabic) servant.
Kadim, Khadeem

Kaden (Arabic) a form of Kadin.
Kadeen, Kadein, Kaidan, Kaiden

Kadin (Arabic) friend, companion.
Caden, Kaden, Kadyn, Kaeden, Kayden

Kadir (Arabic) spring greening.
Kadeer

Kado (Japanese) gateway.

Kaeden (Arabic) a form of Kadin.
Kaedin, Kaedon, Kaedyn

Kaelan, Kaelin (Irish) forms of Kellen.
Kael, Kaelen, Kaelon, Kaelyn

Kaeleb (Hebrew) a form of Kaleb.
Kaelib, Kaelob, Kaelyb, Kailab, Kaileb

Kaemon (Japanese) joyful; right-handed.
Kaeman, Kaemen, Kaemin

Kaenan (Irish) a form of Keenan.
Kaenen, Kaenin, Kaenyn

Ka'eo (Hawaiian) victorious.

Kafele (Nguni) worth dying for.

Kaga (Native American) writer.

Kagan (Irish) a form of Keegan.
Kage, Kagen, Kaghen, Kaigan

Kahale (Hawaiian) home.

Kahil (Turkish) young; inexperienced; naive.
Cahil, Kaheel, Kale, Kayle

Kahlil (Arabic) a form of Khalil.
Kahleal, Kahlee, Kahleel, Kahleil, Kahli, Kahliel, Kahlill, Kalel, Kalil

Kaholo (Hawaiian) runner.

Kahraman (Turkish) hero.

Kai (Welsh) keeper of the keys. (German) a form of Kay. (Hawaiian) sea.
Kae, Kaie, Kaii

Kaikara (Runyoro) Religion: a Banyoro deity.

Kailen (Irish) a form of Kellen.
Kail, Kailan, Kailey, Kailin, Kailon, Kailyn

Kaili (Hawaiian) Religion: a Hawaiian god.
Kailli

Kain (Welsh, Irish) a form of Kane.
Kainan, Kaine, Kainen, Kainin, Kainon

Kainoa (Hawaiian) name.

Kaipo (Hawaiian) sweetheart.

Kairo (Arabic) a form of Cairo.
Kaire, Kairee, Kairi

Kaiser (German) a form of Caesar.
Kaesar, Kaisar, Kaizer

Kaiven (American) a form of Kevin.
Kaivan, Kaiven, Kaivon, Kaivaan

Kaj (Danish) earth.
Kai, Kaje

Kakar (Hindi) grass.

Kala (Hindi) black; phase. (Hawaiian) sun.

Kalama (Hawaiian) torch.
Kalam

Kalan (Irish) a form of Kalen.
Kalane, Kallan

Kalani (Hawaiian) sky; chief.
Kalan

Kale (Arabic) a short form of Kahlil. (Hawaiian) a familiar form of Carl.
Kalee, Kalen, Kaleu, Kaley, Kali, Kalin, Kalle, Kayle

Kaleb (Hebrew) a form of Caleb.
Kaeleb, Kal, Kalab, Kalabe, Kalb, Kale, Kaleob, Kaley, Kalib, Kalieb, Kallb, Kalleb, Kalob, Kaloeb, Kalub, Kalyb, Kilab

Kalen, Kalin (Arabic, Hawaiian) forms of Kellen. (Irish) forms of Kale.
Kalan

Kalevi (Finnish) hero.

Kali (Arabic) a short form of Kalil. (Hawaiian) a form of Gary.

Kalil (Arabic) a form of Khalil. *Kaleel, Kalell, Kali, Kaliel, Kaliil*

Kaliq (Arabic) a form of Khaliq. *Kalic, Kalique*

Kalin (Hindi) tenth. Religion: Kalki is the final incarnation of the Hindu god Vishnu. *Kalki*

Kalle (Scandinavian) a form of Carl. (Arabic, Hawaiian) a form of Kale.

Kallen (Irish) a form of Kellen. *Kallan, Kallin, Kallion, Kallun, Kalun*

Kalon, Kalyn (Irish) forms of Kellen. *Kalone, Kalonn, Kalyen, Kalyne, Kalynn*

Kaloosh (Armenian) blessed event.

Kalvin (Latin) a form of Calvin. *Kal, Kalv, Kalvan, Kalven, Kalvon, Kalvyn, Vinny*

Kamaka (Hawaiian) face.

Kamakani (Hawaiian) wind.

Kamal (Hindi) lotus. (Arabic) perfect, perfection. *Kamaal, Kamel, Kamil*

Kamau (Kikuyu) quiet warrior.

Kamden (Scottish) a form of Camden. *Kamdon*

Kameron (Scottish) a form of Cameron. *Kam, Kamaren, Kamaron, Kameran, Kameren, Kamerin, Kamerion, Kammeren, Kammeron, Kammy, Kamryn, Kamran, Kamron*

Kamil (Arabic) a form of Kamal. *Kameel*

Kami (Hindi) loving.

Kamran, Kamron (Scottish) forms of Kameron. *Kammron, Kamrein, Kamren, Kamrin, Kamryn*

Kamuela (Hawaiian) a form of Samuel.

Kamuhanda (Runyankore) born on the way to the hospital.

Kamukama (Runyankore) protected by God.

Kamuzu (Nguni) medicine.

Kamya (Luganda) born after twin brothers.

Kana (Japanese) powerful; capable. (Hawaiian) Mythology: a demigod.

Kanaiela (Hawaiian) a form of Daniel. *Kana, Kaneii*

Kane (Welsh) beautiful. (Irish) tribute. (Japanese) golden. (Hawaiian) eastern sky. (English) a form of Keene. See Kahan, Kain, Kaney, Kayne.

Kange (Lakota) raven. *Kang, Kanga*

Kaniel (Hebrew) stalk, reed. *Kan, Kani, Kannie, Kanny*

Kannan (Hindi) Religion: another name for the Hindu god Krishna. *Kanaan, Kanan, Kanen, Kanin, Kanine, Kannen*

Kannon (Polynesian) free. (French) A form of Cannon. *Kanon*

Kanoa (Hawaiian) free.

Kantu (Hindi) happy.

Kanu (Swahili) wildcat.

Kaori (Japanese) strong.

Kapila (Hindi) ancient prophet. *Kapil*

Kapono (Hawaiian) righteous. *Kāpena*

Kardal (Arabic) mustard seed. *Karandal, Kardell*

Kare (Norwegian) enormous. *Karee*

Kareem (Arabic) noble; distinguished. *Karee, Karem, Kareme, Karim, Kariem*

Karel (Czech) a form of Carl. *Karell, Karil, Karell*

Karey (Greek) a form of Carey. *Karee, Kari, Karry, Kary*

Karif (Arabic) born in autumn. *Karef*

Kariisa (Runyankore) herdsman.

Karim (Arabic) a form of Kareem.

Karl (German) a form of Carl.
Kaarle, Kaarlo, Kale, Kalle, Kalman, Kálmán, Karcsi, Karel, Kari, Karlen, Karlitis, Karlo, Karlos, Karlton, Karlus, Karol, Kjell

Karlen (Latvian, Russian) a form of Carl.
Karlan, Karlens, Karlik, Karlin, Karlis, Karlon

Karmel (Hebrew) a form of Carmel.

Karney (Irish) a form of Carney.

Karol (Czech, Polish) a form of Carl.
Karal, Karolek, Karolis, Karolos, Károly, Karrel, Karrol

Karr (Scandinavian) a form of Carr.

Karson (English) a form of Carson.
Karrson, Karsen

Karsten (Greek) anointed.
Carsten, Karstan, Karston

Karu (Hindi) cousin.
Karun

Karutunda (Runyankore) little.

Karwana (Rutooro) born during wartime.

Kaseem (Arabic) divided.
Kaseem, Kaseam, Kaseym, Kasim, Kasseem, Kassem, Kazeem

Kaseko (Rhodesian) mocked, ridiculed.

Kasem (Tai) happiness.

Kasen (Basque) protected with a helmet.
Kasean, Kasene, Kaseon, Kasin, Kason, Kassen

Kasey (Irish) a form of Casey.
Kaese, Kaesy, Kasay, Kassey

Kashawn (American) a combination of the prefix Ka + Shawn.
Kashain, Kashan, Kashaun, Kashen, Kashon

Kasib (Arabic) fertile.

Kasim (Arabic) a form of Kaseem.
Kassim

Kasimir (Arabic) peace. (Slavic) a form of Casimir.
Kasim, Kazimierz, Kazimir, Kazio, Kazmer, Kazmér, Kázmér

Kasiya (Nguni) separate.

Kasper (Persian) treasurer. (German) a form of Casper.
Jasper, Kaspar, Kaspero

Kass (German) blackbird.
Kaese, Kasch, Kase

Kassidy (Irish) a form of Cassidy.
Kassady, Kassie, Kassy

Kateb (Arabic) writer.

Kato (Runyankore) second of twins.

Katungi (Runyankore) rich.

Kavan (Irish) handsome.
Cavan, Kavanagh, Kavaugn, Kaven, Kavenaugh, Kavin, Kavon, Kayvan

Kaveh (Persian) ancient hero.

Kavi (Hindi) poet.

Kavin, Kavon (Irish) forms of Kavan.
Kaveon, Kavion, Kavone, Kayvon, Kaywon

Kawika (Hawaiian) a form of David.

Kay (Greek) rejoicing. (German) fortified place. Literature: one of King Arthur's knights of the Round Table.
Kai, Kaycee, Kaye, Kayson

Kayden (Arabic) a form of Kadin.
Kayde, Kaydee, Kaydin, Kaydn, Kaydon

Kayin (Nigerian) celebrated. (Yoruba) long-hoped-for child.

Kayle (Hebrew) faithful dog. (Arabic) a short form of Kahlil.
Kayl, Kayla, Kaylee

Kayleb (Hebrew) a form of Caleb.
Kaylib, Kaylob, Kaylub

Kaylen (Irish) a form of Kellen.
Kaylan, Kaylin, Kaylon, Kaylyn, Kaylynn

Kayne (Hebrew) a form of Cain.
Kaynan, Kaynen, Kaynon

Kayode (Yoruba) he brought joy.

Kayonga (Runyankore) ash.

Kazio (Polish) a form of Casimir, Kasimir. See also Cassidy.
Ka, K.C., Kcee, Keey

Kazuo (Japanese) man of peace.

KC (American) a combination of the initials K. + C. See also Kacey.
Kc, K.C., Kcee, Keey

Keagan (Irish) a form of Keegan.
Keagean, Keagen, Keaghan, Keagyn

Keahi (Hawaiian) flames.

Keaka (Hawaiian) a form of Jack.

Kealoha (Hawaiian) fragrant.
Ke'ala.

Keanan (Irish) a form of Keenan.
Keanen, Keanna, Keannan, Keanon

Keandre (American) a combination of
the prefix Ke + Andre.
*Keandra, Keandray, Keandré, Keandree,
Keandrell, Keondre*

Keane (German) bold; sharp. (Irish)
handsome. (English) a form of
Keene.
Kean

Keanu (Irish) a form of Keenan.
*Keano, Keani, Keanno, Keano, Keanue,
Keeno, Keenu, Kianu*

Kearn (Irish) a short form of Kearney.
Kearne

Kearney (Irish) a form of Carney.
Kar, Karney, Karny, Kearny

Keary (Irish) a form of Kerry.
Kearie

Keaton (English) where hawks fly.
*Keatan, Keaten, Keatin, Keatton,
Keatyn, Keeton, Keetun*

Keaven (Irish) a form of Kevin.
Keavan, Keavon

Keawe (Hawaiian) strand.

Keb (Egyptian) earth. Mythology: an
ancient earth god, also known as
Geb.

Kedar (Hindi) mountain lord. (Arabic)
powerful. Religion: another name for
the Hindu god Shiva.
Kadar, Keddar, Keder

Keddy (Scottish) a form of Adam.
Keddie

Kedem (Hebrew) ancient.

Kedrick (English) a form of Cedric.
*Keddrick, Kedderick, Kedrek, Kedric,
Kiedric, Kiedrick*

Keefe (Irish) handsome; loved.

Keegan (Irish) little; fiery.
*Kagan, Kagan, Keagan, Keegen,
Keeghan, Keegon, Keegun, Kegan,
Keigan*

Keelan (Irish) little; slender.
Keelen, Keelin, Keelyn, Keilan, Kelan

Keeley (Irish) handsome.
*Kealey, Kealy, Keeli, Keelian, Keelie,
Keely*

Keene (German) bold; sharp. (English)
smart. See also Kane.
Kaene, Keane, Keen, Keena

Keenen (Irish) a form of Keenan.
Keenin, Kienen

Keenan (Irish) little Keene.
*Keenan, Keanan, Keena, Keenen,
Keennan, Keenon, Kenan, Keynan,
Kienan, Kienon*

Keegan (Irish) a form of Keegan.
Kegen, Keghan, Kegon, Kegun

Keevon (Irish) a form of Kevin.
*Keevan, Keeven, Keevin, Keevan,
Keevin*

Kees (Dutch) a form of Kornelius.
Keese, Keesee, Keyes

Keevon (Irish) a form of Kevin.
*Keevan, Keeven, Keevin, Keevan,
Keevin*

Kehind (Yoruba) second-born twin.
Kehinde

Keddy (Scottish) a form of Adam.
Keddie

Kedem (Hebrew) ancient.

Keiffer (German) a form of Cooper.
Keefer, Keifer, Kiefer

Keigan (Irish) a form of Keegan.
Keighan, Keighen

Keiji (Japanese) cautious ruler.

Keilan (Irish) a form of Keelan.
*Keiten, Keilin, Keilene, Keillyn, Keilon,
Keilynn*

Keir (Irish) a short form of Kieran.

Keitaro (Japanese) blessed.
Keita

Keith (Welsh) forest. (Scottish) battle
place. See also Kika.
Keath, Keeth, Keithen

Keithen (Welsh, Scottish) a form of
Keith.
Keithan, Keitheon, Keithon

Keivan (Irish) a form of Kevin.
Keiven, Keivn, Keivon, Keivone

Kekapa (Hawaiian) tapa cloth.

Kekipi (Hawaiian) rebel.

Kekoa (Hawaiian) bold, courageous.

Kelby (German) farm by the spring.
Keelby, Kelbee, Kelbey, Kelbi, Kellby

Kele (Hopi) sparrow hawk. (Hawaiian)
a form of Jerry.
Kelle

Kelemen (Hungarian) gentle; kind.
Kellman

Kelevi (Finnish) hero.

Keli (Hawaiian) a form of Terry.

Keli'i (Hawaiian) chief.

Kelile (Ethiopian) protected.

Kell (Scandinavian) spring.

Kellan (Irish) a form of Kellen.
Keillan

Kellen (Irish) mighty warrior.
Kaelan, Kailen, Kalan, Kalen, Kalin, Kallen, Kalon, Kalyn, Kaylen, Keelan, Kelden, Kelin, Kellan, Kelle, Kellin, Kellyn, Kelyn, Kelyn

Keller (Irish) little companion.

Kelly (Irish) warrior.
Kelle, Kellen, Kelley, Kelli, Kellie, Kely

Kelmen (Basque) merciful.
Kelmin

Kelsey (Scandinavian) island of ships.
Kelcy, Kelse, Kelsea, Kelsi, Kelsie, Kelso, Kelsy, Kesley, Kesly

Kelton (English) keel town; port.
Kelden, Keldon, Kelson, Kelston, Kelten, Keltin, Keltonn, Keltyn

Kelvin (Irish, English) narrow river. Geography: a river in Scotland.
Kelvan, Kelven, Kelvon, Kelvyn, Kelwin, Kelwyn

Kemal (Turkish) highest honor.

Kemen (Basque) strong.

Kemp (English) fighter; champion.

Kempton (English) military town.

Ken (Japanese) one's own kind. (Scottish) a short form of Kendall, Kendrick, Kenneth.
Kena, Kenn, Keno

Kenan (Irish) a form of Keenan.

Kenaz (Hebrew) bright.

Kendal (English) a form of Kendall.
Kendale, Kendall, Kendel, Kendul, Kendyl

Kendall (English) valley of the river Kent.
Ken, Kendal, Kendell, Kendrall, Kendryll, Kendyll, Kyndall

Kendarius (American) a combination of Ken + Darius.
Kendarious, Kendarrious, Kendarrius, Kenderious, Kenderius, Kenderyious

Kendell (English) a form of Kendall.
Kendelle, Kendrel, Kendrell

Kendrew (Scottish) a form of Andrew.

Kendrick (Irish) son of Henry. (Scottish) royal chieftain.
Ken, Kenderrick, Kendric, Kendrich, Kendrick, Kendricks, Kendrik, Kendrix, Kendrick, Kendridick, Keondric, Keondrick

Kenley (English) royal meadow.
Kenlea, Kenlee, Kenleigh, Kenlie, Kenly

Kenn (Scottish) a form of Ken.

Kennan (Scottish) little Ken.
Kenna, Kenan, Kenen, Kennen, Kennon

Kennard (Irish) brave chieftain.
Kenner

Kennedy (Irish) helmeted chief. History: John F. Kennedy was the thirty-fifth U.S. president.
Kenedy, Kenidy, Kennady, Kennedey

Kenneth (Irish) handsome. (English) royal oath.
Ken, Keneth, Kenneith, Kennet,

Kennethen, Kennett, Kennieth, Kennith, Kennth, Kenny, Kennyth, Kenya

Kenny (Scottish) a familiar form of Kenneth.
Keni, Kenney, Kenni, Kennie, Kinnie

Kenrick (English) bold ruler; royal ruler.
Kenric, Kenricks, Kenrik

Kent (Welsh) white; bright. (English) a short form of Kenton. Geography: a region in England.

Kentaro (Japanese) big boy.

Kenton (English) from Kent, England.
Kent, Kenten, Kentin, Kentonn

Kentrell (English) king's estate.
Kenreal, Kentrel, Kentrelle

Kenward (English) brave; royal guardian.

Kenya (Hebrew) animal horn. (Russian) a form of Kenneth. Geography: a country in east-central Africa.
Kenyatta

Kenyatta (American) a form of Kenya.
Kenyata, Kenyatae, Kenyatee, Kenyatter, Kenyatti, Kenyotta

Kenyon (Irish) white haired, blond.
Kenyan, Kenynn, Keonyon

Kenzie (Scottish) wise leader. See also Mackenzie.
Kensie

Keoki (Hawaiian) a form of George.

Keola (Hawaiian) life.

Keon (Irish) a form of Ewan.
Keeon, Keion, Keionne, Keondre, Keone, Keonne, Keonte, Keony, Kian, Kion

Keoni (Hawaiian) a form of John.

Keonte (American) a form of Keon.
Keonntay, Keonta, Keontae, Keontay, Keontaye, Keontez, Keontia, Keontis, Keontrae, Keontre, Keontrey, Keontrye

Kerbasi (Basque) warrior.

Kerel (Afrikaans) young.
Kerell

Kerem (Turkish) noble; kind.
Kereem

Kerey (Gypsy) homeward bound.
Ker

Kerman (Basque) from Germany.
Ker

Kermit (Irish) a form of Dermot.
Kermey, Kermie, Kermitt, Kermy

Kern (Irish) a short form of Kieran.
Kearn, Kerne

Kerr (Scandinavian) a form of Carr.
Karr

Kerrick (English) king's rule.

Kerry (Irish) dark; dark haired.
Keary, Keri, Kerrey, Kerri, Kerrie

Kers (Todas) Botany: an Indian plant.

Kersen (Indonesian) cherry.

Kerstan (Dutch) a form of Christian.

Kerwin (Irish) little; dark. (English) friend of the marshlands.
Kervin, Kerwyn, Kerwinn, Kerwyn, Kerwynn, Kirwin, Kirwyn

Kesar (Russian) a form of Caesar.
Kesare

Keshawn (American) a combination of the prefix Ke + Shawn.
Keeshawn, Keeshaun, Keeshon, Kesean, Keshan, Keshane, Keshaun, Keshayne, Keshon, Keshor, Keshone, Keshun, Kishan

Kesin (Hindi) long-haired beggar.

Kesse (Ashanti, Fante) chubby baby.
Kessie

Kester (English) a form of Christopher.

Keung (Chinese) universe.

Kevan (Irish) a form of Kevin.
Kavan, Kevaan, Kevane, Kevann, Keyvan, Kiwan, Kiwane

Keven (Irish) a form of Kevin.
Keve, Keveen, Kiven

Kevin (Irish) handsome. See also Cavan.
Kaiven, Keaven, Keevon, Keivan, Key, Kevan, Keven, Keverne, Kevian, Kevien, Kevin, Kevinn, Kevins, Kevis, Kevm, Kevon, Kevyn, Kyven

Kevon (Irish) a form of Kevin.
Kevoan, Kevion, Kevone, Kevonne, Kevontae, Kevonte, Kevoyn, Kevron, Kevun, Kevone, Keyvon, Kivon

Keyn (Irish) a form of Kevin.
Keeyon

Key (English) key; protected.

Keyon (Irish) a form of Keon.
Keyan, Keyen, Keyin, Keyon

Keyshawn (American) a combination of Key + Shawn.
Keyshan, Keyshaun, Keyshon, Keyshun

Khachig (Armenian) small cross.
Khachik

Khaim (Russian) a form of Chaim.

Khaldun (Arabic) forever.
Khaldoon, Khaldon

Khalfani (Swahili) born to lead.
Khalfan

Khalid (Arabic) eternal.
Khaled, Khallid, Khalyd

Khalil (Arabic) friend.
Kahlil, Kaleel, Kalil, Khahlil, Khaiil, Khalyl, Khalee, Khaleel, Khaleel, Khali, Khalial, Khaliel, Khaliel, Khalil, Khalili, Khalill

Khaliq (Arabic) creative.
Kaliq, Khalique

Khamisi (Swahili) born on Thursday.
Kham

Khan (Turkish) prince.
Kahn

Kharald (Russian) a form of Gerald.

Khayru (Arabic) benevolent.
Khiri, Khiry, Kiry

Khoury (Arabic) priest.
Khory

Khristian (Greek) a form of Christian, Kristian.
Khris, Khristan, Khristin, Khriston, Khrystian

Khristopher (Greek) a form of Kristopher.
Khristofer, Khristophar, Khrystopher

Khristos (Greek) a form of Christos.
Khris, Khristophe, Kristo, Kristos

Kibo (Uset) worldly; wise.

Kibuuka (Luganda) brave warrior. History: a Ganda warrior deity.

Kidd (English) child; young goat.

Kiefer (German) a form of Keifer.
Kief, Kieffer, Kiefor, Kiffer, Kiefer

Kiel (Irish) a form of Kyle.
Kiell

Kiele (Hawaiian) gardenia.

Kieran (Irish) little and dark; little Keir.
Keiran, Keiren, Keiron, Kiaron, Kiarron, Kier, Kieren, Kierian, Kierien, Kierin, Kiernan, Kieron, Kierr, Kierre, Kierron, Kyran

Kiernan (Irish) a form of Kieran.
Kern, Kernan, Kiernen

Kiet (Tai) honor.

Kifeda (Luo) only boy among girls.

Kiho (Rutooro) born on a foggy day.

Kijika (Native American) quiet walker.

Kika (Hawaiian) a form of Keith.

Kiki (Spanish) a form of Henry.

Kile (Irish) a form of Kyle.
Kilee, Kilen, Kiley, Kiyl, Kyle

Killian (Irish) little Kelly.
Kilean, Kilian, Kilien, Killie, Killien, Killiean, Killion, Killy

Kim (English) a short form of Kimball.
Kinnie, Kimmy

Kimball (Greek) hollow vessel. (English) warrior chief.
Kim, Kimbal, Kimbel, Kimbell, Kimble

Kimo (Hawaiian) a form of James.

Kimokeo (Hawaiian) a form of Timothy.

Kin (Japanese) golden.

Kincaid (Scottish) battle chief.
Kincade, Kinkaid

Kindin (Basque) fifth.

King (English) king. A short form of names beginning with "King."

Kingsley (English) king's meadow.
King, Kings, Kingslea, Kingslie, Kingsly, Kingzlee, Kinslea, Kinslee, Kinsley, Kinslie, Kinsly

Kingston (English) king's estate.
King, Kinston

Kingswell (English) king's well.
King

Kini (Hawaiian) a short form of Iukini.

Kinnard (Irish) tall slope.

Kinsey (English) victorious royalty.
Kinze, Kinzie

Kinton (Hindi) crowned.

Kion (Irish) a form of Keon.
Kione, Kionie, Kionne

Kioshi (Japanese) quiet.

Kipp (English) pointed hill.
Kip, Kippar, Kipper, Kippie, Kippy

Kir (Bulgarian) a familiar form of Cyrus.

Kiral (Turkish) king; supreme leader.

Kiran (Sanskrit) beam of light.
Kyran

Kirby (Scandinavian) church village. (English) cottage by the water.
Kerbey, Kerbie, Kerby, Kirbey, Kirbie, Kirkby

Kiri (Cambodian) mountain.

Kiril (Slavic) a form of Cyril.
Kirill, Kiryl, Kyrillos

Kiritan (Hindi) wearing a crown.

Kirk (Scandinavian) church.
Kerk

Kirkland (English) church land.
Kirklin, Kirklind, Kirklynd

Kirkley (English) church meadow.

Kirklin (English) a form of Kirkland.
Kirklan, Kirklen, Kirkline, Kirkloun, Kirklun, Kirklyn, Kirklynn

Kirkwell (English) church well; church spring.

Kirkwood (English) church forest.

Kirton (English) church town.

Kishan (American) a form of
Keshawn.
*Kishaun, Kishawn, Kishen, Kishion,
Kyshon, Kyshun*

Kistna (Hindi) sacred, holy.
Geography: a sacred river in India.

Kistur (Gypsy) skillful rider.

Kit (Greek) a familiar form of
Christian, Christopher, Kristopher.
Kitt, Kitts

Kito (Swahili) jewel; precious child.

Kitwana (Swahili) pledged to live.

Kiva (Hebrew) a short form of Akiva,
Jacob.
Kiba, Kivi, Kiwa

Kiyoshi (Japanese) quiet; peaceful.

Kizza (Luganda) born after twins.
Kizzy

Kjell (Swedish) a form of Karl.
Kjel

Klaus (German) a short form of
Nicholas. A form of Claus.
Klaas, Klaes, Klas, Klause

Klay (English) a form of Clay.

Klayton (English) a form of Clayton.

Kleef (Dutch) cliff.

Klement (Czech) a form of Clement.
*Klema, Klemens, Klemens, Klemet,
Klemo, Klim, Klimek, Kliment, Klimka*

Kleng (Norwegian) claw.

Knight (English) armored knight.
Knighty

Knoton (Native American) a form of
Nodin.

Knowles (English) grassy slope.
Knolls, Nowles

Knox (English) hill.

Knute (Scandinavian) a form of
Canute.
Knud, Knut

Kodi (English) a form of Kody.
Kode, Kodee, Kodie

Kody (English) a form of Cody.
Kodey, Kodi, Kodye, Kory

Kofi (Twi) born on Friday.

Kohana (Lakota) swift.

Koi (Choctaw) panther. (Hawaiian) a
form of Troy.

Kojo (Akan) born on Monday.

Koka (Hawaiian) Scotsman.

Kokayi (Shona) gathered together.

Kolby (English) a form of Colby.
*Kelby, Koalby, Koelby, Kohlbe, Kohlby,
Kolbe, Kolbey, Kolbi, Kolbie, Kolebe,
Koleby, Kollby*

Kole (English) a form of Cole.
Kohl, Kohle

Koleman (English) a form of
Coleman.
Kolemann, Kolemen

Kolin (English) a form of Colin.
Kolen, Koller, Kollin, Kollyn, Kolyn

Koby (Polish) a familiar form of Jacob.
Kobby, Kobe, Kobey, Kobi, Kobia, Kobie

Kolton (English) a form of Colton.
*Kolt, Koltan, Kolte, Kolten, Koltin,
Koltn, Koltyn*

Kolya (Russian) a familiar form of
Nikolai, Nikolos.
Kola, Kolenka, Kolia, Kolja

Kona (Hawaiian) a form of Don.
Konala

Konane (Hawaiian) bright moonlight.

Kondo (Swahili) war.

Kong (Chinese) glorious; sky.

Konner (Irish) a form of Conner,
Connor.
Konar, Koner

Konnor (Irish) a form of Connor.
Kohner, Kohnor, Konor

Kono (Moquelumnan) squirrel eating
a pine nut.

Konrad (German) a form of Conrad.
*Khonrad, Koen, Koenraad, Kon, Konn,
Konney, Konni, Konnie, Konny, Konrád,
Konrade, Konrrado, Kord, Kort, Kunz*

Konstantin (German, Russian) a form
of Constantine. See also Dinos.
*Konstanchi, Konstadine, Konstadino,
Konstandinos, Konstantinos, Konstantine,
Konstantinos, Konstantino, Konstantiny,
Konstantyn, Konstanz, Konstantino,
Kostadino, Kostadinos, Kostadino,
Kostandinos, Kostantin, Kostantino,
Kostas, Kostenka, Kostya, Kotsos*

Kontar (Akan) only child.

Korb (German) basket.

Korbin (English) a form of Corbin.
Korban, Korben, Korbyn

Kordell (English) a form of Cordell.
Kordel

Korey (Irish) a form of Corey, Kory.
Kore, Koree, Korei, Korio, Korre, Korria, Korrye

Kornel (Latin) a form of Cornelius, Kornelius.
Kees, Kornell, Kornell, Korneli, Kornelisz, Kornell, Krelis, Soma

Kornelius (Latin) a form of Cornelius. See also Kees, Kornel.
Karnelius, Kornelius, Korneliaus, Kornelious, Kornellius

Korrigan (Irish) a form of Corrigan.
Korigan, Korigan, Korrigon, Korrigun

Kort (German, Dutch) a form of Cort, Kurt.
Kourt

Kortney (English) a form of Courtney.
Kortni, Kourtney

Korudon (Greek) helmeted one.

Kory (Irish) a form of Corey.
Korey, Kori, Korie, Korrey, Korri, Korrie, Korry

Kosey (African) lion.
Kosse

Kosmo (Greek) a form of Cosmo.
Kosmy, Kozmo

Kostas (Greek) a short form of Konstantin.

Kosti (Finnish) a form of Gustave.

Kosumi (Moquelumnan) spear fisher.

Koukalaka (Hawaiian) a form of Douglas.

Kourtland (English) a form of Courtland.
Kortlan, Kortland, Kortlend, Kortlon, Kourtlin

Kovit (Tai) expert.

Kraig (Irish, Scottish) a form of Craig.
Kraggie, Kraggy, Krayg, Kreg, Kreig, Kreigh

Krikor (Armenian) a form of Gregory.

Kris (Greek) a form of Chris. A short form of Kristian, Kristofer, Kristopher.
Kriss, Krys

Krischan (German) a form of Christian.
Krishan, Krishawn, Krishaun, Krishon, Krishun

Krishna (Hindi) delightful, pleasurable. Religion: the eighth and principal avatar of the Hindu god Vishnu.
Kistna, Kistnah, Krisha, Krishnah

Krispin (Latin) a form of Crispin.
Krispian, Krispino, Krispo

Krister (Swedish) a form of Christian.
Krist, Kristar

Kristian (Greek) a form of Christian, Khristian.
Kerstan, Khristos, Kit, Kris, Krischan, Krist, Kristan, Kristar, Kristek, Kristen, Krister, Kristien, Kristin, Kristine, Kristinn, Kristion, Kristjan, Kristo, Kristos, Krists, Krystek, Krystian, Khrystiyan

Kristo (Greek) a short form of Khristos.

Kristofer (Swedish) a form of Kristopher.
Kris, Kristafer, Kristef, Kristfer, Kristoff, Kristoffer, Kristofo, Kristofor, Kristofyr, Kristufer, Kristus, Krystofer

Kristoff (Greek) a short form of Kristofer, Kristopher.
Kristof, Kristöf

Kristophe (French) a form of Kristopher.

Kristopher (Greek) a form of Christopher. See also Topher.
Khristopher, Kit, Kris, Krisstopher, Kristapher, Kristepher, Kristfer, Kristfor, Krista, Kristofer, Kristoff, Kristoforo, Kristoph, Kristophe, Kristophor, Kristos, Krists, Krisus, Krystopher, Krystupas, Krzysztof

Kruz (Spanish) a form of Cruz.
Kruise, Kruize, Kruse, Kruze

Krystian (Polish) a form of Christian.
Krys, Krystek, Krystien, Krystin

Kuba (Czech) a form of Jacob.
Kubo, Kubus

Kueng (Chinese) universe.

Kugonza (Rutooro) love.

Kuiril (Basque) lord.

Kumar (Sanskrit) prince.

Kunle (Yoruba) home filled with honors.

Kuper (Yiddish) copper.

Kurt (Latin, German, French) a short form of Kurtis. A form of Curt.
Kirt, Kort, Kuno, Kurtt

Kurtis (Latin, French) a form of Curtis.
Kirtis, Kirtus, Kurt, Kurtes, Kurtez, Kurtice, Kurties, Kurtiss, Kurtus, Kurtys

Kuruk (Pawnee) bear.

Kuzih (Carrier) good speaker.

Kwabena (Akan) born on Tuesday.

Kwacha (Nguni) morning.

Kwako (Akan) born on Wednesday.
Kwaku, Kwaku

Kwam (Zuni) a form of John.

Kwame (Akan) born on Saturday.
Kwamen, Kwami, Kwamin

Kwan (Korean) strong.
Kwane

Kwasi (Akan) born on Sunday.
(Swahili) wealthy.
Kwazie, Kwazzi, Kwesi

Kwayera (Nguni) dawn.

Kwende (Nguni) let's go.

Kyele (Irish) a form of Kyle.

Kyle (Irish) narrow piece of land; place where cattle graze. (Yiddish) crowned with laurels.
Cyle, Kiel, Kilan, Kile, Kilen, Kiley, Ky, Kye, Kyel, Kyele, Kylan, Kylee, Kyler, Kyley, Kylie, Kyll, Kylle, Kyrell

Kylan (Irish) a form of Kyle.
Kyelen, Kylen, Kylen, Kylin, Kyline, Kylon, Kylun

Kyler (English) a form of Kyle.
Kylar, Kylor

Kynan (Welsh) chief.

Kyndall (English) a form of Kendall.
Kyndal, Kyndel, Kyndell, Kyndle

Kyne (English) royal.

Kyran (Sanskrit) a form of Kiran.
Kyren, Kyron, Kyrone

Kyros (Greek) master.

Kyven (American) a form of Kevin.
Kyvan, Kyvaun, Kyvon, Kyvon, Kyvynn

Laban (Hawaiian) white.
Labon, Lebaan, Leban, Liban

Labaron (American) a combination of the prefix La + Baron.
Labaren, Labarren, Labarron, Labearon, Labron

Labib (Arabic) sensible; intelligent.

Labrentsis (Russian) a form of Lawrence.
Labhras, Labhruinn, Labrenis

Lachlan (Scottish) land of lakes.
Lache, Lachlann, Lachunn, Lakelan, Lakeland

Ladarian (American) a combination of the prefix La + Darian.
Ladarien, Ladarin, Ladarion, Ladaren, Ladarrian, Ladarrien, Ladarrin,

Laban (Hawaiian) white. — *Ladarrion, Laderion, Laderian, Laderion*

Ladarius (American) a combination of the prefix La + Darius.
Ladarious, Ladaris, Ladarris, Ladauris, Ladarus, Ladrius, Ladrius

Ladarrius (American) a form of Ladarius.
Ladarrius, Ladarrius, Ladarrious, Ladarrious, Laderrius, Laderris

Ladd (English) attendant.
Lad, Laddey, Laddie, Laddy

Laderrick (American) a combination of the prefix La + Derrick.
Ladderrick, Laderrick, Laderic, Laderricks

Ladislav (Czech) a form of Walter.
Laco, Lada, Ladislaus

Lado (Fante) second-born son.

Lafayette (French) History: Marquis de Lafayette was a French soldier and politician who aided the American Revolution.
Lafaette, Lafayett, Lafiette, Laffyette

Laine (English) a form of Lane.
Lain

Laird (Scottish) wealthy landowner.

Lais (Arabic) lion.

Lajos (Hungarian) famous; holy.
Lajci, Laji, Lali

Lake (English) lake.
Lakan, Lakane, Lakee, Laken, Lakin

Lakota (Dakota) a tribal name.
Lakoda

Lal (Hindi) beloved.

Lamar (German) famous throughout the land. (French) sea, ocean.
Lamair, Lamario, Lamaris, Lamarr, Lamarre, Larmar, Lemar

Lambert (German) bright land.
Bert, Lambard, Lamberto, Lambirt, Lampard, Landbert

Lamond (French) world.
Lammond, Lamon, Lamonde, Lamondo, Lamondre, Lamund, Lemond

Lamont (Scandinavian) lawyer.
Lamaunt, Lamonta, Lamonte, Lamontie, Lamonto, Lamount, Lemont

Lance (German) a short form of Lancelot.
Lancy, Lantz, Lanz, Launce

Lancelot (French) attendant.
Literature: the knight who loved King Arthur's wife, Queen Guinevere.
Lance, Lancelott, Launcelet, Launcelot

Landen (English) a form of Landon.
Landenn

Lander (Basque) lion man. (English) landowner.
Landers, Landor

Lando (Portuguese, Spanish) a short form of Orlando, Rolando.

Landon (English) open, grassy meadow.
Landan, Landen, Landin, Landyn

Landry (French, English) ruler.
Landre, Landré, Landrue

Lane (English) narrow road.
Laine, Laney, Lanie, Layne

Lang (Scandinavian) tall man.
Lange

Langdon (English) long hill.
Landon, Langsdon, Langston

Langford (English) long ford.
Lanford, Lankford

Langley (English) long meadow.
Langlea, Langlee, Langleigh, Langly

Langston (English) long, narrow town.
Langsden, Langsdon

Langundo (Native American) peaceful.

Lani (Hawaiian) heaven.

Lanny (American) a familiar form of Lawrence, Laurence.
Lanney, Lannie, Lennie

Lanu (Moquelumnan) running around the pole.

Lanz (Italian) a form of Lance.
Lanzo, Lonzo

Lao (Spanish) a short form of Stanislaus.

Lap (Vietnamese) independent.

Lapidos (Hebrew) torches.
Lapidoth

Laquan (American) a combination of the prefix La + Quan.
Laquain, Laquann, Laquanta, Laquantae, Laquante, Laquawn,

Laquawne, Laquin, Laquinn, Laqun, Laquon, Laquone, Laquwan, Laqwon

Laquintin (American) a combination of the prefix La + Quintin.
Laquentin, Laquenton, Laquintas, Laquinten, Laquintiss, Laquinton

Laramie (French) tears of love. Geography: a town in Wyoming on the Overland Trail.
Larami, Laramy, Laremy

Larenzo (Italian, Spanish) a form of Lorenzo.
Larenz, Larenza, Larinzo, Laurenzo

Larkin (Irish) rough; fierce.
Larklin

Larnell (American) a combination of Larry + Darnell.

Laron (French) thief.
Laran, La'ron, La Ron, Larone, Laronn, Laron, La Ruan

Larrimore (French) armorer.
Larimore, Larmer, Larmor

Larry (Latin) a familiar form of Lawrence.
Larrie, Lary

Lars (Scandinavian) a form of Lawrence.
Laris, Larris, Larse, Larsen, Larson, Larsson, Larz, Lasse, Lawrans, Laurits, Lawrans, Lorens

LaSalle (French) hall.
Lasal, Lasalle, Lasell, Lascelles

Lash (Gypsy) a form of Louis.
Lashi, Lasho

Lashawn (American) a combination of the prefix La + Shawn.
Lasaun, Lasean, Lashajaun, Lashan, Lashane, Lashaun, Lashaun, Lashon, Lashun

Lashon (American) a form of Lashawn.
Lashone, Lashonn

Lasse (Finnish) a form of Nicholas.

László (Hungarian) famous ruler.
Laci, Lacko, Laslo, Lazlo

Lateef (Arabic) gentle; pleasant.
Latif, Letif

Latham (Scandinavian) barn. (English) district.
Laith, Lathe, Lay

Lathan (American) a combination of the prefix La + Nathan.
Lathaniel, Lathen, Lathyn, Leathan

Lathrop (English) barn, farmstead.
Lathe, Lathrope, Lay

Latimer (English) interpreter.
Lat, Latimor, Lottie, Latty, Latymer

Latravis (American) a combination of the prefix La + Travis.
Latavious, Latavius, Lataveus, Latravious, Latravius, Latrayvious, Latrayvous, Latvis

Latrell (American) a combination of the prefix La + Kentrell.
Latreal, Latrail, Latrel, Latrelle, Latread, Letrel, Letrell, Letrelle

Laudalino (Portuguese) praised.
Lino

Laughlin (Irish) servant of Saint Secundinus.
Lanty, Lauchlin, Leachlainn

Laurence (Latin) crowned with laurel. A form of Lawrence. See also Rance, Raulas, Raulo, Renzo.
Lanny, Lauran, Laurance, Laureano, Lauren, Laurencho, Laurenco, Laurens, Lauren, Laurentij, Laurentios, Laurentzi, Laurie, Laurin, Lauris, Lauris, Lauriz, Laurnet, Lauro, Laurus, Lavrenti, Lavrance

Laurencio (Spanish) a form of Laurence.

Laurens (Dutch) a form of Laurence.
Laurenz

Laurent (French) a form of Laurence.
Laurente

Laurie (English) a familiar form of Laurence.
Lauri, Laury, Lorry

Lauris (Swedish) a form of Laurence.

Lauro (Filipino) a form of Laurence.

LaValle (French) valley.
Laval, Laval, Lavalei, Lavalle, Lavell

Lavan (Hebrew) white.
Lavane, Lavaughan, Laven, Lavon, Levan

Lavaughan (American) a form of Lavan.
Lavaughn, Levaughan, Levaughn

Lave (Italian) lava. (English) lord.

Lavi (Hebrew) lion.

Lavon (American) a form of Lavan.
Lavion, Lavone, Lavonn, Lavonne, Lavont, Lavonte

Lavrenti (Russian) a form of Lawrence.
Larenti, Lavrentij, Lavrnsha, Lavrie, Lavro

Lawford (English) ford on the hill.
Ford, Law

Lawler (Irish) soft-spoken.
Lawlor, Lollar, Loller

Lawrence (Latin) crowned with laurel. See also Brencis, Chencho, Labrentsis, Lauwrenty; Lanry, Lanty; Larance, Laren, Larian, Laren, Laris, Larka, Larrance, Larrence, Larry, Lars, Larya, Lawrence, Larrenti, Law, Lawrence, Lawrance, Lawrenti, Law, Lawrie, Lawron, Lawry, Lencho, Lon, Lóránt, Loreca, Loren, Loretto, Lorenzo, Lorne, Lourenco, Lowrance

Lawson (English) son of Lawrence.
Lawsen, Layson

Lawton (English) town on the hill.
Laughton, Law

Layne (English) a form of Lane.
Layn, Laynee

Lavell (French) a form of LaValle.
Lavel, Lavele, Lavelle, Levele, Levell, Levelle

Layton (English) a form of Leighton.
Laydon, Layten, Layth, Laythan, Laython

Lazaro (Italian) a form of Lazarus.
Lazarillo, Lazarito, Lazzaro

Lazarus (Greek) a form of Eleazar. Bible: Lazarus was raised from the dead by Jesus.
Lazar, Lázár, Lazare, Lazarius, Lazaro, Lazaros, Lazorus

Leander (Greek) lion-man; brave as a lion.
Ander, Leandro

Leandro (Spanish) a form of Leander.
Leandra, Léandre, Leandrew, Leandros

Leben (Yiddish) life.
Laben, Lebon

Lebna (Ethiopian) spirit; heart.

Ledarius (American) a combination of the prefix Le + Darius.
Ledarrius, Ledarrius, Lederious, Lederris

Lee (English) a short form of Farley, Leonard, and names containing "lee."
Leigh

Leggett (French) one who is sent; delegate.
Legate, Legette, Leggitt, Liggett

Lei (Chinese) thunder. (Hawaiian) a form of Ray.

Leib (Yiddish) roaring lion.
Leibel

Leif (Scandinavian) beloved.
Laif, Leife, Lief

Leigh (English) a form of Lee.

Leighton (English) meadow farm.
Lay, Layton, Leigh, Leyton

Leith (Scottish) broad river.

Lek (Tai) small.

Lekeke (Hawaiian) powerful ruler.

Leks (Estonian) a familiar form of Alexander.
Leksik, Lekso

Lel (Gypsy) taker.

Leland (English) meadowland; protected land.
Lealand, Lee, Leeland, Leigh, Leighland, Lelan, Lelann, Leland, Lelund, Leyland

Lemar (French) a form of Lamar.
Lemario, Lemarr

Lemuel (Hebrew) devoted to God.
Lem, Lemmie, Lemmy

Len (Hopi) flute. (German) a short form of Leonard.

Lenard (German) a form of Leonard.
Lennard

Lencho (Spanish) a form of Lawrence.
Lenci, Lenzy

Lennart (Swedish) a form of Leonard.
Lennerd

Lenno (Native American) man.

Lennon (Irish) small cloak; cape.
Lenon

Lennor (Gypsy) spring; summer.

Lennox (Scottish) with many elms.
Lennix, Lenox

Lenny (German) a familiar form of Leonard.
Leni, Lennie, Leny

Leo (Latin) lion. (German) a short form of Leon, Leopold.
Lavi, Leão, Lee, Leib, Leibel, Leos, Leosko, Léo, Léocadie, Leos, Leosoko, Lev, Lio, Lion, Liutas, Lyon, Nardek

Leobardo (Italian) a form of Leonard.

Leon (Greek, German) a short form of Leonard, Napoleon.
Leo, Léon, Leonas, Léonce, Leoncio, Leondris, Leone, Leonek, Leonetti, Leoni, Leonid, Leonidas, Leonirez, Leonizio, Leonon, Leons, Leontes, Leontios, Leontrae, Liutas

Leonard (German) brave as a lion.
Leanard, Lee, Len, Lena, Lenard, Lennart, Lenny, Leno, Leobardo, Leon, Léonard, Leonardis, Leonardo, Leonart, Leonerd, Leonhard, Leonidas, Leonnard, Leontes, Leonard, Lienard, Linek, Lnard, Lon, Londard, Lonnard, Lonya, Lynnard

Leonardo (Italian) a form of Leonard.
Leonaldo, Lionardo

Leonel (English) little lion. See also Lionel.
Leonell

Leonhard (German) a form of Leonard.
Leonhards

Leonid (Russian) a form of Leonard.
Leonide, Lyonechka, Lyonya

Leonidas (Greek) a form of Leonard.
Leonida, Leonides

Leopold (German) brave people. *Leo, Leopolde, Leorad, Lipót, Lopolda, Luepold, Luitpold, Poldi*

Leopoldo (Italian) a form of Leopold. *Leory, Lior*

Leor (Hebrew) my light.

Lequinton (American) a combination of the prefix Le + Quinton. *Lequentin, Lequenton, Lequinn*

Leron (French) round, circle. (American) a combination of the prefix Le + Ron. *Leeron, Le Ron, Lerone, Liron, Lyron*

Leroy (French) king. See also Delroy, Elroy. *Lee, Leeroy, LeeRoy, Leigh, Lerai, Leroi, LeRoi, LeRoy, Roy*

Les (Scottish, English) a short form of Leslie, Lester. *Lessie*

Lesharo (Pawnee) chief.

Leshawn (American) a combination of the prefix Le + Shawn. *Lashan, Lesean, Leshaun, Leshon, Leshun*

Leslie (Scottish) gray fortress. *Lee, Leigh, Les, Leslea, Leslee, Lesley, Lesli, Lesly, Lezlie, Lezly*

Lester (Latin) chosen camp. (English) from Leicester, England. *Leicester, Les*

Lev (Hebrew) heart. (Russian) a form of Leo. A short form of Leverett, Levi. *Leb, Leva, Levka, Levko, Levushka*

Leverett (French) young hare. *Lev, Leveret, Leverit, Leveritt*

Levi (Hebrew) joined in harmony. Bible: the third son of Jacob; Levites are the priestly tribe of the Israelites. *Leari, Leevi, Leevie, Lev, Levey, Levie, Levin, Levitis, Levy, Levi, Levvi*

Levin (Hebrew) a form of Levi. *Levine, Levon*

Levon (American) a form of Lavon. *Leevon, Levone, Levonn, Levonne, Levonte, Lyvonne*

Lew (English) a short form of Lewis.

Lewin (English) beloved friend.

Lewis (Welsh) a form of Llewellyn. (English) a form of Louis. *Lew, Lewes, Lewie, Lewy*

Lex (English) a short form of Alexander. *Lexi, Lexie, Lexin*

Lexus (Greek) a short form of Alexander. *Lexis, Lexiis, Lexxus*

Leyati (Moquelumnan) shape of an abalone shell.

Li (Chinese) strong.

Liam (Irish) a form of William. *Liem, Lliam, Lyam*

Liang (Chinese) good, excellent.

Liban (Hawaiian) a form of Laban. *Libaan, Lieban*

Liberio (Portuguese) liberation. *Liberatore, Liborio*

Lidio (Greek, Portuguese) ancient.

Ligongo (Yao) who is this?

Likeke (Hawaiian) a form of Richard. *Like*

Liko (Chinese) protected by Buddha. (Hawaiian) bud.

Lin (Burmese) bright. (English) a short form of Lyndon. *Linh, Linn, Linny, Lyn, Lynn*

Linc (English) a short form of Lincoln. *Link*

Lincoln (English) settlement by the pool. History: Abraham Lincoln was the sixteenth U.S. president. *Linc, Lincon, Lyncoln*

Lindberg (German) mountain where linden grow. *Lindbergh, Lindburg, Lindy*

Lindell (English) valley of the linden. *Lendall, Lendel, Lendell, Lindall, Lindel, Lyndale, Lyndall, Lyndel, Lyndell*

Linden (English) a form of Lyndon.

Lindley (English) linden field. *Lindlea, Lindlee, Lindleigh, Lindly*

Lindon (English) a form of Lyndon. *Lin, Lindan*

Lindsay (English) a form of Lindsey. *Linsay*

Lindsey (English) linden-tree island. *Lind, Lindsay, Lindsee, Lindsie, Lindsy, Lindzy, Linsey, Linzie, Linzy, Lyndsay, Lyndsey, Lyndsie, Lynzie*

Linford (English) linden ford.
Lynford

Linfred (German) peaceful, calm.

Linley (English) flax meadow.
Linlea, Linlee, Linleigh, Linly

Linton (English) flax town.
Lintonn, Lynton, Lyntonn

Linu (Hindi) lily.

Linus (Greek) flaxen haired.
Linas, Linux

Linwood (English) flax wood.

Lio (Hawaiian) a form of Leo.

Lionel (French) lion cub. See also Leonel.
Lional, Lionell, Lionello, Lynel, Lynell, Lyonel

Liron (Hebrew) my song.
Lyron

Lise (Moquelumnan) salmon's head coming out of the water.

Lisimba (Yao) lion.
Simba

Lister (English) dyer.

Litton (English) town on the hill.
Liton

Liu (African) voice.

Liuz (Polish) light.
Lius

Livingston (English) Leif's town.
Livingstone

Liwanu (Moquelumnan) growling bear.

Llewellyn (Welsh) lionlike.
Lewis, Llewelin, Llewellen, Llewelleyn, Llewellin, Llewlyn, Llywellyn, Llywellynn, Llywelyn

Lloyd (Welsh) gray haired; holy. See also Floyd.
Loy, Loyd, Loyde, Loydie

Lobo (Spanish) wolf.

Lochlain (Irish, Scottish) land of lakes.
Laughlin, Lochlan, Lochlann, Lochlin, Locklynn

Locke (English) forest.
Lock, Lockwood

Loe (Hawaiian) a form of Roy.

Logan (Irish) meadow.
Llogan, Logan, Loagen, Loagon, Logann, Logen, Loggan, Loghan, Logon, Logn, Logun, Logunn, Logyn

Lok (Chinese) happy.

Lokela (Hawaiian) a form of Roger.

Lokni (Moquelumnan) raining through the roof.

Lomán (Irish) bare. (Slavic) sensitive.

Lombard (Latin) long bearded.
Bard, Barr

Lon (Irish) fierce. (Spanish) a short form of Alonso, Alonzo, Leonard, Lonnie.
Lonn

Lonato (Native American) flint stone.

London (English) fortress of the moon. Geography: the capital of the

United Kingdom.
Londen, Londyn, Lunden, Lundon

Long (Chinese) dragon. (Vietnamese) hair.

Lonnie (German, Spanish) a familiar form of Alonso, Alonzo.
Lon, Loni, Lonie, Lonnell, Lonney, Lonni, Lonniel, Lonny

Lono (Hawaiian) Mythology: the god of learning and intellect.

Lonzo (German, Spanish) a short form of Alonso, Alonzo.
Lonso

Lootah (Lakota) red.

Lopaka (Hawaiian) a form of Robert.

Loránd (Hungarian) a form of Roland.

Lóránt (Hungarian) a form of Lawrence.
Lorant

Lorcan (Irish) little; fierce.

Lord (English) noble title.

Loren (Latin) a short form of Lawrence.
Lorin, Lorren, Lorrin, Loryn

Lorenzo (Italian, Spanish) a form of Lawrence.
Larenzo, Lerenzo, Leurenzo, Lorenc, Lorence, Lorenco, Lorencz, Lorens, Lorenso, Lorentz, Lorenz, Lorenza, Loretto, Lorinc, Lörinc, Lorinzo, Loritz, Lorrenzo, Lorrie, Lorry, Lourenza, Lourenzo, Lourenzo, Renzo, Zo

Loretto (Italian) a form of Lawrence.
Loreto

Lorimer (Latin) harness maker.
Lorrie, Lorrimer, Lorry

Loring (German) son of the famous warrior.
Lorrie, Lorring, Lorry

Loris (Dutch) clown.

Loritz (Latin, Danish) laurel.
Lauritz

Lorne (Latin) a short form of Lawrence.
Lorn, Lornie

Lorry (English) a form of Laurie.
Lori, Lorri, Lory

Lot (Hebrew) hidden, covered. Bible: Lot fled from Sodom, but his wife glanced back upon its destruction and was transformed into a pillar of salt.
Lott

Lothar (German) a form of Luther.
Lotaire, Lotario, Lothair, Lothaire, Lothario

Lou (German) a short form of Louis.

Loudon (German) low valley.
Louden, Lowden, Loudin, Lowden

Louie (German) a familiar form of Louis.

Louis (German) famous warrior. See also Aloisio, Aloysius, Clovis, Luigi.
Lash, Lashi, Lasho, Lewis, Lou, Loudovicus, Louie, Louies, Louise, Lucho, Lude, Ludek, Ludick, Ludis, Ludko,

Ludvig, Lughaidh, Lui, Luigi, Luis, Luiz, Luki, Lutek

Lourdes (French) from Lourdes, France. Religion: a place where the Virgin Mary was said to have appeared.

Louvain (English) Lou's vanity. Geography: a city in Belgium.
Louvin

Lovell (English) a form of Lowell.
Lovell, Lovel, Lovelle, Lovey

Lowell (French) young wolf. (English) beloved.
Lovell, Love, Lowel

Loyal (English) faithful, loyal.
Loy, Loyall, Loye, Lyall, Lyell

Luboslaw (Polish) lover of glory.
Lubs, Lubz

Lubomir (Polish) lover of peace.

Luca (Italian) a form of Lucius.
Lucca, Luka

Lucas (German, Irish, Danish, Dutch) a form of Lucius.
Lucais, Lucassie, Luccas, Luccas, Luckas, Lucus

Luc (French) a form of Luke.
Luce

Lucian (Latin) a form of Lucius.
Lucan, Lucanus, Luciano, Lucianus, Lucias, Lucjan, Lukianos, Lukyan

Luciano (Italian) a form of Lucian.
Luca, Lucca, Lucino, Lucio

Lucien (French) a form of Lucius.

Lucio (Italian) a form of Lucius.

Lucius (Latin) light; bringer of light.
Loukas, Luc, Luca, Lucais, Lucanus, Luce, Lucian, Lucien, Lucio, Lucius, Luke, Lusio

Lucky (American) fortunate.
Luckee, Luckie, Luckson, Lucson

Ludlow (English) prince's hill.

Ludovic (German) a form of Ludwig.
Ludovick, Ludovico

Ludwig (German) a form of Louis. Music: Ludwig van Beethoven was a famous nineteenth-century German composer.
Ludovic, Ludvig, Ludvik, Ludvik, Luiz

Lui (Hawaiian) a form of Louis.

Luigi (Italian) a form of Louis.
Lui, Luiggi, Luigino, Luigy

Luis, Luiz (Spanish) forms of Louis.
Luise

Lukas, Lukus (Greek, Czech, Swedish) forms of Luke.
Loukas, Lukais, Lukash, Lukasha, Lukass, Lukasz, Lukaus, Lukkas

Luke (Latin) a form of Lucius. Bible: companion of Saint Paul and author of the third Gospel of the New Testament.
Luc, Luchok, Luck, Lucky, Luk, Luka, Lükás, Lukas, Luken, Lukes, Lukes, Lukyan, Luko

Lukela (Hawaiian) a form of Russel.

Luken (Basque) bringer of light.
Lucan, Lucane, Lucano, Luk

Luki (Basque) famous warrior.

Lukman (Arabic) prophet.
Luqman

Lulani (Hawaiian) highest point in heaven.

Lumo (Ewe) born facedown.

Lundy (Scottish) grove by the island.

Lunn (Irish) warlike.
Lon, Lonn

Lunt (Swedish) grove.

Lusila (Hindi) leader.

Lusio (Zuni) a form of Lucius.

Lutalo (Luganda) warrior.

Lutfi (Arabic) kind, friendly.

Luther (German) famous warrior. History: Martin Luther was one of the central figures of the Reformation.
Lothar, Lutero, Luthor

Lutherum (Gypsy) slumber.

Luyu (Moquelumnan) head shaker.

Lyall, lyell (Scottish) loyal.

Lyle (French) island.
Lisle, Ly, Lysle

Lyman (English) meadow.
Leaman, Leeman, Lymon

Lynch (Irish) mariner.
Linch

Lyndal (English) valley of lime trees.
Lyndale, Lyndall, Lyndel, Lyndell

Lyndon (English) linden hill. History: Lyndon B. Johnson was the thirty-sixth U.S. president.
Lin, Linden, Lindon, Lyden, Lydon, Lyn, Lyndan, Lynden, Lynn

Lynn (English) waterfall; brook.
Lyn, Lynell, Lynette, Lynnard, Lynoll

Lyron (Hebrew) a form of Leron, Liron.

Lysander (Greek) liberator.
Lyzander, Sander

Maalik (Punjabi) a form of Malik.
Maalek, Maaliek

Mac (Scottish) son.
Maas

Macadam (Scottish) son of Adam.
MacAdam, McAdam

Macallister (Irish) son of Alistair.
Macalaster, Macalister, MacAlister, McAlister, McAllister

Macario (Spanish) a form of Makarios.

Macarthur (Irish) son of Arthur.
MacArthur, McArthur

Macaulay (Scottish) son of righteousness.
Macaulee, Macauley, Macaully, Macauly, Macauley, Mackauly, Macaulay, McCauley

Macbride (Scottish) son of a follower of Saint Brigid.
Macbryde, Mcbride, McBride

Maccoy (Irish) son of Hugh, Coy.
MacCoy, Mccoy, McCoy

Maccrea (Irish) son of grace.
MacCrae, MacCray, MacCrea, Macrae, Macray, Makray, Mcrea, McCrea

Macdonald (Scottish) son of Donald.
MacDonald, Mcdonald, McDonald, Mcdonna, Mcdonnell, McDonnell

Macdougal (Scottish) son of Dougal.
MacDougal, Mcdougal, McDougal, McDougall, Dougal

Mace (French) club. (English) a short form of Macy, Mason.
Macean, Maceo, Macer, Macey, Macie, Macy

Macgregor (Scottish) son of Gregor.
Macgreggor

Machas (Polish) a form of Michael.

Mack (Scottish) a short form of names beginning with "Mac" and "Mc."
Macke, Mackey, Mackie, Macklin, Macks, Macky

Mackenzie (Irish) son of Kenzie.
Makensy, Mackenxo, Makenze, Makenzey, Mackenzi, MaKenzie, Mackenzly, Mackenzy, Mackienzie, Mackinsey, Mackinzie, Makenzie, McKenzie, Mckenzie

Mackinnley (Irish) son of the learned ruler.
Mackinley, MacKinnley, Mackinnly, Mckinley

Macklain (Irish) a form of Maclean.
Macklaine, Macklane

Maclean (Irish) son of Leander.
Machlin, Macklain, MacLain, MacLean, McLaine, McLean

Macmahon (Irish) son of Mahon.
MacMahon, McMahon

Macmurray (Irish) son of Murray.
McMurray

Macnair (Scottish) son of the heir.
Macnair

Maco (Hungarian) a form of Emmanuel.

Macon (German, English) maker.

Macy (French) Matthew's estate.
Mace, Macey

Maddock (Welsh) generous.
Madoc, Madock, Madog

Maddox (Welsh, English) benefactor's son.
Maddux, Madox

Madhar (Hindi) full of intoxication; relating to spring.

Madison (English) son of Maude; good son.
Maddie, Maddison, Maddy, Madisen, Madisson, Madisyn, Madsen, Son, Sonny

Madongo (Luganda) uncircumcised.

Madu (Ibo) people.

Magar (Armenian) groom's attendant.
Magarios

Magee (Irish) son of Hugh.
MacGee, MacGhee, McGee

Magen (Hebrew) protector.

Magnar (Norwegian) strong; warrior.
Magne

Magnus (Latin) great.
Maghnus, Magnes, Manius, Mayer

Magomu (Luganda) younger of twins.

Maguire (Irish) son of the beige one.
MacGuire, McGuire, McGwire

Mahammed (Arabic) a form of Muhammad.
Mahamad, Mahamed

Mahdi (Arabic) guided to the right path.
Mahde, Mahdee, Mahdy

Mahesa (Hindi) great lord. Religion: another name for the Hindu god Shiva.

Mahi'ai (Hawaiian) a form of George.

Mahir (Arabic, Hebrew) excellent; industrious.
Maher

Mahkah (Lakota) earth.

Mahmoud (Arabic) a form of Muhammad.
Mahamoud, Mahmmoud, Mahmmoud

Mahmúd (Arabic) a form of Muhammad.
Mahmed, Mahmood, Mahmut

Mahomet (Arabic) a form of Muhammad.
Mehemet, Mehmet

Mahon (Irish) bear.

Mahpee (Lakota) sky.

Maimun (Arabic) lucky.
Maimon

Mairtin (Irish) a form of Martin.
Martin, Martainn

Maitias (Irish) a form of Mathias.
Maithias

Maitiú (Irish) a form of Matthew.

Maitland (English) meadowland.

Majid (Arabic) great, glorious.
Majd, Majde, Majdi, Majid, Majed, Majeed

Major (Latin) greater; military rank.
Majar, Maje, Majer, Mayer, Mayor

Makaio (Hawaiian) a form of Matthew.

Makalani (Mwera) writer.

Makani (Hawaiian) wind.

Makarios (Greek) happy; blessed.
Macario, Macarios, Macario, Macarios

Makenzie (Irish) a form of Mackenzie.
Makensie, Makenzy

Makin (Arabic) strong.
Makeen

Makis (Greek) a form of Michael.

Makoto (Japanese) sincere.

Maks (Hungarian) a form of Max.
Makszi

Maksim (Russian) a form of Maximilian.
Maksimka, Maksym, Maxim

Maksym (Polish) a form of Maximilian.
Makimus, Maksim, Maksymilian

Makyah (Hopi) eagle hunter.

Mal (Irish) a short form of names beginning with "Mal."

Malachi (Hebrew) angel of God. Bible: the last canonical Hebrew prophet.
Maeleachlaimn, Mal, Malachai, Malachia, Malachie, Malachy Malakai, Malake, Malaki, Malchija, Malechy, Málik

Malachy (Irish) a form of Malachi.

Malajitm (Sanskrit) garland of victory.

Malcolm (Scottish) follower of Saint Columba who Christianized North Scotland. (Arabic) dove.
Mal, Malcalm, Malcohm, Malcolum, Malcom, Malkolm

Malcom (Scottish) a form of Malcolm.
Malcome, Malcum, Malkom, Malkeum

Malden (English) meeting place in a pasture.
Mal, Maldon

Malek (Arabic) a form of Málik.
Maleek, Maleeke, Maleik, Maleka, Maleke, Mallek

Maleko (Hawaiian) a form of Mark.

Málik (Punjabi) lord, master. (Arabic) a form of Malachi.
Maalik, Malik, Malak, Malic, Malick, Malicke, Maliek, Maliik, Malik, Malike, Malikh, Maliq, Malique, Mallik, Malyk, Malyq

Malin (English) strong, little warrior.
Mal, Mallin, Mallon

Mallory (German) army counselor. (French) wild duck.
Lory, Mal, Mallery, Mallori, Mallorie, Malory

Maloney (Irish) church going.
Malone, Malony

Malvern (Welsh) bare hill.
Malverne

Malvin (Irish, English) a form of Melvin.
Mal, Malvinn, Malvyn, Malvynn

Mamo (Hawaiian) yellow flower; yellow bird.

Manchu (Chinese) pure.

Manco (Peruvian) supreme leader. History: a sixteenth-century Incan king.

Mandala (Yao) flowers.
Manda, Mandela

Mandeep (Punjabi) mind full of light.
Mandieep

Mandel (German) almond.
Mandell

Mandek (Polish) a form of Armand, Herman.
Mandie

Mander (Gypsy) from me.

Manford (English) small ford.

Manfred (English) man of peace. See also Fred.
Manfret, Manfrid, Manfried, Manferd, Mannfred, Mannfryd

Manger (French) stable.

Mango (Spanish) a familiar form of Emmanuel, Manuel.

Manheim (German) servant's home.

Manipi (Native American) living marvel.

Manius (Scottish) a form of Magnus.
Manus, Manyus

Manley (English) hero's meadow.
Manlea, Manleigh, Manly

Mann (German) man.
Manin

Manning (English) son of the hero.

Mannix (Irish) monk.
Mainchin

Manny (German, Spanish) a familiar form of Manuel.
Mani, Manni, Mannie, Marry

Mano (Hawaiian) shark. (Spanish) a short form of Manuel.
Manno, Manolo

Manoj (Sanskrit) cupid.

Mansa (Swahili) king. History: a fourteenth-century king of Mali.

Mansel (English) manse; house occupied by a clergyman.
Mansell

Mansfield (English) field by the river; hero's field.

Man-Shik (Korean) deeply rooted.

Mansūr (Arabic) divinely aided. *Mansoor, Mansour*

Manton (English) man's town; hero's town. *Mannton, Manten*

Manu (Hindi) lawmaker. History: the reputed writer of the Hindi compendium of sacred laws and customs. (Hawaiian) bird. (Ghanaian) second-born son.

Manuel (Hebrew) a short form of Emmanuel. *Maco, Margo, Mannuel, Manny, Mano, Manolón, Manual, Manuale, Manne, Manuelli, Manuelo, Manuil, Manyuil, Minel*

Manville (French) worker's village. (English) hero's village. *Manderville, Manvel, Manvil*

Manzo (Japanese) third son.

Man-Young (Korean) ten thousand years of prosperity.

Maona (Winnebago) creator, earth maker.

Mapira (Yao) millet.

Marc (French) a form of Mark.

Marcel (French) a form of Marcellus. *Marcell, Marsale, Marsel*

Marcelino (Italian) a form of Marcellus. *Marceleno, Marcelin, Marcellin, Marcellino*

Marcelo, Marcello (Italian) forms of Marcellus. *Marchello, Marsello, Marselo*

Marcellus (Latin) a familiar form of Marcus. *Marceau, Marcel, Marceles, Marcelias, Marcelino, Marcelis, Marcelius, Marcelous, Marcelleous, Marcellis, Marcellius, Marcelluas, Marcelo, Marcelus, Marcely, Marciano, Marcilka, Marcsseau, Marquel, Marsalis*

March (English) dweller by a boundness.

Marciano (Italian) a form of Martin. *Marci, Mario*

Marcilka (Hungarian) a form of Marcellus. *Marci, Marcilki*

Marcin (Polish) a form of Martin.

Marco (Italian) a form of Marcus. History: Marco Polo was a thirteenth-century Venetian traveler who explored Asia. *Marko, Marko*

Marcos (Spanish) a form of Marcus. *Marckos, Marcous, Markos, Markose*

Marcus (Latin) martial, warlike. *Marc, Marcas, Marcellus, Marcio, Marcius, Marco, Marcos, Marcous, Marcuss, Marcuus, Marcux, Marek, Mark, Markos, Markus*

Marek (Slavic) a form of Marcus.

Maren (Basque) sea.

Mareo (Japanese) uncommon.

Marian (Polish) a form of Mark. *Marcus, Marchello, Marsalis*

Mariano (Italian) a form of Mark.

Marid (Arabic) rebellious.

Marin (French) sailor. *Marine, Mariner, Marino, Marius, Mariner*

Marino (Italian) a form of Marin. *Marinos, Marinus, Mario, Marino*

Mario (Italian) a form of Marino. *Marios, Marrio*

Marion (French) bitter; sea of bitterness. *Mareon, Mariano*

Marius (Latin) a form of Marin. *Marious*

Mark (Latin) a form of Marcus. Bible: author of the second Gospel in the New Testament. See also Maleko. *Marc, Marek, Marian, Mariano, Marke, Markee, Markel, Markell, Markey, Marko, Markos, Märkus, Markusha, Marque, Martial, Marx*

Markanthony (Italian) a combination of Mark + Anthony.

Marke (Polish) a form of Mark.

Markel, Markell (Latin) forms of Mark. *Markelle, Markelo*

Markes (Portuguese) a form of Marques. *Markess, Markest*

Markese (French) a form of Marquis. *Markease, Markeece, Markees, Markeese, Markei, Markeice, Markeis, Markeise, Markez, Markeez, Markice*

Markham (English) homestead on the boundary.

Markis (French) a form of Marquis.
Markies, Markiese, Markise, Markiss, Markist

Marko (Latin) a form of Marco, Mark.
Markco

Markus (Latin) a form of Marcus.
Markas, Markeus, Markeuss, Markys, Marqus

Marland (English) lake land.

Marley (English) lake meadow.
Marlea, Marleigh, Marly, Marrley

Marlin (English) deep-sea fish.
Marlen, Marlion, Marlyn

Marlon (French) a form of Merlin.

Marlow (English) hill by the lake.
Mar, Marlo, Marlowe

Marmion (French) small.
Marmyon

Marnin (Hebrew) singer; bringer of joy.

Maro (Japanese) myself.

Marquan (American) a combination of Mark + Quan.
Marquane, Marquante

Marquel (American) a form of Marcellus.
Marqueal, Marquelis, Marquell, Marquelle, Marquellis, Marquiel, Marquil, Marquiles, Marquill, Marquille, Marquillus, Marqul, Marqvel, Marqwell

Marques (Portuguese) nobleman.
Markes, Markqes, Markques, Markquese, Marqese, Marqesse, Marqez, Marqeze, Marquees, Marqueso, Marquess, Marquesse, Marquest, Markqueus, Marquez, Marqus

Marquez (Portuguese) a form of Marques.
Marqueze, Marquiez

Marquice (American) a form of Marquis.
Marquaice, Marquece

Marquis, Marquise (French) nobleman.
Marcquis, Marcuis, Markis, Markquis, Markquise, Markuis, Marqise, Marquee, Marqui, Marquice, Marquie, Marquies, Marquiss, Marquist, Marquiz, Marquize

Marquon (American) a combination of Mark + Quon.
Marquin, Marquinn, Marquan, Marquon, Marquyn

Marr (Spanish) divine. (Arabic) forbidden.

Mars (Latin) bold warrior. Mythology: the Roman god of war.

Marsalis (Italian) a form of Marcellus.
Marsalius, Marsallis, Marsellis, Marsellus

Marsden (English) marsh valley.
Marsdon

Marsh (English) swamp land. (French) a short form of Marshall.

Marshal (French) a form of Marshall.
Marschal, Marshel

Marshall (French) caretaker of the horses; military title.
Marsh, Marshal, Marshell

Marshawn (American) a combination of Mark + Shawn.
Marshaine, Marshaun, Marshauwn, Marshean, Marshon, Marshun

Marston (English) town by the marsh.

Martell (English) hammerer.
Martel, Martele, Martellis

Marten (Dutch) a form of Martin.
Maarten, Martein

Martez (Spanish) a form of Martin.
Martaz, Martaze, Martes, Martese, Marteze, Martice, Martiece, Marties, Martiese, Martiez, Martis, Martise, Martize

Marti (Spanish) a form of Martin.
Martee, Martie

Martial (French) a form of Mark.

Martin (Latin, French) a form of Martinus. History: Martin Luther King, Jr. led the Civil Rights movement and won the Nobel Peace Prize. See also Tynek.
Maartin, Mairtin, Marciano, Marcin, Marinos, Marius, Mart, Martan, Marten, Martez, Marti, Martijn, Martinas, Martine, Martinez, Martinho, Martiniano, Martinien, Martinka, Martino, Martins, Marto, Marton, Márton, Marts, Marty, Martyn, Mattin, Mertin, Morten, Moss

Martinez (Spanish) a form of Martin.
Martines

Martinho (Portuguese) a form of
Martin.

Martino (Italian) a form of Martin.
Martinos

Martins (Latvian) a form of Martin.
Martin

Martinus (Latin) martial, warlike.
Martin

Marty (Latin) a familiar form of
Martin.
Martey, Marti, Martie

Marut (Hindi) Religion: the Hindu
god of the wind.

Marv (English) a short form of
Marvin.
Marve, Marvi, Marvis

Marvin (English) lover of the sea.
*Marv, Marvein, Marven, Marvion,
Marvon, Marvyn, Marvin,
Marwynn, Mervin*

Marwan (Arabic) history personage.

Marwood (English) forest pond.

Masaccio (Italian) twin.
Masaki

Masahiro (Japanese) broad-minded.

Masamba (Yao) leaves.

Masao (Japanese) righteous.

Masato (Japanese) just.

Mashama (Shona) surprising.

Maska (Native American) powerful.
(Russian) mask.

Maslin (French) little Thomas.
Maslen, Masling

Mason (French) stone worker.
*Mace, Maison, Masson, Masun, Masyn,
Sonny*

Masou (Native American) fire god.

Massey (English) twin.
Massi

Massimo (Italian) greatest.
Massimiliano

Masud (Arabic, Swahili) fortunate.
Masood, Masoud, Mhasood

Matai (Basque, Bulgarian) a form of
Matthew.
Máté, Matei

Matalino (Filipino) bright.

Mateo (Spanish) a form of Matthew.
Matías, Matteo

Mateusz (Polish) a form of Matthew.
Matejs, Mateus

Mather (English) powerful army.

Mateu (German) a form of Matthew.
Matheau, Mathes, Mathu

Mathew (Hebrew) a form of Matthew.
*Matias, Mathi, Mathia, Mathis, Matias,
Mattia, Matthieus, Mattia, Mattias,
Matus*

Mathias, Matthias (German, Swedish)
forms of Matthew.
*Matias, Mathi, Mathia, Matthis, Matías,
Matthias, Matthias, Matthäus,
Mattheus, Matthews, Matthias, Matty,
Matvey, Matyas, Mayhew*

Mathieu, Matthieu (French) forms of
Matthew.
*Mathie, Mathieux, Mathieu, Matthieu,
Matieu, Mattieux*

Mathis (French) a form of Mathias.

Matías (Spanish) a form of Mathias.
Matias

Mato (Native American) brave.

Matope (Rhodesian) our last child.

Matoskah (Lakota) white bear.

Mats (Swedish) a familiar form of Matt.
Matts, Matz

Matson (Hebrew) son of Matt.
Matison, Matsen, Mattison, Matson

Matt (Hebrew) a short form of
Matthew.
Mat

Matteen (Afghan) disciplined; polite.

Matteus (Scandinavian) a form of
Matthew.

Matthew (Hebrew) gift of God. Bible:
author of the first Gospel of the
New Testament.
*Mads, Makaio, Maitiú, Mata, Matai,
Matek, Mateo, Mateusz, Maffei, Mathe,
Matheson, Matheu, Mathew, Mathian,
Mathias, Mathieson, Mathien, Matro,
Mats, Matt, Mattes, Matthaeus,
Matthaios, Matthias, Matthäus,
Mattheus, Matthews, Matthias, Matty,
Matvey, Matyas, Mayhew*

Matty (Hebrew) a familiar form of
Matthew.
Mattie

Matus (Czech) a form of Mathias.

Matvey (Russian) a form of Matthew.
*Matvij, Matviyko, Matyash, Motka,
Morya*

Matyas (Polish) a form of Matthew.
Mátyás

Mauli (Hawaiian) a form of Maurice.

Maurice (Latin) dark skinned; moor; marshland. See also Seymour.
Mauli, Maur, Maurance, Maureo, Mauricio, Maurids, Mauriece, Maurikas, Maurin, Maurino, Maurise, Mauritz, Maurius, Maurizio, Mauro, Maurrel, Maurtel, Maury, Maurycy, Meurig, Moore, Morice, Moritz, Morel, Morrice, Morrie, Morrill, Morris

Mauricio (Spanish) a form of Maurice.
Mauriccio, Mauriceo, Maurico, Maurisio

Mauritz (German) a form of Maurice.

Maurizio (Italian) a form of Maurice.

Mauro (Latin) a short form of Maurice.
Maur, Maurio

Maury (Latin) a familiar form of Maurice.
Maurey, Maurie, Morrie

Maverick (American) independent.
Maverik, Maveryke, Mavric, Mavrick

Mawuli (Ewe) there is a God.

Max (Latin) a short form of Maximilian, Maxwell.
Mac, Mack, Maks, Maxe, Maxx, Maxy, Miksa

Maxfield (English) Mack's field.

Maxi (Czech, Hungarian, Spanish) a familiar form of Maximilian, Máximo.
Makszi, Maxey, Maxie, Maxis, Maxy

Maxim (Russian) a form of Maxime.

Maxime (French) most excellent.
Maxim, Maxyme

Maximilian (Latin) greatest.
Mac, Mack, Maixim, Maksim, Maksym, Max, Maxamillion, Maximilien, Maxemilion, Maxi, Maximalian, Maximili, Maximilia, Maximiliano, Maximilianus, Maximilien, Maximillian, Máximo, Maximos, Maxmilian, Maxmillion, Maxon, Maxymilian, Maxymillian, Mayheu, Miksa

Maximiliano (Italian) a form of Maximilian.
Massimiliano, Maximiano, Maximino

Maximillian (Latin) a form of Maximilian.
Maximillan, Maximillano, Maximillien, Maximillion, Maxximilian, Maxximillion

Máximo (Spanish) a form of Maximilian.
Massimo, Maxi, Maximiano, Maximiliano, Maximino, Máximo

Maximos (Greek) a form of Maximilian.

Maxwell (English) great spring.
Max, Maxuel, Maxwill, Maxxwell, Maxy

Maxy (English) a familiar form of Max, Maxwell.
Maxi

Mayer (Hebrew) a form of Meir. (Latin) a form of Magnus, Major.
Mahyar, Mayeer, Mayor, Mayur

Mayes (English) field.
Mayo, Mays

Mayhew (English) a form of Matthew.

Maynard (English) powerful; brave. See also Meinhard.
May, Mayne, Maynhard, Maynor, Ménard

Mayo (Irish) yew-tree plain. (English) a form of Mayes. Geography: a county in Ireland.

Mayon (Indian) person of black complexion. Religion: another name for the Indian god Mal.

Mayonga (Luganda) lake sailor.

Mazi (Ibo) sir.
Mazzi

Mazin (Arabic) proper.
Mazen, Mazinn, Mazzin

Mbita (Swahili) born on a cold night.

Mbwana (Swahili) master.

McGeorge (Scottish) son of George.
MacGeorge

Mckade (Scottish) son of Kade.
Mccade

Mckay (Scottish) son of Kay.
Mackay, MacKay, Mckae, Mckai, McKay

McKenzie (Irish) a form of Mackenzie.
Mccenzie, Mckennzie, Mckensey, Mckensie, Mckenson, Mckensson, Mckenzi, Mckenzy, Mckinzie

Mckinley (Irish) a form of Mackinley.
Mckinely, Mckinlley, Mckinnlee, Mckinnley, McKinnley

Mead (English) meadow.
Meade, Meed

Medgar (German) a form of Edgar.

Medwin (German) faithful friend.

Mehetabel (Hebrew) who God benefits.

Mehrdad (Persian) gift of the sun.

Mehtar (Sanskrit) prince.
Mehta

Meinhard (German) strong, firm. See also Maynard.
Meinhardt, Meinke, Meino, Mendar

Meinrad (German) strong counsel.

Meir (Hebrew) one who brightens, shines; enlightener. History: Golda Meir was the prime minister of Israel.
Mayer, Meyer, Muki, Myer

Meka (Hawaiian) eyes.

Mel (English, Irish) a familiar form of Melvin.

Melbourne (English) mill stream.
Melborn, Melburn, Melby, Milborn, Milbourn, Milbourne, Milburn, Millburne

Melchior (Hebrew) king.
Meilseoir, Melchor, Melker, Melkior

Meldon (English) mill hill.
Melden

Melrone (Irish) servant of Saint Ruadhan.

Melvern (Native American) great chief.

Melville (French) mill town. Literature: Herman Melville was a well-known nineteenth-century American writer.
Milville

Melvin (Irish) armored chief. (English) mill friend; council friend. See also Vinny.
Malvin, Mel, Melvino, Melvon, Melvyn, Melwin, Melwyn, Melwynn

Menachem (Hebrew) comforter.
Menahem, Nachman

Menassah (Hebrew) cause to forget.
Menashe, Menashi, Menashia, Menashiah, Menashya, Manasseh

Mendel (English) repairman.
Mendeley, Mendell, Mendie, Mendy

Mengesha (Ethiopian) kingdom.

Menico (Spanish) a short form of Domenico.

Mensah (Ewe) third son.

Menz (German) a short form of Clement.

Mercer (English) storekeeper.

Mered (Hebrew) revolter.

Meredith (Welsh) guardian from the sea.
Meredyth, Merideth, Meridith, Merry

Merion (Welsh) from Merion, Wales.

Merle (French) a short form of Merlin, Merrill.

Merlin (English) falcon. Literature: the magician who served as counselor in King Arthur's court.
Marlon, Merle, Merlen, Merlinn, Merlyn, Merlynn

Merrick (English) ruler of the sea.
Merek, Meric, Merick, Merik, Merric, Merrik, Merryk, Meyrick, Mynug

Merrill (Irish) bright sea. (French) famous.
Meril, Merill, Merle, Merrel, Merrell, Meril, Meryl

Merritt (Latin, Irish) valuable; deserving.
Meri, Meritt, Merrett

Merton (English) sea town.
Murton

Merv (Irish) a short form of Mervin.

Merville (French) sea village.

Mervin (Irish) a form of Marvin.
Merv, Mervyn, Mervynn, Merwin, Merwinn, Merwyn, Murvin, Murvyn, Myrvyn, Myrvynn, Myrwyn

Meshach (Hebrew) artist. Bible: one of Daniel's three friends who emerged unharmed from the fiery furnace of Babylon.

Mesut (Turkish) happy.

Metikla (Moquelumnan) reaching a hand underwater to catch a fish.

Mette (Greek, Danish) pearl.
Almeta, Mete

Meurig (Welsh) a form of Maurice.

Meyer (German) farmer.
Mayer, Meier, Myer

Mhina (Swahili) delightful.

Micah (Hebrew) a form of Michael. Bible: a Hebrew prophet.
Mic, Micaiah, Michiah, Mika, Mikah, Myca, Mycah

Micha (Hebrew) a short form of Michael.
Mica, Micha, Michah

Michael (Hebrew) who is like God? See also Micah, Miguel, Mika, Miles.
Machael, Machas, Mahail, Maichail, Maikal, Makael, Makal, Makel, Makell, Makis, Meikel, Mekal, Mekhail, Mhichael, Micael, Micah, Micahel, Mical, Micha, Michaela, Michaell, Michail, Michak, Michal, Michale, Michalek, Michalel, Michau, Micheal, Micheil, Michel, Michele, Micheler, Michiel, Micho, Michoel, Mick, Mickael, Mickey, Mihail, Mihalje, Mihkel, Mika, Mikael, Mikaele, Mikal, Mike, Mikeal, Mikel, Mikelis, Mikell, Mikhail, Mikkel, Mikko, Miksa, Milko, Miquel, Misael, Misi, Miska, Mitchell, Mychael, Mychajlo, Mychal, Mykal, Mykhas

Michail (Russian) a form of Michael.
Mihas, Mikail, Mikale, Misha

Michal (Polish) a form of Michael.
Michak, Michalek, Michall

Micheal (Irish) a form of Michael.

Michel (French) a form of Michael.
Michaud, Miche, Michee, Michell, Michelle, Michon

Michelangelo (Italian) a combination of Michael + Angelo. Art: Michelangelo Buonarroti was one of the greatest Renaissance painters.
Michelange, Miguelangelo

Michele (Italian) a form of Michael.

Michio (Japanese) man with the strength of three thousand.

Mick (English) a short form of Michael, Mickey.
Mickerson

Mickael (English) a form of Michael.
Mickaele, Mickal, Mickale, Mickeal, Mickel, Mickell, Mickelle, Mickle

Mickenzie (Irish) a form of Mackenzie.
Mickenze, Mickenzy, Mikenzie

Mickey (Irish) a familiar form of Michael.
Mick, Micki, Mickie, Micky, Miki, Mique

Micu (Hungarian) a form of Nick.

Miguel (Portuguese, Spanish) a form of Michael.
Migeel, Migel, Miguelly, Migui

Miguelangel (Spanish) a combination of Miguel + Angel.

Mihail (Greek, Bulgarian, Romanian) a form of Michael.
Mihailo, Mihal, Mihalis, Mikail

Mika (Ponca) raccoon. (Hebrew) a form of Micah. (Russian) a familiar form of Michael.
Miika, Mikah

Mikael (Swedish) a form of Michael.
Mikaeel, Mikaele

Mikáele (Hawaiian) a form of Michael.
Mikele

Mikal (Hebrew) a form of Michael.
Mekal, Mikahl, Mikale

Mikasi (Omaha) coyote.

Mike (Hebrew) a short form of Michael.
Mikey, Myk

Mikeal (Irish) a form of Michael.

Mikel (Basque) a form of Michael.
Mekel, Mikele, Mekell, Mikell, Mikelle

Mikelis (Latvian) a form of Michael.
Mikus, Milkins

Mikhail (Greek, Russian) a form of Michael.
Mekhail, Mihály, Mikhael, Mikhale, Mikhalis, Mikhalka, Mikhall, Mikhel, Mikhial, Mikhos

Miki (Japanese) tree.
Mikio

Mikkel (Norwegian) a form of Michael.
Mikkael, Mikle

Mikko (Finnish) a form of Michael. *Mikek, Mikka, Mikkohl, Mikekol, Miko, Mikol*

Mikolaj (Polish) a form of Nicholas. *Mikolai*

Mikolas (Greek) a form of Nicholas. *Mikelos, Mikek*

Miksa (Hungarian) a form of Max.

Milan (Italian) northerner. Geography: a city in northern Italy. *Milaan, Milano, Milen, Millan, Millen, Mylan, Mylen, Mylon, Mylynn*

Milap (Native American) giving. *Mila*

Milborough (English) middle borough. *Milbrough*

Milek (Polish) a familiar form of Nicholas.

Miles (Greek) millstone. (Latin) soldier. (German) merciful. (English) a short form of Michael. *Milas, Milles, Milo, Mison, Myles*

Milford (English) mill by the ford.

Miliani (Hawaiian) heavenly caress.

Milko (Czech) a familiar form of Michael. (German) a familiar form of Emil. *Milkins*

Millard (Latin) caretaker of the mill. *Mill, Millar, Miller, Millward, Milward, Myller*

Miller (English) miller; grain grinder. *Mellar, Millard, Millen*

Mills (English) mills.

Milo (German) a form of Miles. A familiar form of Emil. *Millo, Mylo*

Milos (Greek, Slavic) pleasant.

Miloslav (Czech) lover of glory. *Milda*

Milt (English) a short form of Milton.

Milton (English) mill town. *Milt, Miltie, Milty, Mylton*

Minis (Greek) a familiar form of Demetrius.

Min (Burmese) king. *Mina*

Mincho (Spanish) a form of Benjamin.

Minel (Spanish) a form of Manuel.

Miner (English) miner.

Mingan (Native American) gray wolf.

Mingo (Spanish) a short form of Domingo.

Minh (Vietnamese) bright. *Minhao, Minhduc, Minhkhan, Minhtong, Minhy*

Minkah (Akan) just, fair.

Minor (Latin) junior; younger. *Mynor*

Minoru (Japanese) fruitful.

Mique (Spanish) a form of Mickey. *Mequel, Mequelin, Miquel*

Miron (Polish) peace.

Miroslav (Czech) peace; glory. *Mirek, Miroslaw, Miroslawy*

Mirwais (Afghan) noble ruler.

Misael (Hebrew) a form of Michael. *Mischael, Mishael, Missael*

Misha (Russian) a short form of Michail. *Misa, Mischa, Mishael, Mishal, Mishe, Mishenka, Mishka*

Miska (Hungarian) a form of Michael. *Misi, Misike, Misko, Miso*

Mister (English) mister. *Mistur*

Misu (Moquelumnan) rippling water.

Mitch (English) a short form of Mitchell.

Mitchel (English) a form of Mitchell. *Mitchel, Mitchal, Mitcheal, Mitchell*

Mitchell (English) a form of Michael. *Mitch, Mitchall, Mitchel, Mitchelle, Mitchem, Mytch, Mytchell*

Mitsos (Greek) a familiar form of Demetrius.

Modesto (Latin) modest.

Moe (English) a short form of Moses. *Mo*

Mogens (Dutch) powerful.

Mohamed (Arabic) a form of Muhammad. *Mohamad, Mohammad, Mohamid*

Mohamed (Arabic) a form of
Muhammad.
Mohamd, Mohameed

Mohamet (Arabic) a form of
Muhammad.
Mahomet, Mehemet, Mehmet

Mohammad (Arabic) a form of
Muhammad.
*Mahammad, Mohammadi, Mohammd,
Mohammid, Mohanad, Mohmad*

Mohammed (Arabic) a form of
Muhammad.
*Mahammed, Mahomet, Mohammad,
Mohamed, Mouhamed, Muhammad*

Mohamud (Arabic) a form of
Muhammad.
Mohammud, Mohamoud

Mohan (Hindi) delightful.

Moises (Portuguese, Spanish) a form
of Moses.
Moices, Moise, Moisés, Moisey, Moisis

Moishe (Yiddish) a form of Moses.
Moshe

Mojag (Native American) crying baby.

Molimo (Moquelumnan) bear going
under shady trees.

Momuso (Moquelumnan) yellow
jackets crowded in their nests for the
winter.

Mona (Moquelumnan) gathering jim-
sonweed seed.

Monahan (Irish) monk.
Monaghan, Monoghan

Mongo (Yoruba) famous.

Monroe (Irish) Geography: the mouth
of the Roe River.
Monro, Munro, Munroe

Montague (French) pointed mountain.
Montagne, Montagu, Monte

Montana (Spanish) mountain.
Geography: a U.S. state.
Montaine, Montanna

Montaro (Japanese) big boy.
Montario, Monterio, Montero

Monte (Spanish) a short form of
Montgomery.
*Montae, Montaé, Montay, Montea,
Montee, Monti, Montoya, Monty*

Montel (American) a form of
Montreal.
Montele, Montell, Montelle

Montez (Spanish) dweller in the
mountains.
Monteiz, Monteze, Montezz, Montisze

Montgomery (English) rich man's
mountain.
Monte, Montgomerie, Monty

Montre (French) show.
*Montra, Montrae, Montray, Montraz,
Montres, Montrey, Montrez, Montreze*

Montreal (French) royal mountain.
Geography: a city in Quebec.
*Montel, Monterial, Monterrell, Montrail,
Montrale, Montrall, Montreall, Montrell,
Montrial*

Montrell (French) a form of
Montreal.
Montral, Montrel, Montrele, Montrelle

Montsho (Tswana) black.

Monty (English) a familiar form of
Montgomery.

Moore (French) dark; moor; marshland.
Moor, Mooro, More

Mordecai (Hebrew) martial, warlike.
Mythology: Marduk was the
Babylonian god of war. Bible: wise
counselor to Queen Esther.
*Mord, Mordachai, Mordechai, Mordie,
Mordy, Mort*

Mordred (Latin) painful. Literature:
the bastard son of King Arthur.
Modred

Morel (French) an edible mushroom.
Morrel

Moreland (English) moor; marshland.
Moorland, Morland

Morell (French) dark; from Morocco.
*Moor, Moore, Morelle, Morelli, Morill,
Morrell, Morrill, Murrel, Murrell*

Morey (Greek) a familiar form of
Moris. (Latin) a form of Morrie.
Morrey, Morry

Morgan (Scottish) sea warrior.
*Mogen, Morghan, Morgin, Morgon,
Morgun, Morgunn, Morgyn, Morgyn,
Morrgan*

Morio (Japanese) forest.

Moris (Greek) son of the dark one.
(English) a form of Morris.
Morey, Morisz, Moriz

Moritz (German) a form of Maurice, Morris. *Morisz*

Morley (English) meadow by the moor. *Moorley, Moorly, Morlee, Morleigh, Morlon, Morly, Mortyn, Morley*

Morrie (Latin) a familiar form of Maurice, Morse. *Maury, Morey, Mori, Morie, Morry, Mory, Morye*

Morris (Latin) dark skinned; moor; marshland. (English) a form of Maurice. *Moris, Morris, Moritz, Morrese, Morrise, Morriss, Morry, Moss*

Morse (English) son of Maurice. *Morresse, Morrie, Morrison, Morrisson*

Mort (French, English) a short form of Morten, Mortimer, Morton. *Morte, Mortey, Mortie, Mortty, Morty*

Morten (Norwegian) a form of Martin. *Mort*

Mortimer (French) still water. *Mort, Mortymer*

Morton (English) town near the moor. *Mort*

Morven (Scottish) mariner. *Morvien, Morvin*

Mose (Hebrew) a short form of Moses.

Moses (Hebrew) drawn out of the water. (Egyptian) son, child. Bible: the Hebrew lawgiver who brought the Ten Commandments down from Mount Sinai. *Moe, Moise, Moïse, Moisei, Moises, Moishe, Mose, Mosee, Moshe, Mosiah, Mosie, Moss, Mosses, Mosya, Mosze, Moszek, Mousa, Moyses, Moze*

Moshe (Hebrew, Polish) a form of Moses. *Mosheh*

Mosi (Swahili) first-born.

Moss (Irish) a short form of Maurice, Morris. (English) a short form of Moses.

Moswen (African) light in color.

Motega (Native American) new arrow.

Mouhamed (Arabic) a form of Muhammad. *Mouhamad, Mouhamadou, Mouhammed, Mouhamoin*

Mousa (Arabic) a form of Moses. *Moussa*

Moze (Lithuanian) a form of Moses. *Mózes, Mózes*

Mpasa (Nguni) mat.

Mposi (Nyakyusa) blacksmith.

Mpoza (Luganda) tax collector.

Msrah (Akan) sixth-born.

Mtima (Nguni) heart.

Muata (Moquelumnan) yellow jackets in their nest.

Mugamba (Runyoro) talks too much.

Mugisa (Rutooro) lucky. *Mugisha, Mukisa*

Muhammad (Arabic) praised. History: the founder of the Islamic religion. See also Ahmad, Hamid, Yasin. *Mahmoud, Mahmud, Mohamad, Mohamed, Mohamet, Mohammad, Mohammed, Mohaned, Mohamad, Muhamad, Muhamed, Muhammadali, Muhammed*

Muhannad (Arabic) sword. *Muhanad*

Muhsin (Arabic) beneficent; charitable.

Muhtadi (Arabic) rightly guided.

Muir (Scottish) moor; marshland.

Mujahid (Arabic) fighter in the way of Allah.

Mukasa (Luganda) God's chief administrator.

Mukhtar (Arabic) chosen. *Mukhtaar*

Mukul (Sanskrit) bud, blossom; soul.

Mulogo (Musoga) wizard.

Mundan (Rhodesian) garden.

Mundo (Spanish) a short form of Edmundo.

Mundy (Irish) from Reamonn.

Mungo (Scottish) amiable.

Mun-Hee (Korean) literate; shiny.

Munir (Arabic) brilliant; shining.

Munny (Cambodian) wise.

Muraco (Native American) white moon.

Murali (Hindi) flute. Religion: the instrument the Hindu god Krishna is usually depicted as playing.

Murat (Turkish) wish come true.

Murdock (Scottish) wealthy sailor.
Murdo, Murdoch, Murtagh

Murphy (Irish) sea warrior.
Murfey, Murfy

Murray (Scottish) sailor.
Macmurray, Moray, Murrey, Murry

Murtagh (Irish) a form of Murdock.
Murtaugh

Musa (Swahili) child.

Musád (Arabic) untied camel.

Musoke (Rukonjo) born while a rainbow was in the sky.

Mustafa (Arabic) chosen; royal.
Mostafa, Mostaffa, Moustafa, Mustafaa, Mustafah, Mustafe, Mustaffa, Mustafo, Mustapha, Mustoffa, Mustofo

Mustapha (Arabic) a form of Mustafa.
Mostapha, Moustapha

Muti (Arabic) obedient.

Mwaka (Luganda) born on New Year's Eve.

Mwamba (Nyakyusa) strong.

Mwanje (Luganda) leopard.

Mwinyi (Swahili) king.

Mwita (Swahili) summoner.

Mychajlo (Latvian) a form of Michael.
Mykhaltso, Mykhas

Mychal (American) a form of Michael.
Mychall, Mychalo, Mycheal

Myer (English) a form of Meir.
Myers, Myur

Mykal, Mykel (American) forms of Michael.
Mykael, Mikele, Mykell

Myles (Latin) soldier. (German) a form of Miles.
Myels, Mylez, Mylles, Mylz

Mynor (Latin) a form of Minor.

Myo (Burmese) city.

Myron (Greek) fragrant ointment.
Mehran, Mehrayan, My, Myran, Myrone, Ron

Myung-Dae (Korean) right; great.

Mzuzi (Swahili) inventive.

N

Naaman (Hebrew) pleasant.

Nabiha (Arabic) intelligent.

Nabil (Arabic) noble.
Nabeel, Nabiel

Nachman (Hebrew) a short form of Menachem.
Nachum, Nahum

Nada (Arabic) generous.

Nadav (Hebrew) generous; noble.
Nadiv

Nadidah (Arabic) equal to anyone else.

Nadim (Arabic) friend.
Nadeem

Nadir (Afghan, Arabic) dear, rare.
Nader

Nadisu (Hindi) beautiful river.

Naeem (Arabic) benevolent.
Naem, Naim, Naiym, Nieem

Naftali (Hebrew) wreath.
Naftalie

Nagid (Hebrew) ruler; prince.

Nahele (Hawaiian) forest.

Nahma (Native American) sturgeon.

Nailah (Arabic) successful.

Nairn (Scottish) river with alder trees.
Nairne

Najee (Arabic) a form of Naji.
Najae, Najée, Najei, Najiee

Naji (Arabic) safe.
Najee, Najih

Najib (Arabic) born to nobility.
Najib, Nejeeb

Naji (Muganda) second child.

Nakia (Arabic) pure.
Nakai, Nakee, Nakeia, Naki, Nakiah, Nakii

Nakos (Arapaho) sage, wise.

Naldo (Spanish) a familiar form of Reginald.

Nalren (Dene) thawed out.

Nam (Vietnamese) scrape off.

Namaka (Hawaiian) eyes.

Namid (Ojibwa) star dancer.

Namir (Hebrew) leopard.
Namer

Nando (German) a familiar form of Ferdinand.
Nandor

Nandin (Hindi) Religion: a servant of the Hindu god Shiva.
Nandan

Nangila (Abaluhya) born while parents traveled.

Nangwaya (Mwera) don't mess with me.

Nansen (Swedish) son of Nancy.

Nantai (Navajo) chief.

Nantan (Apache) spokesman.

Naoko (Japanese) straight, honest.

Napayshni (Lakota) he does not flee; courageous.

Napier (Spanish) new city.
Neper

Napoleon (Greek) lion of the woodland. (Italian) from Naples, Italy. History: Napoleon Bonaparte was a famous nineteenth-century French emperor.
Leon, Nap, Napolean, Napoleón, Napoleone, Nappie, Nappy

Naquan (American) a combination of the prefix Na + Quan.
Naquan, Naquain, Naquen, Naquon

Narain (Hindi) protector. Religion: another name for the Hindu god Vishnu.
Narayan

Narcisse (French) a form of Narcissus.
Narcis, Narciso, Narkis, Narkisso

Narcissus (Greek) daffodil. Mythology: the youth who fell in love with his own reflection.
Narcisse

Nard (Persian) chess player.

Nardo (German) strong, hardy. (Spanish) a short form of Bernardo.

Narve (Dutch) healthy, strong.

Nashashuk (Fox, Sauk) loud thunder.

Nashoba (Choctaw) wolf.

Nasim (Persian) breeze; fresh air.
Naseem, Nassim

Nasser (Arabic) victorious.
Naseer, Naser, Nasier, Nasir, Nasr, Nassir, Nassor

Nat (English) a short form of Nathan, Nathaniel.
Natt, Natty

Natal (Spanish) a form of Noël.
Natale, Natalie, Natalino, Natalio, Nataly

Natan (Hebrew, Hungarian, Polish, Russian, Spanish) God has given.
Naten

Natanael (Hebrew) a form of Nathaniel.
Natanel, Nataniel

Nate (Hebrew) a short form of Nathan, Nathaniel.

Natesh (Hindi) destroyer. Religion: another name for the Hindu god Shiva.

Nathan (Hebrew) a short form of Nathaniel. Bible: a prophet during the reigns of David and Solomon.
Naethan, Nat, Nate, Nathann, Nathean, Nathen, Nathian, Nathin, Nathion, Nathyn, Natthan, Naythan, Nethan

Nathanael (Hebrew) gift of God. Bible: one of the Twelve Apostles. Also known as Bartholomew.
Nathanae, Nathanail, Nathaneal, Nathaneil, Nathanel, Nathaneol

Nathanial (Hebrew) a form of Nathaniel.
Nathanyal, Nathanual

Nathanie (Hebrew) a familiar form of Nathaniel.
Nathania, Nathanni

Nathaniel (Hebrew) gift of God. Bible: one of the Twelve Apostles.
Nat, Natanael, Nate, Nathan, Nathanael, Nathanial, Nathaniele, Nathanil, Nathanile, Nathanielle, Nathaniil, Nathanniel, Nathanyel, Nathanyl, Natheal, Nathel, Nathiniel, Nethaniel, Thaniel

Nathen (Hebrew) a form of Nathan.

Nav (Gypsy) name.

Navarro (Spanish) plains.
Navarre

Navdeep (Sikh) new light.
Navdip

Navin (Hindi) new, novel.
Naveen, Naven

Nawat (Native American) left-handed.

Nawkaw (Winnebago) wood.

Nayati (Native American) wrestler.

Nayland (English) island dweller.

Nazareth (Hebrew) born in Nazareth, Israel.
Nazaire, Nazaret, Nazarie, Nazario, Nazarene, Nazerine

Nazih (Arabic) pure, chaste.
Nazeeh, Nazeem, Nazeer, Nazieh, Nazin, Nazir, Nazz

Ndale (Nguni) trick.

Neal (Irish) a form of Neil.
Neale, Neall, Nealle, Nealon, Nealy

Neci (Latin) a familiar form of Ignatius.

Nectarios (Greek) saint. Religion: a saint in the Greek Orthodox Church.

Ned (English) a familiar form of Edward, Edwin.
Neddie, Neddym, Nedrick

Nehemiah (Hebrew) compassion of Jehovah. Bible: a Jewish leader.
Nahemiah, Nechemya, Nehemias, Nehemie, Nehemyah, Nehimiah, Nehmia, Nehmiah, Nemo, Neyamia

Nehru (Hindi) canal.

Neil (Irish) champion.
Neal, Neel, Neihl, Neile, Neill, Neille, Nels, Niall, Niele, Niels, Nigel, Nil, Niles, Nilo, Nils, Nyle

Neka (Native American) wild goose.

Nelek (Polish) a form of Cornelius.

Nellie (English) a familiar form of Cornelius, Cornell, Nelson.
Nell, Nelly

Nelius (Latin) a short form of Cornelius.

Nelo (Spanish) a form of Daniel.
Nello, Nilo

Nels (Scandinavian) a form of Neil, Nelson.
Nelse, Nelson, Nils

Nelson (English) son of Neil.
Nealson, Neilsen, Neilson, Nellie, Nels, Nelsen, Nilson, Nilsson

Nemesio (Spanish) just.
Nemi

Nemo (Greek) glen, glade. (Hebrew) a short form of Nehemiah.

Nen (Egyptian) ancient waters.

Neptune (Latin) sea ruler. Mythology: the Roman god of the sea.

Nero (Latin, Spanish) stern. History: a cruel Roman emperor.
Neron, Nerone, Nerron

Nesbit (English) nose-shaped bend in a river.
Naisbit, Naisbitt, Nesbitt, Nisbet, Nisbett

Nestor (Greek) traveler; wise.
Nester

Nethaniel (Hebrew) a form of Nathaniel.
Netanel, Netania, Netaniah, Netaniel, Netanya, Nethanel, Nethanial, Nethaniel, Nethanyal, Nethanyel

Neto (Spanish) a short form of Ernesto.

Nevada (Spanish) covered in snow. Geography: a U.S. state.
Navada, Nevade

Nevan (Irish) holy.
Nevean

Neville (French) new town.
Nev, Nevil, Nevile, Nevill, Nevyle

Nevin (Irish) worshiper of the saint. (English) middle; herb.
Nefen, Nev, Nevan, Neven, Nevins, Nevyn, Niven

Newbold (English) new tree.

Newell (English) new hall.
Newall, Newel, Newyle

Newland (English) new land.
Newlan

Newlin (Welsh) new lake.
Newlyn

Newman (English) newcomer.
Neiman, Neimann, Neimon, Newman, Numan, Numen

Newton (English) new town.
Newt

Ngai (Vietnamese) herb.

Nghia (Vietnamese) forever.

Ngozi (Ibo) blessing.

Ngu (Vietnamese) sleep.

Nguyen (Vietnamese) a form of Ngu.

Nhean (Cambodian) self-knowledge.

Niall (Irish) a form of Neil. History: Niall of the Nine Hostages was a famous Irish king.
Nial, Nialle

Nibal (Arabic) arrows.
Nibel

Nibaw (Native American) standing tall.

Nicabar (Gypsy) stealthy.

Nicho (Spanish) a form of Dennis.

Nicholas (Greek) victorious people. Religion: Nicholas of Myra is a patron saint of children. See also Caelan, Claus, Cola, Colar, Cole, Colin, Colson, Klaus, Lasse, Mikolaj, Mikolas, Milek.
Nicolas, Nicholas, Nichelas, Nichele, Niclas, Nichlos, Nichola, Nicholaus, Nicholas, Nicholase, Nicholaus, Nicholace, Nicholoss, Nicholl, Nicholias, Nichole, Nichols, Nicholus, Nicholos, Niclasse, Nickolas, Nicky, Niclas, Niclasse, Nico, Nicola, Nicolai, Nicolas,
Nicoles, Nicolis, Nicoll, Nicolo, Nikhil, Niki, Nikiti, Nikita, Nikko, Niklas, Niko, Nikolai, Nikolas, Nikolaus, Nikolos, Nils, Nicols, Niocol, Nycholas, Nicholaus

Nicholaus (Greek) a form of Nicholas.
Nichalaus, Nichalous, Nichaolas, Nichlaus, Nichlaus, Nichlaus, Nicholaos, Nicholous, Nicholaus

Nichols, Nicholson (English) son of Nicholas.
Nicholes, Nicholis, Niolls, Nickelson, Nickoles

Nick (English) a short form of Dominic, Nicholas. See also Micu.
Nic, Nik

Nickalus (Greek) a form of Nicholas.
Nickalis, Nickalis, Nickalos, Nickelos, Nickelus

Nicklaus, Nicklas (Greek) forms of Nicholas.
Nickelaos, Nickelous, Nickelous, Nickelaus, Nickelos, Nickelous, Nicklos, Nickolaus, Nickelous, Nielaus, Nielaus, Nicklaus

Nickolas (Greek) a form of Nicholas.
Nickelaos, Nickelis, Nickelos, Nickolos, Nickolys, Nickoulas

Nicky (Greek) a familiar form of Nicholas.
Nickey, Nicki, Nickie, Niki, Nikki

Nico (Greek) a short form of Nicholas.
Nico

Nicodemus (Greek) conqueror of the people.
Nicodem, Nicodemus, Nikodem, Nikodema, Nikodemios, Nikodim

Nicola (Italian) a form of Nicholas. See also Cola.
Nicolà, Nikolah

Nicolai (Norwegian, Russian) a form of Nicholas.
Nicholai, Nickolai, Nicolaj, Nicolau, Nicolay, Nicoly, Nikalai

Nicolas (Italian) a form of Nicholas.
Nico, Nicolaas, Nicolás, Nicolaus, Nicoles, Nicolis, Nicolus

Nicolo (Italian) a form of Nicholas.
Niccolò, Niccoló, Nicol, Nicolao, Nicollo

Niels (Danish) a form of Neil.
Niel, Nielsen, Nielson, Niles, Nils

Nien (Vietnamese) year.

Nigan (Native American) ahead.
Nigen

Nigel (Latin) dark night.
Niegel, Nigal, Nigale, Nigele, Nigell, Nigil, Nigil, Nigle, Nijel, Nye, Nygel, Nygel, Nyjil

Nika (Yoruba) ferocious.

Nike (Greek) victorious.
Nikka

Niki (Hungarian) a familiar form of Nicholas.
Nikita, Nikiah, Nikiei, Nikitie, Nykei, Nykey

Nikita (Russian) a form of Nicholas.
Nakita, Nakitas, Nikika

Nikiti (Native American) round and smooth like an abalone shell.

Nikko, Niko (Hungarian) forms of Nicholas.
Nikoe, Nyko

Niklas (Latvian, Swedish) a form of Nicholas.
Niklaas, Niklaus

Nikola (Greek) a short form of Nicholas.
Nikolao, Nikolay, Nykola

Nikolai (Estonian, Russian) a form of Nicholas.
Kolya, Nikolais, Nikolaj, Nikolajs, Nikolay, Nikoli, Nikolia, Nikula, Nikulas

Nikolas (Greek) a form of Nicholas.
Nicanor, Nikalas, Nikalis, Nikalus, Nikholas, Nikolaas, Nikolaos, Nikolis, Nikolos, Nikos, Nilos, Nykolas, Nykolaus

Nikolaus (Greek) a form of Nicholas.
Nikalous, Nikolaos

Nikolos (Greek) a form of Nicholas. See also Kolya.
Nikolos, Nikolaos, Nikolò, Nikolous, Nikolus, Nikos, Nilos

Nil (Russian) a form of Neil.
Nilya

Nila (Hindi) blue.

Niles (English) son of Neil.
Nilesh, Nyles

Nilo (Finnish) a form of Neil.

Nils (Swedish) a short form of Nicholas.

Nimrod (Hebrew) rebel. Bible: a great-grandson of Noah.

Niño (Spanish) young child.

Niran (Tai) eternal.

Nishan (Armenian) cross, sign, mark.
Nishon

Nissan (Hebrew) sign, omen; miracle.
Nisan, Nissim, Nissin, Nisson

Nitis (Native American) friend.
Netis

Nixon (English) son of Nick.
Nixan, Nixson

Nizam (Arabic) leader.

Nkunda (Runyankore) loves those who hate him.

N'namdi (Ibo) his father's name lives on.

Noach (Hebrew) a form of Noah.

Noah (Hebrew) peaceful, restful. Bible: the patriarch who built the ark to survive the Flood.
Noach, Noak, Noe, Noé, Noi

Noam (Hebrew) sweet; friend.

Noble (Latin) born to nobility.
Nobe, Nobie, Noby

Nodin (Native American) wind.
Knoton, Noton

Noe (Czech, French) a form of Noah.

Noé (Hebrew, Spanish) quiet, peaceful. See also Noah.

Noël (French) day of Christ's birth. See also Natal.
Noel, Noël, Noell, Nole, Noli, Nouel, Nouell

Nohea (Hawaiian) handsome.
Noha, Nohe

Nokonyu (Native American) katydid's nose.
Noko, Nokoni

Nolan (Irish) famous; noble.
Noland, Nolande, Nolane, Nolen, Nolin, Nollan, Nolyn

Nollie (Latin, Scandinavian) a familiar form of Oliver.
Noll, Nolly

Norbert (Scandinavian) brilliant hero.
Bert, Norberto, Norbie, Norby

Norberto (Spanish) a form of Norbert.

Norman (French) Norseman. History: a name for the Scandinavians who settled in northern France in the tenth century, and who later conquered England in 1066.
Norm, Normand, Normen, Normie, Normy

Norris (French) northerner. (English) Norman's horse.
Norice, Norie, Noris, Norreys, Norrie, Norry, Norrys

Northcliff (English) northern cliff.
Northcliffe, Northclyff, Northclyffe

Northrop (English) north farm.
North, Northup

Norton (English) northern town.

Norville (French, English) northern town.
Norval, Norvel, Norvell, Norvil, Norvill, Norvylle

Norvin (English) northern friend.
Norvyn, Norvun, Norwin, Norwyn, Norwynn

Norward (English) protector of the north.
Norward

Norwood (English) northern woods.
Norword

Notaku (Moquelumnan) growing bear.

Nowles (English) a short form of Knowles.

Nsoah (Akan) seventh-born.

Numa (Arabic) pleasant.

Numair (Arabic) panther.

Nuncio (Italian) messenger.
Nunzi, Nunzio

Nuri (Hebrew, Arabic) my fire.
Nery, Noori, Nur, Nuris, Nurism, Nury

Nuriel (Hebrew, Arabic) fire of the Lord.

Nuru (Swahili) born in daylight.
Nuria, Nuriah, Nuriya

Nusair (Arabic) bird of prey.

Nwa (Nigerian) son.

Nwake (Nigerian) born on market day.

Nye (English) a familiar form of Aneurin, Nigel.

Nyle (English) island. (Irish) a form of Neil.
Nyal, Nyll

Oakes (English) oak trees.
Oak, Oakie, Oaks, Ochs

Oakley (English) oak-tree field.
Oak, Oakes, Oakie, Oaklee, Oakleigh, Oakly, Oaks

Oalo (Spanish) a form of Paul.

Oba (Yoruba) king.

Obadele (Yoruba) king arrives at the house.

Obadiah (Hebrew) servant of God.
Obadias, Obed, Obediah, Obie, Ovadiach, Ovadiah, Ovadya

Obed (English) a short form of Obadiah.

Obert (German) wealthy; bright.

Obie (English) a familiar form of Obadiah.
Obbie, Obe, Obey, Obi, Oby

Ocan (Luo) hard times.

Octavio (Latin) eighth. See also Tavey, Tavian.
Octave, Octavia, Octaviano, Octavien, Octavino, Octavius, Octavo, Octavous, Octavus, Ottavio

Octavious, Octavius (Latin) forms of Octavio.
Octavius, Octaveous, Octaveus, Octavias, Octavis, Octavous, Octavs

Odakota (Lakota) friendly;
Oda

Odd (Norwegian) point.
Oddvar

Ode (Benin) born along the road. (Irish, English) a short form of Odell.
Odey, Odie, Ody

Oded (Hebrew) encouraging.

Odell (Greek) ode, melody. (Irish) otter. (English) forested hill.
Dell, Odall, Ode

Odin (Scandinavian) ruler. Mythology: the Norse god of wisdom and war.
Oden

Odion (Benin) first of twins.

Odo (Norwegian) a form of Otto.

Odolf (German) prosperous wolf.
Odolff

Odom (Ghanaian) oak tree.

Odon (Hungarian) wealthy protector.
Odi

Odran (Irish) pale green.
Odhran, Oran, Oren, Orin, Orran, Orren, Orrin

Odysseus (Greek) wrathful. Literature: the hero of Homer's epic poem *Odyssey*.

Oberon (German) noble; bearlike. Literature: the king of the fairies in the Shakespearean play *A Midsummer Night's Dream*. See also Auberon, Aubrey.
Oberen, Oberron, Oeberon

Ofer (Hebrew) young deer.

Og (Aramaic) king. Bible: the king of Basham.

Ogaleesha (Lakota) red shirt.

Ogbay (Ethiopian) don't take him from me.

Ogbonna (Ibo) image of his father.
Ogbonnia

Ogden (English) oak valley. Literature: Ogden Nash was a twentieth-century American writer of light verse.
Ogdan, Ogdon

Ogima (Chippewa) chief.

Ogun (Nigerian) Mythology: the god of war.
Ogunkeye, Ogunsanwo, Ogunsheye

Ohanko (Native American) restless.

Ohannes (Turkish) a form of John.

Ohanzee (Lakota) comforting shadow.

Ohin (African) chief.
Ohan

Ohitekah (Lakota) brave.

Oistin (Irish) a form of Austin.
Osten, Ostyn, Ostynn

OJ (American) a combination of the initials O. + J.
O.J., Ojay

Ojo (Yoruba) difficult delivery.

Okapi (Swahili) an African animal related to the giraffe but having a short neck.

Oke (Hawaiian) a form of Oscar.

Okechuku (Ibo) God's gift.

Okeke (Ibo) born on market day.
Okorie

Okie (American) from Oklahoma.
Okee, Okey

Oko (Ghanaian) older twin. (Yoruba) god of war.

Okorie (Ibo) a form of Okeke.

Okpara (Ibo) first son.

Okuth (Luo) born in a rain shower.

Ola (Yoruba) wealthy, rich.

Olaf (Scandinavian) ancestor. History: a patron saint and king of Norway.
Olaff, Olafur, Olav, Ole, Olef, Olof, Oluf

Olajuwon (Yoruba) wealth and honor are God's gifts.
Olajawon, Olajawun, Olajowuan, Olajuan, Olajuanne, Olajuawon, Olajuwa, Olajuwan, Olaujawon, Oljiwoun

Olamina (Yoruba) this is my wealth.

Olatunji (Yoruba) honor reawakens.

Olav (Scandinavian) a form of Olaf.
Ola, Olave, Olavus, Ole, Olen, Olin, Olle, Olov, Olyn

Ole (Scandinavian) a familiar form of Olaf, Olav.
Olay, Oleh, Olle

Oleg (Latvian, Russian) holy.
Olezka

Oleksandr (Russian) a form of Alexander.
Olek, Olesandr, Olesko

Olés (Polish) a familiar form of Alexander.

Olin (English) holly.
Olen, Oliney, Olyn

Olindo (Italian) from Olinthos, Greece.

Oliver (Latin) olive tree. (Scandinavian) kind; affectionate.
Nollie, Oilibhéar, Oliverio, Oliverios, Olivero, Olivier, Oliviero, Oliwa, Ollie, Olliver, Ollivor, Olvan

Olivier (French) a form of Oliver.

Oliwa (Hawaiian) a form of Oliver.

Ollie (English) a familiar form of Oliver.
Olie, Olle, Olley, Olly

Olo (Spanish) a short form of Orlando, Rolando.

Olubayo (Yoruba) highest joy.

Olufemi (Yoruba) wealth and honor favors me.

Olujimi (Yoruba) God gave me this.

Olushola (Yoruba) God has blessed me.

Omar (Arabic) highest; follower of the Prophet. (Hebrew) reverent.
Omair, Omari, Omarr, Omer, Umar

Omari (Swahili) a form of Omar.
Omare, Omaree, Omarey

Omer (Arabic) a form of Omar.
Omeer, Omero

Omolara (Benin) child born at the right time.

On (Burmese) coconut. (Chinese) peace.

Onan (Turkish) prosperous.

Onaona (Hawaiian) pleasant fragrance.

Ondro (Czech) a form of Andrew. *Ondra, Ondre, Ondrea, Ondrey*

O'neil (Irish) son of Neil. *Oneal, O'neal, Oneil, O'neill, Onel, Oniel, Onil*

Onkar (Hindi) God in his entirety.

Onofrio (German) a form of Humphrey. *Oifre, Onfre, Onfrio, Onofre, Onofredo*

Onslow (English) enthusiast's hill. *Ounslow*

Onufry (Polish) a form of Humphrey.

Onur (Turkish) honor.

Ophir (Hebrew) faithful. Bible: an Old Testament people and country.

Opio (Ateso) first of twin boys.

Oral (Latin) verbal speaker.

Oran (Irish) green. *Odhran, Odran, Ora, Orane, Oran*

Oratio (Latin) a form of Horatio. *Orazio*

Orbán (Hungarian) born in the city.

Ordell (Latin) beginning. *Orde*

Oren (Hebrew) pine tree. (Irish) light skinned, white. *Oran, Orin, Oris, Orono, Orren, Orrin*

Orestes (Greek) mountain man. Mythology: the son of the Greek leader Agamemnon. *Aresty, Oreste*

Ori (Hebrew) my light. *Oree, Orie, Orri, Ory*

Orien (Latin) visitor from the east. *Orian, Orie, Orin, Oris, Oron, Orono, Orrin, Oryan*

Orion (Greek) son of fire. Mythology: a giant hunter who was killed by Artemis. See also Zorion.

Orji (Ibo) mighty tree.

Orlando (German) famous throughout the land. (Spanish) a form of Roland. *Lando, Olando, Olo, Orlan, Orland, Orlanda, Orlandas, Orlandes, Orlandis, Orlandos, Orlandus, Orlo, Orlondo*

Orleans (Latin) golden. *Orlean, Orlin*

Orman (German) mariner, seaman. (Scandinavian) serpent, worm. *Ormand*

Ormond (English) bear mountain; spear protector. *Ormande, Ormon, Ormonde*

Orrin (English) river. *Orin, Oryn, Orynn*

Orris (Latin) a form of Horatio. *Oris, Orriss*

Orry (Latin) from the Orient. *Oarrie, Orrey, Orrie*

Orsino (Italian) a form of Orson.

Orson (Latin) bearlike. *Oscino, Orsen, Orsin, Orsini, Orsino, Son, Sonny, Urson*

Orton (English) shore town.

Ortzi (Basque) sky.

Orunjian (Yoruba) born under the midday sun.

Orval (English) a form of Orville. *Orvel*

Orville (French) golden village. History: Orville Wright and his brother Wilbur were the first men to fly an airplane. *Orv, Orvall, Orvell, Orvie, Orvil*

Orvin (English) spear friend. *Orvin, Owynn*

Osahar (Benin) God hears.

Osayaba (Benin) God forgives.

Osaze (Benin) whom God likes.

Osbert (English) divine; bright.

Osborn (Scandinavian) divine bear. (English) warrior of God. *Osbern, Osborn, Osborne, Osbourn, Osbourne, Osburn, Osburne, Oz, Ozzie*

Oscar (Scandinavian) divine spearman.
Oke, Oskar, Osker, Oszkar

Osei (Fante) noble.
Osee

Osgood (English) divinely good.

O'Shea (Irish) son of Shea.
Oshae, Oshai, Oshane, O'Shane, Oshaun, Oshay, Oshaye, Oshe, Oshea, Osheon

Osip (Russian, Ukrainian) a form of Joseph, Yosef. See also Osya.

Oskar (Scandinavian) a form of Oscar.
Osker, Ozker

Osman (Turkish) ruler. (English) servant of God.
Osmanek, Osmen, Osmin, Othmor, Ottmar

Osmar (English) divine; wonderful.

Osmond (English) divine protector.
Osmand, Osmonde, Osmont, Osmund, Osmunde, Osmundo

Osric (English) divine ruler.
Osrick

Ostin (Latin) a form of Austin.
Ostan, Osten, Ostyn

Osvaldo (Spanish) a form of Oswald.
Osbaldo, Osbalto, Osvald, Osvalda

Oswald (English) God's power; God's crest. See also Waldo.
Osvaldo, Oswaldo, Oswall, Oswell, Oswold, Oz, Ozzie

Oswaldo (Spanish) a form of Oswald.

Oswin (English) divine friend.
Osvin, Oswinn, Oswyn, Oswynn

Osya (Russian) a familiar form of Osip.

Ota (Czech) prosperous.
Otik

Otadan (Native American) plentiful.

Otaktay (Lakota) kills many; strikes many.

Otek (Polish) a form of Otto.

Otello (Italian) a form of Othello.

Otem (Luo) born away from home.

Othello (Spanish) a form of Otto. Literature: the title character in the Shakespearean tragedy *Othello*.
Otelo

Othman (German) wealthy.
Ottoman

Otis (Greek) keen of hearing. (German) son of Otto.
Oates, Odis, Otes, Otess, Otez, Otise, Ottis, Otys

Ottah (Nigerian) thin baby.

Ottar (Norwegian) point warrior; fright warrior.

Ottmar (Turkish) a form of Osman.
Otomars, Ottomar

Otto (German) rich.
Odo, Otek, Orello, Offried, Othello, Otho, Othon, Otik, Otilio, Otman, Oto, Otón, Otton, Ottone

Ottokar (German) happy warrior.
Otokars, Ottocar

Otu (Native American) collecting seashells in a basket.

Ouray (Ute) arrow. Astrology: born under the sign of Sagittarius.

Oved (Hebrew) worshiper, follower.

Owen (Irish) born to nobility; young warrior. (Welsh) a form of Evan.
Owain, Owens, Owin, Uaine

Owney (Irish) elderly.
Oney

Oxford (English) place where oxen cross the river.
Ford

Oya (Moquelumnan) speaking of the jacksnipe.

Oystein (Norwegian) rock of happiness.
Ostein, Osten, Ostin, Øystein

Oz (Hebrew) a short form of Osborn, Oswald.

Ozturk (Turkish) pure; genuine Turk.

Ozzie (English) a familiar form of Osborn, Oswald.
Ossie, Ossy, Ozee, Ozi, Ozzi, Ozzy

P

Paavo (Finnish) a form of Paul.
Paaveli

Pablo (Spanish) a form of Paul.
Pable, Paublo

Pace (English) a form of Pascal.
Payce

Pacifico (Filipino) peaceful.

Paco (Italian) pack. (Spanish) a familiar form of Francisco. (Native American) bald eagle. See also Quico.
Pacorro, Panchito, Pancho, Paquito

Paddy (Irish) a familiar form of Padraic, Patrick.
Paddey, Paddi, Paddie

Paden (English) a form of Patton.

Padget (English) a form of Page.
Padgett, Paget, Pagett

Padraic (Irish) a form of Patrick.
Paddrick, Paddy, Padhraig, Padrai, Pádraig, Padraigh, Padraic, Padraic, Padric, Padron, Padruig

Page (French) youthful assistant.
Padget, Paggio, Paige, Payge

Paige (English) a form of Page.

Pakelika (Hawaiian) a form of Patrick.

Paki (African) witness.

Pal (Swedish) a form of Paul.

Pál (Hungarian) a form of Paul.
Pali, Palika

Palaina (Hawaiian) a form of Brian.

Palani (Hawaiian) a form of Frank.

Palash (Hindi) flowery tree.

Palben (Basque) blond.

Palladin (Native American) fighter.
Pallaton, Palleten

Palmer (English) palm-bearing pilgrim.
Pallmer, Palmar

Palti (Hebrew) God liberates.
Palti-el

Panas (Russian) immortal.

Panayiotis (Greek) a form of Peter.
Panagiotis, Panajotis, Panajoti, Panayioti, Panayiotis

Pancho (Spanish) a familiar form of Francisco, Frank.
Panchito

Panos (Greek) a form of Peter.
Petros

Paolo (Italian) a form of Paul.

Paquito (Spanish) a familiar form of Paco.

Paramesh (Hindi) greatest. Religion: another name for the Hindu god Shiva.

Pardeep (Sikh) mystic light.
Pardip

Paris (Greek) lover. Geography: the capital of France. Mythology: the prince of Troy who started the Trojan War by abducting Helen.
Paras, Paree, Pares, Parese, Parie, Parris, Parys

Park (Chinese) cypress tree. (English) a short form of Parker.
Parke, Parkes, Parkey, Parks

Parker (English) park keeper.
Park

Parkin (English) little Peter.
Perkin

Parlan (Scottish) a form of Bartholomew. See also Parthalán.

Parnell (French) little Peter. History: Charles Stewart Parnell was a famous Irish politician.
Nell, Parle, Parnel, Parnell, Pernell

Parr (English) cattle enclosure, barn.

Parrish (English) church district.
Parish, Parrie, Parrisch, Parrysh

Parry (Welsh) son of Harry.
Parrey, Parrie, Pary

Parth (Irish) a short form of Parthalán.
Partha, Parthey

Parthalán (Irish) plowman. See also Parlan, Parth

Parthenios (Greek) virgin. Religion: a Greek Orthodox saint.

Pascal (French) born on Easter or Passover.
Pace, Pascale, Pascalle, Paschal, Paschalis, Pascoe, Pascow, Pascual, Pasquale

Pascual (Spanish) a form of Pascal.
Pascal

Pasha (Russian) a form of Paul.
Pashenka, Pashka

Pasquale (Italian) a form of Pascal.
Pascuale, Pasqual, Pasquali, Pasquel

Pastor (Latin) spiritual leader.

Pat (Native American) fish. (English) a short form of Patrick.
Pattie, Patty

Patakusu (Moquelumnan) ant biting a person.

Patamon (Native American) raging.

Patek (Polish) a form of Patrick.
Patick

Patric (Latin) a form of Patrick.

Patrice (French) a form of Patrick.

Patricio (Spanish) a form of Patrick.
Patricius, Patrizio

Patrick (Latin) nobleman. Religion: the patron saint of Ireland. See also Fitzpatrick, Ticho.
Paddy, Padraic, Pakelika, Pat, Patek, Patric, Patrice, Patricio, Patrickk, Patrik, Patrique, Patrizius, Patryk, Pats, Patsy, Pattrick

Patrin (Gypsy) leaf trail.

Patryk (Latin) a form of Patrick.
Patrycke

Patterson (Irish) son of Pat.
Patteson

Pattin (Gypsy) leaf.

Patton (English) warrior's town.
Paden, Paten, Patin, Paton, Patten, Pattin, Patty, Payton, Peyton

Patwin (Native American) man.

Patxi (Basque, Teutonic) free.

Paul (Latin) small. Bible: Saul, later renamed Paul, was the first to bring the teachings of Christ to the Gentiles.
Oalo, Paavo, Pablo, Pal, Pál, Pall, Paolo, Pasha, Pasko, Pauli, Paulia, Paulin, Paulino, Paulis, Paulo, Pauls, Paulus, Pavel, Pavlos, Pawel, Pol, Poul

Pauli (Latin) a familiar form of Paul.
Pauley, Paulie, Pauly

Paulin (German, Polish) a form of Paul.

Paulino (Spanish) a form of Paul.

Paulo (Portuguese, Swedish, Hawaiian) a form of Paul.

Pavel (Russian) a form of Paul.
Paavel, Pasha, Pavils, Pavlik, Pavlo, Pavlusha, Pavlushenka, Pawl

Pavit (Hindi) pious, pure.

Pawel (Polish) a form of Paul.
Pawelek, Pawl

Pax (Latin) peaceful.
Paz

Paxton (Latin) peaceful town.
Packston, Pax, Paxon, Paxten, Paxtun

Payat (Native American) he is on his way.
Pay, Payatt

Payden (English) a form of Payton.
Paydon

Payne (Latin) from the country.
Paine, Paynn

Paytah (Lakota) fire.
Pay, Payta

Payton (English) a form of Patton.
Paiton, Pate, Payden, Peaton, Peighton, Peyton

Paz (Spanish) a form of Pax.

Pearce (English) a form of Pierce.
Pears, Pearse

Pearson (English) son of Peter. See also Pierson.
Pearsson, Pehrson, Peirson, Peterson

Peder (Scandinavian) a form of Peter.
Peadar, Pedey

Pedro (Spanish) a form of Peter.
Pedrin, Pedrín, Petronio

Peers (English) a form of Peter.
Peems, Piers

Peeter (Estonian) a form of Peter.
Peet

Peirce (English) a form of Peter.
Peirs

Pekelo (Hawaiian) a form of Peter.
Pekka

Peleke (Hawaiian) a form of Frederick.

Pelham (English) tannery town.

Pelí (Latin, Basque) happy.

Pell (English) parchment.
Pall

Pello (Greek, Basque) stone.
Peru, Piarres

Pelton (English) town by a pool.

Pembroke (Welsh) headland. (French) wine dealer. (English) broken fence.
Pembrook

Peniamina (Hawaiian) a form of Benjamin.
Peni

Penley (English) enclosed meadow.

Penn (Latin) pen, quill. (English) enclosure. (German) a short form of Penrod.
Pen, Penna, Penney, Pennie, Penny

Penrod (German) famous commander.
Penn, Pennrod, Rod

Pepa (Czech) a familiar form of Joseph.

Pepe (Spanish) a familiar form of José.
Pepillo, Pepito, Pequin, Pipo

Pepin (German) determined; petitioner. History: Pepin the Short was an eighth-century king of the Franks.
Pepi, Peppie, Peppy

Peppe (Italian) a familiar form of Joseph.
Peppi, Peppo, Pino

Per (Swedish) a form of Peter.

Perben (Greek, Danish) stone.

Percival (French) pierce the valley. Literature: a knight of the Round Table who first appears in Chrétien de Troyes's poem about the quest for the Holy Grail.
Parsefal, Parsifal, Parsifal, Parzival, Perc, Perce, Perceval, Percevall, Percivall, Percy, Perdun, Purcell

Percy (French) a familiar form of Percival.
Pearcy, Pearcy, Percey, Percie, Piercey, Piercy

Peregrine (Latin) traveler; pilgrim; falcon.
Peregrin, Peregryne, Perine, Perry

Pericles (Greek) just leader. History: an Athenian statesman.

Perico (Spanish) a form of Peter.
Pequin, Perquin

Perine (Latin) a short form of Peregrine.
Perino, Perion, Perrin, Perryn

Perkin (English) little Peter.
Perka, Perkins, Perkyn, Perrin

Pernell (French) a form of Parnell.
Perren, Pernall

Perry (English) a familiar form of Peregrine, Peter.
Parry, Perrie, Perrye

Perth (Scottish) thorn-bush thicket. Geography: a burgh in Scotland; a city in Australia.

Pervis (Latin) passage.
Pervez

Pesach (Hebrew) spared. Religion: another name for Passover.
Pessach

Petar (Greek) a form of Peter.

Pete (English) a short form of Peter.
Peat, Peet, Petey, Peti, Petie, Piet, Pit

Peter (Greek, Latin) small rock. Bible: Simon, renamed Peter, was the leader of the Twelve Apostles. See also Boutros, Ferris, Takis.
Panayiotis, Panos, Peadair, Peder, Pedro, Peers, Peeter, Peirce, Pekelo, Per, Perico, Perion, Perkin, Perry, Petar, Pete, Péter, Peterke, Peternus, Petr, Petras, Petros, Pierce, Piero, Pierre, Pieter, Pietrek, Pietro, Piotr, Piter, Piti, Pjeter, Pyotr

Peteri (Shona) where we are.
Peni

Peterson (English) son of Peter.
Peteris, Petersen

Petr (Bulgarian) a form of Peter.
Peni

Petras (Lithuanian) a form of Peter.
Petra, Petrelis

Petros (Greek) a form of Peter.
Petro

Petru (Romanian) a form of Peter.
Petrukas, Petrus, Petruso

Petter (Norwegian) a form of Peter.

Peverell (French) piper.
Peverall, Peverel, Peveril

Peyo (Spanish) a form of Peter.

Peyton (English) a form of Patton, Payton.
Peyt, Peyten, Peython, Peytonn

Pharaoh (Latin) ruler. History: a title for the ancient kings of Egypt.
Faroh, Pharo, Pharoah, Pharoh

Phelan (Irish) wolf.

Phelipe (Spanish) a form of Philip.

Phelix (Latin) a form of Felix.

Phelps (English) son of Phillip.

Phil (Greek) a short form of Philip, Phillip.
Fil, Phill

Philander (Greek) lover of mankind.

Philbert (English) a form of Filbert.
Philibert, Phillbert

Philemon (Greek) kiss.
Phila, Philamina, Phileman, Philemon, Philmon

Philip (Greek) lover of horses. Bible: one of the Twelve Apostles. See also Felipe, Felippo, Filip, Fillipp, Filya, Fischel, Flip.
Phelps, Phelipe, Phil, Philipp, Philippe, Philippo, Philllp, Philllpos, Philly, Philly, Philp, Phylip, Piers, Plilb, Pilipo, Pippo

Philipp (German) a form of Philip.
Phillipp

Philippe (French) a form of Philip.
Philipe, Phillepe, Phillipe, Phillippe, Phillippee, Phyllipe

Phillip (Greek) a form of Philip.
Phil, Phillipos, Phillipp, Phillips, Philly, Phyllip

Phillipos (Greek) a form of Phillip.

Philly (American) a familiar form of Philip, Phillip.
Phillie

Philo (Greek) love.

Phinean (Irish) a form of Finian.
Phinian

Phineas (English) a form of Pinchas.
Fineas, Phinehas, Phinny

Phirun (Cambodian) rain.

Phoenix (Latin) phoenix, a legendary bird.
Phenix, Pheonix, Phynix

Phuoc (Vietnamese) good.
Phuoc

Pias (Gypsy) fun.

Pickford (English) ford at the peak.

Pickworth (English) wood cutter's estate.

Pierce (English) a form of Peter.
Pearce, Pearce, Peers, Peirce, Piercy, Piers

Piero (Italian) a form of Peter.
Pero, Pierro

Pierre (French) a form of Peter.
Peirre, Piere, Pierrot

Pierre-Luc (French) a combination of Pierre + Luc.
Piere Luc

Piers (English) a form of Philip.

Pierson (English) son of Peter. See also Pearson.
Pierson, Piersen, Piersson, Piersun

Pieter (Dutch) a form of Peter.
Pietr

Pietro (Italian) a form of Peter.

Pilar (Spanish) pillar.

Pili (Swahili) second born.

Pilipo (Hawaiian) a form of Philip.

Pillan (Native American) supreme essence.
Pilan

Pin (Vietnamese) faithful boy.

Pinchas (Hebrew) oracle. (Egyptian) dark skinned.
Phineas, Pincas, Pinchos, Pincus, Pinkas, Pinkus, Pinky

Pinky (American) a familiar form of Pinchas.
Pink

Pino (Italian) a form of Joseph.

Piñon (Tupi-Guarani) Mythology: the hunter who became the constellation Orion.

Pio (Latin) pious.

Piotr (Bulgarian) a form of Peter.
Piotrek

Pippin (German) father.

Piran (Irish) prayer. Religion: the patron saint of miners.
Peran, Pieran

Pirro (Greek, Spanish) flaming hair.

Pista (Hungarian) a familiar form of István.
Pisti

Piti (Spanish) a form of Peter.

Pitin (Spanish) a form of Felix.
Pito

Pitney (English) island of the strong-willed man.
Pittney

Pitt (English) pit, ditch.

Placido (Spanish) serene.
Placide, Placidus, Placyd, Placydo

Plato (Greek) broad shouldered.
History: a famous Greek philosopher.
Platon

Platt (French) flatland.
Platte

Pol (Swedish) a form of Paul.
Pól, Pola, Poul

Poldi (German) a familiar form of
Leopold.
Poldo

Pollard (German) close-cropped head.
Poll, Pollerd, Pollyrd

Pollock (English) a form of Pollux.
Art: American artist Jackson Pollock
was a leader of abstract expression-
ism.
Pollack, Polloch

Pollux (Greek) crown. Astronomy: one
of the stars in the constellation
Gemini.
Pollock

Polo (Tibetan) brave wanderer.
(Greek) a short form of Apollo.
Culture: a game played on
horseback. History: Marco Polo was
a thirteenth-century Venetian
explorer who traveled throughout
Asia.

Pomeroy (French) apple orchard.
Pommeray, Pommeroy

Ponce (Spanish) fifth. History: Juan
Ponce de León of Spain searched for
the Fountain of Youth in Florida.

Pony (Scottish) small horse.
Poni

Porfirio (Greek, Spanish) purple stone.
Porphirios, Porphyrios

Porter (Latin) gatekeeper.
Port, Portie, Porty

Poshita (Sanskrit) cherished.

Po Sin (Chinese) grandfather elephant.

Poul (Danish) a form of Paul.
Poulos, Poulus

Pov (Gypsy) earth.

Powa (Native American) wealthy.

Powell (English) alert.
Powel

Pramad (Hindi) rejoicing.

Pravat (Tai) history.

Prem (Hindi) love.

Prentice (English) apprentice.
Prent, Prentis, Prentiss, Printes, Printiss

Prescott (English) priest's cottage. See
also Scott.
Prescot, Prestcot, Prestcott

Presley (English) priest's meadow.
Music: Elvis Presley was an influen-
tial American rock 'n' roll singer.
*Presleigh, Presly, Presslee, Pressley,
Prestley, Priestley, Priestly*

Preston (English) priest's estate.
Prestan, Presten, Prestin, Prestyn

Prewitt (French) brave little one.
*Prewet, Prewett, Prewett, Prewitt, Pruit,
Pruitt*

Price (Welsh) son of the ardent one.
Brice, Bryce, Pryce

Pricha (Tai) clever.

Primo (Italian) first; premier quality.
Preemo, Premo

Prince (Latin) chief; prince.
Prence, Prinz, Prinze

Princeton (English) princely town.
Prenston, Princeston, Princton

Proctor (Latin) official, administrator.
Prockter, Procter

Prokopios (Greek) declared leader.

Prosper (Latin) fortunate.
Prospero, Próspero

Pryor (Latin) head of the monastery;
prior.
Prior, Pry

Pumeet (Sanskrit) pure.

Purdy (Hindi) recluse.

Purvis (French, English) providing
food.
Pervis, Purves, Purviss

Putnam (English) dweller by the
pond.
Putnem

Pyotr (Russian) a form of Peter.
Petenka, Petinka, Petrusha, Petya, Pyatr

Qabil (Arabic) able.

Qadim (Arabic) ancient.

Qadir (Arabic) powerful.
Qaadir, Qadeer, Quaadir, Quadeer, Qudir

Qamar (Arabic) moon.
Quamar, Quamir

Qasim (Arabic) divider.
Quasim

Qimat (Hindi) valuable.

Quaashie (Ewe) born on Sunday.

Quadarius (American) a combination of Quan + Darius.
Quadara, Quadarious, Quadaris, Quadarious, Quandarius, Quandarrius, Qudaris

Quade (Latin) fourth.
Quadell, Quaden, Quadon, Quadre, Quadrie, Quadrine, Quadrion, Quaid, Quayd, Quayde, Qwade

Quamaine (American) a combination of Quan + Jermaine.
Quamain, Quaman, Quamane, Quamayne, Quarmaine

Quan (Comanche) a short form of Quanah.

Quanah (Comanche) fragrant.
Quan

Quandre (American) a combination of Quan + Andre.
Quandrae, Quandré

Quant (Greek) how much?
Quanta, Quantae, Quantai, Quantas, Quantay, Quante, Quantea, Quantey, Quantez, Quantu

Quantavius (American) a combination of Quan + Octavius.
Quantavian, Quantavin, Quantavion, Quantavious, Quantavis, Quantavous, Quatavius

Quashawn (American) a combination of Quan + Shawn.
Quasean, Quashaan, Quashan, Quashawn, Quashaunn, Quashon, Quashone, Quashun, Queshan, Queshon, Queshawn, Qyshawn

Qudamah (Arabic) courage.

Quenby (Scandinavian) a form of Quimby.

Quennell (French) small oak.
Quenell, Quennel

Quenten (Latin) a form of Quentin.
Quienten

Quentin (Latin) fifth. (English) queen's town.
Qentin, Quantin, Quent, Quentan, Quenten, Quentine, Quenton, Quentyn, Quentynn, Quienten, Quienten, Quinten, Quintin, Quinton, Quentin

Quenton (Latin) a form of Quentin.
Quienton

Quico (Spanish) a familiar form of many names.
Paco

Quigley (Irish) maternal side.
Quigly

Quillan (Irish) cub.
Quill, Quillen, Quillin, Quillon

Quimby (Scandinavian) woman's estate.
Quenby, Quimby

Quincy (French) fifth son's estate.
Quenci, Quency, Quince, Quincee, Quincey, Quinci, Quinn, Quinncy, Quinnsy, Quinsey, Quinzy

Quindarius (American) a combination of Quinn + Darius.
Quindarios, Quindarrius, Quinderious, Quinderus, Quindrius

Quinlan (Irish) strong; well shaped.
Quindlen, Quinlen, Quinilin, Quinn, Quinlan, Quinnlin

Quinn (Irish) a short form of Quincy, Quinlan, Quinton.
Quin

Quintavius (American) a combination of Quinn + Octavius.
Quintavious, Quintavis, Quintavus, Quintayvious

Quinten (Latin) a form of Quentin.
Quinten

Quintin (Latin) a form of Quentin.
Quintin, Quintine, Quintyn

Quinton (Latin) a form of Quentin. *Quinn, Quinneton, Quinton, Quintan, Quintann, Quintin, Quinton, Quintus, Quitin, Quito, Quiton, Quinton, Quinton.*

Quiqui (Spanish) a familiar form of Enrique.

Quitin (Latin) a short form of Quinton. *Quiten, Quito, Quiton*

Quito (Spanish) a short form of Quinton.

Quon (Chinese) bright.

Raanan (Hebrew) fresh; luxuriant.

Rabi (Arabic) breeze. *Rabbi, Rabee, Rabeeh, Rabie, Rabih*

Race (English) race. *Racel, Raye*

Racham (Hebrew) compassionate. *Rachaman, Rachamim, Rachim, Rachman, Rachmiel, Rachum, Raham, Rahamim*

Rad (English) advisor. (Slavic) happy. *Raad, Radd, Raddie, Raddy Rade, Radee, Radell, Radey, Radi*

Radbert (English) brilliant advisor.

Radburn (English) red brook; brook with reeds. *Radborn, Radborne, Radbourn, Radbourne, Radburne*

Radcliff (English) red cliff; cliff with reeds. *Radcliffe, Radclyffe*

Radford (English) red ford; ford with reeds.

Radley (English) red meadow; meadow of reeds. *Radlea, Radlee, Radleigh, Radly*

Radman (Slavic) joyful. *Radmen, Radnsha*

Radnor (English) red shore; shore with reeds.

Radomil (Slavic) happy peace.

Radoslaw (Polish) happy glory. *Radie, Rado, Radzmir, Slawek*

Raekwon (American) a form of Raquan. *Raekwan, Raikwan, Rakwane, Rakwon*

Raequan (American) a form of Raquan. *Raequon, Raiquan, Raiquen, Raiqon*

Raeshawn (American) a form of Rashawn. *Raesean, Raeshawn, Raeshon, Raeshun*

Rafael (Spanish) a form of Raphael. See also Falito. *Raffaelle, Rafaello, Rafal, Rafeal, Rafeé, Rafel, Rafello, Raffael, Raffeal, Raffel, Raffeal, Raffelo,*

Rafaele (Italian) a form of Raphael. *Raffaele*

Rafal (Polish) a form of Raphael.

Rafe (English) a short form of Rafferty, Ralph. *Raff*

Rafer (Irish) a short form of Rafferty. *Raffer*

Rafferty (Irish) rich, prosperous. *Rafe, Rafer, Rafferty, Raffarty, Raffer Raffe, Raffee, Raffi, Raffy, Rafi*

Rafi (Arabic) exalted. (Hebrew) a familiar form of Raphael. *Raffi, Raffee, Raffi, Raffy, Rafi*

Rafiq (Arabic) friend. *Raafiq, Rafeeq, Rafi, Rafique*

Raghib (Arabic) desirous. *Raquib*

Raghnall (Irish) wise power.

Ragnar (Norwegian) powerful army. *Ragnor, Rainer, Rainier, Rayner, Raynor, Reinhold*

Rago (Hausa) ram.

Raheem (Punjabi) compassionate God. *Raheem*

Rahim (Arabic) merciful. *Raaheim, Rahaeim, Raheam, Raheim, Rahiem, Rahim, Rahime, Rahium, Rakim*

Rahman (Arabic) compassionate. *Rahmat, Rahmet*

Rahul (Arabic) traveler.

Raid (Arabic) leader.

Raiden (Japanese) Mythology: the thunder god. *Raidan, Rayden*

Raimondo (Italian) a form of Raymond.
Raymondo, Reimundo

Raimund (German) a form of Raymond.
Rajmund

Raimundo (Portuguese, Spanish) a form of Raymond.
Mundo, Raimon, Raimond, Raimonds, Raymundo

Raine (English) lord; wise.
Rain, Raines, Rayne

Rainer (German) counselor.
Rainar, Rainey, Rainier, Rainor, Raynier, Reinier

Rainey (German) a familiar form of Rainer.
Raine, Rainee, Rainie, Rainney, Rainy, Reiny

Raini (Tupi-Guarani) Religion: the god who created the world.

Raishawn (American) a form of Rashawn.
Raishon, Raishun

Rajabu (Swahili) born in the seventh month of the Islamic calendar.

Rajah (Hindi) prince; chief.
Raj, Raja, Rajaah, Rajae, Rajahe, Rajan, Raje, Rajeh, Raji

Rajak (Hindi) cleansing.

Rajan (Hindi) a form of Rajah.
Rajaahn, Rajain, Rajen, Rajin

Rakeem (Punjabi) a form of Raheem.
Rakeeme, Rakeim, Rakem

Rakim (Arabic) a form of Rahim.
Rakiim

Rakin (Arabic) respectable.
Rakeen

Raktim (Hindi) bright red.

Raleigh (English) a form of Rawleigh.
Ralegh

Ralph (English) wolf counselor.
Radolphus, Rafe, Ralf, Ralpheal, Ralphel, Ralphie, Ralston, Raoul, Raul, Rolf

Ralphie (English) a familiar form of Ralph.
Ralph, Ralphy

Ralston (English) Ralph's settlement.

Ram (Hindi) god; godlike. Religion: another name for the Hindu god Rama. (English) male sheep. A short form of Ramsey.
Rami, Ramie, Ramy

Ramadan (Arabic) ninth month of the Arabic year in the Islamic calendar.
Rama

Ramanan (Hindi) god; godlike.
Raman, Ramandeep, Ramanjit, Ramanjot

Rami (Hindi, English) a form of Ram. (Spanish) a short form of Ramiro.
Rane, Ramee, Raney, Ramih

Ramiro (Portuguese, Spanish) supreme judge.
Ramario, Rameer, Rameir, Ramere, Rameriz, Ramero, Rami, Ramires, Ramirez, Ramos

Ramón (Spanish) a form of Raymond.
Ramon, Remon, Remone, Romone

Ramone (Dutch) a form of Raymond.
Raemon, Raemonn, Ramond, Ramone, Remone

Ramsden (English) valley of rams.

Ramsey (English) ram's island.
Ram, Ramsay, Ramsee, Ramsie, Ramsy, Ramzee, Ramzey, Ramzi, Ramzy

Rance (English) a short form of Laurence. (American) a familiar form of Laurence.
Rancel, Rancell, Rances, Rancey, Rancie, Rancy, Ransel, Ransell

Rand (English) shield; warrior.
Randy

Randal (English) a form of Randall.
Randahl, Randale, Randel, Randl, Randle

Randall (English) a form of Randolph.
Randal, Randell, Randy, Randyll

Randolph (English) shield wolf.
Randall, Randol, Randolf, Randolfo, Randolpho, Randy, Ranolph

Randy (English) a familiar form of Rand, Randall, Randolph.
Randdy, Randee, Randey, Randi, Randie, Ranndy

Ranger (French) forest keeper.
Rainger, Range

Rangle (American) cowboy.
Rangler, Wrangle

Rangsey (Cambodian) seven kinds of colors.

Rani (Hebrew) my song; my joy. *Ranen, Ranie, Ranon, Roni*

Ranieri (Italian) a form of Ragnar. *Ranier, Ranier, Rannier*

Ranjan (Hindi) delighted; gladdened.

Rankin (English) small shield. *Randkin*

Ransford (English) raven's ford.

Ransley (English) raven's field.

Ransom (Latin) redeemer. (English) son of the shield. *Rance, Ransome, Ranson*

Raoul (French) a form of Ralph, Rudolph. *Raol, Raul, Raül, Reuel*

Raphael (Hebrew) God has healed. Bible: one of the archangels. Art: a prominent painter of the Renaissance. See also Falito, Rafi. *Rafael, Rafaele, Rafal, Rafel, Raphaël, Raphale, Raphaello, Rapheal, Raphel, Raphello, Raphiel, Ray, Rephael*

Rapheal (Hebrew) a form of Raphael. *Rafel, Raphiel*

Raquan (American) a combination of the prefix Ra + Quan. *Raaquan, Rackwon, Racquan, Raekwon, Raequan, Rahquan, Raquané, Raquon, Raquwan, Raquwn, Raqwuon, Raqwan, Raqwan*

Rapier (French) blade-sharp.

Rashaad (Arabic) a form of Rashad.

Rashaan (American) a form of Rashawn. *Rasan, Rashan, Rashann*

Rashad (Arabic) wise counselor. *Raashad, Rachad, Rachard, Raeshad, Raishard, Rashaad, Rashadd, Rashade, Rashaud, Rasheed, Rashid, Rashod, Reshad, Rhashad, Rishad, Roshad*

Rashard (American) a form of Richard. *Rashard*

Rashaud (Arabic) a form of Rashad. *Rachaud, Rashaude*

Rashaun (American) a form of Rashawn.

Rashawn (American) a combination of the prefix Ra + Shawn. *Raashawn, Raashen, Raeshawn, Rahshawn, Raishawn, Rasawn, Rashaan, Rashaun, Rashaun, Rashun, Rashwan, Rashawn, Rashion, Rhashaun, Rhashawn, Rhashan, Rhashawn, Rhashawn*

Rashean (American) a combination of the prefix Ra + Sean. *Rahsean, Rahseen, Rasean, Rashane, Rasheen, Rashien, Rashiena*

Rasheed (Arabic) a form of Rashad. *Rashead, Rashed, Rasheid, Rhasheed*

Rashid (Arabic) a form of Rashad. *Rasheyd, Rashida, Rashidah, Rashied, Rashieda, Rashaid*

Rashida (Swahili) righteous.

Rashidi (Swahili) wise counselor.

Rashod (Arabic) a form of Rashad. *Rashoda, Rashodd, Rashoud, Rayshod, Rhashod*

Rashon (American) a form of Rashawn. *Rashion, Rashone, Rashorn, Rashuan, Rashun, Rashunn*

Rasmus (Greek, Danish) a short form of Erasmus.

Raul (French) a form of Ralph.

Raulas (Lithuanian) a form of Laurence.

Raulo (Lithuanian) a form of Laurence. *Raulas*

Raven (English) a short form of Ravenel. *Ravin, Ravean, Raven, Ravin, Ravine, Ravon, Ravyn, Reven, Rhaven*

Ravenel (English) raven. *Raven, Ravenell, Revenel*

Ravi (Hindi) sun. *Ravee, Ravijot*

Ravid (Hebrew) a form of Arvid.

Raviv (Hebrew) rain, dew.

Ravon (English) a form of Raven. *Ravon, Ravion, Ravone, Ravonn, Ravone, Rayvon, Revon*

Rawdon (English) rough hill.

Rawleigh (English) deer meadow. *Raleigh, Rawle, Rawley, Rawling, Rawly, Rawlyn*

Rawlins (French) a form of Roland.
Rawlings, Rawlinson, Rawson

Ray (French) kingly, royal. (English) a short form of Rayburn, Raymond. See also Lei.
Rae, Raye

Rayan (Irish) a form of Ryan.
Rayaun

Rayburn (English) deer brook.
Burney, Raeborn, Raeborne, Raebourn, Ray, Raybourn, Raybourne, Rayburne

Rayce (English) a form of Race.

Rayden (Japanese) a form of Raiden.
Raidin, Raydun, Rayedon

Rayhan (Arabic) favored by God.
Rayhaan

Rayi (Hebrew) my friend, my companion.

Raymon (English) a form of Raymond.
Rayman, Raymann, Raymen, Raymone, Raymun, Reamonn

Raymond (English) mighty; wise protector. See also Aymon.
Radmond, Raemond, Raimond, Raimund, Raimundo, Ramón, Ramond, Ramone, Ramone, Ray Raymand, Raymert, Raymon, Raymont, Raymund, Raymunde, Raymundo, Redmond, Reymond, Reymundo

Raymundo (Spanish) a form of Raymond.
Raemondo, Raimundo, Raimundo, Raymondo

Raynaldo (Spanish) a form of Reynold.
Raynal, Raynald, Raynold

Raynard (French) a form of Renard, Reynard.
Raynarde

Rayne (English) a form of Raine.
Raynee, Rayno

Raynor (Scandinavian) a form of Ragnar.
Rainer, Rainor, Ranier, Ranieri, Raynar, Rayner

Rayshawn (American) a combination of Ray + Shawn.
Raysean, Rayshaan, Rayshan, Rayshawn, Raysheen, Rayshon, Rayshone, Rayshonn, Rayshun, Rayshunn

Rayshod (American) a form of Rashad.
Raychard, Rayshad, Rayshard, Rayshaud

Rayvon (American) a form of Ravon.
Rayvan, Rayvaun, Rayven, Rayvone, Reyven, Reyvon

Razi (Aramaic) my secret.
Raz, Raziel, Raziq

Read (English) a form of Reed, Reid.
Raed, Raede, Raeed, Reaad, Reade

Reading (English) son of the red wanderer.
Redding, Reeding, Reiding

Reagan (Irish) little king. History: Ronald Wilson Reagan was the fortieth U.S. president.
Raegan, Reagen, Reaghan, Reegan,

Reegen, Regan, Reigan, Reighan, Reign, Rheagan

Rebel (American) rebel.
Reb

Red (American) red, redhead.
Redd

Reda (Arabic) satisfied.
Ridha

Redford (English) red river crossing.
Ford, Radford, Reaford, Red, Redd

Redley (English) red meadow; meadow with reeds.
Radley, Redlea, Redleigh, Redly

Redmond (German) protecting counselor. (English) a form of Raymond.
Radmund, Radmund, Reddin, Redmund

Redpath (English) red path.

Reece (Welsh) enthusiastic; stream.
Reace, Rece, Reese, Reice, Reyes, Rhys, Rice, Ryese

Reed (English) a form of Reid.
Raeed, Read, Reyde, Rheed

Reese (Welsh) a form of Reece.
Rease, Rees, Reis, Reise, Reiss, Rhys, Riese, Riess

Reeve (English) steward.
Reave, Reaves, Reeves

Reg (English) a short form of Reginald.

Regan (Irish) a form of Reagan.
Regen

Reggie (English) a familiar form of Reginald. *Regi, Regie*

Reginal (English) a form of Reginald. *Reginale, Reginel*

Reginald (English) king's advisor. A form of Reynold. See also Naldo. *Reg, Reggie, Regginald, Reggis, Reginal, Reginaldo, Reginalt, Reginauld, Reginault, Reginold, Reginuld, Regnauld, Ronald*

Regis (Latin) regal.

Rehema (Swahili) second-born.

Rei (Japanese) rule, law.

Reid (English) redhead. *Read, Reed, Reide, Reyd, Ried*

Reidar (Norwegian) nest warrior.

Reilly (Irish) a form of Riley. *Reiley, Reilley, Reily, Rielly*

Reinaldo (Spanish) a form of Reynold.

Reinhold (Swedish) a form of Ragnar. *Reinold*

Reinhart (German) a form of Reynard. *Rainart, Rainhard, Rainhardt, Rainhart, Reinhart, Reinhardt, Renke*

Reku (Finnish) a form of Richard.

Remi, Rémi (French) forms of Remy. *Remie, Remmie*

Remington (English) raven estate. *Rem, Reminton, Tony*

Remus (Latin) speedy, quick. Mythology: Remus and his twin brother, Romulus, founded Rome.

Remy (French) from Rheims, France. *Ramey, Remee, Remi, Rémi, Remmy*

Renaldo (Spanish) a form of Reynold. *Raynaldo, Reynaldo, Rinaldo*

Renard (French) a form of Reynard. *Ranard, Raynard, Reinard, Rennard*

Renardo (Italian) a form of Reynard.

Renato (Italian) reborn.

Renaud (French) a form of Reynard, Reynold. *Renald, Renauld, Renault, Renold*

René (French) reborn. *Renat, Renato, Renatus, Renault, Renay, Renee, Renny*

Rendor (Hungarian) policeman.

Renfred (English) lasting peace.

Renfrew (Welsh) raven woods.

Renjiro (Japanese) virtuous.

Renny (Irish) small but strong. (French) a familiar form of René. *Ren, Renn, Renne, Rennie*

Reno (American) gambler. Geography: a city in Nevada known for gambling. *Renos, Rino*

Renshaw (English) raven woods. *Renishaw*

Renton (English) settlement of the roe deer.

Renzo (Latin) a familiar form of Laurence. (Italian) a short form of Lorenzo. *Renz, Renzy, Renzzo*

Reshad (American) a form of Rashad. *Reshade, Reshard, Reshaud, Reshod*

Reshawn (American) a combination of the prefix Re + Shawn. *Reshaun, Reshaw, Reshon, Reshun*

Reshean (American) a combination of the prefix Re + Sean. *Resean, Reshae, Reshane, Reshay, Reshayne, Reshea, Resheen, Reshey*

Reuben (Hebrew) behold a son. *Reuban, Reubin, Reuven, Rheuben, Rhuben, Rube, Ruben, Rubey, Rubin, Ruby, Rueben*

Reuven (Hebrew) a form of Reuben. *Reuvin, Rouvin, Ruvim*

Rex (Latin) king. *Rexx*

Rexford (English) king's ford.

Rexton (English) king's town.

Rey (Spanish) a short form of Reynaldo, Reynard, Reynold.

Reyes (English) a form of Reece. *Reye*

Reyhan (Arabic) favored by God. *Reyham*

Reymond (English) a form of Raymond. *Reymon, Reymound, Reymund*

Reymundo (Spanish) a form of Raymond.
Reimond, Reimonde, Reimundo, Reymon

Reynaldo (Spanish) a form of Reynold.
Renaldo, Rey, Reynauldo

Reynard (French) wise; bold; courageous.
Raynard, Reinhard, Reinhardt, Reinhart, Renard, Renard, Renaud, Rennard, Rey, Reynards, Reynaud

Reynold (English) king's advisor. See also Reginald.
Rainault, Rainhold, Ranald, Raynald, Raynaldo, Reinald, Reinaldo, Reinaldos, Reinhart, Reinhold, Reinold, Reinwald, Renald, Renaldi, Renaldo, Renaud, Renauld, Rennold, Renold, Rey, Reynald, Reynaldo, Reynaldos, Reynol, Reynolds, Rinaldo, Ronald

Réz (Hungarian) copper; redhead.
Rezso

Rhett (Welsh) a form of Rhys.
Literature: Rhett Butler was the hero of Margaret Mitchell's novel *Gone with the Wind.*
Rhet

Rhodes (Greek) where roses grow. Geography: an island of southeast Greece.
Rhoads, Rhodas, Rodas

Rhyan (Irish) a form of Rian.
Rhian

Rhys (Welsh) a form of Reece, Reese.
Rhett, Rhyce, Rhyse, Rice

Rian (Irish) little king.
Rhyan

Ric (Italian, Spanish) a short form of Rico.
Ricca, Ricci, Ricco

Ricardo (Portuguese, Spanish) a form of Richard.
Racardo, Recard, Ricaldo, Ricard, Ricardoe, Ricardos, Riccardo, Riccarrdo, Ricciardo, Richardo

Rice (English) rich, noble. (Welsh) a form of Reece.
Ryce

Rich (English) a short form of Richard.
Ritch

Richard (English) a form of Richart. See also Aric, Dick, Juku, Likeke.
Rashard, Reku, Ricardo, Rich, Richar, Richards, Richardson, Richart, Richaud, Richer, Richerd, Richie, Richird, Richshard, Rick, Rickard, Rickert, Rickey, Ricky, Rico, Rihards, Rihards, Rikard, Riocard, Riócard, Risa, Risardas, Rishard, Ristéard, Ritchard, Rostik, Rye, Rysio, Ryszard

Richart (German) rich and powerful ruler.

Richie (English) a familiar form of Richard.
Richey, Richi, Richy, Rishi, Ritchie

Richman (English) powerful.

Richmond (German) powerful protector.
Richmon, Richmound

Rick (German, English) a short form of Cedric, Frederick, Richard.
Ric, Ricke, Rickey, Ricks, Ricky, Rik, Riki, Rykk

Rickard (Swedish) a form of Richard.

Ricker (English) powerful army.

Rickey (English) a familiar form of Richard, Rick, Riqui.

Rickie (English) a form of Ricky.
Rickee, Ricki

Rickward (English) mighty guardian.
Rickwerd, Rickwood

Ricky (English) a familiar form of Richard, Rick.
Ricci, Rickie, Riczi, Riki, Rikki, Rikky, Riqui

Rico (Spanish) a familiar form of Richard. (Italian) a short form of Enrico.
Ríc, Ricco

Rida (Arabic) favor.

Riddock (Irish) smooth field.
Riddick

Rider (English) horseman.
Ridder, Ryder

Ridge (English) ridge of a cliff.
Ridgy, Rig, Rigg

Ridgeley (English) meadow near the ridge.
Ridgeleigh, Ridglea, Ridglee, Ridgleigh, Ridgley

Ridgeway (English) path along the ridge.

Ridley (English) meadow of reeds. *Rhidley, Riddley, Ridlea, Ridleigh, Ridly*

Riel (Spanish) a short form of Gabriel.

Rigby (English) ruler's valley.

Rigel (Arabic) foot. Astronomy: one of the stars in the constellation Orion.

Rigg (English) ridge.

Rigoberto (German) splendid; wealthy. *Rigobert*

Rikard (Scandinavian) a form of Richard. *Rikárd*

Riki (Estonian) a form of Rick. *Rikkey, Rikki, Riks, Riky*

Riley (Irish) valiant. *Reilly, Rhiley, Rhyley, Rhyley, Rieley, Rielly, Riely, Rilee, Rilley, Rily, Rilye, Rylee, Ryley*

Rinaldo (Italian) a form of Reynold. *Rinald, Rinaldi*

Ring (English) ring. *Ringo*

Ringo (Japanese) apple. (English) a familiar form of Ring.

Rio (Spanish) river. Geography: Rio de Janeiro is a city in Brazil.

Riordan (Irish) bard, royal poet. *Rearden, Reardin, Reardon*

Rip (Dutch) ripe; full grown. (English) a short form of Ripley. *Ripp*

Ripley (English) meadow near the river. *Rip, Ripleigh, Ripply*

Riqui (Spanish) a form of Rickey.

Rishad (American) a form of Rashad. *Rishaad*

Rishawn (American) a combination of the prefix Ri + Shawn. *Rishan, Rishaun, Rishon, Rishone*

Rishi (Hindi) sage.

Risley (English) meadow with shrubs. *Rislea, Rislee, Risleigh, Risly, Wrisley*

Riston (English) settlement near the shrubs.

Risto (Finnish) a short form of Christopher.

Ritchard (English) a form of Richard. *Ritcherd, Ritchyrd, Ritsherd, Ritsherd*

Ritchie (English) a form of Richie. *Ritchy*

Rithisak (Cambodian) powerful.

Ritter (German) knight; chivalrous. *Rittner*

River (English) river; riverbank. *Rivers, Riviera, Rivor*

Riyad (Arabic) gardens. *Riad, Riyaad, Riyadh, Riyaz, Riyod*

Roald (Norwegian) famous ruler.

Roan (English) a short form of Rowan. *Rhoan*

Roar (Norwegian) praised warrior. *Roary*

Roarke (Irish) famous ruler. *Roark, Rorke, Rourke, Ruark*

Rob (English) a short form of Robert. *Robb, Robe*

Robbie (English) a familiar form of Robert. *Rhobbie, Robbey, Robby, Roby*

Robby (English) a familiar form of Robert.

Robert (English) famous brilliance. See also Bobek, Dob, Lopaka. *Bob, Bobby, Rab, Rabbie, Raby, Riobard, Riobart, Rob, Robars, Robart, Robbie, Robby, Rober, Roberd, Robers, Roberte, Roberto, Roberts, Robin, Robinson, Roibeard, Rosertas, Rubert, Ruberto, Rudbert, Rupert*

Roberto (Italian, Portuguese, Spanish) a form of Robert.

Roberts, Robertson (English) son of Robert. *Roberson, Robertson, Robeson, Robinson, Robson*

Robin (English) a short form of Robert. *Robben, Robbin, Robbins, Robbyn, Roben, Robinet, Robinn, Robins, Robyn, Robyn*

Robinson (English) a form of Roberts. *Robbinson, Robers, Roberson, Robson, Robynson*

Robyn (English) a form of Robin.

Rocco (Italian) rock.
Rocca, Rocio, Rocko, Rocky, Roko, Roque

Rochester (English) rocky fortress.
Chester, Chet

Rock (English) a short form of Rockwell.
Roch, Rocky

Rockford (English) rocky ford.

Rockland (English) rocky land.

Rockledge (English) rocky ledge.

Rockley (English) rocky field.
Rockle

Rockwell (English) rocky spring. Art: Norman Rockwell was a well-known twentieth-century American illustrator.
Rock

Rocky (American) a familiar form of Rocco, Rock.
Rockey, Rockie

Rod (English) a short form of Penrod, Roderick, Rodney.
Rodd

Rodas (Greek, Spanish) a form of Rhodes.

Roddy (English) a familiar form of Roderick.
Roddie, Rody

Roden (English) red valley. Art: Auguste Rodin was an innovative French sculptor.
Rodin

Roderich (German) a form of Roderick.

Roderick (German) famous ruler. See also Broderick.
Rhoderick, Rod, Rodderick, Roddy, Roderic, Roderik, Roderigo, Roderik, Roderrick, Roderyck, Rodgrick, Rodrick, Rodricki, Rodrigo, Rodrigue, Rodrugue, Roodney, Rory, Rurik, Ruy

Rodger (German) a form of Roger.
Rodge, Rodgy

Rodman (German) famous man, hero.
Rodmond

Rodney (English) island clearing.
Rhodney, Rod, Rodnee, Rodnei, Rodni, Rodnie, Rodnne, Rodny

Rodolfo (Spanish) a form of Rudolph.
Rodolpho, Rodulfo

Rodrick (German) a form of Roderick.
Roddrick, Rodric, Rodrich, Rodrik, Rodrique, Rodryck, Rodryk

Rodrigo (Italian, Spanish) a form of Roderick.

Rodriguez (Spanish) son of Rodrigo.
Roddrigues, Rodrigues, Rodriquez

Rodrik (German) famous ruler.

Rodriquez (Spanish) a form of Rodriguez.
Rodriqquez, Rodriques, Rodriquiez

Roe (English) roe deer.
Row, Rowe

Rogan (Irish) redhead.
Rogein, Rogen

Rogelio (Spanish) famous warrior.
Rojelio

Roger (German) famous spearman. See also Lokela.
Rodger, Rog, Rogelio, Rogerick, Rogerio, Rogers, Rogiero, Rojelio, Rüdiger, Ruggerio, Rutger

Rogerio (Portuguese, Spanish) a form of Roger.
Rogerios

Rohan (Hindi) sandalwood.

Rohin (Hindi) upward path.

Rohit (Hindi) big and beautiful fish.

Roi (French) a form of Roy.

Roja (Spanish) red.
Rojay

Roland (German) famous throughout the land.
Lorand, Orlando, Rawlins, Rolan, Rolanda, Rolando, Rolek, Rolland, Rolle, Rollie, Rollin, Rollo, Rowe, Rowland, Ruland

Rolando (Portuguese, Spanish) a form of Roland.
Lando, Olo, Roldan, Roldán, Rolondo

Rolf (German) a form of Ralph. A short form of Rudolph.
Rolfe, Rolle, Rolph, Rolphe

Rolle (Swedish) a familiar form of Roland, Rolf.

Rollie (English) a familiar form of Roland.
Roley, Rolle, Rolli, Rolly

Rollin (English) a form of Roland.
Rolin, Rollins

Rollo (English) a familiar form of Roland.
Rolla, Rolo

Rolon (Spanish) famous wolf.

Romain (French) a form of Roman.
Romaine, Romane, Romanne

Roman (Latin) from Rome, Italy.
Roma, Romain, Romann, Romanos, Romman, Romochka, Romy

Romanos (Greek) a form of Roman.
Romano

Romario (Italian) a form of Romeo.
Romar, Romarius, Romaro, Romarrio

Romel (Latin) a short form of Romulus.
Romele, Romell, Romella, Rommel

Romello (Italian) of Romel.
Romelo, Rommello

Romeo (Italian) pilgrim to Rome; Roman. Literature: the title character of the Shakespearean play *Romeo and Juliet.*
Romario, Roméo, Romero

Romero (Latin) a form of Romeo.
Romario, Rometro, Romer, Romere, Romerio, Romeris, Romeryo

Romney (Welsh) winding river.
Romoney

Romulus (Latin) citizen of Rome. Mythology: Romulus and his twin brother, Remus, founded Rome.
Romel, Romolo, Romono, Romulo

Romy (Italian) a familiar form of Roman.
Rommie, Rommy

Rooney (Irish) redhead.

Roosevelt (Dutch) rose field. History: Theodore and Franklin D. Roosevelt were the twenty-sixth and thirty-second U.S. presidents, respectively.
Roosvelt, Rosevelt

Roper (English) rope maker.

Rory (German) a familiar form of Roderick. (Irish) red king.
Rorey, Rori, Rorie, Rorry

Rosario (Portuguese) rosary.

Roscoe (Scandinavian) deer forest.
Rosco

Roshad (American) a form of Rashad.
Roshard

Roshean (American) a combination of the prefix Ro + Sean.
Roshain, Roshan, Roshane, Roshaun, Roshawn, Roshay, Rosheen, Roshene

Rosito (Filipino) rose.

Ross (Latin) rose. (Scottish) peninsula. (French) red.
Rosse, Rossell, Rossi, Rossie, Rossy

Rosswell (English) springtime of roses.
Rosvel

Rostislav (Czech) growing glory.
Rosta, Rostya

Romain (French) a form of Roman.

Rolland — *[column 2]*

Rolland (English) a familiar form of Roland.

Romanos (Greek) a form of Roman.

Ron (Hebrew) a short form of Aaron, Ronald.

Ronald (Scottish) a form of Reginald.
Ranald, Ron, Ronal, Ronaldo, Ronnald, Ronney, Ronnie, Ronnold, Ronoldo

Ronaldo (Portuguese) a form of Ronald.

Rónán (Irish) seal.
Renan, Ronan, Ronat

Rondel (French) short poem.
Rondal, Rondale, Rondall, Rondeal, Rondell, Rondey, Rondie, Rondrell, Rondy, Ronel

Ronel (American) a form of Rondel.
Ronell, Ronelle, Ronnel, Ronnell, Ronyell

Roni (Hebrew) my song; my joy.
Rani, Roneet, Roney, Ronli, Roni, Rony

Ronnie (Scottish) a familiar form of Ronald.
Roni, Ronie, Ronnie, Ronny

Ronny (Scottish) a form of Ronnie.
Ronney

Ronson (Scottish) son of Ronald.
Ronaldson

Ronté (American) a combination of Ron + the suffix Te.
Rontae, Rontay, Ronte, Rontez

Rosalio (Spanish) rose.
Rosalino

Rosalio (Spanish) rose.

Roswald (English) field of roses.
Ross, Roswell

Roth (German) redhead.

Rothwell (Scandinavian) red spring.

Rover (English) traveler.

Rowan (English) tree with red berries.
Roan, Rowe, Rowen, Rowney, Rowyn

Rowell (English) roe-deer well.

Rowland (English) rough land. (German) a form of Roland.
Rowlando, Rowlands, Rowlandson

Rowley (English) rough meadow.
Rowlea, Rowlee, Rowleigh, Rowly

Rowson (English) son of the redhead.

Roxbury (English) rook's town or fortress.
Roxburghe

Roy (French) king. A short form of Royal, Royce. See also Conroy, Delroy, Fitzroy, Leroy, Loe.
Rey, Roi, Roye, Ruy

Royal (French) kingly, royal.
Roy, Royale, Royall, Royell

Royce (English) son of Roy.
Roice, Roy, Royz

Royden (English) rye hill.
Royd, Roydan

Ruben (Hebrew) a form of Reuben.
Ruban, Rube, Rubean, Rubens, Rubin, Ruby

Rubert (Czech) a form of Robert.

Ruby (Hebrew) a familiar form of Reuben, Ruben.

Rudd (English) a short form of Rudyard.

Ruda (Czech) a form of Rudolph.
Rude, Rudek

Rudi (Spanish) a familiar form of Rudolph.
Ruedi

Rudo (Shona) love.

Rudolf (German) a form of Rudolph.
Rodolf, Rodolfo, Rudolfo

Rudolph (German) famous wolf. See also Dolf.
Raoul, Rezsö, Rodolfo, Rodolph, Rodolphe, Rolf, Ruda, Rudek, Rudi, Rudolf, Rudolpho, Rudolphus, Rudy

Rudolpho (Italian) a form of Rudolph.

Rudy (English) a familiar form of Rudolph.
Roody, Ruddy, Ruddie, Rudey, Rudi, Rudie

Rudyard (English) red enclosure.
Rudd

Rueben (Hebrew) a form of Reuben.
Rueban, Ruebin

Ruff (French) redhead.

Rufin (Polish) redhead.
Rufino

Ruford (English) red ford; ford with reeds.
Rufford

Rufus (Latin) redhead.
Rayfus, Rufe, Ruffis, Ruffus, Rufino, Rufo, Rufous

Rugby (English) rook fortress. History: a famous British school after which the sport of Rugby was named.

Ruggerio (Italian) a form of Roger.
Rogero, Ruggero, Ruggiero

Ruhakana (Rukiga) argumentative.

Ruland (German) a form of Roland.
Rulan, Rulon, Rulondo

Rumford (English) wide river crossing.

Runako (Shona) handsome.

Rune (German, Swedish) secret.

Runrot (Tai) prosperous.

Rupert (German) a form of Robert.
Ruperth, Ruperto, Ruprecht

Ruperto (Italian) a form of Rupert.

Ruprecht (German) a form of Rupert.

Rush (French) redhead. (English) a short form of Russell.
Rushi

Rushford (English) ford with rushes.

Rusk (Spanish) twisted bread.

Ruskin (French) redhead.
Rush, Russ

Russ (French) a short form of Russell.

Russel (French) a form of Russell.

Russell (French) redhead; fox colored.
See also Lukela.
*Roussell, Rush, Russ, Russel, Russelle,
Rusty*

Rusty (French) a familiar form of
Russell.
*Ruste, Rusten, Rustie, Rustin, Ruston,
Rustyn*

Rutger (Scandinavian) a form of
Roger.
Rutger

Rutherford (English) cattle ford.
Rutherfurd

Rutland (Scandinavian) red land.

Rutledge (English) red ledge.

Rutley (English) red meadow.

Ruy (Spanish) a short form of
Roderick.
Rui

Ryan (Irish) little king.
*Rayan, Rhyan, Rhyne, Ryane, Ryann,
Ryen, Ryian, Ryiann, Ryin, Ryne,
Ryon, Ryuan, Ryun, Ryyan*

Rycroft (English) rye field.
Ryecroft

Ryder (English) a form of Rider.
Rydder, Rye

Rye (English) a short form of Ryder.
A grain used in cereal and whiskey.
(Gypsy) gentleman.
Ry.

Ryen (Irish) a form of Ryan.
Ryein, Ryien

Ryerson (English) son of Rider,
Ryder.

Ryese (English) a form of Reece.
Reyse, Ryez, Ryse

Ryker (American) a surname used as a
first name.
Riker, Ryk

Rylan (English) land where rye is
grown.
*Ryland, Rylean, Rylen, Rylin, Rylon,
Rylyn, Rylynn*

Ryland (English) a form of Rylan.
Ryeland, Rylund

Ryle (English) rye hill.
Ryal, Ryel

Rylee (Irish) a form of Riley.
Ryeleigh, Ryleigh, Ryli, Rylie, Rillie

Ryley (Irish) a form of Riley.
Ryely

Ryman (English) rye seller.

Ryne (Irish) a form of Ryan.
Rynn

Ryon (Irish) a form of Ryan.

Sabastian (Greek) a form of
Sebastian.
*Sabastain, Sabastiano, Sabastien,
Sabastin, Sabastion, Sabaston,
Sabastiun, Sabestian*

Saber (French) sword.
Sabir, Sabre

Sabin (Basque) ancient tribe of central
Italy.
Saban, Saben, Sabian, Sabien, Sabino

Sabiti (Rutooro) born on Sunday.

Sabola (Nguni) pepper.

Saburo (Japanese) third-born son.

Sacha (Russian) a form of Sasha.
Sascha

Sachar (Russian) a form of Zachary.

Saddam (Arabic) powerful ruler.

Sadiki (Swahili) faithful.
*Saadiq, Sadeek, Sadek, Sadik, Sadiq,
Sadique*

Sadler (English) saddle maker.
Saddler

Safari (Swahili) born while traveling.
Sefa, Safarian

Safford (English) willow river crossing.

Sage (English) wise. Botany: an herb.
Sagen, Sager, Sage, Saje

Sahale (Native American) falcon.
Sael, Sahal, Sahel, Sahil

Sahen (Hindi) above.
Sahan

Sahil (Native American) a form of
Sahale.
Saheel, Sahel

Sahir (Hindi) friend.

Sa'id (Arabic) happy.
Sa'ad, Saaid, Saed, Sa'eed, Saeed, Sahid, Saide, Sa'ied, Saied, Saiyed, Saiyeed, Sajid, Sajjid, Sayed, Sayeed, Sayid, Seyed, Shahid

Sajag (Hindi) watchful.

Saka (Swahili) hunter.

Sakeri (Danish) a form of Zachary.
Sakarai, Sakari

Sakima (Native American) king.

Sakuruta (Pawnee) coming sun.

Sal (Italian) a short form of Salvatore.

Salam (Arabic) lamb.
Salaam

Salamon (Spanish) a form of Solomon.
Saloman, Salomón

Salaun (French) a form of Solomon.

Sálih (Arabic) right, good.
Saleeh, Saleh, Salehe

Salim (Swahili) peaceful.

Salim (Arabic) peaceful, safe.
Saleem, Salem, Saliym, Salman

Salmalin (Hindi) taloned.

Salman (Czech) a form of Salim, Solomon.
Salmaan, Salmaine, Salmon

Salomon (French) a form of Solomon.
Salomone

Salton (English) manor town; willow town.

Salvador (Spanish) savior.
Salvadore

Salvatore (Italian) savior. See also Xavier.
Sal, Salbatore, Sallie, Sally, Salvator, Salvatore, Salvidor, Sauveur

Sam (Hebrew) a short form of Samuel.
Samm, Sammy, Sern, Shem, Shmuel

Sambo (American) a familiar form of Samuel.
Sambou

Sameer (Arabic) a form of Samír.

Sami, Samy (Hebrew) forms of Sammy.
Sameeh, Sameh, Samie, Samih, Sammi

Samir (Arabic) entertaining companion.
Sameer

Samman (Arabic) grocer.
Saman, Sammon

Sammy (Hebrew) a familiar form of Samuel.
Saamy, Samey, Sami, Sammee, Sammey, Sammie, Samy

Samo (Czech) a form of Samuel.
Samho, Samko

Samson (Hebrew) like the sun. Bible: a judge and powerful warrior betrayed by Delilah.
Sampson, Sansao, Sansom, Sansón, Shem, Shimshon

Samual (Hebrew) a form of Samuel.
Samuael, Samuail

Samuel (Hebrew) heard God; asked of God. Bible: a famous Old Testament prophet and judge. See also Kamuela, Zamiel, Zanvil.
Sam, Samael, Samaru, Samauel, Samaul, Sambo, Sameul, Samiel, Sammail, Sammel, Sammuel, Sammy, Samo, Samouel, Samu, Samual, Samuele, Samuelis, Samuell, Samuello, Samuil, Samuka, Samule, Samuru, Samvel, Sanko, Saumel, Schmuel, Shem, Shmuel, Simão, Simuel, Somhairle, Zamuel

Samuele (Italian) a form of Samuel.
Samille

Samuru (Japanese) a form of Samuel.

Sanat (Hindi) ancient.

Sanborn (English) sandy brook.
Sanborne, Sanbourn, Sanbourne, Sanburn, Sanburne, Sandborn, Sandbourne

Sanchez (Latin) a form of Sancho.
Sanchaz, Sancheze

Sancho (Latin) sanctified; sincere. Literature: Sancho Panza was Don Quixote's squire.
Sanchez, Sauncho

Sandeep (Punjabi) enlightened.
Sandip

Sander (English) a short form of Alexander, Lysander.
Sandor, Sándor, Saunder

Sanders (English) son of Sander.
Sanderson, Saunders, Saunderson

Sándor (Hungarian) a short form of Alexander.
Sanyi

Sandro (Greek, Italian) a short form of Alexander.
Sandero, Sandor, Sandre, Saundro, Shandro

Sandy (English) a familiar form of Alexander.
Sande, Sandey, Sandi, Sandie

Sanford (English) sandy river crossing.
Sandford

Sani (Hindi) the planet Saturn. (Navajo) old.

Sanjay (American) a combination of Sanford + Jay.
Sanjaya, Sanje, Sanjey, Sanjo

Sanjiv (Hindi) long lived.
Sarjeev

Sankar (Hindi) a form of Shankara, another name for the Hindu god Shiva.

Sansón (Spanish) a form of Samson.
Samson, Sansone, Sansun

Santana (Spanish) History: Antonio López de Santa Anna was a Mexican general and political leader.
Santanna

Santiago (Spanish) a form of James.

Santino (Spanish) a form of Santonio.
Santion

Santo (Italian, Spanish) holy.
Santos

Santon (English) sandy town.

Santonio (Spanish) Geography: a short form of San Antonio, a city in Texas.
Santino, Santon, Santoni

Santos (Spanish) saint.
Santo

Santosh (Hindi) satisfied.

Sanyu (Luganda) happy.

Saqr (Arabic) falcon.

Saquan (American) a combination of the prefix Sa + Quan.
Saquané, Saquin, Saquon, Saquan, Saquone

Sarad (Hindi) born in the autumn.

Sargent (French) army officer.
Sargant, Sarge, Sarjant, Sergeant, Sergent, Serjant

Sarito (Spanish) a form of Caesar.
Sarit

Sariyah (Arabic) clouds at night.

Sarngin (Hindi) archer; protector.

Sarojin (Hindi) like a lotus.
Sarojin

Sasha (Russian) a short form of Alexander.
Sacha, Sash, Sashenka, Sashka, Sashok, Sawsha

Sasson (Hebrew) joyful.
Sason

Satchel (French) small bag.
Satch

Satordi (French) Saturn.
Satori

Saul (Hebrew) asked for, borrowed. Bible: in the Old Testament, a king of Israel and the father of Jonathan; in the New Testament, Saint Paul's original name was Saul.
Saül, Shaul, Sol, Solly

Saverio (Italian) a form of Xavier.

Saville (French) willow town.
Savelle, Savil, Savile, Savill, Savylle, Seville, Siville

Savon (Spanish) a treeless plain.
Savan, Savaughn, Saveion, Saveon, Savhon, Saviahn, Savian, Savino, Savo, Savone, Sayon, Sayone, Sayvon, Sayvone

Saw (Burmese) early.

Sawyer (English) wood worker.
Sawyere

Sax (English) a short form of Saxon.
Saxe

Saxon (English) swordsman. History: the Roman name for the Teutonic raiders who ravaged the Roman British coasts.
Sax, Saxen, Saxin, Saxon, Saxxon

Sayer (Welsh) carpenter.
Say, Saye, Sayers, Sayr, Sayre, Sayres

Sayyid (Arabic) master.
Sayed, Sayid, Sayyad, Sayyed

Scanlon (Irish) little trapper.
Scanlan, Scanlen

Schafer (German) shepherd.
Schaefer, Schaffer, Schäffer, Shaffer, Shafer

Schmidt (German) blacksmith.
Schmid, Schmit, Schmitt, Schmydt

Schneider (German) tailor.
Schnieder, Snider, Snyder

Schön (German) handsome.
Schoen, Schönn, Shon

Schuyler (Dutch) sheltering.
Schuylar, Schylar, Scoy, Scy, Skuyler, Sky, Skylar, Skyler, Skylor

Schyler (Dutch) a form of Schuyler.
Schylar, Schylre, Schylur

Scorpio (Latin) dangerous, deadly. Astronomy: a southern constellation near Libra and Sagittarius. Astrology: the eighth sign of the zodiac.
Scorpeo

Scott (English) from Scotland. A familiar form of Prescott.
Scot, Scottie, Scotto, Scotty

Scottie (English) a familiar form of Scott.
Scotie, Scotti

Scotty (English) a familiar form of Scott.
Scottey

Scoville (French) Scott's town.

Scully (Irish) town crier.

Seabert (English) shining sea.
Seabright, Sébert, Seibert

Seabrook (English) brook near the sea.

Seamus (Irish) a form of James.
Seamas, Seumas, Shamus

Sean (Hebrew) God is gracious. (Irish) a form of John.
Seaghan, Séan, Seán, Seanán, Seane,

Seann, Shaan, Shaine, Shane, Shaun, Shawn, Shayne, Shon, Siôn

Searlas (Irish, French) a form of Charles.
Séarlas, Searles, Searlus

Searle (English) armor.

Seasar (Latin) a form of Caesar.
Seasare, Seazar, Sesar, Sesear, Sezar

Seaton (English) town near the sea.
Seeton, Seton

Sebastian (Greek) venerable. (Latin) revered.
Bastian, Sabastian, Sabastien, Sabastian, Sebastain, Sebastiane, Sebastiano, Sebastien, Sebastien, Sebastin, Sebastine, Sebastion, Sebbie, Sebestyén, Sebo, Sepasetiano

Sebastien, Sébastien (French) forms of Sebastian.
Sebasten, Sebastyen

Sebastion (Greek) a form of Sebastian.

Sedgely (English) sword meadow.
Sedgeley, Sedgly

Sedric (Irish) a form of Cedric.
Sedrick, Sedercik, Sedrik, Sedriq

Seeley (English) blessed.
Sealey, Seely, Selig

Sef (Egyptian) yesterday. Mythology: one of the two lions that make up the Akeru, guardian of the gates of morning and night.

Sefton (English) village of rushes.

Sefu (Swahili) sword.

Seger (English) sea spear; sea warrior.
Seager, Seeger, Segar

Segun (Yoruba) conqueror.

Segundo (Spanish) second.

Seibert (English) bright sea.
Seabert, Sebert

Seif (Arabic) religion's sword.

Seifert (German) a form of Siegfried.

Sein (Basque) innocent.

Sekaye (Shona) laughter.

Selby (English) village by the mansion.
Selbey, Shelby

Seldon (English) willow tree valley.
Selden, Sellden

Selig (German) a form of Seeley.
Seligman, Seligmann, Zelig

Selwyn (English) friend from the palace.
Selvin, Selwin, Selwinn, Selwynn, Selwynne, Wyn

Semanda (Luganda) cow clan.

Semer (Ethiopian) a form of George.
Semere, Semier

Semon (Greek) a form of Simon.
Semion

Sempala (Luganda) born in prosperous times.

Sen (Japanese) wood fairy.
Senh

Sener (Turkish) bringer of joy.

Senior (French) lord.

Sennett (French) elderly.
Sennet

Senon (Spanish) living.

Senwe (African) dry as a grain stalk.

Sepp (German) a form of Joseph.
Seppi

Septimus (Latin) seventh.

Serafino (Portuguese) a form of Seraphim.

Seraphim (Hebrew) fiery, burning. Bible: the highest order of angels, known for their zeal and love.
Saraf, Saraph, Serafim, Serafin, Serafino, Seraphimus, Seraphin

Sereno (Latin) calm, tranquil.

Serge (Latin) attendant.
Seargeoh, Serg, Sergei, Sergio, Sergios, Sergius, Sergiusz, Serguei, Sirgio, Sirgios

Sergei (Russian) a form of Serge.
Sergey, Sergeyuk, Serghey, Sergi, Sergie, Sergio, Sergunya, Serhiy, Serhiyko, Serjio, Serzh

Sergio (Italian) a form of Serge.
Serginio, Serjio, Serjio

Servando (Spanish) to serve.
Servan, Servio

Seth (Hebrew) appointed. Bible: the third son of Adam.
Set, Sethan, Sethe, Shet

Setimba (Luganda) river dweller. Geography: a river in Uganda.

Seumas (Scottish) a form of James.
Seamus

Severiano (Italian) a form of Séverin.

Séverin (French) severe.
Seve, Sevé, Severian, Severiano, Severo, Sevrien, Sevrin, Sevryn

Severn (English) boundary.
Sevearn, Severn, Sevrin

Sevilen (Turkish) beloved.

Seward (English) sea guardian.
Seward, Siward

Sewati (Moquelumnan) curved bear claws.

Sexton (English) church official; sexton.

Sextus (Latin) sixth.
Sixtus

Seymour (French) prayer. Religion: name honoring Saint Maur. See also Maurice.
Seamor, Seamore, Seamour, See

Shabouh (Armenian) king, noble. History: a fourth-century Persian king.

Shad (Punjabi) happy-go-lucky.
Shadd

Shadi (Arabic) singer.
Shadde, Shaddi, Shaddy, Shade, Shadee, Shaded, Shadey, Shadie, Shadj, Shydee, Shydi

Shadrach (Babylonian) god; godlike. Bible: one of three companions who emerged unharmed from the fiery furnace of Babylon.
Shad, Shadrack, Shadrick, Sheddrach, Shedrach, Shedrick

Shadwell (English) shed by a well.

Shah (Persian) king. History: a title for rulers of Iran.

Shaheem (American) a combination of Shah + Raheem.

Shahid (Arabic) a form of Sa'id.
Shahed, Shaheed

Shai (Hebrew) a short form of Yeshaya.
Shaie

Shaiming (Chinese) life; sunshine.

Shaine (Irish) a form of Sean.
Shain

Shaka (Zulu) founder, first. History: Shaka Zulu was the founder of the Zulu empire.

Shakeel (Arabic) a form of Shaquille.
Shakeil, Shakel, Shakell, Shakiel, Shakeil, Shakille, Shakyle

Shakir (Arabic) thankful.
Shaker, Shakeer, Shakeir, Shakur

Shakur (Arabic) a form of Shakir.
Shakuur

Shalom (Hebrew) peace.
Shalum, Shlomo, Sholom

Shalya (Hindi) throne.

Shaman (Sanskrit) holy man, mystic, medicine man.
Shamaine, Shamann, Shamin, Shamine, Shammon, Shamon, Shamone

Shamar (Hebrew) a form of Shamir.
Shamaor, Shamare, Shamari

Shamir (Hebrew) precious stone.
Shahmeer, Shahmir, Shamar, Shameer, Shamyr

Shamus (American) slang for detective.
Shamas, Shames, Shamos, Shemus

Shan (Irish) a form of Shane.
Shann, Shanne

Shanahan (Irish) wise, clever.

Shandy (English) rambunctious.
Shandey, Shandie

Shane (Irish) a form of Sean.
Shan, Shayn, Shayne

Shangobunni (Yoruba) gift from Shango.

Shanley (Irish) small; ancient.
Shaneley, Shannley

Shannon (Irish) small and wise.
Shanan, Shannan, Shannen, Shannin, Shannone, Shanon

Shantae (French) a form of Chante.
Shant, Shanta, Shantai, Shante, Shantell, Shantelle, Shanti, Shantia, Shantie, Shanton, Shanty

Shap (English) a form of Shep.

Shaquan (American) a combination of the prefix Sha + Quan.
Shaqaun, Shaquand, Shaquane, Shaquann, Shaquawn, Shaquaun, Shaquian, Shaquian, Shaquin, Shaquan

Shaquell (American) a form of Shaquille.
Shaqueal, Shaquel, Shaquell, Shaquelle, Shaquiel, Shaquiell, Shaquielle

Shaquille (Arabic) handsome.
Shakeel, Shaquell, Shaquil, Shaquile, Shaquill, Shaqul

Shaquon (American) a combination of the prefix Sha + Quon.
Shaikwon, Shaqon, Shaquoin, Shaquoné

Sharad (Pakistani) autumn.
Sharod

Sharif (Arabic) honest; noble.
Shareef, Shareff, Shareif, Sharief, Sharife, Shariff, Shariyf, Sharyf, Sharyf

Sharod (Pakistani) a form of Sharad.
Sharrod

Sharron (Hebrew) flat area, plain.
Sharon, Sharone, Sharonn, Sharonne

Shattuck (English) little shad fish.

Shaun (Irish) a form of Sean.
Shaughan, Shaughn, Shaugn, Shauna, Shaunahan, Shaune, Shaunn, Shaunne

Shavar (Hebrew) comet.
Shavit

Shavon (American) a combination of the prefix Sha + Yvon.
Shavaun, Shavaon, Shavan, Shavaughn, Shaven, Shavin, Shavone, Shawan, Shavon, Shawun

Shaw (English) grove.

Shawn (Irish) a form of Sean.
Shaven, Shawne, Shawnee, Shawnn, Shawon

Shawnta (American) a combination of Shawn + the suffix Ta.
Shawntae, Shawntel, Shawnti

Shay (Irish) a form of Shea.
Shae, Shai, Shaya, Shaye, Shey

Shayan (Cheyenne) a form of Cheyenne.
Shayaan, Shayann, Shayon

Shayne (Hebrew) a form of Sean.
Shayn, Shaynne, Shean

Shea (Irish) courteous.
Shay

Shedrick (Babylonian) a form of Shadrach.
Shadriq, Shederick, Shedric, Shedrique

Sheehan (Irish) little; peaceful.
Shean

Sheffield (English) crooked field.
Field, Shef, Sheff, Sheffie, Sheffy

Shel (English) a short form of Shelby, Sheldon, Shelton.

Shelby (English) ledge estate.
Shel, Shelbe, Shelbey, Shelbie, Shell, Shellby, Shelley, Shelly

Sheldon (English) farm on the ledge.
Shel, Sheldan, Shelden, Sheldin, Sheldyn, Shell, Shelley, Shelly, Shelton

Shelley (English) a familiar form of Shelby, Sheldon, Shelton. Literature: Percy Bysshe Shelley was a nineteenth-century British poet.
Shell, Shelly

Shelton (English) town on a ledge.
Shel, Shelley, Shelten

Shem (Hebrew) name; reputation. (English) a short form of Samuel. Bible: Noah's oldest son.

Shen (Egyptian) sacred amulet. (Chinese) meditation.

Shep (English) a short form of Shepherd.
Shap, Ship, Shipp

Shepherd (English) shepherd.
Shep, Shepard, Shephard, Shepp, Sheppard, Shepperd

Shepley (English) sheep meadow.
Sheplea, Sheplee, Sheppy, Shipley

Sherborn (English) clear brook.
Sherborne, Sherbourn, Sherburn, Sherburne

Sheridan (Irish) wild.
Dan, Sheredan, Sheriden, Sheridon, Sherridan

Sherill (English) shire on a hill.
Sheril, Sherril, Sherrill

Sherlock (English) light haired. Literature: Sherlock Holmes is a famous British detective character, created by Sir Arthur Conan Doyle.
Sherlocke, Shurlock, Shurlocke

Sherman (English) sheep shearer; resident of a shire.
Scherman, Schermann, Sherm, Shermann, Shermaine, Shermann, Shermie, Shermon, Shermy

Sherrod (English) clearer of the land.
Sherod, Sherrad, Sherrard, Sherrodd

Sherwin (English) swift runner, one who cuts the wind.
Sherveen, Shervin, Sherwan, Sherwind, Sherwinn, Sherwyn, Sherwynd, Sherwynne, Win

Sherwood (English) bright forest.
Sherwoode, Shurwood, Woody

Shihab (Arabic) blaze.

Shilin (Chinese) intellectual.
Shilan

Shiloh (Hebrew) God's gift.
Shi, Shile, Shiley, Shilo, Shiloe, Shy, Shyle, Shylo, Shyloh

Shimon (Hebrew) a form of Simon.
Shymon

Shimshon (Hebrew) a form of Samson.
Shimson

Shing (Chinese) victory.
Shingae, Shingo

Shipton (English) sheep village; ship village.

Shiquan (American) a combination of the prefix Shi + Quan.
Shiquane, Shiquann, Shiquawn, Shiquoin, Shiqwan

Shiro (Japanese) fourth-born son.

Shiva (Hindi) life and death. Religion: the most common name for the Hindu god of destruction and reproduction.
Shiv, Shivan, Siva

Shlomo (Hebrew) a form of Solomon.
Shelmo, Shelomo, Shlomi, Shlomot

Shmuel (Hebrew) a form of Samuel.
Shem, Shemuel, Shmelke, Shmiel, Shmulka

Shneur (Yiddish) senior.
Shneiur

Shon (German) a form of Schön. (American) a form of Sean.
Shoan, Shoen, Shondae, Shondale, Shondel, Shore, Shorn, Shonntay, Shontae, Shontarious, Showan, Shown

Shunnar (Arabic) pheasant.

Si (Hebrew) a short form of Silas, Simon.
Sy

Sid (French) a short form of Sidney.
Cyd, Siddie, Siddy, Sidey, Syd

Siddel (English) wide valley.
Siddell

Siddhartha (Hindi) History: Siddhartha Gautama was the original name of Buddha, the founder of Buddhism.
Sida, Siddaartha, Siddhart, Siddhaarth, Sidh, Sidharth, Sidhartha

Sidney (French) from Saint-Denis, France.
Cydney, Sid, Sidnee, Sidny, Sidon, Sidonio, Sydney, Sydny

Sidonio (Spanish) a form of Sidney.

Sidwell (English) wide stream.

Siegfried (German) victorious peace. See also Zigfrid, Ziggy.
Seifert, Seifried, Siegfred, Siffre, Sig, Sigfrid, Sigfried, Sigfroi, Sigfryd, Sig, Sigifredo, Sigvard, Singefrid, Sigfried, Szygfrid

Sierra (Irish) black. (Spanish) saw-toothed.
Siera

Sig (German) a short form of Siegfried, Sigmund.

Sigifredo (German) a form of Siegfried.
Sigfriedo, Sigfrido, Siguefredo

Siggy (German) a familiar form of Siegfried, Sigmund.

Sigmund (German) victorious protector. See also Ziggy, Zsigmond, Zygmunt.
Siegmund, Sig, Siggy, Sigismond, Sigismondo, Sigismund, Sigismundo, Sigismundus, Sigmond, Sigmond, Szygmond

Sigurd (German, Scandinavian) victorious guardian.
Sigord, Sjure, Syver

Sigwald (German) victorious leader.

Silas (Latin) a short form of Silvan.
Si, Sias, Sylas

Silvan (Latin) forest dweller.
Silas, Silvain, Silvano, Silvaon, Silvie, Silvio, Sylvain, Sylvan, Sylvanus, Sylvio

Silvano (Italian) a form of Silvan.
Silvanos, Silvanus, Silvino

Silvester (Latin) a form of Sylvester.
Silvestre, Silvestro, Silvy

Silvestro (Italian) a form of Sylvester.

Silvio (Italian) a form of Silvan.

Simão (Portuguese) a form of Samuel.

Simba (Swahili) lion. (Yao) a short form of Lisimba.
Sim

Simcha (Hebrew) joyful.
Simmy

Simeon (French) a form of Simon.
Simione, Simone

Simms (Hebrew) son of Simon.
Simm, Sims

Simmy (Hebrew) a familiar form of Simcha, Simon.
Simmey, Simmi, Simmie, Symmy

Simon (Hebrew) he heard. Bible: one of the Twelve Disciples. See also Symington, Ximenes.
Saimon, Samien, Semon, Shimon, Si, Sim, Simao, Simen, Simeon, Simion, Simm, Simmon, Simmonds, Simmons, Simn, Simmon, Simonas, Simone, Simon, Simyon, Siomón, Symon, Szymon

Simpson (Hebrew) son of Simon.
Simonson, Simson

Sinclair (French) prayer. Religion: name honoring Saint Clair.
Sinclare, Synclair

Singh (Hindi) lion.
Sing

Sinjon (English) saint, holy man. Religion: name honoring Saint John.
Sinjin, Sinjun, Sjohn, Syngen, Synjen, Synjon

Sipatu (Moquelumnan) pulled out.

Sipho (Zulu) present.

Siraj (Arabic) lamp, light.

Siseal (Irish) a form of Cecil.

Sisi (Fante) born on Sunday.

Siva (Hindi) a form of Shiva.
Siv

Sivan (Hebrew) ninth month of the Jewish year.

Siwatu (Swahili) born during a time of conflict.
Siwazuri

Siwili (Native American) long fox's tail.

Skah (Lakota) white.
Skai

Skee (Scandinavian) projectile.
Ski, Skie

Skeeter (English) swift.
Skeat, Skeet, Skeets

Skelly (Irish) storyteller.
Shell, Skelley, Skellie

Skelton (Dutch) shell town.

Skerry (Scandinavian) stony island.

Skip (Scandinavian) a short form of Skipper.

Skipper (Scandinavian) shipmaster.
Skip, Skipp, Skippie, Skipton

Skiriki (Pawnee) coyote.

Skule (Norwegian) hidden.

Skye (Dutch) a short form of Skylar, Skyler, Skylor.
Sky

Skylar (Dutch) a form of Schuyler. *Skilar, Skkylar, Skye, Skyelar, Skylaar, Skylare, Skylarr, Skylayr*

Skyler (Dutch) a form of Schuyler. *Skieler, Skiler, Skye, Skyeler, Skylee, Skyler*

Skylor (Dutch) a form of Schuyler. *Skye, Skyelor, Skylore, Skylore, Skyloure, Skylour, Skylyr*

Slade (English) child of the valley. *Slaide, Slayde*

Slane (Czech) salty.

Slater (English) roof slater. *Slade, Slate, Slayter*

Slava (Russian) a short form of Stanislav, Vladislav, Vyacheslav. *Slavik, Slavoshka*

Slawek (Polish) a short form of Radoslaw.

Slevin (Irish) mountaineer. *Slaven, Slavin, Slawin*

Sloan (Irish) warrior. *Sloane, Slone*

Smedley (English) flat meadow. *Smedleigh, Smedly*

Smith (English) blacksmith. *Schmidt, Smid, Smidt, Smitt, Smitty, Smyth, Smythe*

Snowden (English) snowy hill. *Snowdon*

Socrates (Greek) wise, learned. History: a famous ancient Greek philosopher. *Socratis, Sokrates, Sokratis*

Sofian (Arabic) devoted.

Sohrab (Persian) ancient hero.

Soja (Yoruba) soldier.

Sol (Hebrew) a short form of Saul, Solomon. *Soll, Sollie, Solly*

Solly (Hebrew) a familiar form of Saul, Solomon. *Sollie, Zollie, Zolly*

Solomon (Hebrew) peaceful. Bible: a king of Israel famous for his wisdom. See also Zalman. *Salaman, Salamon, Salamun, Salaun, Salman, Salomo, Salomon, Selim, Shelomah, Shlomo, Sol, Solamh, Solaman, Solly, Solmon, Soloman, Solomona, Sulaiman*

Solon (Greek) wise. History: a noted ancient Athenian lawmaker.

Somerset (English) place of the summer settlers. Literature: William Somerset Maugham was a well-known British writer. *Sommerset, Somerset, Summerset*

Somerville (English) summer village. *Somerton, Summerton, Summerville*

Son (Vietnamese) mountain. (Native American) star. (English) son, boy. A short form of Madison, Orson. *Sonny*

Songan (Native American) strong. *Song*

Sonny (English) a familiar form of Grayson, Madison, Orson, Son. *Soni, Sonnie, Sony*

Sono (Akan) elephant.

Sören (Danish) thunder; war. *Sorren*

Sorrel (French) reddish brown. *Sorel, Sorell, Sorrell*

Soroush (Persian) happy.

Soterios (Greek) savior. *Soteris, Sotero*

Southwell (English) south well.

Sovann (Cambodian) gold.

Sowande (Yoruba) wise healer sought me out.

Spalding (English) divided field. *Spaulding*

Spangler (German) tinsmith. *Spengler*

Spar (English) happy. *Sparke, Sparkie, Sparky*

Spear (English) spear carrier. *Speare, Spears, Speer, Speers, Spiers*

Speedy (English) quick, successful. *Speed*

Spence (English) a short form of Spencer. *Spense*

Spencer (English) dispenser of provisions. *Spence, Spencar, Spenser*

Spenser (English) a form of Spencer.
Literature: Edmund Spenser was the
British poet who wrote *The Faerie
Queene.*
Spanser, Spense

Spike (English) ear of grain; long nail.
Spyke

Spiro (Greek) round basket; breath.
*Spiridion, Spiridon, Spiros, Spyridon,
Spyros*

Spoor (English) spur maker.
Spoors

Sproule (English) energetic.
Sprowle

Spurgeon (English) shrub.

Spyros (Greek) a form of Spiro.

Squire (English) knight's assistant; large
landholder.

Stacey, Stacy (English) familiar forms
of Eustace.
Stace, Stacee

Stafford (English) riverbank landing.
Staffard, Stafforde, Staford

Stamford (English) a form of
Stanford.

Stamos (Greek) a form of Stephen.
Stamatis, Stamatos

Stan (Latin, English) a short form of
Stanley.

Stanbury (English) stone fortification.
*Stanberry, Stanbery, Stanburghe,
Stansbury*

Stancio (Spanish) a form of
Constantine.
Stancy

Stancliff (English) stony cliff.
Stancliffe, Standcliffe

Standish (English) stony parkland.
History: Miles Standish was a leader
in colonial America.

Stane (Slavic) a short form of
Stanislaus.

Stanfield (English) stony field.
Stansfield

Stanford (English) rocky ford.
*Sandy, Stamford, Stan, Standford,
Stanfield*

Stanislaus (Latin) stand of glory. See
also Lao, Tano.
*Slavik, Stana, Standa, Stane, Stanislao,
Stanislas, Stanislav, Stanislaw, Stanislus,
Stannes, Stano, Stasik, Stasio*

Stanislav (Slavic) a form of Stanislaus.
See also Slava.
Stanislaw

Stanley (English) stony meadow.
*Stan, Stanely, Stanlea, Stanlee, Stanleigh,
Stanly*

Stanmore (English) stony lake.

Stannard (English) hard as stone.

Stanton (English) stony farm.
Stan, Stanten, Staunton

Stanway (English) stony road.

Stanwick (English) stony village.
Stanwicke, Stanwyck

Stanwood (English) stony woods.

Starbuck (English) challenger of fate.
Literature: a character in Herman
Melville's novel *Moby-Dick.*

Stark (German) strong, vigorous.
Starke, Stärke, Starkie

Starling (English) bird.
Sterling

Starr (English) star.
Star, Staret, Starlight, Starlon, Starwin

Stasik (Russian) a familiar form of
Stanislaus.
Stas, Stash, Stashka, Stashko, Stasiek

Stasio (Polish) a form of Stanislaus.
Stas, Stasiek, Stasiu, Staska, Stasko

Stavros (Greek) a form of Stephen.

Steadman (English) owner of a farmstead.
Steadmann, Stedman, Stedmen, Steed

Steel (English) like steel.
Steele

Steen (German, Danish) stone.
Steenn, Stein

Steeve (Greek) a short form of
Steven.

Steeven (Greek) a form of Steven.
*Steaven, Steavin, Steavon, Steevan,
Steeve, Steevn*

Stefan (German, Polish, Swedish) a
form of Stephen.
*Stefaan, Stefeán, Stefan, Stefane,
Stefanson, Stefaun, Stefawn, Steffan*

Stefano (Italian) a form of Stephen.
Stefanos, Steffano

Stefanos (Greek) a form of Stephen.
Stefans, Stefos, Stephano, Stephanos

Stefen (Norwegian) a form of Stephen.
Steffen, Steffin, Stefn

Steffan (Swedish) a form of Stefan.
Staffan

Stefon (Polish) a form of Stephon.
Staffon, Steffon, Steffone, Stefone, Stefonne

Stein (German) a form of Steen.
Steine, Steiner

Steinar (Norwegian) rock warrior.

Stepan (Russian) a form of Stephen.
Stepa, Stepane, Stepanya, Stepka, Stipan

Steph (English) a short form of Stephen.

Stephan (Greek) a form of Stephen.
Stephan, Stephanas, Stephano, Stephanos, Stephanus, Stephaun

Stéphane (French) a form of Stephen.
Stéfane, Stépháne, Stephanne

Stephen (Greek) crowned. See also Estéban, Estebe, Estevan, Estevao, Étienne, István, Szczepan, Tapani, Teb, Teppo, Tiennot.
Stavos, Stavros, Stefan, Stefano, Stefanos, Stéfen, Stenya, Stepan, Stepanos, Steph, Stephan, Stephanas, Stéphane, Stephanos, Stephens, Stephenson, Stephifan, Stephin, Stephon, Stepven, Steve, Steven, Stevie

Stephon (Greek) a form of Stephen.
Stefon, Stephfon, Stephfone, Stephifon, Stephon, Stephone, Stephonne

Sterling (English) valuable; silver penny. A form of Starling.
Sterlen, Sterlin, Stirling

Stern (German) star.

Sterne (English) austere.
Stearn, Stearne, Stearns

Stetson (Danish) stepson.
Steston, Stetsen, Stetzon

Stevan (Greek) a form of Steven.
Stevano, Stevanoe, Stevaughn, Stevean

Steve (Greek) a short form of Stephen, Steven.
Steave, Stevie, Stevy

Steven (Greek) a form of Stephen.
Steeven, Stevan, Stevon, Steve, Stevens, Stevie, Stevin, Stevon, Stiven

Stevens (English) son of Steven.
Stevenson, Stevinson

Stevie, Stevon (Greek) forms of Steven.
Stevion, Stevion, Steryn

Stevie (English) a familiar form of Stephen, Steven.
Stevy

Stewart (English) a form of Stuart.
Steward, Stu

Stian (Norwegian) quick on his feet.

Stig (Swedish) mount.

Stiggur (Gypsy) gate.

Stillman (English) quiet.
Stillmann, Stillmon

Sting (English) spike of grain.

Stockman (English) tree-stump remover.

Stockton (English) tree-stump town.

Stockwell (English) tree-stump well.

Stoddard (English) horse keeper.

Stoffel (German) a short form of Christopher.

Stoker (English) furnace tender.
Stoke, Stokes, Stroker

Stone (English) stone.
Stoen, Stoner, Stoney, Stonie, Stonie, Stonij, Stony

Storm (English) tempest, storm.
Storme, Stormey, Stormi, Stormmie, Stormy

Storr (Norwegian) great.
Story

Stover (English) stove tender.

Stowe (English) hidden; packed away.

Strahan (Irish) minstrel.
Strahan

Stratford (English) bridge over the river. Literature: Stratford-upon-Avon was Shakespeare's birthplace.
Stradford

Stratton (Scottish) river valley town.
Straten, Straton

Strephon (Greek) one who turns.

Strom (Greek) bed, mattress. (German) stream.

Strong (English) powerful.

Stroud (English) thicket.

Struthers (Irish) brook.

Stu (English) a short form of Stewart, Stuart.
Stew

Stuart (English) caretaker, steward. History: a Scottish and English royal family.
Stewart, Stu, Stuarrt

Studs (English) rounded nail heads; shirt ornaments; male horses used for breeding. History: Louis "Studs" Terkel is a famous American journalist.
Stud, Studd

Styles (English) stairs put over a wall to help cross it.
Stiles, Style, Stylz

Subhi (Arabic) early morning.

Suck Chin (Korean) unshakable rock.

Sudi (Swahili) lucky.
Su'ud

Sued (Arabic) master, chief.
Snede

Suffield (English) southern field.

Sugden (English) valley of sows.

Suhail (Arabic) gentle.
Sohail, Sohayl, Souhail, Suhael, Sujal

Suhuba (Swahili) friend.

Sukru (Turkish) grateful.

Sulaiman (Arabic) a form of Solomon.
Salaman, Sulay, Sulaymaan, Sulayman, Saleiman, Suleman, Suleyman, Sulieman, Sulman, Sulomon, Sulyman

Sullivan (Irish) black eyed.
Sullavan, Sullevan, Sully

Sully (Irish) a familiar form of Sullivan. (French) stain, tarnish. (English) south.
Sulleigh, Sulley

Sultan (Swahili) ruler.
Saltaan

Sum (Tai) appropriate.

Summit (English) peak, top.
Sameet, Sumit, Summet, Summitt

Sumner (English) church officer; summoner.
Summer

Sundeep (Punjabi) light; enlightened.
Sandip

Sunny (English) sunny, sunshine.
Sun, Sunni

Sunreep (Hindi) pure.
Sunrip

Sutcliff (English) southern cliff.
Sutcliffe

Sutherland (Scandinavian) southern land.
Southerland, Sutherlan

Sutton (English) southern town.

Sven (Scandinavian) youth.
Svein, Svend, Svenn, Swen, Swenson

Swaggart (English) one who sways and staggers.
Swaggert

Swain (English) herdsman; knight's attendant.
Swaine, Swane, Swanson, Swayne

Swaley (English) winding stream.
Swail, Swailey, Swale, Swales

Sweeney (Irish) small hero.
Sweeny

Swinbourne (English) stream used by swine.
Swinborn, Swinborne, Swinburn, Swinburne, Swinbyrn, Swynborn

Swindel (English) valley of the swine.
Swindell

Swinfen (English) swine's mud.

Swinford (English) swine's crossing.
Swynford

Swinton (English) swine town.

Sy (Latin) a short form of Sylas, Symon.
Si

Sydney (French) a form of Sidney.
Syd, Sydne, Sydnee, Syndey

Syed (Arabic) happy.
Speed, Syid

Sying (Chinese) star.

Sylas (Latin) a form of Silas.
Sy, Syles, Sylus

Sylvain (French) a form of Silvan, Sylvester.
Sylvan, Sylvian

Sylvester (Latin) forest dweller. *Silvestor, Silvestro, Sly, Syl, Sylvain, Sylvester, Sylvestre*

Symington (English) Simon's town, Simon's estate.

Symon (Greek) a form of Simon. *Sy, Syman, Symeon, Symion, Symms, Symon, Symone*

Szczepan (Polish) a form of Stephen. *Szdeo*

Szygfrid (Hungarian) a form of Siegfried. *Szigfrid*

Szymon (Polish) a form of Simon.

Taaveti (Finnish) a form of David. *Taavi, Taavo*

Tab (German) shining, brilliant. (English) drummer. *Tabb, Tabbie, Tabby*

Tabari (Arabic) he remembers. *Tabahri, Tabares, Tabarious, Tabarius, Tabaris, Tabur*

Tabib (Turkish) physician. *Tabeeb*

Tabo (Spanish) a short form of Gustave.

Tabor (Persian) drummer. (Hungarian) encampment. *Tabber, Taber, Taboras, Taibor, Tayber, Taybor, Taver*

Tad (Welsh) father. (Greek, Latin) a short form of Thaddeus. *Tadd, Taddy, Tade, Tadek, Tadey*

Tadan (Native American) plentiful. *Taden*

Tadarius (American) a combination of the prefix Ta + Darius. *Tadar, Tadarious, Tadaris, Tadarrius*

Taddeo (Italian) a form of Thaddeus. *Tadeo*

Taddeus (Greek, Latin) a form of Thaddeus. *Taddeos, Taddeusz, Taddius, Tadeas, Tades, Tadeusz, Tadio, Tadious*

Tadi (Omaha) wind.

Tadzi (Carrier) loon.

Tadzio (Polish, Spanish) a form of Thaddeus. *Taddeusz*

Taffy (Welsh) a form of David. (English) a familiar form of Taft.

Taft (English) river. *Tafft, Tafton*

Tage (Danish) day. *Tag*

Taggart (Irish) son of the priest. *Tegart, Taggert*

Tahir (Arabic) innocent, pure. *Taheer*

Tai (Vietnamese) weather; prosperous; talented.

Taima (Native American) born during a storm.

Tad (Welsh) father. (Greek, Latin) a short form of Thaddeus. *Tadd, Taddy, Tade, Tadek, Tadey*

Taishawn (American) a combination of Tai + Shawn. *Taisen, Taishaun, Taishon*

Tait (Scandinavian) a form of Tate. *Taite, Taitt*

Taiwan (Chinese) island; island dweller. Geography: a country off the coast of China. *Taewon, Tahwan, Taivon, Taiwain, Tawain, Tawan, Tawaun, Tawon, Tywan, Tywan*

Taiwo (Yoruba) first-born of twins.

Taj (Urdu) crown. *Taje, Tajee, Tajeh, Tajh, Taji*

Tajo (Spanish) day. *Taio*

Tajuan (American) a combination of the prefix Ta + Juan. *Tajuan, Taijuan, Taijuon, Tajuan, Tajuan, Tyjuan*

Takeo (Japanese) strong as bamboo. *Takeyo*

Takis (Greek) a familiar form of Peter. *Takius, Taktis*

Takoda (Lakota) friend to everyone.

Tal (Hebrew) dew; rain. *Tali, Talia, Talley, Talor, Talya*

Talbert (German) bright valley.

Talbot (French) boot maker. *Talbott, Tallbot, Tallbott, Tallie, Tally*

Talcott (English) cottage near the lake.

Tale (Tswana) green.

Talen (English) a form of Talon.
Talin, Tallen

Talib (Arabic) seeker.

Taliesin (Welsh) radiant brow.
Tallas, Tallis

Taliki (Hausa) fellow.

Talli (Delaware) legendary hero.

Talmadge (English) lake between two towns.
Talmage

Talmai (Aramaic) mound; furrow.
Telem

Talman (Aramaic) injured; oppressed.
Talmon

Talon (French, English) claw, nail.
Taelon, Taelyn, Talen, Tallin, Tallon, Talyn

Talor (English) a form of Tal, Taylor.
Taelor, Taelur

Tam (Vietnamese) number eight. (Hebrew) honest. (English) a short form of Thomas.
Tama, Tamas, Tamás, Tameas, Tamlane, Tammany, Tammas, Tammen, Tammy

Taman (Slavic) dark, black.
Tama, Tamann, Tamin, Tamon, Tamone

Tamar (Hebrew) date; palm tree.
Tamarie, Tamario, Tamarr, Timur

Tambo (Swahili) vigorous.

Tamir (Arabic) tall as a palm tree.
Taneer

Tammy (English) a familiar form of Thomas.
Tammie

Tamson (Scandinavian) son of Thomas.
Tamsen

Tan (Burmese) million. (Vietnamese) new.
Than

Tanek (Greek) immortal. See also Atek.

Taneli (Finnish) God is my judge.
Tanell, Tanell, Tanella

Taner (English) a form of Tanner.
Tanar

Tanguy (French) warrior.

Tani (Japanese) valley.

Tanmay (Sanskrit) engrossed.

Tanner (English) leather worker; tanner.
Tan, Taner, Tanery, Tann, Tannar, Tannir, Tannor, Tanny

Tannin (English) tan colored; dark.
Tanin, Tannen, Tannon, Tanyen, Tanyon

Tanny (English) a familiar form of Tanner.
Tana, Tannee, Tanney, Tannie, Tany

Tano (Spanish) camp glory. (Ghanaian) Geography: a river in Ghana. (Russian) a short form of Stanislaus.
Tanno

Tanton (English) town by the still river.

Tapan (Sanskrit) sun; summer.

Tapani (Finnish) a form of Stephen.
Tapann, Teppo

Tápko (Kiowa) antelope.

Taquan (American) a combination of the prefix Ta + Quan.
Taquann, Taquawn, Taquon, Taquan

Tarak (Sanskrit) star; protector.

Taran (Sanskrit) heaven.
Tarran

Tarek (Arabic) a form of Táriq.
Tareek, Tareke

Tarell (German) a form of Terrell.
Tarelle, Tarrel, Tarrell, Taryl

Taren (American) a form of Taron.
Taren, Tarrin

Tarif (Arabic) uncommon.
Taref

Tarik (Arabic) a form of Táriq.
Taric, Tarick, Tariek, Tarikh, Tarrick, Tarrik, Taryk

Táriq (Arabic) conqueror. History: Tariq bin Ziyad was the Muslim general who conquered Spain.
Tareck, Tarek, Tarik, Tarique, Tarreq, Tereik

Tarleton (English) Thor's settlement.
Tarlton

Taro (Japanese) first-born male.

Taron (American) a combination of Tad + Ron.
Taeron, Tahron, Taren, Tarone, Tarrion, Tarron, Taryn

Tarrant (Welsh) thunder.
Terrant

Tarun (Sanskrit) young, youth.
Taran

Tarver (English) tower; hill; leader.
Terver

Taryn (American) a form of Taron.
Tavaris, Tavarius, Tavaros, Tavarri,
Tarryn, Taryon

Tas (Gypsy) bird's nest.

Tashawn (American) a combination of
the prefix Ta + Shawn.
Tashaan, Tashan, Tashawn, Tashon,
Tashun

Tass (Hungarian) ancient mythology
name.

Tasunke (Dakota) horse.

Tate (Scandinavian, English) cheerful.
(Native American) long-winded
talker.
Tait, Tayte

Tatius (Latin) king; ruler. History: a
Sabine king.
Tatianus, Tazio, Titus

Tatum (English) cheerful.

Tau (Tswana) lion.

Tauno (Finnish) a form of Donald.

Taurean (Latin) strong; forceful.
Astrology: born under the sign of
Taurus.
Tauraun, Taurein, Taurin, Taurion,
Taurone, Taurus

Taurus (Latin) Astrology: the second
sign of the zodiac.
Taurice, Tauris

Tavares (Aramaic) a form of Tavor.
Tavarres, Tavarese, Taveress

Tavaris (Aramaic) a form of Tavor.
Tavaris, Tavar, Tavaras, Tavari, Tavarian,
Tavarious, Tavarius, Tavarous, Tavarri,
Tavaris, Tavars, Tavarse, Tavaris, Tevaris,
Tevarius, Tevaris

Tavey (Latin) a familiar form of
Octavio.

Tavi (Aramaic) good.

Tavian (Latin) a form of Octavio.
Taveon, Taviann, Tavien, Tavion, Tavin,
Tavio, Tavion, Tavionne, Tavon, Tavyon

Tavish (Scottish) a form of Thomas.
Tav, Tavi, Tavis

Tavo (Slavic) a short form of Gustave.

Tavon (American) a form of Tavian.
Tavonn, Tavonne, Tavonni

Tavor (Aramaic) misfortune.
Tavoris, Tavares, Tavaris, Tavores,
Tavorious, Tavoris, Tavorise, Tavores,
Tavorris, Tavoris

Tawno (Gypsy) little one.
Tawn

Tayib (Hindi) good; delicate.

Tayler (English) a form of Taylor.
Tailer, Taylar, Tayller, Teyler

Taylor (English) tailor.
Tailor, Talor, Tayler, Tayllor, Taylr,
Teylor

Tayshawn (American) a combination
of Taylor + Shawn.
Taysean, Tayshan, Tayshun, Tayson

Tayvon (American) a form of Tavian.
Tayvan, Tayvaughn, Tayven, Tayveon,
Tayvin, Tayvohn, Tayvon

Taz (Arabic) shallow ornamental cup.
Tazz

Tazio (Italian) a form of Tatius.

Teague (Irish) bard, poet.
Teag, Teagan, Teage, Teak, Tegan, Teige

Tearence (Latin) a form of Terrence.
Tearance, Tearce, Tearrance

Tearlach (Scottish) a form of Charles.

Tearle (English) stern, severe.

Teasdale (English) river dweller.
Geography: a river in England.

Teb (Spanish) a short form of Stephen.

Ted (English) a short form of Edward,
Edwin, Theodore.
Tedd, Tedek, Tedik, Tedson

Teddy (English) a familiar form of
Edward, Theodore.
Teddey, Teddie, Tedy

Tedmund (English) protector of the
land.
Tedman, Tedmond

Tedorik (Polish) a form of Theodore.
Teodoor, Teodor, Teodorek

Tedrick (American) a combination of
Ted + Rick.
Tedrick, Tedrick, Tedric

Teetonka (Lakota) big lodge.

Tefere (Ethiopian) seed.

Tegan (Irish) a form of Teague.
Teghan, Tegian, Tiegan

Tej (Sanskrit) light; lustrous.

Tejas (Sanskrit) sharp.

Tekle (Ethiopian) plant.

Telek (Polish) a form of Telford.

Telem (Hebrew) mound; furrow.
Talmai, Tel

Telford (French) iron cutter.
Telek, Telfer, Telfor, Telfour

Teller (English) storyteller.
Tell, Telly

Telly (Greek) a familiar form of Teller, Theodore.

Telmo (English) tiller, cultivator.

Telutci (Moquelumnan) bear making dust as it runs.

Telvin (American) a combination of the prefix Te + Melvin.
Tellvin, Telvan

Tem (Gypsy) country.

Teman (Hebrew) on the right side; southward.

Tembo (Swahili) elephant.

Tempest (French) storm.

Temple (Latin) sanctuary.

Templeton (English) town near the temple.
Temp, Templeten

Tennant (English) tenant, renter.
Tenant, Tennent

Tennessee (Cherokee) mighty warrior. Geography: a southern U.S. state.
Tennesee, Tennesy, Tennysee

Tennyson (English) a form of Dennison. Literature: Alfred, Lord Tennyson was a nineteenth-century British poet.
Tenney, Tenneyson, Tennie, Tennis, Tennison, Tenny, Tenson

Teo (Vietnamese) a form of Tom.

Teobaldo (Italian, Spanish) a form of Theobald.

Teodoro (Italian, Spanish) a form of Theodore.
Teodore, Teodorico

Teppo (French) a familiar form of Stephen.

Tequan (American) a combination of the prefix Te + Quan.
Tequinn, Tequon

Terance (Latin) a form of Terrence.
Terriance

Terell (German) a form of Terrell.
Tarell, Tereall, Terel, Terelle, Tyrel

Teremun (Tiv) father's acceptance.

Terence (Latin) a form of Terrence.
Teren, Teryn

Terencio (Spanish) a form of Terrence.

Terran (Latin) a short form of Terrance.
Teran, Teren, Terran, Terren

Terrance (Latin) a form of Terrence.
Tarrance, Terran

Terrell (German) thunder ruler.
Terell, Terrail, Terral, Terrale, Terrall, Terreal, Terrel, Terrelle, Terrill, Terryal, Terryel, Tirel, Tirell, Tirrell, Turrell, Tyrel, Tyrel

Terrence (Latin) smooth.
Tarrance, Tearance, Tenance, Terence, Terencio, Terrance, Terren, Terrin, Terry, Torrence, Tyreese

Terrick (American) a combination of the prefix Te + Derrick.
Teric, Terick, Terik, Teriq, Terric, Terrik, Tirek, Tirik

Terrill (German) a form of Terrell.
Teriel, Teriell, Teril, Terryl, Terryll, Teryll, Teryl, Tyrill

Terrin (Latin) a short form of Terrence.
Terin, Terrien, Terryn, Teryn, Tiren

Terris (Latin) son of Terry.

Terron (American) a form of Tyrone.
Tereon, Terion, Terione, Teron, Terone, Terrion, Terrione, Terriyon, Terrone, Terronn, Terryon, Tiron

Terry (English) a familiar form of Terrence. See also Keli.
Tarry, Terrey, Terri, Terrie, Tery

Tertius (Latin) third.

Teshawn (American) a combination of the prefix Te + Shawn.
Tesean, Teshaun, Teshon

Teva (Hebrew) nature.

Tevan (American) a form of Tevin.
Tevaughan, Tevaughn, Teven, Tevvan

Tevel (Yiddish) a form of David.

Tevin (American) a combination of the prefix Te + Kevin.
Teavin, Teivon, Tevan, Tevien, Tevinn, Tevon, Tevrin, Tevyn

Tevis (Scottish) a form of Thomas.
Tevish

Tevon (American) a form of Tevin.
Tevion, Tevohn, Tevone, Tevonne, Tevoun, Teyvon

Tewdor (German) a form of Theodore.

Tex (American) from Texas.
Tejas

Thabit (Arabic) firm, strong.

Thad (Greek, Latin) a short form of Thaddeus.
Thadd, Thade, Thadee, Thady

Thaddeus (Greek) courageous. (Latin) praiser. Bible: one of the Twelve Apostles. See also Fadey.
Tad, Taddeo, Taddeus, Thaddis, Thadeaus, Thadeus, Thaddaeus, Thaddaus, Thaddeaus, Thaddeous, Thaddeus, Thaddeos, Thaddeous, Thaddeus, Thaddius, Thadeous, Thaddeus, Thaddeus, Thadius, Thadus

Thady (Irish) praise.
Thaddy

Thai (Vietnamese) many; multiple.

Thaman (Hindi) god; godlike.

Than (Burma) million.
Tan, Thanh

Thane (English) attendant warrior.
Thain, Thaine, Thayne

Thang (Vietnamese) victorious.

Thanh (Vietnamese) finished.

Thaniel (Hebrew) a short form of Nathaniel.

Thanos (Greek) nobleman; bear-man.
Athanasios, Thanasis

Thatcher (English) roof thatcher, repairer of roofs.
Thacher, Thatch, Thaxter

Thaw (English) melting ice.

Thayer (French) nation's army.
Thay

Thel (English) upper story.

Thenga (Yao) bring him.

Theo (English) a short form of Theodore.

Theobald (German) people's prince. See also Dietbald.
Teobaldo, Thebault, Theobald, Thibalt, Tibold, Tiebold, Tiebout, Toiboid, Tybald, Tybalt, Tybault

Theodore (Greek) gift of God. See also Feodor, Fyodor.
Téadóir, Teador, Ted, Teddy, Tedor, Tedorek, Tedorik, Telly, Teodomiro, Teodoro, Teodus, Teos, Tewdor, Theo, Theodor, Theodor, Theodors, Theodorus, Theodosios, Theodreki, Tivadar, Todor, Tolek, Tudor

Theodoric (German) ruler of the people. See also Dedrick, Derek, Dirk.
Teodorico, Thedric, Thedrick, Thierry, Till

Theophilus (Greek) loved by God.
Teofil, Théophile, Theophilos, Theopolis

Theron (Greek) hunter.
Theran, Theren, Thereon, Therin, Therion, Therrin, Therron, Theryn, Theryon

Thian (Vietnamese) smooth.
Thien

Thoma (German) a form of Thomas.

Thom (English) a short form of Thomas.
Thomy

Thibault (French) a form of Theobald.
Thibaud, Thibaut

Thierry (French) a form of Theodoric.
Thierry, Theory

Thom (English) a short form of Thomas.
Thomy

Thoma (German) a form of Thomas.

Thomas (Greek, Aramaic) twin. Bible: one of the Twelve Apostles. See also Chuma, Foma, Maslin.
Tam, Tammy, Tavish, Tevis, Thom, Thoma, Thomason, Thomaz, Thomeson, Thomison, Thommas, Thompson, Thomson, Tom, Toma, Tomas, Tomasso, Tomcy, Tomey, Tomey, Tomi, Tommy, Toomas

Thompson (English) son of Thomas.
Thomason, Thomison, Thomsen, Thomson

Thor (Scandinavian) thunder. Mythology: the Norse god of thunder.
Thorin, Tor, Tyrus

Thorald (Scandinavian) Thor's follower.
Terell, Terrill, Thorold, Torald

Thorbert (Scandinavian) Thor's brightness.
Torbert

Thorbjorn (Scandinavian) Thor's bear.
Thorburn, Thurborn, Thurburn

Thorgood (English) Thor is good.

Thorleif (Scandinavian) Thor's beloved.
Thorlief

Thorley (English) Thor's meadow.
Thorlea, Thorlee, Thorleigh, Thorly, Torley

Thorndike (English) thorny embankment.
Thorn, Thorndyck, Thorndyke, Thorne

Thorne (English) a short form of names beginning with "Thorn."
Thorn, Thornie, Thorny

Thornley (English) thorny meadow.
Thorley, Thorne, Thornlea, Thornleigh, Thornly

Thornton (English) thorny town.
Thorne

Thorpe (English) village.
Thorp

Thorwald (Scandinavian) Thor's forest.
Thorvald

Thuc (Vietnamese) aware.

Thurlow (English) Thor's hill.
Thurlo

Thurmond (English) defended by Thor.
Thormond, Thurmund

Thurston (Scandinavian) Thor's stone.
Thorstan, Thorstein, Thorsten, Thurstain, Thurstan, Thursten, Torsten, Torston

Tiago (Spanish) a form of Jacob.

Tiberio (Italian) from the Tiber River region.
Tiberias, Tiberious, Tiberiu, Tiberius, Tibius, Tyberias, Tyberious, Tyberius, Tyberrius

Tibor (Hungarian) holy place.
Tiburcio

Tichawanna (Shona) we shall see.

Ticho (Spanish) a short form of Patrick.

Tieler (English) a form of Tyler.
Tielar, Tielor, Tielyr

Tiennot (French) a form of Stephen.
Tien

Tiernan (Irish) lord.

Tierney (Irish) lordly.
Tiarnach, Tiernan

Tige (English) a short form of Tiger.
Ti, Tig, Tighe, Ty, Tyg, Tyge, Tygh, Tyghe

Tiger (American) tiger; powerful and energetic.
Tige, Tigger, Tyger

Tiimu (Moquelumnan) caterpillar coming out of the ground.

Tilden (English) tilled valley.
Tildon

Tiktu (Moquelumnan) bird digging up potatoes.

Tilford (English) prosperous ford.

Till (German) a short form of Theodoric.
Thilo, Til, Tillman, Tilman, Tillmann, Tilson

Tilton (English) prosperous town.

Tim (Greek) a short form of Timothy.
Timmie, Timmy

Timin (Arabic) born near the sea.

Timmothy (Greek) a form of Timothy.
Timmathy, Timmithy, Timmoty, Timmthy

Timmy (Greek) a familiar form of Timothy.
Timmie

Timo (Finnish) a form of Timothy.
Timio

Timofey (Russian) a form of Timothy.
Timofei, Timofej, Timofeo

Timon (Greek) honorable.

Timoteo (Portuguese, Spanish) a form of Timothy.

Timothy (Greek) honoring God. See also Kimokeo.
Tadhg, Taidgh, Tiege, Tim, Tima, Timithy, Timka, Timkin, Timmothy, Timmy, Timo, Timofey, Timok, Timon, Timonthee, Timonthy, Timót, Timote, Timotei, Timoteo, Timoteus, Timothé, Timothée, Timotheo, Timotheos, Timotheus, Timothey, Timothie, Timthie, Tiombid, Tisha, Tomothy, Tymon, Tymothy

Timur (Hebrew) a form of Tamar. (Russian) conqueror.
Timour

Tin (Vietnamese) thinker.

Tino (Spanish) venerable, majestic. (Italian) small. A familiar form of Antonio. (Greek) a short form of Augustine.
Tion

Tinsley (English) fortified field.

Tiquan (American) a combination of the prefix Ti + Quan.
Tiquawn, Tiquine, Tiquon, Tiquuan, Tiqwan

Tisha (Russian) a form of Timothy.
Tishka

Tishawn (American) a combination of the prefix Ti + Shawn.
Tishaan, Tishaun, Tishean, Tishon, Tishun

Tito (Italian) a form of Titus.
Titos, Titos, Titos

Titus (Greek) giant. (Latin) hero. A form of Tatius. History: a Roman emperor.
Tite, Titek, Tito, Tytus

Tivon (Hebrew) nature lover.

TJ (American) a combination of the initials T. + J.
Teejay, Tj, TJ, T Jae, Tjayda

Tobal (Spanish) a short form of Christopher.
Tabalito

Tobar (Gypsy) road.

Tobi (Yoruba) great.

Tobias (Hebrew) God is good.
Tobia, Tobiah, Tobiás, Tobiath, Tobin, Tobit, Toby, Tobyas, Twrya

Tobin (Hebrew) a form of Tobias.
Toben, Tobian, Tobyn, Tovin

Toby (Hebrew) a familiar form of Tobias.
Tobbie, Tobby, Tobe, Tobee, Tobey, Tobie

Todd (English) fox.
Tod, Toddie, Toddy

Todor (Basque, Russian) a form of Theodore.
Teodor, Todar, Todas, Todos

Toft (English) small farm.

Tohon (Native American) cougar.

Tokala (Dakota) fox.

Toland (English) owner of taxed land.
Tolan

Tolbert (English) bright tax collector.

Toller (English) tax collector.

Tom (English) a short form of Thomas.
Teo, Thom, Tommey, Tommie, Tommy

Toma (Romanian) a form of Thomas.
Tomah

Tomas (German) a form of Thomas.
Tom, Tomaisin, Tomaz, Tomcio, Tome, Tomek, Tomelis, Tomico, Tomik, Tomislav, Tommas, Tomo, Tomson

Tomás (Irish, Spanish) a form of Thomas.
Tomas, Tómas, Tomasz

Tomasso (Italian) a form of Thomas.
Tomaso, Tommaso

Tombe (Kakwa) northerners.

Tomey (Irish) a familiar form of Thomas.
Tome, Tomi, Tomie, Tomy

Tomi (Japanese) rich. (Hungarian) a form of Thomas.

Tomlin (English) little Tom.
Tomkin, Tomlinson

Tommie (Hebrew) a form of Tommy.
Tommi

Tommy (Hebrew) a familiar form of Thomas.
Tommie, Tomy

Tonda (Czech) a form of Tony.
Tonek

Tong (Vietnamese) fragrant.

Toni (Greek, German, Slavic) a form of Tony.
Tonee, Tonie, Tonio, Tonis, Tonnie

Tonio (Portuguese) a form of Tony. (Italian) a short form of Antonio.
Tono, Tonyo

Tony (Greek) flourishing. (Latin) praiseworthy. (English) a short form of Anthony. A familiar form of Remington.
Tonda, Tonek, Toney, Toni, Tonik, Tonio, Tonry

Tooantuh (Cherokee) spring frog.

Toomas (Estonian) a form of Thomas.
Toomis, Thomas, Tuomo

Topher (Greek) a short form of Christopher, Kristopher.
Tofer, Tophor

Topo (Spanish) gopher.

Topper (English) hill.

Tor (Norwegian) thunder. (Tiv) royalty, king.
Thor

Torian (Irish) a form of Torin.
Toran, Torean, Toriano, Toriaun, Torien, Torrian, Torrien, Torryan

Torin (Irish) chief.
Thorfin, Thorstein, Torian, Iorion, Torrin, Toryn

Torkel (Swedish) Thor's cauldron.

Tormey (Irish) thunder spirit.
Tormé, Tormee

Tormod (Scottish) north.

Torn (Irish) a short form of Torrence.
Toran

Torquil (Danish) Thor's kettle.
Torkel

Torr (English) tower.
Tory

Torrance (Irish) a form of Torrence.
Torance

Torren (Irish) a short form of Torrence.
Torehn, Toren

Torrence (Irish) knolls. (Latin) a form of Terrence.
Taurence, Toreence, Torence, Torenze, Torey, Torin, Torn, Torr, Torrance, Torren, Torreon, Torrin, Torry, Tory, Toryne, Tuarence, Turance

Torrey (English) a form of Tory.
Torey, Torie, Torre, Torri, Torrie, Torry

Toru (Japanese) sea.

Tory (English) familiar form of Torr, Torrence.
Torey, Tori, Torrey

Toshi-Shita (Japanese) junior.

Tovi (Hebrew) good.
Tov

Townley (English) town meadow.
Townlea, Townlee, Townleigh, Townlie, Townly

Townsend (English) town's end.
Town, Townes, Towney, Townie, Townsen, Townshend, Towny

Trace (Irish) a form of Tracy.
Trayce

Tracey (Irish) a form of Tracy.
Traci

Tracy (Greek) harvester. (Latin) courageous. (Irish) battler.
Trace, Tracey, Tracie, Treacy

Trader (English) well-trodden path; skilled worker.

Trae (English) a form of Trey.
Trai, Traie, Tre, Trea

Trahern (Welsh) strong as iron.
Traherne, Tray

Tramaine (Scottish) a form of Tremaine, Tremayne.
Tramain, Traman, Tramane, Tramayne, Traymain, Traymon

Traquan (American) a combination of Travis + Quan.
Traequan, Tragon, Traquon, Traquan, Traquaun, Trayquan, Trayquane, Trayquon

Trashawn (American) a combination of Travis + Shawn.
Trasen, Trashaun, Trasean, Trashon, Trashone, Trashun, Trayshawn, Trayshawn

Traugott (German) God's truth.

Travaris (French) a form of Travers.
Travares, Travaress, Travarious, Travarius, Travarous, Travarus, Travauris, Traveress, Traverez, Traverus, Travoris, Travorus

Travell (English) traveler.
Travail, Travale, Travel, Travelis, Travelle, Trevel, Trevell, Trevelle

Traven (American) a form of Trevon.
Travin, Travine, Trayven

Travers (French) crossroads.
Travaris, Traver, Travis

Travion (American) a form of Trevon.
Traveon, Travian, Travien, Travione, Travioun

Travis (English) a form of Travers.
Travais, Travees, Traves, Traveus, Travious, Traviss, Travious, Travous, Travys, Trayvis, Trevais, Trevis

Travon (American) a form of Trevon.
Traevon, Traivon, Travone, Travonn, Travonne

Tray (English) a form of Trey.
Traye

Trayton (English) town full of trees.
Trayten

Trayon (American) a combination of Tray + Von.
Trayeon, Trayin, Trayion, Trayond, Trayone, Trayoon, Trayyon

Treavon (American) a form of Trevon.
Treavan, Treavin, Treavion

Tredway (English) well-worn road.
Treadway

Tremaine, Tremayne (Scottish) house of stone.
Tramaine, Tremain, Tremane, Treymaine, Trimaine

Trent (Latin) torrent, rapid stream. (French) thirty. Geography: a city in northern Italy.
Trente, Trentino, Trento, Trentonio

Trenton (Latin) town by the rapid stream. Geography: the capital of New Jersey.
Trendun, Trendun, Trenten, Trentin, Trenton, Trentyn, Trinten, Trintin, Trinton

Trequan (American) a combination of Trey + Quan.
Trequanne, Trequann, Trequon, Trequon, Treyquane

Treshawn (American) a combination of Trey + Shawn.
Treshaun, Treshon, Treshun, Treysean, Treyshawn, Treyshon

Treston (Welsh) a form of Tristan.
Trestan, Trestin, Trestton, Trestyn

Trev (Irish, Welsh) a short form of Trevor.

Trevaughn (American) a combination of Trey + Vaughn.
Trevaughan, Trevaugn, Trevaun, Trevaune, Trevaunn, Treyvaughn

Trevelyan (English) Elian's homestead.

Trevin (American) a form of Trevon.
Trevian, Trevien, Trevine, Trevyn, Trevvin

Trevion (American) a form of Trevon.
Trevione, Trevionne, Trevyon, Trevyeon, Treyvion

Trevis (English) a form of Travis.
Treves, Trevez, Treveze, Trevius

Trevon (American) a combination of Trey + Von.
Travon, Treavon, Trebon, Trefon, Tren, Trenat, Trevaes, Trevarious, Trevaris, Trevarius, Trevaros, Trevarus, Trevee, Trevone, Trevores, Trevoris, Trevonn, Trevoun, Trevyn, Treyvor

Trevor (Irish) prudent. (Welsh) homestead.
Travor, Treavor, Trebor, Trefor, Trev, Trevar, Trevares, Trevarious, Trevaris, Trevarius, Trevaros, Trevarus, Trevee, Trevore, Trevores, Trevoris, Trevons, Trevoun, Trevyr, Treyvor

Trey (English) three; third.
Trae, Trai, Tray, Treye, Tri, Trie

Treyvon (American) a form of Trevon.
Treyvan, Treyven, Treyvenn, Treyvone, Treyvonn, Treyvun

Trigg (Scandinavian) trusty.

Trini (Latin) a short form of Trinity.

Trinity (Latin) holy trinity.
Trenedy, Trini, Trinidy

Trip, Tripp (English) traveler.

Tristan (Welsh) bold. Literature: a knight in the Arthurian legends who fell in love with his uncle's wife.
Treston, Tris, Trisan, Tristain, Tristano, Tristen, Tristian, Tristin, Triston, Tristyn, Trystan

Tristano (Italian) a form of Tristan.

Tristen (Welsh) a form of Tristan.
Trisden, Trissten

Tristin (Welsh) a form of Tristan.
Tristian, Tristinn

Triston (Welsh) a form of Tristan.

Tristyn (Welsh) a form of Tristan.
Tristyne

Trot (English) trickling stream.

Trowbridge (English) bridge by the tree.

Troy (Irish) foot soldier. (French) curly haired. (English) water. See also Koi.
Troi, Troye, Troyton

True (English) faithful, loyal.
Tru

Truesdale (English) faithful one's homestead.

Truitt (English) little and honest.
Truett

Truman (English) honest. History: Harry S. Truman was the thirty-third U.S. president.
Trueman, Trumain, Trumaine, Trumann

Trumble (English) strong; bold.
Trumball, Trumbell, Trumbull

Trustin (English) trustworthy.
Tristan, Trusten, Truston

Trygve (Norwegian) brave victor.

Trystan (Welsh) a form of Tristan.
Tryistan, Trysten, Trystian, Trystin, Trystn, Tryston, Trystyn

Tsalani (Nguni) good-bye.

Tse (Ewe) younger of twins.

Tu (Vietnamese) tree.

Tuaco (Ghanaian) eleventh-born.

Tuan (Vietnamese) goes smoothly.

Tucker (English) fuller, tucker of cloth.
Tuck, Tuckie, Tucky, Tuckyr

Tudor (Welsh) a form of Theodore. History: an English ruling dynasty.
Todor

Tug (Scandinavian) draw, pull.
Tugg

Tuketu (Moquelumnan) bear making dust as it runs.

Tukuli (Moquelumnan) caterpillar crawling down a tree.

Tulio (Italian, Spanish) lively.
Tullio

Tullis (Latin) title, rank.
Tullius, Tullos, Tully

Tully (Irish) at peace with God. (Latin) a familiar form of Tullis.
Tull, Tulley, Tullie, Tullio

Tumaini (Mwera) hope.

Tumu (Moquelumnan) deer thinking about eating wild onions.

Tung (Vietnamese) stately, dignified. (Chinese) everyone.

Tungar (Sanskrit) high; lofty.

Tupi (Moquelumnan) pulled up.

Tupper (English) ram raiser.

Turi (Spanish) a short form of Arthur.
Ture

Turk (English) from Turkey.

Turner (Latin) lathe worker; wood worker.

Turpin (Scandinavian) Finn named after Thor.

Tut (Arabic) strong and courageous. History: a short form of Tutankhamen, an Egyptian king.
Tutt

Tutu (Spanish) a familiar form of Justin.

Tuvya (Hebrew) a form of Tobias.
Tevya, Tuvia, Tuviah

Tuwile (Mwera) death is inevitable.

Tuyen (Vietnamese) angel.

Twain (English) divided in two. Literature: Mark Twain (whose real name was Samuel Langhorne Clemens) was one of the most

prominent nineteenth-century American writers.
Tavine, Twaine, Twan, Twane, Tway, Twayn, Twayne

Twia (Fante) born after twins.

Twitchell (English) narrow passage.
Twytchell

Twyford (English) double river crossing.

Txomin (Basque) like the Lord.

Ty (English) a short form of Tyler, Tyrone, Tyrus.
Tye

Tyee (Native American) chief.

Tyger (English) a form of Tiger.
Tige, Tyg, Tygar

Tylar (English) a form of Tyler.
Tyelar, Tylarr

Tyler (English) tile maker.
Tieler, Tiler, Ty, Tyel, Tyeler, Tyelor, Tyhler, Tylar, Tyle, Tylee, Tylere, Tyller, Tylor, Tylyr

Tylor (English) a form of Tyler.
Tylour

Tymon (Polish) a form of Timothy. (Greek) a form of Timon.
Tymain, Tymaine, Tymane, Tymeik, Tymek, Tymen

Tymothy (English) a form of Timothy.
Tymithy, Tymmothy, Tymoteusz, Tymothee, Timothi

Tynan (Irish) dark.
Ty

Tynek (Czech) a form of Martin.
Tynko

Tyquan (American) a combination of Ty + Quan.
Tykwan, Tykwane, Tykwon, Tyquaan, Tyquane, Tyquann, Tyquine, Tyquinn, Tyquon, Tyquone, Tyquwon, Tyqwan

Tyran (American) a form of Tyrone.
Tyraine, Tyrane

Tyree (Scottish) island dweller. Geography: Tiree is an island off the west coast of Scotland.
Tyra, Tyrae, Tyrai, Tyray, Tyre, Tyrea, Tyrée

Tyreese (American) a form of Terrence.
Tyreas, Tyrease, Tyrece, Tyreece, Tyreice, Tyres, Tyrese, Tyresse, Tyrez, Tyreze, Tyrice, Tyrice, Tyriese

Tyrel, Tyrell (American) forms of Terrell.
Tyrelle, Tyrel, Tyrell

Tyrick (American) a combination of Ty + Rick.
Tyreck, Tyreek, Tyreik, Tyrek, Tyreke, Tyric, Tyriek, Tyrik, Tyriq, Tyrique

Tyrin (American) a form of Tyrone.
Tyrinn, Tyrion, Tyrin, Tyryn

Tyron (American) a form of Tyrone.
Tyrohn, Tyronn, Tyronna, Tyronne

Tyrone (Greek) sovereign. (Irish) land of Owen.
Tayron, Tayrone, Teirone, Terron, Ty, Tyerone, Tyhrone, Tyran, Tyrin, Tyron, Tyroney, Tyronne, Tyroon, Tyroun

Tyrus (English) a form of Thor.
Ty, Tyrass, Tyryss

Tyshawn (American) a combination of Ty + Shawn.
Tyshan, Tyshaun, Tyshawun, Tyshian, Tyshien, Tyshion, Tyshon, Tyshone, Tyshonne, Tyshun, Tyshunn, Tyshunn, Tyshyn

Tyson (French) son of Ty.
Tison, Tiszon, Tyce, Tycen, Tyesn, Tyeson, Tysen, Tysie, Tysin, Tysne, Tysone

Tytus (Polish) a form of Titus.
Tytus

Tyvon (American) a combination of Ty + Von.
Tyvan, Tyvin, Tyvinn, Tyvone, Tyvonne

Tywan (Chinese) a form of Taiwan.
Tywain, Tywaine, Tywane, Tywann, Tywaun, Tywen, Tywon, Tywone, Tywonne

Tzadok (Hebrew) righteous.
Tzadik, Zadok

Tzion (Hebrew) sign from God.
Zion

Tzuriel (Hebrew) God is my rock.
Tzuriya

Tzvi (Hebrew) deer.
Tzvi, Zvi

U

Ubadah (Arabic) serves God.

Ubaid (Arabic) faithful.

Uberto (Italian) a form of Hubert.

Uche (Ibo) thought.

Uday (Sanskrit) to rise.

Udell (English) yew-tree valley.
Dell, Eudel, Udale, Udal, Yudell

Udit (Sanskrit) grown; shining.

Udo (Japanese) ginseng plant. (German) a short form of Udolf.

Udolf (English) prosperous wolf.
Udo, Udolfo, Udolph

Ugo (Italian) a form of Hugh, Hugo.

Ugutz (Basque) a form of John.

Uiliam (Irish) a form of William.
Uileog, Uilleam, Ulick

Uinseann (Irish) a form of Vincent.

Uistean (Irish) intelligent.
Uisdean

Uja (Sanskrit) growing.

Uku (Hawaiian) flea, insect; skilled ukulele player.

Ulan (African) first-born twin.

Ulbrecht (German) a form of Albert.

Ulf (German) wolf.

Ulfred (German) peaceful wolf.

Ulger (German) warring wolf.

Ulises (Latin) a form of Ulysses.
Ulishes, Ulisse, Ulisses

Ullock (German) sporting wolf.

Ulmer (English) famous wolf.
Ullmar, Ulmar

Ulmo (German) from Ulm, Germany.

Ulric (German) a form of Ulrich.
Ulrik

Ulrich (German) wolf ruler; ruler of all. See also Alaric.
Uli, Ull, Ulric, Ulrick, Ulrik, Ulrike, Ulu, Ulz, Uwe

Ultman (Hindi) god; godlike.

Ulyses (Latin) a form of Ulysses.
Ulysee, Ulysees

Ulysses (Latin) wrathful. A form of Odysseus.
Eulises, Ulick, Ulises, Ulyses, Ulysse, Ulyssees, Ulysses, Ulyssius

Umang (Sanskrit) enthusiastic.
Umanga

Umar (Arabic) a form of Omar.
Umair, Umarr, Umayr, Umer

Umberto (Italian) a form of Humbert.
Uberto

Umi (Yao) life.

Umit (Turkish) hope.

Unai (Basque) shepherd.
Una

Uner (Turkish) famous.

Unika (Lomwe) brighten.

Unique (Latin) only, unique.
Uneek, Unek, Unikque, Uniqué, Unyque

Unwin (English) nonfriend.
Unwinn, Unwyn

Upshaw (English) upper wooded area.

Upton (English) upper town.

Upwood (English) upper forest.

Urban (Latin) city dweller; courteous.
Urbain, Urbaine, Urbane, Urbano, Urbanus, Urvan, Urvane

Urbane (English) a form of Urban.

Urbano (Italian) a form of Urban.

Uri (Hebrew) a short form of Uriah.
Urie

Uriah (Hebrew) my light. Bible: a soldier and the husband of Bathsheba. See also Yuri.
Uri, Uria, Urias, Urijah

Urian (Greek) heaven.
Urihaan

Uriel (Hebrew) God is my light.
Urie

Urson (French) a form of Orson.
Ursan, Ursus

Urtzi (Basque) sky.

Usamah (Arabic) like a lion.
Usama

Useni (Yao) tell me.
Usene, Usenet

Usi (Yao) smoke.

Ustin (Russian) a form of Justin.

Utatci (Moquelumnan) bear scratching itself.

Uthman (Arabic) companion of the Prophet.
Usman, Uthmaan

Uttam (Sanskrit) best.

Uwe (German) a familiar form of Ulrich.

Uzi (Hebrew) my strength.
Uzzia

Uziel (Hebrew) God is my strength; mighty force.
Uzie, Uzziah, Uzziel

Uzoma (Nigerian) born during a journey.

Uzumati (Moquelumnan) grizzly bear.

Vachel (French) small cow.
Vache, Vachell

Vaclav (Czech) wreath of glory.
Vasek

Vadin (Hindi) speaker.
Vaden

Vail (English) valley.
Vaile, Vaill, Vale, Välle

Val (Latin) a short form of Valentin.

Valborg (Swedish) mighty mountain.

Valdemar (Swedish) famous ruler.

Valentin (Latin) strong; healthy.
Val, Valencio, Valenté, Valentijn, Valentine, Valentino, Valenton, Valentyn, Velentino

Valentino (Italian) a form of Valentin.

Valerian (Latin) strong; healthy.
Valeriano, Valerii, Valerio, Valeryn

Valerii (Russian) a form of Valerian.
Valera, Valerie, Valerij, Valerik, Valery

Valfrid (Swedish) strong peace.

Vain (Hindi) a form of Balin. Mythology: a tyrannical monkey king.

Vallis (French) from Wales.
Valis

Valter (Lithuanian, Swedish) a form of Walter.
Valters, Valther, Valts, Vanda

Van (Dutch) a short form of Vandyke.
Vander, Vane, Vann, Vanno

Vance (English) thresher.

Vanda (Lithuanian) a form of Walter.
Vander

Vandyke (Dutch) dyke.

Vanya (Russian) a familiar form of Ivan.
Vanechka, Vanek, Vanja, Vanka, Vanusha, Wanya

Vardon (French) green knoll.
Vardaan, Varden, Verdan, Verdon, Verdun

Varian (Latin) variable.

Varick (German) protecting ruler.
Varak, Varek, Warrick

Vartan (Armenian) rose producer; rose giver.

Varun (Hindi) rain god.
Varon

Vasant (Sanskrit) spring.

Vashawn (American) a combination of the prefix Va + Shawn.
Vashae, Vashan, Vashann, Vashaun, Vashawnn, Vashon, Vashun, Vishon

Vasilis (Greek) a form of Basil.
Vas, Vasya, Vaselios, Vashon, Vasil, Vasile, Vasileos, Vasileios, Vasilios, Vasilius, Vasilos, Vasilus, Vasily, Vassilios, Vasylko, Vasylko, Vazul

Vasin (Hindi) ruler, lord.

Vasu (Sanskrit) wealth.

Vasyl (German, Slavic) a form of William.
Vasos, Vassily, Vassos, Vasya, Vasyuta, VaVaska, Wassily

Vaughn (Welsh) small.
Vaughan, Vaughen, Vaun, Vaune, Von, Voughn

Veasna (Cambodian) lucky.

Ved (Sanskrit) sacred knowledge.

Vedie (Latin) sight.

Veer (Sanskrit) brave.

Vegard (Norwegian) sanctuary; protection.

Velvel (Yiddish) wolf.

Vencel (Hungarian) a short form of Wenceslaus.
Venci, Vencie

Venedictos (Greek) a form of Benedict.
Venedict, Venediktos, Venka, Venya

Veniamin (Bulgarian) a form of Benjamin.
Venyamin, Verniamin

Venkat (Hindi) god; godlike. Religion: another name for the Hindu god Vishnu.

Venya (Russian) a familiar form of Benedict.
Venedict, Venka

Vere (Latin, French) true.

Vered (Hebrew) rose.

Vergil (Latin) a form of Virgil. Literature: a Roman poet best known for his epic poem *Aenid*.
Verge

Vern (Latin) a short form of Vernon.
Verna, Vernal, Verne, Verneal, Vernel, Vernell, Vernelle, Vernial, Vernine, Vernis, Vernol

Vernon (Latin) springlike; youthful.
Vern, Varnan, Vernen, Verney, Vernin

Verner (German) defending army.
Varner

Verney (French) alder grove.
Verrie

Vernados (German) courage of the bear.

Verrill (German) masculine. (French) loyal.
Verill, Verrall, Verrell, Veroll, Veryl

Vian (English) full of life.

Vic (Latin) a short form of Victor.
Vick, Vicken, Vickenson

Vicente (Spanish) a form of Vincent.
Vicent, Visente

Vicenzo (Italian) a form of Vincent.

Victoir (French) a form of Victor.

Victor (Latin) victor, conqueror.
Vic, Victa, Victer, Victoir, Victoriano, Victorien, Victorin, Victorio, Viktor, Vitin, Vittorio, Vitya, Wikoli, Wiktor, Witek

Victorio (Spanish) a form of Victor.
Victorino

Vidal (Spanish) a form of Vitas.
Vida, Vidale, Vidall, Videll

Vidar (Norwegian) tree warrior.

Vidor (Hungarian) cheerful.

Vidur (Hindi) wise.

Viho (Cheyenne) chief.

Vijay (Hindi) victorious.

Vikas (Hindi) growing.
Vikash, Vikesh

Vikram (Hindi) valorous.
Vikrum

Vikrant (Hindi) powerful.
Vikran

Viktor (German, Hungarian, Russian) a form of Victor.
Viktoras, Viktors

Vilhelm (German) a form of William.
Vilhelms, Vilho, Vilis, Viljo, Villem

Vili (Hungarian) a short form of William.
Villy, Vilmos

Viliam (Czech) a form of William.
Vila, Vilek, Vilém, Viliami, Viliamu, Vilko, Vilous

Viljo (Finnish) a form of William.

Ville (Swedish) a short form of William.

Vimal (Hindi) pure.

Vinay (Hindi) polite.

Vince (English) a short form of Vincent.
Vence, Vint

Vincent (Latin) victor, conqueror. See also Binkentios, Binky.
Uinseann, Vencent, Vicente, Vicenzo, Vikent, Vikenti, Vikesha, Vin, Vince, Vincence, Vincens, Vincente, Vincentius, Vincents, Vincenty, Vincenzo, Vinci, Vincien, Vincient, Vinciente, Vincint, Vinny, Vinsent, Vinsint, Wincent

Vincente (Spanish) a form of Vincent.
Vencente

Vincenzo (Italian) a form of Vincent.
Vincenz, Vincenza, Vincenzio, Vinchenzo, Vinzenz

Vinci (Hungarian, Italian) a familiar form of Vincent.
Vinci, Vinco, Vincze

Vinny (English) a familiar form of Calvin, Melvin, Vincent.
Vinnee, Vinney, Vinni, Vinnie

Vinod (Hindi) happy, joyful.
Vinodh, Vinood

Vinson (English) son of Vincent.
Vinnis

Vipul (Hindi) plentiful.

Viraj (Hindi) resplendent.

Virat (Hindi) very big.

Virgil (Latin) rod bearer, staff bearer.
Vergil, Virge, Virgial, Virgie, Virgilio

Virgilio (Spanish) a form of Virgil.
Virjilio

Virote (Tai) strong, powerful.

Vishal (Hindi) huge; great.
Vishaal

Vishnu (Hindi) protector.

Vitas (Latin) alive, vital.
Vidal, Vitus

Vito (Latin) a short form of Vittorio.
Veit, Vidal, Vital, Vitale, Vitalis, Vitas, Vitin, Vitis, Vitus, Vitya, Vytas

Vittorio (Italian) a form of Victor.
Vito, Vitor, Vitorio, Vittore, Vittorios

Vitya (Russian) a form of Victor.
Vitenka, Vitka

Vivek (Hindi) wisdom.
Vivekinan

Vladimir (Russian) famous prince. See also Dima, Waldemar, Walter.
Bladimir, Vimka, Vlad, Vladamir, Vladik, Vladimar, Vladimeer, Vladimeer, Vladimere, Vladimire, Vladimyr, Vladjimir, Vladka, Vladko, Vladlen, Vladmir, Volodimir, Volodya, Volya, Vova, Wladimir

Vladislav (Slavic) glorious ruler. See also Slava.
Vladie, Vladya, Vlas, Vlatislava, Vyacheslav, Wladislav

Vlas (Russian) a short form of Vladislav.

Vova (Russian) a form of Walter.
Vovka

Vuai (Swahili) savior.

Vyacheslav (Russian) a form of Vladislav. See also Slava.

Waban (Ojibwa) white.
Wabon

Wade (English) ford; river crossing. *Wad, Wadsworth, Wadi, Waide, Waed, Waid, Waide, Wayde, Waydell, Whaid*

Wadley (English) ford meadow.
Wadleigh, Wadly

Wadsworth (English) village near the ford.
Wadsworth

Waban (Ojibwa) white.

Wagner (German) wagoner, wagon maker. Music: Richard Wagner was a famous nineteenth-century German composer.
Waggoner

Wahid (Arabic) single; exclusively unequaled.
Waheed

Wahkan (Lakota) sacred.

Wahkoowah (Lakota) charging.

Wain (English) a short form of Wainwright. A form of Wayne.

Wainwright (English) wagon maker. *Wain, Wainright, Wayne, Wayneright, Waynewright, Waynright, Wright*

Waite (English) watchman.
Waitman, Waiton, Waits, Wayte

Wakefield (English) wet field.
Field, Wake

Wakely (English) wet meadow.

Wakeman (English) watchman.
Wake

Wakiza (Native American) determined warrior.

Walcott (English) cottage by the wall.
Wallcot, Wallcott, Wolcott

Waldemar (German) powerful; famous. See also Vladimir.
Valdemar, Waldemar, Waldo

Walden (English) wooded valley. Literature: Henry David Thoreau made Walden Pond famous with his book *Walden*.
Waldi, Waldo, Waldon, Welti

Waldo (German) a familiar form of Oswald, Waldemar, Walden.
Wald, Waldy

Waldron (English) ruler.

Waleed (Arabic) newborn.
Waled, Walid

Walerian (Polish) strong; brave.

Wales (English) from Wales.
Wael, Wail, Wali, Walie, Waly

Walford (English) Welshman's ford.

Walfred (German) peaceful ruler.
Walfredo, Walfried

Wali (Arabic) all-governing.

Walker (English) cloth walker; cloth cleaner.
Wallie, Wally

Wallace (English) from Wales.
Wallach, Wallas, Wallie, Wallis, Wally, Walsh, Welsh

Wallach (German) a form of Wallace.
Wallace

Waller (German) powerful. (English) wall maker.

Wally (English) a familiar form of Walter.
Walli, Wallie

Walmond (German) mighty ruler.

Walsh (English) a form of Wallace.
Welch, Welsh

Walt (English) a short form of Walter, Walton.
Waltey, Waltii, Walty

Vladislav (Slavic) glorious ruler. See also Slava.
Vladik, Vladya, Vlas, Vlatislava, Vyacheslav, Wladislav

Volker (German) people's guard.
Folke

Volney (German) national spirit.

Von (German) a short form of many German names.

Walter (German) army ruler, general. (English) woodsman. See also Gautier, Gualberto, Gualtiero, Gutierre, Ladislav, Vladimir.
Valter, Vanda, Vova, Walder, Wally, Walt, Walti, Walther, Waltr, Wat, Waterio, Watkins, Watson, Wualter

Walther (German) a form of Walter.

Walton (English) walled town.
Walt

Waltr (Czech) a form of Walter.

Walworth (English) fenced-in farm.

Walwyn (English) Welsh friend.
Waluin, Waluinn, Walwinn, Waluynne, Weluyn

Wamblee (Lakota) eagle.

Wang (Chinese) hope; wish.

Wanikiya (Lakota) savior.

Wanya (Russian) a form of Vanya.
Wanyai

Wapi (Native American) lucky.

Warburton (English) fortified town.

Ward (English) watchman, guardian.
Warde, Warden, Worden

Wardell (English) watchman's hill.

Wardley (English) watchman's meadow.
Wardlea, Wardleigh

Ware (English) wary, cautious.

Warfield (English) field near the weir or fish trap.

Warford (English) ford near the weir or fish trap.

Warley (English) meadow near the weir or fish trap.

Warner (German) armed defender. (French) park keeper.
Werner

Warren (German) general; warden; rabbit hutch.
Ware, Waring, Warrenson, Warrin, Warriner, Worrin

Warton (English) town near the weir or fish trap.

Warwick (English) buildings near the weir or fish trap.
Warick, Warrick

Washburn (English) overflowing river.

Washington (English) town near water. History: George Washington was the first U.S. president.
Wash

Wasili (Russian) a form of Basil.
Wasyl

Wasim (Arabic) graceful; good-looking.
Waseem, Wasseem, Wassim

Watende (Nyakyusa) there will be revenge.

Waterio (Spanish) a form of Walter.
Gualtiero

Watford (English) wattle ford; dam made of twigs and sticks.

Watkins (English) son of Walter.
Watkin

Watson (English) son of Walter.
Wathson, Whatson

Waverly (English) quaking aspen-tree meadow.
Waverlee, Waverley

Wayland (English) a form of Waylon.
Weiland, Weyland

Waylon (English) land by the road.
Wallen, Walon, Way, Waylan, Wayland, Waylen, Waylin, Weylin

Wayman (English) road man; traveler.
Waymon

Wayne (English) wagon maker. A short form of Wainwright.
Wain, Wanye, Wayn, Waynell, Wayne, Wene, Whayne

Wazir (Arabic) minister.

Webb (English) weaver.
Web, Weeb

Weber (German) weaver.
Webber, Webner

Webley (English) weaver's meadow.
Webbley, Webbly, Webby

Webster (English) weaver.

Weddel (English) valley near the ford.

Wei-Quo (Chinese) ruler of the country.
Wei

Welborne (English) spring-fed stream.
Welborn, Welbourne, Welburn, Wellborn, Wellborne, Wellbourn, Wellburn

Welby (German) farm near the well.
Welbey, Welbie, Wellbey, Wellby

Weldon (English) hill near the well.
Weldan

Welfel (Yiddish) a form of William.
Welvel

Welford (English) ford near the well.

Wells (English) springs.
Welles

Welsh (English) a form of Wallace, Walsh.
Welch

Welton (English) town near the well.

Wemilat (Native American) all give to him.

Wemilo (Native American) all speak to him.

Wen (Gypsy) born in winter.

Wenceslaus (Slavic) wreath of honor.
Vencel, Wenceslao, Wenceslas, Wenzel, Wenzell, Wienczyslaw

Wendell (German) wanderer. (English) good dale, good valley.
Wandale, Wendall, Wendel, Wendle, Wendy

Wene (Hawaiian) a form of Wayne.

Wenford (English) white ford.
Wynford

Wentworth (English) pale man's settlement.

Wenutu (Native American) clear sky.

Werner (English) a form of Warner.
Wernhar, Wernher

Wes (English) a short form of Wesley.
Wess

Wesh (Gypsy) woods.

Wesley (English) western meadow.
Wes, Wesley, Wesle, Weslee, Wesleyan, Weslie, Wesly, Wessley, Westleigh, Westley, Wezley

West (English) west.

Westbrook (English) western brook.
Brook, West, Westbrooke

Westby (English) western farmstead.

Westcott (English) western cottage.
Wescot, Wescott, Westcot

Westley (English) a form of Wesley.
Westlee, Westly

Weston (English) western town.
West, Westen, Westin

Wetherby (English) wether-sheep farm.
Weatherbey, Weatherbie, Weatherby, Wetherbey, Wetherbie

Wetherell (English) wether-sheep corner.

Wetherly (English) wether-sheep meadow.

Weylin (English) a form of Waylon.
Weylan, Weylyn

Whalley (English) woods near a hill.
Whaley

Wharton (English) town on the bank of a lake.
Warton

Wheatley (English) wheat field.
Whatley, Wheatlea, Wheatleigh, Wheatly

Wheaton (English) wheat town.

Wheeler (English) wheel maker; wagon driver.

Whistler (English) whistler, piper.

Whit (English) a short form of Whitman, Whitney.
Whitt, Whyt, Whyte, Wit, Witt

Whitby (English) white house.

Whitcomb (English) white valley.
Whitcombe, Whitcomb

Whitelaw (English) small hill.

Whitey (English) white skinned; white haired.

Whitfield (English) white field.

Whitford (English) white ford.

Whitley (English) white meadow.
Whitlea, Whitlee, Whitleigh

Whitman (English) white-haired man.
Witt

Whitmore (English) white moor.
Whitmoor, Whittemore, Witmore, Wittemore

Whitney (English) white island; white water.
Whit, Whitney, Widney, Widny

Whittaker (English) white field.
Whitaker, Whittaker, Whitmaker

Wicasa (Dakota) man.

Wicent (Polish) a form of Vincent.
Wicek, Wicus

Wichado (Native American) willing.

Wickham (English) village enclosure.
Wick

Wickley (English) village meadow.
Wildey

Wid (English) wide.

Wies (German) renowned warrior.

Wikoli (Hawaiian) a form of Victor.

Wiktor (Polish) a form of Victor.

Wilanu (Moquelumnan) pouring water on flour.

Wilbert (German) brilliant; resolute.
Wilberto, Wilburt

Wilbur (English) wall fortification; bright willows.
Wilber, Wilburn, Wilburt, Wilbur, Wilver

Wilder (English) wilderness, wild.
Wylder

Wildon (English) wooded hill.
Wilden, Willdon

Wile (Hawaiian) a form of Willie.

Wiley (English) willow meadow; Will's meadow.
Whiley, Wildy, Willey, Wylie

Wilford (English) willow-tree ford.
Wilferd

Wilfred (German) determined peace-maker.
Wilferd, Wilfredo, Wilfrid, Wilfride,

Wilfried (Spanish) a form of Wilfred.
Fredo, Wifredo, Wifrido, Wilfredo

Wilhelm (German) determined guardian.
Wilhelmus, Willem

Wiliama (Hawaiian) a form of William.
Pila, Wile

Wilkie (English) a familiar form of Wilkins.
Wikie, Wilke

Wilkins (English) William's kin.
Wilkens, Wilkes, Wilkie, Wilkin, Wilks, Wilkes, Willkins

Wilkinson (English) son of little William.
Wilkenson, Willkinson

Will (English) a short form of William.
Wil, Wilm, Wim

Willard (German) determined and brave.
Williard

Willem (German) a form of William.
Willim

William (English) a form of Wilhelm.
See also Gilamu, Guglielmo,
Guilherme, Guillaume, Guillermo,
Gwilym, Liam, Uilliam, Wilhelm.
*Bill, Billy, Vasyl, Vilhelm, Vili, Viliam,
Viljo, Ville, Villiam, Wefel, Wiek, William,
Wiliama, Wiliame, Wiliame, Will, Willaim,
Willam, Willeam, Willem, Williams, Willie,*

Willil, Willis, Willium, Williu, Willyam, Wim

Williams (German) son of William.
Wilams, Willains, Williamson, Wuliams

Willie (German) a familiar form of William.
Wile, Wille, Willi, Willia, Willy

Willis (German) son of Willie.
Willice, Wills, Willus, Wyllis

Willoughby (English) willow farm.
Willoughbey, Willoughbie

Wills (English) son of Will.

Wily (German) a form of Willie.
Willey, Wily

Wilmer (German) determined and famous.
Willmar, Willmer, Wilm, Wilmar, Wylmar, Wylmer

Wilmot (Teutonic) resolute spirit.
Wilmont, Willmont, Wilm, Wilmont

Wilny (Native American) eagle singing while flying.

Wilson (English) son of Will.
Wilkinson, Willson, Wisen, Wolson

Wilt (English) a short form of Wilton.

Wilton (English) farm by the spring.
Will, Wilt

Wilu (Moquelumnan) chicken hawk squawking.

Win (Cambodian) bright. (English) a short form of Winston and names ending in "win."
Winn, Winnie, Winny

Wincent (Polish) a form of Vincent.
Wicek, Wicenty, Wicus, Wince, Wincenty

Winchell (English) bend in the road;
bend in the land.

Windsor (English) riverbank with a
winch. History: the surname of the
British royal family.
Winzer, Winsor, Wyndsor

Winfield (English) friendly field.
*Field, Winfred, Winfrey, Winifield,
Winnfield, Wynfield, Wynnfield*

Winfried (German) friend of peace.

Wing (Chinese) glory.
Wing-Chin, Wing-Kit

Wingate (English) winding gate.

Wingi (Native American) willing.

Winslow (English) friend's hill.

Winston (English) friendly town; vic-
tory town.
*Win, Winsten, Winstin, Winstom,
Winton, Wynstan, Wynston*

Winter (English) born in winter.
Winterford, Wynter

Winthrop (English) victory at the
crossroads.

Winton (English) a form of Winston.
Wynten, Wynton

Winward (English) friend's guardian;
friend's forest.

Wit (Polish) life. (English) a form of
Whit. (Flemish) a short form of
DeWitt.
Witt, Witte, Witty

Witek (Polish) a form of Victor.

Witha (Arabic) handsome.

Witter (English) wise warrior.

Witton (English) wise man's estate.

Wladislav (Polish) a form of Vladislav.
Wladislau

Wolcott (English) cottage in the
woods.

Wolf (German, English) a short form
of Wolfe, Wolfgang.
Wolff, Wolfie, Wolfy

Wolfe (English) wolf.
Wolff, Woolf

Wolfgang (German) wolf quarrel.
Music: Wolfgang Amadeus Mozart
was a famous eighteenth-century
Austrian composer.
Wolf, Wolfgang, Wolfgans

Wood (English) a short form of
Elwood, Garwood, Woodrow.
Woody

Woodfield (English) forest meadow.

Woodford (English) ford through the
forest.

Woodrow (English) passage in the
woods. History: Thomas Woodrow
Wilson was the twenty-eighth U.S.
president.
Wood, Woodman, Woodroe, Woody

Woodruff (English) forest ranger.

Woodson (English) son of Wood.
Woods, Woodsen

Woodward (English) forest warden.
Woodard

Woodville (English) town at the edge
of the woods.

Woody (American) a familiar form of
Elwood, Garwood, Woodrow.
Woody, Woodie

Woolsey (English) victorious wolf.

Worcester (English) forest army camp.

Wordsworth (English) wolf-guardian's
farm. Literature: William Wordsworth
was a famous British poet.

Worie (Ibo) born on market day.

Worth (English) a short form of
Wordsworth.
Worthey, Worthington, Worthy

Worton (English) farm town.

Wouter (German) powerful warrior.

Wrangle (American) a form of
Rangle.
Wrangler

Wray (Scandinavian) corner property.
(English) crooked.
Wreh

Wren (Welsh) chief, ruler. (English)
wren.

Wright (English) a short form of
Wainwright.

Wrisley (English) a form of Risley.
Wrisee, Wrislie, Wrisly

Wriston (English) a form of Riston.
Wryston

Wuliton (Native American) will do well.

Wunand (Native American) God is good.

Wuyi (Moquelumnan) turkey vulture flying.

Wyatt (French) little warrior.
Wiatt, Wyat, Wyatte, Wye, Wyeth, Wyett, Wyitt, Wytt

Wybert (English) battle bright.

Wyborn (Scandinavian) war bear.

Wyck (Scandinavian) village.

Wycliff (English) white cliff; village near the cliff.
Wyckliffe, Wycliffe

Wylie (English) charming.
Wiley, Wye, Wyley, Wyllie, Wyly

Wyman (English) fighter, warrior.

Wymer (English) famous in battle.

Wyn (Welsh) light skinned; white. (English) friend. A short form of Selwyn.
Win, Wyne, Wynn, Wynne

Wyndham (Scottish) village near the winding road.
Windham, Wynndham

Wynono (Native American) first-born son.

Wythe (English) willow tree.

Xabat (Basque) savior.

Xaiver (Basque) a form of Xavier.
Xajavier, Xzaiver

Xan (Greek) a short form of Alexander.
Xane

Xander (Greek) a short form of Alexander.
Xande, Xzander

Xanthus (Latin) golden haired.
Xanthos

Xarles (Basque) a form of Charles.

Xavier (Arabic) bright. (Basque) owner of the new house. See also Exavier, Javier, Salvatore, Saverio.
Xabier, Xaiver, Xavaeir, Xaver, Xavian, Xavian, Xavior, Xavon, Xavyer, Xever, Xizavier, Xxavier, Xzavier, Zavier

Xenophon (Greek) strange voice.
Xeno, Zennie

Xenos (Greek) stranger; guest.
Zenos

Xerxes (Persian) ruler. History: a king of Persia.
Zerk

Ximenes (Spanish) a form of Simon.
Ximenez, Ximon, Ximun, Xymenes

Xylon (Greek) forest.

Xzavier (Basque) a form of Xavier.
Xzavaier, Xzaver, Xzavion, Xzavior, Xzvaier

Yadid (Hebrew) friend; beloved.
Yedid

Yadon (Hebrew) he will judge.
Yadean, Yadin, Yadun

Yael (Hebrew) a form of Jael.

Yafeu (Ibo) bold.

Yagil (Hebrew) he will rejoice.

Yago (Spanish) a form of James.

Yahto (Lakota) blue.

Yahya (Arabic) living.
Yahye

Yair (Hebrew) he will enlighten.
Yahir

Yakecen (Dene) sky song.

Yakez (Carrier) heaven.

Yakov (Russian) a form of Jacob.
Yaacob, Yaacov, Yaakov, Yachov, Yacoub, Yacov, Yakob, Yashko

Yale (German) productive. (English) old.

Yan, Yann (Russian) forms of John.
Yanichek, Yanick, Yanka, Yannick

Yana (Native American) bear.

Yancy (Native American) Englishman, Yankee.
Yan, Yance, Yancey, Yanci, Yansey, Yansy, Yantsey, Yanncy, Yency

Yanick, Yannick (Russian) familiar forms of Yan.
Yanic, Yanik, Yannic, Yannik, Yonic, Yonnik

Yanka (Russian) a familiar form of John.
Yanilem

Yanni (Greek) a form of John.
Ioannis, Yani, Yannakis, Yannis, Yanny, Yiannis, Yoni

Yanton (Hebrew) a form of Johnathon, Jonathon.

Yao (Ewe) born on Thursday.

Yaphet (Hebrew) a form of Japheth.
Yapheth, Yefat, Yephat

Yarb (Gypsy) herb.

Yardan (Arabic) king.

Yarden (Hebrew) a form of Jordan.

Yardley (English) enclosed meadow.
Lee, Yard, Yardlea, Yardlee, Yardleigh, Yardly, Ygor

Yarom (Hebrew) he will raise up.
Yarum

Yaron (Hebrew) he will sing; he will cry out.
Jaron, Yairon

Yasashiku (Japanese) gentle; polite.

Yash (Hindi) victorious; glory.

Yasha (Russian) a form of Jacob, James.
Yascha, Yashka, Yashko

Yashwant (Hindi) glorious.

Yasin (Arabic) prophet.
Yasine, Yasseen, Yassin, Yassine, Yazen

Yasir (Afghan) humble; takes it easy.
(Arabic) wealthy.
Yasar, Yaser, Yashar, Yasser

Yasuo (Japanese) restful.

Yates (English) gates.
Yeats

Yatin (Hindi) ascetic.

Yavin (Hebrew) he will understand.
Jabin

Yawo (Akan) born on Thursday.

Yazid (Arabic) his power will increase.
Yazeed, Yazide

Yechiel (Hebrew) God lives.

Yedidya (Hebrew) a form of Jedidiah.
See also Didi.
Yadad, Yedidia, Yedidiah, Yido

Yegor (Russian) a form of George. See also Egor, Igor.
Ygor

Yehoshua (Hebrew) a form of Joshua.
Yeshua, Yeshuah, Yoshua, Y'shua, Yushua

Yehoyakem (Hebrew) a form of Joachim, Joaquin.
Yakim, Yehayakem, Yokim, Yoyakim

Yehudi (Hebrew) a form of Judah.
Yechudi, Yechudit, Yehuda, Yehudah, Yehudit

Yelutci (Moquelumnan) bear walking silently.

Yeoman (English) attendant; retainer.
Yoeman, Youman

Yeremey (Russian) a form of Jeremiah.

Yervant (Armenian) king, ruler. History: an Armenian king.

Yeshaya (Hebrew) gift. See also Shai.

Yeshurun (Hebrew) right way.

Yeska (Russian) a form of Joseph.
Yesya

Yestin (Welsh) just.

Yevgenyi (Russian) a form of Eugene.
Gena, Yevgeni, Yevgenij, Yevgeniy

Yigal (Hebrew) he will redeem.
Yagel, Yigael

Yirmaya (Hebrew) a form of Jeremiah.
Yirmayahu

Yishai (Hebrew) a form of Jesse.

Yisrael (Hebrew) a form of Israel.
Yesarel, Yisroel

Yitro (Hebrew) a form of Jethro.

Yitzchak (Hebrew) a form of Isaac.
See also Itzak.
Yitzak, Yitzchok, Yitzhak

Yngve (Swedish) ancestor; lord, master.

Yo (Cambodian) honest.

Yoakim (Slavic) a form of Jacob.
Yoackim

Yoan (German) a form of Johan, Johann.
Yoann

Yoav (Hebrew) a form of Joab.

Yochanan (Hebrew) a form of John.
Yohanan

Yoel (Hebrew) a form of Joel.

Yogesh (Hindi) ascetic. Religion: another name for the Hindu god Shiva.

Yohance (Hausa) a form of John.

Yohan, Yohann (German) forms of Johan, Johann.
Yohane, Yohanes, Yohanne, Yohannes, Yohans, Yohn

Yonah (Hebrew) a form of Jonah.
Yona, Yonas

Yonatan (Hebrew) a form of Jonathan.
Yonathan, Yonathon, Yonaton, Yonattan

Yong (Chinese) courageous.
Yonge

Yong-Sun (Korean) dragon in the first position; courageous.

Yoni (Greek) a form of Yanni.
Yonis, Yonnas, Yonny, Yony

Yoofi (Akan) born on Friday.

Yooku (Fante) born on Wednesday.

Yoram (Hebrew) God is high.
Joram

Yorgos (Greek) a form of George.
Yiorgos, Yorgo

York (English) boar estate; yew-tree estate.
Yorick, Yorke, Yorker, Yorkie, Yorrick

Yorkoo (Fante) born on Thursday.

Yosef (Hebrew) a form of Joseph. See also Osip.
Yoceph, Yoosuf, Yoseff, Yoseph, Yosief, Yosif, Yosuf, Yosyf, Yousef, Yusif

Yóshi (Japanese) adopted son.
Yoshiki, Yoshiuki

Yoshiyahu (Hebrew) a form of Josiah.
Yoshia, Yoshiah, Yoshiya, Yoshiyah, Yosiah

Yoskolo (Moquelumnan) breaking off pine cones.

Yosu (Hebrew) a form of Jesus.

Yotimo (Moquelumnan) yellow jacket carrying food to its hive.

Yottoko (Native American) mud at the water's edge.

Young (English) young.
Yung

Young-Jae (Korean) pile of prosperity.

Young-Soo (Korean) keeping the prosperity.

Youri (Russian) a form of Yuri.

Yousef (Yiddish) a form of Joseph.
Yousaf, Youseef, Yousef, Youseph, Yousif, Youssef, Youseff, Yousuf

Youssel (Yiddish) a familiar form of Joseph.
Yussel

Yov (Russian) a short form of Yoakim.

Yovani (Slavic) a form of Jovan.
Yovani, Yovanni, Yovanny, Yovany, Yovni

Yoyi (Hebrew) a form of George.

Yrjo (Finnish) a form of George.

Ysidro (Greek) a short form of Isidore.

Yu (Chinese) universe.
Yue

Yudell (English) a form of Udell.
Yudale, Yudel

Yuki (Japanese) snow.
Yukiko, Yukio, Yuuki

Yul (Mongolian) beyond the horizon.

Yule (English) born at Christmas.

Yuli (Basque) youthful.

Yuma (Native American) son of a chief.

Yunus (Turkish) a form of Jonah.

Yurcel (Turkish) sublime.

Yuri (Russian, Ukrainian) a form of George. (Hebrew) a familiar form of Uriah.
Yehor, Youri, Yura, Yure, Yurii, Yurij, Yurik, Yurko, Yurri, Yury, Yusha

Yusif (Russian) a form of Joseph.
Yuseph, Yusof, Yussof, Yussup, Yuzef, Yuzep

Yustyn (Russian) a form of Justin.
Yusts

Yusuf (Arabic, Swahili) a form of Joseph.
Yusef, Yusuff

Yutu (Moquelumnan) coyote out hunting.

Yuval (Hebrew) rejoicing.

Yves (French) a form of Ivar, Ives.
Yves, Yvon, Yves

Yvon (French) a form of Ivar, Yves.
Ivon, Yuon, Yvan, Yvonne

Zac (Hebrew) a short form of
Zachariah, Zachary.
Zac

Zacarias (Portuguese, Spanish) a form
of Zachariah.
Zaaria, Zacariah

Zacary (Hebrew) a form of Zachary.
Zac, Zacara, Zacari, Zacariah, Zacarias,
Zacarie, Zacarious, Zacary, Zacrye

Zaccary (Hebrew) a form of Zachary.
Zac, Zaccaeus, Zaccari, Zaccaria,
Zaccariah, Zaccary, Zaccea, Zaccharie,
Zachary, Zachery, Zaccury

Zaccheus (Hebrew) innocent, pure.
Zaceus, Zachaeus, Zachious

Zach (Hebrew) a short form of
Zachariah, Zachary.

Zachari (Hebrew) a form of Zachary.
Zacheri

Zacharia (Hebrew) a form of Zachary.
Zacharya

Zachariah (Hebrew) God
remembered.
Zac, Zacarias, Zacarius, Zacary, Zaccary,

Zacharias (German) a form of
Zachariah.
Zacarias, Zacharais, Zacharias,
Zacharius, Zacharias, Zekarias

Zacharie (Hebrew) a form of
Zachary.
Zacharee, Zahurie, Zecharie

Zachary (Hebrew) a familiar form of
Zachariah. History: Zachary Taylor
was the twelfth U.S. president. See
also Sachar, Sakeri.
Xachary, Zac, Zaccary, Zach,
Zacha, Zachaery, Zachaios, Zacharay,
Zachery, Zachari, Zacharia, Zacharias,
Zachary, Zacharry, Zachaury, Zachery,
Zachory, Zacick, Zackary, Zackery,
Zackory, Zakaria, Zakary, Zakery,
Zachary, Zechery, Zecher, Zeke

Zachery (Hebrew) a form of Zachary.
Zacheray, Zacherey, Zacheria, Zacherias,
Zacheriah, Zacherie, Zacherius, Zackery,
Zakkery, Zachary, Zachery, Zeke

Zachry (Hebrew) a form of Zachary.
Zachre, Zachrey, Zachri

Zachory (Hebrew) a form of Zachary.

Zack (Hebrew) a short form of
Zachariah, Zachary.
Zach, Zak, Zaks

Zackary (Hebrew) a form of Zachary.
Zacheray, Zackerey, Zackeria,
Zackeriah, Zacherie, Zacherias, Zackery

Zackery (Hebrew) a form of Zachery.
Zackere, Zackeree, Zackeri, Zackerey,
Zackery, Zackhary, Zackie, Zackree, Zackrey,
Zackry

Zackory (Hebrew) a form of Zachary.
Zackoriah, Zackorie, Zackorry, Zackori,
Zackory, Zackry, Zackory

Zadok (Hebrew) a short form of
Tzadok.
Zaddic, Zadie, Zadoc, Zaydok

Zadornin (Basque) Saturn.

Zafir (Arabic) victorious.
Zafar, Zafer, Zafir, Zaffar

Zahid (Arabic) self-denying, ascetic.
Zaheed

Zahir (Arabic) shining, bright.
Zahair, Zahar, Zaheer, Zahi, Zair, Zaire,
Zayyir

Zahur (Swahili) flower.

Zaid (Arabic) increase, growth.
Zaied, Zaiid, Zayd

Zaide (Hebrew) older.

Zaim (Arabic) brigadier general.

Zain (English) a form of Zane.
Zaine

Zakaria (Hebrew) a form of
Zachariah.
Zakariya, Zakareeya, Zakareeyah,
Zakariah, Zakariya, Zakeria, Zakeriah

Zakariyya (Arabic) prophet. Religion:
an Islamic prophet.

Zakary (Hebrew) a form of Zachery.
Zak, Zakarai, Zakare, Zakaree, Zakari,
Zakarias, Zakarie, Zakarius, Zakariye,
Zake, Zakhar, Zaki, Zakit, Zakkai,
Zako, Zakqary, Zakree, Zakri, Zakris,
Zakry

Zakery (Hebrew) a form of Zachary.
Zakeri, Zakerie, Zakiry

Zaki (Arabic) bright; pure. (Hausa)
lion.
Zakee, Zakia, Zakie, Zakiy, Zakki

Zakia (Swahili) intelligent.

Zakkary (Hebrew) a form of Zachary.
Zakk, Zakkari, Zakkery, Zakkyre

Zako (Hungarian) a form of
Zachariah.

Zale (Greek) sea strength.
Zayle

Zalmai (Afghan) young.

Zalman (Yiddish) a form of Solomon.
Zaloman

Zamiel (German) a form of Samuel.
Zamal, Zamuel

Zamir (Hebrew) song; bird.
Zameer

Zan (Italian) clown.
Zann, Zanni, Zannie, Zanny, Zhan

Zander (Greek) a short form of
Alexander.
Zandore, Zandra, Zandrae, Zandy

Zane (English) a form of John.
Zain, Zayne, Zhane

Zanis (Latvian) a form of Janis.
Zannis

Zanvil (Hebrew) a form of Samuel.
Zanwill

Zaquan (American) a combination of
the prefix Za + Quan.
Zaquain, Zaquon, Zaquwan

Zareb (African) protector.

Zared (Hebrew) ambush.
Zaryd

Zarek (Polish) may God protect the
king.
Zarik, Zarrick, Zereb, Zerick, Zerric,
Zerrick

Zavier (Arabic) a form of Xavier.
Zavair, Zaverie, Zavery, Zavierre, Zavior,
Zavyr, Zayvius, Zxavian

Zayit (Hebrew) olive.

Zayne (English) a form of Zane.
Zayan, Zayin, Zayn

Zdenek (Czech) follower of Saint
Denis.

Zeb (Hebrew) a short form of
Zebediah, Zebulon.
Zev

Zebediah (Hebrew) God's gift.
Zeb, Zebadia, Zebadiah, Zebedee,
Zebedia, Zebidiah, Zedidiah

Zebedee (Hebrew) a familiar form of
Zebediah.
Zebadee

Zebulon (Hebrew) exalted, honored;
lofty house.
Zabulan, Zeb, Zebulan, Zebulen,

Zebulin, Zebulun, Zebulyn, Zev,
Zevlon, Zevulun, Zhebulen, Zubin

Zechariah (Hebrew) a form of
Zachariah.
Zecharia, Zecharian, Zecheriah,
Zechuriah, Zekariah, Zekarias, Zeke,
Zekeria, Zekeriah, Zekerya

Zed (Hebrew) a short form of
Zedekiah.

Zedekiah (Hebrew) God is mighty
and just.
Zed, Zedechiah, Zedekias, Zedikeiah

Zedidiah (Hebrew) a form of
Zebediah.

Zeeman (Dutch) seaman.

Zeév (Hebrew) wolf.
Zeévi, Zeff, Zif

Zeheb (Turkish) gold.

Zeke (Hebrew) a short form of
Ezekiel, Zachariah, Zachary,
Zechariah.

Zeki (Turkish) clever, intelligent.
Zeky

Zelgai (Afghan) heart.

Zelig (Yiddish) a form of Selig.
Zeligman, Zelik

Zelimir (Slavic) wishes for peace.

Zemar (Afghan) lion.

Zen (Japanese) religious. Religion: a
form of Buddhism.

Zenda (Czech) a form of Eugene.
Zhek

Zeno (Greek) cart; harness. History: a Greek philosopher.
Zenon, Zenos, Zeno, Zino, Zinon.

Zephaniah (Hebrew) treasured by God.

Zephyr (Greek) west wind.
Zeferino, Zeffrey, Zephery, Zephire, Zephram, Zephran, Zephrin.

Zero (Arabic) empty, void.

Zeroun (Armenian) wise and respected.

Zeshawn (American) a combination of the prefix Ze + Shawn.
Zeshan, Zeshaun, Zeshon, Zishaan, Zishan, Zshawn.

Zesiro (Luganda) older of twins.

Zeus (Greek) living. Mythology: chief god of the Greek pantheon.

Zeusef (Portuguese) a form of Joseph.

Zev (Hebrew) a short form of Zebulon.

Zevi (Hebrew) a form of Tzvi.
Zhvie, Zhvy, Zvi.

Zhek (Russian) a short form of Evgeny.
Zhenechka, Zhenka, Zhenya.

Zhixin (Chinese) ambitious.
Zhi, Zhihuán, Zhipeng, Zhi-yang, Zhiyuan.

Zhuàng (Chinese) strong.

Zhora (Russian) a form of George.
Zhorik, Zhorka, Zhorz, Zhurka.

Zia (Hebrew) trembling; moving. (Arabic) light.
Ziah.

Zigfrid (Latvian, Russian) a form of Siegfried.
Zegfrid, Zigfrids, Ziggy, Zygfryd, Zigi.

Ziggy (American) a familiar form of Siegfried, Sigmund.
Ziggie.

Zigor (Basque) punishment.

Zikomo (Nguni) thank-you.

Zilaba (Luganda) born while sick.
Zilabamuzale.

Zimra (Hebrew) song of praise.
Zemora, Zimrat, Zimri, Zimria, Zimriah, Zimriya.

Zimraan (Arabic) praise.

Zinan (Japanese) second son.

Zindel (Yiddish) a form of Alexander.
Zindil, Zunde.

Zion (Hebrew) sign, omen; excellent. Bible: the name used to refer to Israel and to the Jewish people.
Tzion, Zyon.

Ziskind (Yiddish) sweet child.

Ziv (Hebrew) shining brightly. (Slavic) a short form of Ziven.

Ziven (Slavic) vigorous, lively.
Zev, Ziv, Zivka, Zivon.

Ziyad (Arabic) increase.
Zayd, Ziyaad.

Zlatan (Czech) gold.
Zlatek, Zlatko.

Zohar (Hebrew) bright light.
Zohair.

Zollie, Zolly (Hebrew) forms of Solly.
Zoilo.

Zoltán (Hungarian) life.

Zorba (Greek) live each day.

Zorion (Basque) a form of Orion.
Zoran, Zoren, Zorian, Zoron, Zorrine, Zorrion.

Zorya (Slavic) star; dawn.

Zotikos (Greek) saintly, holy. Religion: a saint in the Eastern Orthodox Church.

Zotom (Kiowa) a biter.

Zsigmond (Hungarian) a form of Sigmund.
Ziggy, Zigmund, Zsiga.

Zubin (Hebrew) a short form of Zebulon.
Zubeen.

Zuberi (Swahili) strong.

Zuhayr (Arabic) brilliant, shining.
Zyhair, Zuheer.

Zuka (Shona) sixpence.

Zuriel (Hebrew) God is my rock.

Zygmunt (Polish) a form of Sigmund.

Notes

Notes

Also from Meadowbrook Press

◆ **Pregnancy, Childbirth, and the Newborn**
More complete and up-to-date than any other pregnancy guide, this remarkable book is the "bible" for child-birth educators. Now revised with a greatly expanded treatment of pregnancy tests, complications, and infections; an expanded list of drugs and medications (plus advice for uses); and a brand-new chapter on creating a detailed birth plan.

◆ **Eating Expectantly**
Dietitian Bridget Swinney offers a practical and tasty approach to prenatal nutrition, combining nutrition guidelines for each trimester with 200 complete menus, 85 tasty recipes, plus cooking and shopping tips. Cited by *Child* magazine as one of the "10 best parenting books of 1993," *Eating Expectantly* is newly revised with the most current nutrition information.

◆ **Feed Me! I'm Yours**
Parents love this easy-to-use, economical guide to making baby food at home. More than 200 recipes cover everything a parent needs to know about teething foods, nutritious snacks, and quick, pleasing lunches.

◆ **First-Year Baby Care**
This is one of the leading baby-care books to guide you through your baby's first year. It contains complete information on the basics of baby care, including bathing, diapering, medical facts, and feeding your baby. Includes step-by-step illustrated instructions to make finding information easy, newborn screening and immunization schedules, breastfeeding information for working mothers, expanded information on child care options, reference guides to common illnesses, and environmental and safety tips.

We offer many more titles written to delight, inform, and entertain.

To order books with a credit card or browse our full

selection of titles, visit our web site at:

www.meadowbrookpress.com

or call toll-free to place an order, request a free catalog, or ask a question:

1-800-338-2232

 Meadowbrook Press • 5451 Smetana Drive • Minnetonka, MN • 55343